A calendar, a calendar!
look in the almanac;
find out moonshine,
find out moonshine.

Bottom (the weaver), in
A Midsummer Night's Dream,
act III, line 53 (1594)

THE
GREEN BAG
ALMANAC
&
READER

2009

Francis Bacon, 1561-1626

Lawyer, writer, and sometime candidate to be the real author of the plays
attributed to Shakespeare. To learn more, or at least have more fun,
see Jasper Fforde, *The Eyre Affair* 37-40 (Penguin 2002).

THE

GREEN BAG

ALMANAC

OF USEFUL AND ENTERTAINING TIDBITS FOR
LAWYERS FOR THE YEAR TO COME

2009

– AND –

READER

OF EXEMPLARY LEGAL WRITING FROM THE
YEAR JUST PASSED

2008

SELECTED BY THE
LUMINARIES AND SAGES ON OUR BOARD OF ADVISERS

EDITED BY ROSS E. DAVIES

GREEN BAG PRESS
WASHINGTON, DC
2008

Recommended citation form:

[author, title], *in* 2009 GREEN BAG ALM. [page number]

First Elizabethan Edition
limited to 1800 copies

Green Bag Press
6600 Barnaby Street NW
Washington, DC 20015

Green Bag Press is a division of
The Green Bag, Inc., publisher of the
Green Bag, Second Series, an Entertaining Journal of Law.

For more information, please email
editors@greenbag.org or visit
www.greenbag.org.

ISSN: 1931-9711
ISBN 13: 978-1-933658-08-7
ISBN 10: 1-933658-08-8
Library of Congress Control Number: 2008920961

TABLES OF CONTENTS

READER
OF EXEMPLARY LEGAL WRITING 2008

✴ OPINIONS FOR COURTS ✴

✴ BOOKS ✴

★ SHORT ARTICLES ★

★ LONG ARTICLES ★

★ MISCELLANY ★

ALMANAC
OF USEFUL & ENTERTAINING TIDBITS

LAST YEAR & THIS YEAR

SHAKESPEARE

SHAKESPEARIAN FEATURES

OTHER TREASURES

PREFACE

This is the fourth *Green Bag Almanac & Reader*. We recognize that we are a bit late getting this edition off the presses and into your hands, and for that we apologize. We hope you will enjoy this book, off and on, for what is left of 2009. For a reminder of the reasons why the world needs our almanac and our reader, please read the "Preface" to our first (2006) edition. It is available on our web site (www.greenbag.org), in the "Almanac & Reader" section.

OUR DILIGENT BOARD

Our selection process for "Exemplary Legal Writing of 2008" was, like past years', not your typical invitation to competitive self-promotion by authors and their publishers and friends. We did not solicit (or accept) entries from contestants, charge them entry fees, or hand out blue, red, and white ribbons. Rather, we merely sought to:

> (a) organize a moderately vigilant watch for good legal writing, conducted by people (our Board of Advisers) who would know it when they saw it and bring it to our attention;

> (b) coordinate the winnowing of advisers' favorites over the course of the selection season, with an eye to harvesting a crop of good legal writing consisting of those works for which there was the most substantial support (our "Recommended Reading" list);

> (c) ballot our advisers to identify the cream of that already creamy crop; and then

> (d) present the results to you in a useful and entertaining format — this book.

The nitty-gritty of our process for selecting exemplars is a simple but burdensome series of exercises:

Step 1: Our advisers read legal writing as they always have, keeping an eye out for short works and excerpts of longer works that belong in a collection of good legal writing. When they find worthy morsels, they send them to the *Green Bag*. "Good legal writing" is read broadly for our purposes. "Good" means whatever the advisers and the volume editor think it does. As one experienced scholar and public servant on our board put it, "there is good writing in the sense of what is being said and also in the sense of how it is being said." Our advisers are looking for works that have something of each. "Legal" means anything written about law — opinions, briefs, articles, orders, statutes, books, motions, letters, emails, contracts, regulations, reports, speeches, and so on. "Writing" means ink-on-paper or characters-on-screen.

Step 2: The *Green Bag* organizes the advisers' favorites into categories, and then sends a complete set to every adviser. Advisers' names are not attached to the works they nominate. In other words, everything is anonymized. Advisers vote without knowing who nominated a piece. Similarly, their rankings are secret. No one but the volume editor ever sees individual advisers' rankings or knows who voted in which categories. And the editor destroys all individualized records once the *Almanac* is in print.

Advisers are free to vote in as many categories — or as few — as they desire. That is, although there may be scores of nominated works in total, they are free to select the types of writing they want to evaluate. Almost all — but invariably not all — advisers vote in each category.[1]

Step 3: The volume editor tallies the rankings and compiles the "Reader" portion of the *Almanac & Reader* based on the results, reserving, as editors tend to do, the right to add, subtract, and reorganize within reason. Nominated works not published in the book are listed in the "Recommended Reading" section.

Step 4: The advisers and the editor start all over again for next year's edition — a process which has been underway since last Halloween (recall that our annual cycle for selection of exemplary legal writing begins and ends on October 31), with dozens of nominees already in the queue for the 2010 *Almanac*.

Despite the substantial work involved in this business, most of our advisers seem to enjoy participating. Those who don't enjoy it appear to view this business as some sort of professional duty. Either way, we're glad to have them. But these are people with day jobs, other substantial commitments, and minimum sleep requirements. So not everyone can pitch in every year. Being listed as an adviser implies that a body has

---

[1] Given the caliber of our advisers, it should come as no surprise that several of them are also authors of exemplars appearing in this volume or included in our list of "Recommended Reading." Perhaps it should also come as no surprise — in a group that consists almost entirely of people who either work under the authority of, or engage from time to time in the contemplation of, 28 U.S.C. § 455(a) ("Any justice, judge, or magistrate of the United States shall disqualify himself in any proceeding in which his impartiality might reasonably be questioned.") or its state-law equivalents — that none of the advisers whose works are published in this volume voted for themselves.

done some advising, however, and it just doesn't seem right to burden someone with some small slice of the collective responsibility (or credit, if there is any) for a project in which they did not participate, at least this time around. So the list of board members published on the inside and the outside of this *Almanac* has changed since last year and will, we expect, continue to change from year to year. The fact that people come and go from the board does not necessarily indicate anything about their ongoing commitment to the *Almanac*, other than when they have had the time and inclination to participate. Of course, we hope they always will.

WHERE ARE THE BLOGS?

Last year I explained why we had not yet seen nominations from the blogosphere, and expressed hope that we would receive more over time. This year we took a small step. One blog entry made it into the packet of nominees sent to our board of sagacious and luminous advisers, and they selected it for inclusion in this year's *Almanac & Reader* (see page 491). Congratulations to the author — Judge Richard G. Kopf of the United States District Court for the District of Nebraska — and to the publisher — the *Ohio State Journal of Criminal Law*, which posts *OSJCL Amici: Views from the Field* at osjcl.blogspot.com.

JUST WHAT IS LEGAL WRITING?

We do not have an entirely satisfying answer. (Recall Justice Ronald Nehring's thoughtful letter on this subject on pages 9-10 of the 2007 *Almanac*.) As I explained above,

> "Good legal writing" is read broadly for our purposes. . . . "Legal" means anything written about law — opinions, briefs, articles, orders, statutes, books, motions, letters, emails, contracts, regulations, reports, speeches, and so on. . . .

But that does not mean all of our readers are quite so loosey-goosey. David Roe, an accomplished lawyer and an *Almanac* adviser, recently expressed his concerns:

> To the Editor:
> It's a pleasure to read through the Almanac nominations, and flattering to do it as one of your judges. But I find myself not voting for some of the best-written pieces in the bunch. They are *writing*, but they are not *legal writing* — written about legal subjects, but not written for legal purposes, and therefore not examples of the limited and technically demanding craft

that lawyers and judges must exercise in their professional roles.

Why niggle over the Almanac's definition of "legal writing," which now includes *New Yorker* and *Vanity Fair* pieces, front-page newspaper articles, and books of history and current affairs? They're certainly welcome leavening in the stack of reading you send us judges every fall, and nearly always better writing, as writing, than the best of opinions and briefs.

My sense of the Almanac's purpose, however, is to highlight and encourage excellent writing within the legal profession — to remind lawyers as they go about their written craft, fitting complex points and materials onto the page in as unassailable form as possible, that grace and pith also count. Legal writing in this sense operates within tight boundaries, and writing well within those boundaries is different from writing well in general.

What tighter definition of "legal writing" would I offer the Almanac? Not just documents with a file stamp, and not just articles in law reviews. Instead, how about writing that has primarily a professional legal purpose, or is meant for primarily a professional legal audience? This would exclude *New York Times* coverage of the U.S. Supreme Court but would include Stern & Gressman, or a do-it-yourself divorce manual, or a Scalia speech to the Federalist Society.

It's still a fuzzy line, and it would cut out some of the most pleasurable of your materials. But otherwise doesn't the slippery slope go all the way to the best writers in the world, whenever their subject matter happens to stray into legal territory — Merchant of Venice, The Trial, Bleak House?

Faithfully, and with thanks that this worthy exercise exists,

David Roe

Mr. Roe makes some good points and offers some promising suggestions. What do you think? Where would you draw the lines between what we should and should not consider, and how would you define the categores into which we ought to divide those things that fall inside the lines? The *Green Bag* would like to know. Please write to us at editors@greenbag.org.

And Homer Keeps on Nodding . . .

We continue to struggle, and fail, to produce a flawless big fat book in a hurry. Here are the errors we are sure we made in the 2008 *Almanac*:

Pages 5-6: Last year we said this:

> "Bob Berring extolled the wisdom of Meredith Wilson, not 'Mary Willson.' *See* Mary Whisner, *Almanac Errata Errata*, 10

Green Bag 2d 277 (2007). Professor Berring tactfully asks, 'Could this lead to an infinite series of corrections, like something drawn from M.C. Escher or perhaps based on Steven Colbert's portrait of Steven Colbert standing in front of a portrait of Steven Colbert . . . ?'"

Alas, the answer to Professor Berring's question is increasingly appearing to be "yes." In February Adam Sachs of San Francisco wrote to us:

> "Erratum again, in the 2008 Almanac on page 5: Re the note about page 7 of the 2007 Almanac, Bob Berring was probably extolling the wisdom of Meredith Willson, whose last name was also, I believe, misspelled in the last issue. To answer Bob's question, perhaps it would lead to an infinite series of corrections. When will they mesh back together is the question I'd ask Bob to answer."

To which Professor Berring replied:

> "There is something perfect about this one."

Page 252: And in March Jack Metzler of Washington, DC sent us this helpful email:

> "I write to note that the reprint of *The Adventure of Silver Blaze* in the 2008 Almanac appears to have a typo on page 252, third paragraph. The sentence that begins, 'But if falls away towards Mapleton' should, I believe, read, 'But _it_ falls away towards Mapleton . . . .'"

Mr. Metzler is correct.

Page 589: We put "Page 145-180" where "Pages 145-180" would have been better.

Page 591: We included a credit for a little treasure from Michael Stokes Paulsen that we decided to save for some other rainy day.

We will keep trying.

IN OTHER BUSINESS

Our goals remain the same: to present a useful and entertaining, perhaps even inspiring, monthly dose of our stock in trade — good legal reasoning and reporting, well-written — with moderate amounts of the traditional almanac potpourri of useful and distracting information thrown in. Like the law itself, the 2008 exemplars republished in this volume are wide-ranging in subject, form, and style. This year most of the potpourri has to do with Shakespeare; next year the mix will be mostly baseball-related.

With any luck we'll deliver some reading pleasure, a few role models, and some reassurance that the nasty things some people say about legal writing are not entirely accurate.

• • • •

Finally, the *Green Bag* proffers the traditional, and in our case deep and sincere, gratitude to you, our readers. Your continuing kind remarks about the *Almanac* are inspiring. Our hearts are replete with thankfulness. The *Green Bag* also thanks our Board of Advisers for nominating and selecting the works recognized here; the George Mason University School of Law and the George Mason Law & Economics Center for their continuing generous support of the *Green Bag*; Susan Davies, whose pains to improve this book we commend, as should everyone who shares in the gains; Susan Birchler, Ofemi Cadmus, Rachel Davies, Amy Flanagan, Paul Haas, Andrew Heger, Jeff Newman, Don Rebstock, and David Van Zandt; and Green Bag Fellow Patrick Foltz.

Ross E. Davies
December 25, 2008

[I would not] give one
scene in Shakespeare for
1000 Harringtons, Lockes
and [John] Adams.

Robert R. Livingston (1776)

RECOMMENDED READING

We have tallied the ballots and printed the top vote-getters in this book. They are the ones listed in the Table of Contents above and marked on the list below by a little *✶*. There were plenty of other good works on the ballot. We list them here. Congratulations to all.[1]

• • • •

OPINIONS FOR COURTS

Carlos Bea, *Navajo Nation v. U.S. Forest Service*, 535 F.3d 1058 (9th Cir. 2008)

Franklin D. Elia, *Krinsky v. Doe 6*, 159 Cal. App. 4th 1154 (6th Dist. 2008)

✶ Frank H. Easterbrook, *FTC v. QT, Inc.*, 512 F.3d 858 (7th Cir. 2008)

Ronald M. George, *In re Marriage Cases*, 43 Cal.4th 757 (2008)

Ruth Bader Ginsburg, *Taylor v. Sturgell*, 128 S. Ct. 2161 (2008)

Ronald Gould, *Witt v. Dep't of the Air Force*, 527 F.3d 806 (9th Cir. 2008)

Patrick E. Higginbotham, *In re Katrina Canal Litigation Breaches*, 524 F.3d 700 (5th Cir. 2008)

✶ Robert A. Katzmann, *Aris v. Mukasey*, 517 F.3d 595 (2d Cir. 2008)

Alex Kozinski, *Garcia-Aguilar v. U.S. District Court for the Southern Dist. of California*, 535 F.3d 1021 (9th Cir. 2008)

Michael McConnell, *Colorado Christian University v. Weaver*, 534 F.3d 1245 (10th Cir. 2008)

✶ M. Margaret McKeown, *Anderson v. Terhune*, 516 F.3d 781 (9th Cir. 2008) (en banc)

Antonin Scalia, *District of Columbia v. Heller*, 128 S. Ct. 2783 (2008)

J. Harvie Wilkinson III, *EEOC v. Sunbelt Rentals, Inc.*, 521 F.3d 306 (4th Cir. 2008)

William G. Young, *Situation Management Systems v. ASP Consulting Group*, 535 F. Supp. 2d 231 (D. Mass. 2008)

William J. Zloch, *In re Beck*, 526 F. Supp. 2d 1291 (S.D. Fla. 2007)

---

[1] Some publishers require consideration for republication that exceeds our modest resources. It was publishers' demands for money, not low supplies of votes, that precluded our presentation of Adam Liptak's article, *Illegal Globally, Bail for Profit Remains in U.S.*, and an extract from H. Jefferson Powell's book, *Constitutional Conscience: The Moral Dimension of Judicial Decision*.

Opinions Concurring, Dissenting, etc.

Samuel A. Alito Jr., *Kennedy v. Louisiana*, 128 S. Ct. 2641 (2008)

William A. Fletcher, *Navajo Nation v. U.S. Forest Service*, 535 F.3d 1058 (9th Cir. 2008)

Thomas Reavley, *Wheeler v. Pilgrim's Pride Corp.*, 536 F.3d 455 (5th Cir. 2008)

Robert Sack, *Arar v. Ashcroft*, 532 F.3d 157 (2d Cir. 2008)

Antonin Scalia, *Boumediene v. Bush*, 128 S. Ct. 2229 (2008)

David Souter, *United States v. Williams*, 128 S. Ct. 1830 (2008)

John Paul Stevens, *New York State Board of Elections v. Lopez Torres*, 128 S. Ct. 791 (2008)

John Paul Stevens, *Baze v. Rees*, 128 S. Ct. 1520 (2008)

Books

(including articles more than 25,000 words long)

Thomas B. Colby, *The Federal Marriage Amendment and the False Promise of Originalism*, 108 Columbia Law Review 529 (2008)

Mary L. Dudziak, *Exporting American Dreams* (Oxford University Press 2008)

Oona A. Hathaway, *Treaties End*, 117 Yale Law Journal 1236 (2008)

✯ Charles Lane, *The Day Freedom Died* (Henry Holt & Co. 2008)

✯ Victoria F. Nourse, *In Reckless Hands* (W.W. Norton & Co. 2008)

Nicholas Parrillo, *The De-Privatization of American Warfare*, 19 Yale Journal of Law & Humanities 1 (2007)

Justin Peacock, *A Cure for Night* (Doubleday Press 2008)

William D. Popkin, *Evolution of the Judicial Opinion: Institutional and Individual Styles* (New York University Press 2007)

H. Jefferson Powell, *Constitutional Conscience: The Moral Dimension of Judicial Decision* (University of Chicago Press 2008)

✯ Antonin Scalia & Bryan A. Garner, *Making Your Case: The Art of Persuading Judges* (Thomson/West 2008)

William J. Stuntz, *Unequal Justice*, 121 Harvard Law Review 1969 (2008)

Steven M. Teles, *The Rise of the Conservative Legal Movement* (Princeton University Press 2008)

Laurence H. Tribe, *The Invisible Constitution* (Oxford University Press 2008)

✭ Benjamin Wittes, *Law and the Long War: The Future of Justice in the Age of Terror* (Penguin Press 2008)

Jonathan Zittrain, *The Future of the Internet and How to Stop It* (Yale University Press 2008)

SHORT ARTICLES

Neil Kinkopf, *The Congress as Surge Protector*, www.acslaw.org/pdf/Kinkopf-Surge.pdf (2007)

Michael J. Klarman, *Conclusion, in Unfinished Business: Racial Equality in American History* (Oxford University Press 2007)

Adam Liptak, *If Your Hard Drive Could Testify . . .*, New York Times, January 7, 2008

Adam Liptak, *Illegal Globally, Bail for Profit Remains in U.S.*, New York Times, January 29, 2008

Theodore B. Olson, *Clinton v. Obama: The Lawsuit*, Wall Street Journal, February 11, 2008

✭ Norman Otto Stockmeyer, *To Err Is Human, To Moo Bovine: The Rose of Aberlone Story*, 24 Thomas M. Cooley Law Review 491 (2007)

✭ Jeffrey Toobin, *Death in Georgia*, The New Yorker, Feb. 4, 2008

Henry Weinstein, *Supreme Court takes up lethal injection battle*, Los Angeles Times, January 7, 2008

✭ J. Harvie Wilkinson III, *Toward One America: A Vision in Law*, 83 New York University Law Review 323 (2008)

LONG ARTICLES

Rachel E. Barkow, *The Ascent of the Administrative State and the Demise of Mercy*, 121 Harvard Law Review 1333 (2008)

✭ Michael Boudin, *Judge Henry Friendly and the Mirror of Constitiutional Law*, 82 New York University Law Review 975 (2007)

Jose Cabranes, *International Law By Consent of the Governed*, 42 Valparaiso University Law Review 119 (2007)

Scott Dodson, *Mandatory Rules*, 61 Stanford Law Review 1 (2008)

Lisa Eichhorn, *Clarity and the Rules of Civil Procedure: A Lesson from the Style Project*, 5 Journal of ALWD 1 (2008)

✶ Lee Epstein, Kevin Quinn, Andrew D. Martin & Jeffrey A. Segal, *On the Perils of Drawing Inferences About Supreme Court Justices from Their First Few Years of Service*, 91 Judicature 168 (2008)

Robert George, *Natural Law*, 31 Harvard Journal of Law & Public Policy 171 (2008)

Jamal Greene, *Giving the Constitution to the Courts*, 117 Yale Law Journal 886 (2008)

Steven G. Kalar and Jon M. Sands, *An Object All Sublime – Let the Punishment Fit the Crime*, The Champion 20 (March 2008)

Jamie Gibbs Pleune, *Is Scalian Standing the Latest Sighting . . . ?*, 38 Lewis & Clark Law School's Environmental Law Online

✶ James Robertson, *Quo Vadis, Habeas Corpus?*, 55 Buffalo Law Review 1063 (2008)

✶ Philippe Sands, *The Green Light*, Vanity Fair (May 2008)

Joseph W. Singer, *Things that We Would Like to Take for Granted*, 2 Harvard Law & Policy Review 139 (2008)

John Yoo, *Jefferson and Executive Power*, 88 Boston University Law Review 421 (2008)

MISCELLANY

✶ Richard G. Kopf, *The Top Ten Things I Learned From Apprendi, Blakely, Booker, Rita, Kimbrough and Gall*, osjcl.blogspot.com (2008)

Ronald B. Leighton, *Presidio Group LLC v. GMAC Mortgage LLC*, 2008 WL 2595675 (W.D. Wash. 2008)

Benjamin C. Mizer, *Application for a Stay*, *Brunner v. Ohio Republican Party*, 129 S. Ct. 5 (2008)

James R. Nowlin, *Waggoner v. Wal-Mart Stores, Inc.*, No. A-07-CA-703-JRN (W.D. Tex., June 3, 2007)

✶ John G. Roberts, Jr., *Pennsylvania v. Dunlap*, 129 S. Ct. 448 (2008)

Chris Satullo, *A not-so-glorious Fourth*, Philadelphia Inquirer, July 1, 2008

THE YEAR 2008 IN
GRAMMAR, USAGE &
WRITING

Bryan A. Garner†

JANUARY

The *Philadelphia Weekly* reported that "drive-by lexicologists nearly wet themselves last week as word spread about the burgeoning use of *yo* as a gender-neutral singular pronoun among Baltimore schoolchildren." It seems they are using *yo* not to replace the awkward *his or her* constructions, but instead primarily as a singular subject: "Yo sucks at magic tricks." "Yo handin' out papers." "Yo look like a sackass gump." (That is, "He sucks at magic tricks," "She's handing out papers," etc.) One hardly knows about the looking, but these sentences, some might think, make the speaker sound like a sackass gump (whatever that is). • According to *USA Today*, John Breen's website www.freerice.com, founded in October 2007, continued to gain popularity among Internet users. The vocabulary game presents a word and four possible definitions. Pick right, and the cash equivalent of 20 grains of rice is donated by site advertisers to the United Nation's World Food Program. In barely three months, the site produced donations of about $258,000. The *USA Today* article reported that Breen has now hired professional lexicographers to add 1,000 more words and five more levels of difficulty. • In the *Chicago Tribune*, Mary Schmich wrote an opinion piece that summed up an important grammatical truth: "Grammar is beautifully bipartisan. Whether you're for Clinton or Obama, Romney or McCain, you can be outraged by people who say 'between you and I' instead of, correctly, 'between you and me.'" But year by year, more and more of the electorate seems less and less outraged than ever about the barbarism *between you and I*. • *The Economist* reported that Udachkuax*a'a'ch, also known as Marie Smith, had died on January 21 —

---

† Bryan Garner is the author of more than a dozen books about words and their uses, including *Garner's Modern American Usage* (Oxford 2d ed. 2003). He is also the editor in chief of *Black's Law Dictionary* (West 8th ed. 2004) and president of Law-Prose, Inc. Copyright © 2008 Bryan A. Garner.

["

and with her another language. Mrs. Smith was the last speaker of Eyak, the tongue native to the tribe of the same name in southeastern Alaska. After her last sister died in the 1990s, Mrs. Smith had no one else to use it with. The language had been dying even in her youth, the magazine reported: in 1933 there were only 38 Eyaks left, and the language was forbidden in schools and salmon factories. She bore nine children, but none of them was interested in learning more than a few Eyak words. Mrs. Smith generally shunned visitors, but she took a liking to Michael Krauss with the University of Alaska at Fairbanks, who with her help compiled an Eyak dictionary and grammar.

FEBRUARY

In the *Boston Globe*, worry was expressed about the impending National Grammar Day (March 4) — a "holiday" sponsored by the Society for the Promotion of Good Grammar. The estimable John McIntyre of the *Baltimore Sun* was quoted as fretting over whether the day might "bring out the strident, self-appointed guardians of the language and judges of everyone else's speech and prose." Instead, McIntyre suggested, we should use the day as an opportunity to "reflect on our own use of language, to try to use words more carefully, and to cut everyone else a little slack." Sound advice. • The *Monterey County Herald* in California editorialized about an attempt by the Venezuelan government to stamp out English words that have crept into general use. Spanish, the Communications and Information Ministry reported, is "threatened by sectors that have started a battle for the cultural domination of our nations." The recently nationalized telecommunications company, CANTV, was ordered to avoid English words in business dealings and computer technology. "Say it in Spanish. Say it with pride," the ministry urged on stickers and banners. So *marketing, staff,* and *meeting* become *cercadeo, equipo,* and *reunion.* On the computer, enter your *contrasena* (password) and click your *raton* (mouse). The *Herald* opines: "It's probably only fair to warn Hugo Chavez of this, but the French tried the same thing he's trying, and it didn't work for them, either." • The Associated Press reported that punctuation in surnames "can stop you from voting, destroy your dental appointments, make it difficult to rent a car or book a flight, even interfere with your college exams." Despite 50 years of advances in computer programming, many computer systems cannot recognize punctuation such as apostrophes (as in O'Connor) or hyphens (as in Al-Athari), or recognize a space between parts of surnames (as in Van Kemp), leading to many identification problems. The problem famously arose during the 2004 Michigan caucuses when thousands of eligible voters' ballots weren't counted.

Things went more smoothly in Michigan this year, but surname-recognition problems persist. Some people just give up and surrender to technology, the AP reported. For example, Iraqi immigrant Lina Al-Athari dropped her hyphen and is now known as Lina Alathari. "There is no pronunciation difference," she said, "so I'm fine with it." • The *New York Times* reported that Senator John McCain's nomination could revive debates about the meaning of "natural-born citizen" as used in the U.S. Constitution. Does the term apply only to citizens born in the United States or does it include citizens (like McCain) born outside the U.S. (Panama Canal Zone) to parents who are U.S. citizens? It wasn't the first time the question had been raised, but it has never been definitively answered. The term wasn't in common use in the 18th century, and the Constitution's drafters didn't leave much evidence about their intended meaning. Barack Obama's election in November didn't end the debate either — although Obama was born in Hawaii after it gained statehood, his father was not a U.S. citizen. A new question arose about whether "natural-born citizen" covers a person born in the U.S. but who has only one American parent. The U.S. Supreme Court refused to hear that challenge, so there is still no definitive answer. • The *New York Times* extolled the use of a semicolon in a New York City Transit public-service placard that asked subway riders not to leave newspapers on the trains. The placard read, "Please put it in a trash can; that's good news for everyone." The *Times* considered the sighting of a semicolon significant because Americans prefer shorter sentences without them: "in literature and journalism, not to mention advertising, the semicolon has been largely jettisoned as a pretentious anachronism." In fact, when the *Times* asked the transit agency who was responsible, the writer expected a complaint rather than a punctuational plaudit.

MARCH

In England, the *Western Mail* reported that business leaders are warning that "Wales' future prosperity is at risk unless children are taught how to communicate in good, accurate English in the Internet age." This came as officials in England unveiled plans to clamp down on poor punctuation by exam candidates: England's Qualifications and Curriculum Authority is piloting a "functional literacy" test this year, with the aim of requiring students to punctuate accurately with commas, apostrophes, and inverted commas (quotation marks). They have a point there. • Lake Superior State University unveiled its 33rd annual List of Words Banished from the Queen's English for Misuse, Overuse, and General Uselessness. The winners (ahem, losers) were *organic* ("The possibility of a food item being inorganic, i.e., not being composed of carbon atoms, is nil."), *it is what it is*

("It accomplishes the dual feat of adding nothing to the conversation while also being phonetically and thematically redundant."), *under the bus* ("Please, just 'blame' them."), and *emotional* ("Reporters, short on vocabulary, often describe a scene as 'emotional.' Well sure, but which emotion?"). • The *Hartford Courant* reported that the Noah Webster House, birthplace of the famous lexicographer, will receive $100,000 in state money for renovations to prepare for the 250th anniversary of his birth in October. About 18,000 to 20,000 people visit the house each year. • Forty years after the publication of *The New Language of Politics,* William Safire came out with a fourth revised edition in time for the marathon 2008 presidential campaign. Reviewing *Safire's Political Dictionary* for *Newsweek,* Katie Baker noted how this revision — the latest since 1993 — reflects the fertile linguistic ground of the Bubba years (with Bill and Hillary Clinton's *bridge to the 21st century, soccer moms,* and *vast right-wing conspiracy*) and the Dubya years (with George W. Bush's *compassionate conservatism, decider,* and *misunderestimate*). The 862-page compilation features historical and etymological insight into well over a thousand words and phrases dear to the hearts of political junkies. Safire, who writes the weekly "On Language" column for the *New York Times Magazine,* no doubt collected many new tidbits from the 2008 campaigns, from *Joe the Plumber* to *lipstick on a pig* to *yes we can.* As Safire notes in his "prolegomenon" (= prefatory essay), quoting Disraeli, "Finality is not the language of politics."

APRIL

The *West Australian* reported that school exams are being dumbed down, noting that "a sample of next year's Year 12 English exam has fueled fears [that] education has gone off the rails." Whereas a 1965 paper required students to study Shakespeare and Chaucer and emphasized spelling and punctuation, the 2009 exam allows the study of Spiderman and film posters and also allows answers using mind maps, tables, and "dot points." A University of Western Australia lecturer sighed: "You have to entertain them somehow. If you gave them just the conventional literature approach most of them wouldn't know where to start." • The *Albany Times Union* reported that Erin McKean, author of *Weird and Wonderful Words* (2002) and editor in chief of *The New Oxford American Dictionary* (2005), asked John Linnell — songwriter for the rock band They Might Be Giants — to write a song using some imperiled words. And so he did: "Contrecoup," a ballad about a brain-damaged man on the romantic rebound. The song contains *contrecoup* (= an injury that is the result of a secondary blow), *limerent* (= possessing an intense romantic desire for another person), and *craniosophic* (= of or relating to an expertise in skulls). •

The Australian newspaper *Courier Mail* reported that "swearing is increasingly prevalent today." The reporter, Graham Readfearn, asked: "Just how flippin' offended would you be if every third freaking word in this story was obscene? Not at all? Just a bit, or would you be really friggin' peed-off about the whole damn thing?" A Queensland University linguist, Ghil'ad Zuckerman, opined that "there is a generational gap in language — things that we were forbidden to say in the past have now become common." Alas. ● Eugene Ehrlich, the self-educated lexicographer who wrote 40 dictionaries, thesauruses, and phrase books, died on April 5 at his home in Mamaroneck, N.Y., at the age of 85. As reported by the *New York Times*, someone said "To who?" while in the presence of Mr. Ehrlich on his deathbed. "To whom!" he exclaimed, with a weak voice but great authority.

MAY

In his widely read language column in the *New York Times Magazine*, William Safire emoted about emoticons, noting that "language is in its third phase of compression." First came contractions, then portmanteau words, and now emoticons. Safire recommended an article by Sali Tagliamonte and Derek Denis in the spring 2008 *American Speech*: "Linguistic Ruin? LOL! Instant Messaging and Teen Language." Like so many of Safire's columns, this one made us :-). ● In the *New York Times*, Virginia Heffernan reported on the *Oxford English Dictionary* and the possibility that the "book" may never again appear in a print version. "As of now," she wrote, "Oxford University Press has no official plans to publish a new print edition." Further: "Oxford gave us the modern dictionary; now it gives us the modern lexicographical Web site — if a subscriber-only site can still be described as 'modern.' . . . If you're smitten, $300 a year, or $30 a month, will get you unrivaled elegant and stylish entries. Geek out at OED.com." ● In an extended article on cultural "appropriacy," Kate Elwood wrote in the *Daily Yomiuri* of Japan that both teachers and learners of English as a second language "recognized grammatical errors more often than errors related to cultural appropriacy." But she concluded with the idea that "hopefully" something can be learned from the experience: "After all this time, when I'm the one on the receiving end, I may still react strongly to inappropriate speech acts." A better sense of appropriacy might lead everyone to recoil from inappropriate speech acts. Yet one wonders about the appropriacy of the word *appropriacy*. ● The *Patriot News* in Harrisburg, Pennsylvania, reported that some students of Middletown Area High School recognized the faces in their 2008 yearbook, but not all the names. Max Zupanovic, for example, was nowhere to be found, although "Max Supernova" bore a striking resemblance to him. Likewise, "Cameron Bandage" looked a lot like classmate Cameron Bendgen, "Kathy Airbag" looked like Kathy Carbaugh, "Alexandria Impolite" looked like Alessandra Ippolito, and so on. The book's printer, Taylor Publishing, blamed its computer spell-checker and said such errors are common. The company provided free stickers with the corrected names and accepted full responsibility, said Ed Patrick, a Taylor spokesman. Unfortunately, when the *Patriot News* broke the story, it misspelled *Patrick*.

JUNE

In the *Times Higher Education Supplement*, Professor Tim Birkhead of Sheffield University reported on "Writing Matters," a recent report by the Royal Literary Fund, which acknowledges the widespread nature of illiteracy. RLF fellows enter British universities to explore the way students write and then to work with them on improving their writing skills. Birkhead estimated that 70% of his tutorial time with students involves correcting undergraduate English. • The *New Zealand Herald* reported that there can be pragmatic reasons for using the adjective *alternate* where the adjective *alternative* is called for: When an offramp is closed or closing, signs urge motorists to use "alternate offramps" instead of "alternative offramps," because the variable message signs can hold only 10 characters per line — so *alternative* won't fit. Hence the poor usage is subliminally reinforced in the minds of all New Zealand motorists. • According to the *New York Times*, the International Astronomical Union, which two years ago took away a planet (Pluto), gave us a new word. On June 11, the IAU officially inaugurated the word *plutoid* to denote a dwarf planet outside the orbit of Neptune. Pluto is one of two known plutoids, the other being the slightly bigger Eris, discovered in 2003. Having downgraded Pluto to a "dwarf planet" and thereby provoking a small furor, the IAU was apparently seeking to quell some of the upset with its neologism.

JULY

The publisher Perigree Trade released Ammon Shea's *Reading the OED: One Man, One Year, 21,730 Pages*. It soon became a bestseller — not quite approaching the popularity of Simon Winchester's *The Professor and the Madman*, but demonstrating yet again the broad appeal of the world's greatest feat of lexicography, the *Oxford English Dictionary*. The book's 26 chapters (A–Z) chronicle Shea's trudge through the 137-pound tome, focusing on the most startling, amusing, shocking, and useless words in each letter of the alphabet, such as *acnestis* (= the point of the back between the shoulders and the lower back, which cannot be reached to be scratched); *agelastic* (= a person who never laughs); *bed-swerver* (= an unfaithful spouse); *elumbated* (= weakened in the loins); *grinagog* (= a person who is always grinning); *kakistocracy* (= government by the worst citizens); *natiform* (= buttock-shaped); *unasinous* (= being equal to another in stupidity); and *wonderclout* (= something showy but worthless). ● After two years of increasingly popular podcasts on grammar, Mignon Fogarty, aka Grammar Girl, did an interview with the *Atlanta Journal-Constitution* upon the publication of her book *Quick and Dirty Tips for Better Writing*. Q: "How do you feel about spell-checker or grammar-check?" Fogarty: "I think spell-check is a good thing. I don't think you should ever send off a document without running it through spell-check. Grammar-check is not as useful. . . . I would never trust one." ● In the *Times* of Trenton, New Jersey, Peter G. Verniero wrote an op-ed piece about *District of Columbia v. Heller*, the Supreme Court's gun-rights decision. Of Justice Scalia's 64-page majority opinion, Verniero writes that it is "clearly written, scholarly, and meticulous in its treatment of the relevant issues." Then he adds: "[Justice Scalia] traces the history of the Second Amendment from before we were a country, using readable language resembling a David McCullough narrative. He parses the amendment's text, phrase by phrase, like a professional grammarian, which judges sometimes have to become when they are called on to interpret statutes and regulations." ● The linguist David Crystal's newest book, *txtng: the gr8 db8*, was released. In it, Crystal looks into the common concerns that text-messaging and similar short-form communications are eroding standards in the English language. Despite fears of declining literacy, Crystal argues that texting actually depends on good verbal skills to create and use abbreviated forms that communicate effectively and wittily. As support, he points to Coventry University research showing that adolescents who text score higher on reading and vocabulary tests than their peers who don't. Crystal also argues that texting is a sign of healthy linguistic evolution. Nonstandard spellings are also a part of English literary tradition (the *Oxford English Dictionary* has recorded *cos* from 1828, *wot* from 1829, *luv* from 1898, *thanx* from 1936, and *ya* from 1941). Both change and complaints about change are themselves unchanging. As Crystal notes, "The English essayist Joseph Addison complained about the way words were being 'miserably curtailed.' That was in 1711."

AUGUST

Laurence Urdang, the prolific lexicographer who helped write and publish more than 100 dictionaries and other reference books, died in Branford, Connecticut, at the age of 81. He was the founding editor of *Verbatim* magazine, a scholarly quarterly with a wry sense of humor. As managing editor of the first edition of the *Random House Dictionary of the English Language*, Urdang brought lexicography into the digital age, being the first to use computers to help compile dictionary entries. • The London *Times* reported that lexicographers at the Collins publishing house had isolated the English word most commonly misspelled (10% of the time) in published documents and on the Internet: *supersede*, which represents a bold departure from the etymologically unrelated words *cede, intercede, precede,* and *secede*. The article also named the top five misspellings resulting from a pronunciation that differs from the spelling: *conscience, foreign, indict, mortgage,* and *phlegm*. • The *Toronto Star* reported on the voguishness of the insulting term *douchebag* (= a stupid, contemptible, despicable man). The word dates from the 1940s, but it has now spread to new heights of popularity — even as the device literally denoted by the word is in steep decline. Increasingly, too, the term is shortened to *douche* or *d-bag*. • The *Mississauga News* reported that 17-year-old Mark Breiva was crowned the fastest text-messenger in Canada, for which honor he won a $25,000 first prize in the inaugural Canadian Texting Championships. According to the *News*, "His correctly spelled, fastest-entered winning phrase in the regionals, done in just 7.401 seconds, was, 'my hom is on da dnc flor.'" What is meant by "correctly spelled" — or indeed what is meant by the winning message itself — remains a mystery to many readers (including me).

SEPTEMBER

In her convention acceptance speech as the Republican vice-presidential candidate, Sarah Palin referred to herself as a "pitbull with lipstick." Soon after, Democratic presidential candidate Barack Obama said of GOP promises to change policies: "You can put lipstick on a pig, but it's still a pig." That provoked a flurry of Republican dudgeon about a sexist insult (even though Palin's running mate, John McCain, had used the folksy metaphor himself several times). Lexicologists soon traced the origins of the catchphrase to a 1985 San Francisco radio program, in which the host was condemning a plan to build a new sports stadium. The next year, Texas Democrat Jim Hightower used the phrase to describe a reshuffle of President Ronald Reagan's Cabinet. But it was Texas Governor Ann Richards who, in 1991, used a variation on the phrase most memorably. Producing her first budget, she declared, "This is not another one of those deals where you put lipstick on a hog and call it a princess." • In the *Hindu*, Snigdha Poonam editorialized in favor of Britain's "New Literacy" movement, which holds that the teaching of correct spelling is an elitist imposition that discriminates against the disadvantaged. He quoted a professor at Buckinghamshire New University who argues that academics should grant a spelling amnesty to the 20 most common slips, such as "Febuary" and "ignor," and start treating them as variants of standard spellings. Poonam dismissed arguments that accepting misspellings "will only legitimize inferior standards of literacy in this already philistine intellectual climate of our times." • On September 24, National Punctuation Day, Craig Wilson devoted his *USA Today* column to reflecting on the fact that (1) a semicolon is not a medical problem; (2) good punctuation brings periods of happiness; and (3) an exclamation point should never appear unless the sentence is about the end of the world, and the end of the world is tomorrow. • The *Sunday Telegraph* reported that the British publishing house Penguin has produced a dictionary of "Indlish" called *Entry from Backside Only* — an Indian phrase commonly used on signposts to indicate the rear entrance of a building. The author-lexicographer of *Backside*, Binoo John, said he was inspired by years of reading newspaper reports of politicians "air-dashing" to destinations, "issueless" couples (those without children), and people "preponing" (bringing forward) meetings. And a typical Indlish opening for correspondence: "Dear Sir, with reference to your above see my below." • The celebrated novelist and essayist David Foster Wallace committed suicide by hanging himself — causing wide and profound bereavement within the literary world. The obituary in the *New York Times* described his writing as "prodigiously observant, exuberantly plotted, grammatically and etymologically challenging, philosophically probing, and culturally hypercontemporary." Wallace was 46.

OCTOBER

The *Toronto Star* reported that Canadian English spelling, a sort of British–American hybrid, is being "denationalized by stealth" through spellcheckers and American online dictionaries. The newspaper also reported that Oxford University Press had laid off all four staff members of *The Oxford Canadian Dictionary*, citing decreased demand for print dictionaries. • The *San Jose Mercury News* reported that the economic downturn has had lexicographic ramifications: "fashionistas" who buy handbags with four-digit price tags are reforming themselves into "recessionistas" who buy imitations for under $100. *Recessionista* is defined as a style maven on a tight budget. • In the *Independent* (London), John Walsh reviewed Jonathon Green's new book the *Chambers Slang Dictionary* (2008) as a phenomenal compendium of nonstandard usages. Noting that Green has a "soft spot for rude words" — especially terms for body parts, sexual activities, disease, and bathroom practices that are not discussed in the presence of children and the clergy, much less great-aunts — Walsh hailed

Green as Britain's "indefatigable lexicographer of filth, a tireless troweller in the slurry of the unsayable." • John Morse, president and publisher of Merriam-Webster Inc., delivered a lecture at the U.S. Embassy in Tokyo to commemorate the 250th anniversary of the birth of Noah Webster. Morse argued that Webster's three urgent aims as a lexicographer in the early 19th century were to educate (thus building a competent electorate for the fledgling democracy), to unify (by creating a linguistic standard), and to inspire (by legitimizing American English). • Writing in the *New York Times*, Simon Winchester elucidated the sad development of the vogue word *subprime* (*pre-slime*, as he gingerly put it). It seems that until recently the *OED* had recorded only the 1976 sense "of or relating to a loan offered below the prime rate and typically offered only to the most desirable borrowers." Now a new definition has been added: "of or designating a loan, typically having relatively unfavorable terms, made to a borrower who does not qualify for other loans because of a poor credit history." As Winchester noted, "You can usually tell that a period of human disquietude has evolved into something of historical significance when the lexicographers become involved."

NOVEMBER

The *Columbus Dispatch* ran an interview with Roy Blount Jr. about his newly released *Alphabet Juice*, whose subtitle is *The Energies, Gists, and Spirits of Letters, Words, and Combinations Thereof; Their Roots, Bones, Innards, Piths, Pips, and Secret Parts, Tinctures, Tonics, and Essences; with Examples of Their Usage Foul and Savory.* In the interview, Blount says that the subtitle is a tribute to his ancestor, Sir Thomas Blount, whose 1656 *Glossographia* likewise had a voluble subtitle. • On November 24, it was announced that 33-year-old Henry Hitching won a top British literary award, the John Llewellyn Rhys Prize, for his new book *The Secret Life of Words*. The book is a fascinating account of how the English language has adapted words from around the world and through the ages. • Upon leaving the school board in Richmond, Virginia, Keith West wrote a thoughtful commentary for the *Richmond Times-Dispatch* pointing out that tucking in shirts has become a point of contention in the Richmond school district. West argued that "students who can't be convinced to tuck their shirttails in are unlikely to grasp how important it is to use good grammar." • Karen Duncan of Eugene, Oregon, laid into her local newspaper, the *Register-Guard*, in a letter to the editor objecting to the editors' failure to enforce the distinction between *lie* and *lay*: "Usually, I ignore it when I come across this bad construction in the *Register-Guard*, but the Nov. 10 paper was too much. In the City/Region section there were two articles describing people being forced to 'lay' on the floor." The articles had nothing to do with nonconsensual sex. • HarperCollins announced that the word *meh* has been included in the 30th anniversary edition of the *Collins English Dictionary*. Although the origins of *meh* (a verbal shrug) are murky, according to a report of the *Press of Atlantic City*, "the term grew in popularity after being used in a 2001 episode of 'The Simpsons' in which Homer suggests a day trip to his children, Bart and Lisa." They both just reply "Meh" and keep watching TV.

DECEMBER

In Australia, the *Brisbane News* reported that "textese," the language of instant messaging, benefits the senders more than the receivers. In a study of 55 students, almost half of them took twice as long to read text messages using the slangy shorthand, as opposed to standard English versions. Among the abbreviations that are spreading: *143* means "I love you" (from the number of letters in each word), *404* means "clueless" (from the error message when a browser can't find a webpage), and *book* means "cool" (for reasons unclear to this writer). • England's *Western Morning News* reported that Oxford University Press has issued the latest version of the *Oxford Junior Dictionary*, which has become multicultural and therefore removed references to Christmas — as a result of which there are now no entries for *carol, holly, manger,* and *mistletoe*. Other Christian words are gone, too: *abbey, aisle, altar, bishop, chapel, christen, disciple, minister, monastery, monk, nun, parish, pew, psalm, saint, sin, devil,* and *vicar* are, according to the report, "no longer deemed to be a necessary part of a child's vocabulary." • London's *Daily Mail* reported on a rather different aspect of historical lexicography: according to a new biography by Jeffrey Meyers (*Samuel Johnson: The Struggle*), Samuel Johnson "enjoyed being thrashed by his mistress, Hester Thrale," whose "ritualistic whippings" gave Johnson "masochistic pleasure in pain and humiliation." • In Singapore, the *Straits Times* reported that the Speak Good English Movement, which promotes the use of standard English as opposed to Singlish (a dialectal form of Singapore English), is the bane of local linguists. The linguists favor allowing Singlish to flourish. According to sociolinguist Anthea Fraser Gupta, Singapore "is the equivalent of a really well-equipped laboratory for a chemist." • In the *Daily Press* of Newport News, Virginia, Tony Gabriele proposed that the legislature should enact an "I'm like" Regulatory Revenue Act. It refers, of course, to taxing the spreading practice of people saying "I'm like such-and-such" instead of "I said such-and-such." Gabriele opined that "if we all cooperate, we can collect billions to send to the federal government."

NOTABLE LANDMARKS

250 years ago: On 16 October 1758, Noah Webster was born in West Hartford, Connecticut. **245 years ago:** On May 16, 1763, the English lexicographer, author, and wit Samuel Johnson first met his future biographer, James Boswell. **180 years ago:** Noah Webster published his magnum opus, the two-volume unabridged *American Dictionary of the English Language*. **140 years ago:** The most scurrilous, fly-specking, stricture-ridden book ever written on English usage was published in London: George Washington Moon's *The Bad English of Lindley Murray and Other Writers on the English Language: A Series of Criticisms*. **100 years ago:** One of the most important books in English-usage circles was published in New York: Thomas R. Lounsbury's *The Standard of Usage in English*. **80 years ago:** The first edition of *The Oxford English Dictionary* was completed. **50 years ago:** Theodore M. Bernstein's first usage book, *Watch Your Language*, was published.

One-half the doubts in life arise
from the defects of language.

William Johnson (1824)

THE YEAR IN LAW
2007-2008

John P. Elwood[†]

2007

Nov. 8: By a vote of 53-40, the Senate confirms former federal judge Michael Mukasey as the 81st Attorney General of the United States.

Nov. 15: Home run king Barry Bonds is indicted for perjury and obstruction of justice for telling a federal grand jury he did not knowingly use performance-enhancing drugs.

Nov. 16: The Senate announces that it will hold a series of "pro forma sessions" at which no business will be conducted during the upcoming recess in an effort to prevent President Bush from making recess appointments, the first use of such sessions for that purpose.

Dec. 1: According to a determination made by the Business Cycle Dating Committee, the U.S. economy enters a recession during December 2007.

Dec. 6: The Bush Administration announces a plan for a five-year freeze in qualifying home loan rates to address a looming mortgage crisis.

Dec. 7: Newspapers report that the CIA destroyed videotapes of the interrogation of high-value al Qaeda detainees; the agency states that it did so to protect the identity of investigators. The next day, the Justice Department announces that it has opened an investigation. ● After mailed summonses are returned because the addresses are "incomplete," a judge in India uses a newspaper ad to summon Hindu gods Ram and Hanuman to testify in a property dispute involving two temples.

Dec. 9: The *Washington Post* reports that several members of Congress, including Speaker of the House Nancy Pelosi (D-CA), were briefed in 2002

---

on the use of "waterboarding" and other interrogation techniques on high-value al Qaeda detainees and either did not object or supported it.

Dec. 10: Former Vice President Al Gore and the Intergovernmental Panel on Climate Change receive the Nobel Peace Prize for their work on global warming. • Former Atlanta Falcons quarterback Michael Vick is sentenced to 23 months in federal prison for his involvement in a dog-fighting ring.

Dec. 11: In a rare public opinion, the Foreign Intelligence Surveillance Court holds that it will not make public documents regarding the Bush Administration's warrantless NSA wiretapping program because of a "real risk of harm to national security interests." • The U.S. Sentencing Commission unanimously decides to make a reduction to the crack cocaine sentencing guidelines retroactive, giving thousands of inmates an opportunity to reduce their sentences.

Dec. 12: For the second time, President Bush vetoes legislation to expand the SCHIP government-provided health insurance program for children.

Dec. 13: The Senate Judiciary Committee finds former presidential adviser Karl Rove and current Chief of Staff Joshua B. Bolten in contempt of Congress for refusing to testify and to turn over documents in the investigation of the 2006 removal of nine U.S. Attorneys. • Former Sen. George Mitchell releases his report on the use of performance-enhancing drugs in Major League Baseball. The 409-page report implicates 86 players, including such prominent players as Roger Clemens and Barry Bonds. • Liberty City Seven defendant Lyglenson Lemorin is acquitted of federal charges that he plotted to join forces with al Qaeda to blow up Chicago's Sears Tower; the judge declares a mistrial for six codefendants.

Dec. 17: New Jersey abolishes the death penalty, the first state to do so in more than 40 years.

Dec. 18: Aruba authorities, saying there is insufficient evidence to charge anyone in the 2005 disappearance of American teenager Natalee Holloway, close their investigation.

Dec. 19: Congress passes a $555 billion bill that funds the Iraq war well into 2008. • The EPA denies California's application to adopt greenhouse gas emission standards for cars. The same day, President Bush signs legislation requiring production of more fuel-efficient vehicles and wider ethanol use.

Dec. 21: A New York appeals court, citing evidence implicating others in the crime, overturns the murder conviction of Martin H. Tankleff, imprisoned 17 years for killing his parents.

Dec. 26: Newspapers report that oil services company VECO Corp. provided more than $150,000 worth of labor renovating the home of Sen. Ted Stevens (R-AK).

Dec. 31: President Bush pocket vetoes a defense bill containing a provision that would expose the Iraqi government to lawsuits for wrongdoing during the Saddam Hussein era, saying it would imperil Iraq's financial health at a critical juncture. • After more than three decades in prison for attempting to assassinate President Gerald R. Ford, Sara Jane Moore is released on parole.

2008

Jan. 2: Attorney General Mukasey appoints career federal prosecutor John Durham to investigate whether CIA officials broke the law by destroying interrogation videotapes. • California and 15 other states sue the EPA for denying their application to regulate vehicular greenhouse gas emissions. • Oil prices briefly pass the $100 per-barrel mark for the first time in history. By July, the per-barrel U.S. price has hit $145.29; by late November, it has tumbled to $49.62.

Jan. 3: First-term Illinois Sen. Barack Obama wins the Iowa caucuses among Democrats; former Arkansas Gov. Mike Huckabee wins among Republicans.

Jan. 4: Convicted terrorist Jose Padilla sues former Office of Legal Counsel attorney John C. Yoo, based on allegations that he was tortured as a result of memoranda Yoo prepared.

Jan. 8: In what is widely seen as a dual comeback, Sen. Hillary Clinton wins the New Hampshire primary among Democrats and Sen. John McCain wins among Republicans.

Jan. 11: Three former leaders of an Islamic charity are convicted in Boston on federal tax and fraud charges for using tax exemptions to hide support for alleged terrorists overseas. • Former Olympic gold medalist Marion Jones is sentenced to six months in prison for lying to investigators about using performance-enhancing drugs.

Jan. 12: Iraq's Parliament passes a law allowing some former Baath Party members to take government jobs or receive pensions, a key legislative benchmark the U.S. had long sought to promote reconciliation. Former Baathists express skepticism.

Jan. 16: Former Rep. Mark Siljander (R-MI) is indicted on federal charges stemming from alleged ties to an Islamic charity that sent money to suspected terrorists.

Jan. 17: The White House discloses that it recycled its backup computer tapes of e-mail before October 2003, and acknowledges the possibility that electronic messages have been lost. In March, it is disclosed that some old hard drives were destroyed. ● The D.C. Circuit vacates the conviction of former General Services Administration official David Safavian, convicted as part of the Abramoff lobbying investigation, on the ground that the charges were legally insufficient.

Jan. 18: Mohammed Mansour Jabarah is sentenced in Manhattan federal court to life in prison for his participation in a plot to bomb U.S. embassies in Singapore and the Philippines.

Jan. 22: Convicted terrorist Jose Padilla is sentenced to more than 17 years' imprisonment.

Feb. 1: A jury finds actor Wesley Snipes guilty on three misdemeanor charges for failing to file federal income tax returns but acquits him of felony charges of conspiracy to defraud the IRS. In April, he is sentenced to three years' imprisonment.

Feb. 5: Super Tuesday. Sen. Obama wins 13 states, Sen. Clinton 9. Obama goes on to win 11 straight contests, building a delegate lead from which Clinton never recovers.

Feb. 6: Chinese and U.S. businesses and executives are indicted for manufacturing and importing a tainted pet food ingredient, which killed and sickened countless pets in 2007.

Feb. 8: The Nebraska Supreme Court rules that executing convicted murderers in the electric chair is cruel and unusual punishment.

Feb. 11: The Defense Department announces that Khalid Sheikh Mohammed, Walid Muhammad Salih Mubarek bin 'Attash, Ramzi Binalshibh, Ali Abdul Aziz Ali, Mustafa Ahmed Adam al Hawsawi, and Mohamed al Kahtani have been charged for the 9/11 attacks. At arraignment, Mohammed says he welcomes martyrdom. ● Plaintiffs' lawyer Bill Lerach is sentenced to two years in federal prison for giving plaintiffs kickbacks to gain control of lawsuits and win larger fees.

Feb. 13: The Senate Ethics Committee rebukes Sen. Larry Craig (R-ID) for his 2007 conviction for disorderly conduct in an airport men's restroom. • Iraqi lawmakers pass three key measures: a $48-billion national budget, an amnesty bill, and legislation paving the way for provincial elections.

Feb. 14: The House of Representatives holds Joshua Bolten and Harriet Miers in contempt for failing to produce documents and testify regarding the removal of nine U.S. Attorneys.

Feb. 21: Three former employees of the British bank National Westminster Bank are sentenced to 37 months in prison for fraud arising from a transaction with former Enron executives.

Feb. 29: Dawn Wells, who played "Mary Ann" on the television series Gilligan's Island, is sentenced to five days in jail after being arrested with marijuana in her car.

Mar. 3: Federal District Judge Mark R. Filip is confirmed as Deputy Attorney General.

Mar. 4: Sen. Clinton wins contests in Texas and Ohio, denting Sen. Obama's delegate lead. • James Clark, chief of staff to former Alaska Gov. Frank H. Murkowski, pleads guilty to accepting nearly $70,000 in illegal polling and consulting expenses from VECO Corp. for Murkowski's 2006 re-election campaign.

Mar. 8: President Bush vetoes legislation that would have limited CIA interrogations to methods authorized in the Army Field Manual, saying that it is important that al Qaeda and other terrorists not know the techniques they may face upon capture.

Mar. 10: The House Judiciary Committee files suit to force Joshua Bolten and Harriet Miers to provide information about the removal of nine U.S. Attorneys. • Newspapers report that New York Gov. Eliot Spitzer patronized a high-priced prostitution ring. Spitzer publicly apologizes; two days later, he resigns.

Mar. 14: Bear Stearns turns to rival JP Morgan Chase and the Federal Reserve Bank for an emergency bailout. Days later, JP Morgan Chase announces it is buying Bear Stearns.

Mar. 18: Sen. Obama delivers a speech on race, in part to distance himself from controversial remarks by his longtime pastor, the Rev. Jeremiah Wright.

Mar. 20: Melvyn Weiss becomes the fourth Milberg Weiss partner to admit criminal conduct, when he pleads guilty to racketeering stemming from concealed payments to plaintiffs.

Mar. 24: Federal prosecutors charge Puerto Rico Gov. Aníbal Acevedo Vilá and associates with conspiracy, false statements, fraud, and tax crimes related to campaign financing. In December, a judge dismisses 15 of 24 charges, all but two of them with prejudice. • Chi Mak, a former defense contractor engineer, is sentenced to 293 months in prison for conspiring to export military technology to the People's Republic of China.

Mar. 25: The Supreme Court rules 6-3 in *Medellin v. Texas* that neither the President nor the International Court of Justice has the authority to order a Texas court to reopen a death penalty case involving a foreign national. Texas executes Medellin in August, drawing a formal protest from Mexico.

Mar. 27: The Eleventh Circuit orders convicted former Alabama Gov. Don Siegelman released pending the appeal of his corruption case. The same day, the House Judiciary Committee seeks his testimony on claims of selective prosecution by the Justice Department.

Mar. 31: Former Defense Department official Gregg William Bergersen pleads guilty to conspiring to disclose national defense information to the People's Republic of China.

April 2: Mose Jefferson, brother of indicted Rep. William Jefferson (D-LA), is charged with bribery to help secure $14 million in public contracts. • Arkansas Gov. Mike Beebe signs a technical correction bill establishing 18 as the minimum age for marriage; a scrivener's error had removed the minimum age.

Apr. 15: Colorado physicist Daniel Max Sherman pleads guilty to seeking to transmit export controlled technical data to a foreign national from the People's Republic of China.

Apr. 16: The Supreme Court rules 7-2 in *Baze v. Rees* that Kentucky's method of lethal injection does not violate the Eighth Amendment's prohibition on cruel and unusual punishment. • Roger Von Bergendorff is charged with possession of ricin after being found unconscious in a Las Vegas hotel room with the toxin, firearms, and a silencer.

Apr. 22: Former Justice Department official Robert Coughlin II pleads guilty to accepting meals and golf outings from an Abramoff associate in exchange for helping his clients.

Apr. 28: The Supreme Court rules 6-3 in *Crawford v. Marion County Election Board* that Indiana's voter ID law does not violate the Constitution. • David M. Fish is sentenced to 30 months in prison for illegally distributing newly released movies, games, software and music online.

May 3: In response to a request for a protective order to avoid having to be deposed in another state, federal District Judge James Nowlin orders the deposition to occur on the Texas-Arkansas state line on the steps of the Texarkana federal courthouse.

May 8: The former highest-ranking Qantas Airways cargo executive in the U.S. pleads guilty to conspiring to fix international air cargo rates. • Former Alaska state representative Victor H. Kohring is sentenced to 42 months in federal prison for soliciting financial benefits from VECO Corp.

May 12: The trial of R&B star R. Kelly begins on charges that he videotaped himself having sex with an underage girl. One potential juror is excused for stating, "R. Kelly may have led the Taliban in attacking us on 9/11, but you can't prove it." R. Kelly is acquitted.

May 13: Businessman Tai Shen Kuo pleads guilty to federal charges of conspiring to deliver national defense information to the People's Republic of China.

May 15: By a 4-3 vote, the California Supreme Court holds that a voter-approved ban on gay marriage violates the state constitution. • Lori Drew of Missouri is indicted for fraudulently using a MySpace account to pose as a teenage boy to torment a 13 year-old female neighbor, who later committed suicide. In November, Drew is convicted of three misdemeanors, but acquitted of felony charges. • Celebrity private investigator Anthony Pellicano is convicted of racketeering charges for using unlawful methods to dig up dirt for use in lawsuits, divorces, and business disputes.

May 19: The Supreme Court by a 7-2 vote in *United States v. Williams* upholds Congress's effort to combat child pornography on the Internet, concluding that criminalizing "pandering" of real or purported obscene material does not violate free-speech guarantees.

May 20: A divided panel of the D.C. Circuit holds in *American Council of the Blind v. Paulson* that U.S. paper money must be modified to enable the blind to determine denominations. • A divided panel of the Fourth Circuit strikes down Virginia's "partial-birth infanticide" statute. The court grants rehearing en banc on July 28. • In Iowa, 85 defendants arrested during a major sting operation against illegal immigrants working at

Agriprocessors Inc. plead guilty to immigration offenses. In November, federal authorities indict Agriprocessors for harboring undocumented aliens.

May 21: President Bush vetoes the farm bill. Congress later overrides the veto, but inadvertently omits a 34-page section when sending it to the White House, so that the President vetoes a different bill from the one it passed. Congress re-passes the entire bill, the President vetoes it again, and, in June, Congress successfully overrides the President's second veto. ● The Ninth Circuit holds that the military cannot automatically discharge people because they are gay, but must show that an individual's dismissal furthers troop readiness and unit cohesion.

May 27: Barry Gitarts is the fifteenth person convicted of copyright infringement as part of the largest criminal music piracy prosecution in U.S. history.

May 29: New York Gov. David A. Paterson directs that same-sex marriages "legally performed elsewhere will be recognized in New York state." ● The Texas Supreme Court holds that officials should not have seized children from a polygamist sect's compound because the state failed to show they were in danger. ● Track coach Trevor Graham is convicted of lying to agents in a federal steroids probe.

May 30: A three-judge District Court holds that Congress acted constitutionally when it extended for another 25 years the Voting Rights Act's requirement that areas with a history of racial discrimination obtain federal preclearance for any changes in voting procedures.

June 3: Sen. Obama obtains commitments of sufficient "superdelegates" to clinch the Democratic Party nomination for President. ● Christopher Paul, aka "Abdul Malek," pleads guilty to conspiring to use a weapon of mass destruction against targets in Europe and the United States.

June 5: Antoin 'Tony' Rezko, a former Obama fundraiser, is convicted of mail and wire fraud. ● A brother, sister, and niece of indicted Rep. William Jefferson are charged with pocketing more than $600,000 intended for charitable and educational projects. ● More than 800 black farmers file a new lawsuit against the Department of Agriculture after Congress enacted a law that authorized reopening a 1999 discrimination settlement. ● Patricia Vincent, convicted of chopping down trees on national forest land to improve her view of Lake Tahoe, is sentenced to approximately four minutes of probation. (Before sentencing, Vincent performed community service and paid $100,000 in restitution.)

June 12: The Supreme Court holds 5-4 in *Boumediene v. Bush* that terrorism suspects held at Guantanamo Bay have a right to habeas corpus under the Constitution and that a provision of the Military Commissions Act is an unconstitutional suspension of that right.

June 13: A federal jury in Ohio convicts Mohammad Zaki Amawi, Marwan Othman El-Hindi, and Wassim I. Mazloum of conspiring to commit terrorist acts against Americans overseas.

June 18: Software engineer Xiaodong Sheldon Meng is sentenced to 24 months in prison for selling stolen military-application trade secrets to the People's Republic of China.

June 19: Former Bear Sterns managers Ralph Cioffi and Matthew Tannin are charged with misleading investors into holding hedge funds heavily exposed to subprime mortgages. Deputy Attorney General Mark Filip announces that a nationwide law enforcement effort against mortgage fraud has brought charges against more than 400 individuals involving losses of more than $1 billion.

June 20: President Bush invokes executive privilege in withholding documents from a congressional investigation into whether the White House pressured EPA to weaken decisions on smog and greenhouse gases. • In the first merits case under the Detainee Treatment Act, the D.C. Circuit holds that there was insufficient basis for the Pentagon's classification of Guantanamo Bay detainee Huzaifa Parhat, a Chinese Muslim known as a Uighur, as an enemy combatant.

June 24: The Justice Department's Inspector General releases a report concluding that some officials broke civil service laws by rejecting applicants to the Department's Honors Program and law intern program who had ties to Democrats or liberal organizations.

June 25: The Supreme Court holds by a 5-4 margin in *Kennedy v. Louisiana* that the Eighth Amendment's prohibition on cruel and unusual punishment prohibits executing a person for raping a child. The Court relied on the absence of a national consensus that the offense warranted imposition of the death penalty, but failed to note that Congress had recently enacted a provision authorizing the death penalty for the offense. When that fact is brought to the Court's attention, it orders briefing, but denies rehearing by a 5-4 vote. • The Supreme Court holds by a 5-3 vote in *Exxon Shipping v. Baker* that a $2.5 billion punitive damages award against Exxon for the Exxon Valdez oil spill was excessive.

June 26: By a 5-4 vote, the Supreme Court holds in *District of Columbia v. Heller* that the D.C. handgun ban violates the Second Amendment, which protects an individual right to gun ownership. • By a 5-4 vote, the Supreme Court holds in *Davis v. Federal Election Commission* that the "millionaire's amendment" to the McCain-Feingold campaign finance law, which increased contribution limits for opponents of wealthy, self-funded candidates, is unconstitutional. • North Korea agrees to submit for outside inspection a long-delayed declaration of its nuclear program. The Bush Administration announces it will take steps to remove the country from the State Department's list of state sponsors of terrorism. • Air France, Cathay Pacific Airways, KLM Royal Dutch Airlines, and SAS plead guilty and pay $504 million in criminal fines for conspiring to fix air cargo rates.

June 27: Plaintiffs' lawyer Dickie Scruggs is sentenced to five years in federal prison for conspiring to bribe a judge; Scruggs reportedly nearly faints during sentencing.

June 30: U.S. military prosecutors charge Guantanamo Bay detainee Abd al Rahim al-Nashiri with planning the October 2000 attack on the USS Cole. • The Second Circuit holds in *Arar v. Ashcroft* that foreign nationals may not sue U.S. officials for damages for capturing them and sending them to foreign countries where they were tortured. On August 14, the court orders rehearing en banc.

July 2: Actress Tatum O'Neal pleads guilty to disorderly conduct stemming from her June arrest in New York during an alleged crack cocaine purchase.

July 8: The G8 agrees to support cuts of 50% in greenhouse gas emissions by 2050.

July 9: After a GAO report criticized the Air Force's February award of a $35 billion contract for midair refueling tankers to a partnership of Northrop Grumman and Airbus, the Pentagon announces it will reopen bidding, allowing Boeing a second chance to win the contract.

July 10: The FISA Amendments Act of 2008 is enacted. • Alaska Sen. John Cowdery is indicted for bribery and conspiracy involving VECO Corp.

July 12: The federal government takes control of IndyMac Bank in what regulators call the second-largest bank failure in U.S. history.

July 13: Treasury Secretary Henry Paulson asks Congress to approve a plan to shore up Fannie Mae and Freddie Mac by authorizing Treasury to take an ownership position in the firms.

July 14: Three men accused of plotting to bomb trans-Atlantic passenger jets with liquid explosives plead guilty to planning to set off bombs, but maintain they did not seek to destroy airliners. • The board of Anheuser-Busch agrees to sell the company to Belgian giant InBev for $52 billion; the merger will create the world's largest brewer. • President Bush lifts the executive ban on offshore oil and gas drilling and criticizes Congress for not lifting a congressional ban that has been in place since 1981.

July 15: The en banc Fourth Circuit holds by a 5-4 margin in *Al-Marri v. Pucciarelli* that President Bush may order the indefinite military detentions of civilians captured in the United States, but holds that al-Marri must be given an additional opportunity to challenge his detention. • Congress overrides President Bush's veto of the Medicare Improvements for Patients and Providers Act, which would forestall pay cuts to doctors who treated seniors, the disabled, and military personnel.

July 16: President Bush invokes executive privilege in response to a congressional subpoena seeking an FBI memorandum recounting a confidential 2004 interview with Vice President Cheney about the Valerie Plame matter.

July 25: California becomes the first state in the country to ban trans fats in restaurants and retail baked goods.

July 28: The Justice Department's Inspector General and Office of Professional Responsibility conclude that some former Department officials violated civil service laws by considering political affiliation in hiring.

July 29: Sen. Ted Stevens is indicted on seven counts of making false statements on financial disclosure forms for failing to disclose his receipt of more than $250,000 from VECO Corp., principally involving remodeling of his house. • President Bush signs legislation to freeze assets of Myanmar's ruling regime and ban imports of its rubies and jade. • Former Newark Mayor Sharpe James is sentenced to 27 months in prison for his role in the cut-rate sales of city land to his former mistress. • A 5.4-magnitude earthquake interrupts the first day of the California bar exam. Reportedly, at least at one location, concerned test-takers are told "this happens all the time in California," and they should continue with the test.

July 30: A House panel votes to cite former presidential adviser Karl Rove for contempt of Congress for failing to testify about the removal of nine U.S. Attorneys and the prosecution of former Alabama Gov. Don Siegelman. • President Bush signs a housing-rescue bill in an effort to head off rising foreclosures and stabilize jittery financial markets. • Senate Republicans block a vote on a media-shield law that would protect reporters from having to testify about their confidential sources. • The Tenth Circuit grants en banc review of a panel's decision ordering a new trial in the insider trading case of former Qwest CEO Joe Nacchio.

July 31: The D.C. federal district court holds that Harriet Miers and Joshua Bolten are not immune from compelled congressional testimony (but may invoke executive privilege in response to specific questions) and orders them to produce non-privileged subpoenaed documents. • Massachusetts repeals a 1913 law that prohibited marrying out-of-state couples whose marriages would not be legal in their home states, which had prevented out-of-state same-sex couples from marrying. • President Bush revises Executive Order 12333 concerning intelligence activities to align with 2004 intelligence reform legislation and implement certain recommendations of the 9/11 Commission. • Bruce E. Ivins, a top government scientist who helped the FBI analyze samples from the 2001 anthrax attacks, commits suicide just as the Justice Department is about to charge him for the attacks. Days later, DOJ officials publicly lay out the evidence that Bruce Ivins committed the attacks.

Aug. 5: Federal prosecutors charge 11 people with the theft and sale of more than 40 million credit and debit card numbers in one of the largest-ever identity-theft prosecutions.

Aug. 6: In the first U.S. war crimes trial since the end of World War II, a jury convicts Osama bin Laden's former driver, Salim Ahmed Hamdan, of supporting terrorism, but acquits him of conspiring to carry out terrorist attacks. With credit for time served, he will be released in five months.

Aug. 12: The D.C. Circuit upholds the dismissal of former CIA analyst Valerie Plame's lawsuit against Vice President Cheney and former Bush Administration officials for disclosing her identity.

Aug. 15: Don Webster is sentenced to 30 years in prison for sex trafficking in children and adults, with some of the victims he forced into prostitution as young as 13. His prosecution is part of a significant Justice Department initiative begun in 2006 to crack down on the sexual exploitation of children that has resulted in a 27.8% increase in such prosecutions.

Aug. 19: Charles Morrison of Greensburg, Pa., is convicted of aggravated assault with a garden gnome.

Aug. 22: A divided panel of the D.C. Circuit holds in *Free Enterprise Fund v. Public Companies Accounting Oversight Board* that provisions of the Sarbanes-Oxley Act that created the accounting oversight body do not violate the Appointments Clause. Judge Brett Kavanaugh files a 58-page dissent.

Aug. 24: Sen. Obama announces that he has chosen Sen. Joe Biden (D-DE) to be his running mate.

Aug. 27: Barack H. Obama is nominated to be the Democratic Party candidate for President of the United States.

Aug. 28: The Second Circuit affirms the dismissal of charges against former executives of accounting firm KPMG for marketing illegal tax shelters, holding that prosecutors had improperly coerced KPMG to refuse to pay their legal costs by saying it would consider KPMG's payment of their legal fees in determining the extent of the firm's cooperation. • Deputy Attorney General Mark Filip announces that the Justice Department has revised its corporate charging guidelines, which no longer consider a company's waiver of privileges, payment of attorney's fees, or entry into joint defense agreements. • Federal District Judge Samuel B. Kent is indicted for attempted aggravated sexual abuse and for abusive sexual touching of a court employee.

Aug. 29: Sen. McCain announces he has selected Gov. Sarah Palin (R-AK) to be his running mate.

Sept. 3: John S. McCain III is nominated to be the Republican Party candidate for President of the United States. • A federal jury convicts retired University of Tennessee professor J. Reece Roth of illegally exporting military technology relating to aerial drones to the People's Republic of China.

Sept. 4: Former lobbyist Jack Abramoff is sentenced to 48 months in prison and ordered to pay $23 million in restitution for fraud and related charges. • Detroit Mayor Kwame Kilpatrick pleads guilty to obstruction of justice charges stemming from an affair with his former chief of staff.

Sept. 5: The Third Circuit holds that former Allegheny County Coroner Dr. Cyril H. Wecht can be retried on 41 criminal charges against him, but orders that District Judge Arthur J. Schwab be removed from the case because proceedings were pervaded by "rancor."

Sept. 7: The federal government places Freddie Mac and Fannie Mae in receivership.

Sept. 8: A London court convicts three of eight defendants who had been charged in a plan to destroy commercial airliners over the mid-Atlantic using liquid explosives. • Kevin A. Ring, a former lobbyist who worked with Jack Abramoff, is arrested on conspiracy, fraud, and obstruction of justice charges for his alleged role in giving gifts to lawmakers and officials in return for help for his clients.

Sept. 9: The Fifth Circuit overturns the three life sentences James Ford Seale is serving for the 1964 abduction and murder of two black teenagers, holding that his prosecution 40 years after the killings violated the statute of limitations.

Sept. 10: The Department of the Interior's Inspector General reports widespread ethics abuses in the office that collects oil and gas royalties, including financial self-dealing, accepting gifts from energy companies, cocaine use, and sexual misconduct. • Prominent lawyer Robert Simels is arrested on federal charges that he attempted to have the main witness against a client murdered.

Sept. 11: Rep. Charles B. Rangel (D-NY) says that he had failed to pay several thousand dollars in taxes owed on rental income from a beach house he owns in the Dominican Republic because "cultural and language barriers" prevented him from understanding its finances.

Sept. 14: Actor George Takei, who played "Sulu" on the television series *Star Trek*, is married to Brad Altman in California.

Sept. 15: Lehman Brothers files for bankruptcy. Bank of America agrees to buy Merrill Lynch. • The Dow Jones Industrial Average ("DJIA") falls 500 points.

Sept. 16: The government takes control of insurance giant AIG. • News reports indicate that Rep. Rangel failed to report the $70,000 profit from the 2006 sale of a Florida condominium.

Sept. 17: The DJIA plunges 449 points.

Sept. 18: The Bush Administration proposes a plan to purchase distressed debt. • The DJIA gains 410 points, its biggest one-day rally since October 2002.

Sept. 19: The U.S. Treasury offers temporary insurance for money market funds, while the SEC imposes a two-week ban on short-selling the stocks of 799 financial firms.

Sept. 22: West Virginia police charge Jose Cruz with battery of an officer for offensive flatulence while being fingerprinted on a DUI charge.

Sept. 24: Sen. McCain suspends his campaign to return to Washington to join talks over a proposed financial bailout package and states he will not participate in the presidential debate two days later unless a deal is struck.

• Iraq's parliament unanimously approves a provincial elections law. • The House ethics panel votes to probe Rep. Rangel's financial disclosures. • Physicist Shu Quan-Sheng is charged with illegally exporting space launch technical data to the People's Republic of China. • California enacts a law making it illegal to read or send text messages while driving.

Sept. 25: Federal regulators seize Washington Mutual. • FBI agents arrest evangelist Tony Alamo, alleging that he took minors across state lines for sexual purposes.

Sept. 26: Sen. McCain says talks have progressed to the point that he will participate in the presidential debate.

Sept. 29: The Administration-endorsed bailout bill fails in the House of Representatives; the DJIA plunges 778 points, the biggest one-day drop in history. • The Justice Department's Inspector General and Office of Professional Responsibility conclude that top Department officials failed properly to supervise subordinates during the removal of nine U.S. Attorneys in 2006 and that there was "significant evidence" that politics played a role in some of the dismissals.

Sept. 30: The SEC and the Financial Accounting Standards Board relax the "mark-to-market rule," requiring that securities be assigned their current market value, and permit other factors to be taken into account in valuing illiquid securities. • The DJIA gains 485 points on news that Congress is expected to enact a bailout plan. • President Bush signs legislation making $25 billion in low-interest loans available to aid U.S. auto makers' transition to building more fuel-efficient vehicles. • Prompted by $4/gallon gasoline, the Democratic leadership of Congress allows the quarter-century congressional ban on offshore oil drilling to expire. • Keith Packer, former commercial general manager for British Airways World Cargo, pleads guilty to conspiring to fix rates for international air cargo shipments. • Four U.S. shipping company executives plead guilty to conspiring to fix prices and allocate market shares for the U.S.-Puerto Rico market.

Oct. 1: The Russian Supreme Court holds that the nation's last czar, Nicholas II, and his family were victims of "groundless repression."

Oct. 3: President Bush signs the Emergency Economic Stabilization Act of 2008. • Thirteen years to the day after his acquittal for the murder of his ex-wife, O.J. Simpson is convicted of robbery and kidnapping for a confrontation over sports memorabilia.

Oct. 6: The D.C. Circuit stays the district court order requiring Harriet Miers and Joshua Bolten to appear before Congress and produce records. • The DJIA drops nearly 370 points, falling below 10,000 for the first time in five years.

Oct. 7: D.C. District Judge Ricardo Urbina orders that 17 Uighurs detained at Guantanamo Bay be released into the United States. • David C. Kernell, the son of a Democratic Memphis legislator, is indicted on charges that he hacked into the personal email of Republican vice presidential candidate Sarah Palin. • The DJIA falls 508 points.

Oct. 8: President Bush signs legislation approving a nuclear deal with India, permitting fuel and technology sales in exchange for safeguards and inspections of civilian nuclear plants. • A federal judge postpones sentencing of Tony Rezko; his lawyer indicates that he is cooperating with prosecutors in the hopes of receiving a reduced sentence.

Oct. 9: The temporary SEC short-selling restriction expires; the DJIA falls 679 points, with shares of General Motors hard hit on fears the auto industry will collapse.

Oct. 10: The *New York Times* reports that an analysis of Obama campaign finance records found that nearly 3,000 donations were made in the names of fictitious donors. • A former prostitute alleges that District Judge Edward Nottingham encouraged her to lie to hide from investigators that he paid her for sex.

Oct. 11: The United States removes North Korea from its list of state sponsors of terrorism. • An inquiry by the Alaska legislature concludes that Sarah Palin abused her authority by pressuring subordinates to fire a state trooper involved in a dispute with her family. • The DJIA drops 128 points.

Oct. 13: The Department of the Treasury announces it will take equity stakes in nine major U.S. banks. • The DJIA gains 936 points, its highest-ever one-day gain.

Oct. 15: The DJIA falls 733 points as retail sales figures spark fears of deeper global recession.

Oct. 20: The DJIA gains 413 points. • A divided panel of the D.C. Circuit blocks the release into the U.S. of 17 Uighurs detained at Guantanamo Bay until it can hear further legal arguments in the case.

Oct. 21: The DJIA falls 514 points on disappointing corporate earnings reports. • A Los Angeles federal judge grants an injunction barring members of the Mongol motorcycle gang from wearing patches bearing the gang's trademarked logo.

Oct. 23: According to press accounts, the White House forces Scott J. Bloch, controversial head of the government's employee watchdog office, the Office of Special Counsel, to take administrative leave until the end of his 5-year term; the action essentially ends his tenure.

Oct. 27: U.S. District Judge Emmet Sullivan substitutes a new juror for the panel deliberating in the trial of Sen. Ted Stevens, after dismissing a juror who said she was going to her father's funeral; later that day, the jury convicts Stevens. The dismissed juror later admits she left to go to a horse race.

Oct. 28: The DJIA gains 889 points, correctly anticipating that the Federal Reserve will announce a rate cut the next day.

Oct. 29: The Justice Department approves the proposed merger of Delta and Northwest Airlines.

Oct. 30: A federal jury convicts Charles McArthur Emmanuel, the son of former Liberian President Charles Taylor, of torture, the first prosecution under a federal torture law.

Nov. 3: The Alaska state personnel board concludes that Gov. Sarah Palin violated no ethics laws when she fired her public safety commissioner. • Ali Hamza al-Bahlul is sentenced to life in prison after being convicted at Guantanamo Bay of solicitation to commit murder and material support for terrorism.

Nov. 4: Barack Obama is elected the 44th President of the United States. Democrats pick up at least seven seats in the Senate, and at least 20 seats in the House of Representatives. • Seven congressional elections remain undecided more than a week after Election Day, including four House races and three Senate races (Alaska, Georgia, Minnesota); as this goes to press, the race for the Minnesota Senate seat is still undergoing a recount. • It takes over two weeks to determine the winner of the presidential race in Missouri; for the first time since 1956, Missouri backs the losing candidate. • Despite widespread predictions of record turnout, roughly the same portion of eligible voters cast ballots as in 2004. • All three states that have ballot questions on same-sex marriage enact restrictions. California voters adopt a state constitutional amendment outlawing same-sex marriage only months after the state's highest court concluded the constitution required allowing gays to marry. Similar amendments also pass in Florida and Arizona. • Voters in Colorado, South Dakota, and California reject anti-abortion ballot measures. • Massachusetts voters approve an initiative to eliminate criminal penalties for possessing small amounts of marijuana, but a similar proposal fails in California; Michigan voters approve allowing gravely ill patients to use marijuana with a physician's approval. • The Federal Circuit strikes down a statute that sets a goal that 5% of defense contracting dollars be awarded to small businesses owned by the socially and economically disadvantaged, saying it violates the Due Process Clause of the Fifth Amendment. • The FCC approves the merger of Verizon Wireless and Alltel Corp, and the merger of Sprint Nextel's WiMax with Clearwire Corp.

Nov. 5: Daniel Cowart and Paul Schlesselman are indicted for conspiring to assassinate Barack Obama. • Yahoo! and Google abandon their advertising agreement after the Department of Justice states that it would sue to block its implementation. • The DJIA drops 486 points, the worst post-election performance in history.

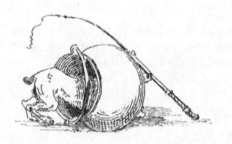

[Of Mr. Baron Parke:] He loved
the law, and probably, like lovers
of more material things, could see
no fault in the object of his love.

William Ballantine (1882)

A TERM IN THE LIFE OF THE

SUPREME COURT

Tony Mauro[†]

Some developments involving the Supreme Court of the United States from November 1, 2007 to October 31, 2008 that are not likely to be memorialized in the United States Reports.

2007

Nov. 4: Justice John Paul Stevens takes the rare step of writing to the *New York Times Magazine* to "correct certain misunderstandings" in its profile of Stevens published Sept. 23. In the letter Stevens says that while he did serve in the Navy communications intelligence unit at Pearl Harbor in World War II, he did not "help break the code" on a Japanese operation as the story suggested. The justice also counters the article's suggestion that he once joined good-government forces in Chicago. "I was never active in politics," Stevens writes.

Nov. 15: During an appearance before the Federalist Society in Washington, D.C., Justice Clarence Thomas is asked, "Why do your colleagues ask so many questions during oral arguments?" Thomas replies, "I did not plant that question," adding, "When you figure it out, let me know." Thomas, who rarely asks questions from the bench, says, "One thing I've demonstrated in the last 16 years is that you can do this job without asking a single question."

Dec. 3: During oral arguments in *Sprint/United Management Co. v. Mendelsohn*, Justice Samuel Alito Jr. asks Deputy Solicitor General Gregory Garre a question, and Garre addresses him as Justice (Antonin) Scalia in response. Other lawyers have made the same error, in the same way that, years earlier, oral advocates occasionally addressed Justice Sandra Day O'Connor as Justice Ruth Bader Ginsburg, and vice versa.

Dec. 8: The Senate Judiciary Committee votes 11-8 in favor of S. 344, which would require the Supreme Court to allow broadcast coverage of its open sessions, unless a majority of justices in a particular case votes

---

† Tony Mauro is Supreme Court correspondent for *Legal Times*, American Lawyer Media, and law.com.

that such coverage would violate due process. Leading sponsor Sen. Arlen Specter (R-Pa.) says the time has come: "If information can be safely made open and broadcast to the public, it should be." No further action on the bill takes place during the rest of the session.

2008

Jan. 1: In his annual report on the state of the judiciary, Chief Justice John Roberts Jr. states, "Americans should take enormous pride in our judicial system." He notes that Great Britain, Japan and South Korea have recently adopted changes that bring their legal systems close to that of the United States. Roberts repeats his perennial call on Congress to increase compensation for the federal judiciary. "This salary restoration legislation is vital now that the denial of annual increases over the years has left federal trial judges — the backbone of our system of justice — earning about the same as (and in some cases less than) *first-year lawyers* at firms in major cities, where many of the judges are located." (Emphasis in the original.)

Mid-Jan.: Raw, unscripted videotaped interviews with eight of the nine justices (all but David Souter) are posted on the Web site of LawProse, Inc., operated by legal writing expert Bryan Garner. The justices were asked about their preferences and pet peeves when it comes to the legal briefs they receive and the oral arguments they hear. Chief Justice Roberts calls the newly fashionable citations to web sites "an obscene distraction, with all those letters strung together." Justice Anthony Kennedy hates showy, made-up verbs like "incentivize," which he compares to "wearing a very ugly cravat."

Jan. 15: The Supreme Court shatters a glass ceiling by appointing the first female special master in the Court's history: Kristin Linsley Myles of San Francisco, litigation partner in the firm Munger, Tolles & Olson and a former law clerk to Justice Scalia. She is named special master in the case of *South Carolina v. North Carolina*, a dispute between the states over distribution of water from the Catawba River, which came to the Court under its original jurisdiction.

Mar. 17: Following his argument in *Republic of Philippines v. Pimentel*, Deputy Solicitor General Edwin Kneedler is summoned back to the podium to receive the Court's congratulations for arguing his 100th case before the justices. Chief Justice Roberts notes Kneedler is the first advocate to reach this milestone in the new century. "We look forward to hearing you many more times," Roberts tells Kneedler, 62, who argued his first case in 1979.

Apr. 22: The television series "Boston Legal" airs an episode that is sharply critical of the current Court, an unusual example of the treatment of the Court in popular culture. The show's lawyers argue before look-alike justices in a case modeled after the pending case *Kennedy v. Louisiana* on the constitutionality of the death penalty for child rapists. "Who are you people?" asks actor James Spader as Alan Shore, also attacking the justices to their faces as "overtly and shamelessly pro-business."

Apr. 28: Accompanied by a rare burst of publicity for the usually camera-shy Justice Scalia, a book he co-authored is published by Thomson West. Entitled *Making Your Case: The Art of Persuading Judges,* the book offers extensive advice for lawyers on winning their cases through brief-writing and oral advocacy. The co-author is legal writing expert Bryan Garner. In addition to obvious advice such as "Know your case," the book suggests lawyers research the background of the judges before whom they will argue. "At the very least, these details will humanize the judge before you, so that you will be arguing to a human being instead of a chair." It also tells male lawyers with ponytails, "We don't recommend this coiffure if advocacy before elderly judges is your day job." Scalia's promotional efforts include extensive interviews with CBS News' "60 Minutes" and National Public Radio, as well as a continuing legal education program July 25 at the Kennedy Center for the Performing Arts.

May 12: Because four justices recuse in the Court's consideration of a case called *American Isuzu Motors v. Ntsebeza,* the Court lacks a quorum to grant or deny review of the case. A class of South Africans is seeking compensation from more than 50 American and foreign companies for their role in perpetuating apartheid. The Court's lack of a quorum means the lower court ruling, which allowed the suit to proceed, is affirmed. Three who recuse — Chief Justice Roberts and Justices Stephen Breyer and Alito — have reported on their financial disclosure forms that they own stock in defendant companies. Kennedy, the fourth justice to recuse, has a son Gregory who is a managing partner at Credit Suisse, another named defendant.

June 6: Speaking before the conference of the U.S. Court of Appeals for the D.C. Circuit, Chief Justice Roberts announces adjustments to the Supreme Court's argument calendar for the coming term. Instead of the usual two arguments per day when the Court is sitting, Roberts says three will be scheduled on argument days in October and November, with possibly fewer than two in April, its final month for arguments. The aim of frontloading the calendar, Roberts says, is to give justices more time to write more opinions earlier in the term, thereby alleviating the usual end-of-term crunch in May and June.

June 11: Seven justices — all but Scalia and Thomas — attend a reception at the Court in honor of journalist Linda Greenhouse, who is leaving the Supreme Court beat after 30 years of Pulitzer Prize-winning coverage for the *New York Times*. Chief Justice Roberts offers congratulations, joking that commenting on Greenhouse's work is like "asking a corpse to comment on the work of the coroner." Her byline, he says, has been in the *Times* 2,800 times — tribute to "the brilliance of her career." The event is sponsored by Greenhouse's colleagues in the press corps.

July 14: Isaac Lidsky, the first blind Supreme Court law clerk, begins work for retired Justice O'Connor. A onetime child actor — he played Weasel on the NBC show "Saved By the Bell: The New Class" in 1993 — Lidsky suffers from retinitis pigmentosa, which left him going blind while at Harvard Law School. He created Hope for Vision, a non-profit to fund eye disease research. Lidsky is undaunted by the prospect of the reading-intensive job of law clerk, telling *Legal Times* that with new software that "reads" documents to him, "I can listen to things as fast as people can read them. I can do the functional equivalent of skimming."

Sept. 25: The *New York Times* reports that Justice Alito has decided to withdraw from the Court's so-called "cert pool," a pooling arrangement under which the law clerks of participating justices split up incoming petitions so that each petition is summarized by one clerk, and that clerk's report goes to all the justices in the pool. The pool, begun in 1972 to cope with the rising number of petitions, has been criticized as giving too much power over the docket to individual clerks. Before Alito's withdrawal, Justice Stevens was the only justice outside the pool. On Oct. 31, Alito explains his decision to *Legal Times*. "I wanted to simulate it in my own chambers, but it never worked. So I decided to give it a try."

Oct. 2: Chief Justice Roberts tells a Drake University audience that because of the ongoing "comprehensive renovation" of the Supreme Court, the justices have been temporarily unable to hold their private conferences in their traditional conference room behind the court room but have had to meet "elsewhere in the building" for the first time, away from the rewiring and infrastructure work in that section of the building.

Oct. 14: Chief Justice Roberts dissents from the denial of certiorari in *Pennsylvania v. Dunlap*, adopting an unusually literary writing style borrowed from the noir or pulp crime fiction genre. An excerpt: "Officer Sean Devlin, Narcotics Strike Force, was working the morning shift. Undercover surveillance. The neighborhood? Tough as a three dollar steak. Devlin knew." The dissent wins generally favorable notice, though a lawyer for Nathan Dunlap, the defendant in the Fourth Amendment probable cause arrest case, says Roberts' tone "makes a bit light" of Dunlap's side of the story.

Oct. 22: The Hoover Institution Archives announces that the family of the late Chief Justice William Rehnquist has donated his papers to the Stanford University-affiliated institution. Under the arrangement with Hoover, case files won't be released while any of the justices on the Court at the time are still alive. As a result, case files from Rehnquist's early years on the Court, 1972 to 1975, are set for release Nov. 17, along with correspondence and other material from his Court and pre-Court days.

[B]ecause the life of the laws lies in the due execution and administration of them, let your eye be, in the first place, upon the choice of good judges.

Francis Bacon (1616)

MEASURE FOR MEASURE

William Shakespeare[†]

WITH

INTRODUCTION & NOTES

John V. Orth, with the assistance of Joseph L. Hyde[*]

Editor's note: This year, each month begins with an installment of Professor Orth's commentary on *Measure for Measure*.

W hen John Mortimer, the famous English barrister and creator of the even more famous Rumpole of the Bailey, was asked to name his five favorite fictional portraits of the legal world, he listed three classic nineteenth-century novels — *Bleak House* and *Great Expectations* by Charles Dickens and *Orley Farm* by Anthony Trollope — one modern crime novel, *A Certain Justice* by P.D. James, and a play, *Measure for Measure* by William Shakespeare. Finding the play "the most perturbing study of lawyers and the law," Mortimer described it as a dramatized debate "between the law and natural justice."[1]

Like all good legal dramas, *Measure for Measure* ends with a trial scene, but — as we would expect from Shakespeare — one with an unusual twist. Charges of corruption are brought against Angelo, the deputy who ruled Vienna during the temporary absence of its Duke Vincentio. The newly returned Duke, even then making his triumphal entry at the city gates, orders an immediate trial: *Come, cousin Angelo / In this I'll be impartial; be you judge / Of your own cause.*[2]

As the theater audience knows, the Duke's absence from the city was feigned, not real; he had remained in Vienna, disguised as a friar, to observe the effects of Angelo's governance. The Duke's avowed purpose

---

[†] Elizabethan actor and author.

[*] Professor Orth is the William Rand Kenan, Jr. Professor of Law at the University of North Carolina School of Law. Mr. Hyde is a student at the University of North Carolina School of Law. He expects to graduate in 2009.

[1] *Wall St. Journal* (Feb. 24-25, 2007).

[2] 5.1.184-86. The Duke and Angelo are not actually cousins, but powerful persons have long maintained the fiction that they are all related. The lingering practice of judges describing themselves as "brethren" is a modern example. For further discussion of the legal issue raised by letting the defendant serve as the judge, see the preface to September, *A Judge in his Own Case: "Judex in propria causa."*

had been to allow Angelo, whose reputation for righteousness seemed unimpeachable, to restore respect for the law, which had declined under the Duke's too indulgent rule. But he had discovered while incognito that Angelo, after sentencing Claudio to death under a long-ignored law against fornication, succumbed to temptation himself when petitioned by Claudio's beautiful sister, Isabella, an aspiring nun, and offered to pardon her brother in return for sex, demanding fornication by the sister in return for pardoning it in the brother. By convenient happenstance, the Duke had discovered the hitherto overlooked fact that years earlier Angelo had jilted Mariana, his intended bride, after her dowry had been lost and arranged to substitute one maiden for another in the dark to satisfy Angelo's desire.

Compounding his offense, Angelo had actually ordered the execution of Claudio to go ahead even as his sexual demand on Isabella was (seemingly) being satisfied. Working in the background, the Duke managed to spare Claudio, deceiving both Angelo and Isabella, so that on his reemergence in his true character at the end of the play, he could stage-manage the trial of Angelo on the charges brought by the aggrieved young woman. Knowing the truth of the matter, the Duke is not in fact impartial as he claims, but by letting Angelo be the judge in his own cause, he is setting a trap for the unjust deputy, who willingly falls in. When his corruption is publicly exposed, Angelo recognizes that he should die the death he intended for another. On the plea of Mariana, Angelo's abandoned bride with whom he had unwittingly consummated his marriage — joined dramatically by the wronged Isabella — the Duke is moved to mercy, and the play manages a happy ending, complete with all the obligatory marriages, qualifying it technically for inclusion among Shakespeare's comedies.

Long recognized as a "law play," Shakespeare's *Measure for Measure* differs from his other plays, and from plays by his contemporaries, in the degree of attention it pays to law and legalism.[3] As the influential nineteenth-century German critic, A.W. Schlegel, observed: "In *Measure for Measure* Shakespeare was compelled, by the nature of the subject, to make

---

[3] It is estimated that a third or more of Elizabethan and Jacobean plays included a trial, an arraignment, or a lawsuit. Tim Stretton, *Women Waging Law in Elizabethan England* 63 (1998). Less well known than Shakespeare's earlier "law play," *The Merchant of Venice*, *Measure for Measure* contains a plea for mercy that rivals Portia's more famous speech. And unlike *The Merchant of Venice* or the later *Winter's Tale*, the third of Shakespeare's legal dramas, *Measure for Measure* is more completely focused on the dilemmas of the administration of justice.

his poetry more familiar with criminal justice than is usual with him."[4] Law, legal terms, and legal officers abound in the play, and — as John Mortimer observed — the deeper problems of justice are probed as well. Perhaps that explains why the play has attracted the particular attention of lawyers and judges over the years. In the eighteenth century, Sir William Blackstone, author of the famous *Commentaries on the Laws of England*, contributed notes on the play, and over the last ninety years American judges have quoted from it in their judicial opinions 49 times.[5]

Also unlike his other plays, Shakespeare's *Measure for Measure* deals openly with religious, specifically Christian, themes.[6] The Duke worries about executing Barnardine, a convicted murderer, who is not ready to meet his maker: *A creature unprepared, unmeet for death, / And to transport him in the mind he is / Were damnable.*[7] And Isabella's moving plea for her brother invokes Christ's atonement: *Why, all the souls that were were forfeit once, / And He that might the vantage best have took, / Found out the remedy.*[8] The play's title is an obvious reference to a passage from Jesus' Sermon on the Mount. Although the now classic English translation of the Bible known as the King James' (or Authorized) Version was still a few years in the future when Shakespeare wrote *Measure for Measure*, he was familiar with the so-called Geneva Bible, which translated the passage in identical language: "Judge not, that ye be not judged. / For with what judgement ye judge, ye shall be judged, and with what measure ye mete, it shall be measured to you againe."[9] When at the play's climax the Duke orders Angelo to be the judge of his own cause, he is inviting the deputy to measure out his own punishment. And Shakespeare is forcing us all to confront the dilemma of judgment by flawed and failing human judges.

---

[4] A.W. Schlegel, *Lectures on Dramatic Art and Literature* 387 (1811) (based on lectures originally delivered in Vienna) (John Black trans., 2d ed. rev. by A.J.W. Morrison) (1889).

[5] Selected notes by Blackstone, taken from 1 Edmond Malone, *Supplement to the Edition of Shakespeare's Plays Published in 1778 by Samuel Johnson and George Steevens* (1780), appear in footnotes to the text of the play. Footnotes also indicate passages quoted in American cases. In an additional seven cases the play is referred to in general terms. See *Measure for Measure in Court*, at page 566 below. For modern academic legal commentary, see Daniel J. Kornstein, *Kill All the Lawyers? Shakespeare's Legal Appeal* 35-51 (1994). A contemporary application of the play is attempted in Robert Batey, Kenneth Starr — Among Others — Should (Re)Read *Measure for Measure*, 26 Okla. City U. L. Rev. 261 (2001).

[6] See generally Darryl Gless, *Measure for Measure, the Law, and the Convent* (1979).

[7] 4.3.63-65.

[8] 2.2.95-97.

[9] Matt. 7:1-2 (Geneva Bible).

MEASURE FOR MEASURE

Editor's note: This edition of *Measure for Measure* is based on
the one found in the *Complete Moby Shakeaspeare*, which is in
the public domain and freely available online.

THE SCENE: VIENNA[1]

THE NAMES OF ALL THE ACTORS

Vincentio, the Duke
Angelo, the Deputy
Escalus, an ancient Lord
Claudio, a young Gentleman
Lucio, a fantastic
2 Other like Gentlemen
Provost
Thomas
Peter
2 Friars

Elbow, a simple Constable
Froth, a foolish Gentleman
Clown [Pompey, a Tapster]
Abhorson, an Executioner
Barnardine, a dissolute prisoner
Isabella, sister to Claudio
Mariana, betrothed to Angelo
Juliet, beloved of Claudio
Francisca, a Nun
Mistress Overdone, a Bawd

ACT I
SCENE I. AN APARTMENT IN THE DUKE'S PALACE.

Enter DUKE VINCENTIO, ESCALUS, Lords and Attendants

DUKE VINCENTIO
Escalus.

ESCALUS
My lord.

DUKE VINCENTIO
Of government the properties to unfold,
Would seem in me t'affect speech and discourse;
Since I am put to know that your own science   5
Exceeds, in that, the lists of all advice

---

[1] By setting his play outside England, Shakespeare could not only use religious
characters like friars and nuns, absent from England since Henry VIII's dissolution
of the monasteries in the 1530s, but could also address legal issues without concern
for the particularities of English law. The time of the action is not indicated, but the
Vienna of the play seems to be just another Renaissance city, like the Venice of *The
Merchant of Venice* and the London of Shakespeare's own day.

My strength can give you: then no more remains,
But that to your sufficiency as your worth is able,
And let them work.[2] The nature of our people,
Our city's institutions, and the terms   10
For common justice, you're as pregnant in
As art and practise hath enriched any
That we remember.[3] There is our commission,
From which we would not have you warp. Call hither,
I say, bid come before us Angelo.   15

                                          Exit an Attendant

What figure of us think you he will bear?
For you must know, we have with special soul
Elected him our absence to supply,
Lent him our terror, dress'd him with our love,
And given his deputation all the organs   20
Of our own power: what think you of it?

ESCALUS
    If any in Vienna be of worth
    To undergo such ample grace and honour,
    It is Lord Angelo.

DUKE VINCENTIO
    Look where he comes.   25

                                            Enter ANGELO

ANGELO
    Always obedient to your grace's will,
    I come to know your pleasure.

---

[2] If you are having difficulty parsing this sentence, you are in good company.
Shakespeare scholars think one or more lines are missing.

[3] The Duke recognizes that law is not abstract but related to society's customs and
traditions (*the nature of our people*), its *institutions*, and its legal language (*the terms
for common justice*) — what the ethnologist Clifford Geertz described as the "thick
description" of a culture. See Clifford Geertz, *The Interpretation of Cultures* (1973).
Sir William Blackstone glossed this passage: "*Terms* means the technical language
of the courts. An old book called *Les Termes de la Ley,* (written in Henry the Eighth's
time) was in Shakespeare's days, and is now, the accidence [sic] of young students
of the law." A later commentator suggested that *common justice* means justice as
administered in the Duke's Courts as opposed to the inferior courts. Alfred Edward
Thiselton, *Some Textual Notes on Measure for Measure* 5 (1901). There may, in other
words, be a reference to the English Court of Common Pleas.

DUKE VINCENTIO
Angelo,
There is a kind of character in thy life,
That to the observer doth thy history   30
Fully unfold. Thyself and thy belongings
Are not thine own so proper as to waste
Thyself upon thy virtues, they on thee.
Heaven doth with us as we with torches do,
Not light them for themselves; for if our virtues   35
Did not go forth of us, 'twere all alike
As if we had them not. Spirits are not finely touch'd
But to fine issues, nor Nature never lends
The smallest scruple of her excellence
But, like a thrifty goddess, she determines   40
Herself the glory of a creditor,
Both thanks and use. But I do bend my speech
To one that can my part in him advertise;
Hold therefore, Angelo:--
In our remove be thou at full ourself;   45
Mortality and mercy in Vienna
Live in thy tongue and heart: old Escalus,
Though first in question, is thy secondary.
Take thy commission.

ANGELO
Now, good my lord,   50
Let there be some more test made of my metal,
Before so noble and so great a figure
Be stamp'd upon it.

DUKE VINCENTIO
No more evasion:
We have with a leaven'd and prepared choice   55
Proceeded to you; therefore take your honours.
Our haste from hence is of so quick condition
That it prefers itself and leaves unquestion'd
Matters of needful value. We shall write to you,
As time and our concernings shall importune,   60
How it goes with us, and do look to know
What doth befall you here. So, fare you well;
To the hopeful execution do I leave you
Of your commissions.

ANGELO
> Yet give leave, my lord,   65
> That we may bring you something on the way.

DUKE VINCENTIO
> My haste may not admit it;
> Nor need you, on mine honour, have to do
> With any scruple; your scope is as mine own
> So to enforce or qualify the laws   70
> As to your soul seems good.[4] Give me your hand:
> I'll privily away. I love the people,
> But do not like to stage me to their eyes:
> Though it do well, I do not relish well
> Their loud applause and Aves vehement;   75
> Nor do I think the man of safe discretion
> That does affect it. Once more, fare you well.

ANGELO
> The heavens give safety to your purposes!

ESCALUS
> Lead forth and bring you back in happiness!

DUKE
> I thank you. Fare you well.   80

> *Exit*

ESCALUS
> I shall desire you, sir, to give me leave
> To have free speech with you; and it concerns me
> To look into the bottom of my place:
> A power I have, but of what strength and nature
> I am not yet instructed.   85

ANGELO
> 'Tis so with me. Let us withdraw together,
> And we may soon our satisfaction have
> Touching that point.

ESCALUS
> I'll wait upon your honour.

---

[4] While on the one hand the grant of authority to *qualify the laws* seems to confer on Angelo equitable jurisdiction; on the other, it seems to conflict with the Duke's plan for strict enforcement of the law, stated later in this Act.

SCENE II. A STREET.

Enter LUCIO and two Gentlemen

LUCIO

If the duke with the other dukes come not to
composition with the King of Hungary, why then all
the dukes fall upon the king.

FIRST GENTLEMAN

Heaven grant us its peace, but not the King of
Hungary's!   5

SECOND GENTLEMAN

Amen.

LUCIO

Thou concludest like the sanctimonious pirate, that
went to sea with the Ten Commandments, but scraped
one out of the table.[5]

SECOND GENTLEMAN

'Thou shalt not steal'?   10

LUCIO

Ay, that he razed.

FIRST GENTLEMAN

Why, 'twas a commandment to command the captain and
all the rest from their functions: they put forth
to steal. There's not a soldier of us all, that, in
the thanksgiving before meat, do relish the petition   15
well that prays for peace.

SECOND GENTLEMAN

I never heard any soldier dislike it.

LUCIO

I believe thee; for I think thou never wast where
grace was said.

SECOND GENTLEMAN

No? a dozen times at least.   20

FIRST GENTLEMAN

What, in metre?

---

[5] *Quoted in* Denlinger v. Brennan, 87 F.3d 214, 215 (7th Cir. 1996) (Easterbrook, J).

LUCIO
In any proportion or in any language.

FIRST GENTLEMAN
I think, or in any religion.

LUCIO
Ay, why not? Grace is grace, despite of all
controversy: as, for example, thou thyself art a   25
wicked villain, despite of all grace.

FIRST GENTLEMAN
Well, there went but a pair of shears between us.

LUCIO
I grant; as there may between the lists and the
velvet. Thou art the list.

FIRST GENTLEMAN
And thou the velvet: thou art good velvet; thou'rt   30
a three-piled piece, I warrant thee: I had as lief
be a list of an English kersey as be piled, as thou
art piled, for a French velvet. Do I speak
feelingly now?

LUCIO
I think thou dost; and, indeed, with most painful   35
feeling of thy speech: I will, out of thine own
confession, learn to begin thy health; but, whilst I
live, forget to drink after thee.

FIRST GENTLEMAN
I think I have done myself wrong, have I not?

SECOND GENTLEMAN
Yes, that thou hast, whether thou art tainted or free.   40

LUCIO
Behold, behold, where Madam Mitigation comes! I
have purchased as many diseases under her roof as come to--

SECOND GENTLEMAN
To what, I pray?

LUCIO
Judge.

SECOND GENTLEMAN
 To three thousand dolours a year.   45

FIRST GENTLEMAN
 Ay, and more.

LUCIO
 A French crown more.

FIRST GENTLEMAN
 Thou art always figuring diseases in me; but thou
 art full of error; I am sound.

LUCIO
 Nay, not as one would say, healthy; but so sound as   50
 things that are hollow: thy bones are hollow;
 impiety has made a feast of thee.
            Enter MISTRESS OVERDONE

FIRST GENTLEMAN
 How now! which of your hips has the most profound sciatica?

MISTRESS OVERDONE
 Well, well; there's one yonder arrested and carried
 to prison was worth five thousand of you all.   55

SECOND GENTLEMAN
 Who's that, I pray thee?

MISTRESS OVERDONE
 Marry, sir, that's Claudio, Signior Claudio.

FIRST GENTLEMAN
 Claudio to prison? 'tis not so.

MISTRESS OVERDONE
 Nay, but I know 'tis so: I saw him arrested, saw
 him carried away; and, which is more, within these   60
 three days his head to be chopped off.

LUCIO
 But, after all this fooling, I would not have it so.
 Art thou sure of this?

MISTRESS OVERDONE
 I am too sure of it: and it is for getting Madam
 Julietta with child.   65

LUCIO
Believe me, this may be: he promised to meet me two
hours since, and he was ever precise in
promise-keeping.

SECOND GENTLEMAN
Besides, you know, it draws something near to the
speech we had to such a purpose.   70

FIRST GENTLEMAN
But, most of all, agreeing with the proclamation.

LUCIO
Away! let's go learn the truth of it.
Exeunt LUCIO and Gentlemen

MISTRESS OVERDONE
Thus, what with the war, what with the sweat, what
with the gallows and what with poverty, I am
custom-shrunk.   75

Enter POMPEY

How now! what's the news with you?

POMPEY
Yonder man is carried to prison.

MISTRESS OVERDONE
Well; what has he done?

POMPEY
A woman.

MISTRESS OVERDONE
But what's his offence?   80

POMPEY
Groping for trouts in a peculiar river.

MISTRESS OVERDONE
What, is there a maid with child by him?

POMPEY
No, but there's a woman with maid by him. You have
not heard of the proclamation, have you?

MISTRESS OVERDONE
What proclamation, man?   85

POMPEY
All houses in the suburbs of Vienna must be plucked down.

MISTRESS OVERDONE
And what shall become of those in the city?

POMPEY
They shall stand for seed: they had gone down too,
but that a wise burgher put in for them.[6]

MISTRESS OVERDONE
But shall all our houses of resort in the suburbs be   90
pulled down?

POMPEY
To the ground, mistress.

MISTRESS OVERDONE
Why, here's a change indeed in the commonwealth!
What shall become of me?

POMPEY
Come; fear you not: good counsellors lack no   95
clients:[7] though you change your place, you need not
change your trade; I'll be your tapster still.
Courage! there will be pity taken on you: you that
have worn your eyes almost out in the service, you
will be considered.   100

MISTRESS OVERDONE
What's to do here, Thomas tapster? let's withdraw.

---

[6] Keeping a house of prostitution, traditionally called a bawdy house, was an offense at common law, indictable as a common nuisance. See Brayne v. Cooper, 5 M. & W. 249, 151 Eng. Rep. 106 (Exch. 1839). Because some bawdy houses were spared while others were *plucked down,* this seems to be an instance where Angelo exercised the authority given him by the Duke to *qualify the laws* on the advice of a *wise burgher* (Escalus?), although it compromised the Duke's plan for strict enforcement of the law. The blatant class-bias demonstrated by targeting the suburban brothels and sparing those in the city was one of the aspects of the play that attracted Bertold Brecht to attempt a German adaptation. See the preface to January, *Unequal Law: A Marxist Measure for Measure.*
[7] *Quoted in* United States v. Matsumara, 244 F.3d 1092, 1096 (9th Cir. 2001) (Trott, J.). If *counsellors* refers to lawyers, the legal profession is here analogized to prostitution.

POMPEY

    Here comes Signior Claudio, led by the provost to
    prison; and there's Madam Juliet.

Exeunt
Enter Provost, CLAUDIO, JULIET, and Officers

CLAUDIO

    Fellow, why dost thou show me thus to the world?
    Bear me to prison, where I am committed.   105

PROVOST

    I do it not in evil disposition,
    But from Lord Angelo by special charge.

CLAUDIO

    Thus can the demigod Authority
    Make us pay down for our offence by weight
    The words of heaven; on whom it will, it will;   110
    On whom it will not, so; yet still 'tis just.

Re-enter LUCIO and two Gentlemen

LUCIO

    Why, how now, Claudio! whence comes this restraint?

CLAUDIO

    From too much liberty, my Lucio, liberty:
    As surfeit is the father of much fast,
    So every scope by the immoderate use   115
    Turns to restraint. Our natures do pursue,
    Like rats that ravin down their proper bane,
    A thirsty evil; and when we drink we die.

LUCIO

    If I could speak so wisely under an arrest, I would
    send for certain of my creditors: and yet, to say   120
    the truth, I had as lief have the foppery of freedom
    as the morality of imprisonment. What's thy
    offence, Claudio?

CLAUDIO

    What but to speak of would offend again.

LUCIO

    What, is't murder?   125

CLAUDIO

    No.

LUCIO
Lechery?

CLAUDIO
Call it so.[8]

PROVOST
Away, sir! you must go.

CLAUDIO
One word, good friend. Lucio, a word with you.   130

LUCIO
A hundred, if they'll do you any good.
Is lechery so look'd after?

CLAUDIO
Thus stands it with me: upon a true contract
I got possession of Julietta's bed:
You know the lady; she is fast my wife,   135
Save that we do the denunciation lack
Of outward order: this we came not to,
Only for propagation of a dower
Remaining in the coffer of her friends,
From whom we thought it meet to hide our love   140
Till time had made them for us. But it chances
The stealth of our most mutual entertainment
With character too gross is writ on Juliet.

LUCIO
With child, perhaps?

CLAUDIO
Unhappily, even so.   145
And the new deputy now for the duke--
Whether it be the fault and glimpse of newness,
Or whether that the body public be
A horse whereon the governor doth ride,
Who, newly in the seat, that it may know   150
He can command, lets it straight feel the spur;
Whether the tyranny be in his place,

---

[8] Although Shakespeare often refers in the play to the law against fornication, he makes no attempt to reproduce its terms. That was left to Richard Wagner who attempted a musical adaptation of the play. See the preface to February, *The Law Against Love: An Operatic Measure for Measure*.

Or in his eminence that fills it up,
I stagger in:--but this new governor
Awakes me all the enrolled penalties   155
Which have, like unscour'd armour, hung by the wall
So long that nineteen zodiacs have gone round
And none of them been worn; and, for a name,
Now puts the drowsy and neglected act
Freshly on me: 'tis surely for a name.   160

LUCIO
I warrant it is: and thy head stands so tickle on
thy shoulders that a milkmaid, if she be in love,
may sigh it off. Send after the duke and appeal to
him.

CLAUDIO
I have done so, but he's not to be found.   165
I prithee, Lucio, do me this kind service:
This day my sister should the cloister enter
And there receive her approbation:
Acquaint her with the danger of my state:
Implore her, in my voice, that she make friends   170
To the strict deputy; bid herself assay him:
I have great hope in that; for in her youth
There is a prone and speechless dialect,
Such as move men; beside, she hath prosperous art
When she will play with reason and discourse,   175
And well she can persuade.

LUCIO
I pray she may; as well for the encouragement of the
like, which else would stand under grievous
imposition, as for the enjoying of thy life, who I
would be sorry should be thus foolishly lost at a   180
game of tick-tack. I'll to her.

CLAUDIO
I thank you, good friend Lucio.

LUCIO
Within two hours.

CLAUDIO
Come, officer, away!

                                                        Exeunt

SCENE III. A MONASTERY.

Enter DUKE VINCENTIO and FRIAR THOMAS

DUKE VINCENTIO
No, holy father; throw away that thought;
Believe not that the dribbling dart of love
Can pierce a complete bosom. Why I desire thee
To give me secret harbour, hath a purpose
More grave and wrinkled than the aims and ends   5
Of burning youth.[9]

FRIAR THOMAS
May your grace speak of it?

DUKE VINCENTIO
My holy sir, none better knows than you
How I have ever loved the life removed
And held in idle price to haunt assemblies   10
Where youth, and cost, and witless bravery keeps.
I have deliver'd to Lord Angelo,
A man of stricture and firm abstinence,
My absolute power and place here in Vienna,
And he supposes me travell'd to Poland;   15
For so I have strew'd it in the common ear,
And so it is received. Now, pious sir,
You will demand of me why I do this?

FRIAR THOMAS
Gladly, my lord.

DUKE VINCENTIO
We have strict statutes and most biting laws.[10]   20
The needful bits and curbs to headstrong weeds,[11]
Which for this nineteen years we have let slip;

---

[9] Friar Thomas assumes the Duke wants to use the friary as a place of assignation, an indication of the level of sexual activity in Vienna during the Duke's reign — and perhaps of the ducal reputation. See Lucio's later description of the Duke and the Duke's indignant denial in Act III.

[10] *Quoted in* Leigh v. Perdue Farms, Inc., 2001 U.S. Dist. LEXIS 11986, 4 (M.D. Ala. 2001) (DeMent, J.).

[11] "According to a standard legal-theoretic story, Strict Law is conceived as reason's check on pleasure's unruly promptings — an essential check for populace and rulers alike." Thomas C. Grey, *The Wallace Stevens Case: Law and the Practice of Poetry* 87 (1991).

Even like an o'ergrown lion in a cave,
That goes not out to prey. Now, as fond fathers,
Having bound up the threatening twigs of birch,   25
Only to stick it in their children's sight
For terror, not to use, in time the rod
Becomes more mock'd than fear'd; so our decrees,
Dead to infliction, to themselves are dead;[12]
And liberty plucks justice by the nose;[13]   30
The baby beats the nurse, and quite athwart
Goes all decorum.

FRIAR THOMAS
  It rested in your grace
To unloose this tied-up justice when you pleased:
And it in you more dreadful would have seem'd   35
Than in Lord Angelo.

DUKE VINCENTIO
  I do fear, too dreadful:
Sith 'twas my fault to give the people scope,
'Twould be my tyranny to strike and gall them
For what I bid them do: for we bid this be done,   40
When evil deeds have their permissive pass
And not the punishment. Therefore indeed, my father,
I have on Angelo imposed the office;
Who may, in the ambush of my name, strike home,
And yet my nature never in the fight   45
To do in slander. And to behold his sway,
I will, as 'twere a brother of your order,
Visit both prince and people: therefore, I prithee,
Supply me with the habit and instruct me
How I may formally in person bear me   50
Like a true friar. More reasons for this action
At our more leisure shall I render you;
Only, this one: Lord Angelo is precise;
Stands at a guard with envy; scarce confesses
That his blood flows, or that his appetite   55

---

[12] On the question whether long non-enforcement of a law can be considered an implied repeal, see the preface to March, *Desuetude: "Dormiunt aliquando leges, numquam moriuntur."*

[13] *Quoted in* Connecticut Gen'l Life Ins. Co. v. Chicago Title & Trust Co., 690 F.2d 115, 116 (7th Cir. 1982) (Posner, J.).

Is more to bread than stone: hence shall we see,
If power change purpose, what our seemers be.

Exeunt

SCENE IV. A NUNNERY.

Enter ISABELLA and FRANCISCA

ISABELLA
And have you nuns no farther privileges?

FRANCISCA
Are not these large enough?

ISABELLA
Yes, truly; I speak not as desiring more;
But rather wishing a more strict restraint
Upon the sisterhood, the votarists of Saint Clare.   5

LUCIO
[Within] Ho! Peace be in this place!

ISABELLA
Who's that which calls?

FRANCISCA
It is a man's voice. Gentle Isabella,
Turn you the key, and know his business of him;
You may, I may not; you are yet unsworn.   10
When you have vow'd, you must not speak with men
But in the presence of the prioress:
Then, if you speak, you must not show your face,
Or, if you show your face, you must not speak.
He calls again; I pray you, answer him.   15

Exit

Peace and prosperity! Who is't that calls

Enter LUCIO

LUCIO
Hail, virgin, if you be, as those cheek-roses
Proclaim you are no less! Can you so stead me
As bring me to the sight of Isabella,
A novice of this place and the fair sister   20
To her unhappy brother Claudio?

ISABELLA
    Why 'her unhappy brother'? let me ask,
    The rather for I now must make you know
    I am that Isabella and his sister.

LUCIO
    Gentle and fair, your brother kindly greets you: 25
    Not to be weary with you, he's in prison.

ISABELLA
    Woe me! for what?

LUCIO
    For that which, if myself might be his judge,
    He should receive his punishment in thanks:
    He hath got his friend with child.   30

ISABELLA
    Sir, make me not your story.

LUCIO
    It is true.
    I would not--though 'tis my familiar sin
    With maids to seem the lapwing and to jest,
    Tongue far from heart--play with all virgins so: 35
    I hold you as a thing ensky'd and sainted.
    By your renouncement an immortal spirit,
    And to be talk'd with in sincerity,
    As with a saint.

ISABELLA
    You do blaspheme the good in mocking me.   40

LUCIO
    Do not believe it. Fewness and truth, 'tis thus:
    Your brother and his lover have embraced:
    As those that feed grow full, as blossoming time
    That from the seedness the bare fallow brings
    To teeming foison, even so her plenteous womb   45
    Expresseth his full tilth and husbandry.

ISABELLA
    Some one with child by him? My cousin Juliet?

LUCIO
    Is she your cousin?

ISABELLA
Adoptedly; as school-maids change their names
By vain though apt affection.   50

LUCIO
She it is.

ISABELLA
O, let him marry her.

LUCIO
This is the point.
The duke is very strangely gone from hence;
Bore many gentlemen, myself being one,   55
In hand and hope of action: but we do learn
By those that know the very nerves of state,
His givings-out were of an infinite distance
From his true-meant design. Upon his place,
And with full line of his authority,   60
Governs Lord Angelo; a man whose blood
Is very snow-broth; one who never feels
The wanton stings and motions of the sense,
But doth rebate and blunt his natural edge
With profits of the mind, study and fast.   65
He--to give fear to use and liberty,
Which have for long run by the hideous law,
As mice by lions--hath pick'd out an act,
Falls into forfeit: he arrests him on it;   70
And follows close the rigour of the statute,
To make him an example. All hope is gone,
Unless you have the grace by your fair prayer
To soften Angelo: and that's my pith of business
'Twixt you and your poor brother.   75

ISABELLA
Doth he so seek his life?

LUCIO
Has censured him
Already; and, as I hear, the provost hath
A warrant for his execution.

ISABELLA
Alas! what poor ability's in me   80
To do him good?

LUCIO
    Assay the power you have.

ISABELLA
    My power? Alas, I doubt--

LUCIO
    Our doubts are traitors
    And make us lose the good we oft might win   85
    By fearing to attempt. Go to Lord Angelo,
    And let him learn to know, when maidens sue,
    Men give like gods; but when they weep and kneel,
    All their petitions are as freely theirs
    As they themselves would owe them.   90

ISABELLA
    I'll see what I can do.

LUCIO
    But speedily.

ISABELLA
    I will about it straight;
    No longer staying but to give the mother
    Notice of my affair. I humbly thank you: 95
    Commend me to my brother: soon at night
    I'll send him certain word of my success.

LUCIO
    I take my leave of you.

ISABELLA
    Good sir, adieu.

Exeunt

ACT II
SCENE I. A HALL IN ANGELO'S HOUSE.

Enter ANGELO, ESCALUS,
and a Justice, Provost, Officers,
and other Attendants, behind

ANGELO
    We must not make a scarecrow of the law,
    Setting it up to fear the birds of prey,
    And let it keep one shape, till custom make it

Their perch and not their terror.[14]

ESCALUS

    Ay, but yet   5
    Let us be keen, and rather cut a little,
    Than fall, and bruise to death. Alas, this gentleman
    Whom I would save, had a most noble father!
    Let but your honour know,
    Whom I believe to be most strait in virtue,   10
    That, in the working of your own affections,
    Had time cohered with place or place with wishing,
    Or that the resolute acting of your blood
    Could have attain'd the effect of your own purpose,
    Whether you had not sometime in your life   15
    Err'd in this point which now you censure him,
    And pull'd the law upon you.

ANGELO

    'Tis one thing to be tempted, Escalus,
    Another thing to fall. I not deny,
    The jury, passing on the prisoner's life,   20
    May in the sworn twelve have a thief or two
    Guiltier than him they try.[15] What's open made to justice,
    That justice seizes: what know the laws
    That thieves do pass on thieves? 'Tis very pregnant,
    The jewel that we find, we stoop and take't   25
    Because we see it; but what we do not see
    We tread upon, and never think of it.
    You may not so extenuate his offence
    For I have had such faults; but rather tell me,

---

[14] *Quoted in* Collazo v. Estelle, 940 F.2d 411, 433 (9th Cir. 1991) (O'Scannlain, J., dissenting); United States v. Lynch, 499 F.2d 1011, 1032 (D.C. Cir. 1974) (MacKinnon, J., dissenting); In re Finley, Kumble, Wagner, Heine, Underberg, Manley, Myerson & Casey, 160 B.R. 882, 897 (Bankr. S.D.N.Y. 1993) (Conrad, J.); Fields v. Luther, 1988 U.S. Dist. LEXIS 5405, 34 (D. Md. 1988) (Blake, Mag.); Nigido v. First Nat. Bank of Baltimore, 288 A.2d 127, 128 (Md. 1972) (McWilliams, J.).

[15] *Quoted in* State v. Serra, 529 So.2d 1262, 1263 (Fla. Dist. Ct. App. 1988) (per curiam); State v. Lanier, 273 S.E.2d 746, 749 (N.C. App. 1981) (Whichard, J.); Application of Allan S., 387 A.2d 271, 277 (Md. 1978) (Digges, J., dissenting); Ford Motor Credit Co. v. Amodt, 139 N.W.2d 6, 9 (Wis. 1966) (Gordon, J.). In Vienna, a civil law jurisdiction, there would have been no jury. Concerning the problem of one criminal condemning another, see the preface to April, *Judge Not: The jury . . . may in the sworn twelve have a thief or two.*

When I, that censure him, do so offend, 30
Let mine own judgment pattern out my death,
And nothing come in partial. Sir, he must die.

ESCALUS
Be it as your wisdom will.

ANGELO
Where is the provost?

PROVOST
Here, if it like your honour. 35

ANGELO
See that Claudio
Be executed by nine to-morrow morning:
Bring him his confessor, let him be prepared;
For that's the utmost of his pilgrimage.

Exit Provost

ESCALUS
[Aside] Well, heaven forgive him! and forgive us all! 40
Some rise by sin, and some by virtue fall:
Some run from brakes of ice, and answer none:
And some condemned for a fault alone.

Enter ELBOW, and Officers with FROTH and POMPEY

ELBOW
Come, bring them away: if these be good people in
a commonweal that do nothing but use their abuses in 45
common houses, I know no law: bring them away.

ANGELO
How now, sir! What's your name? and what's the matter?

ELBOW
If it please your honour, I am the poor duke's
constable, and my name is Elbow: I do lean upon
justice, sir, and do bring in here before your good 50
honour two notorious benefactors.

ANGELO
Benefactors? Well; what benefactors are they? are
they not malefactors?

ELBOW

    If it please your honour, I know not well what they
are: but precise villains they are, that I am sure   55
of; and void of all profanation in the world that
good Christians ought to have.

ESCALUS

    This comes off well; here's a wise officer.

ANGELO

    Go to: what quality are they of? Elbow is your
name? why dost thou not speak, Elbow?   60

POMPEY

    He cannot, sir; he's out at elbow.

ANGELO

    What are you, sir?

ELBOW

    He, sir! a tapster, sir; parcel-bawd; one that
serves a bad woman; whose house, sir, was, as they
say, plucked down in the suburbs; and now she   65
professes a hot-house, which, I think, is a very ill house too.

ESCALUS

    How know you that?

ELBOW

    My wife, sir, whom I detest before heaven and your honour,--

ESCALUS

    How? thy wife?

ELBOW

    Ay, sir; whom, I thank heaven, is an honest woman,--   70

ESCALUS

    Dost thou detest her therefore?

ELBOW

    I say, sir, I will detest myself also, as well as
she, that this house, if it be not a bawd's house,
it is pity of her life, for it is a naughty house.

ESCALUS

    How dost thou know that, constable?   75

ELBOW

    Marry, sir, by my wife; who, if she had been a woman
    cardinally given, might have been accused in
    fornication, adultery, and all uncleanliness there.

ESCALUS

    By the woman's means?

ELBOW

    Ay, sir, by Mistress Overdone's means: but as she   80
    spit in his face, so she defied him.

POMPEY

    Sir, if it please your honour, this is not so.

ELBOW

    Prove it before these varlets here, thou honourable
    man; prove it.

ESCALUS

    Do you hear how he misplaces?   85

POMPEY

    Sir, she came in great with child; and longing,
    saving your honour's reverence, for stewed prunes;
    sir, we had but two in the house, which at that very
    distant time stood, as it were, in a fruit-dish, a
    dish of some three-pence; your honours have seen   90
    such dishes; they are not China dishes, but very
    good dishes,--

ESCALUS

    Go to, go to: no matter for the dish, sir.

POMPEY

    No, indeed, sir, not of a pin; you are therein in
    the right: but to the point. As I say, this   95
    Mistress Elbow, being, as I say, with child, and
    being great-bellied, and longing, as I said, for
    prunes; and having but two in the dish, as I said,
    Master Froth here, this very man, having eaten the
    rest, as I said, and, as I say, paying for them very   100
    honestly; for, as you know, Master Froth, I could
    not give you three-pence again.

FROTH
No, indeed.

POMPEY
Very well: you being then, if you be remembered,
cracking the stones of the foresaid prunes,--   105

FROTH
Ay, so I did indeed.

POMPEY
Why, very well; I telling you then, if you be
remembered, that such a one and such a one were past
cure of the thing you wot of, unless they kept very
good diet, as I told you,--   110

FROTH
All this is true.

POMPEY
Why, very well, then,--

ESCALUS
Come, you are a tedious fool: to the purpose. What
was done to Elbow's wife, that he hath cause to
complain of? Come me to what was done to her.   115

POMPEY
Sir, your honour cannot come to that yet.

ESCALUS
No, sir, nor I mean it not.

POMPEY
Sir, but you shall come to it, by your honour's
leave. And, I beseech you, look into Master Froth
here, sir; a man of four-score pound a year; whose   120
father died at Hallowmas: was't not at Hallowmas,
Master Froth?

FROTH
All-hallond eve.

POMPEY
Why, very well; I hope here be truths. He, sir,
sitting, as I say, in a lower chair, sir; 'twas in   125
the Bunch of Grapes, where indeed you have a delight
to sit, have you not?

FROTH
I have so; because it is an open room and good for winter.

POMPEY
Why, very well, then; I hope here be truths.

ANGELO
This will last out a night in Russia,   130
When nights are longest there: I'll take my leave.
And leave you to the hearing of the cause;
Hoping you'll find good cause to whip them all.

ESCALUS
I think no less. Good morrow to your lordship.

Exit ANGELO

Now, sir, come on: what was done to Elbow's wife, once more?   135

POMPEY
Once, sir? there was nothing done to her once.

ELBOW
I beseech you, sir, ask him what this man did to my wife.

POMPEY
I beseech your honour, ask me.

ESCALUS
Well, sir; what did this gentleman to her?

POMPEY
I beseech you, sir, look in this gentleman's face.   140
Good Master Froth, look upon his honour; 'tis for a
good purpose. Doth your honour mark his face?

ESCALUS
Ay, sir, very well.

POMPEY
Nay; I beseech you, mark it well.

ESCALUS
Well, I do so.   145

POMPEY
Doth your honour see any harm in his face?

ESCALUS
Why, no.

POMPEY

    I'll be supposed upon a book, his face is the worst
    thing about him. Good, then; if his face be the
    worst thing about him, how could Master Froth do the   150
    constable's wife any harm? I would know that of
    your honour.

ESCALUS

    He's in the right. Constable, what say you to it?

ELBOW

    First, an it like you, the house is a respected
    house; next, this is a respected fellow; and his   155
    mistress is a respected woman.

POMPEY

    By this hand, sir, his wife is a more respected
    person than any of us all.

ELBOW

    Varlet, thou liest; thou liest, wicked varlet! the
    time has yet to come that she was ever respected   160
    with man, woman, or child.

POMPEY

    Sir, she was respected with him before he married with her.

ESCALUS

    Which is the wiser here? Justice or Iniquity? Is
    this true?

ELBOW

    O thou caitiff! O thou varlet! O thou wicked   165
    Hannibal! I respected with her before I was married
    to her! If ever I was respected with her, or she
    with me, let not your worship think me the poor
    duke's officer. Prove this, thou wicked Hannibal, or
    I'll have mine action of battery on thee.   170

ESCALUS

    If he took you a box o' the ear, you might have your
    action of slander too.[16]

---

[16] These are common law terms (*the terms for common justice*), which may explain why the Viennese Elbow confuses them, but Escalus is better informed and makes a joke of the mistake. If an *action of battery* would lie for a slander, then an *action of slander* would lie for a battery.

ELBOW

> Marry, I thank your good worship for it. What is't
> your worship's pleasure I shall do with this wicked caitiff?

ESCALUS

> Truly, officer, because he hath some offences in him   175
> that thou wouldst discover if thou couldst, let him
> continue in his courses till thou knowest what they
> are.

ELBOW

> Marry, I thank your worship for it. Thou seest, thou
> wicked varlet, now, what's come upon thee: thou art   180
> to continue now, thou varlet; thou art to continue.

ESCALUS

> Where were you born, friend?

FROTH

> Here in Vienna, sir.

ESCALUS

> Are you of fourscore pounds a year?

FROTH

> Yes, an't please you, sir.   185

ESCALUS

> So. What trade are you of, sir?

POMPEY

> Tapster; a poor widow's tapster.

ESCALUS

> Your mistress' name?

POMPEY

> Mistress Overdone.

ESCALUS

> Hath she had any more than one husband?   190

POMPEY

> Nine, sir; Overdone by the last.

ESCALUS

> Nine! Come hither to me, Master Froth. Master
> Froth, I would not have you acquainted with
> tapsters: they will draw you, Master Froth, and you

will hang them.[17] Get you gone, and let me hear no   195
more of you.

FROTH
I thank your worship. For mine own part, I never
come into any room in a tap-house, but I am drawn
in.

ESCALUS
Well, no more of it, Master Froth: farewell.   200

Exit FROTH

Come you hither to me, Master tapster. What's your
name, Master tapster?

POMPEY
Pompey.

ESCALUS
What else?

POMPEY
Bum, sir.   205

ESCALUS
Troth, and your bum is the greatest thing about you;
so that in the beastliest sense you are Pompey the
Great. Pompey, you are partly a bawd, Pompey,
howsoever you colour it in being a tapster, are you
not? come, tell me true: it shall be the better for you.   210

POMPEY
Truly, sir, I am a poor fellow that would live.

ESCALUS
How would you live, Pompey? by being a bawd? What
do you think of the trade, Pompey? is it a lawful trade?

POMPEY
If the law would allow it, sir.[18]

---

[17] Escalus' warning to Froth that tapsters *will draw you* and *you will hang them* is a
punning allusion to the historic punishment for aggravated felonies: "being drawn
or dragged to the place of execution" and there "being hanged by the neck till
dead." 4 William Blackstone, *Commentaries on the Laws of England* 370 (1769).
[18] Pompey's reasoning is reminiscent of the answer a student gave to the classic question: What, sir, is the Rule in Shelley's Case?: "The rule in Shelley's case is very simple

ESCALUS

But the law will not allow it, Pompey; nor it shall   215
not be allowed in Vienna.

POMPEY

Does your worship mean to geld and splay all the
youth of the city?

ESCALUS

No, Pompey.

POMPEY

Truly, sir, in my poor opinion, they will to't then.   220
If your worship will take order for the drabs and
the knaves, you need not to fear the bawds.[19]

ESCALUS

There are pretty orders beginning, I can tell you:
it is but heading and hanging.

POMPEY

If you head and hang all that offend that way but   225
for ten year together, you'll be glad to give out a
commission for more heads: if this law hold in
Vienna ten year, I'll rent the fairest house in it
after three-pence a bay: if you live to see this
come to pass, say Pompey told you so.   230

ESCALUS

Thank you, good Pompey; and, in requital of your
prophecy, hark you: I advise you, let me not find
you before me again upon any complaint whatsoever;
no, not for dwelling where you do: if I do, Pompey,
I shall beat you to your tent, and prove a shrewd   235
Caesar to you; in plain dealing, Pompey, I shall
have you whipt: so, for this time, Pompey, fare you well.

POMPEY

I thank your worship for your good counsel:

Aside

---

if you understand it. It means that the same law which was applied in that case applies equally to every other case just like it." Welch v. Gibson, 138 S.E. 25, 28 (N.C.
1927) (Stacy, C.J.).

[19] Had illegal drugs been the problem in Vienna, Pompey might have argued that if
you can suppress the demand, you need not worry about the supply.

but I shall follow it as the flesh and fortune shall
better determine. 240
Whip me? No, no; let carman whip his jade:
The valiant heart is not whipt out of his trade.

Exit

ESCALUS
    Come hither to me, Master Elbow; come hither, Master
    constable. How long have you been in this place of constable?

ELBOW
    Seven year and a half, sir. 245

ESCALUS
    I thought, by your readiness in the office, you had
    continued in it some time. You say, seven years together?

ELBOW
    And a half, sir.

ESCALUS
    Alas, it hath been great pains to you. They do you
    wrong to put you so oft upon 't: are there not men 250
    in your ward sufficient to serve it?

ELBOW
    Faith, sir, few of any wit in such matters: as they
    are chosen, they are glad to choose me for them; I
    do it for some piece of money, and go through with
    all.[20] 255

ESCALUS
    Look you bring me in the names of some six or seven,
    the most sufficient of your parish.

ELBOW
    To your worship's house, sir?

ESCALUS
    To my house. Fare you well.

Exit ELBOW

    What's o'clock, think you? 260

---

[20] Petty constables were usually appointed in rotation to serve for one year. They
were unpaid and often hired substitutes. See 2 Leon Radzinowicz, *A History of English Criminal Law* 183-85 (1957). Elbow is being paid by other men in the parish to
serve in their place.

JUSTICE
Eleven, sir.

ESCALUS
I pray you home to dinner with me.

JUSTICE
I humbly thank you.

ESCALUS
It grieves me for the death of Claudio;
But there's no remedy.   265

JUSTICE
Lord Angelo is severe.

ESCALUS
It is but needful:
Mercy is not itself, that oft looks so;
Pardon is still the nurse of second woe:
But yet,--poor Claudio! There is no remedy.   270
Come, sir.

Exeunt

SCENE II. ANOTHER ROOM IN THE SAME.

Enter Provost and a Servant

SERVANT
He's hearing of a cause; he will come straight
I'll tell him of you.

PROVOST
Pray you, do.

Exit Servant

I'll know
His pleasure; may be he will relent. Alas,   5
He hath but as offended in a dream!
All sects, all ages smack of this vice; and he
To die for't!

Enter ANGELO

ANGELO
Now, what's the matter. Provost?

PROVOST
Is it your will Claudio shall die tomorrow?   10

ANGELO
Did not I tell thee yea? hadst thou not order?
Why dost thou ask again?

PROVOST
Lest I might be too rash:
Under your good correction, I have seen,
When, after execution, judgment hath   15
Repented o'er his doom.[21]

ANGELO
Go to; let that be mine:
Do you your office, or give up your place,
And you shall well be spared.

PROVOST
I crave your honour's pardon.   20
What shall be done, sir, with the groaning Juliet?
She's very near her hour.

ANGELO
Dispose of her
To some more fitter place, and that with speed.[22]

Re-enter Servant

SERVANT
Here is the sister of the man condemn'd   25
Desires access to you.

ANGELO
Hath he a sister?

PROVOST
Ay, my good lord; a very virtuous maid,
And to be shortly of a sisterhood,
If not already.   30

ANGELO
Well, let her be admitted.

Exit Servant

See you the fornicatress be removed:
Let have needful, but not lavish, means;
There shall be order for't.

---

[21] This is a standard argument against the death penalty.
[22] It is not clear in *Measure for Measure* whether Juliet was ever intended to suffer Claudio's fate. See the preface for May, *Pleading the Belly: the groaning Juliet*.

Enter ISABELLA and LUCIO

PROVOST

God save your honour! 35

ANGELO

Stay a little while.

To ISABELLA

You're welcome: what's your will?

ISABELLA

I am a woeful suitor to your honour,
Please but your honour hear me.

ANGELO

Well; what's your suit? 40

ISABELLA

There is a vice that most I do abhor,
And most desire should meet the blow of justice;
For which I would not plead, but that I must;
For which I must not plead, but that I am
At war 'twixt will and will not. 45

ANGELO

Well; the matter?

ISABELLA

I have a brother is condemn'd to die:
I do beseech you, let it be his fault,
And not my brother.

PROVOST

[Aside] Heaven give thee moving graces! 50

ANGELO

Condemn the fault and not the actor of it?
Why, every fault's condemn'd ere it be done:
Mine were the very cipher of a function,
To fine the faults whose fine stands in record,
And let go by the actor. 55

ISABELLA

O just but severe law!
I had a brother, then. Heaven keep your honour!

LUCIO

Aside to ISABELLA

Give't not o'er so: to him

again, entreat him;
Kneel down before him, hang upon his gown: 60
You are too cold; if you should need a pin,
You could not with more tame a tongue desire it:
To him, I say!

ISABELLA
Must he needs die?

ANGELO
Maiden, no remedy.   65

ISABELLA
Yes; I do think that you might pardon him,
And neither heaven nor man grieve at the mercy.

ANGELO
I will not do't.

ISABELLA
But can you, if you would?

ANGELO
Look, what I will not, that I cannot do.   70

ISABELLA
But might you do't, and do the world no wrong,
If so your heart were touch'd with that remorse
As mine is to him?

ANGELO
He's sentenced; 'tis too late.

LUCIO
                                                Aside to ISABELLA

You are too cold.   75

ISABELLA
Too late? why, no; I, that do speak a word.
May call it back again. Well, believe this,
No ceremony that to great ones 'longs,
Not the king's crown, nor the deputed sword,
The marshal's truncheon, nor the judge's robe,   80
Become them with one half so good a grace
As mercy does.[23]

---

[23] This speech is reminiscent of the more famous speech of Portia in *The Merchant of*

If he had been as you and you as he,
You would have slipt like him; but he, like you,
Would not have been so stern.[24]   85

ANGELO

Pray you, be gone.

ISABELLA

I would to heaven I had your potency,
And you were Isabel! should it then be thus?
No; I would tell what 'twere to be a judge,
And what a prisoner.   90

LUCIO

Aside to ISABELLA

Ay, touch him; there's the vein.
ANGELO
Your brother is a forfeit of the law,
And you but waste your words.

ISABELLA

Alas, alas!
Why, all the souls that were were forfeit once;   95
And He that might the vantage best have took
Found out the remedy. How would you be,
If He, which is the top of judgment, should
But judge you as you are? O, think on that;
And mercy then will breathe within your lips,   100
Like man new made.

ANGELO

Be you content, fair maid;
It is the law, not I condemn your brother:[25]
Were he my kinsman, brother, or my son,
It should be thus with him: he must die tomorrow.[26]   105

Venice, beginning *The quality of mercy is not strained* (4.1.184).

[24] *Quoted in* Wollman v. Gross 637 F.2d 544, 550 (8th Cir. 1980) (Adams, J., dissenting).

[25] *Quoted in* United States v. Chischilly, 30 F.3d 1144, 1163 (9th Cir. 1994) (Noonan, J., dissenting). For the conflicting uses of the concept of separating the law from the men who enforce it, see the preface for June, *Laws not Men: "Not under man but under God and the law."*

[26] The elder Brutus in 580 B.C. as first consul refused to pardon his two sons, guilty of conspiring to restore the hated Tarquins. This image of republican virtue is im-

ISABELLA

To-morrow! O, that's sudden! Spare him, spare him!
He's not prepared for death. Even for our kitchens
We kill the fowl of season: shall we serve heaven
With less respect than we do minister
To our gross selves? Good, good my lord, bethink you;   110
Who is it that hath died for this offence?
There's many have committed it.

LUCIO

Aside to ISABELLA

Ay, well said.

ANGELO

The law hath not been dead, though it hath slept:[27]
Those many had not dared to do that evil,   115
If the first that did the edict infringe
Had answer'd for his deed: now 'tis awake
Takes note of what is done; and, like a prophet,
Looks in a glass, that shows what future evils,
Either new, or by remissness new-conceived,   120
And so in progress to be hatch'd and born,
Are now to have no successive degrees,
But, ere they live, to end.

ISABELLA

Yet show some pity.

ANGELO

I show it most of all when I show justice;   125
For then I pity those I do not know,
Which a dismiss'd offence would after gall;
And do him right that, answering one foul wrong,
Lives not to act another. Be satisfied;
Your brother dies to-morrow; be content.   130

---

mortalized in Jacques-Louis David's painting *Brutus Seeing the Bodies of His Sons* (1789), now in the Louvre.

[27] *Quoted in* Labat v. Bennett, 365 F.2d 698, 701 (5th Cir. 1956) (Wisdom, J.); Farr v. Designer Phosphate and Premix Int'l, Inc., 804 F.Supp. 1190, 1198 (D. Neb. 1992) (Kopf, J.); United States v. Elliott, 266 F.Supp. 318, 326 (S.D.N.Y. 1967) (Cooper, J.); Waldron v. British Petroleum Co., 231 F.Supp. 72, 95 (S.D.N.Y. 1964) (Herlands, J.); Committee on Legal Ethics of the W.Va. State Bar v. Printz, 416 S.E.2d 720, 725 (W.Va. 1992) (Neely, J.); Commonwealth v. Blessing, 29 Pa. D. & C.3d 356, 366 (1984) (Dowling, J.).

ISABELLA

So you must be the first that gives this sentence,
And he, that suffer's. O, it is excellent
To have a giant's strength; but it is tyrannous
To use it like a giant.[28]

LUCIO

Aside to ISABELLA

That's well said.   135

ISABELLA

Could great men thunder
As Jove himself does, Jove would ne'er be quiet,
For every pelting, petty officer
Would use his heaven for thunder;
Nothing but thunder! Merciful Heaven,   140
Thou rather with thy sharp and sulphurous bolt
Split'st the unwedgeable and gnarled oak
Than the soft myrtle: but man, proud man,
Drest in a little brief authority,[29]
Most ignorant of what he's most assured,   145
His glassy essence, like an angry ape,

---

[28] *Quoted in* New York v. Microsoft Corp., 224 F.Supp.2d 76, 103 (D.C. Cir. 2002) (Kollar-Kotelly, J.); Gardiner v. A.H. Robins Co., Inc., 747 F.2d 1180, 1194 (8th Cir. 1990) (Lay, C.J.); Davis v. Ohio Barge Line, Inc., 697 F.2d 549, 558 (3d Cir. 1983) (Aldisert, J.); Air Terminal Services, Inc. v. United States, 330 F.2d 974, 984 (Ct. Cl. 1964) (Jones, C.J., dissenting); United States v. Worcester, 190 F.Supp. 548, 561 (D.C. Mass. 1960) (Wyzanski, J.) (quoting but not citing play); Ford v. Ford, 727 A.2d 254, 259 (Conn. App. 1999) (Landau, J.); Cooney v. Park County, 792 P.2d 1287, 1301 (Wyo. 1990) (Urbigkit, J., dissenting); People v. Fatone, 165 Cal.App.3d 1164, 1180-81 (1985) (Crosby, J.); Lewis v. Bill Robertson & Sons, Inc., 162 Cal.App.3d 650, 657 (1984) (Feinerman, J.). American judges agree with Lucio, *That's well said*; they have quoted these lines more than any other.

[29] *Quoted in* Michigan State UAW Community Action Program Council (CAP) v. Austin, 198 N.W.2d 385, 404 (Mich. 1972) (Black, J., dissenting); Magreta v. Ambassador Steel Co., 158 N.W.2d 473, 476 (Mich. 1968) (Black, J., concurring); In re Apportionment of Mich. Legislature, 140 N.W.2d 436, 439 (Mich. 1966) (Black, J.); Taylor v. Auditor General, 103 N.W.2d 769, 786 (Mich. 1960) (Black, J., dissenting); Fritts v. Krugh, 92 N.W.2d 604, 619 (Mich. 1958) (Black, J., dissenting); Matteson v. Board of Education, 286 P. 482, 484 (Cal. App. 1930) (Burnell, J.). *In Brief Authority* (1962) was the title of the second volume of the autobiography of Francis Biddle, who served as U.S. Attorney General from 1941to 1945 and as the primary American judge at the Nuremberg Trials.

Plays such fantastic tricks before high heaven
As make the angels weep; who, with our spleens,
Would all themselves laugh mortal.

LUCIO

Aside to ISABELLA

O, to him, to him, wench! He   150
will relent;
He's coming; I perceive 't.

PROVOST
[Aside] Pray heaven she win him!

ISABELLA
We cannot weigh our brother with ourself:
Great men may jest with saints; 'tis wit in them,   155
But in the less foul profanation.

LUCIO
Thou'rt i' the right, girl; more o, that.

ISABELLA
That in the captain's but a choleric word,
Which in the soldier is flat blasphemy.

LUCIO

Aside to ISABELLA

Art avised o' that? more on 't.   160

ANGELO
Why do you put these sayings upon me?

ISABELLA
Because authority, though it err like others,
Hath yet a kind of medicine in itself,
That skins the vice o' the top. Go to your bosom;
Knock there, and ask your heart what it doth know   165
That's like my brother's fault: if it confess
A natural guiltiness such as is his,
Let it not sound a thought upon your tongue
Against my brother's life.

ANGELO
[Aside] She speaks, and 'tis   170
Such sense, that my sense breeds with it. Fare you well.

ISABELLA
    Gentle my lord, turn back.

ANGELO
    I will bethink me: come again tomorrow.

ISABELLA
    Hark how I'll bribe you: good my lord, turn back.

ANGELO
    How! bribe me?   175

ISABELLA
    Ay, with such gifts that heaven shall share with you.

LUCIO
                                                    Aside to ISABELLA

    You had marr'd all else.

ISABELLA
    Not with fond shekels of the tested gold,
    Or stones whose rates are either rich or poor
    As fancy values them; but with true prayers   180
    That shall be up at heaven and enter there
    Ere sun-rise, prayers from preserved souls,
    From fasting maids whose minds are dedicate
    To nothing temporal.

ANGELO
    Well; come to me to-morrow.   185

LUCIO
                                                    Aside to ISABELLA

    Go to; 'tis well; away!

ISABELLA
    Heaven keep your honour safe!

ANGELO
    [*Aside*] Amen:
    For I am that way going to temptation,
    Where prayers cross.   190

ISABELLA
    At what hour to-morrow
    Shall I attend your lordship?

ANGELO
At any time 'fore noon.

ISABELLA
'Save your honour!

Exeunt ISABELLA, LUCIO, and Provost

ANGELO
From thee, even from thy virtue!   195
What's this, what's this? Is this her fault or mine?
The tempter or the tempted, who sins most?
Ha!
Not she: nor doth she tempt: but it is I
That, lying by the violet in the sun,   200
Do as the carrion does, not as the flower,
Corrupt with virtuous season. Can it be
That modesty may more betray our sense
Than woman's lightness? Having waste ground enough,
Shall we desire to raze the sanctuary   205
And pitch our evils there? O, fie, fie, fie!
What dost thou, or what art thou, Angelo?
Dost thou desire her foully for those things
That make her good? O, let her brother live!
Thieves for their robbery have authority   210
When judges steal themselves.[30] What, do I love her,
That I desire to hear her speak again,
And feast upon her eyes? What is't I dream on?
O cunning enemy, that, to catch a saint,
With saints dost bait thy hook! Most dangerous   215
Is that temptation that doth goad us on
To sin in loving virtue: never could the strumpet,
With all her double vigour, art and nature,
Once stir my temper; but this virtuous maid
Subdues me quite. Even till now,   220
When men were fond, I smiled and wonder'd how.

Exit

---

[30] Sir Edward Coke described a corrupt judge as "the grievance of grievances." Catherine Drinker Bowen, *Francis Bacon: The Temper of Man* 189 (1963). Judge Noonan thinks the character of Angelo was "probably modeled on Bacon." John T. Noonan, Making the Case One's Own, 32 Hofstra L. Rev. 1139, 1139 (2004). See John T. Noonan, *Bribes* 327-65 (1984).

SCENE III. A ROOM IN A PRISON.

Enter, severally, DUKE VINCENTIO disguised as a friar, and Provost

DUKE VINCENTIO
Hail to you, provost! so I think you are.
Provost
I am the provost. What's your will, good friar?

DUKE VINCENTIO
Bound by my charity and my blest order,
I come to visit the afflicted spirits
Here in the prison. Do me the common right   5
To let me see them and to make me know
The nature of their crimes, that I may minister
To them accordingly.

PROVOST
I would do more than that, if more were needful.

Enter JULIET

Look, here comes one: a gentlewoman of mine,   10
Who, falling in the flaws of her own youth,
Hath blister'd her report: she is with child;
And he that got it, sentenced; a young man
More fit to do another such offence
Than die for this.   15

DUKE VINCENTIO
When must he die?

PROVOST
As I do think, to-morrow.
I have provided for you: stay awhile,

To JULIET

And you shall be conducted.

DUKE VINCENTIO
Repent you, fair one, of the sin you carry?   20

JULIET
I do; and bear the shame most patiently.

DUKE VINCENTIO
I'll teach you how you shall arraign your conscience,
And try your penitence, if it be sound,
Or hollowly put on.

JULIET
    I'll gladly learn.   25

DUKE VINCENTIO
    Love you the man that wrong'd you?

JULIET
    Yes, as I love the woman that wrong'd him.

DUKE VINCENTIO
    So then it seems your most offenceful act
    Was mutually committed?

JULIET
    Mutually.   30

DUKE VINCENTIO
    Then was your sin of heavier kind than his.

JULIET
    I do confess it, and repent it, father.

DUKE VINCENTIO
    'Tis meet so, daughter: but lest you do repent,
    As that the sin hath brought you to this shame,
    Which sorrow is always towards ourselves, not heaven,   35
    Showing we would not spare heaven as we love it,
    But as we stand in fear,--

JULIET
    I do repent me, as it is an evil,
    And take the shame with joy.

DUKE VINCENTIO
    There rest.   40
    Your partner, as I hear, must die to-morrow,
    And I am going with instruction to him.
    Grace go with you, Benedicite!

                                                                            Exit

JULIET
    Must die to-morrow! O injurious love,
    That respites me a life, whose very comfort   45
    Is still a dying horror!

PROVOST
    'Tis pity of him.

                                                                          Exeunt

Scene IV. A room in Angelo's house.

Enter ANGELO

ANGELO

When I would pray and think, I think and pray
To several subjects. Heaven hath my empty words;
Whilst my invention, hearing not my tongue,
Anchors on Isabel: Heaven in my mouth,
As if I did but only chew his name;   5
And in my heart the strong and swelling evil
Of my conception. The state, whereon I studied
Is like a good thing, being often read,
Grown fear'd and tedious; yea, my gravity,
Wherein--let no man hear me--I take pride,   10
Could I with boot change for an idle plume,
Which the air beats for vain. O place, O form,
How often dost thou with thy case, thy habit,
Wrench awe from fools and tie the wiser souls
To thy false seeming! Blood, thou art blood: 15
Let's write good angel on the devil's horn:
'Tis not the devil's crest.

Enter a Servant

How now! who's there?

SERVANT

One Isabel, a sister, desires access to you.

ANGELO

Teach her the way.   20

Exit Servant

O heavens!
Why does my blood thus muster to my heart,
Making both it unable for itself,
And dispossessing all my other parts
Of necessary fitness?   25
So play the foolish throngs with one that swoons;
Come all to help him, and so stop the air
By which he should revive: and even so
The general, subject to a well-wish'd king,
Quit their own part, and in obsequious fondness   30
Crowd to his presence, where their untaught love
Must needs appear offence.

Enter ISABELLA

How now, fair maid?

ISABELLA
I am come to know your pleasure.

ANGELO
That you might know it, would much better please me   35
Than to demand what 'tis. Your brother cannot live.

ISABELLA
Even so. Heaven keep your honour!

ANGELO
Yet may he live awhile; and, it may be,
As long as you or I
yet he must die.   40

ISABELLA
Under your sentence?

ANGELO
Yea.

ISABELLA
When, I beseech you? that in his reprieve,
Longer or shorter, he may be so fitted
That his soul sicken not.   45

ANGELO
Ha! fie, these filthy vices! It were as good
To pardon him that hath from nature stolen
A man already made, as to remit
Their saucy sweetness that do coin heaven's image
In stamps that are forbid: 'tis all as easy   50
Falsely to take away a life true made
As to put metal in restrained means
To make a false one.

ISABELLA
'Tis set down so in heaven, but not in earth.

ANGELO
Say you so? then I shall pose you quickly.   55
Which had you rather, that the most just law
Now took your brother's life; or, to redeem him,
Give up your body to such sweet uncleanness
As she that he hath stain'd?

ISABELLA

Sir, believe this, 60

I had rather give my body than my soul.

ANGELO

I talk not of your soul: our compell'd sins

Stand more for number than for accompt.

ISABELLA

How say you?

ANGELO

Nay, I'll not warrant that; for I can speak 65

Against the thing I say. Answer to this:

I, now the voice of the recorded law,[31]

Pronounce a sentence on your brother's life:

Might there not be a charity in sin

To save this brother's life? 70

ISABELLA

Please you to do't,

I'll take it as a peril to my soul,

It is no sin at all, but charity.

ANGELO

Pleased you to do't at peril of your soul,

Were equal poise of sin and charity. 75

ISABELLA

That I do beg his life, if it be sin,

Heaven let me bear it! you granting of my suit,

If that be sin, I'll make it my morn prayer

To have it added to the faults of mine,

And nothing of your answer. 80

ANGELO

Nay, but hear me.

Your sense pursues not mine: either you are ignorant,

Or seem so craftily; and that's not good.

---

[31] Blackstone described the common law judges as "the depositary of the laws, the living oracles, who must decide in all cases of doubt, and who are bound by an oath to decide according to the law of the land." 1 William Blackstone, *Commentaries on the Laws of England* 69 (1765).

ISABELLA
Let me be ignorant, and in nothing good,
But graciously to know I am no better. 85

ANGELO
Thus wisdom wishes to appear most bright
When it doth tax itself; as these black masks
Proclaim an enshield beauty ten times louder
Than beauty could, display'd. But mark me;
To be received plain, I'll speak more gross: 90
Your brother is to die.

ISABELLA
So.

ANGELO
And his offence is so, as it appears,
Accountant to the law upon that pain.

ISABELLA
True. 95

ANGELO
Admit no other way to save his life,--
As I subscribe not that, nor any other,
But in the loss of question,--that you, his sister,
Finding yourself desired of such a person,
Whose credit with the judge, or own great place, 100
Could fetch your brother from the manacles
Of the all-building law; and that there were
No earthly mean to save him, but that either
You must lay down the treasures of your body
To this supposed, or else to let him suffer; 105
What would you do?

ISABELLA
As much for my poor brother as myself:
That is, were I under the terms of death,
The impression of keen whips I'ld wear as rubies,
And strip myself to death, as to a bed 110
That longing have been sick for, ere I'ld yield
My body up to shame.

ANGELO
Then must your brother die.

ISABELLA
 And 'twere the cheaper way:
 Better it were a brother died at once,   115
 Than that a sister, by redeeming him,
 Should die for ever.

ANGELO
 Were not you then as cruel as the sentence
 That you have slander'd so?

ISABELLA
 Ignomy in ransom and free pardon   120
 Are of two houses: lawful mercy
 Is nothing kin to foul redemption.

ANGELO
 You seem'd of late to make the law a tyrant;
 And rather proved the sliding of your brother
 A merriment than a vice.   125

ISABELLA
 O, pardon me, my lord; it oft falls out,
 To have what we would have, we speak not what we mean:
 I something do excuse the thing I hate,
 For his advantage that I dearly love.

ANGELO
 We are all frail.   130

ISABELLA
 Else let my brother die,
 If not a feodary, but only he
 Owe and succeed thy weakness.

ANGELO
 Nay, women are frail too.

ISABELLA
 Ay, as the glasses where they view themselves;   135
 Which are as easy broke as they make forms.
 Women! Help Heaven! men their creation mar
 In profiting by them. Nay, call us ten times frail;
 For we are soft as our complexions are,
 And credulous to false prints.   140

ANGELO
 I think it well:
 And from this testimony of your own sex,--

Since I suppose we are made to be no stronger
Than faults may shake our frames,--let me be bold;
I do arrest your words. Be that you are, 145
That is, a woman; if you be more, you're none;
If you be one, as you are well express'd
By all external warrants, show it now,
By putting on the destined livery.

ISABELLA

I have no tongue but one: gentle my lord, 150
Let me entreat you speak the former language.

ANGELO

Plainly conceive, I love you.

ISABELLA

My brother did love Juliet,
And you tell me that he shall die for it.

ANGELO

He shall not, Isabel, if you give me love. 155

ISABELLA

I know your virtue hath a licence in't,
Which seems a little fouler than it is,
To pluck on others.

ANGELO

Believe me, on mine honour,
My words express my purpose. 160

ISABELLA

Ha! little honour to be much believed,
And most pernicious purpose! Seeming, seeming!
I will proclaim thee, Angelo; look for't:
Sign me a present pardon for my brother,
Or with an outstretch'd throat I'll tell the world aloud 165
What man thou art.

ANGELO

Who will believe thee, Isabel?
My unsoil'd name, the austereness of my life,
My vouch against you, and my place i' the state,
Will so your accusation overweigh, 170
That you shall stifle in your own report
And smell of calumny. I have begun,
And now I give my sensual race the rein:

Fit thy consent to my sharp appetite;
Lay by all nicety and prolixious blushes, 175
That banish what they sue for; redeem thy brother
By yielding up thy body to my will;
Or else he must not only die the death,
But thy unkindness shall his death draw out
To lingering sufferance. Answer me to-morrow, 180
Or, by the affection that now guides me most,
I'll prove a tyrant to him. As for you,
Say what you can, my false o'erweighs your true.

Exit

ISABELLA
To whom should I complain? Did I tell this,
Who would believe me? O perilous mouths, 185
That bear in them one and the self-same tongue,
Either of condemnation or approof;
Bidding the law make court'sy to their will:
Hooking both right and wrong to the appetite,
To follow as it draws! I'll to my brother: 190
Though he hath fallen by prompture of the blood,
Yet hath he in him such a mind of honour
That, had he twenty heads to tender·down
On twenty bloody blocks, he'ld yield them up,
Before his sister should her body stoop 195
To such abhorr'd pollution.
Then, Isabel, live chaste, and, brother, die:
More than our brother is our chastity.
I'll tell him yet of Angelo's request,
And fit his mind to death, for his soul's rest. 200

Exit

ACT III
SCENE I. A ROOM IN THE PRISON.

Enter DUKE VINCENTIO disguised as before,
CLAUDIO, and Provost

DUKE VINCENTIO
So then you hope of pardon from Lord Angelo?

CLAUDIO
The miserable have no other medicine
But only hope:
I've hope to live, and am prepared to die.

DUKE VINCENTIO
Be absolute for death; either death or life   5
Shall thereby be the sweeter. Reason thus with life:
If I do lose thee, I do lose a thing
That none but fools would keep: a breath thou art,
Servile to all the skyey influences,
That dost this habitation, where thou keep'st,   10
Hourly afflict: merely, thou art death's fool;
For him thou labour'st by thy flight to shun
And yet runn'st toward him still. Thou art not noble;
For all the accommodations that thou bear'st
Are nursed by baseness. Thou'rt by no means valiant;   15
For thou dost fear the soft and tender fork
Of a poor worm. Thy best of rest is sleep,
And that thou oft provokest; yet grossly fear'st
Thy death, which is no more. Thou art not thyself;
For thou exist'st on many a thousand grains   20
That issue out of dust. Happy thou art not;
For what thou hast not, still thou strivest to get,
And what thou hast, forget'st. Thou art not certain;
For thy complexion shifts to strange effects,
After the moon. If thou art rich, thou'rt poor;   25
For, like an ass whose back with ingots bows,
Thou bear's thy heavy riches but a journey,
And death unloads thee. Friend hast thou none;
For thine own bowels, which do call thee sire,
The mere effusion of thy proper loins,   30
Do curse the gout, serpigo, and the rheum,
For ending thee no sooner. Thou hast nor youth nor age,
But, as it were, an after-dinner's sleep,
Dreaming on both;[32] for all thy blessed youth
Becomes as aged, and doth beg the alms   35
Of palsied eld; and when thou art old and rich,
Thou hast neither heat, affection, limb, nor beauty,
To make thy riches pleasant. What's yet in this
That bears the name of life? Yet in this life
Lie hid moe thousand deaths: yet death we fear,   40
That makes these odds all even.

---

[32] T.S. Eliot used this passage as the epigraph for his poem *Gerontion* (1920), where
the dreaming has little to do with youth: "Here I am, an old man in a dry month."

CLAUDIO
> I humbly thank you.
> To sue to live, I find I seek to die;
> And, seeking death, find life: let it come on.

ISABELLA
> *[Within]* What, ho! Peace here; grace and good company!   45

PROVOST
> Who's there? come in: the wish deserves a welcome.

DUKE VINCENTIO
> Dear sir, ere long I'll visit you again.

CLAUDIO ·
> Most holy sir, I thank you.

> *Enter ISABELLA*

ISABELLA
> My business is a word or two with Claudio.

PROVOST
> And very welcome. Look, signior, here's your sister.   50

DUKE VINCENTIO
> Provost, a word with you.

Provost
> As many as you please.

DUKE VINCENTIO
> Bring me to hear them speak, where I may be concealed.

> *Exeunt DUKE VINCENTIO and Provost*

CLAUDIO
> Now, sister, what's the comfort?

ISABELLA
> Why,   55
> As all comforts are; most good, most good indeed.
> Lord Angelo, having affairs to heaven,[33]
> Intends you for his swift ambassador,
> Where you shall be an everlasting leiger:

---

[33] Sir William Blackstone read Isabella's answer differently: "*As all comforts are: most good. / Indeed Lord Angelo, having affairs to heaven . . . .*" And thought he heard an echo of legal argumentation: "*Indeed* is the same as *in truth*, or *truly*, the common beginning of speeches in Shakspeare's [sic] age. See Charles the First's Trial. The king and Bradshaw seldom say any thing without this preface: 'Truly, Sir -----.'"

Therefore your best appointment make with speed;   60
To-morrow you set on.

CLAUDIO
Is there no remedy?

ISABELLA
None, but such remedy as, to save a head,
To cleave a heart in twain.

CLAUDIO
But is there any?   65

ISABELLA
Yes, brother, you may live:
There is a devilish mercy in the judge,
If you'll implore it, that will free your life,
But fetter you till death.

CLAUDIO
Perpetual durance?   70

ISABELLA
Ay, just; perpetual durance, a restraint,
Though all the world's vastidity you had,
To a determined scope.
CLAUDIO
But in what nature?

ISABELLA
In such a one as, you consenting to't,   75
Would bark your honour from that trunk you bear,
And leave you naked.

CLAUDIO
Let me know the point.

ISABELLA
O, I do fear thee, Claudio; and I quake,
Lest thou a feverous life shouldst entertain,   80
And six or seven winters more respect
Than a perpetual honour. Darest thou die?
The sense of death is most in apprehension;
And the poor beetle, that we tread upon,
In corporal sufferance finds a pang as great   85
As when a giant dies.

CLAUDIO
> Why give you me this shame?
> Think you I can a resolution fetch
> From flowery tenderness? If I must die,
> I will encounter darkness as a bride,   90
> And hug it in mine arms.

ISABELLA
> There spake my brother; there my father's grave
> Did utter forth a voice. Yes, thou must die:
> Thou art too noble to conserve a life
> In base appliances. This outward-sainted deputy,   95
> Whose settled visage and deliberate word
> Nips youth i' the head and follies doth emmew
> As falcon doth the fowl, is yet a devil
> His filth within being cast, he would appear
> A pond as deep as hell.   100

CLAUDIO
> The prenzie Angelo!

ISABELLA
> O, 'tis the cunning livery of hell,
> The damned'st body to invest and cover
> In prenzie guards! Dost thou think, Claudio?
> If I would yield him my virginity,   105
> Thou mightst be freed.

CLAUDIO
> O heavens! it cannot be.

ISABELLA
> Yes, he would give't thee, from this rank offence,
> So to offend him still. This night's the time
> That I should do what I abhor to name,   110
> Or else thou diest to-morrow.

CLAUDIO
> Thou shalt not do't.

ISABELLA
> O, were it but my life,
> I'ld throw it down for your deliverance
> As frankly as a pin.   115

CLAUDIO
> Thanks, dear Isabel.

ISABELLA
Be ready, Claudio, for your death tomorrow.

CLAUDIO
Yes. Has he affections in him,
That thus can make him bite the law by the nose,
When he would force it? Sure, it is no sin,   120
Or of the deadly seven, it is the least.

ISABELLA
Which is the least?

CLAUDIO
If it were damnable, he being so wise,
Why would he for the momentary trick
Be perdurably fined? O Isabel!   125

ISABELLA
What says my brother?

CLAUDIO
Death is a fearful thing.

ISABELLA
And shamed life a hateful.

CLAUDIO
Ay, but to die, and go we know not where;
To lie in cold obstruction and to rot;   130
This sensible warm motion to become
A kneaded clod; and the delighted spirit
To bathe in fiery floods, or to reside
In thrilling region of thick-ribbed ice;
To be imprison'd in the viewless winds,   135
And blown with restless violence round about
The pendent world;[34] or to be worse than worst
Of those that lawless and incertain thought
Imagine howling: 'tis too horrible!
The weariest and most loathed worldly life   140
That age, ache, penury and imprisonment
Can lay on nature is a paradise
To what we fear of death.[35]

---

[34] *Quoted in* Hopkinson v. State, 632 P.2d 79, 209 (Wyo. 1981) (Rose, C.J., dissenting in part and concurring in part); District Attorney for the Suffolk Dist. v. Watson, 411 N.E.2d 1274, 1292 (Mass. 1980) (Liacos, J., concurring).

ISABELLA
Alas, alas!

CLAUDIO
Sweet sister, let me live: 145
What sin you do to save a brother's life,
Nature dispenses with the deed so far
That it becomes a virtue.

ISABELLA
O you beast!
O faithless coward! O dishonest wretch! 150
Wilt thou be made a man out of my vice?
Is't not a kind of incest, to take life
From thine own sister's shame? What should I think?
Heaven shield my mother play'd my father fair!
For such a warped slip of wilderness 155
Ne'er issued from his blood. Take my defiance!
Die, perish! Might but my bending down
Reprieve thee from thy fate, it should proceed:
I'll pray a thousand prayers for thy death,
No word to save thee. 160

CLAUDIO
Nay, hear me, Isabel.

ISABELLA
O, fie, fie, fie!
Thy sin's not accidental, but a trade.[36]
Mercy to thee would prove itself a bawd:
'Tis best thou diest quickly. 165

CLAUDIO
O hear me, Isabella!

Re-enter DUKE VINCENTIO

DUKE VINCENTIO
Vouchsafe a word, young sister, but one word.

---

[35] *Quoted in* Grasso v. State, 857 P.2d 802, 811 (Okla. Crim. App. 1993) (Chapel, J., concurring).

[36] *Quoted in* Aguirre v. State, 22 S.W.3d 463, 475 (Tex. Crim. App. 1999) (Womack, J.). Also quoted in Glanville Williams, *Criminal Law* 235 (2d ed.1961) (on "public welfare offenses" or "regulatory offenses") ("if the law is broken there will be a suspicion that it was a deliberate breach due to self-interest").

ISABELLA
What is your will?

DUKE VINCENTIO
Might you dispense with your leisure, I would by and
by have some speech with you: the satisfaction I   170
would require is likewise your own benefit.

ISABELLA
I have no superfluous leisure; my stay must be
stolen out of other affairs; but I will attend you awhile.

Walks apart

DUKE VINCENTIO
Son, I have overheard what hath passed between you
and your sister. Angelo had never the purpose to   175
corrupt her; only he hath made an essay of her
virtue to practise his judgment with the disposition
of natures: she, having the truth of honour in her,
hath made him that gracious denial which he is most
glad to receive. I am confessor to Angelo, and I   200
know this to be true; therefore prepare yourself to
death: do not satisfy your resolution with hopes
that are fallible: tomorrow you must die; go to
your knees and make ready.

CLAUDIO
Let me ask my sister pardon. I am so out of love   205
with life that I will sue to be rid of it.

DUKE VINCENTIO
Hold you there: farewell.

Exit CLAUDIO

Provost, a word with you!

Re-enter Provost

PROVOST
What's your will, father

DUKE VINCENTIO
That now you are come, you will be gone. Leave me   210
awhile with the maid: my mind promises with my
habit no loss shall touch her by my company.

PROVOST
In good time.

Exit Provost. ISABELLA comes forward

103

DUKE VINCENTIO

    The hand that hath made you fair hath made you good:

    the goodness that is cheap in beauty makes beauty   215

    brief in goodness; but grace, being the soul of

    your complexion, shall keep the body of it ever

    fair. The assault that Angelo hath made to you,[37]

    fortune hath conveyed to my understanding; and, but

    that frailty hath examples for his falling, I should   220

    wonder at Angelo. How will you do to content this

    substitute, and to save your brother?

ISABELLA

    I am now going to resolve him: I had rather my

    brother die by the law than my son should be

    unlawfully born. But, O, how much is the good duke   225

    deceived in Angelo! If ever he return and I can

    speak to him, I will open my lips in vain, or

    discover his government.

DUKE VINCENTIO

    That shall not be much amiss: Yet, as the matter

    now stands, he will avoid your accusation; he made   230

    trial of you only. Therefore fasten your ear on my

    advisings: to the love I have in doing good a

    remedy presents itself. I do make myself believe

    that you may most uprighteously do a poor wronged

    lady a merited benefit; redeem your brother from   235

    the angry law; do no stain to your own gracious

    person; and much please the absent duke, if

    peradventure he shall ever return to have hearing of

    this business.

ISABELLA

    Let me hear you speak farther. I have spirit to do   240

    anything that appears not foul in the truth of my spirit.

DUKE VINCENTIO

    Virtue is bold, and goodness never fearful. Have

    you not heard speak of Mariana, the sister of

    Frederick the great soldier who miscarried at sea?

---

[37] Assault, in law, did not require physical contact, so Angelo's proposition could be loosely called an *assault*, but in Shakespeare's day *assault* could also mean "a love-proposal, a wooing." 1 *Oxford English Dictionary* 702 (2d ed. 1989).

ISABELLA

I have heard of the lady, and good words went with her name.   245

DUKE VINCENTIO

She should this Angelo have married; was affianced
to her by oath, and the nuptial appointed: between
which time of the contract and limit of the
solemnity, her brother Frederick was wrecked at sea,
having in that perished vessel the dowry of his   250
sister. But mark how heavily this befell to the
poor gentlewoman: there she lost a noble and
renowned brother, in his love toward her ever most
kind and natural; with him, the portion and sinew of
her fortune, her marriage-dowry; with both, her   255
combinate husband, this well-seeming Angelo.

ISABELLA

Can this be so? did Angelo so leave her?

DUKE VINCENTIO

Left her in her tears, and dried not one of them
with his comfort; swallowed his vows whole,
pretending in her discoveries of dishonour:[38] in few,   260
bestowed her on her own lamentation, which she yet
wears for his sake; and he, a marble to her tears,
is washed with them, but relents not.[39]

ISABELLA

What a merit were it in death to take this poor maid
from the world! What corruption in this life, that   265
it will let this man live! But how out of this can she avail?

DUKE VINCENTIO

It is a rupture that you may easily heal: and the

---

[38] Angelo seems to have charged Mariana with unchastity. If so, it was slander per
se; that is, it was actionable without the need to allege and prove damages. See
Prosser & Keeton on the Law of Torts 788 (5th ed. 1984).

[39] Many readers of *Measure for Measure* have wondered how the Duke knew of
Mariana's mistreatment and why in light of that knowledge he trusted Angelo to
be the deputy in his apparent absence. Sir William Blackstone speculated that "the
duke probably had learnt of the story of Mariana in some of his former retirements,
'having ever loved the life removed.' And he had a suspicion that Angelo was but a
seemer and therefore stays to watch him." Perhaps Lucio was referring to this aspect
of the Duke's character when he describes him in the next Act as *the old fantastical
Duke of dark corners.*

cure of it not only saves your brother, but keeps
you from dishonour in doing it.

ISABELLA

Show me how, good father. 270

DUKE VINCENTIO

This forenamed maid hath yet in her the continuance
of her first affection: his unjust unkindness, that
in all reason should have quenched her love, hath,
like an impediment in the current, made it more
violent and unruly. Go you to Angelo; answer his 275
requiring with a plausible obedience; agree with
his demands to the point; only refer yourself to
this advantage, first, that your stay with him may
not be long; that the time may have all shadow and
silence in it; and the place answer to convenience. 280
This being granted in course,--and now follows
all,--we shall advise this wronged maid to stead up
your appointment, go in your place; if the encounter
acknowledge itself hereafter, it may compel him to
her recompense: and here, by this, is your brother 285
saved, your honour untainted, the poor Mariana
advantaged, and the corrupt deputy scaled. The maid
will I frame and make fit for his attempt. If you
think well to carry this as you may, the doubleness
of the benefit defends the deceit from reproof. 290
What think you of it?

ISABELLA

The image of it gives me content already; and I
trust it will grow to a most prosperous perfection.

DUKE VINCENTIO

It lies much in your holding up. Haste you speedily
to Angelo: if for this night he entreat you to his 295
bed, give him promise of satisfaction. I will
presently to Saint Luke's: there, at the moated
grange, resides this dejected Mariana.[40] At that

---

[40] Tennyson used *Mariana in the moated grange*, citing *Measure for Measure*, as the
epigraph for his poem, *Mariana* (1830), which depicts a more than merely *dejected*
woman. "Then, said she, 'I am very dreary, / He will not come,' she said; / She
wept, 'I am aweary, aweary, / Oh God, that I were dead!'"

place call upon me; and dispatch with Angelo, that
it may be quickly.   300

ISABELLA
I thank you for this comfort. Fare you well, good father.

Exeunt severally

SCENE II. THE STREET BEFORE THE PRISON.

Enter, on one side, DUKE VINCENTIO disguised as before;
on the other, ELBOW, and Officers with POMPEY

ELBOW
Nay, if there be no remedy for it, but that you will
needs buy and sell men and women like beasts, we
shall have all the world drink brown and white bastard.

DUKE VINCENTIO
O heavens! what stuff is here?

POMPEY
'Twas never merry world since, of two usuries, the   5
merriest was put down, and the worser allowed by
order of law a furred gown to keep him warm; and
furred with fox and lamb-skins too, to signify, that
craft, being richer than innocency, stands for the facing.[41]

ELBOW
Come your way, sir. 'Bless you, good father friar.   10

DUKE VINCENTIO
And you, good brother father. What offence hath
this man made you, sir?

ELBOW
Marry, sir, he hath offended the law: and, sir, we
take him to be a thief too, sir; for we have found
upon him, sir, a strange picklock, which we have   15
sent to the deputy.[42]

---

[41] The *two usuries* seem to be prostitution and the taking of interest. The former was
outlawed; the latter was allowed up to a maximum rate of interest, but even that
restriction could be avoided by disguising a loan as a sale. See the preface for August, *A Rogues' Gallery: all great doers in our trade.*
[42] Possession of burglar's tools is a criminal offence. See, e.g., N.C. Gen. Stat. § 14-55
("If any person . . . shall be found having in his possession, without lawful excuse,

DUKE VINCENTIO

    Fie, sirrah! a bawd, a wicked bawd!
    The evil that thou causest to be done,
    That is thy means to live. Do thou but think
    What 'tis to cram a maw or clothe a back   20
    From such a filthy vice: say to thyself,
    From their abominable and beastly touches
    I drink, I eat, array myself, and live.
    Canst thou believe thy living is a life,
    So stinkingly depending? Go mend, go mend.   25

POMPEY

    Indeed, it does stink in some sort, sir; but yet,
    sir, I would prove--

DUKE VINCENTIO

    Nay, if the devil have given thee proofs for sin,
    Thou wilt prove his. Take him to prison, officer:
    Correction and instruction must both work   30
    Ere this rude beast will profit.

ELBOW

    He must before the deputy, sir; he has given him
    warning: the deputy cannot abide a whoremaster: if
    he be a whoremonger, and comes before him, he were
    as good go a mile on his errand.   35

DUKE VINCENTIO

    That we were all, as some would seem to be,
    From our faults, as faults from seeming, free!

ELBOW

    His neck will come to your waist,--a cord, sir.

POMPEY

    I spy comfort; I cry bail. Here's a gentleman and a
    friend of mine.   40

                         Enter LUCIO

LUCIO

    How now, noble Pompey! What, at the wheels of
    Caesar? art thou led in triumph? What, is there

---

any picklock, key, bit, or other implement of housebreaking . . . , such person shall
be punished as a Class I felon.").

none of Pygmalion's images, newly made woman, to be
had now, for putting the hand in the pocket and
extracting it clutch'd? What reply, ha? What   45
sayest thou to this tune, matter and method? Is't
not drowned i' the last rain, ha? What sayest
thou, Trot? Is the world as it was, man? Which is
the way? Is it sad, and few words? or how? The
trick of it?   50

DUKE VINCENTIO
Still thus, and thus; still worse!

LUCIO
How doth my dear morsel, thy mistress? Procures she
still, ha?

POMPEY
Troth, sir, she hath eaten up all her beef, and she
is herself in the tub.   55

LUCIO
Why, 'tis good; it is the right of it; it must be
so: ever your fresh whore and your powdered bawd:
an unshunned consequence; it must be so. Art going
to prison, Pompey?

POMPEY
Yes, faith, sir.   60

LUCIO
Why, 'tis not amiss, Pompey. Farewell: go, say I
sent thee thither. For debt, Pompey? or how?[43]

ELBOW
For being a bawd, for being a bawd.

---

[43] Judgment creditors had the power at common law to cause debtors to be kept in prison till the debt was paid, as anyone knows who has read the novels of Charles Dickens. See William S. Holdsworth, *Charles Dickens as Legal Historian* 136-43 (1929). After the Revolution, American states moved to abolish the practice. The Pennsylvania Constitution of 1776 led the way, prohibiting it, in the absence of evidence of fraud, if the debtor turned over all his assets, a primitive form of bankruptcy. See J. Paul Selsam, *The Pennsylvania Constitution of 1776: A Study in Revolutionary Democracy* 203 (1936) (current provision in Pa. Const. art. I, § 16). A large majority of the states still have constitutional provisions against imprisonment for debt. See, e.g., John V. Orth, *The North Carolina State Constitution, With History and Commentary* 70-71 (1993) (commenting upon N.C. Const. art. I, § 28).

LUCIO

Well, then, imprison him: if imprisonment be the
due of a bawd, why, 'tis his right: bawd is he   65
doubtless, and of antiquity too; bawd-born.
Farewell, good Pompey. Commend me to the prison,
Pompey: you will turn good husband now, Pompey; you
will keep the house.

POMPEY

I hope, sir, your good worship will be my bail.   70

LUCIO

No, indeed, will I not, Pompey; it is not the wear.
I will pray, Pompey, to increase your bondage: If
you take it not patiently, why, your mettle is the
more. Adieu, trusty Pompey. 'Bless you, friar.

DUKE VINCENTIO

And you.   75

LUCIO

Does Bridget paint still, Pompey, ha?

ELBOW

Come your ways, sir; come.

POMPEY

You will not bail me, then, sir?

LUCIO

Then, Pompey, nor now. What news abroad, friar?
what news?   80

ELBOW

Come your ways, sir; come.

LUCIO

Go to kennel, Pompey; go.

                                  Exeunt ELBOW, POMPEY and Officers
What news, friar, of the duke?

DUKE VINCENTIO

I know none. Can you tell me of any?

LUCIO

Some say he is with the Emperor of Russia; other   85
some, he is in Rome: but where is he, think you?

DUKE VINCENTIO
I know not where; but wheresoever, I wish him well.

LUCIO
It was a mad fantastical trick of him to steal from
the state, and usurp the beggary he was never born
to. Lord Angelo dukes it well in his absence; he   90
puts transgression to 't.

DUKE VINCENTIO
He does well in 't.

LUCIO
A little more lenity to lechery would do no harm in
him: something too crabbed that way, friar.

DUKE VINCENTIO
It is too general a vice, and severity must cure it.   95

LUCIO
Yes, in good sooth, the vice is of a great kindred;
it is well allied: but it is impossible to extirp
it quite, friar, till eating and drinking be put
down. They say this Angelo was not made by man and
woman after this downright way of creation: is it   100
true, think you?

DUKE VINCENTIO
How should he be made, then?

LUCIO
Some report a sea-maid spawned him; some, that he
was begot between two stock-fishes. But it is
certain that when he makes water his urine is   105
congealed ice; that I know to be true: and he is a
motion generative; that's infallible.

DUKE VINCENTIO
You are pleasant, sir, and speak apace.

LUCIO
Why, what a ruthless thing is this in him, for the
rebellion of a codpiece to take away the life of a   110
man! Would the duke that is absent have done this?
Ere he would have hanged a man for the getting a
hundred bastards, he would have paid for the nursing
a thousand: he had some feeling of the sport: he
knew the service, and that instructed him to mercy.   115

DUKE VINCENTIO
> I never heard the absent duke much detected for
> women; he was not inclined that way.

LUCIO
> O, sir, you are deceived.

DUKE VINCENTIO
> 'Tis not possible.

LUCIO
> Who, not the duke? yes, your beggar of fifty; and   120
> his use was to put a ducat in her clack-dish: the
> duke had crotchets in him. He would be drunk too;
> that let me inform you.

DUKE VINCENTIO
> You do him wrong, surely.

LUCIO
> Sir, I was an inward of his. A shy fellow was the   125
> duke: and I believe I know the cause of his
> withdrawing.

DUKE VINCENTIO
> What, I prithee, might be the cause?

LUCIO
> No, pardon; 'tis a secret must be locked within the
> teeth and the lips: but this I can let you   130
> understand, the greater file of the subject held the
> duke to be wise.

DUKE VINCENTIO
> Wise! why, no question but he was.

LUCIO
> A very superficial, ignorant, unweighing fellow.

DUKE VINCENTIO
> Either this is the envy in you, folly, or mistaking: 135
> the very stream of his life and the business he hath
> helmed must upon a warranted need give him a better
> proclamation. Let him be but testimonied in his own
> bringings-forth, and he shall appear to the
> envious a scholar, a statesman and a soldier.   140
> Therefore you speak unskilfully: or if your
> knowledge be more it is much darkened in your malice.

LUCIO
Sir, I know him, and I love him.

DUKE VINCENTIO
Love talks with better knowledge, and knowledge with
dearer love. 145

LUCIO
Come, sir, I know what I know.

DUKE VINCENTIO
I can hardly believe that, since you know not what
you speak. But, if ever the duke return, as our
prayers are he may, let me desire you to make your
answer before him. If it be honest you have spoke, 150
you have courage to maintain it: I am bound to call
upon you; and, I pray you, your name?

LUCIO
Sir, my name is Lucio; well known to the duke.

DUKE VINCENTIO
He shall know you better, sir, if I may live to
report you. 155

LUCIO
I fear you not.

DUKE VINCENTIO
O, you hope the duke will return no more; or you
imagine me too unhurtful an opposite. But indeed I
can do you little harm; you'll forswear this again.

LUCIO
I'll be hanged first: thou art deceived in me, 160
friar. But no more of this. Canst thou tell if
Claudio die to-morrow or no?

DUKE VINCENTIO
Why should he die, sir?

LUCIO
Why? For filling a bottle with a tundish. I would
the duke we talk of were returned again: the 165
ungenitured agent will unpeople the province with
continency; sparrows must not build in his
house-eaves, because they are lecherous. The duke
yet would have dark deeds darkly answered; he would

never bring them to light: would he were returned!　　　　170
Marry, this Claudio is condemned for untrussing.
Farewell, good friar: I prithee, pray for me. The
duke, I say to thee again, would eat mutton on
Fridays. He's not past it yet, and I say to thee,
he would mouth with a beggar, though she smelt brown　　175
bread and garlic: say that I said so. Farewell.

Exit

DUKE VINCENTIO

No might nor greatness in mortality
Can censure 'scape; back-wounding calumny
The whitest virtue strikes. What king so strong
Can tie the gall up in the slanderous tongue?[44]　　　　180
But who comes here?

Enter ESCALUS, Provost, and Officers
with MISTRESS OVERDONE

ESCALUS

Go; away with her to prison!

MISTRESS OVERDONE

Good my lord, be good to me; your honour is accounted
a merciful man; good my lord.

ESCALUS

Double and treble admonition, and still forfeit in　　　185
the same kind! This would make mercy swear and play
the tyrant.

PROVOST

A bawd of eleven years' continuance, may it please
your honour.

MISTRESS OVERDONE

My lord, this is one Lucio's information against me.　　　190
Mistress Kate Keepdown was with child by him in the
duke's time; he promised her marriage: his child
is a year and a quarter old, come Philip and Jacob:
I have kept it myself; and see how he goes about to abuse me!

ESCALUS

That fellow is a fellow of much licence: let him be　　　195
called before us. Away with her to prison! Go to;
no more words.

---

[44] *Quoted in* Commonwealth v. Vallone, 32 A.2d 889, 894 (Pa. 1943) (Maxey, C.J.).

Exeunt Officers with MISTRESS OVERDONE

Provost, my brother Angelo will not be altered;
Claudio must die to-morrow: let him be furnished
with divines, and have all charitable preparation.   200
if my brother wrought by my pity, it should not be
so with him.

PROVOST
So please you, this friar hath been with him, and
advised him for the entertainment of death.

ESCALUS
Good even, good father.   205

DUKE VINCENTIO
Bliss and goodness on you!

ESCALUS
Of whence are you?

DUKE VINCENTIO
Not of this country, though my chance is now
To use it for my time: I am a brother
Of gracious order, late come from the See   210
In special business from his holiness.

ESCALUS
What news abroad i' the world?

DUKE VINCENTIO
None, but that there is so great a fever on
goodness, that the dissolution of it must cure it:
novelty is only in request; and it is as dangerous   215
to be aged in any kind of course, as it is virtuous
to be constant in any undertaking. There is scarce
truth enough alive to make societies secure; but
security enough to make fellowships accurst: much
upon this riddle runs the wisdom of the world. This   220
news is old enough, yet it is every day's news. I
pray you, sir, of what disposition was the duke?

ESCALUS
One that, above all other strifes, contended
especially to know himself.

DUKE VINCENTIO
What pleasure was he given to?   225

115

ESCALUS
Rather rejoicing to see another merry, than merry at
any thing which professed to make him rejoice: a
gentleman of all temperance. But leave we him to
his events, with a prayer they may prove prosperous;
and let me desire to know how you find Claudio   230
prepared. I am made to understand that you have
lent him visitation.

DUKE VINCENTIO
He professes to have received no sinister measure
from his judge, but most willingly humbles himself
to the determination of justice: yet had he framed   235
to himself, by the instruction of his frailty, many
deceiving promises of life; which I by my good
leisure have discredited to him, and now is he
resolved to die.

ESCALUS
You have paid the heavens your function, and the   240
prisoner the very debt of your calling. I have
laboured for the poor gentleman to the extremest
shore of my modesty: but my brother justice have I
found so severe, that he hath forced me to tell him
he is indeed Justice.[45]   245

DUKE VINCENTIO
If his own life answer the straitness of his
proceeding, it shall become him well; wherein if he
chance to fail, he hath sentenced himself.

ESCALUS
I am going to visit the prisoner. Fare you well.

DUKE VINCENTIO
Peace be with you!   250

Exeunt ESCALUS and Provost

He who the sword of heaven will bear
Should be as holy as severe;[46]

---

[45] Angelo has become *Justice* personified, but his harsh justice recalls the maxim:
"*Summum jus, summa injuria*" (More law, less justice). See Pits v. James, Hob. 121,
125, 80 Eng. Rep. 271, 274 (K.B. 1615) (quoting Cicero, *De officiis* I: 10). See Walter
Miller trans., Loeb Classical Library vol. 30 (1913).
[46] *Quoted in* Summerlin v. Stewart, 267 F.3d 926, 948 (9th Cir. 2001) (Silver, J.) (judicial impairment caused by use of marijuana).

Pattern in himself to know,
Grace to stand, and virtue go;
More nor less to others paying   255
Than by self-offences weighing.
Shame to him whose cruel striking
Kills for faults of his own liking!
Twice treble shame on Angelo,
To weed my vice and let his grow!   260
O, what may man within him hide,
Though angel on the outward side!
How may likeness made in crimes,
Making practise on the times,
To draw with idle spiders' strings   265
Most ponderous and substantial things!
Craft against vice I must apply:
With Angelo to-night shall lie
His old betrothed but despised;
So disguise shall, by the disguised,   270
Pay with falsehood false exacting,
And perform an old contracting.

Exit

ACT IV
SCENE I. THE MOATED GRANGE AT ST. LUKE'S.

Enter MARIANA and a Boy

BOY sings
　　Take, O, take those lips away,
　　That so sweetly were forsworn;
　　And those eyes, the break of day,
　　Lights that do mislead the morn:
　　But my kisses bring again, bring again;   5
　　Seals of love, but sealed in vain, sealed in vain.

MARIANA
　　Break off thy song, and haste thee quick away:
　　Here comes a man of comfort, whose advice
　　Hath often still'd my brawling discontent.

Exit Boy
Enter DUKE VINCENTIO disguised as before

　　I cry you mercy, sir; and well could wish   10
　　You had not found me here so musical:

Let me excuse me, and believe me so,
My mirth it much displeased, but pleased my woe.

DUKE VINCENTIO
'Tis good; though music oft hath such a charm
To make bad good, and good provoke to harm.   15
I pray, you, tell me, hath any body inquired
for me here to-day? Much upon this time have
I promised here to meet.

MARIANA
You have not been inquired after:
I have sat here all day.   20

Enter ISABELLA

DUKE VINCENTIO
I do constantly believe you. The time is come even
now. I shall crave your forbearance a little: may
be I will call upon you anon, for some advantage to yourself.

MARIANA
I am always bound to you.

Exit

DUKE VINCENTIO
Very well met, and well come.   25
What is the news from this good deputy?

ISABELLA
He hath a garden circummured with brick,
Whose western side is with a vineyard back'd;
And to that vineyard is a planched gate,
That makes his opening with this bigger key: 30
This other doth command a little door
Which from the vineyard to the garden leads;
There have I made my promise
Upon the heavy middle of the night
To call upon him.   35

DUKE VINCENTIO
But shall you on your knowledge find this way?

ISABELLA
I have ta'en a due and wary note upon't:
With whispering and most guilty diligence,
In action all of precept, he did show me
The way twice o'er.   40

DUKE VINCENTIO
    Are there no other tokens
    Between you 'greed concerning her observance?

ISABELLA
    No, none, but only a repair i' the dark;[47]
    And that I have possess'd him my most stay
    Can be but brief; for I have made him know   45
    I have a servant comes with me along,
    That stays upon me, whose persuasion is
    I come about my brother.

DUKE VINCENTIO
    'Tis well borne up.
    I have not yet made known to Mariana   50
    A word of this. What, ho! within! come forth!

                                    Re-enter MARIANA

    I pray you, be acquainted with this maid;
    She comes to do you good.

ISABELLA
    I do desire the like.

DUKE VINCENTIO
    Do you persuade yourself that I respect you?   55

MARIANA
    Good friar, I know you do, and have found it.

DUKE VINCENTIO
    Take, then, this your companion by the hand,
    Who hath a story ready for your ear.
    I shall attend your leisure: but make haste;
    The vaporous night approaches.   60

MARIANA
    Will't please you walk aside?
                        Exeunt MARIANA and ISABELLA
DUKE VINCENTIO
    O place and greatness! millions of false eyes

---

[47] The "bed trick," substituting one woman for another in the dark, has ancient precedent; for example, Leah substituted for her sister Rachel in the bed of the patriarch Jacob in Genesis (29:21-27). The masculine reality was summed up by Benjamin Franklin in his notorious *Advice to a Young Man on the Choice of a Mistress:* "In the dark all cats are grey," in 3 *Papers of Benjamin Franklin* 27, 31 (Leonard W. Larabee ed. 1961).

Are stuck upon thee: volumes of report
Run with these false and most contrarious quests
Upon thy doings: thousand escapes of wit   65
Make thee the father of their idle dreams
And rack thee in their fancies.
                                    Re-enter MARIANA and ISABELLA
Welcome, how agreed?

ISABELLA
She'll take the enterprise upon her, father,
If you advise it.   70

DUKE VINCENTIO
It is not my consent,
But my entreaty too.

ISABELLA
Little have you to say
When you depart from him, but, soft and low,
'Remember now my brother.'   75

MARIANA
Fear me not.

DUKE VINCENTIO
Nor, gentle daughter, fear you not at all.
He is your husband on a pre-contract:[48]
To bring you thus together, 'tis no sin,
Sith that the justice of your title to him   80
Doth flourish the deceit. Come, let us go:
Our corn's to reap, for yet our tithe's to sow.

                                                    Exeunt

SCENE II. A ROOM IN THE PRISON.

                                        Enter Provost and POMPEY
PROVOST
Come hither, sirrah. Can you cut off a man's head?

POMPEY
If the man be a bachelor, sir, I can; but if he be a

---

[48] On the question how (if at all) Claudio's consensual sex with Juliet differs from Angelo's unintended intercourse with Mariana, see the preface for July, *The Marriage Contract: a pre-contract / a true contract.*

married man, he's his wife's head, and I can never
cut off a woman's head.

PROVOST

Come, sir, leave me your snatches, and yield me a   5
direct answer. To-morrow morning are to die Claudio
and Barnardine. Here is in our prison a common
executioner, who in his office lacks a helper: if
you will take it on you to assist him, it shall
redeem you from your gyves; if not, you shall have   10
your full time of imprisonment and your deliverance
with an unpitied whipping, for you have been a
notorious bawd.

POMPEY

Sir, I have been an unlawful bawd time out of mind;
but yet I will be content to be a lawful hangman. I   15
would be glad to receive some instruction from my
fellow partner.

PROVOST

What, ho! Abhorson! Where's Abhorson, there?

Enter ABHORSON

ABHORSON

Do you call, sir?

PROVOST

Sirrah, here's a fellow will help you to-morrow in   20
your execution. If you think it meet, compound with
him by the year, and let him abide here with you; if
not, use him for the present and dismiss him. He
cannot plead his estimation with you; he hath been a bawd.

ABHORSON

A bawd, sir? fie upon him! he will discredit our mystery.   25

PROVOST

Go to, sir; you weigh equally; a feather will turn
the scale.   *Exit*

POMPEY

Pray, sir, by your good favour,--for surely, sir, a
good favour you have, but that you have a hanging
look,--do you call, sir, your occupation a mystery?   30

ABHORSON

Ay, sir; a mystery[49]

POMPEY

Painting, sir, I have heard say, is a mystery; and
your whores, sir, being members of my occupation,
using painting, do prove my occupation a mystery:
but what mystery there should be in hanging, if I   35
should be hanged, I cannot imagine.

ABHORSON

Sir, it is a mystery.

POMPEY

Proof?

ABHORSON

Every true man's apparel fits your thief: if it be
too little for your thief, your true man thinks it   40
big enough; if it be too big for your thief, your
thief thinks it little enough: so every true man's
apparel fits your thief.

Re-enter Provost

PROVOST

Are you agreed?

POMPEY

Sir, I will serve him; for I do find your hangman is   45
a more penitent trade than your bawd; he doth
oftener ask forgiveness.

PROVOST

You, sirrah, provide your block and your axe
to-morrow four o'clock.

ABHORSON

Come on, bawd; I will instruct thee in my trade; follow.   50

POMPEY

I do desire to learn, sir: and I hope, if you have

---

[49] *Mystery* was formerly used to refer to a profession, but already in Shakespeare's
day, it was ripe for Pompey's punning. Oliver Wendell Holmes in the first sentence
of his famous lecture *The Path of the Law* echoed the word play: "When we study
law we are not studying a mystery but a well known profession." 10 *Harv. L. Rev.*
457, 457 (1897).

occasion to use me for your own turn, you shall find
me yare; for truly, sir, for your kindness I owe you
a good turn.

PROVOST
Call hither Barnardine and Claudio: 55

Exeunt POMPEY and ABHORSON

The one has my pity; not a jot the other,
Being a murderer, though he were my brother.

Enter CLAUDIO

Look, here's the warrant, Claudio, for thy death:
'Tis now dead midnight, and by eight to-morrow
Thou must be made immortal. Where's Barnardine?   60

CLAUDIO
As fast lock'd up in sleep as guiltless labour
When it lies starkly in the traveller's bones:
He will not wake.

PROVOST
Who can do good on him?
Well, go, prepare yourself.   65

Knocking within

But, hark, what noise?
Heaven give your spirits comfort!

Exit CLAUDIO

By and by.
I hope it is some pardon or reprieve
For the most gentle Claudio.   70

Enter DUKE VINCENTIO disguised as before

Welcome father.

DUKE VINCENTIO
The best and wholesomest spirits of the night
Envelope you, good Provost! Who call'd here of late?

PROVOST
None, since the curfew rung.

DUKE VINCENTIO
Not Isabel?   75

PROVOST
No.

DUKE VINCENTIO
They will, then, ere't be long.

PROVOST
What comfort is for Claudio?

DUKE VINCENTIO
There's some in hope.

PROVOST
It is a bitter deputy.   80

DUKE VINCENTIO
Not so, not so; his life is parallel'd
Even with the stroke and line of his great justice:
He doth with holy abstinence subdue
That in himself which he spurs on his power
To qualify in others: were he meal'd with that   85
Which he corrects, then were he tyrannous;
But this being so, he's just.

Knocking within

Now are they come.

Exit Provost

This is a gentle provost: seldom when
The steeled gaoler is the friend of men.   90

Knocking within

How now! what noise? That spirit's possessed with haste
That wounds the unsisting postern with these strokes.

Re-enter Provost

PROVOST
There he must stay until the officer
Arise to let him in: he is call'd up.

DUKE VINCENTIO
Have you no countermand for Claudio yet,   95
But he must die to-morrow?

PROVOST
None, sir, none.

DUKE VINCENTIO
As near the dawning, provost, as it is,
You shall hear more ere morning.

PROVOST
Happily   100

You something know; yet I believe there comes
No countermand; no such example have we:
Besides, upon the very siege of justice
Lord Angelo hath to the public ear
Profess'd the contrary.   105

Enter a Messenger

This is his lordship's man.

DUKE VINCENTIO
And here comes Claudio's pardon.

MESSENGER

Giving a paper

My lord hath sent you this note; and by me this
further charge, that you swerve not from the
smallest article of it, neither in time, matter, or   110
other circumstance. Good morrow; for, as I take it,
it is almost day.

PROVOST
I shall obey him.

Exit Messenger

DUKE VINCENTIO
[*Aside*] This is his pardon, purchased by such sin
For which the pardoner himself is in.   115
Hence hath offence his quick celerity,
When it is born in high authority:
When vice makes mercy, mercy's so extended,
That for the fault's love is the offender friended.
Now, sir, what news?   120

PROVOST
I told you. Lord Angelo, belike thinking me remiss
in mine office, awakens me with this unwonted
putting-on; methinks strangely, for he hath not used it before.

DUKE VINCENTIO
Pray you, let's hear.

PROVOST
[*Reads*]
'Whatsoever you may hear to the contrary, let   125
Claudio be executed by four of the clock; and in the
afternoon Barnardine: for my better satisfaction,

let me have Claudio's head sent me by five. Let
this be duly performed; with a thought that more
depends on it than we must yet deliver. Thus fail   130
not to do your office, as you will answer it at your peril.'
What say you to this, sir?

DUKE VINCENTIO
What is that Barnardine who is to be executed in the
afternoon?

PROVOST
A Bohemian born, but here nursed up and bred; one   135
that is a prisoner nine years old.

DUKE VINCENTIO
How came it that the absent duke had not either
delivered him to his liberty or executed him? I
have heard it was ever his manner to do so.

PROVOST
His friends still wrought reprieves for him: and,   140
indeed, his fact, till now in the government of Lord
Angelo, came not to an undoubtful proof.

DUKE VINCENTIO
It is now apparent?

PROVOST
Most manifest, and not denied by himself.

DUKE VINCENTIO
Hath he borne himself penitently in prison? How   145
seems he to be touched?

PROVOST
A man that apprehends death no more dreadfully but
as a drunken sleep; careless, reckless, and fearless
of what's past, present, or to come; insensible of
mortality, and desperately mortal.   150

DUKE VINCENTIO
He wants advice.

PROVOST
He will hear none: he hath evermore had the liberty
of the prison; give him leave to escape hence, he
would not: drunk many times a day, if not many days

entirely drunk. We have very oft awaked him, as if 155
to carry him to execution, and showed him a seeming
warrant for it: it hath not moved him at all.

DUKE VINCENTIO
More of him anon. There is written in your brow,
provost, honesty and constancy: if I read it not
truly, my ancient skill beguiles me; but, in the 160
boldness of my cunning, I will lay myself in hazard.
Claudio, whom here you have warrant to execute, is
no greater forfeit to the law than Angelo who hath
sentenced him. To make you understand this in a
manifested effect, I crave but four days' respite; 165
for the which you are to do me both a present and a
dangerous courtesy.

PROVOST
Pray, sir, in what?

DUKE VINCENTIO
In the delaying death.

PROVOST
A lack, how may I do it, having the hour limited, 170
and an express command, under penalty, to deliver
his head in the view of Angelo? I may make my case
as Claudio's, to cross this in the smallest.

DUKE VINCENTIO
By the vow of mine order I warrant you, if my
instructions may be your guide. Let this Barnardine 175
be this morning executed, and his head born to Angelo.

PROVOST
Angelo hath seen them both, and will discover the favour.

DUKE VINCENTIO
O, death's a great disguiser; and you may add to it.
Shave the head, and tie the beard; and say it was
the desire of the penitent to be so bared before his 180
death: you know the course is common. If any thing
fall to you upon this, more than thanks and good
fortune, by the saint whom I profess, I will plead
against it with my life.

PROVOST

   Pardon me, good father; it is against my oath.   185

DUKE VINCENTIO

   Were you sworn to the duke, or to the deputy?

PROVOST

   To him, and to his substitutes.

DUKE VINCENTIO

   You will think you have made no offence, if the duke
   avouch the justice of your dealing?

PROVOST

   But what likelihood is in that?   190

DUKE VINCENTIO

   Not a resemblance, but a certainty. Yet since I see
   you fearful, that neither my coat, integrity, nor
   persuasion can with ease attempt you, I will go
   further than I meant, to pluck all fears out of you.
   Look you, sir, here is the hand and seal of the   195
   duke: you know the character, I doubt not; and the
   signet is not strange to you.

PROVOST

   I know them both.

DUKE VINCENTIO

   The contents of this is the return of the duke: you
   shall anon over-read it at your pleasure; where you   200
   shall find, within these two days he will be here.
   This is a thing that Angelo knows not; for he this
   very day receives letters of strange tenor;
   perchance of the duke's death; perchance entering
   into some monastery; but, by chance, nothing of what   205
   is writ. Look, the unfolding star calls up the
   shepherd. Put not yourself into amazement how these
   things should be: all difficulties are but easy
   when they are known. Call your executioner, and off
   with Barnardine's head: I will give him a present   210
   shrift and advise him for a better place. Yet you
   are amazed; but this shall absolutely resolve you.
   Come away; it is almost clear dawn.   *Exeunt*

Scene III. Another Room in the Same.

Enter POMPEY

POMPEY

I am as well acquainted here as I was in our house
of profession: one would think it were Mistress
Overdone's own house, for here be many of her old
customers. First, here's young Master Rash; he's in
for a commodity of brown paper and old ginger,   5
ninescore and seventeen pounds; of which he made
five marks, ready money: marry, then ginger was not
much in request, for the old women were all dead.
Then is there here one Master Caper, at the suit of
Master Three-pile the mercer, for some four suits of   10
peach-coloured satin, which now peaches him a
beggar. Then have we here young Dizy, and young
Master Deep-vow, and Master Copperspur, and Master
Starve-lackey the rapier and dagger man, and young
Drop-heir that killed lusty Pudding, and Master   15
Forthlight the tilter, and brave Master Shooty the
great traveller, and wild Half-can that stabbed
Pots, and, I think, forty more; all great doers in
our trade, and are now 'for the Lord's sake.'[50]

Enter ABHORSON

ABHORSON

Sirrah, bring Barnardine hither.   20

POMPEY

Master Barnardine! you must rise and be hanged.
Master Barnardine!

ABHORSON

What, ho, Barnardine!

BARNARDINE

[Within] A pox o' your throats! Who makes that
noise there? What are you?   25

POMPEY

Your friends, sir; the hangman. You must be so
good, sir, to rise and be put to death.

---

[50] The play provides a parade of criminals, not just bawds like Pompey and prostitutes like Mistress Overdone. See the preface for August, *A Rogues' Gallery: all great doers in our trade.*

BARNARDINE

[*Within*] Away, you rogue, away! I am sleepy.

ABHORSON

Tell him he must awake, and that quickly too.

POMPEY

Pray, Master Barnardine, awake till you are   30
executed, and sleep afterwards.

ABHORSON

Go in to him, and fetch him out.

POMPEY

He is coming, sir, he is coming; I hear his straw rustle.

ABHORSON

Is the axe upon the block, sirrah?

POMPEY

Very ready, sir.   35

Enter BARNARDINE

BARNARDINE

How now, Abhorson? what's the news with you?

ABHORSON

Truly, sir, I would desire you to clap into your
prayers; for, look you, the warrant's come.

BARNARDINE

You rogue, I have been drinking all night; I am not
fitted for 't.   40

POMPEY

O, the better, sir; for he that drinks all night,
and is hanged betimes in the morning, may sleep the
sounder all the next day.

ABHORSON

Look you, sir; here comes your ghostly father: do
we jest now, think you?   45

Enter DUKE VINCENTIO disguised as before

DUKE VINCENTIO

Sir, induced by my charity, and hearing how hastily
you are to depart, I am come to advise you, comfort
you and pray with you.

BARNARDINE
> Friar, not I: I have been drinking hard all night,
> and I will have more time to prepare me, or they   50
> shall beat out my brains with billets: I will not
> consent to die this day, that's certain.

DUKE VINCENTIO
> O, sir, you must: and therefore I beseech you
> Look forward on the journey you shall go.

BARNARDINE
> I swear I will not die to-day for any man's   55
> persuasion.

DUKE VINCENTIO
> But hear you.

BARNARDINE
> Not a word: if you have any thing to say to me,
> come to my ward; for thence will not I to-day.

> *Exit*

DUKE VINCENTIO
> Unfit to live or die: O gravel heart!   60
> After him, fellows; bring him to the block.

> *Exeunt ABHORSON and POMPEY*
> *Re-enter Provost*

PROVOST
> Now, sir, how do you find the prisoner?

DUKE VINCENTIO
> A creature unprepared, unmeet for death;
> And to transport him in the mind he is
> Were damnable.   65

PROVOST
> Here in the prison, father,
> There died this morning of a cruel fever[51]
> One Ragozine, a most notorious pirate,[52]

---

[51] The insanitary conditions of English prisons gave rise to a particularly dangerous illness known as "gaol [jail] fever" from which many prisoners died. It was equally fatal to all who came in contact with them. At Oxford in 1577 the chief baron, the sheriff, and about 300 others succumbed within 40 hours. 11 William Holdsworth, *A History of English Law* 567 (1938).

[52] Piracy was certainly a crime, defined by Blackstone as "robbery and depredation upon the high seas," 4 William Blackstone, *Commentaries on the Laws of England* 71

A man of Claudio's years; his beard and head
Just of his colour. What if we do omit   70
This reprobate till he were well inclined;
And satisfy the deputy with the visage
Of Ragozine, more like to Claudio?

DUKE VINCENTIO

O, 'tis an accident that heaven provides!
Dispatch it presently; the hour draws on   75
Prefix'd by Angelo: see this be done,
And sent according to command; whiles I
Persuade this rude wretch willingly to die.

PROVOST

This shall be done, good father, presently.
But Barnardine must die this afternoon: 80
And how shall we continue Claudio,
To save me from the danger that might come
If he were known alive?

DUKE VINCENTIO

Let this be done.
Put them in secret holds, both Barnardine and Claudio: 85
Ere twice the sun hath made his journal greeting
To the under generation, you shall find
Your safety manifested.

PROVOST

I am your free dependant.

DUKE VINCENTIO

Quick, dispatch, and send the head to Angelo.   90

Exit Provost

Now will I write letters to Angelo,--
The provost, he shall bear them, whose contents
Shall witness to him I am near at home,
And that, by great injunctions, I am bound
To enter publicly: him I'll desire   95
To meet me at the consecrated fount
A league below the city; and from thence,
By cold gradation and well-balanced form,

(1769), but pirates must have been far fewer in the prisons of an inland city like
Vienna than in those of a great port like London.

We shall proceed with Angelo.

Re-enter Provost

PROVOST
Here is the head; I'll carry it myself.   100

DUKE VINCENTIO
Convenient is it. Make a swift return;
For I would commune with you of such things
That want no ear but yours.

PROVOST
I'll make all speed.

Exit

ISABELLA
[Within] Peace, ho, be here!   105

DUKE VINCENTIO
The tongue of Isabel. She's come to know
If yet her brother's pardon be come hither:
But I will keep her ignorant of her good,
To make her heavenly comforts of despair,
When it is least expected.   110

Enter ISABELLA

ISABELLA
Ho, by your leave!

DUKE VINCENTIO
Good morning to you, fair and gracious daughter.

ISABELLA
The better, given me by so holy a man.
Hath yet the deputy sent my brother's pardon?

DUKE VINCENTIO
He hath released him, Isabel, from the world: 115
His head is off and sent to Angelo.

ISABELLA
Nay, but it is not so.

DUKE VINCENTIO
It is no other: show your wisdom, daughter,
In your close patience.

ISABELLA
O, I will to him and pluck out his eyes!   120

DUKE VINCENTIO
You shall not be admitted to his sight.

ISABELLA
Unhappy Claudio! wretched Isabel!
Injurious world! most damned Angelo!

DUKE VINCENTIO
This nor hurts him nor profits you a jot;
Forbear it therefore; give your cause to heaven.   125
Mark what I say, which you shall find
By every syllable a faithful verity:
The duke comes home to-morrow; nay, dry your eyes;
One of our convent, and his confessor,
Gives me this instance: already he hath carried   130
Notice to Escalus and Angelo,
Who do prepare to meet him at the gates,
There to give up their power. If you can, pace your wisdom
In that good path that I would wish it go,
And you shall have your bosom on this wretch,   135
Grace of the duke, revenges to your heart,
And general honour.

ISABELLA
I am directed by you.

DUKE VINCENTIO
This letter, then, to Friar Peter give;
'Tis that he sent me of the duke's return: 140
Say, by this token, I desire his company
At Mariana's house to-night. Her cause and yours
I'll perfect him withal, and he shall bring you
Before the duke, and to the head of Angelo
Accuse him home and home. For my poor self,   145
I am combined by a sacred vow
And shall be absent. Wend you with this letter:
Command these fretting waters from your eyes
With a light heart; trust not my holy order,
If I pervert your course. Who's here?   150

Enter LUCIO

LUCIO
Good even. Friar, where's the provost?

DUKE VINCENTIO
Not within, sir.

LUCIO

O pretty Isabella, I am pale at mine heart to see
thine eyes so red: thou must be patient. I am fain
to dine and sup with water and bran; I dare not for   155
my head fill my belly; one fruitful meal would set
me to 't. But they say the duke will be here
to-morrow. By my troth, Isabel, I loved thy brother:
if the old fantastical duke of dark corners had been
at home, he had lived.   160

Exit ISABELLA

DUKE VINCENTIO

Sir, the duke is marvellous little beholding to your
reports; but the best is, he lives not in them.

LUCIO

Friar, thou knowest not the duke so well as I do:
he's a better woodman than thou takest him for.

DUKE VINCENTIO

Well, you'll answer this one day. Fare ye well.   165

LUCIO

Nay, tarry; I'll go along with thee
I can tell thee pretty tales of the duke.

DUKE VINCENTIO

You have told me too many of him already, sir, if
they be true; if not true, none were enough.

LUCIO

I was once before him for getting a wench with child.   170

DUKE VINCENTIO

Did you such a thing?

LUCIO

Yes, marry, did I but I was fain to forswear it;
they would else have married me to the rotten medlar.

DUKE VINCENTIO

Sir, your company is fairer than honest. Rest you well.

LUCIO

By my troth, I'll go with thee to the lane's end: 175
if bawdy talk offend you, we'll have very little of
it. Nay, friar, I am a kind of burr; I shall stick.

Exeunt

SCENE IV. A ROOM IN ANGELO'S HOUSE.

Enter ANGELO and ESCALUS

ESCALUS

Every letter he hath writ hath disvouched other.

ANGELO

In most uneven and distracted manner. His actions
show much like to madness: pray heaven his wisdom be
not tainted! And why meet him at the gates, and
redeliver our authorities there?   5

ESCALUS

I guess not.

ANGELO

And why should we proclaim it in an hour before his
entering, that if any crave redress of injustice,
they should exhibit their petitions in the street?

ESCALUS

He shows his reason for that: to have a dispatch of   10
complaints, and to deliver us from devices
hereafter, which shall then have no power to stand
against us.

ANGELO

Well, I beseech you, let it be proclaimed betimes
i' the morn; I'll call you at your house: give   15
notice to such men of sort and suit as are to meet
him.

ESCALUS

I shall, sir. Fare you well.

ANGELO

Good night.

Exit ESCALUS

This deed unshapes me quite, makes me unpregnant   20
And dull to all proceedings. A deflower'd maid!
And by an eminent body that enforced
The law against it! But that her tender shame
Will not proclaim against her maiden loss,
How might she tongue me! Yet reason dares her no;   25
For my authority bears of a credent bulk,
That no particular scandal once can touch

But it confounds the breather. He should have lived,
Save that riotous youth, with dangerous sense,
Might in the times to come have ta'en revenge,   30
By so receiving a dishonour'd life
With ransom of such shame. Would yet he had lived!
A lack, when once our grace we have forgot,
Nothing goes right: we would, and we would not.

Exit

SCENE V. FIELDS WITHOUT THE TOWN.

Enter DUKE VINCENTIO in his own habit,
and FRIAR PETER

DUKE VINCENTIO
These letters at fit time deliver me

Giving letters

The provost knows our purpose and our plot.
The matter being afoot, keep your instruction,
And hold you ever to our special drift;
Though sometimes you do blench from this to that,   5
As cause doth minister. Go call at Flavius' house,
And tell him where I stay: give the like notice
To Valentinus, Rowland, and to Crassus,
And bid them bring the trumpets to the gate;
But send me Flavius first.   10

FRIAR PETER
It shall be speeded well.

Exit; enter VARRIUS

DUKE VINCENTIO
I thank thee, Varrius; thou hast made good haste:
Come, we will walk. There's other of our friends
Will greet us here anon, my gentle Varrius.

Exeunt

SCENE VI. STREET NEAR THE CITY GATE.

Enter ISABELLA and MARIANA

ISABELLA
To speak so indirectly I am loath:
I would say the truth; but to accuse him so,
That is your part: yet I am advised to do it;
He says, to veil full purpose.

MARIANA

 Be ruled by him.   5

ISABELLA

 Besides, he tells me that, if peradventure
 He speak against me on the adverse side,
 I should not think it strange; for 'tis a physic
 That's bitter to sweet end.

MARIANA

 I would Friar Peter--   10

ISABELLA

 O, peace! the friar is come.

            Enter FRIAR PETER

FRIAR PETER

 Come, I have found you out a stand most fit,
 Where you may have such vantage on the duke,
 He shall not pass you. Twice have the trumpets sounded;
 The generous and gravest citizens   15
 Have hent the gates, and very near upon
 The duke is entering: therefore, hence, away!

               Exeunt

ACT V
SCENE I. THE CITY GATE.

MARIANA veiled, ISABELLA, and FRIAR PETER, at their stand.
Enter DUKE VINCENTIO, VARRIUS, Lords,
ANGELO, ESCALUS, LUCIO,
Provost, Officers, and Citizens, at several doors

DUKE VINCENTIO

 My very worthy cousin, fairly met!
 Our old and faithful friend, we are glad to see you.

ANGELO, ESCALUS

 Happy return be to your royal grace!

DUKE VINCENTIO

 Many and hearty thankings to you both.
 We have made inquiry of you; and we hear   5
 Such goodness of your justice, that our soul
 Cannot but yield you forth to public thanks,
 Forerunning more requital.

ANGELO
> You make my bonds still greater.

DUKE VINCENTIO
> O, your desert speaks loud; and I should wrong it,   10
> To lock it in the wards of covert bosom,
> When it deserves, with characters of brass,
> A forted residence 'gainst the tooth of time
> And razure of oblivion. Give me your hand,
> And let the subject see, to make them know   15
> That outward courtesies would fain proclaim
> Favours that keep within. Come, Escalus,
> You must walk by us on our other hand;
> And good supporters are you.

>   *FRIAR PETER and ISABELLA come forward*

FRIAR PETER
> Now is your time: speak loud and kneel before him.   20

ISABELLA
> Justice, O royal duke! Vail your regard
> Upon a wrong'd, I would fain have said, a maid!
> O worthy prince, dishonour not your eye
> By throwing it on any other object
> Till you have heard me in my true complaint   25
> And given me justice, justice, justice, justice!

DUKE VINCENTIO
> Relate your wrongs; in what? by whom? be brief.
> Here is Lord Angelo shall give you justice:
> Reveal yourself to him.

ISABELLA
> O worthy duke,   30
> You bid me seek redemption of the devil:
> Hear me yourself; for that which I must speak
> Must either punish me, not being believed,
> Or wring redress from you. Hear me, O hear me, here!

ANGELO
> My lord, her wits, I fear me, are not firm: 35
> She hath been a suitor to me for her brother
> Cut off by course of justice,--

ISABELLA
> By course of justice!

ANGELO

And she will speak most bitterly and strange.

ISABELLA

Most strange, but yet most truly, will I speak: 40
That Angelo's forsworn; is it not strange?
That Angelo's a murderer; is't not strange?
That Angelo is an adulterous thief,
An hypocrite, a virgin-violator;
Is it not strange and strange?   45

DUKE VINCENTIO

Nay, it is ten times strange.

ISABELLA

It is not truer he is Angelo
Than this is all as true as it is strange:
Nay, it is ten times true; for truth is truth
To the end of reckoning.   50

DUKE VINCENTIO

Away with her! Poor soul,
She speaks this in the infirmity of sense.

ISABELLA

O prince, I conjure thee, as thou believest
There is another comfort than this world,
That thou neglect me not, with that opinion   55
That I am touch'd with madness! Make not impossible
That which but seems unlike: 'tis not impossible
But one, the wicked'st caitiff on the ground,
May seem as shy, as grave, as just, as absolute
As Angelo; even so may Angelo,   60
In all his dressings, characts,[53] titles, forms,
Be an arch-villain;[54] believe it, royal prince:
If he be less, he's nothing; but he's more,
Had I more name for badness.

---

[53] Blackstone glossed *characts* as follows: "*Charact* signifies an inscription. The stat. I Edw. VI. c. 2. directed the seals of office of every bishop to have 'certain *characts* under the king's arms for the knowledge of the diocese.' *Characters* are the letters in which an inscription is written. *Charactery* is the materials of which the characters are composed. 'Fairies use flowers for their *charactery.*' *Merry Wives of Windsor.*"

[54] *Quoted in* Grant v. Pendley, 39 S.W.2d 596, 597 (Tex. Comm'n App. 1931) (Leddy, J.).

DUKE VINCENTIO
By mine honesty,   65
If she be mad,--as I believe no other,--
Her madness hath the oddest frame of sense,
Such a dependency of thing on thing,
As e'er I heard in madness.

ISABELLA
O gracious duke,   70
Harp not on that, nor do not banish reason
For inequality; but let your reason serve
To make the truth appear where it seems hid,
And hide the false seems true.[55]

DUKE VINCENTIO
Many that are not mad   75
Have, sure, more lack of reason. What would you say?

ISABELLA
I am the sister of one Claudio,
Condemn'd upon the act of fornication
To lose his head; condemn'd by Angelo:
I, in probation of a sisterhood,   80
Was sent to by my brother; one Lucio
As then the messenger,--

LUCIO
That's I, an't like your grace:
I came to her from Claudio, and desired her
To try her gracious fortune with Lord Angelo   85
For her poor brother's pardon.

ISABELLA
That's he indeed.

DUKE VINCENTIO
You were not bid to speak.

LUCIO
No, my good lord;
Nor wish'd to hold my peace.   90

DUKE VINCENTIO
I wish you now, then;

---

[55] *Quoted in* People v. Lalka, 449 N.Y.S.2d 579, 582 (N.Y. City Ct. 1982) (Bristol, J.).

Pray you, take note of it: and when you have
A business for yourself, pray heaven you then
Be perfect.

LUCIO
    I warrant your honour.   95

DUKE VINCENTIO
    The warrant's for yourself; take heed to't.

ISABELLA
    This gentleman told somewhat of my tale,--

LUCIO
    Right.

DUKE VINCENTIO
    It may be right; but you are i' the wrong
    To speak before your time. Proceed.   100

ISABELLA
    I went
    To this pernicious caitiff deputy,--

DUKE VINCENTIO
    That's somewhat madly spoken.

ISABELLA
    Pardon it;
    The phrase is to the matter.   105

DUKE VINCENTIO
    Mended again. The matter; proceed.

ISABELLA
    In brief, to set the needless process by,
    How I persuaded, how I pray'd, and kneel'd,
    How he refell'd me, and how I replied,--
    For this was of much length,--the vile conclusion   110
    I now begin with grief and shame to utter:
    He would not, but by gift of my chaste body
    To his concupiscible intemperate lust,
    Release my brother; and, after much debatement,
    My sisterly remorse confutes mine honour,   115
    And I did yield to him: but the next morn betimes,
    His purpose surfeiting, he sends a warrant
    For my poor brother's head.

DUKE VINCENTIO
This is most likely!

ISABELLA
O, that it were as like as it is true! 120

DUKE VINCENTIO
By heaven, fond wretch, thou know'st not what thou speak'st,
Or else thou art suborn'd against his honour
In hateful practise. First, his integrity
Stands without blemish. Next, it imports no reason
That with such vehemency he should pursue 125
Faults proper to himself: if he had so offended,
He would have weigh'd thy brother by himself
And not have cut him off. Some one hath set you on:
Confess the truth, and say by whose advice
Thou camest here to complain. 130

ISABELLA
And is this all?
Then, O you blessed ministers above,
Keep me in patience, and with ripen'd time
Unfold the evil which is here wrapt up
In countenance! Heaven shield your grace from woe, 135
As I, thus wrong'd, hence unbelieved go!

DUKE VINCENTIO
I know you'ld fain be gone. An officer!
To prison with her! Shall we thus permit
A blasting and a scandalous breath to fall
On him so near us? This needs must be a practise. 140
Who knew of your intent and coming hither?

ISABELLA
One that I would were here, Friar Lodowick.

DUKE VINCENTIO
A ghostly father, belike. Who knows that Lodowick?

LUCIO
My lord, I know him; 'tis a meddling friar;
I do not like the man: had he been lay, my lord 145
For certain words he spake against your grace
In your retirement, I had swinged him soundly.

143

DUKE VINCENTIO
    Words against me? This is a good friar, belike!
    And to set on this wretched woman here
    Against our substitute! Let this friar be found.   150

LUCIO
    But yesternight, my lord, she and that friar,
    I saw them at the prison: a saucy friar,
    A very scurvy fellow.

FRIAR PETER
    Blessed be your royal grace!
    I have stood by, my lord, and I have heard   155
    Your royal ear abused. First, hath this woman
    Most wrongfully accused your substitute,
    Who is as free from touch or soil with her
    As she from one ungot.

DUKE VINCENTIO
    We did believe no less.   160
    Know you that Friar Lodowick that she speaks of?

FRIAR PETER
    I know him for a man divine and holy;
    Not scurvy, nor a temporary meddler,
    As he's reported by this gentleman;
    And, on my trust, a man that never yet   165
    Did, as he vouches, misreport your grace.

LUCIO
    My lord, most villainously; believe it.

FRIAR PETER
    Well, he in time may come to clear himself;
    But at this instant he is sick my lord,
    Of a strange fever. Upon his mere request,   170
    Being come to knowledge that there was complaint
    Intended 'gainst Lord Angelo, came I hither,
    To speak, as from his mouth, what he doth know
    Is true and false; and what he with his oath
    And all probation will make up full clear,   175
    Whensoever he's convented. First, for this woman.
    To justify this worthy nobleman,
    So vulgarly and personally accused,
    Her shall you hear disproved to her eyes,
    Till she herself confess it.   180

DUKE VINCENTIO
Good friar, let's hear it.

ISABELLA is carried off guarded;
and MARIANA comes forward

Do you not smile at this, Lord Angelo?
O heaven, the vanity of wretched fools!
Give us some seats. Come, cousin Angelo;
In this I'll be impartial; be you judge   185
Of your own cause.[56] Is this the witness, friar?
First, let her show her face, and after speak.

MARIANA
Pardon, my lord; I will not show my face
Until my husband bid me.

DUKE VINCENTIO
What, are you married?   190

MARIANA
No, my lord.

DUKE VINCENTIO
Are you a maid?

MARIANA
No, my lord.

DUKE VINCENTIO
A widow, then?

MARIANA
Neither, my lord.   195

DUKE VINCENTIO
Why, you are nothing then: neither maid, widow, nor wife?

LUCIO
My lord, she may be a punk; for many of them are
neither maid, widow, nor wife.

DUKE VINCENTIO
Silence that fellow: I would he had some cause
To prattle for himself.   200

---

[56] As the Duke himself shortly admits when he returns in his disguise as a friar,
there is something fundamentally unjust about putting Isabella's trial *in the villain's
mouth / Which here you come to accuse.* See the preface to September, *A Judge in his
Own Case: "Judex in propria causa."*

LUCIO
> Well, my lord.

MARIANA
> My lord; I do confess I ne'er was married;
> And I confess besides I am no maid:
> I have known my husband; yet my husband
> Knows not that ever he knew me.   205

LUCIO
> He was drunk then, my lord: it can be no better.

DUKE VINCENTIO
> For the benefit of silence, would thou wert so too!

LUCIO
> Well, my lord.

DUKE VINCENTIO
> This is no witness for Lord Angelo.

MARIANA
> Now I come to't my lord   210
> She that accuses him of fornication,
> In self-same manner doth accuse my husband,
> And charges him my lord, with such a time
> When I'll depose I had him in mine arms
> With all the effect of love.   215

ANGELO
> Charges she more than me?

MARIANA
> Not that I know.

DUKE VINCENTIO
> No? You say your husband.

MARIANA
> Why, just, my lord, and that is Angelo,
> Who thinks he knows that he ne'er knew my body,   220
> But knows he thinks that he knows Isabel's.

ANGELO
> This is a strange abuse. Let's see thy face.

MARIANA
> My husband bids me; now I will unmask.

Unveiling

This is that face, thou cruel Angelo,
Which once thou swor'st was worth the looking on;   225
This is the hand which, with a vow'd contract,
Was fast belock'd in thine; this is the body
That took away the match from Isabel,
And did supply thee at thy garden-house
In her imagined person.   230

DUKE VINCENTIO
Know you this woman?

LUCIO
Carnally, she says.

DUKE VINCENTIO
Sirrah, no more!

LUCIO
Enough, my lord.

ANGELO
My lord, I must confess I know this woman: 235
And five years since there was some speech of marriage
Betwixt myself and her; which was broke off,
Partly for that her promised proportions
Came short of composition, but in chief
For that her reputation was disvalued   240
In levity: since which time of five years
I never spake with her, saw her, nor heard from her,
Upon my faith and honour.

MARIANA
Noble prince,
As there comes light from heaven and words from breath,   245
As there is sense in truth and truth in virtue,
I am affianced this man's wife as strongly
As words could make up vows: and, my good lord,
But Tuesday night last gone in's garden-house
He knew me as a wife. As this is true,   250
Let me in safety raise me from my knees
Or else for ever be confixed here,
A marble monument!

ANGELO
I did but smile till now:
Now, good my lord, give me the scope of justice   255

147

My patience here is touch'd. I do perceive
These poor informal women are no more
But instruments of some more mightier member
That sets them on: let me have way, my lord,
To find this practise out.   260

DUKE VINCENTIO
Ay, with my heart
And punish them to your height of pleasure.
Thou foolish friar, and thou pernicious woman,
Compact with her that's gone, think'st thou thy oaths,
Though they would swear down each particular saint,   265
Were testimonies against his worth and credit
That's seal'd in approbation? You, Lord Escalus,
Sit with my cousin; lend him your kind pains
To find out this abuse, whence 'tis derived.
There is another friar that set them on;   270
Let him be sent for.

FRIAR PETER
Would he were here, my lord! for he indeed
Hath set the women on to this complaint:
Your provost knows the place where he abides
And he may fetch him.   275

DUKE VINCENTIO
Go do it instantly.

                                                    Exit Provost

And you, my noble and well-warranted cousin,
Whom it concerns to hear this matter forth,
Do with your injuries as seems you best,
In any chastisement: I for a while will leave you;   280
But stir not you till you have well determined
Upon these slanderers.

ESCALUS
My lord, we'll do it throughly.

                                                      Exit DUKE

Signior Lucio, did not you say you knew that
Friar Lodowick to be a dishonest person?   285

LUCIO
'Cucullus non facit monachum:' honest in nothing
but in his clothes; and one that hath spoke most
villainous speeches of the duke.

ESCALUS
We shall entreat you to abide here till he come and
enforce them against him: we shall find this friar a   290
notable fellow.

LUCIO
As any in Vienna, on my word.

ESCALUS
Call that same Isabel here once again; I would speak with her.

Exit an Attendant

Pray you, my lord, give me leave to question; you
shall see how I'll handle her.   295

LUCIO
Not better than he, by her own report.

ESCALUS
Say you?

LUCIO
Marry, sir, I think, if you handled her privately,
she would sooner confess: perchance, publicly,
she'll be ashamed.   300

ESCALUS
I will go darkly to work with her.

LUCIO
That's the way; for women are light at midnight.

Re-enter Officers with ISABELLA;
and Provost with the DUKE VINCENTIO in his friar's habit

ESCALUS
Come on, mistress: here's a gentlewoman denies all
that you have said.

LUCIO
My lord, here comes the rascal I spoke of; here with   305
the provost.

ESCALUS
In very good time: speak not you to him till we
call upon you.

LUCIO
Mum.

ESCALUS
>Come, sir: did you set these women on to slander   310
>Lord Angelo? They have confessed you did.

DUKE VINCENTIO
>'Tis false.

ESCALUS
>How! know you where you are?

DUKE VINCENTIO
>Respect to your great place! and let the devil
>Be sometime honour'd for his burning throne!   315
>Where is the duke? 'tis he should hear me speak.

ESCALUS
>The duke's in us; and we will hear you speak:
>Look you speak justly.

DUKE VINCENTIO
>Boldly, at least. But, O, poor souls,
>Come you to seek the lamb here of the fox?   320
>Good night to your redress! Is the duke gone?
>Then is your cause gone too. The duke's unjust,
>Thus to retort your manifest appeal,
>And put your trial in the villain's mouth
>Which here you come to accuse.   325

LUCIO
>This is the rascal; this is he I spoke of.

ESCALUS
>Why, thou unreverend and unhallow'd friar,
>Is't not enough thou hast suborn'd these women
>To accuse this worthy man, but, in foul mouth
>And in the witness of his proper ear,   330
>To call him villain? and then to glance from him
>To the duke himself, to tax him with injustice?
>Take him hence; to the rack with him! We'll touse you
>Joint by joint, but we will know his purpose.
>What, 'unjust'!   335

DUKE VINCENTIO
>Be not so hot; the duke
>Dare no more stretch this finger of mine than he
>Dare rack his own: his subject am I not,
>Nor here provincial. My business in this state

Made me a looker on here in Vienna,   340
Where I have seen corruption boil and bubble
Till it o'er-run the stew; laws for all faults,
But faults so countenanced, that the strong statutes
Stand like the forfeits in a barber's shop,
As much in mock as mark.[57]   345

ESCALUS
Slander to the state![58] Away with him to prison!

ANGELO
What can you vouch against him, Signior Lucio?
Is this the man that you did tell us of?

LUCIO
'Tis he, my lord. Come hither, goodman baldpate:
do you know me?   350

DUKE VINCENTIO
I remember you, sir, by the sound of your voice: I
met you at the prison, in the absence of the duke.

LUCIO
O, did you so? And do you remember what you said of the duke?

DUKE VINCENTIO
Most notedly, sir.

LUCIO
Do you so, sir? And was the duke a fleshmonger, a   355
fool, and a coward, as you then reported him to be?

DUKE VINCENTIO
You must, sir, change persons with me, ere you make
that my report: you, indeed, spoke so of him; and
much more, much worse.

LUCIO
O thou damnable fellow! Did not I pluck thee by the   360
nose for thy speeches?

DUKE VINCENTIO
I protest I love the duke as I love myself.

---

[57] *Quoted in* Tomasi v. Wayne, 313 A.2d 229, 233 (N.J. Super. 1973) (Schwartz, J.).
[58] Writing against the government was punishable as the crime of seditious libel, but seditious words (*slander to the state*) were also criminal. See 8 William Holdsworth, *A History of English Law* 336-40 (2d ed. 1937).

ANGELO

    Hark, how the villain would close now, after his
    treasonable abuses!

ESCALUS

    Such a fellow is not to be talked withal. Away with   365
    him to prison! Where is the provost? Away with him
    to prison! lay bolts enough upon him: let him
    speak no more. Away with those giglots too, and
    with the other confederate companion!

DUKE VINCENTIO

To Provost

    Stay, sir; stay awhile.   370

ANGELO

    What, resists he? Help him, Lucio.

LUCIO

    Come, sir; come, sir; come, sir; foh, sir! Why, you
    bald-pated, lying rascal, you must be hooded, must
    you? Show your knave's visage, with a pox to you!
    show your sheep-biting face, and be hanged an hour!   375
    Will't not off?

Pulls off the friar's hood,
and discovers DUKE VINCENTIO

DUKE VINCENTIO

    Thou art the first knave that e'er madest a duke.
    First, provost, let me bail these gentle three.

To LUCIO

    Sneak not away, sir; for the friar and you
    Must have a word anon. Lay hold on him.   380

LUCIO

    This may prove worse than hanging.

DUKE VINCENTIO

To ESCALUS

    What you have spoke I pardon: sit you down:
    We'll borrow place of him.

To ANGELO

    Sir, by your leave.
    Hast thou or word, or wit, or impudence,   385
    That yet can do thee office? If thou hast,

Rely upon it till my tale be heard,
And hold no longer out.

ANGELO
    O my dread lord,
    I should be guiltier than my guiltiness,   390
    To think I can be undiscernible,
    When I perceive your grace, like power divine,
    Hath look'd upon my passes. Then, good prince,
    No longer session hold upon my shame,
    But let my trial be mine own confession:[59]   395
    Immediate sentence then and sequent death
    Is all the grace I beg.

DUKE VINCENTIO
    Come hither, Mariana.
    Say, wast thou e'er contracted to this woman?

ANGELO
    I was, my lord.   400

DUKE VINCENTIO
    Go take her hence, and marry her instantly.
    Do you the office, friar; which consummate,
    Return him here again. Go with him, provost.

                    Exeunt ANGELO, MARIANA, FRIAR PETER and Provost
ESCALUS
    My lord, I am more amazed at his dishonour
    Than at the strangeness of it.   405

DUKE VINCENTIO
    Come hither, Isabel.
    Your friar is now your prince: as I was then
    Advertising and holy to your business,
    Not changing heart with habit, I am still
    Attorney'd at your service.   410

ISABELLA
    O, give me pardon,
    That I, your vassal, have employ'd and pain'd
    Your unknown sovereignty!

---

[59] Even in constitutional systems that guarantee trial by jury, in case of a defendant's confession, there is no need for a trial. See, e.g., Patton v. United States, 281 U.S. 276 (1930).

DUKE VINCENTIO
  You are pardon'd, Isabel:
  And now, dear maid, be you as free to us.   415
  Your brother's death, I know, sits at your heart;
  And you may marvel why I obscured myself,
  Labouring to save his life, and would not rather
  Make rash remonstrance of my hidden power
  Than let him so be lost. O most kind maid,   420
  It was the swift celerity of his death,
  Which I did think with slower foot came on,
  That brain'd my purpose. But, peace be with him!
  That life is better life, past fearing death,
  Than that which lives to fear: make it your comfort,   425
  So happy is your brother.

ISABELLA
  I do, my lord.

                    Re-enter ANGELO, MARIANA, FRIAR PETER, and Provost

DUKE VINCENTIO
  For this new-married man approaching here,
  Whose salt imagination yet hath wrong'd
  Your well defended honour, you must pardon   430
  For Mariana's sake: but as he adjudged your brother,--
  Being criminal, in double violation
  Of sacred chastity and of promise-breach
  Thereon dependent, for your brother's life,--
  The very mercy of the law cries out   435
  Most audible, even from his proper tongue,
  'An Angelo for Claudio, death for death!'
  Haste still pays haste, and leisure answers leisure;
  Like doth quit like, and MEASURE still FOR MEASURE.[60]
  Then, Angelo, thy fault's thus manifested;   440
  Which, though thou wouldst deny, denies thee vantage.
  We do condemn thee to the very block
  Where Claudio stoop'd to death, and with like haste.
  Away with him!

MARIANA
  O my most gracious lord,   445
  I hope you will not mock me with a husband.

---

[60] Images of weight, measure, and boundaries pervade the play, as its title implies.
See the preface for October, *Measure for Measure: "the golden metwand."*

DUKE VINCENTIO
It is your husband mock'd you with a husband.
Consenting to the safeguard of your honour,
I thought your marriage fit; else imputation,
For that he knew you, might reproach your life   450
And choke your good to come; for his possessions,
Although by confiscation they are ours,[61]
We do instate and widow you withal,
To buy you a better husband.

MARIANA
O my dear lord,   455
I crave no other, nor no better man.

DUKE VINCENTIO
Never crave him; we are definitive.

MARIANA
Gentle my liege,--
Kneeling

DUKE VINCENTIO
You do but lose your labour.
Away with him to death!   460

To LUCIO

Now, sir, to you.

MARIANA
O my good lord! Sweet Isabel, take my part;
Lend me your knees, and all my life to come
I'll lend you all my life to do you service.

DUKE VINCENTIO
Against all sense you do importune her: 465
Should she kneel down in mercy of this fact,
Her brother's ghost his paved bed would break,
And take her hence in horror.

MARIANA
Isabel,
Sweet Isabel, do yet but kneel by me;   470
Hold up your hands, say nothing; I'll speak all.

---

[61] A felon's land escheated to his lord; a traitor's land was forfeited to the Crown. 2 Frederick Pollock & Frederic William Maitland, *The History of English Law* 500 (2d ed. 1898). By which means the Duke was entitled to Angelo's estate is not clear.

They say, best men are moulded out of faults;
And, for the most, become much more the better
For being a little bad: so may my husband.
O Isabel, will you not lend a knee?   475

DUKE VINCENTIO
He dies for Claudio's death.

ISABELLA
Most bounteous sir,
Kneeling
Look, if it please you, on this man condemn'd,
As if my brother lived: I partly think
A due sincerity govern'd his deeds,   480
Till he did look on me: since it is so,
Let him not die. My brother had but justice,
In that he did the thing for which he died:
For Angelo,
His act did not o'ertake his bad intent,   485
And must be buried but as an intent
That perish'd by the way: thoughts are no subjects;
Intents but merely thoughts.[62]

MARIANA
Merely, my lord.

DUKE VINCENTIO
Your suit's unprofitable; stand up, I say.   490
I have bethought me of another fault.
Provost, how came it Claudio was beheaded
At an unusual hour?

PROVOST
It was commanded so.

DUKE VINCENTIO
Had you a special warrant for the deed?   495

---

[62] *Quoted in* United States v. Apfelbaum, 445 U.S. 115, 132 n. 13 (1980) (Rehnquist, C.J.) (citing Glanville Williams, *Criminal Law* 6 (2d ed. 1961)). The quotation is repeated in United States v. Alkhabaz, 104 F.3d 1492, 1494 (6th Cir. 1997) (Martin, J.) and in State v. Spicer, 2005 WL 742071 (Kan. App. 2005). Its use to refer to the requirement of *mens rea* was anticipated by North Carolina's learned Chief Justice Walter Clark. State v. Sykes, 104 S.E. 83, 84 (N.C. 1920). See the preface for November, *Mens Rea: bad intent.*

PROVOST
No, my good lord; it was by private message.

DUKE VINCENTIO
For which I do discharge you of your office:
Give up your keys.

PROVOST
Pardon me, noble lord:
I thought it was a fault, but knew it not;   500
Yet did repent me, after more advice;
For testimony whereof, one in the prison,
That should by private order else have died,
I have reserved alive. .

DUKE VINCENTIO
What's he?   505

PROVOST
His name is Barnardine.

DUKE VINCENTIO
I would thou hadst done so by Claudio.
Go fetch him hither; let me look upon him.

Exit Provost

ESCALUS
I am sorry, one so learned and so wise
As you, Lord Angelo, have still appear'd,   510
Should slip so grossly, both in the heat of blood.
And lack of temper'd judgment afterward.

ANGELO
I am sorry that such sorrow I procure:
And so deep sticks it in my penitent heart
That I crave death more willingly than mercy;   515
'Tis my deserving, and I do entreat it.

Re-enter Provost, with BARNARDINE,
CLAUDIO muffled, and JULIET

DUKE VINCENTIO
Which is that Barnardine?

PROVOST
This, my lord.

DUKE VINCENTIO

There was a friar told me of this man.

Sirrah, thou art said to have a stubborn soul.   520

That apprehends no further than this world,

And squarest thy life according. Thou'rt condemn'd:

But, for those earthly faults, I quit them all;

And pray thee take this mercy to provide

For better times to come. Friar, advise him;   525

I leave him to your hand. What muffled fellow's that?

PROVOST

This is another prisoner that I saved.

Who should have died when Claudio lost his head;

As like almost to Claudio as himself.

Unmuffles CLAUDIO

DUKE VINCENTIO

To ISABELLA

If he be like your brother, for his sake   530

Is he pardon'd; and, for your lovely sake,

Give me your hand and say you will be mine.[63]

He is my brother too: but fitter time for that.

By this Lord Angelo perceives he's safe;

Methinks I see a quickening in his eye.   535

Well, Angelo, your evil quits you well:

Look that you love your wife; her worth worth yours.

I find an apt remission in myself;

And yet here's one in place I cannot pardon.

To LUCIO

You, sirrah, that knew me for a fool, a coward,   540

One all of luxury, an ass, a madman;

Wherein have I so deserved of you,

That you extol me thus?

LUCIO

'Faith, my lord. I spoke it but according to the

trick. If you will hang me for it, you may; but I   545

had rather it would please you I might be whipt.

---

[63] Readers of the play have noticed that Isabella never replies to the Duke's proposal, or is given any chance to. In a live performance her reaction depends on the director's preference.

DUKE VINCENTIO
Whipt first, sir, and hanged after.
Proclaim it, provost, round about the city.
Is any woman wrong'd by this lewd fellow,
As I have heard him swear himself there's one   550
Whom he begot with child, let her appear,
And he shall marry her: the nuptial finish'd,
Let him be whipt and hang'd.

LUCIO
I beseech your highness, do not marry me to a whore.
Your highness said even now, I made you a duke: 555
good my lord, do not recompense me in making me a cuckold.

DUKE VINCENTIO
Upon mine honour, thou shalt marry her.
Thy slanders I forgive; and therewithal
Remit thy other forfeits. Take him to prison;
And see our pleasure herein executed.   560

LUCIO
Marrying a punk, my lord, is pressing to death,[64]
whipping, and hanging.

DUKE VINCENTIO
Slandering a prince deserves it.

Exit Officers with LUCIO

She, Claudio, that you wrong'd, look you restore.
Joy to you, Mariana! Love her, Angelo: 565
I have confess'd her and I know her virtue.
Thanks, good friend Escalus, for thy much goodness:

---

[64] *Pressing to death* refers to the archaic punishment *peine forte et dure*, by which an accused felon who refused to plead to the charge was pressed under heavy weights until he either pleaded or died. The Statute of Westminster, 3 Edw. I, c. 12 (1275), had provided that a person who refused to plead should be committed to a "hard and strong prison" (*prison forte et dure*). In time, this was transformed into the torture *peine forte et dure*. See Andrea McKenzie, 'This Death Some Strong and Stout Hearted Man Doth Choose': The Practice of *Peine Forte et Dure* in Seventeenth- and Eighteenth-Century England, 23 *Law & Hist. Rev.* 279 (2005). Some prisoners preferred to die rather than plead because without a conviction, their estates were not forfeited but passed to their heirs or devisees. Giles Corey, one of the accused in the Salem witch trials, refused to subject himself to trial by jury and was pressed to death. His death is referred to in Arthur Miller's play, *The Crucible* act 4 (1953).

There's more behind that is more gratulate.
Thanks, provost, for thy care and secrecy:
We shall employ thee in a worthier place.   570
Forgive him, Angelo, that brought you home
The head of Ragozine for Claudio's:
The offence pardons itself. Dear Isabel,
I have a motion much imports your good;
Whereto if you'll a willing ear incline,   575
What's mine is yours and what is yours is mine.
So, bring us to our palace; where we'll show
What's yet behind, that's meet you all should know.[65]

Exeunt

---

[65] From time out of mind, justice has been administered at the city gates. See the
preface to December, *The Measure of Justice: Meet him at the gates.*

January

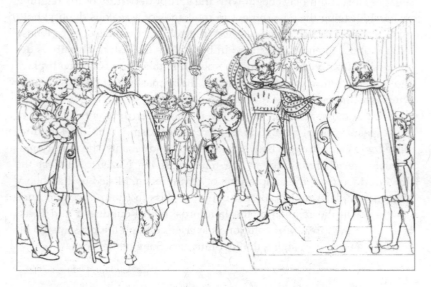

Unequal Law: A Marxist Measure for Measure

By John V. Orth, with the assistance of Joseph L. Hyde

Bawdy houses in the suburbs are to be *plucked down*, but those in the city are spared. Angelo expedites the execution of Claudio for an offense he has himself committed. Escalus would spare the condemned man because he had *a most noble father*. While in disguise, Duke Vincentio discovered that his city was *a stew of corruption*. It was as an *exposé* of class bias that *Measure for Measure* attracted the German playwright Bertolt Brecht, who prepared a contemporary version of the play in 1932. Brecht had earlier re-worked other classic English dramas. In 1923 he had turned Christopher Marlowe's historical tragedy *Edward II* into *Leben Eduards des Zweiten von England*, and in 1928 he had converted John Gay's *The Beggar's Opera* into *Die Dreigroschenoper* with music by Kurt Weill, known in English translation as *The Threepenny Opera* in which Gay's highwayman Macheath becomes Mack the Knife.

Although Brecht had originally considered naming his version of Shakespeare's play *Mass für Mass*, a literal rendering of *Measure for Measure*, he finally settled on the title *Die Rundköpfe und die Spitzköpfe*, or *Roundheads and Peakheads*.[1] The title refers to the costuming that distinguishes

---

[1] Bertolt Brecht, *Roundheads and Peakheads: Rich and Rich Make Good Company*

two races in the mythical kingdom of Jahoo, a name doubtless derived from *Gulliver's Travels*. Brecht retained the general outline of Shakespeare's story: both plays begin with the abrupt departure of the reigning monarch, leaving the government in the hands of a zealous deputy; both plays feature a character condemned to death for a morals offence whose sister is about to enter a nunnery; in both plays the sister's chastity is demanded but not yielded because a substitute takes her place; both plays end with the return of the absent ruler, the unmasking of disguised characters, and the salvation of the condemned man.

But the message of Brecht's play is altogether different. In place of Shakespeare's moral ambiguity is a crude Marxism.[2] With the kingdom locked in a class struggle between landlords and tenants, the deputy manipulates racial differences in the manner of the Nazis to distract the downtrodden from the temptations of communism. Misled by the theory of economic determinism, Brecht expected class to trump race and ends his play with the reunion of the landlords, both Roundhead and Peakhead, once the threat of revolution is averted, though the peasants go off to the gallows softly singing the revolutionary Song of the Sickle.

continued on page 205 . . .

IN RE WRUBLESKI
380 B.R. 635, 636-37 (S.D. Fla. January 11, 2008)

John K. Olson, Bankruptcy Judge

This case presents the curious tale of a Chapter 13 Debtor who apparently believes that the United States Treasury owes him at least $10 million and so, *mirabile dictu*, he can draw on this glorious balance to setoff and thus satisfy $163,517.65 which the Internal Revenue Service asserts he owes for income taxes, penalties and interest. How exactly it is that the United States came to owe Mr. Wrubleski $10 million (or more) is never made perfectly clear but perhaps, as Thomas Carlyle exclaimed in his *History of the French Revolution* (1837), "The Age of Miracles is forever here!" Or more likely, at least as far as this Debtor is concerned, "miracles are past." William Shakespeare, *All's Well That Ends Well*, Act II, Scene iii.

(N.Goold-Verschoyle trans. 1937), in *Jungle of Cities and Other Plays* 167-283 (1966).

[2] For a more sympathetic assessment of Brecht's adaptation and an argument that he correctly understood Shakespeare's meaning, see Louise Halper, *Measure for Measure*: Law, Prerogative, Subversion, 13 Cardozo Stud. L. & Lit. 221 (2001). Daniel J. Kornstein has his doubts. See A Comment on Professor Halper's Reading of *Measure for Measure*, id. 265.

❧ JANUARY ❧

SUN	MON	TUES	WED	THUR	FRI	SAT
				1	2	3
4	5	6	7	8	9	10
11	12	13	14	15	16	17
18	19	20	21	22	23	24
25	26	27	28	29	30	31

LAW REVIEW CIRCULATION

Many law reviews take advantage of the U.S. Postal Service's low rates for qualifying periodicals. In return, they are expected to share some barebones "Ownership, Management, and Circulation" information:

> The publisher of each publication authorized Periodicals mailing privileges ... must publish a complete statement of ownership, containing all information required by Form 3526, in an issue of the publication to which that statement relates ....[1]

It is not difficult. Form 3526 is straightforward, and a journal can simply paste its completed form into the back of an issue. See, for example, the form published in 2004 by the *University of Chicago Law Review* and reprinted on pages 167 and 168 below.

In the tables on pages 165 and 166 below we present the "Total Paid Circulation" data from line 15c of the completed Form 3526s[2] published in the flagship law reviews of the 15 "Best Law Schools" ranked by *U.S. News* in 2008.[3]

Some journals are more compliant than others. The *Columbia Law Review*, for example, has done a good job for a long time, as has the *California Law Review* (Boalt's flagship). The *Stanford Law Review*, on the other hand, got out of the habit of reporting in the 1980s and '90s, as did the *NYU Law Review* for much of that period. And the *University of Chicago Law Review* appears to be in the same boat nowadays. Other journals report numbers that are not plausible. The *Yale Law Journal*, for example, laid claim to a run of remarkably round and stable circulation numbers in the 1980s and '90s, and recently the *Vanderbilt Law Review* has done the same.

The price of non-reporting can be substantial:

> If a publisher does not comply with the filing or publishing standards of [Domestic Mail Manual § 707.]8.3 and, after notice from the postmaster, further fails to comply within 10 days, that publisher's eligibility for Periodicals prices is suspended until compliance occurs.[4]

On the other hand, we know of no case in which a postmaster has expressed any concern about, let alone issued notice to, any law review that has failed to comply with § 707.8.3. So perhaps negligent law reviews can rest easy, at least until they hear from a postmaster. For law review edi-

---

[1] USPS, Domestic Mail Manual § 707.8.3.3.
[2] Line 15c in old versions of Form 3526 was labeled "Total Paid and/or Requested Circulation." We treat all 15c data as the same.
[3] http://grad-schools.usnews.rankingsandreviews.com/grad/law/search.
[4] USPS, Domestic Mail Manual § 707.8.3.4.

tors whose noncompliance goes beyond negligence, however, the price of false reporting could be steeper and more personal under, for example, 18 U.S.C. § 1722:

> Whoever knowingly submits to the Postal Service or to any officer or employee of the Postal Service, any false evidence relative to any publication for the purpose of securing the admission thereof at the second-class rate, for transportation in the mails, shall be fined under this title.

In any event, it would be wise to comply. First, because obeying the rules is generally a good idea. And second, because accurate reporting will enable the *Green Bag* to produce more useful and interesting tables.

"TOTAL PAID CIRCULATION"
1979-2008 FOR THE FLAGSHIPS OF THE U.S. NEWS TOP 15

	Yale	Harvard	Stanford	Columbia	NYU	Boalt	Chicago	Penn
1979-80	*	8760	*	3795	2100	2549	2068	2176
1980-81	4051	8836	*	3790	*	2342	1827	2150
1981-82	4126	9767	2056	3790	2092	2342	1993	2150
1982-83	4199	8389	2350	3561	2074	2342	*	1900
1983-84	4092	8762	*	4046	2069	2200	2150	2080
1984-85	3950	7390	*	3227	*	2168	2300	1996
1985-86	3755	7705	*	3164	*	2014	2617	*
1986-87	3755	7694	*	2938	*	1990	*	1708
1987-88	3700	7325	*	2947	*	1990	*	1762
1988-89	3700	6995	*	2337	*	1816	*	1628
1989-90	3700	7016	*	2913	*	*	2229	1864
1990-91	3700	7768	*	2676	*	1740	*	1719
1991-92	3700	6517	*	2798	*	1694	2205	1781
1992-93	3600	6070	*	2525	*	1690	2454	1672
1993-94	3500	6018	*	2463	*	1701	*	*
1994-95	3300	5204	*	2381	*	1696	1979	1551
1995-96	3300	5029	*	2497	*	1595	2048	1446
1996-97	3300	5454	*	2365	*	1507	1959	1408
1997-98	3300	4367	*	2273	1362	*	1922	1334
1998-99	3300	4574	*	2227	1222	1639	1875	1347
1999-00	2705	4223	8850	2174	1200	*	1872	1191
2000-01	2705	4013	*	2082	1183	1305	2062	1043
2001-02	2677	3735	1434	*	1159	1253	1769	*
2002-03	2577	3491	1280	2029	1211	1196	1845	*
2003-04	2579	3451	1112	1875	1209	1045	*	1180
2004-05	2712	*	1112	1743	867	1040	*	1056
2005-06	2296	2837	1112	1638	999	992	*	1101
2006-07	1915	2853	1089	1578	*	1178	*	1093
2007-08	*	2610	1008	*	*	884	*	923

* Form 3526 report not found for this year.

There is a related pedagogical concern: What are we to make of the fact that at the best law schools, some of the best and the brightest students struggle to comply with what probably qualifies as one of the simplest bureaucratic mandates most *Green Bag* readers have ever seen? For that matter, what of the faculty advisers to (and administrative monitors of) all those bright students?

Is it ignorance? Possibly. Incompetence? Indolence? Insolence? Much less likely. Or maybe it is a kind of unconscsious puffery by neglect, an unwillingness — revealed in the failure to accurately report falling circulation numbers — to confront the possibility that a drop in circulation

"TOTAL PAID CIRCULATION"
1979-2008 FOR THE FLAGSHIPS OF THE U.S. NEWS TOP 15

	Michigan	N'western	Virginia	Cornell	Duke	G'town	Vanderbilt
1979-80	2950	1771	*	3350	1326	3197	1995
1980-81	2979	1610	2396	3350	*	3058	2046
1981-82	2985	1520	2387	*	1411	2950	2046
1982-83	2844	1416	2443	3603	1440	3100	1995
1983-84	*	1440	2400	*	1378	3200	*
1984-85	2727	*	2161		1412	3000	2001
1985-86	2657	1251	*	3682	1445	1116	2020
1986-87	2604	1268	*	*	1469	1116	1996
1987-88	2535	1264	2029	*	1335	*	1550
1988-89	2481	1223	1958	*	1295	*	1359
1989-90	*	1178	*	*	1268	3043	1253
1990-91	2382	951	1882	*	1255	2782	1281
1991-92	2332	*	*	*	1253	2260	1330
1992-93	*	887	1840	*	1187	3955	1220
1993-94	2256	*	*	3250	*	1514	1252
1994-95	2227	723	1670	*	*	*	1252
1995-96	2125	*	1550	2958	*	*	1267
1996-97	*	*	1552	2890	*	1536	1287
1997-98	1925	*	1536	2803	*	1487	1265
1998-99	2010	*	*	2805	*	1471	1165
1999-00	1841	*	*	2859	*	*	952
2000-01	1697	*	*	2845	*	1398	960
2001-02	1654	*	1849	2816	*	*	855
2002-03	1571	1017	1068	2288	*	*	*
2003-04	1419	997	644	1766	*	*	800
2004-05	1207	660	616	1827	*	1027	850
2005-06	925	466	483	1712	*	*	850
2006-07	862	575	526	1497	*	924	850
2007-08	783	*	530	*	957	*	850

* Form 3526 report not found for this year.

might be connected to a drop in influence or status. There are signs. The *Harvard Law Review,* for example, boasts on its website that, "A circulation of about 8,000 enables the *Review* to pay all of its own expenses."[5] We doubt this is one of those forgot-to-upate-the-website oversights. The last time the *HLR* had 8,000 subscribers was in 1985. But who knows?

On the other hand, while our tables do show declines in law-review circulation, they do not account for any rise in web-based consumption

---

United States Postal Service

Statement of Ownership, Management, and Circulation

1. Publication Title	2. Publication Number									3. Filing Date
University of Chicago Law Review	6	5	0	.	9	6 .	0			1-28-04

4. Issue Frequency	5. Number of Issues Published Annually	6. Annual Subscription Price
Quarterly	4	$45.00

7. Complete Mailing Address of Known Office of Publication *(Not printer) (Street, city, county, state, and ZIP+4)*
1111 E. 60th Street, Chicago, Il 60637

Contact Person
D. Matthews

Telephone
(773) 702-9593

8. Complete Mailing Address of Headquarters or General Business Office of Publisher *(Not printer)*

1111 E. 60th St., Chicago, IL 60637

9. Full Names and Complete Mailing Addresses of Publisher, Editor, and Managing Editor *(Do not leave blank)*
Publisher *(Name and complete mailing address)*
University of Chicago Law Review
1111 E. 60th Street.
Chicago, IL 60637
Editor *(Name and complete mailing address)*
Aditya Bamzai
1111 E. 60th St.
Chicago, IL 60637
Managing Editor *(Name and complete mailing address)*
Brad A. Russo
1111 E. 60th St.
Chicago, IL 60637

10. Owner *(Do not leave blank. If the publication is owned by a corporation, give the name and address of the corporation immediately followed by the names and addresses of all stockholders owning or holding 1 percent or more of the total amount of stock. If not owned by a corporation, give the names and addresses of the individual owners. If owned by a partnership or other unincorporated firm, give its name and address as well as those of each individual owner. If the publication is published by a nonprofit organization, give its name and address.)*

Full Name	Complete Mailing Address
University of Chicago Law School	1111 E. 60th St., Chicago, IL 60637

11. Known Bondholders, Mortgagees, and Other Security Holders Owning or Holding 1 Percent or More of Total Amount of Bonds, Mortgages, or Other Securities. If none, check box ▸ ☒ None

Full Name	Complete Mailing Address

12. Tax Status *(For completion by nonprofit organizations authorized to mail at nonprofit rates) (Check one)*
The purpose, function, and nonprofit status of this organization and the exempt status for federal income tax purposes:
☒ Has Not Changed During Preceding 12 Months
☐ Has Changed During Preceding 12 Months *(Publisher must submit explanation of change with this statement)*

PS Form 3526, October 1999   *(See Instructions on Reverse)*

---

[5] www.harvardlawreview.org/ about.shtml (visited Dec. 7, 2008).

that might roughly correspond to, and at least partly explain, those declines. Westlaw, Lexis, HeinOnline, Findlaw, etc. — and more recently even the law reviews themselves[6] — have made it easy to read journals without a subscription. Perhaps the net consumption of law reviews is actually on the rise, along with their influence and status. Who knows?

3. Publication Title University of Chicago Law Review		4. Issue Date for Circulation Data Below Volume 70:4 December 2003	
15.	Extent and Nature of Circulation	Average No. Copies Each Issue During Preceding 12 Months	No. Copies of Single Issue Published Nearest to Filing Date
a. Total Number of Copies (Net press run)		2250	2250
b. Paid and/or Requested Circulation	(1) Paid/Requested Outside-County Mail Subscriptions Stated on Form 3541 (include advertiser's proof and exchange copies)	1315	1315
	(2) Paid In-County Subscriptions Stated on Form 3541 (Include advertiser's proof and exchange copies)		
	(3) Sales Through Dealers and Carriers, Street Vendors, Counter Sales, and Other Non-USPS Paid Distribution		
	(4) Other Classes Mailed Through the USPS	530	530
c. Total Paid and/or Requested Circulation (Sum of 15b. (1), (2),(3),and (4))		1845	1845
d. Free Distribution by Mail (Samples, compliment ary, and other free)	(1) Outside-County as Stated on Form 3541		
	(2) In-County as Stated on Form 3541		
	(3) Other Classes Mailed Through the USPS	115	115
e. Free Distribution Outside the Mail (Carriers or other means)		110	110
f. Total Free Distribution (Sum of 15d. and 15e.)		225	225
g. Total Distribution (Sum of 15c. and 15f)		2070	2070
h. Copies not Distributed		180	180
i. Total (Sum of 15g. and h.)		2250	2250
j. Percent Paid and/or Requested Circulation (15c. divided by 15g. times 100)		89%	

16. Publication of Statement of Ownership
☐ Publication required. Will be printed in the 71:1 Feb. 2004 issue of this publication ☐ Publication not required.

17. Signature and Title of Editor, Publisher, Business Manager, or Owner

Brad A. Russo — Managing Editor | Date 01/28/04

I certify that all information furnished on this form is true and complete. I understand that anyone who furnishes false or misleading information on this form or who omits material or information requested on the form may be subject to criminal sanctions (including fines and imprisonment) and/or civil sanctions (including civil penalties).

Instructions to Publishers

1. Complete and file one copy of this form with your postmaster annually on or before October 1. Keep a copy of the completed form for your records.

2. In cases where the stockholder or security holder is a trustee, include in items 10 and 11 the name of the person or corporation for whom the trustee is acting. Also include the names and addresses of individuals who are stockholders who own or hold 1 percent or more of the total amount of bonds, mortgages, or other securities of the publishing corporation. In item 11, if none, check the box. Use blank sheets if more space is required.

3. Be sure to furnish all circulation information called for in item 15. Free circulation must be shown in items 15d, e, and f.

4. Item 15h., Copies not Distributed, must include (1) newsstand copies originally stated on Form 3541, and returned to the publisher, (2) estimated returns from news agents, and (3), copies for office use, leftovers, spoiled, and all other copies not distributed.

5. If the publication had Periodicals authorization as a general or requester publication, this Statement of Ownership, Management, and Circulation must be published; it must be printed in any issue in October or, if the publication is not published during October, the first issue printed after October.

6. In item 16, indicate the date of the issue in which this Statement of Ownership will be published.

7. Item 17 must be signed.

Failure to file or publish a statement of ownership may lead to suspension of Periodicals authorization.

PS Form 3526, October 1999 (Reverse)

---

[6] See, e.g., THE FORUM, www.harvardlawreview.org (visited Dec. 7, 2008).

FTC v. QT, INC.

Frank H. Easterbrook[†]

WIRED Magazine recently put the Q-Ray Ionized Bracelet on its list of the top ten Snake-Oil Gadgets. *See* http://blog.wired.com/gadgets/2007 /11/10-awesome-gadg.html.

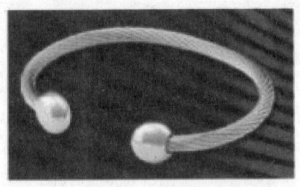

The "Gold Deluxe" Q-Ray Ionized Bracelet

The Federal Trade Commission has an even less honorable title for the bracelet's promotional campaign: fraud. In this action under 15 U.S.C. §§ 45(a), 52, 53, a magistrate judge, presiding by the parties' consent, concluded after a bench trial that the bracelet's promotion has been thoroughly dishonest. The court enjoined the promotional claims and required defendants to disgorge some $16 million (plus interest) for the FTC to distribute to consumers who have been taken in. 448 F.Supp.2d 908 (N.D. Ill.2006), *modified in part by* 472 F.Supp.2d 990 (N.D. Ill.2007).

According to the district court's findings, almost everything that defendants have said about the bracelet is false. Here are some highlights:

[†] Chief Judge of the United States Court of Appeals for the Seventh Circuit, joined by Judges William J. Bauer and Ann Claire Williams. This opinion is reported at 512 F.3d 858 (7th Cir. 2008).

- Defendants promoted the bracelet as a miraculous cure for chronic pain, but it has no therapeutic effect.

- Defendants told consumers that claims of "immediate, significant or complete pain relief" had been "test-proven"; they hadn't.

- The bracelet does not emit "Q-Rays" (there are no such things) and is not ionized (the bracelet is an electric conductor, and any net charge dissipates swiftly). The bracelet's chief promoter chose these labels because they are simple and easily remembered — and because Polaroid Corp. blocked him from calling the bangle "polarized".

- The bracelet is touted as "enhancing the flow of bio-energy" or "balancing the flow of positive and negative energies"; these empty phrases have no connection to any medical or scientific effect. Every other claim made about the mechanism of the bracelet's therapeutic effect likewise is techno-babble.

- Defendants represented that the therapeutic effect wears off in a year or two, despite knowing that the bracelet's properties do not change. This assertion is designed to lead customers to buy new bracelets. Likewise the false statement that the bracelet has a "memory cycle specific to each individual wearer" so that only the bracelet's original wearer can experience pain relief is designed to increase sales by eliminating the second-hand market and "explaining" the otherwise-embarrassing fact that the buyer's friends and neighbors can't perceive any effect.

- Even statements about the bracelet's physical composition are false. It is sold in "gold" and "silver" varieties but is made of brass.

The magistrate judge did not commit a clear error, or abuse his discretion, in concluding that the defendants set out to bilk unsophisticated persons who found themselves in pain from arthritis and other chronic conditions.

Defendants maintain that the magistrate judge subjected their statements to an excessively rigorous standard of proof. Some passages in the opinion could be read to imply that any statement about a product's therapeutic effects must be deemed false unless the claim has been verified in a placebo-controlled, double-blind study: that is, a study in which some persons are given the product whose effects are being investigated while others are given a placebo (with the allocation made at random), and neither the person who distributes the product nor the person who measures the effects knows which received the real product. Such studies are expensive, not only because of the need for placebos and keeping the experimenters in the dark, but also because they require large numbers of participants to achieve statistically significant results. Defendants observe that requiring vendors to bear such heavy costs may keep useful products off the market (this has been a problem for drugs that are subject to the FDA's testing protocols) and prevent vendors from making truthful statements that will help consumers locate products that will do them good.

Nothing in the Federal Trade Commission Act, the foundation of this litigation, requires placebo-controlled, double-blind studies. The Act forbids false and misleading statements, and a statement that is plausible but has not been tested in the most reliable way cannot be condemned out of hand. The burden is on the Commission to prove that the statements are false. (This is one way in which the Federal Trade Commission Act differs from the Food and Drug Act.) Think about the seller of an adhesive bandage treated with a disinfectant such as iodine. The seller does not need to conduct tests before asserting that this product reduces the risk of infection from cuts. The bandage keeps foreign materials out of the cuts and kills some bacteria. It may be debatable *how much* the risk of infection falls, but the direction of the effect would be known, and the claim could not be condemned as false. Placebo-controlled, double-blind testing is not a legal requirement for consumer products.

But how could this conclusion assist defendants? In our example the therapeutic claim is based on scientific principles. For the Q-Ray Ionized Bracelet, by contrast, all statements about how the product works — Q-Rays, ionization, enhancing the flow of bio-energy, and the like — are blather. Defendants might as well have said: "Beneficent creatures from the 17th Dimension use this bracelet as a beacon to locate people who need pain relief, and whisk them off to their homeworld every night to provide help in ways unknown to our science."

Although it is true, as Arthur C. Clarke said, that "[a]ny sufficiently advanced technology is indistinguishable from magic" by those who don't understand its principles ("Profiles of the Future" (1961)), a person who promotes a product that contemporary technology does not understand must establish that this "magic" actually works. Proof is what separates an effect new to science from a swindle. Defendants themselves told customers that the bracelet's efficacy had been "test-proven"; that statement was misleading unless a reliable test had been used and statistically significant results achieved. A placebo-controlled, double-blind study is the best test; something less may do (for there is no point in spending $1 million to verify a claim worth only $10,000 if true); but defendants have no proof of the Q-Ray Ionized Bracelet's efficacy. The "tests" on which they relied were bunk. (We need not repeat the magistrate judge's exhaustive evaluation of this subject.) What remain are testimonials, which are not a form of proof because most testimonials represent a logical fallacy: post hoc ergo propter hoc. (A person who experiences a reduction in pain after donning the bracelet may have enjoyed the same reduction without it. That's why the "testimonial" of someone who keeps elephants off the streets of a large city by snapping his fingers is the basis of a joke rather than proof of cause and effect.)

To this defendants respond that one study shows that the Q-Ray Ionized Bracelet *does* reduce pain. This study, which the district court's opinion describes in detail, compared the effects of "active" and "inactive" bracelets (defendants told the experimenter which was which), with the "inactive" bracelet serving as a control. The study found that both "active" and "inactive" bracelets had a modest — and identical — effect on patients' reported levels of pain. In other words, the Q-Ray Ionized Bracelet exhibits the placebo effect. Like a sugar pill, it alleviates symptoms even though there is no apparent medical reason. The placebo effect is well established. *See, e.g.*, Anne Harrington, *The Placebo Effect: An Interdisciplinary Exploration* (1999); Asbjorn Hrobjartsson & Peter C. Gotzsche, *Is the Placebo Powerless? An Analysis of Clinical Trials Comparing Placebo with No Treatment*, 344 New England J. Medicine 1594 (2001); Ted Kaptchuk, *Intentional Ignorance: A History of Blind Assessment and Placebo Controls in Medicine*, 72 Bulletin of the History of Medicine 389 (1998). Defendants insist that the placebo effect vindicates their claims, even though they are false — indeed, especially *because* they are false, as the placebo effect depends on deceit. Tell the patient that the pill contains nothing but sugar, and there is no pain relief; tell him (falsely) that it contains a powerful analgesic, and the perceived level of pain falls. A product that confers this benefit cannot be excluded from the market, defendants insist, just because they told the lies necessary to bring the effect about.

Yet the Federal Trade Commission Act condemns material falsehoods in promoting consumer products; the statute lacks an exception for "beneficial deceit." We appreciate the possibility that a vague claim — along the lines of "this bracelet will reduce your pain without the side effects of drugs" — could be rendered true by the placebo effect. To this extent we are skeptical about language in *FTC v. Pantron I Corp.*, 33 F.3d 1088 (9th Cir. 1994), suggesting that placebo effects always are worthless to consumers. But our defendants advanced claims beyond those that could be supported by a placebo effect. They made statements about Q-Rays, ionization, and bio-energy that they knew to be poppycock; they stated that the bracelet remembers its first owner and won't work for anyone else; the list is extensive.

One important reason for requiring truth is so that competition in the market will lead to appropriate prices. Selling brass as gold harms consumers independent of any effect on pain. Since the placebo effect can be obtained from sugar pills, charging $200 for a device that is represented as a miracle cure but works no better than a dummy pill is a form of fraud. That's not all. A placebo is necessary when scientists are searching for the marginal effect of a new drug or device, but once the study is over a reputable professional will recommend whatever works best.

Medicine aims to do *better* than the placebo effect, which any medieval physician could achieve by draining off a little of the patient's blood. If no one knows how to cure or ameliorate a given condition, then a placebo is the best thing going. Far better a placebo that causes no harm (the Q-Ray Ionized Bracelet is inert) than the sort of nostrums peddled from the back of a wagon 100 years ago and based on alcohol, opium, and wormwood. But if a condition responds to treatment, then selling a placebo as if it had therapeutic effect directly injures the consumer. *See Kraft, Inc. v. FTC,* 970 F.2d 311, 314 (7th Cir. 1992) (a statement violates the FTC Act "if it is likely to mislead consumers, acting reasonably under the circumstances, in a material respect").

Physicians know how to treat pain. Why pay $200 for a Q-Ray Ionized Bracelet when you can get relief from an aspirin tablet that costs 1¢? Some painful conditions do not respond to analgesics (or the stronger drugs in the pharmacopeia) or to surgery, but it does not follow that a placebo at any price is better. Deceit such as the tall tales that defendants told about the Q-Ray Ionized Bracelet will lead some consumers to avoid treatments that cost less and do more; the lies will lead others to pay too much for pain relief or otherwise interfere with the matching of remedies to medical conditions. That's why the placebo effect cannot justify fraud in promoting a product. Doctor Dulcamara was a charlatan who harmed most of his customers even though Nemorino gets the girl at the end of Donizetti's *L'elisir d'amore.*

Now for the remedy. Defendants do not contest the terms of the injunction. They do, however, say that the financial award was excessive. The magistrate judge set as his goal the disgorgement of the profits that defendants made while the Q-Ray Ionized Bracelet was heavily promoted with infomercials on late-night television. Disgorging profits is an appropriate remedy. *See FTC v. Febre,* 128 F.3d 530, 534 (7th Cir. 1997); *FTC v. Amy Travel Service, Inc.,* 875 F.2d 564, 571-72 (7th Cir. 1989). But defendants say that the record does not contain evidence about their profits. True, the FTC compiled balance sheets showing profits running in the millions every year. These should not be considered, defendants insist, because when Que Te Park (defendants' principal investor and CEO) testified about the subject, he was asked only whether he could "see" the enterprise's net income (he conceded that he could), not whether the figures are correct, and the FTC's lawyer then forgot to offer the balance sheets themselves as evidence.

This is too clever by half. The FTC made estimates of profits from the Q-Ray Ionized Bracelet business and gave defendants an opportunity to respond. They chose not to do so. Park's noncommittal answers avoided any risk of prosecution for perjury but did not meet the FTC's prima facie showing. The magistrate judge was entitled to treat the evasion as an admission that the FTC's computation is in the ballpark. A monetary award often depends on estimation, for defendants may not keep (or may conceal) the data required to make an exact calculation. Defendants' business was a profitable one; that much, at least, they concede. (It is so profitable that they continue to carry it on despite the injunction that requires them to stop making most of their old claims for its efficacy. Today it is sold with testimonials and vaporous statements.) A court is entitled to proceed with the best available information; if defendants thought that their profits for these years were below $16 million, they should have produced their own figures — for once the FTC produces a reasonable estimate, the defendants bear the burden of showing that the estimate is inaccurate. *Febre,* 128 F.3d at 536.

Although defendants complain that the magistrate judge failed to separate ill-got gains from legitimate profits, they offer no reason to think that *any* of their profits are "legitimate." Defendants' sole business is the sale of Q-Ray products.

On top of paying $16 million (plus interest) into a fund for distribution to all of their customers, defendants must refund the full purchase price of some bracelets purchased over the Internet. Defendants' infomercials promised buyers that the purchase price would be refunded any time during 30 days after the sale if the buyers were not satisfied with their bracelets. Defendants honored that promise for bracelets purchased by telephone but not for bracelets purchased from their web sites. Internet purchasers were allowed only 10 days to return their bracelets. The district court held that defendants must refund the purchase price of anyone who bought from the web sites and returned the merchandise between days 11 and 30. Defendants protest that their web sites disclosed the 10-day refund period, but this does not meet the FTC's point. The infomercials promised a 30-day return period, then suggested that customers purchase online. Anyone who followed that advice received only a 10-day return period. The disclosure of this shorter period was buried several clicks away in the web site. The district court was entitled to conclude the switch deceived reasonable persons who relied on what the infomercials told them.

Finally, Park contends that he should not have been held jointly and severally responsible for the financial aspects of the judgment. Yet he not only participated in the false promotional activities but also had the authority to control them. Either participation or control suffices. *Amy Travel*, 875 F.2d at 573. Park insists that he believed the representations to be accurate (or at least thought them to be such transparent prattle that they could not be false), but the district court found otherwise — and sensibly.

AFFIRMED

Othello is disagreeable to me because his villain comes down front and tells you he is a villain and what nasty things he means to do, and chance favors him unfairly, but the talk is so tremendous that you forgive that.

Oliver Wendell Holmes, Jr. (1922)

Clown, in *Measure for Measure*.

SHAKESPEARE'S LEGAL ACQUIREMENTS CONSIDERED

IN A LETTER TO J. PAYNE COLLIER, ESQ., F.S.A.

John Lord Campbell, LL.D., F.R.S.E.[†]

> "Thou art *clerkly*, thou art *clerkly!*"
> *Merry Wives of Windsor*

Editor's note: Campbell's entire book is scattered through this year's *Almanac*, with only the slightest of tweaks to the format (but not the content) and, surely, a smattering of innocent, or at worst negligent, editorial and typographical errors.

PREFACE

When my old and valued friend, Mr. Payne Collier, received the following Letter, which I wrote with a view to assist him in his Shakespearian lucubrations, he forthwith, in terms which I should like to copy if they were not so complimentary, strongly recommended me to print and publish it in my own name—intimating that I might thus have "the glory of placing a *stone* on the lofty *cairn* of our immortal bard." If he had said a *"pebble,"* the word would have been more appropriate. But the hope of making any addition, even if infinitesimally small, to this great national monument, is enough to induce me to follow my friend's advice, although I am aware that by the attempt I shall be exposed to some peril. In pointing out Shakespeare's frequent use of law-phrases, and the strict propriety with which he always applies them, the *Chief Justice* may be likened to the *Cobbler*, who, when shown the masterpiece of a great painter, representing the Pope surrounded by an interesting historical group, could not be prevailed upon to notice any beauty in the painting, except the skilful structure of a slipper worn by his Holiness.

Nevertheless I may meet with kinder critics, and some may think it right to countenance any effort to bring about a "fusion of Law and Lit-

---

[†] John Campbell (1779-1861), was Chief Justice, Queen's Bench, when this work was first published by John Murray of Albemarle Street, London, in 1859.

erature," which, like "Law and Equity," have too long been kept apart in England.

Stratheden House, Jan. 1, 1859.

INTRODUCTION

To J. Payne Collier, Esq.,
Riverside, Maidenhead, Berks.

Hartrigge, Jedburgh, N.B.
September 15th, 1858.

My dear Mr. *Payne Collier,*

Knowing that I take great delight in Shakespeare's plays, and that I have paid some attention to the common law of this realm, and recollecting that both in my 'Lives of the Chancellors,' and in my 'Lives of the Chief Justices,' I have glanced at the subject of Shakespeare's legal acquirements, you demand rather peremptorily my opinion upon the question keenly agitated of late years, whether Shakespeare was a clerk in an attorney's office at Stratford before he joined the players in London?

From your indefatigable researches and your critical acumen, which have thrown so much new light upon the career of our unrivalled dramatist, I say, with entire sincerity, that there is no one so well qualified as yourself to speak authoritatively in this controversy, and I observe that in both the editions of your 'Life of Shakespeare' you are strongly inclined to the belief that the author of 'Hamlet' was employed some years in engrossing deeds, serving writs, and making out bills of costs.

However, as you seem to consider it still an open question, and as I have a little leisure during this long vacation, I cannot refuse to communicate to you my sentiments upon the subject, and I shall be happy if, from my professional knowledge and experience, I can afford you any information or throw out any hints which may be useful to you hereafter. I myself, at any rate, must derive some benefit from the task, as it will for a while drive from my mind the recollection of the wranglings of Westminster Hall. In literary pursuits should I have wished ever to be engaged, —

"Me si fata meis paterentur ducere vitam
Anspiciis, et sponte mea componere curas."

Having read nearly all that has been written on Shakespeare's *ante-Londinensian* life, and carefully examined his writings with a view to obtain internal evidence as to his education and breeding, I am obliged to say that to the question you propound no positive answer can very safely be given.

Were an issue tried before me as Chief Justice at the Warwick assizes, "whether William Shakespeare, late of Stratford-upon-Avon, gentleman, ever was clerk in an attorney's office in Stratford-upon-Avon aforesaid," I should hold that there is evidence to go to the jury in support of the affirmative, but I should add that the evidence is very far from being conclusive, and I should tell the twelve gentlemen in the box that it is a case entirely for their decision,— without venturing even to hint to them, for their guidance, any opinion of my own. Should they unanimously agree in a verdict either in the affirmative or negative, I do not think that the court, sitting *in banco*, could properly set it aside and grant a new trial. But the probability is (particularly if the trial were by a special jury of Fellows of the Society of Antiquaries) that, after they had been some hours in deliberation, I should receive a message from them — "*there is no chance of our agreeing, and therefore we wish to be discharged;*" that having sent for them into court, and read them a lecture on the duty imposed upon them by law of being unanimous, I should be obliged to order them to be locked up for the night; that having sat up all night without eating or drinking, and "without fire, candle-light excepted,"* they would come into court next morning pale and ghastly, still saying "*we cannot agree,*" and that, according to the rigour of the law, I ought to order them to be again locked up as before till the close of the assizes, and then sentence them to be put into a cart, to accompany me in my progress towards the next assize town, and to be shot into a ditch on the confines of the county of Warwick.

Yet in the hope of giving the gentlemen of the jury a chance of escaping these horrors, to which, according to the existing state of the law, they would be exposed, and desiring, without departing from my impartiality, to assist them in coming to a just conclusion, I should not hesitate to state, with some earnestness, that there has been a great deal of misrepresentation and delusion as to Shakespeare's opportunities when a youth of acquiring knowledge, and as to the knowledge he had acquired. From a love of the incredible, and a wish to make what he afterwards accomplished actually miraculous, a band of critics have conspired to lower the condition of his father, and to represent the son, when approaching man's estate, as still almost wholly illiterate. We have been told that his father

---

* These are the words of the oath administered to the bailiff into whose custody the jurymen are delivered. I had lately to determine whether gas-lamps could be considered "candle-light." *In favorem vitæ*, I ventured to rule in the affirmative; and, the night being very cold, to order that the lamps should be liberally supplied with gas, so that, directly administering *light* according to law, they might, contrary to law, incidentally administer *heat*.

was a butcher in a small provincial town; that "pleasant Willy" was bred to his father's business; that the only early indication of genius which he betrayed was his habit, while killing a calf, eloquently to harangue the bystanders; that he continued in this occupation till he was obliged to fly the country for theft; that arriving in London a destitute stranger, he at first supported himself by receiving pence for holding gentlemen's horses at the theatre; that he then contrived to scrape an acquaintance with some of the actors, and being first employed as prompter, although he had hardly learned to read, he was allowed to play some very inferior parts himself;— and that without any further training he produced 'Richard III.,' 'Othello,' 'Macbeth,' and 'King Lear.' But, whether Shakespeare ever had any juridical education or not, I think it is established beyond all doubt that his father was of a respectable family, had some real property by descent, married a coheiress of an ancient house, received a grant of armorial bearings from the Heralds with a recognition of his lineage, was for many years an Alderman of Stratford, and, after being intrusted by the Corporation to manage their finances as Chamberlain, served the office of Chief Magistrate of the town. There are entries in the Corporation books supposed to indicate that at one period of his life he was involved in pe-cuniary difficulties; but this did not detract from his gentility, as is proved by the subsequent confirmation of his armorial bearings, with a slight alteration in his quarterings;— and he seems still to have lived respectably in Stratford or the neighbourhood.* That he was, as has been recently as-serted, a glover, or that he ever sold wool or butcher's meat, is not proved by anything like satisfactory evidence;— and, at any rate, according to the usages of society in those times, occasional dealings whereby the owner of land disposed of part of the produce of it by retail were reckoned quite consistent with the position of a squire. At this day, and in our own coun-try, gentlemen not unfrequently sell their own hay, corn, and cattle, and

---

* I am aware of your suggestion in your 'Life of Shakespeare,' that the first grant of arms to the father was at a subsequent time, when the son, although he had ac-quired both popularity and property, was, on account of his profession (then sup-posed to be unfit for a gentleman), not qualified to bear arms. But the "Confirma-tion" in 1596 recites that a patent had been before granted by Clarencieux Cooke to John Shakespeare, when chief magistrate of Stratford, and, as a ground for the Confirmation, that this original patent had been sent to the Heralds' Office when Sir William Dethick was Garter King-at-Arms. Against this positive evidence we lawyers should consider the negative evidence, that, upon search, an entry of the first grant is not found, to be of no avail: and there could be no object in forging the first grant, as an original grant in 1596 would have been equally beneficial both to father and son.

on the Continent the high nobility are well pleased to sell by the bottle the produce of their vineyards.

It is said that the worthy Alderman could not write his own name. But the fac simile of the document formerly relied upon to establish this [an order, dated 29th Sept., 7 Eliz., for John Wheeler to take upon himself the office of Bailiff, signed by nineteen aldermen and burgesses] appears to me to prove the contrary, for the name of *John Shakespeare* subscribed in a strong, clear hand, and the *mark*, supposed to be his, evidently belongs to the name of *Thomas Dyrun* in the line below.* You tell us, in your latest edition, of the production of two new documents before the Shakespeare Society, dated respectively 3rd and 9th Dec., 11 Eliz., which, it is said, if John Shakespeare could have written, would have been signed by him, — whereas they only bear his mark. But in my own experience I have known many instances of documents bearing a mark as the signature of persons who could write well, and this was probably much more common in illiterate ages, when documents were generally authenticated by a seal. Even if it were demonstrated that John Shakespeare had not been "so well brought up that he could write his name," and that "he had a mark to himself like an honest, plain-dealing man," — considering that he was born not very long after the wars of the Roses, this deficiency would not weigh much in disproving his wealth or his gentility. Even supposing him to have been a genuine marksman, he was only on a par in this respect with many persons of higher rank, and with several of the most influential of his fellow townsmen. Of the nineteen Aldermen and burgesses who signed the order referred to, only seven subscribe their names with a pen, and the High Bailiff and Senior Alderman are among the marksmen.

Whatever may have been the clownish condition of John Shakespeare, that the "Divine Williams" (as the French call our great dramatist) received an excellent school education can hardly admit of question or doubt. We certainly know that he wrote a beautiful and business-like hand, which he probably acquired early. There was a free grammar school at Stratford, founded in the reign of Edward IV., and reformed by a charter of Edward VI. This school was supplied by a succession of competent masters to teach Greek and Latin; and here the sons of all the members of the corporation were entitled to gratuitous instruction, and mixed with the sons of the neighbouring gentry. At such grammar schools, generally speaking, only a smattering of Greek was to be acquired, but the boys were thoroughly grounded in Latin grammar, and were rendered familiar with the most popular Roman classics. Shakespeare must have been at

---

* See that most elaborate and entertaining book, Knight's 'Life of Shakspere,' 1st ed., p. 16.

this school at least five years. His father's supposed pecuniary difficulties, which are said to have interrupted his education, did not occur till William had reached the age of 14 or 15, when, according to the plan of education which was then followed, the sons of tradesmen were put out as apprentices or clerks, and the sons of the more wealthy went to the university. None of his school compositions are preserved, and we have no authentic account of his progress; but we know that at these schools boys of industry and genius have become well versed in classical learning. Samuel Johnson said that he acquired little at Oxford beyond what he had brought away with him from Lichfield Grammar School, where he had been taught, like Shakespeare, as the son of a burgess; and many from such schools, without further regular tuition, have distinguished themselves in literature.

It is said that "the boy is the father of the man;" and knowing the man, we may form a notion of the tastes and habits of the boy. Grown to be a man, Shakespeare certainly was most industrious, and showed an insatiable thirst for knowledge. We may therefore fairly infer that from early infancy he instinctively availed himself of every opportunity of mental culture, —

> "What time, where lucid Avon stray'd,
> To him the mighty mother did unveil
> Her awful face:— the dauntless child
> Stretched forth his little arms, and smiled."

The grand difficulty is to discover, or to conjecture with reasonable probability, how Shakespeare was employed from about 1579, when he most likely left school, till about 1586, when he is supposed to have gone to London. That during this interval he was merely an *operative*, earning his bread by manual labour, in stitching gloves, sorting wool, or killing calves, no sensible man can possibly imagine. At twenty-three years of age, although he had not become regularly learned as if he had taken the degree of M.A. at Oxford or Cambridge, after disputing in the schools *de omni scibili et quolibet ente*,— there can be no doubt that, like our Scottish *Burns*, his mind must have been richly cultivated, and that he had laid up a vast stock of valuable knowledge and of poetical imagery, gained from books, from social intercourse, and from the survey of nature. Whoever believes that when Shakespeare was first admitted to play a part in the Blackfriars Theatre his mind was as unfurnished as that of the stolid 'Clown' in the 'Winter's Tale,' who called forth a wish from his own father that "there were no age between ten and three and twenty," will readily give credit to all the most extravagant and appalling marvels of mesmerism, clairvoyance, table-turning, and spirit-rapping.

Of Shakespeare's actual occupations during these important years, when his character was formed, there is not a *scintilla* of contemporary proof; and the vague traditionary evidence which has been resorted to was picked up many years after his death, when the object was to startle the world with things strange and supernatural respecting him.— That his time was engrossed during this interval by labouring as a mechanic, is a supposition which I at once dismiss as absurd.

Aubrey asserts that from leaving school till he left Warwickshire Shakespeare was a schoolmaster. If this could be believed, it would suffi- ciently accord with the phenomena of Shakespeare's subsequent career, except the familiar, profound, and accurate knowledge he displayed of juridical principles and practice. Being a schoolmaster in the country for some years (as Samuel Johnson certainly was), his mental cultivation would have certainly advanced, and so he might have been prepared for the arena in which he was to appear on his arrival in the metropolis.

Unfortunately, however, the pedagogical theory is not only quite un- supported by evidence, but it is not consistent with established facts. From the registration of the baptism of Shakespeare's children, and other well authenticated circumstances, we know that he continued to dwell in Stratford, or the immediate neighbourhood, till he became a citizen of London: there was no other school in Stratford except the endowed grammar school, where he had been a pupil; of this he certainly never was master, for the unbroken succession of masters from the reign of Edward VI. till the reign of James I. is on record; none of the mob who stand out for Shakespeare being quite illiterate will allow that he was qualified to be usher; and there is no trace of there having been any usher employed in this school.

It may likewise be observed that if Shakespeare really had been a schoolmaster, he probably would have had some regard for the "order" to which he belonged. In all his dramas we have three schoolmasters only, and he makes them all exceedingly ridiculous. First we have Holofernes in 'Love's Labour's Lost,' who is brought on the stage to be laughed at for his pedantry and his bad verses; then comes the Welshman, Sir Hugh Evans, in the 'Merry Wives of Windsor,' who, although in holy orders, has not yet learned to speak the English language; and last of all, Pinch, in the 'Comedy of Errors,' who unites the bad qualities of a pedagogue and a conjuror.

By the process of exhaustion, I now arrive at the only other occupation in which it is well possible to imagine that Shakespeare could be engaged during the period we are considering — that of an attorney's clerk — first suggested by Chalmers, and since countenanced by Malone, yourself and others, whose opinions are entitled to high respect, but impugned by nearly an equal number of biographers and critics of almost equal author-ity,— without any one, on either side, having as yet discussed the ques-tion very elaborately.

It must be admitted that there is no established fact with which this supposition is not consistent. At Stratford there was, by royal charter, a court of record, with jurisdiction over all personal actions to the amount of 30*l*., equal, at the latter end of the reign of Elizabeth, to more than 100*l*. in the reign of Victoria. This court, the records of which are extant, was regulated by the course of practice and pleading which prevailed in the superior courts of law at Westminster, and employed the same barbarous dialect, composed of Latin, English, and Norman-French. It sat every fort-night, and there were belonging to it, besides the Town-clerk, six attor-neys, some of whom must have practised in the Queen's Bench and in Chancery, and have had extensive business in conveyancing. An attorney, steward of the Earl of Warwick, lord of the manor of Stratford, twice a year held a court-leet and view of frankpledge there, to which a jury was summoned, and at which constables were appointed and various pre-sentments were made.

If Shakespeare had been a clerk to one of these attorneys, all that fol-lowed while he remained at Stratford, and the knowledge and acquire-ments which he displayed when he came to London, would not only have been within the bounds of possibility, but would seem almost effect from cause — in a natural and probable sequence.

From the moderate pay allowed him by his master he would have been able decently to maintain his wife and children; vacant hours would have been left to him for the indulgence of his literary propensity; and this temporary attention to law might have quickened his fancy,— although a systematic, lifelong devotion to it, I fear, may have a very different ten-dency. Burke eloquently descants upon the improvement of the mental faculties by juridical studies; and Warburton, Chatterton, Pitt the younger, Canning, Disraeli, and Lord Macaulay are a few out of many instances which might be cited of men of brilliant intellectual career who had early become familiar with the elements of jurisprudence.

Here would be the solution of Shakespeare's *legalism* which has so perplexed his biographers and commentators, and which Aubrey's tradi-tion leaves wholly unexplained. We should only have to recollect the maxim that "the vessel long retains the flavour with which it has been once imbued." Great as is the knowledge of law which Shakespeare's writings display, and familiar as he appears to have been with all its forms and proceedings, the whole of this would easily be accounted for if for some years he had occupied a desk in the office of a country attorney in good business,— attending sessions and assizes,— keeping leets and law days,— and perhaps being sent up to the metropolis in term time to conduct suits before the Lord Chancellor or the superior courts of common law at Westminster, according to the ancient practice of country attorneys, who would not employ a London agent to divide their fees.*

On the supposition of Shakespeare having been an attorney's clerk at Stratford we may likewise see how, when very young, he contracted his taste for theatricals, even if he had never left that locality till the unlucky affair of Sir Thomas Lucy's deer. It appears from the records of the Corporation of Stratford, that nearly every year the town was visited by strolling companies of players, calling themselves "the Earl of Derby's servants," "the Earl of Leicester's servants," and "Her Majesty's servants." These companies are most graphically represented to us by the strolling players in 'Hamlet' and in the 'Taming of the Shrew.' The custom at Stratford was for the players on their arrival to wait upon the Bailiff and Al-

---

* If Shakespeare really was articled to a Stratford attorney, in all probability during the five years of his clerkship he visited London several times on his master's business, and he may then have been introduced to the green room at Blackfriars by one of his countrymen connected with that theatre.

Even so late as Queen Anne's reign there seems to have been a prodigious influx of all ranks from the provinces into the metropolis in term time. During the preceding century Parliament sometimes did not meet at all for a considerable number of years; and being summoned rarely and capriciously, the "London season" seems to have been regulated, not by the session of Parliament, but by the law terms,—

"—and prints before Term ends." —*Pope.*

While term lasted, Westminster Hall was crowded all the morning, not only by lawyers, but by idlers and politicians, in quest of news. Term having ended, there seems to have been a general dispersion. Even the Judges spent their vacations in the country, having when in town resided in their chambers in the Temple or Inns of Court. The Chiefs were obliged to remain in town a day or two after term for Nisi Prius sittings; but the Puisnes were entirely liberated when proclamation was made at the rising of the court on the last day of term, in the form still preserved, that "all manner of persons may take their ease, and give their attendance here again on the first day of the ensuing term." An old lady very lately deceased, a daughter of Mr. Justice Blackstone, who was a puisne judge of the Common Pleas and lived near Abingdon, used to relate that the day after term ended, the family coach, with four black long-tailed horses, used regularly to come at an early hour to Serjeants' Inn to conduct them to their country house; and there the Judge and his family remained till they travelled to London in the same style on the essoin-day of the following term. When a student of law, I had the honour of being presented to the oldest of the judges, Mr. Justice Grose, famous for his beautiful seat in the Isle of Wight, where he leisurely spent a considerable part of the year, *more majorem*. To his question to me, "Where do you live?" I answered, "I have chambers in Lincoln's Inn, my Lord." "Ah!" replied he, "but I mean — *when term is over.*"

dermen to obtain a licence to perform in the town. The Guildhall was generally allotted to them, and was fitted up as a theatre according to the simple and rude notions of the age. We may easily conceive that Will Shakespeare, son of the chief magistrate who granted the licence, now a bustling attorney's clerk, would actually assist in these proceedings when his master's office was closed for the day; and that he might thus readily become intimate with the manager and the performers, some of whom were said to be his fellow-townsmen. He might well have officiated as prompter, the duty said to have been first assigned to him in the theatre at the Black-friars. The travelling associations of actors at that period consisted generally of not more than from five to ten members; and when a play to be performed in the Guildhall at Stratford contained more characters than individuals in the list of strollers, it would be no great stretch of imagination to suppose that, instead of mutilating the piece by suppression, or awkwardly assigning two parts to one performer, "pleasant Willy's" assistance was called in; and our great dramatist may thus have commenced his career as an actor in his native town.

To prove that he had been bred in an attorney's office, there is one piece of direct evidence. This is an alleged libel upon him by a contemporary — published to the world in his lifetime — which, if it do actually refer to him, must be considered as the foundation of a very strong inference of the fact.

Leaving Stratford and joining the players in London in 1586 or 1587, there can be no doubt that his success was very rapid; for, as early as 1589, he had actually got a share in the Blackfriars Theatre, and he was a partner in managing it with his townsman Thomas Green and his countryman Richard Burbadge. I do not imagine that when he went up to London he carried a tragedy in his pocket to be offered for the stage as Samuel Johnson did "Irene." The more probable conjecture is, that he began as an actor on the London boards, and being employed, from the cleverness he displayed, to correct, alter, and improve dramas written by others, he went on to produce dramas of his own, which were applauded more loudly than any that had before appeared upon the English stage.

> "Envy does merit as its shade pursue;"

and rivals whom he surpassed not only envied Shakespeare, but grossly libelled him. Of this we have an example in 'An Epistle to the Gentlemen Students of the Two Universities, by Thomas Nash,' prefixed to the first edition of Robert Greene's 'Menaphon' (which was subsequently called 'Greene's Arcadia') — according to the title-page, published in 1589. The alleged libel on Shakespeare is in the words following, viz.:—

"I will turn back to my first text of studies of delight, and talk a little in friendship with a few of our trivial translators. It is a common
practice now-a-days, amongst a sort of shifting companions that
run through every art and thrive by none, to leave the trade of
Noverint whereto they were born, and busy themselves with the
endeavours of art, that could scarcely Latinize their neck-verse if
they should have need; yet English Seneca, read by candle-light,
yields many good sentences, as *blood is a beggar*, and so forth; and if
you intreat him fair, in a frosty morning, he will afford you whole
Hamlets; I should say handfuls of tragical speeches. But O grief!
Tempus edax rerum — what is that will last always? The sea exhaled
by drops will in continuance be dry; and Seneca, let blood, line by
line, and page by page, at length must needs die to our stage."

Now, if the *innuendo* which would have been introduced into the declaration in an action, "*Shakespeare* v. *Nash*," for this libel (—"thereby then
and there meaning the said William Shakespeare"—) be made out, there
can be no doubt as to the remaining *innuendo* "thereby then and there
meaning that the said William Shakespeare had been an attorney's clerk,
or bred an attorney."

In Elizabeth's reign deeds were in the Latin tongue; and all deeds poll,
and many other law papers, began with the words "NOVERINT universi
per presentes" — "Be it known to all men by these presents that, &c." The
very bond which was given in 1582, prior to the grant of a licence for
Shakespeare's marriage with Ann Hathaway, and which Shakespeare
most probably himself drew, commences "NOVERINT *universi per presentes.*" The business of an attorney seems to have been then known as
"the trade of NOVERINT." Ergo, "these shifting companions" are charged
with having abandoned the legal profession, to which they were bred;
and, although most imperfectly educated, with trying to manufacture
tragical speeches from an English translation of Seneca.

For completing Nash's testimony (*valeat quantum*) to the fact that
Shakespeare had been bred to the law, nothing remains but to consider
whether Shakespeare is here aimed at? Now, independently of the expressions "whole Hamlets" and "handfuls of tragical speeches," which,
had Shakespeare's '*Hamlet*' certainly been written and acted before the
publication of Nash's letter, could leave no doubt as to the author's intention, there is strong reason to believe that the intended victim was the
young man from Warwickshire, who had suddenly made such a sensa-
tion and such a revolution in the theatrical world. Nash and Robert
Greene, the author of 'Menaphon' or 'Arcadia,' the work to which Nash's
Epistle was appended, were very intimate. In this very epistle Nash calls
Greene "sweet friend." It is well known that this Robert Greene (who, it
must always be remembered, was a totally different person from Thomas

Green, the actor and part proprietor of the Blackfriars Theatre) was one of the chief sufferers from Shakespeare being engaged by the Lord Chamberlain's players to alter stock pieces for the Blackfriars Theatre, to touch up and improve new pieces proposed to the managers, and to supply original pieces of his own. Robert Greene had been himself employed in this department, and he felt that his occupation was gone. Therefore, by publishing Nash's Epistle in 1589, when Shakespeare, and no one else, had, by the display of superior genius, been the ruin of Greene, the two must have combined to denounce Shakespeare as having abandoned "the trade of Noverint" in order to "busy himself with the endeavours of art," and to furnish tragical speeches from the translation of Seneca.

In 1592 Greene followed up the attack of 1589 in a tract called 'The Groatsworth of Wit.' Here he does not renew the taunt of abandoning "the trade of *Noverint*," which with Nash he had before made, but he pointedly upbraids Shakespeare by the nickname of *Shake-scene*, as "an upstart crow beautified with our feathers," having just before spoken of himself as "the man to whom actors had been previously beholding." He goes on farther to allude to Shakespeare as one who "supposes he is as well able to bombast out a blank verse as the best of his predecessors," as "an absolute Johannes Factotum," and "in his own conceit the only *Shake-scene* in a country." In 1592 Robert Greene frankly complains that *Shake-scene* had undeservedly met with such success as to be able to drive him (Greene) and others similarly circumstanced from an employment by which they had mainly subsisted.[*] This evidence, therefore, seems amply sufficient to prove that there was a conspiracy between the two libellers, Nash and Robert Greene, and that Shakespeare was the object of it.

But I do not hesitate to believe that Nash, in 1589, directly alludes to 'Hamlet' as a play of Shakespeare, and wishes to turn it into ridicule. I am aware that an attempt has been made to show that there had been an edition of 'Menaphon' before 1589; but no copy of any prior edition of it, with Nash's Epistle appended to it, has been produced. I am also aware that 'Hamlet,' in the perfect state in which we now behold it, was not finished till several years after; but I make no doubt that before the publication of Nash's Epistle Shakespeare's first sketch of his play of 'Hamlet,' taken probably from some older play with the same title, had been produced upon the Blackfriars stage and received with applause which generated envy.

---

[*] You no doubt recollect that Robert Greene actually died of starvation before his 'Groatsworth of Wit,' in which he so bitterly assailed *Shakespeare* as "Shake-scene," was published.

From the saying of the players, recorded by *Ben Jonson*, that Shakespeare never blotted a line, an erroneous notion has prevailed that he carelessly sketched off his dramas, and never retouched them or cared about them after. So far from this (contrary to modern practice), he often materially altered, enlarged, and improved them subsequently to their having been brought out upon the stage and having had a successful run. There is clear proof that he wrote and rewrote 'Hamlet,' 'Romeo and Juliet,' 'The Merry Wives of Windsor,' and several other of his dramas, with unwearied pains, making them at last sometimes nearly twice as long as they were when originally represented.

With respect to these dates it is remarkable that an English translation of Seneca, from which Shakespeare was supposed to have plagiarised so freely, had been published several years before Nash's Epistle;— and in the scene with the players on their arrival at Elsinore (if this scene appeared in the first sketch of the tragedy, as it probably did, from being so essential to the plot), Shakespeare's acquaintance with this author was proclaimed by the panegyric of Polonius upon the new company, for whom "*Seneca* could not be too heavy nor Plautus too light."

Therefore, my dear Mr. Payne Collier, in support of your opinion that Shakespeare had been bred to the profession of the law in an attorney's office, I think you will be justified in saying that the fact was asserted publicly in Shakespeare's lifetime by two contemporaries of Shakespeare, who were engaged in the same pursuits with himself, who must have known him well, and who were probably acquainted with the whole of his career.

I must likewise admit that this assertion is strongly corroborated by internal evidence to be found in Shakespeare's writings. I have once more perused the whole of his dramas, that I might more satisfactorily answer your question, and render you some assistance in finally coming to a right conclusion.

In 'The Two Gentlemen of Verona,' 'Twelfth Night,' 'Julius Caesar,' 'Cymbeline,' 'Timon of Athens,' 'The Tempest,' 'King Richard II.,' 'King Henry V.,' 'King Henry VI. Part I.,' 'King Henry VI. Part III.,' 'King Richard III.,' 'King Henry VIII.,' 'Pericles of Tyre,' and 'Titus Andronicus' — fourteen of the thirty-seven dramas generally attributed to Shakespeare — I find nothing that fairly bears upon this controversy. Of course I had only to look for expressions and allusions that must be supposed to come from one who has been a professional lawyer. Amidst the seducing beauties of sentiment and language through which I had to pick my way, I may have overlooked various specimens of the article of which I was in quest, which would have been accidentally valuable, although intrinsically worthless.

189

However, from each of the remaining twenty-three dramas I have made extracts which I think are well worth your attention. These extracts I will now lay before you, with a few explanatory remarks,— which perhaps you will think demonstrably prove that your correspondent is a *lawyer, and nothing but a lawyer.*

I thought of grouping the extracts as they may be supposed to apply to particular heads of law or particular legal phrases, but I found this impracticable; and I am driven to examine *seriatim* the dramas from which the extracts are made. I take them in the order in which they are arranged, as "Comedies," "Histories," and "Tragedies," in the folio of 1623, the earliest authority for the whole collection.

THE MERRY WIVES OF WINDSOR

In Act II. Sc. 2, where Ford, under the name of Master Brook, tries to induce Falstaff to assist him in his intrigue with Mrs. Ford, and states that from all the trouble and money he had bestowed upon her he had had no beneficial return, we have the following question and answer:—

> *Fal.* Of what quality was your love, then?
>
> *Ford.* Like a fair house built upon another man's ground; so that *I have lost my edifice by mistaking the place where I erected it.*

Now this shows in Shakespeare a knowledge of the law of real property, not generally possessed. The unlearned would suppose that if, by mistake, a man builds a fine house on the land of another, when he discovers his error he will be permitted to remove all the materials of the structure, and particularly the marble pillars and carved chimney-pieces with which he has adorned it; but Shakespeare knew better. He was aware that, being fixed to the freehold, the absolute property in them belonged to the owner of the soil, and he recollected the maxim, *Cujus est solum, ejus est usque ad cœlum.*

Afterwards, in writing the second scene of Act IV., Shakespeare's head was so full of the recondite terms of the law, that he makes a lady thus pour them out, in a confidential *tête-à-tête* conversation with another lady, while discoursing of the revenge they two should take upon an old gentleman for having made an unsuccessful attempt upon their virtue:—

> *Mrs. Page.* I'll have the cudgel hallowed, and hung o'er the altar: it hath done meritorious service.
>
> *Mrs. Ford.* What think you? May we, with the warrant of womanhood, and the *witness* of a good conscience, pursue him with any farther revenge?

> *Mrs. Page.* The spirit of wantonness is, sure, scared out of him: if the devil have him not *in fee simple, with fine and recovery,* he will never, I think, in the way of waste, attempt us again.

This Merry Wife of Windsor is supposed to know that the highest estate which the devil could hold in any of his victims was *a fee simple,* strengthened by *fine and recovery.* Shakespeare himself may probably have become aware of the law upon the subject, when it was explained to him in answer to questions he put to the attorney, his master, while engrossing the deeds to be executed upon the purchase of a Warwickshire estate with a doubtful title.

MEASURE FOR MEASURE

In Act I. Sc. 2, the old lady who had kept a *lodging-house* of a disreputable character in the suburbs of Vienna being thrown into despair by the proclamation that all such houses in the suburbs must be plucked down, the Clown thus comforts her:—

> *Clo.* Come; fear not you: *good counsellors lack no clients.*

This comparison is not very flattering to the bar, but it seems to show a familiarity with both the professions alluded to.

In Act II. Sc. 1, the ignorance of special pleading and of the nature of actions at law betrayed by Elbow, the constable, when slandered, is ridiculed by the Lord Escalus in a manner which proves that the composer of the dialogue was himself fully initiated in these mysteries:—

> *Elbow.* Oh, thou caitiff! Oh, thou varlet! Oh, thou wicked Hannibal! I respected with her, before I was married to her?— If ever I was respected with her, or she with me, let not your worship think me the poor duke's officer.— Prove this, thou wicked Hannibal, or I'll have *mine action of battery* on thee.
>
> *Escal.* If he took you a box o' th' ear, you might have your *action of slander* too.

The manner in which, in Act III. Sc. 2, Escalus designates and talks of Angelo, with whom he was joined in commission as Judge, is so like the manner in which one English Judge designates and talks of another, that it countenances the supposition that Shakespeare may often, as an attorney's clerk, have been in the presence of English Judges:—

Escal. Provost, *my brother Angelo* will not be altered; Claudio must die to-morrow. . . . If *my brother* wrought by my pity, it should not be so with him. . . . I have laboured for the poor gentleman to the extremest shore of my modesty; but *my brother justice* have I found so severe, that he hath forced me to tell him, he is indeed — *Justice.**

Even where Shakespeare is most solemn and sublime, his sentiments and language seem sometimes to take a tinge from his early pursuits, — as may be observed from a beautiful passage in this play, — which, lest I should be thought guilty of irreverence, I do not venture to comment upon: —

Angelo. Your brother is a forfeit to the law.

Isabella. — Alas! alas!
Why, all the souls that were, were forfeit once;
And He that might the vantage best have took
Found out the remedy: How would you be
If He, which is the top of judgment, should
But judge you as you are? O, think on that;
And mercy then will breathe within your lips,
Like man new made.

(Act II. Sc. 2.)

continued on page 227 . . .

---

* I am glad to observe that our "brethren" in America adhere to the old phraseology of Westminster Hall. A Chief Justice in New England thus concludes a very sound judgment:— "My brother Blannerhasset, who was present at the argument, but is prevented by business at chambers from being here to-day, authorises me to say that he has read this judgment, and that he entirely concurs in it."

DEATH IN GEORGIA

THE HIGH PRICE OF TRYING TO SAVE
AN INFAMOUS KILLER'S LIFE.

Jeffrey Toobin[†]

On the morning of March 11, 2005, Brian Nichols embarked on one of
the most notorious crime sprees in recent American history. Nichols, a
thirty-three-year-old African-American, was being retried on rape charges
in Atlanta and was in custody at the Fulton County Courthouse, where his
first trial had ended in a hung jury. In a holding cell on the eighth floor,
where he was changing into the street clothes that he was to wear in court,
he overpowered a sheriff's deputy and stole her gun. Then Nichols entered the courtroom and shot and killed Judge Rowland Barnes as well as
the court reporter, Julie Ann Brandau, before escaping down a stairwell.
On the sidewalk outside the building, he shot and killed another deputy
sheriff, Hoyt Teasley.

Nichols immediately became the object of a frenzied manhunt in the
Atlanta area. Over the next few hours, he hijacked as many as five cars
and, apparently while looking for shelter, murdered a federal agent, David
Wilhelm. Finally, Nichols took as hostage a woman named Ashley Smith
and held her in her apartment in the suburb of Duluth for seven hours,
until she persuaded him to surrender to the authorities.

Paul L. Howard, Jr., the district attorney of Fulton County, announced that he would seek the death penalty against Nichols. The case
appeared to be open-and-shut: the first two murders, of the Judge and the
court reporter, took place in front of several witnesses, and Nichols confessed to all four of the killings in statements to police. But almost three
years later the case has stalled, caught in a bitter dispute over funding for
Nichols's defense team, which has so far been paid about $1.2 million by

---

[†] This article originally appeared in the February 4, 2008 issue of *The New Yorker*. Copyright
© 2008 by Jeffrey Toobin. Reprinted by permission of the author and the publisher.

the state of Georgia. The state agency responsible for indigent defense has run out of money, and other cases are at risk of being delayed or derailed. Jury selection in Nichols's trial, which began more than a year ago, has not been, and may never be, completed. The prosecutor has petitioned, so far unsuccessfully, to have the trial judge removed from the case and to change the defense team. During a recent hearing, the judge, Hilton Fuller, implored members of the public to "write me an anonymous letter" with suggestions about how to bring the case to trial. Some Georgia legislators, furious about the delays, have advocated impeaching Judge Fuller.

The Nichols case illustrates a troubling paradox in death-penalty jurisprudence: the more heinous a crime — and the more incontrovertible the evidence of a defendant's guilt — the greater the cost of the defense may be. Death-penalty trials require juries not only to determine whether the defendant is guilty but also to make other complex moral judgments — why a defendant committed a crime, whether he is likely to do so again, what punishment fits the crime. Defendants are entitled to often costly expert assistance, including the services of psychiatrists, as they prepare their cases. Yet spending large sums of public money on the defense of capital cases is politically incendiary, and in Georgia the consequences may be cataclysmic. According to Stephen B. Bright, the senior counsel for the Southern Center for Human Rights, in Atlanta, "We are just now starting to see the ripple effect of Nichols. The question now is whether the whole thing is going to come crashing down."

In 1963, the Supreme Court ruled, in Gideon v. Wainwright, that indigent criminal defendants must be provided with lawyers free of charge. But the Court allowed local officials to decide whether to establish full-time staffs of defense lawyers for the poor or to assign private lawyers on a case-by-case basis, as well as to determine how much the government should pay for them. Until 2005, Georgia, like many states, lacked a coherent plan for providing attorneys. "Georgia has a hundred and fifty-nine counties, and each one had a different system of hiring lawyers for the poor," Bright told me.

For decades, Bright fought to change the system in Georgia and, over the years, developed the weary patience of a liberal in a conservative state. He has led the small, tenuously financed Southern Center for Human Rights for twenty-six years, overseeing a staff of nine lawyers who fight against the death penalty and for improved prison conditions. By the nineteen-nineties, the indigent-defense system, hobbled by cronyism, incompetence, and under-funding, had become an embarrassment for the state, and there was a broad consensus for reform. In the spring of 2003, the state legislature, with Bright's help, created public-defense offices for most of the state's forty-nine judicial circuits and a new agency, the Georgia Public Defender Standards Council, to oversee them. An office in Atlanta, now known as the Georgia Capital Defenders, was established to provide attorneys, all trained in the intricacies of death-penalty law, for indigent defendants in capital cases. In order to avoid the spectre of taxpayer money being used to pay for such an unpopular cause, the new law required that the defense lawyers' compensation be derived from fees assessed on plaintiffs in lawsuits and other participants in the court system.

The new regime went into effect on January 1, 2005. Ten weeks later, Brian Nichols was taken to the holding cell near the courtroom to change his clothes.

Over three decades, Nichols's life took a steady, then precipitous, descent from middle-class respectability to incomprehensible violence. He grew up in Baltimore, where his mother worked for the Internal Revenue Service and his father owned various small businesses. In 2003, Nichols's parents, who had retired, moved to Africa, and his mother, Claritha, took a job with the Tanzania Revenue Authority. The couple were in Africa when they learned that their son had been charged with four murders.

Brian was a football player in high school, and his skills as a linebacker won him admission to Kutztown University, in rural Pennsylvania. Nichols left during his sophomore year, after three arrests for minor charges, including disorderly conduct. He eventually enrolled in Newberry College, in South Carolina, but was asked not to return to school when, two years later, he was charged with stealing audio equipment from a dorm room. In 1995, he moved to the Atlanta area, where again he got into trouble with the law: he was caught with marijuana and was on probation from 1996 to 1999. For a time, Nichols worked for UPS.

During his years in Atlanta, Nichols had a steady girlfriend, a corporate executive with an M.B.A., who was as accomplished as Nichols was feckless. At one point, Nichols lived with her in the suburb of Sandy Springs; he drove a BMW that she gave him, and they worshipped together at a Word of God church in nearby Suwanee.

In April, 2004, the couple broke up, but started dating again that summer. Nichols had been seeing another woman, who became pregnant. News of the pregnancy was apparently enough to persuade Nichols's girlfriend to end their relationship for good. She began dating a minister at their church, which enraged Nichols. On two occasions in August, he confronted the minister outside the woman's apartment. After Nichols threatened to commit suicide, his ex-girlfriend sent his mother an e-mail, in which she wrote, "Things between Brian and I are spiraling out of control." Early on the morning of August 19th, Nichols again appeared at her apartment and, she later told police, raped her.

Nichols was arrested and held without bail. His first trial, before Judge Barnes, began on February 21, 2005, and he testified in his own defense. "From a defense perspective he was a very good witness," Ash Joshi, the assistant district attorney who cross-examined Nichols, told me. "He would take my question and then turn toward the jury and give the answer, the way you would teach a witness to do it. He was a charismatic individual." Nichols acknowledged that he was upset about his ex-girlfriend's relationship with the minister. "There's a section of the Bible that talks about qualifications for a pastor," he testified. "It says that a pastor should be blameless, you know. A person not covetous, merciful." But the core of Nichols's defense was his claim that the sex had been consensual. "We ended up being intimate," Nichols told the court. "It was with her consent, you know, which is why we're here. And, you know, let me say this: as a man, I've never put my hands on a woman." The jury could not agree on a verdict, splitting eight-to-four in favor of acquittal.

Judge Barnes ordered a retrial, which began on Monday, March 7th. The prosecutors called more witnesses this time, and the government lawyers felt confident that they would win the case. Nichols apparently agreed. At the lunch break on Wednesday, March 9th, he told Joshi, "You're doing a much better job this time." That evening, sheriff's deputies found two shanks — thick pieces of metal — in Nichols's shoes, and the next morning Judge Barnes called the lawyers into his chambers to discuss the matter. "We all decided that at the time of the verdict there would be a great deal more security in the courtroom," Joshi said. "When that verdict comes out, the Judge said he wanted nothing on the defense table — no pens, no pencils, nothing he could use as a weapon. But the sad part was we mistakenly thought that, once we got the shanks away from him, his plot had been foiled."

Most courts in Atlanta are housed in one of two buildings connected by sky bridges: the old Fulton County Courthouse, a Beaux Arts building dating from 1914, and, directly behind it, the Justice Center Tower, which was completed in 1995. By 2005, virtually all of the judges had moved to courtrooms in the tower, but Judge Barnes preferred the homier charms of the older building.

Barnes, who was sixty-four at the time of his death, was a popular judge, a bearded, genial man who had been on the bench since 1998. At

8:30 A.M., on Friday, March 11th, an hour before Nichols's trial was to resume, Barnes heard a legal argument on a motion in a contract dispute. Richard Robbins, a partner in a large Atlanta law firm, who had argued many cases before Judge Barnes, was representing the plaintiff. "As soon as he took the bench that morning, I could tell I was going to win — just the look on his face," Robbins told me. One of the lawyers for the defendant spoke first. "She was going on and on, and I was watching the clock," Robbins recalled. "It was within a moment or two of nine. She said I had argued a contrary position in an earlier case. And Judge Barnes looked at me and smiled, and said, 'Wait a minute, you mean our Mr. Robbins?' And he winked at me.

"Then I heard a loud sound. Nichols had come into the courtroom and shot the Judge and shot the court reporter, but I honestly don't have a memory of seeing him do that. The first thing I have a memory of is seeing the Judge slump over. I knew he was dead. Then Nichols was standing right in front of me. I remember thinking he was very nice-looking. He looked like a law clerk, not the usual kind of thug you see around the courthouse. And I remember thinking, He's going to kill the prosecutor, too, and I am at the prosecution table. He had this totally calm, methodical look on his face. There was no point in lying down or hiding. I thought, He's going to shoot me next."

Almost three years later, Judge Barnes's courtroom remains a crime scene, its main door locked and shielded from view by a large folding screen. Robbins took me to the hall to describe what happened next. "I ran straight ahead, right here, to one of the sky bridges to the new building," he said. "Nichols didn't follow me, but turned left and went down the stairs. As I was running in one direction, I saw a deputy running after Nichols to the stairs. That was Hoyt Teasley, and Nichols killed him when they got to the sidewalk. When I got to the new tower, I pushed through a locked security door like it wasn't even there. After about an hour, I realized that I had broken my hand on it."

The response by law-enforcement officials to Nichols's crimes was marred by terrible errors. After the shanks were discovered, Judge Barnes said he wanted the sheriff's department, which handles security in the courthouse, to provide Nichols with additional guards, yet he was escorted to court by a single female deputy sheriff. Part of his attack on the deputy was captured by surveillance cameras, but no one was monitoring them. The Atlanta police, who did not begin searching for Nichols until forty minutes after the first shootings, failed to seal off access to two parking garages where Nichols had been seen; he escaped from both. During a subsequent investigation, five sheriff's deputies were found to have lied about their actions with regard to Nichols. Eight deputies were fired for misconduct, all but two of whom were later rehired.

The courts have done little better in handling Nichols's case. In the nineteen-seventies, the Supreme Court struck down mandatory death-penalty laws passed by many states. Instead, after jurors in a capital case find a defendant guilty, there is now a separate mini-trial, known as the penalty phase, in which they decide whether to impose a death sentence. "Ever since the Court started allowing the death penalty again, it has been trying to make it a rational process — make sure that jurors have legitimate reasons for imposing death," Carol Steiker, a professor at Harvard Law School, said. "So the Court says the state must list any of the so-called 'aggravating factors' that justify a death sentence, like murder of more than one person, or murder of a law-enforcement officer." At the same time, the Court ruled that defendants may present evidence — known as mitigating factors — suggesting why they do not deserve the death penalty. "The jury has to be free to consider anything about the defendant that might call for a sentence of less than death," Steiker said.

The Court took an additional step in 1985, ruling that the state must pay for experts who could present mitigating evidence about capital defendants to juries. "This is partly why death-penalty cases are so much more expensive than other cases," Steiker said. "It's not just that there is a separate penalty-phase proceeding, but the defense has the right, even the obligation, to go find mitigating evidence."

Given the complexity of Nichols's case, Georgia Capital Defenders, the organization created by the 2003 reform, assigned four lawyers to it. (The state usually assigns two defense lawyers in death-penalty cases.) But in May, 2005, two months into the assignment, Nichols's lawyers learned that one member of their team had moved to Georgia from out of state and let his bar membership lapse. On the theory that further representation by any one of them could taint Nichols's defense, all four lawyers asked for, and got, Judge Fuller's permission to withdraw.

Fuller, a judge from DeKalb County, had retired in 2004, but agreed to return and take on the case after the judges in Fulton County recused themselves, on the ground that they had been colleagues of Judge Barnes. Fuller, who is sixty-five and still has a boyish cowlick, won election to his judgeship in 1980 and had developed a reputation as a moderate. His current chambers are behind an unmarked door in the Fulton County Justice Center Tower, not far from the stairs by which Nichols escaped. Fuller does not hide his bewilderment at how he has become an object of contempt and ridicule.

"This case is different from any other case that anyone has tried anywhere in the world," he told me in December. He said that he wished he hadn't allowed the entire Georgia Capital Defenders' team to resign, but that at the time he believed there were satisfactory replacements. In July, 2005, he approved the Georgia Public Defender Standards Council's selection of Henderson Hill, an accomplished criminal-defense lawyer from Charlotte, North Carolina, who specializes in death-penalty cases, to lead a new team of four. "I felt that this case was difficult enough that we needed someone away from the local Atlanta legal community," Fuller said. "The indictment was fifty-four counts, there are eleven different crime scenes, and it was just a complicated case. The local criminal-defense bar did not come flocking to this case. I went to one of the best defense lawyers in Atlanta to ask him about taking this case, and he said, 'Heavens, no. I knew Judge Barnes too well.' Judge Barnes was loved by everyone here. That decision — hiring the lawyers from North Carolina — has been the thing that caused the most trouble, because it's been expensive to have people come in from out of state."

Defense costs for travel and lodging have been substantial, though Hill cut his usual hourly rate from three hundred and fifty dollars to a hundred and seventy-five dollars, and his colleagues — Jacob Sussman, from Hill's North Carolina firm, and Robert L. McGlasson, a veteran death-penalty specialist in Atlanta — are working for less. A fourth lawyer, Penny Marshall, volunteers her time. Still, there is no doubt that using the salaried Capital Defenders would have been cheaper, and the council's open-ended commitment to pay hourly rates to private lawyers remains at the heart of the controversy.

Hill and his team work out of an office in the Capital Defenders' headquarters, in downtown Atlanta, in a mock courtroom that is normally used for training. The prosecution has indicated that it may call as many as four hundred witnesses, and in Hill's office are twenty-seven black binders, spanning eight feet of floor space, containing witness statements and other evidence gathered by the district attorney. The prosecution has also produced more than forty thousand pages of other material, and there are more than four hundred hours of tapes of telephone calls that Nichols has made from jail. On the wall are twenty sheets of yellow paper, each one representing a location relevant to the case.

Hill, a fifty-one-year-old alumnus of Harvard Law School, has an easy manner and the melodic voice of a soft-rock d.j., but few lawyers in the country have more experience trying death-penalty cases. After examining the evidence against Nichols, he sought to make a deal. In a letter to Paul Howard, the Fulton County district attorney, on December 12, 2006, he wrote:

> Surely it is stating the obvious to say that the violence on March 11 [was] utterly without justification or excuse. Words fail. On an occasion such as this, however, it is both healthy and important to articulate fundamental truths. In contemplating what justice system response would reduce the burdens on surviving family members and maximize opportunities for emotional, physical and spiritual recovery, I suggest that a marathon, contested capital trial and sentencing proceeding may be the least well designed judicial intervention.

Instead, Hill wrote, Nichols was prepared to plead guilty to every count in the indictment and accept a sentence of life in prison if Howard agreed to abandon his quest for the death penalty.

Howard said no. As an elected official, he had little to lose by taking a hard line against one of the most notorious criminals in the country. The long wait to bring Nichols to trial has been frustrating for Howard, who works in an office in the old courthouse, five floors beneath the murder scene. Defending his decision to reject Hill's plea offer, Howard told me, "My belief is that punishment is a question that should be decided by the community. It is not appropriate to kill four people and outline for the citizens what his punishment should be. I don't think the defendant should choose his own punishment."

Howard has assigned five lawyers to work on the case, and has hired at least eight independent experts to assist them. These include a crime-scene specialist, two psychiatrists, and a psychologist. Of course, the D.A. has also been assisted by the local sheriff, the Atlanta police, and the F.B.I.

The defense has attempted to respond in kind. An early round of litigation concerned a motion by the defense to disqualify Howard's office. (Several members of the D.A.'s staff are expected to be witnesses at the upcoming trial.) Fuller allowed Howard to remain. The defense also filed an unusual motion to change the "situs," or site, of the trial: Hill wanted to move the trial from the courthouse where the crime took place, while still drawing on the Fulton County jury pool, which is substantially black and, he believed, reluctant to impose the death penalty. Fuller tried to find another courtroom, but the local federal court and Fort McPherson, a nearby Army base, refused his entreaties to host the trial. "The concept of trying it in this complex is something I would like to avoid if I could,"

Fuller told me. "We rode around to several little municipal courthouses, seeing if we could do it there. But these other places didn't just say no — they said hell, no." Eventually, he denied the defense motion.

If the case ever gets to trial, the defense will offer an even more contentious argument: that Nichols, who has pled not guilty, acted out of a "delusional compulsion" (a version of the insanity defense allowed under Georgia law). "That's their only defense, because everyone in the world knows he did it," Judge Fuller told me. In court papers, the defense cited, among other things, Nichols's "peculiar thinking and behavior at or about the time he was charged with rape in August 2004." Such a defense requires the testimony of expert witnesses, especially forensic psychiatrists, to which Nichols is entitled.

The Supreme Court has recently established another expensive entitlement for defendants in capital cases. In a 2003 case, Justice Sandra Day O'Connor's opinion overturned a death sentence against a Maryland man because of his attorneys' "failure to investigate his background and present mitigating evidence of his unfortunate life history." O'Connor noted that "among the topics counsel should consider presenting are medical history, educational history, employment and training history, family and social history, prior adult and juvenile correctional experience, and religious and cultural influences." It is now more or less mandatory for defense attorneys to hire social workers and investigators to compile mini-biographies of their clients, known as "social histories." In general, the investigators pay particular attention to a defendant's childhood, in an effort to determine whether he suffered abuse. Of course, such research is expensive.

By the beginning of 2007, Hill's team had been at work for almost a year and a half, and told the Judge that it needed still more time. Fuller felt that the only way to keep the case moving was to schedule jury selection and force the trial to start. On January 11, 2007, he brought the first round of prospective jurors to the courthouse, to fill out a questionnaire. But in March, with no jurors selected, the Georgia Public Defender Standards Council informed the court that its funds were running low and that it had to petition the state legislature for more, and the Judge suspended the proceedings. The legislature turned the request down. In July, the council announced that, having paid Hill's team $1.2 million, it was now out of money.

The lawyers kept working anyway, and on October 10th Fuller ordered the council to start paying the defense lawyers again, to no avail. Still, five days later, Fuller began to question prospective jurors. After two days of jury selection, Nichols's lawyers filed a motion to stop the process, asserting, "The defense simply cannot continue coming to court on a daily basis without financial backing."

That day, Fuller stopped jury selection. "This case is not going to go on long, no matter what stage we're in, without adequate funding if I'm the presiding judge," he said in open court. "It affects every aspect of this case, and I don't know what else I can say about that."

Fuller's handling of jury selection caused outrage in Georgia. Craig L. Schwall, a Fulton County judge, sent an e-mail to his colleagues on the bench, in which he wrote that Fuller was a "fool" and a "disgrace." Howard, the district attorney, filed a highly unusual motion in the Georgia Supreme Court questioning whether Fuller and the defense team should remain on the case. On November 30th, the court said that Howard's gambit was premature, but the chief justice, in a concurring opinion, registered her impatience with all sides, including Fuller.

Fuller has frequently been criticized in the State Capitol, where the political balance has shifted toward the Republican Party since the 2003 reform was passed. The budget for the Georgia Capital Defenders has been cut each year since 2005, although the revenue from the fees that are supposed to finance the council keeps rising. The Speaker of the Georgia House has appointed a committee to investigate grounds for impeaching Judge Fuller, and the majority whip wrote, in a letter to Fuller, "The people of Georgia are entitled to know if the Court's approval of the excessive expenditure of public funds is being used to indirectly subvert the ends of justice." And last week Fuller, who has refused to step down, granted Howard's request to appeal to the Georgia Supreme Court to throw him off the case. In his brief, Howard wrote, "The Court has exhibited a course of conduct that can only be described as advocacy for the defendant's trial strategy in this case."

Mack Crawford, a former Republican state legislator who was appointed director of the Georgia Public Defender Standards Council last July, told me, "I live out in the country, sixty miles south of Atlanta. Every morning, I get a sausage and biscuit in a country store. The people there are all pissed off that the state spent the money. The question I get is 'What is the cost of a reasonable defense?'"

It's a question without a clear answer. The 2003 reform in Georgia established a comparatively generous, open-ended compensation system for defense lawyers in capital cases. By contrast, Florida caps legal fees in death-penalty cases at fifteen thousand dollars, and South Carolina and Oklahoma allocate twenty-five thousand. Expenses for experts, however, often push the total cost in those states to six figures; in Georgia the average death-penalty defense costs about three hundred thousand dollars, and so it is not surprising that a case as complicated as Nichols's has cost a great deal more.

Last month, Fulton County allocated a hundred and twenty-five thousand dollars for a psychiatric evaluation of Nichols and for other defense experts, but the standoff over the other costs of his defense remains unresolved. On January 18th, the Georgia council asked Judge Fuller to assign the case back to the state Capital Defenders. Hill would not comment, but Stephen Bright, of the Southern Center for Human Rights, called the move "a gross violation of the right to counsel." Both Judge Fuller and Nichols's defense team have argued that changing lawyers at this point would violate Nichols's rights. Ironically, the refusal of state authorities to continue to pay Nichols's legal fees has only increased the chances that he will avoid the death penalty. ("If this case was properly funded, it would have been over a year ago," Fuller told me.) And, in the meantime, the Georgia council's financial problems are beginning to affect other trials. In November, a judge in a murder case in rural Pike County removed two private attorneys because the council could no longer afford to pay them.

Nichols himself continues to make his lawyers' jobs even more difficult. In 2005, he began exchanging letters and phone calls with Lisa Meneguzzo, a thirty-eight-year-old woman from Beacon Falls, Connecticut, who visited him in jail. She has since told authorities that Nichols asked her to help him escape. According to investigators' records obtained by the Associated Press, Nichols asked Meneguzzo to go to a Home Depot and buy a masonry saw, a circular saw, and other tools for cutting through cinder block. In a letter to Meneguzzo, Nichols said that, once he was outside the walls, a van driven by a friend who would pose as a Red Cross volunteer would pick him up. A special prosecutor is investigating Meneguzzo's story as a basis for adding additional charges to Nichols's indictment.

One witness to Nichols's crimes who is certain to testify at his trial is Ashley Smith, who briefly became famous following his arrest. After Nichols took Smith hostage in her apartment, he tied her up with masking tape and an extension cord. Smith convinced Nichols to untie her and directed him to a stash of methamphetamine she had in her room, and, after he snorted the powder, they talked all night. Smith told him about her husband, who was stabbed to death in 2001, and her daughter, of whom she had given up custody because of her drug use. In the morning, she made pancakes for Nichols and read to him from Rick Warren's inspirational best-seller "The Purpose-Driven Life." Smith co-wrote a book of her own about her ordeal, "Unlikely Angel," and her daughter is now living with her again. "I hoped Brian knew he had done the right thing" by surrendering, she wrote. "And that his heavenly Father was pleased with the choice he made to give himself up." In an e-mail to me, Smith said, "My opinions of Brian Nichols haven't changed."

Smith's heroism stands in quiet counterpoint to the noisy failure of the legal system to bring any kind of resolution to Nichols's case. Judge Fuller seems to despair of finding a way forward. "I've been floundering," he said, when we spoke in his chambers. "A lot of people say just bring out the gallows." His voice trembling, Fuller went on, "It's about got me to the point that I am frustrated by it. My demeanor is someone who can hold his cool and not get flustered. I am about to get flustered."

———— ◆ ————

For myself the delay [in taking office as President] may be compared with a reprieve; for in confidence I assure you, with the world it would obtain little credit that my movements to the chair of Government will be accompanied by feelings not unlike those of a culprit who is going to the place of his execution: so unwilling am I, in the evening of a life nearly consumed in public cares, to quit a peaceful abode for an Ocean of difficulties, without that competency of political skill, abilities and inclination which is necessary to manage the helm.

George Washington (1789)

FEBRUARY

THE LAW AGAINST LOVE:
AN OPERATIC MEASURE FOR MEASURE

By John V. Orth, with the assistance of Joseph L. Hyde

If Bertold Brecht saw *Measure for Measure* as a demonstration of law as a tool of the ruling class, the great German composer, Richard Wagner, saw it as an attempt by a hypocritical legal establishment to suppress sexual freedom. Wagner's early opera based on Shakespeare's play highlights the law — *Das Liebesverbot*, the "ban on love" — which Shakespeare repeatedly refers to, but never quotes. The King of Sicily turns over temporary control of his kingdom to his German deputy who promptly bans the carnival, closes the taverns, and declares that *"jedes Vergehen des Trunkes, sowie der Liebe, werde fortan mit dem Tode bestraft"* (any violator of drink or love will immediately be punished by death). Claudio is condemned. Isabella leaves the convent to plead for her brother. The deputy propositions her, but thanks to an elaborate plot, is exposed, and a happy ending is arranged.[1] The opera's style is out of keeping with Wagner's grandiose

---

[1] Wagner's own plot summary of *Das Liebesverbot* (1836) is in his autobiography, *My Life* 113-18 (Andrew Gray trans., Mary Whittall ed. 1983). For a critical analysis of the opera, see Charles Osborne, *The Complete Operas of Wagner* 40 (1990) (describing Wagner's libretto as "a travesty of Shakespeare's play").

later operas and is rarely performed.[2]

While Wagner turned the law against love into a romantic opera, the English barrister W.S. Gilbert turned it into a musical joke. In *The Mikado*, the town of Titipu is turned upside down when the Emperor of Japan "decreed, in words succinct, / That all who flirted, leered or winked, / (Unless connubially linked), / Should forthwith be beheaded."[3] Not one to pass up the chance to make a pun, Gilbert has one law breaker enthusiastically declare: "To flirt is capital."[4]

But the "ban on love," more accurately the ban on fornication, raises a serious legal question: Does *Measure for Measure* condemn the attempt to use law to regulate morality? According to one legal scholar, the answer is Yes. Daniel J. Kornstein thinks Shakespeare comes out firmly against "laws seeking to enforce private morality,"[5] but it seems unwise to try to pin Shakespeare down in this way. In any event, the law against fornication is left unrepealed at the end of the play.

continued on page 231 . . .

VENTENBERGS V. CITY OF SEATTLE
163 Wash.2d 92, 133 (Wash. February 21, 2008)

Richard B. Sanders, Justice

This case presents a textbook example of governmental corporate favoritism to advance the profits of the privileged few at the expense, and the extinction, of any potential competitors. . . . The majority today embraces a devil the framers banished with article I, section 12. As William Shakespeare put it, "tell truth and shame the devil." William Shakespeare, *The First Part of King Henry the Fourth*, act 3, sc. 1.

---

[2] *Das Liebesverbot* received one of its rare public performances at the Glimmerglass Opera in Cooperstown, N.Y., July 19-Aug. 22, 2008. Reviews appeared in the *New York Times* (Aug. 12, 2008), *Wall St. Journal* (Aug. 13, 2008), and *Financial Times* (Aug. 15, 2008).

[3] W.S. Gilbert, *The Mikado*, act I, ll. 91-94 (1885), in *The Complete Annotated Gilbert and Sullivan* 563 (Ian Bradley ed. 1996).

[4] Id. at l. 493, in *Annotated Gilbert and Sullivan* at 585.

[5] Daniel J. Kornstein, *Kill All the Lawyers? Shakespeare's Legal Appeal* 35-51 (1994) (drawing parallels between legal issues raised in *Measure for Measure* and the U.S. Supreme Court decision in Bowers v. Hardwick, 478 U.S. 186 (1986), upholding the Georgia anti-sodomy statute). *Bowers* was overruled by Lawrence v. Texas, 529 U.S. 558 (2003).

✎ FEBRUARY ✎

SUN	MON	TUES	WED	THUR	FRI	SAT
1	2	3	4	5	6	7
8	9	10	11	12	13	14
15	16	17	18	19	20	21
22	23	24	25	26	27	28

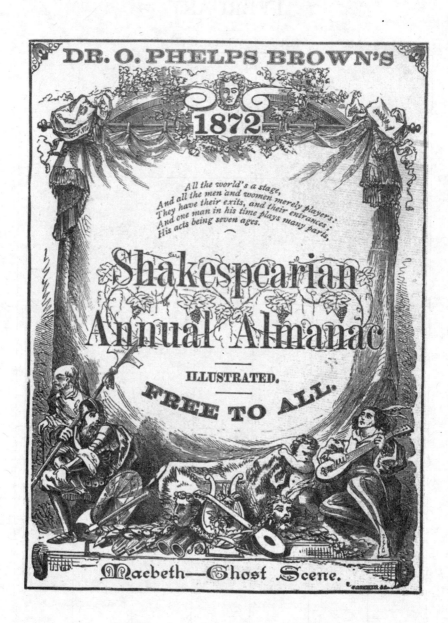

DR. O. PHELPS BROWN'S

1872

All the world's a stage,
And all the men and women merely players;
They have their exits, and their entrances;
And one man in his time plays many parts,
His acts being seven ages.

Shakespearian Annual Almanac

ILLUSTRATED.

FREE TO ALL.

Macbeth—Ghost Scene.

WRITING STYLE

from

MAKING YOUR CASE:
THE ART OF PERSUADING JUDGES

Antonin Scalia and Bryan A. Garner[†]

Editor's note: Scalia and Garner's book is divided into four big sections — "General Prnciples of Argumentation," "Legal Reasoning," "Briefing," and "Oral Argument." Those four are divided into a total of 17 subsections, which are in turn divided into 115 principles. The portion of the book reproduced here is the "Writing Style" subsection in the "Briefing" section, consisting of principles 39–54.

39. VALUE CLARITY ABOVE ALL OTHER ELEMENTS OF STYLE.

In brief-writing, one feature of a good style trumps all others. Literary elegance, erudition, sophistication of expression — these and all other qualities must be sacrificed if they detract from clarity. This means, for example, that the same word should be used to refer to a particular key concept, even if elegance of style would avoid such repetition in favor of various synonyms. It means that you must abandon interesting and erudite asides if they sidetrack the drive toward the point you are making. It means that you should never use a word that the judge may have to look up. It means that nothing important to your argument should appear in a footnote.

Further, it means shunning puffed-up, legalistic language. Make your points and ask for your relief in a blunt, straightforward manner.

[†] Antonin Scalia is a member of the Supreme Court of the United States. Bryan Garner is president of LawProse, Inc. Copyright © 2008 by Antonin Scalia and Bryan A. Garner. This excerpt of *Making Your Case — The Art of Persuading Judges* (Thomson/West 2008) is reprinted with permission from the authors and the publisher. For more information about this publication please visit www.west.thomson.com.

Wrong: The undersigned counsel do hereby for and on behalf of their clients, for the reasons explained hereinbelow, respectfully request that this Honorable Court consider and hereby rule that no issues of material fact do exist in the instant controversy, and that a final judgment be entered in favor of the client of the undersigned counsel (sometimes herein referred to as "Defendant" or "Cross-Plaintiff") and against Plaintiff.

Right: Johnson requests entry of summary judgment.

Clarity is amply justified on the ground that it ensures you'll be understood. But in our adversary system it performs an additional function. The clearer your arguments, the harder it will be for your opponent to mischaracterize them. Put yourself in the shoes of a lawyer confronting an opposing brief that is almost incomprehensible. You struggle to figure out what it means — and so does the court. What an opportunity to characterize the opposing argument in a way that makes it weak! This can't happen to you — your opponent will not be able to distort what you say — if you are clear.

40. USE CAPTIONED SECTION HEADINGS.

Many court opinions dispense with captions for sections and subsections, relying on numbers and letters alone (I, II, and III; A, B, and C within each). Whatever the value of that practice in opinions (and even that is questionable), it's not a good approach for briefs. Since clarity is the all-important objective, it helps to let the reader know in advance what topic you're about to discuss. Headings are most effective if they're full sentences announcing not just the topic but your position on the topic: Not "I. Statute of Limitations" but "I. The statute of limitations was tolled while the plaintiff suffered from amnesia."

The section headings in a typical appellant's brief might read as follows:

1. The four-year statute of limitations bars this action because Bartleby waited six years to file suit.

2. Two essential elements of fraud — intent to deceive and detrimental reliance — were not established.

   A. The record contains no evidence of an intent to deceive.

   B. The record contains no evidence of detrimental reliance.

3. Conclusion.

Theoretically, each of these headings could be further broken down into subheadings. Every argument, for example, could be divided into (1) major premise, (2) minor premise, (3) conclusion, and (4) refutation of opposing arguments. But such excessive subdivision clutters more than clarifies. Avoid overkill.

41. USE PARAGRAPHS INTELLIGENTLY; SIGNPOST YOUR ARGUMENTS.

Section headings are not the only means of mapping your argument. Within each captioned section, paragraph breaks perform the same function. The first sentences of paragraphs (your fifth-grade teacher called them "topic sentences") are as important as captioned section headings in guiding your readers through your brief — telling them what next thought is about to be discussed. Paragraph breaks should not occur randomly, inserted simply because the last paragraph was getting too long. They should occur when you are moving on to a new subpoint and wish to signal a change of topic.

One writer on brief-writing (who must remain nameless) suggests that no paragraph should be more than five sentences long. We think that's bad advice. Your readers didn't make it to the bench by reading only Classic Comics. Judges are accustomed to legal argumentation, which often — indeed, usually — requires more than five sentences to develop an idea. Use as many sentences as the thought demands. If the paragraph is becoming unusually long (say a page of your brief), break the idea into two paragraphs if possible. (¶ "Another factor leading to the same conclusion . . . .") Some ideas will take only five sentences — indeed, some may take only three. But a brief with paragraphs of rigidly uniform length is almost sure to be a bad brief. Use what it takes.

In helping the reader follow the progression of thought — both between and within paragraphs — guiding words are essential. Consider the difference between the following two progressions: (1) "He is not a great sprinter. He came in third." (2) "He is not a great sprinter. But he came in third." The word "but" signals that the next thought will somehow qualify the point just made. Or your second sentence might have been "After all, he came in third" — the "After all" signifies that the upcoming thought will affirm the previous one. Or you might have used a subordinating conjunction: "Although he is not a great sprinter, he came in third."

There are many such guiding words and phrases: *moreover, however* (preferably not at the head of a sentence), *although, on the other hand, nonetheless, to prove the point,* etc. These words and phrases turn the reader's head, so to speak, in the direction you want the reader to look. Good writers use them abundantly.

Normally, the very best guiding words are monosyllabic conjunctions: *and*, *but*, *nor*, *or*, *so*, and *yet*. Professional writers routinely put them at the head of a sentence, and so should you. There's a myth abroad that you should never begin a sentence with a conjunction. But look at any species of reputable writing — whether it's a good newspaper, journal, novel, or nonfiction work — and you're likely to find several sentences per page beginning with one of those little connectives. You can hardly achieve a flowing narrative or argument without them.

42. TO CLARIFY ABSTRACT CONCEPTS, GIVE EXAMPLES.

Legal briefs are necessarily filled with abstract concepts that are difficult to explain. Nothing clarifies their meaning as well as examples. One can describe the interpretive canon *noscitur a sociis* as the concept that a word is given meaning by the words with which it is associated. But the reader probably won't really grasp what you're talking about until you give an example similar to the one we gave earlier: "pins, staples, rivets, nails, and spikes." In that context, "pins" couldn't refer to lapel ornaments, "staples" couldn't refer to standard foodstuffs, "nails" couldn't refer to fingernails, and "spikes" couldn't refer to hairstyles.

43. MAKE IT INTERESTING.

To say that your writing must be clear and brief is not to say that it must be dull. Of course, you should employ the usual devices of effective writing: simile, metaphor, understatement, analogy, and antithesis. But you shouldn't use these or other devices of style for their own sake. They are helpful only if they cause the serious legal points you're making to be more vivid, more lively, and hence more memorable.

Three simple ways to add interest to your writing are to enliven your word choices, to mix up your sentence structures, and to vary your sentence lengths. With words, ask yourself whether there's a more colorful way to put it. With sentences, guard against falling into a monotonous subject–verb–object rut — especially when it's the same subject, sentence after sentence. And remember that an occasional arrestingly short sentence can deliver real punch ("This wolf comes as a wolf").

44. BANISH JARGON, HACKNEYED EXPRESSIONS, AND NEEDLESS LATIN.

By "jargon" we mean the words and phrases used almost exclusively by lawyers in place of plain-English words and phrases that express the same thought. Jargon adds nothing but a phony air of expertise. A *nexus*, for example, is nothing more or less than a link or a connection. And what is *the instant case?* Does it have anything to do with instant coffee? Alas, to tell the truth, it's no different from *this case* or even *here*. Write normal English. *Such* as a demonstrative adjective (*such action*) can almost always be replaced with the good old normal English *this* or *that*. And *hereinbefore* with *earlier*. And *pursuant to* with *under*. The key is to avoid words that would cause people to look at you funny if you used them at a party. Pretend that you're telling your story to some friends in your living room; that's how you should tell it to the court.

Give the reader credit for having a brain — and show that you have one, too. Don't leave your common sense at the door. If your brief repeatedly refers to the Secretary of Transportation and mentions no other Secretary, it is silly to specify parenthetically, the first time you mention the Secretary of Transportation, "(hereinafter 'the Secretary')." No one will think that your later references to "the Secretary" denote the Secretary of Defense, or perhaps your own secretary.

Hackneyed expressions are verbal formulations that were wonderfully vivid when first used, but whose vividness, through overuse, no longer pleases but bores. Such-and-such a case "and its progeny" is a good example. Or the assertion that an argument is "fatally flawed" or "flies in the face of" something; that your adversary is "painting with a broad brush"; that a claim isn't "viable"; that the "parameters" of a rule aren't settled; or that something is true "beyond peradventure of doubt." The test is: have you seen the vivid phrase a lot? If so, odds are it's a cliché.

Some Latin expressions are convenient shorthand for rules or principles that have no English shorthand equivalent (*res ipsa loquitur*, for example, or *inclusio unius est exclusio alterius*). But avoid using other Latin phrases, such as *ceteris paribus*, *inter alia*, *mutatis mutandis*, and *pari passu*. Judges are permitted to show off in this fashion, but lawyers must not. And the judge who does not happen to know the obscure Latin phrase you have flaunted will think you a twit.

45. CONSIDER USING CONTRACTIONS OCCASIONALLY — OR NOT.

The Garner view: In a book I wrote in 1991, this advice appeared: "Contractions are usually out of place in legal writing. Instead of *can't*, prefer *cannot*; instead of *won't*, *will not*; and so forth. . . . Common contractions such as *hasn't* and *didn't* may be perfectly appropriate in correspondence, but not in court papers."[1] Eleven years later, in the second edition, the relevant passage was dramatically changed: "You might well have heard that contractions don't belong in legal writing. The view seems to be that they aren't professional. But that's just a shibboleth. In fact, the decision whether to use a contraction often boils down to this: do I want to sound natural, or do I want to sound stuffy?"[2]

What accounted for the about-face? Mostly the influence of John R. Trimble, author of a classic book on writing,[3] who urged a change of position on grounds that contractions help you achieve a more conversational rhythm in your writing. He's not the only respected expert advocating contractions.[4] Unsurprisingly, empirical studies have shown that frequent contractions enhance readability.[5] And then, of course, there are the respected legal writers who've used contractions as a way of making their writing more readable, such as Clarence Darrow, Griffin B. Bell, Richard A. Posner, Frank Easterbrook, and Alex Kozinski. And consider that every President since President Ford in 1975 has used contractions in the State of the Union Address. Did these contractions diminish the perceived "dignity" of the addresses? Seemingly not.

Contractions ought to become more widespread in legal writing. That includes briefs and judicial opinions. But they shouldn't appear at every single turn — only when, in speaking, one would most naturally use a contraction.

As for the idea that contractions may arouse negativity in the judicial mind, it doesn't square with experience. If contractions are distractingly beneath the judicial reader's dignity, then what kind of reaction occurs when judges' eyes are accosted with contractions on virtually every page of the *New Yorker*, *Time*, *Newsweek*, and the *Economist*? In some sentences, are not contractions all but obligatory? Do you not think?

(Aside: In his ensuing discussion of contractions, Justice Scalia dispar-

---

[1] Garner, *The Elements of Legal Style* 81 (1991).

[2] Garner, *The Elements of Legal Style* 81 (2d ed. 2000).

[3] John R. Trimble, *Writing with Style: Conversations on the Art of Writing* (2d ed. 2000).

[4] *See* William Zinsser, *On Writing Well* 75 (6th ed. 1998) ("Your style will be warmer and truer to your own personality if you use contractions like *won't* and *can't* when they fit comfortably into what you're writing."); David W. Ewing, *Writing for Results in Business, Government, and the Professions* 358 (1974) ("Such common contractions as *it's, that's, they're*, and *she'll* are correct in almost all written communications in business and the professions."); Rudolf Flesch, *The Art of Readable Writing* 82 (1949) ("[t]he most conspicuous and handiest device of [writing readably] is to use contractions.").

[5] Wayne A. Danielson & Dominic L. Lasorsa, *A New Readability Formula Based on the Stylistic Age of Novels*, 33 J. Reading 194, 196 (1989).

ages my insistence that we make this text gender-neutral. He yielded on the point in part, I think, because my usage books recommend this strategy in extended entries entitled "Sexism," and I'm grateful that he did so. In my view, that's an instance of adopting a convention to avoid distracting readers. So I advocate "invisible gender-neutrality."[6] In a way it's similar to the debate on contractions: I think the uncontracted words will distract or subliminally repel readers, and he thinks the contraction will distract or subliminally repel readers. It's an empirical issue that will no doubt be tested in years to come.)

The Scalia view: Clarence Darrow and Griffin Bell may well have made their "legal writings" more readable by occasional use of contractions. But I doubt that the legal writings thus vulgarized (look the word up before you consider it too strong) included their briefs filed in court. As for Judges Posner, Easterbrook, and Kozinski, life tenure is a wonderful thing; neither they nor any client of theirs pays a price for their contractions. (Kozinski, for Pete's sake, has been known to write an opinion with 200 movie titles embedded within it.) And the State of the Union Address is not writing but (hello!) an address. The rules for oral communication are different. A proper test would be whether Presidents use contractions in their signing statements, veto messages, and executive orders. (They do not.)

The issue before us here, however, in this advice-giving treatise on legal argumentation, is quite simply whether contractions are (1) *more* or (2) *less* likely to advance your cause. I have no doubt that (2) is the answer. All of us employ different styles of speech, and of writing, for different occasions. Some words perfectly proper in some circumstances are jarringly inapt in others. That is why good dictionaries have the designation "*colloq.*" Written forensic presentations have always been thought demanding of more formal expression, just as oral forensic presentations are demanding (see § 73) of more formal attire.

Formality bespeaks dignity. I guarantee that if you use contractions in your written submissions, some judges — including many who are not offended by the use of contractions in the *New Yorker*, *Time*, *Vogue*, the *Rolling Stone*, *Field and Stream*, and other publications not addressed to black-robed judges engaged in the exercise of their august governmental powers — will take it as an affront to the dignity of the court. ("Why next, to ensure a more 'conversational' environment, this cheeky fellow

---

[6] *See* Garner, "Bias-Free Language," in *The Chicago Manual of Style* § 5.204, at 233 (15th ed. 2003).

will have us shed our robes, and start calling us by our first names!") And those judges who don't take offense will not understand your brief, or vote for your case, one whit more readily. There is, in short, something to be lost, and nothing whatever to be gained. Unless, of course, you and your client share with my esteemed coauthor the Jacobin passion to bring written discourse in the forum down to the level of spoken discourse in the marketplace.

As for the telling example "Do you not think?": that sounds klutzy for two reasons. First, because it is colloquial in dropping the last word, "so," and the combination of informality and formality is absurd. And second, because it is almost impossible to conjure up an example of formal writing that asks the reader a direct question; the very act of asking is *inherently* informal, so couching the question in formal terms seems absurd. (Yes, formal writings sometimes contain rhetorical questions that answer themselves; they are not seeking the reader's opinion, but are addressed, so to speak, to the Spirit of Reason.) Moreover, surely writings that use contractions also confront clumsy patches that must be written around — unless my coauthor employs the unacceptable "ain't" or suddenly inserts among his folksy contractions the very formal "am I not."

Which suggests another comment that is almost a point of personal privilege: I find it incomprehensible that my esteemed coauthor, who has displayed the inventiveness of a DaVinci and the imagination of a Tolkien in devising circumlocutions that have purged from my contributions to this volume (at some stylistic cost) all use of "he" as the traditional, generic, unisex reference to a human being — incomprehensible, I say, that this same coauthor should speak disparagingly of "shibboleths," and feign inability to come up with an acceptable substitute for the clumsy "Do you not think?" (Try "Is that not so?" or "Would you not agree?")

(Response to aside: Invisible, my eye. I'll bet you can spot the places where force or simplicity has been sacrificed to second-best circumlocution. As for distraction: To those of us who believe that "he" means, and has always meant, "he or she" when not referring to a male antecedent, the ritual shunning of it to avoid giving offense to gender-neutralizers is . . . well, distracting.)

46. AVOID ACRONYMS. USE THE PARTIES' NAMES.

Acronyms are mainly for the convenience of the writer or speaker. Don't burden your reader or listener with many of them, especially unfamiliar ones. FBI and IRS are OK, but not CPSC and FHLBB. You may be surprised how easy it is to avoid a brief of alphabet soup — and from the reader's point of view (which is the only point of view that counts) it is worth the effort. If the Consumer Product Safety Commission plays a prominent role in your case, and no other agency has any part at all, call it "the Commission," or even simply "the agency." If the case concerns the Prosecutorial Remedies and Other Tools to end the Exploitation of Children Today Act of 2003 (117 Stat. 650), foil the drafters by refusing to call it "the PROTECT Act"; just "the Act" will do.

The reason for avoiding acronyms is well exemplified in a fictional passage devised by Judge Daniel Friedman:

> [I]t is not unusual to read a sentence such as this in a brief: "The Port Association of Freight Forwarders (PAFF) entered into an Agreement Covering Loading Practices in the Inner Harbor (ACLPIH) with the Seattle Chapter of the Union of Warehousemen and Stevedores (SCUWS)." Two pages later, the following appears: "Under the ACLPIH, SCUWS was required to consult with PAFF before taking that action." This problem could be avoided if, instead of using these initials, the writer employed shorthand terms, such as "Association," "Agreement," and "Union." In place of the gibberish just quoted, the sentence would be fully comprehensible and succinct: "Under the Agreement, the Union was required to consult with the Association before taking that action."[7]

Refer to the parties by their names rather than their status in the litigation (plaintiff, respondent, etc.). There are good reasons for this. Sometimes, in reading briefs, judges will get confused about who is on the up-side and who on the down-side — and will have to flip back to the cover to see who "Petitioner" is. Moreover, the petitioner here may have been the defendant at trial, and the respondent on the first appeal. This can make the record on appeal confusing if status-names are used in the briefing and argument at each level. Everett Jones, however, is always and everywhere, at all stages of the litigation, Jones.

Some mistakenly advise that you should try to personalize your client and depersonalize the opposing party by calling the former "Jones" and the latter "Defendant." This is much too cute; rather than depersonalizing the defendant, it will annoy the court and ruin the story.

Sometimes each side of the case has multiple parties, so it is impossible to use a single name. No problem. If they are all railroads, refer to them as

---

[7] Hon. Daniel M. Friedman, "Winning on Appeal," in *Appellate Practice Manual* 129, 134 (Priscilla Anne Schwab ed., 1992).

"the railroads"; or if all debtors, call them "the debtors." If they are a mish-mash, pick the name of one of them and define that to include the entire group. For example, "The petitioners (collectively, 'Exxon') claimed below that . . . ."

Here, as everywhere, clarity governs all. It sometimes makes sense to use terms like "general contractor," "owner," and "subcontractor" if that will identify the cast of characters in a way that makes the story more comprehensible.

47. DON'T OVERUSE ITALICS; DON'T USE BOLD TYPE EXCEPT IN HEADINGS; DON'T USE UNDERLINING AT ALL.

Italicize to emphasize, but do it sparingly. Remember that when too much is emphasized, nothing is. Constant italicizing gives your brief the tone of an adolescent diary, which is not what you should be striving for.

Whenever possible, replace your italics with the device that provides the usual means of emphasis in written English: word order. In phrasing sentences, try to put the punch word at the end. Instead of writing "She held *a knife* in her hand," write "What she held in her hand was a knife." The latter formulation gives equivalent prominence to the desired word but sounds less excited. But when the only means of making your thought clear is to italicize a word or phrase, do it.

Some brief-writers ill-advisedly use boldface type within normal text. The result is visually repulsive. Reserve boldface for headings.

As for underlining, it's a crude throwback: that's what writers used in typewriting — when italics weren't possible. Nobody using a computer in the 21st century should be underlining text. To the extent that *The Bluebook* suggests otherwise, it should be revised.

48. DESCRIBE AND CITE AUTHORITIES WITH SCRUPULOUS ACCURACY.

Persuasive briefing induces the court to draw favorable conclusions from accurate descriptions of your authorities. It never distorts cases to fit the facts. The impression you want to make on the court — that you're knowledgeable and even expert — will be compromised by any misdescription that opposing counsel brings to the court's attention. If a case is only close but not completely in point, say so. Then explain why the difference is insubstantial and should not affect the outcome.

Make faithful and accurate use of the conventional introductory signals, as set forth in *The Bluebook*[8] or the *ALWD Citation Manual*[9] — one of which should always be on your desk. If another style manual is required in your state courts, use it. When you cite a case with no introductory signal, you're affirming to the court that this case explicitly *holds* what you have just said. If it is an alternative holding, say so with the parenthetical "(alternative holding)." If the proposition you have propounded is not stated in the case but necessarily follows from its holding, introduce the case by *See*. When the case you cite is merely analogous authority for the proposition you have stated, introduce it with the signal *Cf*. Show a contrary holding with *Contra*, and a case from whose reasoning a contrary holding necessarily follows with *But see*. And so forth. Consult your citation guide.

When even one of your citations fails to live up to your introductory signal, or is not parenthetically qualified when necessary, all the rest of your citations inevitably become suspect. Remember the evidentiary maxim, which pretty well describes the way people (including judges) generally react to intentional or even careless distortion: *falsus in uno, falsus in omnibus*. False in one respect, false in all.

And put your citations in the form most convenient for the generalist judge. In referring to a governing text, cite the official code. Some briefs cite sections of the original enactment as contained in session laws (in the federal system, "Stat." cites) rather than the sections as codified (e.g., the United States Code). For example, a brief may refer to "section 502(a)(3) of ERISA" to identify a provision of the Employee Retirement Income Security Act of 1974, Pub. L. No. 93-406, Tit. I, 88 Stat. 829, even though that provision is now codified at 29 U.S.C. § 1132(a)(3). It's easy to understand why this practice arises, since before codification the *only* source for citation is the session law; all the early law-review articles and commentaries refer to "section __ of the Act," and practitioners specializing in that field become accustomed to using that form of reference. But once codification has occurred, this practice can do nothing but confuse. Since proper citation form requires the Code section, we end up with a brief that refers to § 502(a)(3), followed (at least the first time that designation is used) by a citation of § 1132(a)(3). Worse, sometimes a brief that does this then adds an appendix using only the Code sections, leaving it to the reader to figure out which one is § 502. Once an act has been

---

[8] *The Bluebook: A Uniform System of Citation* § 1.2, at 46–48 (18th ed. 2005).
[9] *ALWD Citation Manual: A Professional System of Citation* § 44.3, at 324–25 (3d ed. 2006).

codified, refer to the Code sections; to do otherwise is to frustrate the whole purpose of codification. The judges may not be as familiar with the original act as you are, and they are accustomed to working from the Code. Make their job easier by using Code references consistently.

Professionalism is largely a matter of thwarting Murphy's Law: if something can go wrong, it will. Anyone who has ever written a book or article knows that errors can creep in with alarming ease. So you create safeguards that prevent things from going awry. Verify your quotations and citations as you enter them into a draft. Ensure that someone other than the researcher verifies them a second time. Ensure that others read the brief — not just those who collaborated in producing it. You yourself proofread it two more times than you think necessary. And KeyCite or Shepardize the citations once again before filing the brief — perhaps while creating the Table of Authorities.

49. CITE AUTHORITIES SPARINGLY.

You're not writing a treatise, a law-review article, or a comprehensive *Corpus Juris* annotation. You are trying to persuade one court in one jurisdiction. And what you're trying to persuade it of is not your (or your junior associate's) skill and tenacity at legal research. You will win no points, therefore, for digging out and including in your brief every relevant case. On the contrary, the glut of authority will only be distracting. What counts is not how many authorities you cite, but how well you use them.

As for governing authority, if the point you are making is relevant to your reasoning but is neither controversial nor likely to be controverted, a single citation (the more recent the better) will suffice. Anything more is just showing off to an unappreciative audience. But if the point is central to your case and likely to be contested, not only cite the case but concisely describe its facts and its holding. And follow that description by citing other governing cases *(Accord Smith v. Jones, Roe v. Doe)*.

If there is no governing authority in point, your resort to persuasive authority may require more extensive citation to show that the rule you are urging has been accepted in other jurisdictions. (For example: "Every other jurisdiction that has confronted this question has reached the same conclusion. *See Smith v. Jones*, 972 P.2d 1294 (Cal. 1998); *Roe v. Doe*, 649 N.E.2d 1391 (N.Y. 1995); *Riley v. Silberman*, 593 S.E.2d 930 (Va. 2003).") If persuasive authority is overwhelmingly in your favor but not uniformly so, you may have to resort to a footnote showing all the courts in your favor, followed by a *But see* citation of the few courts that are opposed. And citing an ALR annotation on point will be helpful.

Secondary authorities (treatises, law-review articles, case annotations) help confirm your analysis of trends in the law, general background (supporting, for example, your statement that before the statute at issue was adopted, the law was thus-and-so), and your view about what is the "best" rule with the most desirable policy consequences. It's superfluous — and hence harmful — to cite a secondary authority for a proposition clearly established by governing authority.

Don't expect the court, or even the law clerks, to read your secondary authority; they will at most check to see that it supports the point you make. They will therefore be persuaded not by the *reasoning* of your secondary authority but only by the *fact* that its author agrees with you. And the force of the persuasion will vary directly with the prominence of the author. Thus, except as a convenient way to refer the court to a compendium of cases, it's not much help to bring to the court's attention the fact that a student law-review note is on your side. Use it only when you have nothing else.

50. QUOTE AUTHORITIES MORE SPARINGLY STILL.

We've said that it pays to quote directly from a case setting forth your major premise. But it doesn't pay to string along quotation after quotation for the rest of the paragraph. A remarkably large number of lawyers seem to believe that their briefs are improved if each thought is expressed in the words of a governing case. The contrary is true. After you have established your major premise, it will be your reasoning that interests the court, and this is almost always more clearly and forcefully expressed in your own words than in the stringing together of quotations from various cases. Such a cut-and-paste approach also produces an air of artificiality, even of lack of self-assurance. You want the court to develop confidence in your reasoning — not in your ability to gopher up supporting quotations. Say what you know to be the law, and support it by citing a case that holds precisely that.

Be especially loath to use a lengthy, indented quotation. It invites skipping. In fact, many block quotes have probably never been read by anyone. So never let your point be made only in the indented quotation. State the point, and then support it with the quotation ("As Chief Justice Marshall expressed it: . . ."). This is, to be sure, iteration (yet another reason to avoid block quotes). But iteration that simultaneously buttresses with authority is sometimes effective.

If you can't weave quotations deftly into the fabric of your prose — especially the block quotations — abjure them altogether and paraphrase instead. If you ever use a series of quotations, remember that you must supply connective tissue between them — words to take the reader smoothly from one quotation to the next. Back-to-back quotations with no connectives are verboten.

51. SWEAR OFF SUBSTANTIVE FOOTNOTES — OR NOT.

The Garner view: Put no substantive point in a footnote — none, at least, that you consider important to your argument. There are several reasons for this, but the best is that many judges don't read footnotes. Some courts have even announced that they won't consider any argument raised exclusively in a footnote.[10] Ah, yes, you are accustomed to seeing lengthy footnotes in judicial opinions and in law-review articles. But the authors of judicial opinions don't win or lose by keeping their audience's attention. And law-review writers are generally most interested in demonstrating their scholarship. Whatever the value of substantive footnotes in those contexts — and many think they ought to be seriously curbed there as well — they have no place in a brief. If the point is not important enough to be in the text, it's not important enough to be in the brief.

You may recoil from the blackletter admonition here. But a year or two after deciding that you'll never put a sentence in a footnote (reference notes containing only bibliographical material are okay), you'll probably be surprised at how easy that resolution is to keep.

---

[10] *E.g.*, *NSTAR Elec. & Gas Corp. v. FERC*, 481 F.3d 794, 799–800 (D.C. Cir. 2007) ("[T]his argument is found in a single footnote in NSTAR's opening brief, and such a reference is not enough to raise an issue for our review."); *Smithkline Beecham Corp. v. Apotex Corp.*, 439 F.3d 1312, 1320 (Fed. Cir. 2006) ("[A]rguments raised in footnotes are not preserved."); *Lutwin v. Thompson*, 361 F.3d 146, 148 n.1 (2d Cir. 2004) ("We decline to consider this argument because '[a] contention is not sufficiently presented for appeal if it is conclusorily asserted only in a footnote.'" [quoting *Tolbert v. Queens College*, 242 F.3d 58, 75 (2d Cir. 2001)]); *U.S. v. Dairy Farmers of Am., Inc.*, 426 F.3d 850, 856 (6th Cir. 2005) ("An argument contained only in a footnote does not preserve an issue for our review."); *Sledd v. Lindsay*, 102 F.3d 282, 288 (7th Cir. 1996); *Equipment Mfrs. Inst. v. Janklow*, 300 F.3d 842, 848 n.2 (8th Cir. 2002) ("[T]his Court will not consider a claim improperly presented in a footnote."); *Bakalis v. Golembeski*, 35 F.3d 318, 326 n.8 (7th Cir. 1994) (An argument "made only in a footnote in the opening brief" and "not fully developed until the reply brief . . . is deemed waived."); *People v. Crosswhite*, 124 Cal. Rptr. 2d 301, 306 n.5 (Ct. App. 2001) ("This argument is waived by raising it only in a footnote under an argument heading which gives no notice of the contention."); *Roberts v. Worcester Redev. Auth.*, 759 N.E.2d 1220, 1227 n.11 (Mass. App. Ct. 2001) ("We are not required to address an argument raised in a footnote.").

A Scalia qualification: In my view, the preceding advice is too categorical. The Solicitor General of the United States, after all, is a highly skilled and experienced advocate, and the briefs of that office almost always contain substantive footnotes.

It is assuredly true that nothing really important to the decision should be in a footnote. And it's even true that, in most courts before which you are likely to appear, nothing of substance should be in a footnote. But in those courts with a relatively limited docket, accustomed to issuing detailed and exhaustive opinions, some relatively unimportant matters are worth discussing below the text. As Chief Judge Frank Easterbrook of the Seventh Circuit, himself a former Deputy Solicitor General, has told us in a letter:

> The SG's style, at least when I was there, was to write two briefs: one for all the Justices as they prepared for oral argument, and another for the Justice assigned to write the opinion. The straightforward, punchy argument appeared in the text of the brief. The extra details were in the footnotes. The office also used footnotes to anticipate the other side's weaker arguments and to address arguments that the other side never made — but that the Justices or their clerks might think up.
>
> It is bad to waste space in the text of a brief addressing arguments never made, but it is worse to know that a bright person might come up with an argument, have a ready answer, omit it from the brief, and then find from the opinion that the judge has thought up the argument *but not the answer.* Putting such information in footnotes makes it possible to file a cogent and streamlined brief, the sort of thing that will persuade on first reading, while keeping potentially helpful elaboration available for the judge to consult later.

I know of no court that will categorically not consider substantive footnotes. The citations contained in my coauthor's scary footnote pertain to the raising of fundamentally new claims or new arguments — for example, making a Due Process Clause argument in a footnote when all the rest of the brief relies on the Sixth Amendment. That shouldn't be done anyway. But providing useful (though less than essential) support for an argument made in text is quite different. And more different still is a footnoted response to a weak argument made by the other side. These footnotes may not be read; but if read they will be considered.

52. CONSIDER PUTTING CITATIONS IN FOOTNOTES — OR NOT.

The Garner view: I've made it something of a cause célèbre to reform the way citations are interlarded in lawyers' texts.[11] Since 1992, I've recommended putting all bibliographic material (volume numbers and page numbers) in footnotes but avoiding putting any substantive text (complete sentences) there. Nothing should appear in a footnote that anyone should have to read — only what someone might consult for looking up a reference.[12] Under this system of subordinating citations, readers should never be asked to look down at footnotes — there's nothing significant there because the important authorities have been named and discussed in the text ("Three years ago in *Flom v. Baumgartner*, this Court held that . . .").

Using this system, while describing in the text the major authorities you're relying on, has several advantages: (1) visually, the important material on the page, the discussion of authorities through close reasoning, is most prominent instead of the least important information, namely, the volume and page numbers; (2) disjointed thoughts, which are rampant in briefs, are immediately exposed for what they are; (3) poor paragraphing gets exposed; (4) discussion of governing and persuasive authorities is enhanced because it can no longer be buried in parentheticals following citations; and (5) the prose more closely follows the practices of the most accomplished nonfiction writers of our day. Although this technique improves the prose, it concededly makes greater demands on the writer, who must maintain a tighter train of thought. Readers need no longer skip over long swaths of bibliographic characters in the middle of the page (a holdover of typewriting style). Meanwhile, those readers who are critically evaluating your cited authorities — your adversaries and judges — can still see what you've cited.

Whether this system will gain widespread acceptance within the profession remains to be seen. Many judges and lawyers have adopted it,[13] and their numbers are increasing. We should measure progress in decades. It is with no small degree of sadness that I note my inability to persuade my coauthor to use this method for the improvement of judicial writing generally. One of his favorite sayings is that "whatever doesn't help hurts," and it's inconceivable that 535 U.S. 274, 276, 122 S.Ct. 1414, 1416, 152 L.Ed.2d 437, 439 helps anyone who's trying to get through a paragraph.

---

[11] *See* William Glaberson, *Legal Citations on Trial in Innovation v. Tradition*, N.Y. Times, 8 July 2001, at 1, 16.

[12] *See Garner on Language and Writing* 436–55, 460–71 (2008).

[13] For cited examples, see Garner, *Legal Writing in Plain English* (2001).

Meanwhile, his worries about "crabby judges" have rarely if ever been borne out among the many hundreds of lawyers who years ago adopted my recommendation and continue to follow it. Quite the opposite: they report that they routinely meet with positive outcomes — in part because they write more compellingly as a result of this technique.

The Scalia view: Alas, I disapprove this novel suggestion. You cannot make your product more readable to the careful lawyer by putting the entire citation material (case name, court, date, volume, and page) in a footnote — because the careful lawyer wants to know, while reading along, what the authority is for what you say. So, far from enabling the reader's eyes to run smoothly across a text uninterrupted by this ugly material, you would force the eyes to bounce repeatedly from text to footnote.

My coauthor's solution to this problem is to "weave" the name of the court and the case name (and the date?) into the text ("As the Supreme Court of the United States said in the 1959 case of *Schwarz v. Schwarz*,[1] . . ."). I doubt that this can be done (without sounding silly) for all the citations that a brief contains. But if it can, it will surely place undue emphasis upon, and inflate the text with, details inessential to the reasoning. I will rarely want the court, name, and date of a case thrust in my face, so to speak, by inclusion in the narrative text as though it's really important. Ordinarily, such information can better be conveyed, almost subliminally, in a running citation. Lawyers are used to skipping over these signals quickly and moving on to the next sentence. If in this respect legal-writing style differs from other writing style, it is only because lawyers must evaluate statements not on the basis of whether they make sense but on the basis of whether some governing authority said so.

Of course, whatever the merits of this debate, the conclusive reason not to accept Garner's novel suggestion is that it is novel. Judges are uncomfortable with change, and it is a sure thing that some crabby judges will dislike this one. You should no more try to convert the court to citation-free text at your client's expense than you should try to convert it to colorful ties or casual-Friday attire at oral argument. Now if Garner wanted to make a really useful suggestion, he might suggest avoiding, wherever possible, the insertion of lengthy citations in the middle of a sentence. That is easy to achieve, and certain not to offend.

53. MAKE THE RELEVANT TEXT READILY AVAILABLE TO THE COURT.

A text worth discussing is a text worth reading. Make sure that the *entirety* of the text you are relying on (or that your adversary is mistakenly relying on) appears somewhere in your brief. This is an exception to our caution against block quotations. If the statutory or other material is lengthy, put it in an appendix to the brief. (Placing some or most of it in a Joint Appendix is not enough; judges are distracted and annoyed by having to flip back and forth between volumes for material that is central to the case.) By the *entirety* of the text we mean not only the dispositive provision but also other portions that you claim bear on interpretation of the dispositive provision. Whatever text forms part of your argument should be not merely cited but reproduced in your brief.

And reproduce the text of the statute, ordinance, or regulation as it existed at the relevant time. If it has been amended since, that should be indicated in a citation. Sometimes earlier or later versions of the text are relevant to its interpretation. When that is so, reproduce the other versions — with the differences shown in italics or redlining.

54. DON'T SPOIL YOUR PRODUCT WITH POOR TYPOGRAPHY.

When business consultants make a presentation to a prospective client, they come forward with a professionally produced, bound proposal. They understand that to get business they must persuade, and that good visuals help. The same is true for persuading judges. A brief that is in an ugly typeface, with crowded lines, will not invite careful perusal. In the days when briefs had to be printed, counsel (and the court) could rely on a knowledgeable printer to produce a readily legible product. Now that lawyers can produce their own briefs using desktop-publishing software, the filed product is often disastrous.

The Supreme Court of the United States has set forth printing requirements in its rule 33. If the court in which you're filing has no such requirements, or significantly less rigorous ones, you should consider using the Supreme Court rules as a model. Better still, the United States Court of Appeals for the Seventh Circuit has posted on its website detailed, sage guidance for proper printing.

If necessary, hire someone to do the job right.

SHAKESPEARE'S LEGAL ACQUIREMENTS

(continued from page 192)

John Lord Campbell

THE COMEDY OF ERRORS

The following is part of the dialogue between Antipholus of Syracuse and his man Dromio, in Act II. Sc. 2:—

> *Dro. S.* There's no time for a man to *recover* his hair, that grows bald by nature.
>
> *Ant. S.* May he not do it by *fine and recovery?*
>
> *Dro. S.* Yes, to pay a *fine* for a periwig, and *recover* the lost hair of another man.

These jests cannot be supposed to arise from anything in the laws or customs of Syracuse; but they show the author to be very familiar with some of the most abstruse proceedings in English jurisprudence.

In Act IV. Sc. 2, Adriana asks Dromio of Syracuse, "Where is thy master, Dromio? Is he well?" and Dromio replies—

> No, he's in Tartar limbo, worse than hell:
> A devil in an everlasting garment hath him,
> One whose hard heart is button'd up with steel;
> A fiend, a fairy, pitiless and rough;
> A wolf; nay worse, a fellow all in buff;
> A back-friend, a shoulder-clapper, one that countermands
> The passages and alleys, creeks, and narrow lands:
> A hound that runs counter, and yet draws dry-foot well;
> One that *before the judgment* carries poor souls to hell.

> *Adr.* Why, man, what is the matter?
>
> *Dro. S.* I do not know the matter; he is *'rested on the case.*
>
> *Adr.* What, is he arrested? tell me at whose suit.
>
> *Dro. S.* I know not at whose suit he is arrested, well,
> But he's in a suit of buff which 'rested him, that can I tell. . . .
>
> *Adr.* . . . . This I wonder at:
> That he, unknown to me, should be in debt.
> Tell me, was he arrested on a *bond?*
>
> *Dro. S.* Not on a *bond*, but on a stronger thing:
> A *chain*, a *chain!*

Here we have a most circumstantial and graphic account of an English arrest on *mesne process* ["before judgment"], in an action *on the case*, for the price of a gold chain, by a sheriff's officer, or bum-bailiff, in his buff costume, and carrying his prisoner to a sponging-house — a spectacle which might often have been seen by an attorney's clerk. A fellow-student of mine (since an eminent Judge), being sent to an attorney's office, as part of his legal education, used to accompany the sheriff's officer when making captions on mesne process, that he might enjoy the whole feast of a lawsuit from the egg to the apples — and he was fond of giving a similar account of this proceeding,— which was then constantly occurring, but which, like "Trial by Battle," may now be considered obsolete.

As You Like It

In Act I. Sc. 2, Shakespeare makes the lively Rosalind, who, although well versed in poesy and books of chivalry, had probably never seen a bond or a law-paper of any sort in her life, quite familiar with the commencement of all deeds poll, which in Latin was, *Noverint universi per presentes*, in English, "Be it known to all men by these presents":—

> *Le Beau.* There comes an old man and his three sons,—
>
> *Cel.* I could match this beginning with an old tale.
>
> *Le Beau.* Three proper young men, of excellent growth and presence;—
>
> *Ros.* With bills on their necks,— *"Be it known unto all men by these presents,"* —

This is the technical phraseology referred to by Thomas Nash in his "Epistle to the Gentlemen Students of the two Universities," in the year 1589, when he is supposed to have denounced the author of "Hamlet" as one of those who had "left the trade of *Noverint*, whereto they were born, for handfuls of tragical speeches" — that is, an attorney's clerk become a poet, and penning a stanza when he should engross.

"As You Like It" was not brought out until shortly before the year 1600, so that Nash's *Noverint* could not have been suggested by it. Possibly Shakespeare now introduced the "Be it known unto all men," &c., in order to show his contempt for Nash's sarcasm.

In Act. II. Sc. 1, there are illustrations which would present themselves rather to the mind of one initiated in legal proceedings, than of one who had been brought up as an apprentice to a glover, or an assistant to a butcher or a woolstapler:— for instance, when it is said of the poor wounded deer, weeping in the stream:—

> "— thou makest a *testament*
> As worldlings do, giving thy sum of more
> To that which hath too much."

And again where the careless herd, jumping by him without greeting him, are compared to "fat and greasy citizens," who look

> "Upon that poor and broken *bankrupt* there,"—

without pitying his sufferings or attempting to relieve his necessities.

It may perhaps be said that such language might be used by any man of observation. But in Act III. Sc. 1, a deep technical knowledge of law is displayed, howsoever it may have been acquired.

The usurping Duke, Frederick, wishing all the real property of Oliver to be seized, awards a writ of *extent* against him, in the language which would be used by the Lord Chief Baron of the Court of Exchequer—

> *Duke Fred.* Make an *extent upon his house and lands*—

an *extendi facias* applying to house and lands, as a *fieri facias* would apply to goods and chattels, or a *capias ad satisfaciendum* to the person.

So in "King Henry VIII." we have an equally accurate statement of the *omnivorous* nature of a writ of *Præmunire*. The Duke of Suffolk, addressing Cardinal Wolsey, says,—

> "Lord Cardinal, the King's further pleasure is,
> Because all those things you have done of late
> By your power legatine within this kingdom
> Fall into the compass of a *præmunire*,
> That therefore such a writ be sued against you,
> *To forfeit all your goods, lands, tenements,*
> *Chattels, and whatsoever, and to be*
> *Out of the King's protection.*

In the next scene of "As You Like It," Shakespeare shows that he was well acquainted with lawyers themselves and the vicissitudes of their lives. Rosalind having told "who Time ambles withal, who Time trots withal, who Time gallops withal," being asked, "Who Time stands still withal?" answers—

> With lawyers in the vacation; for *they sleep between term and term,* and then they perceive not how Time moves.

Our great poet had probably observed that some lawyers have little enjoyment of the vacation after a very few weeks, and that they again long for the excitement of arguing demurrers end pocketing fees.

———

In the first scene of Act IV. Shakespeare gives us the true legal meaning of the word "attorney," viz. *representative* or *deputy*. [Celui qui vient à tour d'autrui; Qui alterius vices subit; Legatus; Vakeel.]

> *Ros.* Well, in her person I say — I will not have you.
>
> *Orl.* Then, in my own person, I die.
>
> *Ros.* No, faith, *die by attorney*. The poor world is almost six thousand years old, and in all this time there was not any man died in his own person, *videlicet*, in a love-cause.*

I am sorry to say that in our time the once most respectable word "attorney" seems to have gained a new meaning, viz. "a disreputable legal practitioner;" so that attorneys at law consider themselves treated discourteously when they are called "Attorneys." They now all wish to be called *Solicitors*, when doing the proper business of attorneys in the Courts of Common Law. Most sincerely honouring this branch of our profession, if it would please them, I am ready to support a bill "to prohibit the use of the word attorney, and to enact that on all occasions the word Solicitor shall be used instead thereof."

Near the end of the same scene Shakespeare again evinces his love for legal phraseology and imagery by converting Time into an aged Judge of Assize, sitting on the Crown side: —

> *Ros.* Well, Time is the old *Justice* that examines all such offenders, and let Time try.

As in "Troilus and Cressida" (Act IV. Sc. 5) Shakespeare makes Time an *Arbitrator*: —

> And that old common *Arbitrator*, Time,
> Will one day end it.

continued on page 272 . . .

---

* So in 'Richard III.,' Act IV. Sc. 4, the crook-backed tyrant, after murdering the infant sons of Edward IV., audaciously proposes to their mother to marry the Princess Elizabeth, their sister, and wishing the queen to intercede with her in his favour, says—

Be the *attorney* of my love to her.

Again in the same play (Act V. Sc. 3) Lord Stanley, meeting Richmond on the field at Bosworth, says—

I by *attorney* bless thee from thy mother.

MARCH

DESUETUDE: "DORMIUNT ALIQUANDO LEGES, NUMQUAM MORIUNTUR"

By John V. Orth, with the assistance of Joseph L. Hyde

Duke Vincentio ruefully admits that for many years he had failed to enforce Vienna's *strict statutes and most biting laws . . . , so our decrees, / Dead to infliction, to themselves are dead.* But his deputy has a different idea: *The law hath not been dead, though it hath slept . . . , now 'tis awake, / Takes note of what is done.* Among the passages in *Measure for Measure* most often quoted by American judges are those that concern the disuse of the law. Desuetude, the legal doctrine that if a statute is left unenforced long enough, the courts will regard it as having no effect, is recognized in Roman law and legal systems derived from it — as in the real-world Vienna of Shakespeare's time. A well educated West Virginia judge confronting "the problem of a statute that produces such absurd results that it has long been ignored" was reminded not only of Angelo's words, but also of a passage in the Digest of the Emperor Justinian: *"leges non solum suffragio legis latoris, sed etiam tacito consensu omnium per desuetudinem abrogentur"* (statutes may be repealed not only by vote of the legislature but also by the silent agreement of everyone expressed through desuetude).[1]

---

[1] Committee on Legal Ethics of the W.Va. State Bar v. Printz, 416 S.E.2d 720, 725

Desuetude also occurred to two legal scholars, Alexander Bickel and Robert Bork, as a possible approach to the birth control cases, Poe v. Ullman[2] and Griswold v. Connecticut.[3] Bickel in his classic study of judicial review, *The Least Dangerous Branch,* observed that statutes too unpopular to be enforced but not unpopular enough to be repealed "present a deadlock of wills, from which the Court [is] asked to extricate the state"[4] and suggested that desuetude was a possible judicial alternative to a constitutional ruling. Bork in his best-selling book, *The Tempting of America,* similarly observed:

> There is a problem with laws . . . [that] are kept on the books as precatory statements, affirmations of moral principle. It is quite arguable that this is an improper use of law, most particularly of criminal law, that statutes should not be on the books if no one intends to enforce them. It has been suggested that if anyone tried to enforce a law that had moldered in disuse for many years, the statute should be declared void by reason of desuetude or that the defendant should go free because the law had not provided fair warning.[5]

Duke Vincentio recognizes the problem — *Sith 'twas my fault to give the people scope, / 'Twould be my tyranny to strike and gall them* — but incongruously concludes, *I have on Angelo imposed the office.*

continued on page 275 . . .

ANCHOR SAVINGS BANK, FSB V. UNITED STATES
81 Fed.Cl. 1 (March 14, 2008)

Lawrence J. Block, Judge

[T]he very history of the savings and loan crisis, including the market forces that contributed to it and the regulatory and market responses . . . are critical to understanding Anchor's long-term business plans and the impetus for the bank's diversification. Both of these, in turn, are essential to the court's subsequent lost profit analysis because each goes to the heart of Anchor's claim for damages. Shakespeare was indeed prescient when he wrote that the "past is prologue." *The Tempest,* act 2, sc. 1.

(W.Va. 1992) (Neely, J.) (quoting Digest 1.3.32). See 1 *The Digest of Justinian* 13 (trans. Alan Watson 1985).

[2] 367 U.S. 497 (1961).

[3] 381 U.S. 479 (1965).

[4] Alexander M. Bickel, *The Least Dangerous Branch: The Supreme Court at the Bar of Politics* 147 (1962).

[5] Robert H. Bork, *The Tempting of America: The Political Seduction of the Law* 96 (1990).

≈ MARCH ≈

SUN	MON	TUES	WED	THUR	FRI	SAT
1	2	3	4	5	6	7
8	9	10	11	12	13	14
15	16	17	18	19	20	21
22	23	24	25	26	27	28
29	30	31				

left on the cheekes will make the owner looke big like a bowdled hen.

Bowdlerize (bau·dlərəiz), *v.* [f. the name of *Dr. T. Bowdler*, who in 1818 published an edition of Shakspere, 'in which those words and expressions are omitted which cannot with propriety be read aloud in a family': see -IZE.] *trans.* To expurgate (a book or writing), by omitting or modifying words or passages considered indelicate or offensive; to castrate.

1836 GEN. P. THOMPSON *Let.* in *Exerc.* (1842) IV. 124 Among the names..are many, like Hermes, Nereus..which modern ultra-christians would have thought formidably heathenish; while Epaphroditus and Narcissus they would probably have *Bowdler*ized. 1869 *Westm. Rev.* Jan., It is gratifying to add that Mr. Dallas has resisted the temptation to Bowdlerize. 1881 SAINTSBURY *Dryden* 9 Evil counsellors who wished him to bowdlerise glorious John. 1883 *Ch. Times* 703/4 It [Henry IV] is Bowdlerized, to be sure, but that is no evil for school purposes.

Hence **Bow·dlerism, Bow:dleriza·tion, Bow·dlerized** *ppl. a.*, **Bow·dlerizer, Bow·dlerizing,** *vbl. sb.* and *ppl. a.*

1869 *Pall Mall G.* 4 Aug. 12 We doubt whether Juvenal.. can be read with advantage at the age when Bowdlerism, as a moral precaution, would be desirable. 1878 *Athenæum* 6 Apr., False squeamishness or inclination to Bowdlerism. 1882 *Westm. Rev.* Apr. 583 The bowdlerization..is done in an exceedingly awkward and clumsy fashion. 1879 F. HARRISON *Choice Bks.* (1886) 63 A Bowdlerised version of it would be hardly intelligible as a tale. 1886 HUXLEY in *19th Cent.* Apr. 489 We may fairly inquire whether editorial Bowdlerising has not prevailed over historic truth.

† **Bow·-draught.** *Obs.* [f. BOW *sb.*1 + DRAUGHT from the phrase *to draw a bow.*] A

Oxford English Dictionary 1031 (1888).

HOW NOT TO BOWDLERIZE

In his useful and entertaining book *How Not to Write*, William Safire tells us where the verb "to bowdlerize" comes from:

> Dr. Thomas Bowdler, eager to make Shakespeare "fit for the perusal of our virtuous females," cut out what he considered the naughty and profane words. In his sanitized version, Lady Macbeth's "Out, damn'd spot!" was changed to "Out, crimson spot!", which earned the censor a place in the dictionaries in the verb *to bowdlerize*.[1]

Safire is referring to *The Family Shakspeare*,[2] a 10-volume collection of cleaned-up versions of Shakespeare's works brought out in London in 1818 by Thomas Bowdler (1754-1825), whose work was an extension of the earlier efforts of his sister and fellow-expurgator Henrietta (1750-1830).[3] But alas, Safire is not quoting from *The Family Shakspeare*, although apparently he thinks he is. Instead, in the course of describing how Bowdler doctored Shakespeare, Safire has doctored Bowdler.

BOWDLER AND THE BULFINCHES

Let us begin by acknowledging the accuracy of the general thrust of Safire's story. Thomas Bowdler, hell-bent on making Shakespeare safe for consumption by all humanity, did in fact thoroughly butcher the Bard in *The Family Shakspeare*. (There is, after all, much naughtiness and profanity in Shakespeare.) And Bowdler's name and –ism have long been epithets to be wielded by the cosmopolitan and the libertarian against the puritan and the censor.

According to the *Oxford English Dictionary*, Thomas Perronet Thompson coined the term "bowdlerism" in a June 8, 1836 letter to his constituents. Thompson, who represented Kingston upon Hull in the House of

---

[1] HOW NOT TO WRITE: THE ESSENTIAL MISRULES OF GRAMMAR 100 (1990; 2005 prtg.).

[2] Yes, that is the way Bowdler spelled the name. *See* THOMAS BOWDLER, 1 THE FAMILY SHAKSPEARE title page (1818).

[3] NOEL PERRIN, DR. BOWDLER'S LEGACY: A HISTORY OF EXPURGATED BOOKS IN ENGLAND AND AMERICA ch. 3 (1969) (hereafter PERRIN); *see also* M. Clare Loughlin-Chow, *Bowdler, Henrietta Maria (1750-1830)*, and *Bowdler, Thomas (1754-1825)*, *in* OXFORD DICTIONARY OF NATIONAL BIOGRAPHY (2004), www.oxforddnb.com/view/article/3028 and www.oxforddnb.com/view/article/3032. A second edition of Perrin's book appeared in 1971, and a third in 1992. All citations are to the 1969 edition because it is the one most likely to be at the root of the confusion discussed in this article and the relevant passages are unchanged in the later editions.

Commons at the time, was deriding a Parliamentary act of discrimination on the basis of religion:

> I should like to know on what particular portion of either the letter or the spirit of anything left by the founders of Christianity, the Anglican sect undertakes to found a right of cutting men off from civil advantages, as the engine of increasing the number of baptisms. . . . There may be reason for believing, that when the early Christians baptized a full-grown heathen, they sometimes gave him a new name, as a token probably of the newness of life to which he was called. But even this, it is plain, they did not always do. For among the names preserved in the writings of the apostles, are many, like Hermes, Nereus, Olympas, Silvanus, and perhaps Phebe our sister, which modern ultra-christians would have thought formidably heathenish; while Epaphroditus and Narcissus they would probably have *Bowdler*ized.[4]

Since then, Bowdler's name has been tied — quite appropriately — to those who would, as the *American Heritage Dictionary* puts it, "remove material that is considered offensive or objectionable from (a book, for example)."[5] Safire has occasionally used Bowdler as Thompson did, in moderately epithetical ways in his famous *New York Times* "On Language" column and in other writings.[6] Lawyers, too, do their part to carry on the tradition begun by Thompson of associating Bowdler with self-righteous, moralizing censorship.[7]

The sharp point of Safire's story in *How Not to Write*, however, is wrong. Recall that as an example of the extremity of Bowdler's prudish editing, Safire cites his transformation of Lady Macbeth's famous profanity "Out, damn'd spot!" into the less colorful "Out, crimson spot!" At first blush this seems like a great illustration of bowdlerism at its worst: the

---

[4] *Letters of a Representative to his Constituents, during the session of 1836, reprinted in* T. PERRONET THOMPSON, 4 EXERCISES, POLITICAL AND OTHERS 61, 123-124 (2d ed. 1843) (emphasis in the original), *cited in* 2 OXFORD ENGLISH DICTIONARY 454 (2d ed. 1989); OXFORD ENGLISH DICTIONARY 1031 (1888); *see also* THE RANDOM HOUSE DICTIONARY OF THE ENGLISH LANGUAGE 248 (2d ed. 1987).

[5] THE AMERICAN HERITAGE DICTIONARY OF THE ENGLISH LANGUAGE 218 (4th ed. 2006).

[6] *See, e.g.,* note 1 above and accompanying text; *Patriotic Gore*, N.Y. TIMES, Mar. 16, 1984, at A25; *Clone Clone Clone Clone*, N.Y. TIMES, Apr. 6, 1997, at SM18; *Sexy Lexies*, N.Y. TIMES, June 29, 2003, at SM18.

[7] *See, e.g., U.S. v. American Library Ass'n, Inc.,* 539 U.S. 194, 237-38 (2003) (Souter, J., dissenting); *U.S. v. 12 200-Foot Reels of Super 8mm Film*, 413 U.S. 123, 133 (1973) (Douglas, J., dissenting); Brief for Petitioners at 33, *Denver Area Educational Telecommunications Consortium, Inc. v. F.C.C.*, 518 U.S. 727 (1996); Richard A. Posner, *A Political Court*, 119 HARV. L. REV. 31, 101 (2005).

perfect and original language, composed by an accomplished and respected author, has been disfigured and reduced by a sanctimonious editor who thinks himself a superior character if not a superior writer. But
look at page 238. That is a picture of page 234 of volume 4 of Bowdler's
The Family Shakspeare — the page containing the passage that Safire claims
to be quoting. But the "crimson" passage isn't there. Instead, Lady Macbeth quite conventionally (for her and for Shakespeare) says, "Out,
damned spot!" In other words, Bowdler did not change "damn'd" (or
"damned") to "crimson." Well, who did?

The culprits are two Bostonians, Thomas Bulfinch (1796-1867) and his
brother Stephen Greenleaf Bulfinch (1809-1870). Thomas was a famous
bowdlerizer, as the *New York Times* reported in his obituary:

> He was the author of several books of decided usefulness, which
> he prepared with great painstaking and taste. Among these are
> some that may be regarded as manuals, such as *The Age of Fable*,
> *The Age of Chivalry*, [and] *Legends of Charlemagne*, in which, expur-
> gated of all that would be offensive, he presented in a succinct and
> lucid manner a large amount of information needed by readers,
> and especially by young readers, in regards to the beliefs, supersti-
> tions and traditions of the past.[8]

After his death Thomas's three "manuals" were often published in one-
volume editions as *Bulfinch's Mythology*. They are still in print in that form
today.[9] His brother Stephen was also a prominent figure in his own time,
known as a respectable Unitarian minister and the author of numerous
religious tracts.[10]

In 1865, the brothers Bulfinch collaborated on their own bowdlerized
Shakespeare — an edition "Adapted for Reading Classes, and for the Family Circle." As they explained in the introduction,

> There is in the writings of this great author a degree of coarseness,
> consistent with the manners of his age, but disapproved by the
> higher refinement of the present day. This fact, as well as the num-
> ber and unequal merit of his works, renders a selection allowable,
> and we think desirable. In the present volume an attempt is made

---

[8] *Death of Mr. Thomas Bulfinch*, N.Y. TIMES, May 31, 1867, at 2; *see also, e.g., Author's
Preface, in* THOMAS BULFINCH, 1 THE AGE OF FABLE OR BEAUTIES OF MYTHOLOGY vii
(Rev. of Revs. ed. 1914) ("Such stories and parts of stories as are offensive to pure
taste and good morals are not given.").

[9] *See, e.g.,* BULFINCH'S MYTHOLOGY (Barnes & Noble Classics 2006).

[10] 1 APPLETON'S CYCLOPÆDIA OF AMERICAN BIOGRAPHY 444 (James Grant Wilson &
John Fiske eds., 1888); *Death of Prominent Citizens*, N.Y. TIMES, Oct. 14, 1870, at 1.

234 . MACBETH. [ACT V.

Gent. Since his majesty went into the field, I
have seen her rise from her bed, throw her night-
gown upon her, unlock her closet, take forth paper,
fold it, write upon it, read it, afterwards seal it, and
again return to bed; yet all this while in a most fast
sleep.

Doct. A great perturbation in nature! to receive
at once the benefit of sleep, and do the effects of
watching. — In this slumbry agitation, besides her
walking, and other actual performances, what, at
any time, have you heard her say?

Gent. That, sir, which I will not report after her.

Doct. You may, to me; and 'tis most meet you
should.

Gent. Neither to you, nor any one; having no
witness to confirm my speech.

Enter Lady MACBETH, *with a Taper.*

Lo you, here she comes! This is her very guise;
and, upon my life, fast asleep. Observe her; stand
close.

Doct. How came she by that light?

Gent. Why, it stood by her: she has light by her
continually; 'tis her command.

Doct. You see, her eyes are open.

Gent. Ay, but their sense is shut.

Doct. What is it she does now? Look, how she
rubs her hands.

Gent. It is an accustomed action with her, to seem
thus washing her hands; I have known her continue
in this a quarter of an hour.

Lady M. Yet here's a spot.

Doct. Hark, she speaks: I will set down what
comes from her, to satisfy my remembrance the
more strongly.

Lady M. Out, damned spot! out, I say! — One;
Two; Why, then 'tis time to do't: —— Hell is

Bowdler, 4 *The Family Shakspeare* 234 (1818).

to present such a selection, in a compact and elegant form. . . . Such scenes and passages have been omitted as were objectionable on the score of morals or taste, or could be spared without serious loss.[11]

And on page 382 of the Bulfinches' *Shakespeare Adapted for Reading Classes*: "*Lady M.* Out, crimson spot!" (See page 240.)

How certain can we be that the Bulfinches are the original authors of the "crimson"-for-"damn'd" bowdlerization that Safire attributes to Bowdler? Pretty — but not absolutely — certain.

Noel Perrin was, until his recent death, a professor of English at Dartmouth and a leading authority on bowdlerism. He appears to have been the first modern scholar to note the Bulfinches' extreme expurgation of Lady Macbeth. In his book *Dr. Bowdler's Legacy: A History of Expurgated Books in England and America*, Perrin reports,

> Compared to the weeding done by Thomas Bulfinch of Boston, [a contemporary's bowdlerizing] may actually be a trifle lax. Bulfinch, son of the great architect and himself the well-known author of Bulfinch's *Mythology*, published *Shakespeare Adapted for Reading Classes and the Family Circle* in 1865. In it he carried delicacy so far as to deny Lady Macbeth what is the most famous and least-mutilated blasphemy in Shakespeare. In his version she looks at her hand and says, "Out, crimson spot." I have found no other case of this.[12]

We have had no more success than Perrin finding another instance of "crimson"-for-"damn'd" bowdlerization.[13] We are confident that Thomas Bowdler himself never did it. The last edition of Bowdler's bowdlerization of Shakespeare — published in 1825 — is the same as the first when it comes to that damn'd spot. Other than the failure to mention Stephen Bulfinch's co-bowdlerizership, Perrin's story seems correct.

---

[11] THOMAS BULFINCH & REV. S.G. BULFINCH, SHAKESPEARE ADAPTED FOR READING CLASSES, AND FOR THE FAMILY CIRCLE xi (1865).

[12] PERRIN at 108-09.

[13] William Cusack Smith, a prominent and controversial Irish judge, did use "Out, crimson spot" in a poem published in 1836, but he used "Out, damned spot!" on the same page and attributed both versions to Lady Macbeth, making his fiddling with her words an exercise in poetic rather than expurgatorial license. *To Sleep, in* THE GOBLINS OF NEAPOLIS 108, 109 & n.‡ (1836) (Paul P. Peeradeal (pseud.), ed.); Brigitte Anton, *Smith, Sir William Cusack, second baronet (1766–1836), in* OXFORD DICTIONARY OF NATIONAL BIOGRAPHY (2004), www.oxforddnb.com/view/article/25936.

Gent. Ay, but their sense is shut.

Doct. What is it she does now? Look, how she rubs her hands.

Gent. It is an accustomed action with her to seem thus washing her hands: I have known her continue in this a quarter of an hour.

Lady M. Yet here's a spot.

Doct. Hark! she speaks. I will set down what comes from her, to satisfy my remembrance the more strongly.

Lady M. Out, crimson spot! out, I say!—One; two: why, then 'tis time to do 't. — Fie, my lord, fie! a soldier, and afeard? What need we fear who knows it, when none can call our power to account? — Yet who would have thought the old man to have had so much blood in him?

Doct. Do you mark that?

Lady M. The Thane of Fife had a wife: where is she now? — What, will these hands ne'er be clean? — No more o' that, my lord; no more o' that; you mar all with this starting.

Doct. Go to, go to; you have known what you should not.

Gent. She has spoke what she should not, I am sure of that. Heaven knows what she has known.

Lady M. Here's the smell of the blood still: all the perfumes of Arabia will not sweeten this little hand. O! O! O!

Doct. What a sigh is there! The heart is sorely charged.

Gent. I would not have such a heart in my bosom for the dignity of the whole body.

Doct. Well, well, well, —

Bulfinch, *Shakespeare Adapted for Reading Classes, and for the Family Circle* 382 (1865).

HOW THE BULFINCHES BECAME BOWDLER

As language guru Bryan Garner has observed, "heavy borrowing" was not unusual among lexicographers in bygone days, but it is "suspect today."[14] Suspect but, perhaps, not absent. How else can we explain the fact that William Safire is not alone in his particular mistreatment of Bowdler? For example, Morton Freeman's *A New Dictionary of Eponyms* — published by the Oxford University Press in 1997, seven years after the first printing of Safire's *How Not to Write* — includes the following in its definition of "bowdler, bowdlerize":

> In 1818 Bowdler published a diluted ten-volume edition of Shakespeare's works "in which nothing is added to the original text; but those words are omitted that cannot with propriety be read aloud in a family." He had toned down suggestive dialogue and snipped off scenes that he thought were too explicit, insisting that only references that might "raise a blush on the cheek of modesty" had been excised.
>
> Bowdler believed that the language of the seventeenth century was not necessarily acceptable in the nineteenth. For example, . . . Lady Macbeth's poignant "Out, damn'd spot!" became "Out, crimson spot!"[15]

Among Safire's other successors-in-error have been lexicographer Nigel Rees,[16] and test-prep author Suzee Vlk.[17] Surely they did not all independently, mistakenly put quotation marks around the same line that is not in Bowdler's *Family Shakspeare*, and attribute the quote to that work.

But that still leaves us with the question of how Safire made the mistake in the first place.

It turns out that Safire had predecessors-in-error as well as successors. The *Green Bag* has no expertise in the field of lexicographical sleuthing,

---

[14] *See* Bryan A. Garner, *Preface to the First Pocket Edition of Black's Law Dictionary, in* GARNER ON LANGUAGE AND WRITING 351, 352 (2008).

[15] MORTON S. FREEMAN, A NEW DICTIONARY OF EPONYMS 28-29 (1997) (Freeman's description of Bowdler and his edition of Shakespeare contains several other inaccuracies, most of which are not strictly relevant here).

[16] NIGEL REES, CASSELL'S DICTIONARY OF WORD AND PHRASE ORIGINS 35 (2002) (describing the work of "Thomas Bowdler[,] who published *The Family Shakespeare* (1818)": "'Out damn'd spot' became 'Out crimson spot', and so on.").

[17] SUZEE VLK, THE GRE TEST FOR DUMMIES 69 (5th ed. 2002) ("Dr. Thomas Bowdler, an English physician, published in 1818 a ten-volume edition of Shakespeare's plays called The Family Shakespeare. He left out all the dirty parts. For example, instead of 'Out, damn'd spot!' the line reads, 'Out, crimson spot!'").

but that did not stop us from doing a little amateurish work. Here is the story as best we have been able to piece it together. It all began with the *New York Times*.

In 1969, in his book *Dr. Bowdler's Legacy*, Noel Perrin correctly reported that Thomas Bulfinch — not Thomas Bowdler — substituted "Out, crimson spot!" for "Out, damn'd spot!" in Shakespeare's *Macbeth*.

The *New York Times* reviewed *Dr. Bowdler's Legacy* in the autumn of that year. The review's description of Bowdler's work included this passage — "one editor, who should be everyone's favorite, changed Lady Macbeth's famous line to 'Out, crimson spot'" — without mentioning one or more Bulfinches or making it clear that Bowdler was not the "one editor."[18] A few days later, a *Time* magazine reviewer, noting that Perrin "takes as his point of departure Dr. Thomas Bowdler," asked, "What could prompt an educated man to change Lady Macbeth's most famous line to 'Out, crimson spot'?" — without mentioning one or more Bulfinches or making it clear that Bowdler was not the "educated man."[19] And a few weeks after that, a *Christian Science Monitor* review sporting the title *'Out, crimson spot'* included this line — "that state of overrefinement which leads editors to rewrite Lady Macbeth's most famous speech as, 'Out, crimson spot'" — also without mentioning one or more Bulfinches.[20]

Over the next 20 years, a variety of authors — holding themselves out as experts on a range of topics including sex,[21] language,[22] and the Scho-

---

[18] Thomas Lask, *Notes on Castrati*, N.Y. TIMES, Sept. 27, 1969, at 31.

[19] *"Knows Where!"*, TIME, Oct. 3, 1969.

[20] Melvin Maddocks, *'Out, crimson spot'*, CHRISTIAN SCIENCE MONITOR, Nov. 20, 1969, at 16.

[21] JAMES LESLIE MCCARY, HUMAN SEXUALITY: PHYSIOLOGICAL, PSYCHOLOGICAL, AND SOCIOLOGICAL FACTORS 380 (2d ed. 1973) ("That prototype of the self-appointed guardian of public morals, Dr. Thomas Bowdler, was heard to say, 'Shakespeare, Madam, is obscene, and thank God, we are sufficiently advanced to have found it out!' Lady Macbeth's famous cry, 'Out, damned spot' spot was therefore rendered, 'Out, crimson spot.'"). There was no mention of Bowdler in the first edition of *Human Sexuality* (JAMES LESLIE MCCARY, HUMAN SEXUALITY: PHYSIOLOGICAL AND PSYCHOLOGICAL FACTORS OF SEXUAL BEHAVIOR (1967)), suggesting McCary learned of the "crimson"-for-"damn'd" bowdlerization between 1967 and 1973.

[22] LORETO TODD & IAN HANCOCK, INTERNATIONAL ENGLISH USAGE 94 (1986) (". . . Bowdler removed anything that he felt might cause embarrassment. He cut out large sections and modified others, causing Lady Macbeth, for example, to proclaim 'Out, crimson spot' instead of 'Out, damned spot.'"); ROSIE BOYCOTT, BATTY, BLOOMERS & BOYCOTT: A LITTLE ETYMOLOGY OF EPONYMOUS WORDS 24 (1983) ("In The Family Shakespeare, . . . the famous line 'Out damn'd spot!' becomes 'Out crimson spot!'"); Quentin Letts, *NS Profile: Rosie Boycott*, NEW STATESMAN, June 24, 2002, www. newstatesman.com/200206240013 (visited January 9, 2009).

lastic Aptitude Test[23] — took the *Times'* (and *Time's*, and *Monitor's*) elisions and ran with them, indicting Thomas Bowdler for Thomas (and Stephen) Bulfinch's "crimson"-for-"damn'd" bowdlerization of Lady Macbeth. This is not to say that what Perrin had written in 1969 was lost on everyone. In his 1978 book *Whatever Happened to Shakespeare?*, for example, Kenneth McClellan recommends Perrin's book, and — proving that he actually read it — provides an accurate synopsis of Perrin's Bulfinch discovery: "Thomas Bulfinch, of *Mythology* fame, had Lady Macbeth say, 'Out, crimson spot'."[24]

Which brings us down to 1990, and William Safire.

Some stories are so obviously true they do not need to be checked — or at least they can seem that way, says Harvard's Cass Sunstein:

> Rumor transmission often involves the rational processing of information, in a way that leads people, quite sensibly in light of their existing knowledge, to believe and to spread falsehoods. . . . [R]umors often arise and gain traction because of their relationship with the prior convictions of those who accept them.[25]

Our best guess, or the first part of it, is that by the time Safire sat down to write *How Not to Write*, almost everyone in the circles in which he traveled had read the *New York Times* review of Perrin's book — or talked to someone who had read it, or read a book written by someone who had read it, or read a book written by someone who had talked to someone who had read it, or talked to someone who had read a book written by someone who had read it, or something of the sort.

The second part of our best guess is that almost none of those people had actually read the Perrin book, even fewer had ever seen Bowdler's *Family Shakspeare*, and yet fewer even knew of the existence of the Bulfinches' *Shakespeare Adapted for Reading Classes.*

The third part of our best guess is that, as Sunstein might say, everyone already had good reason to know what bowdlerism was, and they knew that it was and remains a bad thing, and as a result, they knew that Bowdler was the one who put "Out, crimson spot!" in Lady Macbeth's mouth.

---

[23] JOAN DAVENPORT CARRIS, WILLIAM R. MCQUADE & MICHAEL R. CRYSTAL, SAT SUCCESS: PETERSON'S STUDY GUIDE TO ENGLISH AND MATH SKILLS FOR COLLEGE ENTRANCE EXAMINATIONS 94 (1987) ("He rewrote Lady Macbeth's famous cry, 'Out, damned spot!' to read 'Out, crimson spot!'").

[24] KENNETH MCCLELLAN, WHATEVER HAPPENED TO SHAKESPEARE? 84, 85 (1978).

[25] Cass R. Sunstein, *"She Said What?" "He Did That?" Believing False Rumors*, Harvard Pub. L. Working Paper 08-56 (prelim. draft 11/21/08), ssrn.com/abstract=1304268 (citations omitted).

And there was no need to waste time digging hard at the roots of facts that everyone knew to be true.

Perrin would have winced at this strange and unfortunate offshoot of his disclosure of the Bulfinches' bowdlerization of Lady Macbeth. Perrin writes with gentle, perhaps excessive charity that when Bowdler butchered Shakespeare's works he sought to "revise them into innocence"[26] — treating Bowdler's enterprise as good-hearted, though misguided. But when reporting allegations that an editor added extra spice to the already racy poems of John Wilmot, 2nd Earl of Rochester, Perrin is less forgiving: "the forty genuine poems were doctored to make them dirtier than Rochester had already . . . [in] one of the rare cases of anti-bowdlerism."[27] It is one thing, Perrin might have summed-up, to fiddle with an auther's work in an effort (however arrogant or misguided) to make that author look good; it is quite another to fiddle with an author's work in an effort (wilful, reckless, or negligent) to make that author look bad.

HOW NOT TO BOWDLERIZE

How not to bowdlerize? You could look it up, before you write it down. But a perfect commitment to that rule would require not only superhuman discipline (because "it's hard . . . suspecting everyone, everything, it wears you down"[28]), but also access to research resources that are probably beyond the reach even of the *New York Times* or the Oxford University Press. Moreover, recent studies of brain function suggest that our brains drive us to adopt as truth what those about us claim as truth, even in the absence of evidence of truth.[29] A perpetual, independent return to first facts as well as first principles is a labor for gods, not humans.

Like it or not, we all have to choose some people and authorities to trust in this world, if we are ever going to get anything done. Making those choices is not easy, and finding fault in those we do choose is dis-

---

[26] PERRIN at 63.

[27] *Id.* at 45. This characterization might reflect the limited scope of Perrin's study. Doctoring the words of others to make them naughtier than they really are — anti-bowdlerism, as Perrin calls it — is part of the literature of politics. *See, e.g.,* Cindy Richards, *Fighting A Lie That Just Won't Die,* CHI. TRIB., May 30, 1999, at C1; Al Kamen, *In The Loop: Another White House Tale,* WASH. POST, Sept. 25, 1998, at A23; *see generally* snopes.com/politics/politics.asp. All the better that the term "bowdlerism" was coined by a politician. *See* note 4 above and accompanying text.

[28] Fox Mulder, *in Little Green Men,* THE X-FILES (air date Sept. 16, 1994); *see also, e.g.,* THOMAS S. KUHN, THE STRUCTURE OF SCIENTIFIC REVOLUTIONS ch. 6 (3d ed. 1996).

[29] *See, e.g.,* Vasily Klucharev et al., *Reinforcement Learning Signal Predicts Social Conformity,* 61 NEURON 140, 140, 147-48 (2009).

comfiting. But perfectionism — while it might be a charming aspiration and a too-clever job-interview answer ("What do you see as your greatest weakness, young man?" "Oh, I've been told I invest too much effort in trying to do everything perfectly." Jeez!) — is as fruitless as looking everything up. We get on well in life by going with what is excellent, not by holding out for what is perfect. The former is in short enough supply and hard enough to find. The latter, when it does turn up, tends to be in a form that falls under the jurisdiction of the Federal Trade Commission. [30]

Knowing Safire from long readership, we still trust him, in no small part because he is that rare public intellectual who seems to care enough about accuracy to value, even relish, corrections not only of others' work, but also of his own.[31] How many writers subsidize corrections and criticisms of their own work by publishing the critics — in their own words — in the company of the writer's own work?[32] How many would or plausibly could publish a book titled "I Stand Corrected"?[33] He isn't perfect, but he is excellent, and reassuringly accountable. And wrong about Bowdler.

EPILOGUE

Rumor-mongering is a slippery slope. Once we free ourselves from the obligation to check our facts, we are free to write imaginatively. Consider, for example, Morton Freeman, the author of A New Dictionary of Eponyms. Having borrowed (in all likelihood) from someone else the story pinning the "crimson"-for-"damn'd" bowdlerization on Bowdler, and having failed (without a doubt) to note that he has not looked at Bowdler's work himself, Freeman then proceeds to carry on extravagantly for nearly a full page about the scope of Bowdler's bowdlerization of Shakespeare, concluding his indictment as follows: "Bowdler's eraser skipped none of Shakespeare's works. He expurgated all of them."[34]

Thomas Bowdler would have been surprised to learn that he had been so thorough. Take Measure for Measure, for example. According to Bowdler, the "indecent" parts were so deeply embedded in the play that its reduction-and-redemption was a task that exceeded even his capacity for expurgation. And he provided a lengthy and public explanation — right there in the pages of The Family Shakspeare — of his decision not to cut into Measure for Measure:

---

[30] See, e.g., FTC v. QT, Inc., 512 F.3d 858 (7th Cir. 2008) & 2009 GREEN BAG ALM. 169.

[31] See generally RICHARD A. POSNER, PUBLIC INTELLECTUALS (2001; 2004 prtg.).

[32] See generally, e.g., WILLIAM SAFIRE, YOU COULD LOOK IT UP (1988); WILLIAM SAFIRE, NO UNCERTAIN TERMS (2003).

[33] WILLIAM SAFIRE, I STAND CORRECTED (1984).

[34] FREEMAN, A NEW DICTIONARY OF EPONYMS at 29.

PREFACE TO THE FOLLOWING THEATRE COPY OF

MEASURE FOR MEASURE

Thomas Bowdler
2 The Family Shakspeare 1-3 (1818)

This comedy contains scenes which are truly worthy of the first of dramatic poets. Isabella pleading with Angelo in behalf of mercy to her brother, and afterwards insisting that his life must not be purchased by the sacrifice of her chastity, is an object of such interest, as to make the reader desirous of overlooking the many great defects which are to be found in other parts of this play. The story is little suited to a comedy. The wickedness of Angelo is so atrocious, that I recollect only one instance of a similar kind being recorded in history; and that is considered by many persons as of doubtful authority.[1] His crimes indeed, are not completed, but he supposed them to be so; and his guilt is as great as it would have been if the person of Isabella had been violated, and the head of Ragozine had been Claudio's. This monster of iniquity appears before the Duke, defending his cause with unblushing boldness; and after the detection of his crimes, he can scarcely be said to receive any punishment. A hope is even expressed that he will prove a good husband, but for no good reason — namely, because he *has been a little bad*. Angelo betrayed the trust reposed in him by the Duke, he threatened Isabella that if she would not surrender her virtue, he would not merely put her brother to death, but make his death drawn out to lingering sufferance; and finally, when he thought his object accomplished, he ordered Claudio to be murdered in violation of his most solemn engagement. These are the crimes which, in the language of Mariana, are expressed by the words *a little bad*; and, with a perfect knowledge of Angelo's having committed them, she

"Craves no other nor no better man."

Claudio's life having been preserved by the Provost, it would not, perhaps have been lawful to have put Angelo to death; but the Duke might, with great propriety, have addressed him in the words of Bolingbroke to Exton,

"Go wander through the shade of night,
"And never show thy head by day or light."

---

[1] Kirk.

Other parts of the play are not without faults. The best characters act too much on a system of duplicity and falsehood; and the Duke, in the fifth act, trifles curly with the feelings of Isabella, allowing her to suppose her brother to be dead, much longer than the story of the play required. Lucio is inconsistent as well as profligate. He appears, in the first act, as the friend of Claudio, and in the fifth, he assists the cause of Angelo, whom he supposes to have been his murderer. Lastly, the indecent expressions with which many of the scenes abound, are so interwoven with the story, that it is extremely difficult to separate the one from the other.[2]

Feeling my own inability to render this play sufficiently correct for family-reading, I have thought it advisable to print it (without presuming to alter a single word) from the published copy, as performed at the Theatre Royal, Covent Garden.

The alterations, as I am informed, are the work of that gentleman, to whose theatrical talents and laudable exertions, untied to those of his unrivalled sister, our dramatic writers in general, and Shakespeare in particular, are more indebted than to any person since the death of Mr. Garrick.

If my Readers should think (and I confess myself to be of that opinion) that "Measure for Measure" is not yet an unobjectionable play, I would request them to peruse it attentively in its original form; and I am fully persuaded that there is no person, who will not then bestow praise on the ability with which Mr. Kemble has improved it, rather than express surprise at its not being entirely freed from those defects which are inseparably connected with the story.

---

[2] It is gratifying to me to perceive that Mrs. Inchbald, the respectable Editor of "The British Theatre," in her preface to this play, has expressed her sentiments respecting Angelo and the comic characters, in terms exactly corresponding with my own.

ON THE PERILS OF DRAWING INFERENCES

ABOUT SUPREME COURT JUSTICES FROM THEIR FIRST FEW YEARS OF SERVICE

Lee Epstein, Kevin Quinn, Andrew D. Martin & Jeffrey A. Segal[†]

Even before the start of their second year in office, commentators were already reading the tea leaves on Samuel A. Alito, Jr. and John G. Roberts, Jr. According to the prominent legal scholar Erwin Chemerinsky, the two new justices "were every bit as conservative as conservatives had hoped and progressives had feared. [Their] willingness to overrule decades-old precedents certainly gives a sense that major changes are likely ahead in constitutional law *in the years to come*."[1] Chemerinsky was hardly alone; similar forecasts appeared on the editorial pages of newspapers as ideological disparate as the *Wall Street Journal* and the *New York Times*, as well as hundreds, if not thousands, of blogs across the country.

Forecasting of this sort — a veritable cottage industry each time a new justice completes a term or two of service — may seem harmless enough and sufficiently divorced from the concerns of empirical legal studies to ignore. Nonetheless, the entire enterprise rests on a strong empirical assumption, which, in fact, has important implications for systematic schol-

---

[†] Lee Epstein is Beatrice Kuhn Professor, School of Law and Department of Political Science, Northwestern University. (lee-epstein@northwestern.edu) Kevin Quinn is an Associate Professor in the Department of Government at Harvard University. (kquinn@gov. harvard.edu) Andrew D. Martin is a Professor in the School of Law and Department of Political Science, Washington University in St. Louis. (admartin@wustl.edu) Jeffrey A. Segal is SUNY Distinguish Professor, Department of Political Science, Stony Brook University. (jeffrey.segal@stonybrook.edu) This article originally appeared at 91 JUDICATURE 168 (Jan.-Feb. 2008). Copyright © 2008 by American Judicature Society. Reprinted by permission of the authors and of *Judicature*, the journal of the American Judicature Society.
[1] Erwin Chemerinsky, *The Kennedy Court: October Term 2005*, 9 GREEN BAG 335, at 346 (2006). Our emphasis.

arship: that one can draw high-quality inferences about the justices' long-term ideological tendencies from their first few terms in office.

Is this a plausible assumption? Unfortunately, and despite decades of study, we cannot offer a conclusive answer. To some, most notably Hagle, reliance on initial voting records to predict future behavior borders on the absurd.[2] Most justices, he empirically demonstrated, manifest unstable behavior in their "freshman" year relative to the balance of their career. To other scholars, most recently Shipan, predictions based on the first term are not particularly troubling.[3] The instability identified by Hagle, they say, appears insufficiently widespread to be "considered a general phenomenon."[4] In between comes work by Wood et al., which found that roughly half the justices under analysis experienced "acclimation" effects.[5]

In what follows, we hope to bring a fresh eye to this seemingly age-old but nonetheless on-going debate.[6] Drawing on methodological strategies that we used to examine ideological drift on the Supreme Court,[7] we first contemplate the literature's primary concern: to what extent do new justices evince different or unstable behavior in their first year relative to all others? Or, to frame it in more contemporary terms, to what extent can we reach high-quality inferences about the justices' long-term ideological preferences based on one-year's — the first-year's — worth of observations?

Finding that Hagle and others in his camp have the better case — all but 4 of the 26 justices we investigated exhibited statistically significant ideological drift from their *initial* preferences — we turn to questions of substantive importance. Specifically, we demonstrate that movement away from first-year ideal points occasionally manifests itself in consequential doctrinal change — so consequential that a vote in favor of, say, restricting privacy rights or permitting prayer in school in the first term might translate into a vote in opposition before the justice concludes his or her first decade of service. These findings, compatible with our previous work documenting extensive ideological movement on the part of Court

---

[2] Timothy Hagle, *Freshman Effects for Supreme Court Justices*, 37 AM. J. POL. SCI. 1142 (1993).

[3] Charles R. Shipan, *Acclimation Effects Revisited*, 40 JURIMETRICS J. 243 (2000).

[4] *Id.*

[5] Sandra L.Wood, et al., *'Acclimation Effects' for Supreme Court Justices: A Cross-Validation, 1888-1940*, 42 AM. J. POL. SCI. 690 (1998).

[6] *See, e.g.*, Mark S. Hurwitz and Joseph V. Stefko, *Acclimation and Attitudes: 'Newcomer' Justices and Precedent Conformance on the Supreme Court*, 57 POL. RES. Q. 121 (2004).

[7] Lee Epstein, Andrew D. Martin, Kevin Quinn, and Jeffrey Segal, *Ideological Drift on the U.S. Supreme Court*, 101 NW. U. L. Rev. 1483 (2007).

members throughout their careers,[8] continue to demonstrate that the ideological boxes into which policy makers, scholars, and lawyers place justices at the time of their appointment are not so tightly sealed.

INFERRING FUTURE BEHAVIOR

Inferring future behavior from a justice's first few years in office hardly began with John Roberts and Samuel Alito; in fact, the legal historian George L. Haskins supplies compelling evidence that the practice dates nearly as far back as the Court itself.[9] Surely, though, the most (in)famous modern-day example came after Harry A. Blackmun's first year of service. The Minneapolis-born Blackmun was so closely aligned with his boyhood friend, the conservative Chief Justice Warren Burger, that commentators of the day tagged him a "Minnesota Twin."

While this turned out to be a stunning misnomer, it hardly put the brakes on future forecasting. Quite the opposite. Since Blackmun, virtually every justice has been the object of prediction. After examining Lewis F. Powell's first term in office, one columnist opined that the new justice is emerging "as the conservative's strong man," who will ultimately help "write some pretty good law."[10] Five years later, Justice Scalia was quickly branded Chief Justice Rehnquist's "ideological compatriot."[11] Of David Souter, the chair of the Democratic National Committee declared that he "is slowly demonstrating his loyalty to Republican extremism."[12] Analysts too tried to draw inferences about Justice Kennedy from his first-year record, even though Kennedy (much like Alito) had served for only six months. Bruce Fein, the conservative commentator, declared "there was a clear showing that Justice Kennedy will be in the conservative bloc."[13] The editors of the *New York Times* agreed, as did a host of other long-time Court observers.[14]

---

[8] *Id.*

[9] George Lee Haskins, FOUNDATIONS OF POWER: JOHN MARSHALL, 1805-15, VOL. II OF HISTORY OF THE SUPREME COURT OF THE UNITED STATES 152 (New York: Macmillan, 1982).

[10] James J. Kilpatrick, *High Court: Proof the System Works*, Los Angeles Times, July 23, 1972, at F6.

[11] Charles M. Haar and Jerald S. Kayden, *Private Property vs. Public Use*, New York Times, July 29, 1987, at 23A.

[12] Quoted in Steve Daley, *Friends, Foes Hunting Thomas' 'Paper Trail'*, Chicago Tribune, July 4, 1991, at 1.

[13] Quoted in Joseph Tybor and Glen Elsasser, *Judging Rehnquist's Court*, Chicago Tribune, July 3, 1988, at 1.

[14] *See, e.g.*, Stuart Taylor, *High Court Rulings Hint Move to Right*, New York Times, July 3,

Nonetheless, it is hard to deny that tasseography may have reached new heights with Roberts' and Alito's ascensions to the high Court. What with bloggers now joining journalists and scholars, forecasting future ideological tendencies based on a year or less of service has become something of a cottage industry. And a fast-moving cottage industry at that. Attracting substantial attention just a year after Alito and Roberts took their seats was Greenburg's *Supreme Conflict*, famous for its punchline that the two Bush appointees have succeeded in moving the Court to the right.[15]

But what inferences can we really draw? Linda Greenhouse, the astute *New York Times* reporter, suggests we should refrain from the practice altogether. "A Justice's first year on the Court, or even first few years," she once observed, "are notoriously poor indicators of that Justice's eventual role."[16] No doubt, a non-trivial fraction of justices would agree. As William J. Brennan, Jr. once said,

> There is nothing that you do that prepares you for this job. Even Felix Frankfurter used to say that his lifelong study of the Court never really prepared him for this job. You simply cannot study it from afar and expect to know it. You simply cannot know how you will respond to the legal issues as a Justice, as opposed to a law professor, or a judge on a court of appeals or even a state supreme court. *I know that was certainly true of me.*[17]

Social scientists are less certain but hardly for lack of effort. In a line of inquiry dating back to the 1950s,[18] though picking up considerable steam in the 1970s into the 2000s, nearly countless analysts sought to determine whether new justices evince different or unstable behavior during their first year or so — a period of acclimation on the Court — than in the years to follow.[19] Their findings, as we noted at the outset, have been

---

1988, at 1; Lyle Denniston, *This Term, Supreme Court Had New Look*, St. Petersburg Times, July 3, 1988, at 1A.

[15] Jan Crawford Greenburg, SUPREME CONFLICT: THE INSIDE STORY OF THE STRUGGLE FOR CONTROL OF THE UNITED STATES SUPREME COURT (New York: Penguin Press, 2007).

[16] Linda Greenhouse, *The Conservative Majority Solidifies*, New York Times, June 30, 1991, at 1, Sec. 4.

[17] Quoted in Jeffrey T. Leeds, *A Life on the Court*, New York Times, October 5, 1986 (Sunday magazine). Our emphasis.

[18] Elois Snyder, *The Supreme Court as a Small Group*, 36 SOC. FORCES 232 (1958). *See also* J. Woodford Howard, *Justice Murphy: The Freshman Years*, 18 VAND. L. REV. 473 (1968); John D. Sprague, VOTING PATTERNS OF THE UNITED STATES SUPREME COURT: CASES IN FEDERALISM, 1889-1959 (New York: Bobbs-Merrill, 1968).

[19] *See, e.g.*, Terry Bowen, *Consensual Norms and the Freshman Effect on the United States Supreme Court*, 76 SOC. SCI. Q. 222 (1995); John M. Scheb and Lee W. Ailshie, *Justice Sandra*

mixed to say the least. Even if we confine ourselves exclusively to studies of voting,[20] empirical results run the gamut from nearly complete agreement with the Greenhouse/Brennan sentiment to nearly complete disagreement.[21]

Why the mixed findings is a question with many possible answers.[22] Far more relevant here is a commonalty, not a point of distinction, among the existing work: Regardless of their conclusions, recent disciplinary developments have rendered features of the extant studies problematic at best and obsolete at worst. Of particular concern are the measurement strategies they deploy; we are also troubled by their approach to research design.

Let us elaborate, beginning with design — specifically with the issue of how to determine whether new justices are unstable in their voting. While approaches vary from study to study, a prominent one is to compare, say, the percentage of conservative votes cast in the justice's first term, with the mean percentage of conservative votes cast thereafter.[23] If a difference emerges, then analysts claim they have found evidence of a freshman effect — meaning, to use our terminology, that it would be a mistake to draw inferences about the long term based on observations from the first year.

Because this design has its share of intuitive appeal, we understand why scholars have invoked it. Nonetheless, as Shipan correctly observed, it can inadvertently lead to rather severe errors of inference. To see the why, consider Figure 1, in which we present the voting patterns in the area of constitutional criminal procedure for two hypothetical justices, L(eft Panel) and R(ight Panel). Notice that the left panel appears to present few problems for the conventional approach: Because Justice L cast

---

Day O'Connor and the Freshman Effect, 69 JUDICATURE 9 (1985); Thea F. Rubin and Albert P. Melone, *Justice Antonin Scalia: A First Year Freshman Effect?*, 72 JUDICATURE 98 (1988); Albert P. Melone, *Revisiting the Freshman Effect Hypothesis: The First Two Terms of Anthony Kennedy*, 74 JUDICATURE 6 (1990); Wood et al., *supra* n. 5; Hurwitz and Stefko, *supra* n. 6; Shipan, *supra* n. 3; Hagle, *supra* n. 2.

[20] To determine if new justices exhibit acclimation or newcomer effects, scholars have looked at a wide range of behavior (e.g., opinion writing, bloc formation, and adherence to stare decisis). While interesting, our emphasis here is on voting behavior, as it is in most contemporary studies.

[21] For literature reviews, see, e.g., Hagle, *supra* n. 2; Shipan, *supra* n. 3; Hurwitz and Stefko, *supra* n. 6; Christopher F. Smith and S. Thomas Read, *The Performance and Effectiveness of New Appointees to the Rehnquist Court*, 20 OHIO N. U. L. REV. 205 (1993).

[22] See, e.g., Hagle, *supra* n. 2; Shipan, *supra* n. 3.

[23] See, e.g., Hagle, *supra* n. 2; Wood, *supra* n. 5.

only 10 percent of her votes in favor of defendants in her first term and 60 percent in all others (*p* .05), scholars would likely conclude that L's first-term behavior reveals little about the balance of her career.[24]

FIGURE 1: HYPOTHETICAL VOTING PATTERNS OF TWO JUSTICES IN CONSTITUTIONAL CRIMINAL PROCEDURE CASES

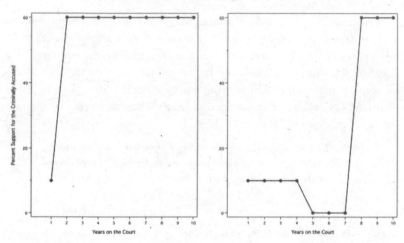

Justice L, depicted in the left panel, cast 10 percent of her votes in favor of defendants in her first year and 60 percent in all others. In his first term, Justice R, in the right panel, also cast 10 peercent of his votes in support of defendants. The mean for the rest of his career is 20 percent.

But what of the right panel? Would we be able to make high-quality inferences about Justice R's career based on his freshman preferences? Under conventional methods, the answer is yes: Because no significant difference emerges between R's voting in Term 1 (10 percent) versus the mean of all others (20 percent), first-year behavior provides a plausible predictor of future behavior. The obvious problem with this, the conventional response, is that it fails to attend Justice R's dramatic move to the left even before the end of his first decade of service. Only by developing a design plan capable of capturing the fact that for both R and L evidence of unstable behavior emerges — in fact, evidence sufficiently ample to suggest that inferences based on the first year would provide misinformation about overall career patterns — can we hurdle this obstacle.

---

[24] Actually, given that the percentages displayed in Figure 1 fail to control for changes in case content (i.e., changes in issue or case stimuli), this conclusion may not hold. We return to this point shortly.

Momentarily, we propose such a plan. For now, though, it is worth considering a second, even more fundamental concern with the existing literature — one that Figure 1 also brings to light. Note that in creating the panels· we follow the conventional strategy, and depict votes as raw, term-by-term percentages (here, percent support for defendants). That approach, however, fails to attend to changes in the content of litigation ("case stimuli") over time.[25]

Conceptually, the problem is straightforward enough. Absent controls for case stimuli we might incorrectly assume that a justice evinces ideo-logical change after her first term when it well may be the content of the litigation that changed.[26] As a result, we cannot attribute the alteration's source, whether to instability during a justice's early years or to the cases themselves. Greenhouse recognized as much when she wrote of the new justice David Souter,

> While [he] appeared firmly in the conservative camp this term, that impression is due in part to the unusually high proportion of the term's cases that dealt with criminal law and procedure, the area in which he voted most consistently with Chief Justice Rehnquist."[27]

Greenhouse's commentary well captures the flavor of the problem but, because case stimuli can vary in discrete areas of law, it is likely more severe than even she cast it. To provide but one example, consider a jus-tice — call her Justice M(oderate) — who has served on the Court for two terms. Suppose that in her first term, Justice M was quite unsuppor-tive of defendants in Fourth Amendment cases casting only one out of every ten votes in their favor. In the next term, however, Justice M voted to support defendants in nine of ten cases.

If we looked only at these votes, we might conclude that Justice M in-deed exhibited unstable, freshman-like, behavior — moving from 10 per-cent support of defendants in her first term to 90 percent support in her second. But Figure 2 raises another possibility. Here, the horizontal lines represent a single issue, Fourth Amendment search and seizure cases, for two terms (1 and 2). For each term, we have arrayed the ruling of the relevant lower court (labeled O), the alternative policies that could be

---

[25] We are not the first to recognize this problem. For a review of previous efforts to deal with it, along with their inadequacies, see Shipan, *supra* n. 3.

[26] *See, e.g.*, Harold Spaeth, *The Attitudinal Model*, in Lee Epstein (ed.) CONTEMPLATING COURTS (Washington, D.C.: CQ Press, 1995); Lawrence Baum, *Measuring Policy Change on the United States Supreme Court*, 82 AM. POL. SCI. REV. 905 (1988).

[27] Greenhouse, *supra* n. 16.

formulated by a group of justices (labeled A), and the ideal points of hypothetical Justice M, along with Justices L(iberal) and C(onservative).

FIGURE 2: HYPOTHETICAL FOURTH AMENDMENT SEARCH AND SEIZURE CASES AND JUSTICES IN IDEOLOGICAL SPACE AT TWO TIME PERIODS (TERM 1 AND TERM 2)

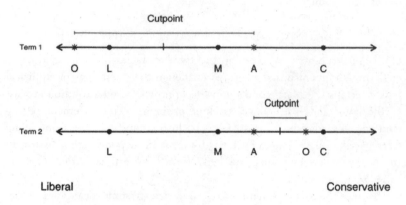

L, M. and C are the ideal points of the three justices — a liberal, a moderate, and a conservative. O represents the status quo policy from a lower court ruling. A is the alternative policy (that could be) formulated by a group of justices. The cutpoint is the location halfway between O and A such that the justices to the left would choose the more liberal outcome, and those on the right the more conservative option.

Suppose that in Term 1 the justices review a lower court decision excluding evidence from a house search on the ground that the judge lacked probable cause to issue the warrant (indicated in Figure 2 by the fairly leftward-located value of O). Further assume, as is standard in the social science literature, that each justice will cast a vote for the more ideologically proximate outcome. If this is so, then — given the choice between the status quo policy O and an alternative policy A, which would, say, allow the introduction of the evidence on a good faith exception — Justice L will vote to uphold the lower court ruling O. Justices M and C, in contrast, will vote for the good faith exception A. Indeed, any justice to the left of the cutpoint — the middle location between the status quo O and alternative A — will vote to uphold, and any justice to the right will vote to overturn.

Now suppose that in Term 2 the lower court rules that a warrantless search is valid, thereby producing the more rightward-located value of O in Term 2. If, once again, the justices make a choice between the lower court ruling O and an alternative A, Justice C will again vote for the more conservative alternative and Justice L for the more liberal one, A. Note, though, that Justice M will now also support the liberal policy, even though her underlying preferences remained stable between the two terms. This implies that just comparing percentages of votes can be profoundly misleading.

A BAYESIAN DYNAMIC IDEAL POINT APPROACH

Until quite recently, overcoming the twin obstacles of design and especially measurement posed a serious challenge to generations of empirical legal specialists.[28] Martin and Quinn have now devised a solution at least to the latter and, we believe, trickier problem of measurement. Using data derived from the votes cast by the justices and a Bayesian modeling strategy, they have generated term-by-term ideal point estimates for all the justices appointed since the 1937 term[29] — estimates that *attend to variation in case content.*[30]

Because the Martin-Quinn (M-Q) Bayesian dynamic ideal point model has been described[31] and applied elsewhere,[32] only a few words are in order here. First, not only does their model allow for ideal points to change over time but the estimates are also directly comparable over time. That is, owing to M-Q's approach, we can compare, e.g., Justice Souter's revealed preferences in his first term with his second, third, fourth, and so on. Second, as we suggest above, the M-Q method typically will not conflate changes in case content and in ideal points: their model estimates

---

[28] Some scholars, most notably Segal, have developed area-specific solutions; in Segal's case, Fourth Amendment search and seizure litigation. *See* Jeffrey Segal, *Measuring Change on the Supreme Court: Examining Alternative Models*, 29 AM. J. POL. SCI. 461 (1985). But we know of no work that satisfactorily tackles the problem across the range of legal areas.

[29] The Martin-Quinn scores, though theoretically unbounded, range from about -6 (Douglas) on the left to about +4 (Thomas) on the right. Across all justices in all terms, the standard deviation of the scores is approximately 2.

[30] Andrew D. Martin and Kevin Quinn, *Dynamic Ideal Point Estimation via Markov Chain Monte Carlo for the U.S. Supreme Court, 1953-1999*, 10 POL. ANALYSIS 134 (2002).

[31] *See, e.g.*, Martin and Quinn, *id.*; Andrew D. Martin, Kevin Quinn, and Lee Epstein, *The Median Justice on the U.S. Supreme Court*, N. CAR. L. REV. 1275 (2005); Epstein et al., *supra* n. 7.

[32] *See, e.g.*, Theodore W. Ruger, *Justice Harry Blackmun and the Phenomenon of Judicial Preference Change*, 70 MO. L. REV. 1209 (2005); Barry Friedman and Anna L. Harvey, *Electing the Supreme Court*, 78 IND. L.J. 123 (2005); Paul Wahlbeck, *The Chief Justice and the Institutional Judiciary: Strategy and Constraints on Supreme Court Opinion Assignment*, 154 U. PA. L. REV. 1729 (2006).

them separately. In other words, using M-Q's approach we can squarely confront the question we pose here — to what extent can we make high-quality inferences about justices based on their first-year record — without having to consider whether any changes we observe are the result of fluctuations in the case content or in the justice's revealed preferences.

Martin and Quinn have dealt with the problem of measurement, but what of design? Certainly, for the reasons we suggest above, we must avoid the extant literature's trap of relying exclusively on a comparison of a justice's revealed preferences (here, measured by the M-Q estimates) in Term 1 with the mean of all others. We rather require an approach that is capable of juxtaposing a justice's initial preferences against the preferences she expresses in each term remaining in her career. Only in this way can we assess the quality of inferences we can draw about a justice's future preferences based on the first years of service.

Our solution to this design quandary follows from our work on ideological drift.[33] For each of the 26 justices appointed since 1937 and who served 10 or more terms, we calculate the (posterior) probability that the justice's revealed preferences (i.e., the M-Q ideal point estimates) were more conservative[34] in each subsequent term than her first term.[35] A finding that a justice exhibits statistically significant differences between her freshman year and more than half of her remaining years ought, we believe, raise serious concerns about the ability to forecast future preferences from the initial term of service.[36]

Applying these calculations to each justice readily enables us to accomplish our primary goal of determining the extent to which she or he, in any given term, exhibited significantly different preferences than in the first year. To supply a straightforward example, consider Figure 3. There

---

[33] Epstein, et al., *supra* n. 7.

[34] Because the ideal points are continuous, the probability that any two ideal points will be exactly equal is 0. Thus, 1 minus the probability that a justice's revealed preferences are more conservative at some later time is exactly equal to the probability that the justice's later preferences are more liberal. Put another way, knowing the probability of a move to the right allows one to easily calculate the probability of a move to the left.

[35] In other words, we use the first term as our primary baseline. For more on question of the appropriate baseline, see Hagle, *supra* n. 2.

[36] As we describe in previous work, generating these posterior probabilities presents no major difficulties. It is simply a matter of calculating the fraction of samples generated by the M-Q procedures for which the justice's ideal point in later terms was to the right of the baseline value, the first term. *See* Epstein, et al., *supra* n. 7; Andrew D. Martin and Kevin Quinn, *Assessing Preference Change on the U.S. Supreme Court*, 23 J. L. ECON. & ORG. 365 (2007).

we visually depict the results of our calculations for Harry Blackmun, specifically, the estimated probability that he was more conservative (or liberal) in each subsequent term than in his first. Note that if the probability is greater than 0.975 (i.e., Blackmun's ideal point estimate is above the top dotted horizontal line), then we can conclude that he was significantly more conservative in that term than in his first year. Alternatively, if the estimated probability is less than 0.025 (i.e., Blackmun's ideal point estimate is below the bottom dotted line), then we can conclude that he was significantly more liberal in that term than in his first. For purposes of making statistical and substantive inferences, we have added a vertical line representing Blackmun's tenth year of service.

FIGURE 3: THE PROBABILITY THAT JUSTICE BLACKMUN WAS MORE CONSERVATIVE IN SUBSEQUENT TERMS THAN IN HIS FIRST TERM

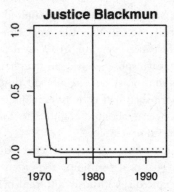

The vertical axis denotes the estimated probability. If the solid line is above the top dotted line, then Blackmun was significantly more conservative. If that line is below the bottom dotted line, then Blackmun was significantly more liberal. The vertical line represents Blackmun's tenth year of service.

The takeaway from Figure 3 is inescapable: Blackmun moved so far from his first-year ideal point that, despite their best efforts, even the most astute observers of the day could not possibly have drawn accurate inferences about his subsequent behavior based on his first year. Actually, because in no term after his third was he as conservative as he was in his first, even conventional approaches to assessing unstable voting would have picked up the effect; that is, a statistically significant difference emerges between Blackmun's M-Q ideal point estimate in his first term (1.86) and the mean M-Q estimate for the rest of his career (-.19).

STATISTICAL DANGERS OF DRAWING INFERENCES

Given the spate of commentary on Blackmun's judicial "journey,"[37] Figure 3 is likely to come to the surprise of no one. But what of the other justices? Is Blackmun the anomaly — the rare justice for whom inferences based on first-year behavior would have been seriously flawed — or the rule? From a statistical vantage point, the answer is clear. By their tenth year of service, 22 of the 26 justices moved, significantly so, away from their first-term ideal point estimate in the majority of their subsequent terms on the Court. Blackmun, in short, is clearly unexceptional.

Let us begin, though, with the exceptions, the four justices — Potter Stewart, Anthony Kennedy, Warren Burger, and especially Frank Murphy — whose observed behavior might encourage the forecasters. While it is true, as we can see in Figure 4, that Stewart and Kennedy eventually grew significantly more liberal, our approach shows that inferences about their ideology based on their freshman term would not have been too far off the mark — at least not for their first decade in office.

FIGURE 4: FOUR JUSTICES, APPOINTED SINCE 1937, WHO WERE NO MORE LIBERAL OR CONSERVATIVE IN MORE THAN HALF THEIR SUBSEQUENT TERMS THAN IN THEIR FIRST TERM

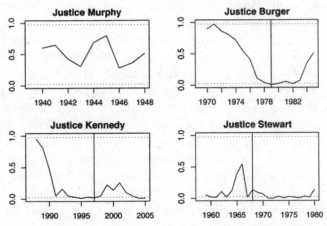

The vertical axis denotes the estimated probability of being more conservative in a future term. If the solid line in each panel is above the top dotted line, then the justice is significantly more conservative. If that line is below the bottom dotted line, then the justice is significantly more liberal. The vertical line within each panel represents the tenth term of service.

---

[37] See, e.g., Ruger, supra n. 32; Linda Greenhouse, BECOMING JUSTICE BLACKMUN: HARRY BLACKMUN'S SUPREME COURT JOURNEY (New York: Holt, 2005).

The same holds for both Burger and Murphy but their preferences were even more stable.[38] Only in the Chief's ninth and tenth terms — falling near the end of the Carter presidency — was he significantly more liberal than in his freshman year. By the time Ronald Reagan took office, Burger had drifted back to the right, revealing preferences that were statistically indistinguishable from his earlier years. As for Murphy, he represents the true anomaly in our database: the only justice who exhibits no significant preference change between his first year and any of his remaining terms.

In direct juxtaposition come the 22 justices, who — *compared to their first term* — moved to the left, to the right, or in both directions in more than half their subsequent terms. Beginning with the largest subset (see Figure 5), 11 justices, or roughly half those in our database, were significantly more liberal before or at their tenth term than in their first. For the majority, movement came almost immediately. By their second terms, David Souter and Earl Warren, for example, had turned sharply to the left, never to move back. Inferring much about Tom Clark's and, of course, Harry Blackmun's eventual preferences based on their first term too would be deeply problematic in light of the patterns revealed in Figure 5. On the other hand, Justice O'Connor's preferences remained relatively stable until her first decade of service approached, at which point she grew significantly more liberal.

Composing a somewhat smaller, though nonetheless notable group are the nine justices who exhibited movement in the opposite direction. As we depict in Figure 6, Black, Burton, Frankfurter, Harlan, Jackson, Reed, Scalia, Thomas, and White were significantly more conservative by their tenth term than in their first. But the trends, once again, differ. For the majority, rightward movement was not long in coming. Frankfurter, for example, was on the Court but two short terms before his revealed preferences grew quite distinct from those in his freshman year. For others, especially White, change came later — closer to the decade mark — but it nonetheless came. Either way, significant movement renders perilous efforts to characterize even their early career stages based on their first years.

---

[38] Murphy and Burger are the only two justices, who, even under the conventional test, show no signs of voting instability. That is, a comparison of their first-year ideal point estimate and the mean of their remaining terms reveals no statistically significant difference. We cannot say the same for any other justice in our database, including Stewart and Kennedy.

FIGURE 5: ELEVEN JUSTICES, APPOINTED SINCE 1937, WHO WERE MORE
LIBERAL IN SUBSEQUENT TERMS THAN IN THEIR FIRST TERM

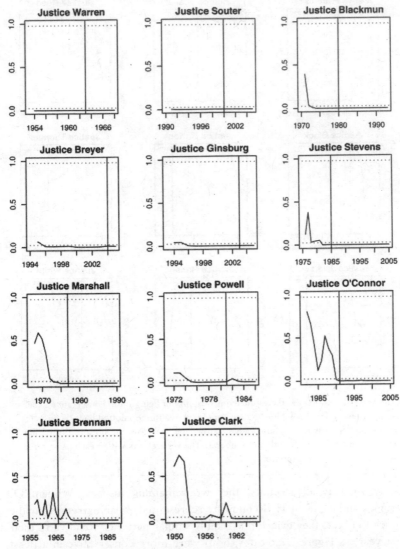

The vertical axis denotes the estimated probability of being more conservative in subsequent terms. If the solid line in each panel is above the top dotted line, then the justice is significantly more conservative. If that line is below the bottom dotted line, then the justice is significantly more liberal. The vertical line within each panel represents the tenth term of service.

FIGURE 6: NINE JUSTICES, APPOINTED SINCE 1937, WHO WERE MORE
CONSERVATIVE IN SUBSEQUENT TERMS THAN IN THEIR FIRST TERM

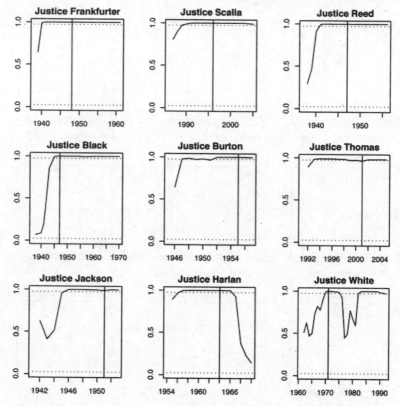

The vertical axis denotes the estimated probability of being more conservative in subsequent terms. If the solid line in each panel is above the top dotted line, then the justice is significantly more conservative. If that line is below the bottom dotted line,
then the justice is significantly more liberal. The vertical line within each panel represents the tenth term of service.

By virtually all accounts, the two remaining justices, William O.
Douglas and William H. Rehnquist, represented polar extremes on the
Court and, yet, they evince remarkably similar patterns. Relative to their
first year, as Figure 7 indicates, both were more conservative in at least
some of the years prior to their tenth. And, by their eighteenth, both were
significantly more liberal relative to their freshman year. In other words,
for only a few terms apiece were their revealed preferences indistinct
from their first-year behavior.

FIGURE 7: TWO JUSTICES, APPOINTED SINCE 1937, WHO WERE BOTH
MORE CONSERVATIVE AND MORE LIBERAL IN SUBSEQUENT TERMS THAN
IN THEIR FIRST TERM

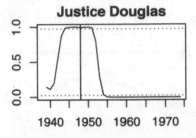
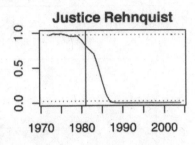

The vertical axis denotes the estimated probability of being more conservative in subsequent terms. If the solid line in each panel is above the top dotted line, then the justice is significantly more conservative. If that line is below the bottom dotted line,
then the justice is significantly more liberal. The vertical line within each panel represents the tenth term of service.

SUBSTANTIVE DANGERS OF DRAWING INFERENCES

From a statistical vantage point, it would be difficult to observe the patterns in Figures 4 through 7 and reach any conclusion other than the one
we have stressed throughout: Regardless of whether we analyze preferences on term-by-term basis, as we have done in the figures, or via the
more conventional approach,[39] most justices reveal behavior in subsequent years that differs significantly from their first.

But are the statistical findings compelling enough to dissuade commentators from reaching inferences about Alito, Roberts, and any future justices? Likewise, are they sufficiently persuasive to dispel any doubts about
unstable behavior among the justices?

Because statistical significance may not translate into substantive importance, we suspect the answer in both instances is no. Scalia provides a
case in point. To be sure, as Figure 6 indicates, he was significantly less
conservative in his first term than in the balance of his career. But we cannot say that commentators of the day were in error to tag the justice a
"conservative," and Figure 8 shows why. There we display Scalia's term-
by-term (Martin & Quinn) ideal point estimates. (For purposes of comparison, we also plot the estimates for O'Connor, a more moderate justice, and for Stevens, a more liberal justice.) To be sure, Scalia drifts to

---

[39] See id.

the right, but only in his first two most "liberal" terms does he even approximate O'Connor (at her most conservative); and his liberalism comes nowhere near Stevens', even in Stevens' early, most right-leaning days.

FIGURE 8: JUSTICES SCALIA'S, O'CONNOR'S, AND STEVENS' ESTIMATED IDEAL POINTS

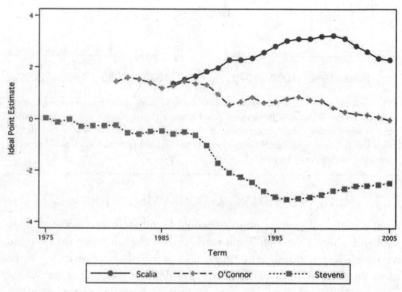

The vertical axis is the justice's estimated ideal point. Higher values are more conservative.

Antonin Scalia, in short, revealed conservative preferences at the outset of his career, and simply grew more reliably conservative with time. Even more to the point, Scalia's rightward departure was likely of little substantive (doctrinal) consequence, as Figure 9 depicts. Here we again plot Scalia's term-by-term ideal point estimates, along with the cut point lines for three cases implicating different areas of the law: *Dickerson v. United States* (holding that *Miranda v. Arizona* was a constitutional decision that Congress could not overrule by simple legislation); *Adarand Constructors v. Pena* (ruling that all racial classifications must be subjected to strict scrutiny); and *Lawrence v. Texas* (striking down sodomy laws). The cut points provide information about the likely behavior of justices above and below it, such that if a justice's ideal point is above the line, the

FIGURE 9: TIME SERIES PLOT OF JUSTICE SCALIA'S ESTIMATED IDEAL POINTS, 1986-2005 TERMS

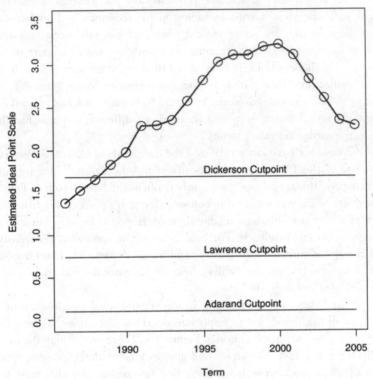

The vertical axis is the estimated ideal point scale, such that higher values are more conservative. The horizaontal lines are the cut points for *Dickerson v. United States*, *Adarand Constructors v. Pena*, and *Lawrence v. Texas* such that points above the line indicate a probability of greater than .50 of voting conservatively; those below the line indicate a greater than .50 probability of voting in the liberal direction (as the Court did in *Dickerson* and *Lawrence* but not in *Adarand*).

probability is greater than .50 that she or he will cast a conservative vote (i.e., against *Dickerson* and *Lawrence*, and in favor of *Adarand*).[40]

---

[40] We derive these cut points using the Quinn-Martin method. Under their approach, the data and modeling assumptions determine the joint distribution of the ideal points and the cut points. While this joint distribution is large and complex, it is possible to use the conditional distributions of the ideal points-given the cut points-and the cut points-given the ideal points-to fit the model. For more details, see Quinn and Martin, *supra* n. 36; Epstein,

In the case of *Adarand*, we know that five justices ruled against the government's set-aside program; we also know that Scalia was among this group. His estimated ideal point in 1995 was above the line and, in fact, he was in the majority in *Adarand*. But also note the location of his ideal points in all previous terms, including in his freshman and sophomore years. Because they are above the cut point, we can safely conclude that even at his most moderate moment — coinciding with the start of his tenure — Scalia would likely have voted to apply strict scrutiny to all racial classifications formulated by the government. More generally, in looking at all three cases depicted in Figure 9, in only *Dickerson* — and for only three terms at that — would we predict a different response had the case come earlier in Scalia's tenure.

Of course we have not scrutinized the cut points of all 1,937 cases resolved since the 1986 term when Scalia joined the Court.[41] But we suspect that additional analyses would only confirm the basic lesson of Figure 8. Because Scalia was sufficiently conservative in his preferences from the start of his service, his turn to the right corresponds to only a marginal change in his jurisprudence. For Scalia, to put it somewhat differently, analyses of statistical and substantive significance depart. The latter implies that any inferences based on Scalia's first term are not necessarily as defective as the former suggests.[42]

For the balance of our justices, however, statistical significant movement, in all likelihood, led to important doctrinal alterations. To provide a few extreme examples, consider Figure 10. There we display the ideal points for Souter and Warren — two justices who made 180-degree turns from the preferences revealed in their first few terms. We also show the cut point lines for three decisions, all in the areas of rights and liberties: for Souter, *Rust v. Sullivan* (upholding regulations that prohibit the use of public funds for abortion counseling) and *Lee v. Weisman* (prohibiting a clergy-led prayer during a public high school graduation); for Warren, the landmark *Miranda v. Arizona*.

---

et al., *supra* n. 7.

[41] We derive the figure of 1,937 from the July 2007 release of Harold J. Spaeth's U.S. Supreme Court Judicial Database, with analu=0 and dec type=1, 6, or 7.

[42] We could probably say the same of other extremists who grew only more extreme over time (e.g., Brennan and Marshall). For these justices, as for Scalia, their ideological transformations, from liberals (conservatives) in their first year to more extreme liberals (conservatives) in later terms, likely failed to translate into consequential doctrinal change.

FIGURE 10: TIME SERIES PLOTS OF CHIEF JUSTICE WARREN'S (LEFT PANEL)
AND JUSTICE SOUTER'S (RIGHT PANEL) ESTIMATED IDEAL POINTS

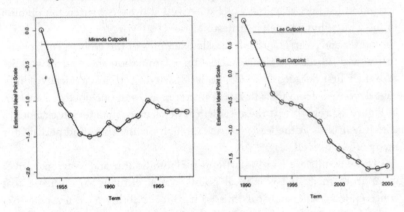

The horizontal lines are the cut points for *Rust v. Sullivan*, *Lee v. Weisman*, and *Miranda v. Arizona* such that points above the line indicate a probability of greater than .50 of voting for the government (as the Court did in *Rust*); those below the line indicate a greater than .50 probability of voting for the defendant/plaintiff (as the Court did in *Lee* and *Miranda*).

Turning first to Souter's panel, note that when the Court decided to uphold the regulations at issue in *Rust*, Souter was in the majority. Given that his revealed preferences for the 1990 term — his first on the Court — were north of the *Rust* cutpoint line, his vote was not a surprise. Nor, for that matter, was his concurrence in *Lee* supporting the Court's (5-4) decision to prohibit clergy-led prayers at public school graduations. His ideal point in the 1991 term was slightly below the *Lee* cutpoint line.

Far more relevant, and troubling for inference, however, is that Souter's dramatic doctrinal move to the left would have led to mispredictions in the case of *Rust* within three terms of the justice's first year and in the case of *Lee*, just one term thereafter. Indeed, if the Court had heard *Lee* during Souter's freshman — instead of sophomore — year, in all likelihood he would have voted to uphold the prayer. That vote, in turn, may have been enough to convert a five-person majority to strike the prayer into a five-person majority to uphold it (a step many commentators of the day had expected the Court to take). With little doubt forecasts of Souter's "loyalty to Republican extremism" based on his initial period of service were doomed to statistical and jurisprudential failure.[43]

---

[43] Quoted in *Daley*, supra n. 12.

The same likely holds about inferences of Earl Warren's preferences in the area of criminal law — or, at minimum, in the landmark opinion, his opinion, in *Miranda*. As the right panel of Figure 10 shows, had *Miranda* arrived in his first year, the Chief may well still have written the opinion of the Court, but not one in Ernesto Miranda's favor.

Souter and Warren provide classic examples of the convergence of statistical and substantive significance. Our examination shows that well before their first decade of service, both departed — to a statistically significant degree — from their first year preferences; and our doctrinal analysis in Figure 10 reveals that those statistical departures manifest in changes of consequence — at the least, for several high-profile cases and perhaps for many others as well.

These results are hardly startling: for both Souter and Warren, movement from their first-year ideal points was eventually so dramatic that contemporary scholars hardly missed it. But instability need not be as extreme for substantive change to result. In a paper on the Court's median justice, Martin, Quinn, and Epstein demonstrate as much about Sandra Day O'Connor's gradual drift to the left (also documented in Figure 5).[44] They show that had Justice O'Connor's freshman preferences remained stable, odds are that she would not have provided the fifth vote to uphold Michigan Law School's affirmative action program in the 2003 case, *Grutter v. Bollinger*.

An even more surprising example may be Chief Justice Rehnquist, whose ideal points we depict in Figure 11. Displayed as well are the cut points for *Lawrence*, *Adarand*, and *Dickerson*, along with *Wiggins v. Smith* (holding that the defendant's attorney had failed to provide effective counsel during the sentencing phase of his capital case). Observe that in neither *Adarand* nor *Lawrence* did Rehnquist's leftward trend translate into doctrinal change: Odds are that at no point in his career would he have voted to invalidate the sodomy law at issue in *Lawrence* or uphold the affirmative action program in *Adarand*. And, in fact, he dissented in both. The criminal cases present a different picture. Had either appeared in Rehnquist's first term, we predict that the then-associate justice would have ruled for the government. It was only in the latter part of his career, when he moved sufficiently to the center, that the odds shifted in favor of the defendant. And, in fact, in both *Dickerson* and *Wiggins* Rehnquist cast votes against the government.

---

[44] Martin, Quinn, and Epstein, *supra* n. 31.

FIGURE 11: TIME SERIES PLOT OF CHIEF JUSTICE REHNQUIST'S ESTIMATED
IDEAL POINTS, 1971-2004 TERMS

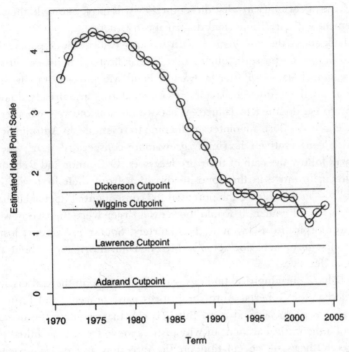

The horizontal lines are the cut points for *Adarand Constructors v. Pena*, *Lawrence v. Texas*,
Dickerson v. United States, and *Wiggins v. Smith* such that points above the line indicate a
probability of greater than .50 of voting conservatively; those below the line indicate a
greater than .50 probability of voting in the liberal direction (as the Court did in all
but *Adarand*).

CONCLUDING THOUGHTS

In the conclusion of his important 1993 study, Hagle reported evidence of
"significant voting instability" among the justices he examined.[45] While his
results have not lacked for challengers, our study provides strong cor-
roborating evidence. Exploiting statistical tools unavailable to Hagle in
1993 or even his adversaries, we find that virtually all Supreme Court
justices exhibit significant drift from their first-term preferences; and that
drift occasionally manifests in doctrinal change of consequence.

These are the primary lessons of our study, and ones, we hope, that

---

[45] Hagle, *supra* n. 2.

work to resolve a long standing debate in the field. But important challenges remain. While we can say with a high degree of certainty that most justices will move from their first-term preferences, we can specify with no degree of certainty in what direction they will move, nor whether their movement will carry important doctrinal consequences.

Think about the two justices with whom we started our paper, Alito and Roberts. To be sure, our results here indicate that unless either is highly anomalous — a Potter Stewart or Frank Murphy — drawing inferences about their future behavior, as commentators are already doing, is an enterprise doomed to failure. What we do not know is whether the two George W. Bush appointees will come to resemble an Antonin Scalia, that is, a conservative who simply grew more conservative. Or, whether they will follow the path of their predecessors, O'Connor and Rehnquist, and gradually move in the opposite direction from their first-year ideal points[46] — in which case the potential for consequential doctrinal change looms large. Of course, it would loom even larger were the two new justices to morph into Blackmuns, Frankfurters, Souters, Warrens, justices whose first-term behavior actually provided misinformation about their future preferences.

In light of our empirical findings, gaining leverage on these alternatives — whether for Roberts, Alito, or justices past, present, and future — strikes us as a crucial next step. But it is one that requires the development of a theoretical account of why justices move from their initial preferences. Otherwise, speculation on the direction and consequences of instability is just as perilous as inferences that assume a lack of instability.

If we have provided scholars with some incentive to take on the task of developing such an account, as we hope we have, they need not pursue it blindly. Conceptually, several contemporary writers have provided some tantalizing leads. Michael Dorf, for example, argues that justices who come to the Court with executive branch experience are unlikely to move from their initial preferences;[47] and, perhaps not unrelatedly, Lawrence Baum suggests that Republican appointees from outside the beltway are more likely to shift to the left than Republican appointees who are D.C. residents.[48] Another possibility is that justices ascending to the Court from

---

[46] According to Martin and Quinn's estimates (available at: http://mqscores.wustl.edu/) both Alito and Roberts are to the right of the Court's median, Justice Kennedy.

[47] Michael Dorf, *Does Federal Executive Branch Experience Explain Why Some Republican Supreme Court Justices 'Evolve' and Others Don't*, HARV. L. & POL'Y REV., forthcoming (2007).

[48] Lawrence Baum, JUDGES AND THEIR AUDIENCES: A PERSPECTIVE ON JUDICIAL BEHAVIOR (Princeton, NJ: Princeton University Press, 2006).

the federal circuits should exhibit relatively weak newcomer effects. If Baum is right, this effect may be even less still for those coming from the D.C. court of appeals.

Turning to methods, analysts could deploy the data developed here to construct an indicator of the "on average" deviation (from a first-year baseline), thereby adding a "how much" dimension to the "either/or" that we explore in this paper. With this measure in hand, assessing explanations of the influences of variability from freshman behavior should pose few problems.

Whether scholars pursue these leads or develop their own approaches is, of course, less the point than the need to undertake the mission in the first place. Given the empirical findings here, the time seems especially ripe to move beyond description and towards the crucial, yet still unrealized, goal of devising an explanation of instability and its impact on doctrinal development.

We thank the Center for Empirical Research in the Law, the National Science Foundation, and the Northwestern University School of Law Beatrice Kuhn Research Fund for supporting our research. Quinn also wishes to acknowledge the Center for Advanced Study in the Behavioral Sciences for its hospitality and support. The project's web site [epstein.law.northwestern.edu/research/firstyear.html] houses a full replication archive, including the data and documentation necessary to reproduce our results. Please send all correspondence to Andrew Martin, Washington University School of Law, Campus Box 1120, St. Louis MO 63130. admartin@wustl.edu; 314.935.5863.

I have heard something said
about allegiance to the South.
I know no South, no North,
no East, no West, to which I owe
any allegiance . . . The Union, sir,
is my country.

Henry Clay (1848)

SHAKESPEARE'S LEGAL ACQUIREMENTS

(continued from page 230)

John Lord Campbell

MUCH ADO ABOUT NOTHING

It has been generally supposed that Shakespeare, in the characters of Dogberry and Verges, only meant to satirize the ignorance and folly of parish constables — a race with which we of this generation were familiar till the establishment of the metropolitan and rural police; but I cannot help suspecting that he slyly aimed at higher legal functionaries — Chairmen at Quarter-sessions, and even Judges of assize — with whose performances he may probably have become acquainted at Warwick and elsewhere.

There never has been a law or custom in England to "*give a charge*" to constables; but from times immemorial there has been "*a charge to grand juries*" by the presiding judge. This charge, we are bound to believe, is now-a-days always characterised by simplicity, pertinence, and correctness, although, according to existing etiquette, in order that it may not be too severely criticised, the barristers are not admitted into the Crown Court till the charge is over. But when Justice Shallow gave the charge to the grand jury at sessions in the county of Gloucester, we may conjecture that some of his doctrines and directions were not very wise; and Judges of the superior courts in former times made themselves ridiculous by expatiating, in their charges to grand juries, on vexed questions of manners, religion, politics, and political economy. Dogberry uses the very words of the oath administered by the Judges' marshal to the grand jury at the present day:—

> Keep your fellows' counsels and your own.
>
> (Act III. Sc. 3.)

If the different parts of Dogberry's charge are strictly examined, it will be found that the author of it had a very respectable acquaintance with crown law. The problem was to save the constables from all trouble, danger, and responsibility, without any regard to the public safety:—

> *Dogb.* If you meet a thief, you may suspect him, by virtue of your office, to be no true man; and for such kind of men, the less you meddle or make with them, why, the more is for your honesty.

> 2 *Watch.* If we know him to be a thief, shall we not lay hands on
> him?
>
> *Dogb.* Truly, by your office you may; but, I think, they that touch
> pitch will be defiled. The most peaceable way for you, if you
> do take a thief, is to let him show himself what he is, and steal
> out of your company.

Now there can be no doubt that Lord Coke himself could not more accurately have defined the power of a peace-officer.

I cannot say as much for the law laid down by Dogberry and Verges in Act IV. Sc. 2, that it was *"flat perjury"* to call a prince's brother villain; or *"flat burglary* as ever was committed" to receive a thousand ducats "for accusing a lady wrongfully." But the dramatist seems himself to have been well acquainted with the terms and distinctions of our criminal code, or he could not have rendered the blunders of the parish officers so absurd and laughable.

LOVE'S LABOUR'S LOST

In Act I. Sc. 1, we have an extract from the Report by Don Adriano de Armado of the infraction he had witnessed of the King's proclamation by Costard with Jaquenetta; and it is drawn up in the true lawyerlike, tautological dialect,— which is to be paid for at so much a folio:—

> Then for the place where; where, I mean, I did encounter that obscene and most preposterous event that draweth from my snow-white pen the ebon-coloured ink, which here thou viewest, beholdest, surveyest, and seest.... Him I (as my ever-esteemed duty pricks me on) have sent to thee to receive the meed of punishment, by thy sweet Grace's officer, Antony Dull, a man of good repute, carriage, bearing, and estimation.

The gifted Shakespeare might perhaps have been capable, by intuition, of thus imitating the conveyancer's jargon; but no ordinary man could have hit it off so exactly, without having *engrossed* in an attorney's office.

MIDSUMMER NIGHT'S DREAM

Egeus makes complaint to Theseus, in Act I. Sc. 1, against his daughter Hermia, because, while he wishes her to marry Demetrius, she prefers Lysander; and he seeks to enforce the law of Athens, that a daughter, who refuses to marry according to her father's directions, may be put to death by him:—

And, my gracious duke,
Be it so, she will not here, before your grace,
Consent to marry with Demetrius
I beg the ancient privilege of Athens,
As she is mine, I may dispose of her,
Which shall be either to this gentleman,
Or to her death, according to our law
Immediately provided in that case.

Commenting on this last line, Steevens observes,— "Shakespeare is grievously suspected of having been placed, while a boy, in an attorney's office. The line before us has an undoubted smack of legal commonplace: Poetry disclaims it."

The precise formula — "In such case made and provided" — would not have stood in the verse. There is certainly no nearer approach in heroic measure to the technical language of an indictment; and there seems no motive for the addition made to the preceding line, except to show a familiarity with legal phraseology, which Shakespeare, whether he ever were an attorney's clerk or not, is constantly fond of displaying.

continued on page 292 . . .

APRIL

JUDGE NOT: THE JURY . . . MAY IN THE SWORN TWELVE HAVE A THIEF OR TWO

By John V. Orth, with the assistance of Joseph L. Hyde

Pressed by Escalus to be less strict — *Let us be keen and rather cut a little, / Than fall and bruise to death.* — Angelo admits that *the jury passing on the prisoner's life / May in the sworn twelve have a thief or two / Guiltier than him they try,* but pragmatically concludes that the law must concern itself with what it knows: *What knows the laws / That thieves do pass on thieves?* Of course, the lesson is misplaced in Renaissance Vienna, a civil law jurisdiction, where there were no juries.[1] In the play, there is no mention of a jury trial for Claudio and Juliet at the beginning, and none for Angelo (or Lucio) at the end.

But the reminder that one wrongdoer can pass sentence on another is central to *Measure for Measure.* It was a counsel of humility for one American judge who wrote concerning a criminal appeal:

---

[1] On juror disqualification in America, see Brian C. Kalt, The Exclusion of Felons From Jury Service, 53 Am. U. L. Rev. 65 (2003).

The sum of the evidence against this defendant is that one and one-half to two hours after a breaking occurred and one and one-half to two miles away, he was found on a "little sandbar" by a creek watching the rippling of the brook on a Sunday afternoon. If this constitutes criminal conduct, the author of this opinion pleads guilty to repeated offenses; and he only regrets the infrequency of their occurrence. Further, this may be the type of case Shakespeare had in mind . . . .[2]

In the deadly context of the play, the passage sets the stage for Angelo's fall. *Tell me, / When I that censure him do so offend, / Let mine own judgment pattern out my death / And nothing come in partial.* In the play's climactic trial scene, the Duke tells his deputy: *Come, cousin Angelo / In this I'll be impartial; be you judge / Of your own cause.* And the deputy enthusiastically seizes the opportunity to *come in partial.*

continued on page 309 . . .

PERLA V. REAL PROPERTY SOLUTIONS CORP.
19 Misc.3d 1125 (N.Y. Sup. Ct., 2nd Jud. Dist. April 28, 2008) (Table)

Arthur M. Schack, Justice

[Wells Fargo Bank] blames [Impac Funding Corporation] for its default and Richmond Abstract Company for failing to promptly record the earlier mortgage, which resulted in their junior position to the Perla mortgage. The Court reminds [Wells Fargo] of Cassius['s] advice to Brutus, in Act I, Scene 2 of William Shakespeare's *Julius Caesar*:

> The fault, dear Brutus, is not in our stars,
> But in ourselves.

---

[2] State v. Lanier, 273 S.E.2d 746, 749 (N.C. App. 1981) (Whichard, J.).

❧ APRIL ❧

SUN	MON	TUES	WED	THUR	FRI	SAT
			1	2	3	4
5	6	7	8	9	10	11
12	13	14	15	16	17	18
19	20	21	22	23	24	25
26	27	28	29	30		

Antonio and Shylock, in *Merchant of Venice*.

ANDERSON V. TERHUNE

M. Margaret McKeown[†]

It is likely that few Americans can profess fluency in the Bill of Rights, but the Fifth Amendment is surely an exception. From television shows like "Law & Order" to movies such as "Guys and Dolls," we are steeped in the culture that knows a person in custody has "the right to remain silent." *Miranda* is practically a household word. And surely, when a criminal defendant says, "I plead the Fifth," it doesn't take a trained linguist, a Ph.D, or a lawyer to know what he means. Indeed, as early as 1955, the Supreme Court recognized that "in popular parlance and even in legal literature, the term 'Fifth Amendment' in the context of our time is commonly regarded as being synonymous with the privilege against self-incrimination." *Quinn v. United States*, 349 U.S. 155, 163 (1955); *accord In re Johnny V.*, 149 Cal. Rptr. 180, 184, 188 (1978) (holding that the statement "I'll take the fifth" was an assertion of the Fifth Amendment privilege). More recently, the Court highlighted that "*Miranda* has become embedded in routine police practice to the point where the warnings have become part of our national culture." *Dickerson v. United States*, 530 U.S. 428, 443 (2000).

We granted rehearing en banc[1] in this appeal from the district court's denial of Jerome Alvin Anderson's petition for writ of habeas corpus. Anderson challenges his conviction of special circumstances murder on the grounds that he was denied his constitutional right to remain silent and that admission of his involuntary confession into evidence violated his right to due process. Specifically, Anderson claims that he invoked his Fifth

---

[†] Judge on the United States Court of Appeals for the Ninth Circuit, joined by Judges Mary M. Schroeder, Stephen Reinhardt, Sidney R. Thomas, Kim McLane Wardlaw, William A. Fletcher, Ronald M. Gould, Richard A. Paez, Richard R. Clifton, and Sandra S. Ikuta. This opinion is reported at 516 F.3d 781 (9th Cir. 2008) (en banc).

[1] *Anderson v. Terhune*, 467 F.3d 1208 (9th Cir.2006), *reh'g en banc granted*, 486 F.3d 1155 (9th Cir.2007).

Amendment right to terminate his police interrogation and that the police officer's continued questioning violated that right.

Anderson twice attempted to stop police questioning, stating "I don't even wanna talk about this no more," and "Uh! I'm through with this." After questioning continued, Anderson stated unequivocally, "I plead the Fifth." Instead of honoring this unambiguous invocation of the Fifth Amendment, the officer queried, "Plead the Fifth. What's that?" and then continued the questioning, ultimately obtaining a confession. It is rare for the courts to see such a pristine invocation of the Fifth Amendment and extraordinary to see such flagrant disregard of the right to remain silent.

The state court held that Anderson's statement, "I plead the Fifth," was ambiguous and that the officer asked a legitimate clarifying question. Under even the narrowest construction of the Antiterrorism and Effective Death Penalty Act, 28 U.S.C. § 2254(d) ("AEDPA"), the state court erred in failing to recognize this constitutional violation. The continued questioning violated the Supreme Court's bright-line rule established in *Miranda*. Once a person invokes the right to remain silent, all questioning must cease:

> If the individual indicates in any manner, at any time prior to or during questioning, that he wishes to remain silent, the interrogation must cease. At this point he has shown that he intends to exercise his Fifth Amendment privilege; any statement taken after the person invokes his privilege cannot be other than the product of compulsion, subtle or otherwise.

Miranda v. Arizona, 384 U.S. 436, 473-74 (1966); *see also Michigan v. Mosley*, 423 U.S. 96, 103 (1975) (explaining that once a defendant has invoked his right to remain silent, that right must be "scrupulously honored") (quoting *Miranda*, 384 U.S. at 479).

An examination of the interrogation transcript[2] reveals that the state court's conclusion that Anderson's invocation was ambiguous was an unreasonable application of *Miranda* and based on an unreasonable determination of the facts. *See* 28 U.S.C. § 2254(d)(1), (2). Only one reasonable conclusion can be gleaned from his statements, especially his last declaration, "I plead the Fifth": Anderson invoked his right to remain silent and

---

[2] Anderson filed a motion requesting that the en banc panel take judicial notice of the entire transcript of the interrogation. We asked the parties to clarify whether either the complete transcript or the audio tape of the interrogation was part of the record before the state appellate court. The answer is unclear, although it is undisputed that both were available to the court. Thus, we consider both to be part of the record in this appeal. Nonetheless, whether one considers the transcript or the audio tape, the result is the same.

wanted to end the interrogation. Construing the officer's statement, "Plead the Fifth? What's that?", as asking what Anderson meant is also an unreasonable determination of the facts. *Id.* § 2254(d)(2). These errors were not harmless and, accordingly, we reverse the judgment of the district court and remand with directions to grant the writ of habeas corpus.

I. BACKGROUND

Anderson and the victim, Robert Clark, were friends. On the morning of July 9, 1997, a mutual acquaintance, Patricia Kuykendall, discovered that her car had been stolen. Anderson and Kuykendall suspected that Clark was involved and later that morning confronted him at Kuykendall's house. Kuykendall began yelling at Clark, but Anderson remained calm. When Clark denied that he stole the car, he appeared edgy and nervous. As Kuykendall left the room to call the police, Clark left the house. Anderson and Kuykendall's roommate, Abe Santos, left ten minutes later, stating they were going to follow Clark.

Clark's body was discovered by the side of a road later that afternoon. He had been shot in the head four times. Investigators found a methamphetamine pipe lying between Clark's arm and body. A cigarette lighter was resting on Clark's stomach under his right hand. Pieces of a partially-eaten hamburger and a fresh cigarette butt were also near the body, as well as spent .22 caliber shell casings.

The police asked Anderson to come in for an interview two days later, July 11. During the interview, Anderson explained that on the day of the murder he saw Clark at Kuykendall's apartment in the morning, but that he and Santos left to buy some hamburgers, after which they went to Santos's father's house and to a car wash.

The police took Anderson into custody for a parole violation on July 12. Four officers interviewed Anderson for approximately three and a half hours. Despite clear and repeated invocations of his right to remain silent, the officer continued to question Anderson about the murder:

> Officer: You act like you're cryin' like a baby, an' you can't cry for someone that was a no good . . . an' you killed him for a good reason.
>
> Anderson: No, way! No, way. I — You know what, I don't even wanna talk about this no more. We can talk about it later or whatever. I don't want to talk about this no more. That's wrong. That's wrong.
>
> Officer: Right now, you show your remorse.

Immediately after this exchange, the officer continued to interrogate Anderson regarding his drug use on the day of the murder, including whether Anderson had used pipes. This questioning is significant because the murder victim was found with a pipe next to him. The entire conversation was about the murder. In response to this questioning, Anderson unambiguously indicated that he wanted to end the interrogation by stating that he was "through with this," wanted to "be taken into custody" and "I plead the Fifth." The relevant portion of the transcript is so extraordinary that it bears repeating.

> Anderson: I have nothin' to worry about, nothin' to hide. That's why I show no remorse. Nothin' to worry about, nothin' to hide. He was my friend, an' there's no way I would do it. No, way I would do it.
>
> Officer: Were you high that day?
>
> Anderson: No, sir. I – probably was later on. Yes.
>
> Officer: Did you have any dope with you that . . . that day?
>
> Anderson: No, sir.
>
> Officer: No, dope at all? What do you smoke with?
>
> Anderson: I smoke with my . . . my fingers.
>
> Officer: When you smoke your dope what do you do with that? How do you smoke that?
>
> Anderson: You smoke it with pipes and stuff like that.
>
> Officer: Okay. What kind of pipes?
>
> Anderson: Lines.
>
> Officer: What kind of pipes?
>
> Anderson: N'ah . . . I would – I –
>
> Officer: Well, what kind of pipes?
>
> Anderson: Uh! I'm through with this. I'm through. I wanna be taken into custody, with my parole . . .
>
> Officer: Well, you already are. I wanna know what kinda pipes you have?
>
> Anderson: I plead the [F]ifth.
>
> Officer: Plead the [F]ifth. What's that?
>
> Anderson: No, you guys are wrong. You guys are wrong. You guys have – I've tried to tell you everything I know. As far as I know, you guys are lying, uh, making things up, extenuating and that's not right. It's not right.
>
> Officer: We're not makin' anything up.
>
> Anderson: Sir, sure you are.

Officer: What are we makin' up?

Anderson: You're tellin' me that I didn't have tears in my eyes.

Officer: Yeah.

Anderson: You're tellin' me, okay, that, uh, uh, Abe said I kilt
   him. That's a lie.

The questioning continued until Anderson asked for a lawyer: "I'd like
to have an attorney present." At that juncture, an officer turned off the
tape recorder and, somewhat suspiciously, following this hiatus, the officers concluded that Anderson wanted to reinitiate the discussion. The
further questioning, which took place over a three-hour period, led to a
confession by Anderson.

Anderson was convicted of special circumstances murder. On appeal,
as in the trial court, he challenged the admissibility of his confession, arguing that it was obtained in violation of *Miranda* and of his Fifth Amendment
right to remain silent. The California Court of Appeal rejected Anderson's
argument. The court concluded that Anderson's invocation of his right to
remain silent was ambiguous and that the officer asked a legitimate clarifying question when he responded to Anderson's statement, "I plead the
[F]ifth," with "Plead the [F]ifth. What's that?" The state appellate court
reasoned that Anderson could have been refusing to talk about his drug
use, and did not intend to terminate the interview. The state court further
held that Anderson waived any invocation of the right to silence or to
counsel when he re-initiated the interrogation after the officers turned off
the tape.

II. STANDARD OF REVIEW

Under AEDPA, a writ of habeas corpus may not be granted unless the
state court's decision (1) resulted in a decision that was contrary to, or
involved an unreasonable application of, clearly established federal law, as
determined by the Supreme Court of the United States; or (2) resulted in
a decision that was based on an unreasonable determination of the facts in
light of the evidence presented in the state court proceeding. 28 U.S.C.
§ 2254(d)(1), (2). Although this standard requires us to give considerable
deference to the state courts, AEDPA deference is not a rubber stamp. *See
Miller-El v. Dretke*, 545 U.S. 231, 240, 265 (2005) (refusing to accept a
state court's "dismissive and strained interpretation" of the prisoner's evidence on habeas review and, noting that "[d]eference does not by definition preclude relief"). The state court decision here collides with AEDPA
on all grounds. It reflects both an unreasonable application of *Miranda,*

which is clearly established federal law, and an unreasonable determination of the facts.

III. IN CONTRAVENTION OF *MIRANDA*, THE STATE COURT UNREASONABLY CONCLUDED THAT ANDERSON'S INVOCATION ("I PLEAD THE FIFTH") WAS AMBIGUOUS

Following the issuance of *Miranda* in 1966 and the literally thousands of cases that repeat its rationale, we rarely have occasion to address a situation in which the defendant not only uses the facially unambiguous words "I plead the Fifth," but surrounds that invocation with a clear desire not to talk any more. The state court accurately recognized that under *Miranda,* "if [an] individual indicates in any manner, at any time prior to or during questioning, that he wishes to remain silent, the interrogation must cease," 384 U.S. at 473-74, but then went on to eviscerate that conclusion by stating that the comments were "ambiguous in context":

> In the present case, the defendant's comments were ambiguous in context because they could have been interpreted as not wanting officers to pursue the particulars of his drug use as opposed to not wanting to continue the questioning at all. By asking defendant what he meant by pleading the fifth, the officer asked a legitimate clarifying question.

Using "context" to transform an unambiguous invocation into open-ended ambiguity defies both common sense and established Supreme Court law. It is not that context is unimportant, but it simply cannot be manufactured by straining to raise a question regarding the intended scope of a facially unambiguous invocation of the right to silence. As the Supreme Court has observed, in invoking a constitutional right, "a suspect need not 'speak with the discrimination of an Oxford don.'" *Davis v. United States*, 512 U.S. 452, 459 (1994)[3] (quoting *id.* at 476 (Souter, J., concurring in judgment)). Anderson would meet even this erudite standard. *Miranda* requires only that the suspect "indicate[] in any manner . . . that he wishes to remain silent." *Miranda*, 384 U.S. at 473-74.

---

[3] We acknowledge that *Davis* is an invocation of counsel case under *Miranda,* not a Fifth Amendment right to silence case. We rely on *Miranda* and *Mosley,* not *Davis,* as "clearly established" law. *See Evans v. Demosthenes,* 98 F.3d 1174, 1176 (9th Cir. 1996) (declining to address whether *Davis* applies to right to silence cases). Nonetheless, the general principles from cases involving the clarity of invocation of rights during custodial interrogation are instructive as to common sense interpretation of language.

This is not a case where the officers or the court were left scratching their heads as to what Anderson meant.[4] Nothing was ambiguous about the statement "I plead the Fifth." Ambiguity means "admitting more than one interpretation or reference" or "having a double meaning or reference." The New Shorter Oxford English Dictionary (1993). Even if the preliminary statements "I don't even wanna talk about this no more" and "I'm through with this. I'm through. I wanna be taken in custody," were viewed as somewhat equivocal — a dubious conclusion at best — "I plead the Fifth" left no room for doubt.

As we recently observed, "neither the Supreme Court nor this court has required that a suspect seeking to invoke his right to silence provide any statement more explicit or more technically-worded than 'I have nothing to say.'" *Arnold v. Runnels*, 421 F.3d 859, 865 (9th Cir.2005). We went on to underscore that Arnold's statement easily met the Fifth Amendment standard: "Indeed, it is difficult to imagine how much more clearly a layperson like Arnold could have expressed his desire to remain silent." *Id.* at 866.

Anderson did not equivocate in his invocation by using words such as "maybe" or "might" or "I think." *See id.* at 865-66 (distinguishing cases in which the court concluded that a qualified invocation was ambiguous from cases in which the invocation of the right to silence was specific and unambiguous). Nor was there anything ambiguous in Anderson declaring, "I plead the Fifth." Anderson had already *twice* attempted to stop the police questioning using crystal-clear language: "I don't want to talk about this no more" and "Uh! I'm through with this. I'm through. I wanna be taken into custody . . . ." Saying that he wanted to be taken into custody was an indication that Anderson did not want to talk about the murder, his drug use, or anything else. Thus, the state court was unreasonable in concluding that the invocation was ambiguous in context because the context, in fact, makes it clear that Anderson wanted to end the interrogation in all respects. Anderson had the right to end the interrogation at any point and the fact that Anderson had answered the officers' questions for over two

---

[4] The trial court stated, "while the defendant articulated words *that could, in the isolation* [sic], *be viewed as an invocation of his right to remain silent*, the defendant did not intend to terminate the interview." (emphasis added). Similarly, the state court of appeal stated, "In the present case, the defendant's comments were ambiguous in context because they could have been interpreted as not wanting officers to pursue the particulars of his drug use *as opposed to not wanting to continue the questioning at all*." (emphasis added). Obviously, the court recognized that "I plead the Fifth" was an invocation of the right to silence; it detected ambiguity only as to the scope of the invocation.

hours does not somehow undermine or cast doubt on an unambiguous invocation. Whether these were "statements of frustration," as the government posited at oral argument, misses the point. A suspect can both be frustrated with an interrogation and seek to terminate it. "Taking the Fifth" is as unequivocal as one can get in invoking the right to remain silent.

IV. THE STATE COURT'S CONCLUSION THAT THE OFFICER ASKED A LEGITIMATE CLARIFYING QUESTION WAS AN UNREASONABLE DETERMINATION OF THE FACTS

Anderson's unambiguous, unequivocal invocation should have brought an immediate end to questioning. Notably, the Supreme Court's commitment to *Miranda*'s fundamental tenet — that police must "*scrupulously honor*[]" a suspect's right to remain silent by immediately ceasing questioning when the suspect invokes this right, 384 U.S. at 479 (emphasis added) — has never wavered. See *Mosley*, 423 U.S. at 103 (*Miranda*'s "critical safeguard" is "a person's 'right to cut off questioning'"); *see also Arizona v. Roberson*, 486 U.S. 675, 683 (1988); *Kolender v. Lawson*, 461 U.S. 352, 368 n.6 (1983) (Brennan, J., concurring); *cf. Dickerson*, 530 U.S. at 440 (reaffirming constitutional requirement that "the exercise of [*Miranda*] rights must be fully honored").

Instead of scrupulously honoring the request, the interrogating officer decided to "play dumb," hoping to keep Anderson talking by inquiring, "Plead the Fifth. What's that?" This effort to keep the conversation going was almost comical. At best, the officer was mocking and provoking Anderson. The officer knew what "I plead the Fifth" meant. It is thus baffling that the state court determined that "[b]y asking defendant what he meant by pleading the Fifth, the officers asked a legitimate clarifying question." The need for clarification presumes some ambiguity or uncertainty. Nothing needed clarification.

This situation brings to mind the phrase attributed to a Canadian judge — "won't take no for an answer" — and later popularized in country music as "What part of 'no' don't you understand?"[5] What about the words "I plead the Fifth" is unclear, ambiguous, or confusing to a reasonable officer? Nothing. *See Connecticut v. Barrett*, 479 U.S. 523, 529 (1987) (holding

---

[5] *See* The Phrase Finder, What part of no don't you understand?, http://www.phrases.org. uk/meanings/what-part-of-no.html (last visited Nov. 30, 2007); LORRIE MORGAN, *What Part of No* (words and music by Wayne Perry and Gerald Smith), on WATCH ME (BNA Records 1992).

in the context of the invocation of the right to counsel that "[i]nterpretation is only required where the defendant's words, understood as ordinary people would understand them, are ambiguous"). Rather, the officer hoped Anderson would explain more about the murder, the exact topic Anderson did not want to talk about. The officer thought that continuing the interrogation was "reasonably likely to elicit an incriminating response" from Anderson. *Rhode Island v. Innis*, 446 U.S. 291, 303 (1980). And he was right.

In the right-to-counsel context, the Supreme Court has countenanced clarifying questions only to ascertain whether a suspect's ambiguous or equivocal statement is actually an invocation of his Fifth Amendment right. *See Davis*, 512 U.S. at 461; *Miranda*, 384 U.S. at 445 (focusing only on the threshold question of whether the accused "indicate[d] in any manner that he d[id] not wish to be interrogated" when deciding whether police had honored the accused's Fifth Amendment rights); *cf. Smith v. Illinois*, 469 U.S. 91, 95 (1984) (holding that "[t]his case concerns the threshold inquiry: whether Smith invoked his right to counsel in the first instance"). Ignoring this principle, the state court found that the comments were ambiguous "because they could have been interpreted as not wanting officers to pursue the particulars of his drug use as opposed to not wanting to continue the questioning at all."

The state court's rationale collapses beneath its own weight, because the officer's comment showed that the interrogating officers did not believe that Anderson's statement was ambiguous. The officer did not ask Anderson what subject he did not want to discuss; nor did any of his follow-up questioning address this topic. Similarly, the officer did not ask him if he wished to remain silent or whether he simply did not want to talk about the drug issue. The officer did not even ask Anderson what he meant. No reasonable officer could legitimately be in doubt about the meaning of "I plead the Fifth." The state court's characterization is a fanciful re-imagining of the colloquy between Anderson and the officer, and under AEDPA, an unreasonable determination of the facts.

The state court's conclusion that "[i]t was the defendant, not the interrogators, who continued the discussion," ignores the bedrock principle that the interrogators should have stopped all questioning.[6] A statement taken after the suspect invoked his right to remain silent "cannot be other

---

[6] As the Third Circuit aptly stated, "[u]nder *Miranda*, the onus was not on [the suspect] to be persistent in her demand to remain silent. Rather, the responsibility fell to the law enforcement officers to scrupulously respect her demand." *United States v. Lafferty*, 503 F.3d 293, 304 (3d Cir.2007).

than the product of compulsion, subtle or otherwise." *Miranda*, 384 U.S. at 474.

Finally, it makes no sense to split hairs and say that maybe, just maybe, Anderson wanted to talk about the murder and not about his drug use because, in fact, the drug use was inextricably intertwined with the murder. The victim's body was found next to a methamphetamine pipe. Anderson's drug use that day could well tie him to the murder. He was taken in for questioning about the murder, not on a potential drug charge.

It is precisely this kind of conjecture and hair-splitting that the Supreme Court wanted to avoid when it fashioned the bright-line rule in *Miranda*. *Cf. Davis*, 512 U.S. at 461 (noting that, where the suspect asks for counsel, the benefit of the bright-line rule is the "clarity and ease of application" that "can be applied by officers in the real world without unduly hampering the gathering of information" by forcing them "to make difficult judgment calls" with a "threat of suppression if they guess wrong"). No guess work was required here.

Under the state court's application of *Miranda* and its progeny, every time a suspect unequivocally invokes the right to remain silent, the police can ask follow-up questions to clarify whether he really, *really* wants to invoke the right and to parse the subject matter — "what specifically do you not want to talk about?" Such a practice is tantamount to endless re-interrogation.

The Sixth Circuit's decision in *McGraw v. Holland*, 257 F.3d 513 (6th Cir.2001), where the defendant stated "I don't want to talk about it," illustrates the error of the state court's approach:

> In the criminal proceeding against Tina McGraw, the state trial court declined to hold the confession inadmissible under *Miranda* since Tina 'never demanded or requested to terminate the interview.' Although Tina said that she did not want to talk about the rape itself, in other words, her confession that she assisted in the rape was held to be admissible under *Miranda* because she never said that she did not want to talk about subjects other than the rape. This, in our view, was an unreasonable application of *Miranda* and its progeny.

Id. at 518.

Here, the state court's loose paraphrasing of the officer's question — "Plead the [F]ifth. What's that?" — as "asking defendant *what he meant* by pleading the Fifth" is unconvincing and an unreasonable determination of the facts. As the transcript reveals, the officer did not even pretend not to understand what Anderson meant. Instead, incredibly, he feigned ignorance of the Fifth Amendment.

Where the initial request to stop the questioning is clear, "the police may not create ambiguity in a defendant's desire by continuing to question him or her about it." *Barrett*, 479 U.S. at 535 n.5 (Brennan, J., concurring). By parsing Anderson's invocation into specific subjects, "the police failed to honor a decision of a person in custody to cut off questioning, either by refusing to discontinue the interrogation upon request or by persisting in repeated efforts to wear down his resistance and make him change his mind." *Mosley*, 423 U.S. at 105-06. The net result is that such follow-up questions allowed the officer to avoid honoring the Fifth Amendment and, as in a right to counsel situation, enabled "the authorities through 'badger[ing]' or 'overreaching' — explicit or subtle, deliberate or unintentional — [to] wear down the accused and persuade him to incriminate himself." *Smith*, 469 U.S. at 98.

Looking at this case through the AEDPA lens of deference, as we must, does nothing to change these conclusions. The state court's decision to ignore an unambiguous declaration of the right to remain silent is an unreasonable application of *Miranda*, as was the decision to allow continued questioning. *See Runnels*, 421 F.3d at 867. Finally, the state court's labeling of Anderson's statements as ambiguous and characterizing the officer's response as a legitimate clarifying inquiry were unreasonable determinations of fact.

V. THE STATE COURT'S DECISION WAS CONTRARY TO SUPREME COURT PRECEDENT BY FINDING A WAIVER BASED ON ANDERSON'S RESPONSES TO RE-INTERROGATION

The state appellate court attempted to bolster its conclusion about Anderson's statements by claiming that he waived his right to remain silent in continuing to answer police questions after he stated, "I plead the Fifth":

> [W]hile words of invocation were spoken by the defendant, the court concludes that, in any case, he effectively waived the right to remain silent by what followed . . . . By continuing to talk to the police officers, defendant demonstrated a willingness to continue to discuss the case.

Put another way, the state court endorses the principle that once the officers ignored Anderson's unequivocal invocation of the Fifth Amendment, their questioning kept him talking and resulted in a waiver of his right to remain silent. This analysis directly contravenes Supreme Court precedent: "[U]nder the clear logical force of settled precedent, an accused's *postrequest* responses to further interrogation may not be used to cast retrospective doubt on the clarity of the initial request itself." *Smith*, 469 U.S. at 100 (emphasis in original).

Smith mandates that all questioning must immediately cease once the right to remain silent is invoked, and that any subsequent statements by the defendant in response to continued interrogation cannot be used to find a waiver or cast ambiguity on the earlier invocation. The Supreme Court's somewhat lengthy recitation of this principle is particularly instructive in this case:

> Where nothing about the request for counsel or the circumstances leading up to the request would render it ambiguous, all questioning must cease. In these circumstances, an accused's subsequent statements are relevant only to the question whether the accused waived the right he had invoked. Invocation and waiver are entirely distinct inquiries, and the two must not be blurred by merging them together . . . .
>
> With respect to the waiver inquiry, we accordingly have emphasized that a valid waiver "cannot be established by showing only that [the accused] responded to further police-initiated custodial interrogation." Using an accused's subsequent responses to cast doubt on the adequacy of the initial request *itself* is even more intolerable. "No authority, and no logic, permits the interrogator to proceed . . . on his own terms and as if the defendant had requested nothing, in the hope that the defendant might be induced to say something casting retrospective doubt on his initial statement that he wished to speak through an attorney or not at all."

Id. at 98-99 (internal citations omitted) (emphasis, alteration and second ellipsis in original).

We are not faced with a situation where there was a break in questioning after the *Miranda* invocation. Instead, police simply continued the conversation up to the point that Anderson said, "I'd like to have an attorney present." Only at that point did they stop the interrogation and turn off the recorder. But it was too late.

We cannot simply suppress the portion of the interrogation that occurred after the invocation of the right to silence and before Anderson's purported re-initiation of the interrogation. Doing so would eviscerate the mandate to "scrupulously honor[]" the invocation of *Miranda* rights. We understand the phrase "scrupulously honor" to have practical meaning. For the "right to remain silent" to have currency, there must be some silence. The interrogation must stop for some period of time. *See Miranda*, 384

U.S. at 473-74; *Mosley*, 423 U.S. at 103-04. Although the Supreme Court has yet to tell us how long the break in questioning must last, in this case there was no cessation at all. Because the interrogation was continuous to that point, we need not determine whether Anderson waived his right to counsel after viewing a videotape of his alleged accomplice nor do we need to address his coercion claim.

The prejudice from Anderson's confession cannot be soft pedaled, and the error was not harmless. *Brecht v. Abrahamson*, 507 U.S. 619, 623 (1993). The confession was central to the conviction. *See Arizona v. Fulminante*, 499 U.S. 279, 296 (1991) ("A confession is like no other evidence. Indeed, the defendant's own confession is probably the most . . . damaging evidence that can be admitted against him." (internal quotation marks omitted)). Although deference must be given to state court determinations under AEDPA, we would be abdicating our responsibility to abide by Supreme Court precedent and to police the Constitution's boundaries were we to permit such an egregious violation of *Miranda* to go unchecked.

The judgment of the district court is reversed and the case is remanded with instructions to grant the writ.

Reversed and remanded.

Education makes a people easy to lead, but difficult to drive; easy to govern, but impossible to enslave.

Henry Peter Brougham

Shakespeare's Legal Acquirements

(continued from page 274)

John Lord Campbell

The Merchant of Venice

In Act I. Sc. 3, and Act II. Sc. 8, Antonio's bond to Shylock is prepared and talked about according to all the forms observed in an English attorney's office. The distinction between a "single bill" and a "bond with a condition" is clearly referred to; and *punctual payment* is expressed in the technical phrase — "Let good Antonio *keep his day*."

———

It appears by Act III. Sc. 3, between Shylock, Salarino, Antonio, and a Jailer, that the action on the bond had been commenced, and Antonio had been arrested on *mesne process*. The trial was to come on before the Doge; and the question was, whether Shylock was entitled to judgment specifically for his pound of flesh, or must be contented with pecuniary damages.

———

Shylock threatens the Jailer with an action for "escape" for allowing Antonio to come for a short time beyond the walls of the prison:—

> I do wonder,
> Thou naughty Jailer, that thou art so fond
> To come abroad with him at his request.

Antonio is made to confess that Shylock is entitled to the pound of flesh, according to the plain meaning of the bond and condition, and the rigid strictness of the common law of England:—

> *Salarino.* I am sure the Duke
>   Will never grant this forfeiture to hold.
>
> *Antonio.* The Duke cannot deny the course of law.

All this has a strong odour of Westminster Hall.

———

The trial comes on in Act IV. Sc. 1, and it is duly conducted according to the strict forms of legal procedure. Portia, the *Podesta* or judge called in to act under the authority of the Doge, first inquires if there be any plea of *non est factum*.

She asks Antonio, "Do you confess the bond?" and when he answers, "I do," the judge proceeds to consider how the damages are to be assessed. The plaintiff claims the penalty of the bond, according to the words of the condition; and Bassanio, who acts as counsel for the defendant, attempting on equitable grounds to have him excused by paying twice the sum of money lent, or "ten times o'er," judgment is given:—

> *Portia.* It must not be. There is no power in Venice
> Can alter a decree established.
> 'Twill be recorded for a precedent,
> And many an error by the same example
> Will rush into the state. . . .
> This bond is forfeit,
> And lawfully by this the Jew may claim
> A pound of flesh to be by him cut off
> Nearest the merchant's heart.

However, *oyer* of the bond being demanded, the judge found that it gave "no jot of blood;" and the result was that Shylock, to save his own life, was obliged to consent to make over all his goods to his daughter Jessica and her Christian husband Lorenzo, and himself to submit to Christian baptism.

Shakespeare concludes this scene with an ebullition which might be expected from an English lawyer, by making Gratiano exclaim,—

> In christening thou shalt have *two godfathers*:
> Had I been judge, thou shouldst have had *ten more*,
> To bring thee to the *gallows*, not the *font*—

meaning a jury of twelve men, to find him guilty of the capital offence of *an attempt to murder*;— whereupon he must have been hanged.

I may further observe that this play, in the last scene of the last act, contains another palpable allusion to English legal procedure. In the court of Queen's Bench, when a complaint is made against a person for a "*contempt*," the practice is that before sentence is finally pronounced, he is sent into the Crown Office, and being there "*charged upon interrogatories*," he is made to swear that he will "answer all things faithfully." Accordingly, in the moonlight scene in the garden at Belmont, after a partial explanation between Bassanio, Gratiano, Portia, and Nerissa, about their rings, some farther inquiry being deemed necessary, Portia says,—

> Let us go in,
> And *charge us there upon inter'gatories*,
> And *we will answer all things faithfully*.

Gratiano assents, observing, —

> Let it be so: the first inter'gatory
> That my Nerissa shall be sworn on is,
> Whether till the next night she had rather stay,
> Or go to bed now, being two hours to day.

THE TAMING OF THE SHREW

In the *"Induction"* Shakespeare betrays an intimate knowledge of the matters which may be prosecuted as offences before the *Court Leet*, the lowest court of criminal judicature in England. He puts this speech into the mouth of a servant, who is trying to persuade Sly that he is a great lord, and that he had been in a dream for fifteen years, during which time he thought he was a frequenter of alehouses: —

> For though you lay here in this goodly chamber,
> Yet would you say, ye were beaten out of door,
> And rail upon the hostess of the house,
> And say you would *present her at the leet,*
> *Because she brought stone jugs, and no sealed quarts.*

Now, in the reigns of Elizabeth and James I., there was a very wholesome law, that, for the protection of the public against "false measures," ale should be sold only in sealed vessels of the standard capacity; and the violation of the law was to be presented at the "Court Leet," or "View of Frankpledge," held in every hundred, manor, or lordship, before the steward of the leet.

Malone, in reference to this passage, cites the well-known treatise of "Kitchen on Courts," and also copies a passage from a work with which I am not acquainted — "Characterismi, or Lenton's Leasures," 12mo. 1631 — which runs thus: — "He [an informer] transforms himselfe into several shapes, to avoid suspicion of *inneholders*, and inwardly joyes at the sight of a blacke pot or *jugge*, knowing that their sale by *sealed quarts* spoyles his market."

In Act I. Sc. 2, the proposal of Tranio that the rival lovers of Bianca, while they eagerly in her presence should press their suit, yet, when she is absent, should converse freely as friends, is illustrated in a manner to induce a belief that the author of Tranio's speech had been accustomed to see the contending counsel, when the trial is over, or suspended, — on very familiar and friendly terms with each other: —

> *Tra.* Sir, I shall not be slack: in sign whereof

Please ye, we may contrive this afternoon,
And quaff carouses to our mistress' health;
And do as adversaries do in law,
Strive mightily, but eat and drink as friends.

This clearly alludes not to the *parties litigating*, who, if they were to eat and drink together, would generally be disposed to poison each other but to the *counsel* on opposite sides, with whom, notwithstanding the fiercest contests in court, when they meet in private immediately after, it is "All hail, fellow, and well met."

In the first encounter of wits between Katherine and Petruchio, Shakespeare shows that he was acquainted with the law for regulating "trials by battle" between champions, one of which had been fought in Tothill Fields before the judges of the Court of Common Pleas in the reign of Elizabeth.

> *Kath.* What is your crest? a coxcomb?
> *Pet.* A combless cock, so Kate will be my hen.
> *Kath.* No cock of mine; you crow too like a *craven.*

(Act II. Sc. 1.)

This all lawyers know to be the word spoken by a champion who acknowledged that he was beaten, and declared that he would fight no more:— whereupon judgment was immediately given against the side which he supported, and he bore the infamous name of *Craven* for the rest of his days.

We have like evidence in "Hamlet" (Act IV. Sc. 4) of Shakespeare's acquaintance with the legal meaning of this word, where the hero says—

> Now, whether it be
> Bestial oblivion, or some *craven* scruple
> Of thinking too precisely on th' event.

continued on page 338 . . .

TOWARD ONE AMERICA

A VISION IN LAW

J. Harvie Wilkinson III[†]

INTRODUCTION

The present age will go down in American history as a partisan and polarizing one. Indeed, that may be its defining characteristic. America has had deeply divisive eras before — the Federalist-Republican period and the Civil War spring to mind — but those eras divided over deeply consequential principles. The partisan differences of the present era are hardly insignificant, but these differences do not justify what can be described without exaggeration as the sheer magnitude of mutual hate. Thus again we have an America defined by colors — red and blue states — less portentous than the Civil War's blue and gray, but in their own way sapping the nation's common bonds and sense of strength.

It would be surprising if the acrimony of the political system had left the courts unscathed. Still no one anticipated *Bush v. Gore*.[1] "Although we may never know with complete certainty the identity of the winner of this year's Presidential election," reads the impassioned coda of Justice Stevens's dissent, "the identity of the loser is perfectly clear. It is the Nation's confidence in the judge as an impartial guardian of the rule of law."[2] The expression capped a judicial era of deep factional divisions, contrary to the founding years of our Republic, when the partisan strife in the political

---

[†] Copyright © 2008 by J. Harvie Wilkinson III. U.S. Circuit Judge, United States Court of Appeals for the Fourth Circuit. An earlier version of this essay was delivered as the James Madison Lecture at the New York University School of Law on October 2, 2007. I wish to thank Dean Richard Revesz, Professor Norman Dorsen, and the entire law school community for the warm and gracious welcome I received during my visit. This article originally appeared at 83 N.Y.U. L. REV. 323 (2008). Reprinted by permission of the author and the publisher.

[1] 531 U.S. 98 (2000).

[2] *Id.* at 128-29 (Stevens, J., dissenting).

arena was met by an extraordinary degree of unanimity in the Third Branch.[3]

If law is part of the problem of polarization, it should likewise be part of the solution. In other words, law should consciously aspire to promote a stronger sense of national cohesion and unity. We have not traditionally thought of law in these terms. The great purposes of law have historically been the preservation of order in which freedom may flourish and the protection of liberty itself from overreaching by the State.

To these must now be added a third great purpose — that of maintaining a concept of American nationhood in a divisive and rapidly evolving age. It is hard to overstate the need for a national purpose in law. The gravity of our divisions demands it. The structural manifestations of our divisions — the gerrymandering of congressional districts to reflect each party's political base; the constant electioneering that leaves less time and opportunity for governance; the twenty-four-hour news cycle replete with cable, blogs, talk radio, and online news sites; the bitter judicial confirmation battles; the willingness of partisans to impeach, to destroy character, or to criminalize political differences — all these have led to the disintegration of civility and the ascendancy of partisanship.

The divisions in the body politic tell but part of the story. The changing demographics of this country augur a future of rich and challenging diversity, in which no ethnic group is a majority and the boundaries of race and ethnicity may become increasingly less distinct. In an age of varied national origins and ethnic heritages, it becomes important for law to celebrate commonality as well as to appreciate difference.

And in a nation where liberal and conservative, secular and sectarian, sunbelt and rustbelt, senior and junior, manual and informational, expose ever sharper fault lines, it becomes imperative that law bridge, not broaden, America's new gaps.

It is much easier to posit the need for a unifying role for law than to say how the law should unify. Where one person sees unity, another may see only division. Perhaps then it is best to draw prescriptions from various sides of the current legal debate. Even then, suggesting how national identity might thrive among competing racial, ethnic, regional, generational, religious, and other loyalties is a perilous task.

I nonetheless have seven recommendations. I arrived at seven not because it is the number of the wonders of the ancient world or even the

---

[3] See, e.g., Gibbons v. Ogden, 22 U.S. (9 Wheat.) 1 (1824); McCulloch v. Maryland, 17 U.S. (4 Wheat.) 316 (1819); Marbury v. Madison, 5 U.S. (1 Cranch) 137 (1803).

first number of the famous convenience store, but because seven imperatives naturally suggest themselves to me as prerequisites to maintaining
even a modest sense of national identity throughout the twenty-first century. I recognize that many of you may dispute this or that point in my
talk. My hope, however, is that these suggestions, taken as a whole, will
make us a stronger and healthier country.

I

Let's respect judicial restraint. By restraint, I mean a healthy judicial regard for the roles and enactments of the coordinate branches of the federal
government and the proper functioning of the states. Judicial restraint
promotes the pursuit of national unity. The corollary is that judicial activism tends to undermine it.

In advancing this thesis, I have no wish to point a finger. Both right and
left have had their fling. *Lochner v. New York* advanced the notion of a personal freedom of contract as part of the liberty protected by the Fourteenth Amendment.[4] *Roe v. Wade* transported substantive due process
from the economic to the personal realm.[5] The Rehnquist Court did not
break with the notion that substantive due process applied to state legislation,[6] and the Court struck down federal legislation as well under the
commerce power[7] and Section 5 of the Fourteenth Amendment.[8] The
point here is not whether some forms of activism are more or less justifiable than others. That question is surely debatable, but what is not debatable is that all forms of activism gild the scepter of judicial power.

But why is activism so inimical to national unity? One could argue that
a national constitutional standard actually serves a unifying function on
occasion by reminding us of the fundamental personal freedoms and governmental structures for which we stand. This is true to some extent —
the invalidation of the poll tax, for example, is a valuable reminder that
the franchise is something that is open to all.[9]

---

[4] 198 U.S. 45, 53 (1905).

[5] 410 U.S. 113, 153-54 (1973).

[6] *See, e.g.*, *Lawrence v. Texas*, 539 U.S. 558 (2003); *Planned Parenthood of Se. Pa. v. Casey*, 505 U.S. 833 (1992).

[7] *E.g.*, *United States v. Morrison*, 529 U.S. 598 (2000) (striking down civil damages provision of Violence Against Women Act); *United States v. Lopez*, 514 U.S. 549 (1995) (striking down federal statute regulating gun use).

[8] *E.g.*, *City of Boerne v. Flores*, 521 U.S. 507 (1997) (holding that Religious Freedom Restoration Act exceeds Congress's power under Section 5).

[9] *See Harper v. Va. Bd. of Elections*, 383 U.S. 663 (1966) (holding that poll tax imposes unconstitutional restriction on franchise).

Taken sufficiently far, however, the idea of a unifying constitutionalism is nothing more than a neat rationalization for judicial supremacy. Such supremacy is deeply divisive, and not just because of the commonly given reason that unelected judges serving for life should not lightly displace the will of the people's chosen representatives.[10]

The underlying reason for the divisiveness of judicial activism is as much cultural as it is legal or political. Judges are drawn from the ranks of one profession only. There are no plumbers or flight attendants or school teachers or investment bankers or firefighters or insurance salesmen in our midst. It is odd, to say the least, that the members of one privileged profession should be making the most intimate and important decisions for the family and the workplace of all other professions. That one entire branch of government has been populated by the members of one profession only is no testament to the innate superiority of lawyers. It is a reminder that with great responsibility goes greater humility, lest the arrogance of legal authority drive resentments through our national heart.

Nor does the divisive potential of an activist bench end there. The courts reflect not only one profession, but the elite reaches of that profession to boot. Many judges — and I do not exempt myself — have been educated at the most exclusive colleges and law schools, have spent their careers in the upper ethers of legal practice or academia, and have served in the upper echelons of state and national government.

This training is superb in several respects. It may acquaint us with the workings of government and it may hone first-rate analytical and intellectual skills. It equips us well to perform the important interpretative and courtroom tasks we do. But our backgrounds have not by and large given birth to a breadth of human experience. We judges are as a class bereft of acquaintance with the variegated and pluralistic country that we serve. While we may project and empathize, that is no substitute for first-hand life experience or even the eye-and-ear contact with the electorate that a career in elective politics can bring. The courtroom and the bar conventions and the symposia and those proverbial embassy parties provide detachment and impartiality of a sort, but they regrettably shelter us from the bumps and bruises that attend our fellow citizens' daily lives. Those who enjoy the habit of deference should not acquire the taste for dictation. Judicial activism is no long-run strategy for national wholeness; the inevi-

---

[10] *See, e.g., Connor v. Finch*, 431 U.S. 407, 431 (1977) (Powell, J., dissenting) ("[L]egislative plans are likely to reflect a State's political policy and the will of its people more accurately than a decision by unelected federal judges.").

table elitism of a judicial ruling class will spawn a populist rancor in America that will frustrate the attempt to bridge our most basic divides.

II

My next three recommendations have to do with how we regard our Constitution. This is critical, because how citizens regard their founding charter will influence how they view America itself.

Let's be sparing in what we seek to constitutionalize. Our Constitution sets forth a structure of governance and those basic rights the state may not abridge. It is a document of inclusion that welcomes all citizens into the American fold. Perhaps that is what makes the recent spate of same-sex marriage amendments (federal and state)[11] so at odds with the generous and unifying spirit any constitution must achieve. To forbid same-sex marriage through legislation is one thing. To assign second-class status to gay citizens in our founding charters is something else. Passing amendments whose character will so plainly be perceived as punitive is not the way to One America. Our constitutions must bind wounds, not rub them raw.

If law is to express a national purpose, a constitution must cover very few things. The Second Amendment doesn't need to be read to assign judges the final say over questions of gun control. The Equal Rights Amendment doesn't need to be passed to give judges the final word over relations between the sexes. National unity means a Constitution that embodies only surpassing common values around which citizens can unite. In fact, the Framers bequeathed a document that did not partake of most particulars because each generation must be free to seek its own way and because the most difficult subjects — volatile social issues, tax and budgetary disputes, even war and peace — are most amenable to political compromise which promises today's losers the prospect of tomorrow's change.

To constitutionalize our differences is to up the ante gravely. Legislation implies temporary winners and temporary losers. Constitutionalizing implies permanent winners and permanent losers, the most divisive of all

---

[11] *See, e.g.,* Kevin Simpson, *Marriage, Gay Rights: Amend. 43 Supporters Revel in Double Victory,* DENVER POST, Nov. 9, 2006, at B06 (noting that seven states passed constitutional amendments banning same-sex marriages in 2006). While the proposed Federal Marriage Amendment has not passed, the fact that it has been so vigorously debated as a constitutional option was bound to deepen social division. *See* Alan Cooperman, *Gay Marriage as 'the New Abortion': Debate Becomes Polarizing as Both Sides Become Better Organized, Spend Millions,* WASH. POST, July 26, 2004, at A03 (describing debate).

worlds. Constitutionalizing tampers with our legal birthright and common heritage — with what we as a nation hold most dear. It is thus unfortunate when judges decree unenumerated rights to privacy or when legislators seek constitutional status for restrictions on personal rights. The American Constitution should not reflect the agenda of the NRA or NOW or Focus on the Family or NARAL Pro-Choice America. Interest-group politics are fine for Congress, but they threaten to tarnish our national constitutional trust.

III

Let's value the nationalism in our Constitution. It is, of course, too simple to say the Constitution is a nationalistic document. It is rather a charter of tensions, most notably between the three branches of federal government and between the federal government and the states. But the Constitution has a strong nationalist component — it was, after all, "to form a more perfect Union" that "[w]e the People of the United States" did "ordain and establish" the Constitution in the first place.[12]

At the core of constitutional nationalism are the enumerated powers of Congress in Article I, Section 8. And at the core of the enumerated powers are the commerce and spending powers, the latter being couched as a provision "for the common Defence and general Welfare."[13] The commerce power in particular has recently been the subject of debate, and its exercise by Congress has not received complete deference from the courts.[14]

So far, so good — a reminder that Congress's powers are enumerated, not residual, is a salutary thing. But there is also a danger here, best illustrated by efforts to weaken Congress's authority to protect the national environment. It is tempting, I suppose, to see the states as sovereigns of their own resources, be they lands or animal species or bodies of water that have their chief locus within a single state. It is further tempting to say such things are not really commerce, at least in the sense that trucks and trains and roads and canals or production processes are. It is tempting finally to see federal officials as far-off policemen, out to handcuff property owners and developers from exercising basic rights.

---

[12] U.S. Const. pmbl.

[13] U.S. Const. art. I, § 8, cl. 1.

[14] The Rehnquist Court invalidated the civil damages provision of the Violence Against Women Act and the entire Gun-Free School Zones Act as exceeding Congress's Commerce Clause powers. *United States v. Morrison*, 529 U.S. 598 (2000); *United States v. Lopez*, 514 U.S. 549 (1995). *But see Gonzales v. Raich*, 545 U.S. 1 (2005) (holding that federal Controlled Substances Act does not exceed Commerce Clause).

There is force to these arguments, but pushed too aggressively, they unwind the fabric of national life. The scarce and migratory quality of natural resources surely permits the constitutional exercise of national conservation measures. Inimical to national unity are judicial decrees that resources which all America may cherish are constitutionally beyond the power of Congress to preserve.

The issue, in fact, goes far beyond the environment. Imagine a scarce mineral or medicinal property found largely within the borders of one state. Imagine Congress further deems such resources important to the national defense or prevention of pandemic. The happenstance of property location should not place it beyond the power of Congress to protect: The same Constitution that rightly limits government's ability to take property[15] likewise furnishes government the tools to guard against its dissipation and to preserve it for the longer haul and larger good.

And while we are at the business of constitutional nationalism, let's raise a toast to the dormant commerce clause. Often maligned as lacking an explicit textual basis or requiring judges to subjectively balance burdens against benefits,[16] the silent commerce clause is an indispensable ingredient of national unity. It has in fact persevered for generations,[17] a testament to its enduring utility as a unifying instrument. The last thing we need in a more global marketplace is a revival of efforts to parochialize at home. The vision of American states compelled to negotiate their own little NAFTAs with one another is no doubt an exaggerated fear. And yet it should sensitize us to the danger of burdening free trade within our national marketplace.[18]

It is the genius of our system that even a strong dose of constitutional nationalism will not enfeeble the states. The Supremacy Clause of Article VI and the preemption doctrines derived from it[19] provide a hefty boost

---

[15] U.S. Const. amend. V.

[16] *See, e.g., Okla. Tax Comm'n v. Jefferson Lines, Inc.*, 514 U.S. 175, 200 (1995) (Scalia, J., concurring) ("[T]he 'negative Commerce Clause' . . . is 'negative' not only because it negates state regulation of commerce, but also because it does not appear in the Constitution.").

[17] *See Cooley v. Bd. of Wardens*, 53 U.S. (12 How.) 299, 319 (1851) (recognizing dormant aspect of Commerce Clause).

[18] *See Gen. Motors Corp. v. Tracy*, 519 U.S. 278, 287 (1997) ("The negative or dormant implication of the Commerce Clause prohibits state taxation or regulation that discriminates against or unduly burdens interstate commerce and thereby impedes free private trade in the national marketplace." (internal citations and quotations omitted)).

[19] *See Gade v. Nat'l Solid Wastes Mgmt. Ass'n*, 505 U.S. 88, 108 (1992) ("[U]nder the Supremacy Clause, from which our pre-emption doctrine is derived, 'any state law, however

for economic nationalism; it is far less certain that they should be utilized to assert a federal cultural supremacy or to erode the benefits of diversity and experimentation within our federal system. Constitutional nationalism will be most effective if, like good parenting, it does not attempt to regulate every subject under the sun.

IV

Let's restore a constitutional respect for community. It is futile to expect a healthy nation in the absence of a healthy sense of community. Community instills within us the sense that we live for something larger and more meaningful than just ourselves. This sense of something larger than the self underlies the successful formation of all communities, be they the village or the nation. Communities are built around shared purposes and values, one of which is surely a respect and appreciation for individual rights. But there must likewise be the sense that individuals contribute to, as well as take from, this larger whole of which we as single persons are but parts.

Today the adjective "constitutional" is invariably associated with the noun "rights." The linkage itself is hardly automatic (the noun might be "structure" or "governance," for example), and the rights revolution that began not coincidentally in the 1960s has left the balance between the individual and society out of whack. For quite a while now, constitutional law has placed a strong emphasis upon rights, often at the expense of community, whether the rights be those of the accused or the victims of discrimination or the practitioners of intimate choice. The Warren Court began the constitutional rights revolution; the Burger Court extended it; and the Rehnquist Court did not curtail it, at least not in any significant way.

Much of this development was decidedly good, because a society that fails to accord respect and dignity to each of its members is not a society worthy of the name. It must still be asked whether the notion of free-floating, i.e., non-textual, constitutional rights of personal autonomy has not helped to deprive us of a sense of connectedness that is indispensable to the formation of collective identity. There is a limit to which individual intimacies should be at the sufferance of majorities, but there are likewise limits to the extent that democratic majorities in a state or nation can be deprived of the communal right to promote cherished values. To enshrine a sanctity of self in our founding charter without textual or historical warrant may be just as pernicious as the attempt to enshrine discrimination

---

clearly within a State's acknowledged power, which interferes with or is contrary to federal law, must yield.'" (quoting *Felder v. Casey*, 487 U.S. 131, 138 (1988))).

against those whose personal choices may for good and legitimate reason fail to conform to the majority's own.

On many of the great questions of the day, our Constitution is consciously agnostic. Its enumeration of rights is significant, but finite. Its grant of powers to representative government is formidable, but it does not prescribe what substantive ends the exercise of those powers must embody. To bend our Constitution in the direction of autonomy or collectivity is detrimental to our national health. I have argued earlier that the rash of constitutional bans on same-sex marriage risks the destruction of the spirit of welcome and inclusiveness on which a sound republic rests.[20] Similarly, the judicially spearheaded rights revolution has left America in too much of a vacuum, where "I" and "me" trump all else.

Each of us can without much trouble compose a lengthy list of rights. But wish lists of rights may be grounded less in law than in desire. So while one might not wish to wear a seat belt, a community is not constitutionally precluded from asserting its prerogative to save others the costs of serious accidents.

When we next drive through the countryside or take a moment's pause, we might reflect on what we get from living in society: We did not build our own home; make our own car or clothes; or invent the computers, phones, lights, or appliances we now take so much for granted. Left alone, we could not enjoy a concert, educate our children, put out a fire, raise capital, or take a trip. We would, in short, be both miserable and helpless. So this unmoored, evolving constitutional notion of the supremacy of the individual is really quite at odds with reality as we experience it. The great exhortation in President Kennedy's inaugural address[21] may seem to some an obsolete plea, but if so, the fault is not that of our forebears. It is not somehow anti-constitutional to think in terms of obligation and responsibility. That document protects democratic prerogative as well as individual liberty. In so doing, it enhances the collective consciousness on which a vital nation must in the end depend.

V

The search for One America requires less polarization, but not necessarily less partisanship. The two must be distinguished. Polarization is the accumulation of personal animosities that is presently tearing us apart. Parti-

---

[20] *See supra* Part II.

[21] "[A]sk not what your country can do for you — ask what you can do for your country." John F. Kennedy, *Presidential Inaugural Address* (Jan. 20, 1961) (transcript available at http://www.yale.edu/lawweb/avalon/presiden/inaug/kennedy.htm).

sanship is more of a mixed bag. It can easily proceed too far, but it can also promote vigorous debate and frame electoral choices.

In a polarized age, the judiciary must assume the duty of lowering national temperatures. National unity requires that courts counteract both partisanship and polarization in the body politic. The judiciary fulfills this mission not only through allegiance to principles of law that transcend political division, but in its demeanor and approach, which should consciously lower volume as political discourse raises it.

It is good for a vital nation to be noisy; it is good for appellate courts to be places of some quiet. By quiet, I do not mean agreement, but civility, decorum, and restraint. The civility and restraint that should mark the judicial calling help satisfy the yearning for some institution of governance that serves the national interest in a non-ideological way.

Are we in the courts fulfilling our charge of counteracting the tendencies of a polarizing age? The answer would depend on whom you ask. On the one hand, it is reassuring that the rank partisanship of the day has not permeated judicial deliberation to a greater degree. On the other hand, the rhetoric in judicial opinions is sometimes personalized to an extent that obscures rather than clarifies real differences. The media identify judges as Republican or Democrat; the confirmation process sends nominees through bruising partisan disputes in which underlying merit is obscured; law clerks are too often chosen with their ideological proclivities uppermost in mind; and new statutes on controversial subjects, as well as eras of past activism, have brought an unprecedented level of interest-group participation in cases as well as confirmations.

All this makes it more difficult for courts to speak calmly, and to fulfill the civilizing and conciliatory function that national strength and unity require.

VI

My sixth recommendation involves the reaffirmation that a unified nation cannot be one in which public allocations and benefits are premised on ethnicity and race. This principle should not be unfamiliar to us. Neutrality as to speech, neutrality as to faith, neutrality as to race. Our country rests on the pillars of neutrality that are the First and Fourteenth Amendments.

The temptations to compromise this principle are ever-present. In the Michigan higher-education cases, the Supreme Court took notice of the need to develop diversity in the nation's future ranks of leadership.[22] And

---

[22] *Gratz v. Bollinger*, 539 U.S. 244, 268-71 (2003); *Grutter v. Bollinger*, 539 U.S. 306, 332

in the challenges to pupil assignment plans in the Louisville and Seattle public school systems, it was argued that race could be contemplated in non-meritocratic settings, and especially in elementary schools where the need to experience the benefits of diversity at a young age was undeniable.[23]

I respect this view. Many good people contend that affirmative action is unifying, not divisive, and that it will help America become a more integrated whole.[24] And others who may subscribe to the general or ultimate value of race neutrality nonetheless find compelling reasons to deviate from the principle in particular contexts,[25] including those noted above.

The need for contextual deviation is often argued sensibly in the singular, but the cumulation of contextual exceptions threatens to swallow the rule of race neutrality whole. Where does that leave us as a nation? It is the rapid diversification of our demographic profile that should render race-based preferences obsolete. Seeking to identify preferred groups and to parcel preferences among them will be a dangerous and divisive enterprise in our multi-ethnic nation. It will become a path to balkanization that America can ill afford. In fact, the increasing numbers of interracial and interethnic marriages make it ever more difficult to ascertain who belongs in what category. And the effort to categorize will prove in itself to be uncomfortably reminiscent of racial engineering efforts undertaken in the darkest hours of human history.

How much better to repair to the bright text and clear command of the Fourteenth Amendment, designed to rejoin us after the searing conflict of the Civil War. It says, ever so simply, that the State shall not "deny to any person within its jurisdiction the equal protection of the laws."[26] It does not speak of groups or of group entitlements. We should not suppose, however, that the Framers meant to embrace through this language a vision of radical individualism. Instead, the Amendment's explicit prohibition of the denial of equal protection to any person reflects the view that

---

(2003).

[23] *Parents Involved in Cmty. Sch. v. Seattle Sch. Dist. No. 1*, 127 S. Ct. 2738, 2755 (2007).

[24] For example, Justice Breyer predicated much of his dissent in *Parents Involved* on the idea that affirmative action would produce "one America." *Id.* at 2824 (Breyer, J., dissenting).

[25] See *Grutter*, 539 U.S. at 343 ("We expect that 25 years from now, the use of racial preferences will no longer be necessary to further the interest approved today."); *Regents of the Univ. of Cal. v. Bakke*, 438 U.S. 265, 403 (1978) (Blackmun, J., concurring) ("At some time, however, beyond any period of what some would claim is only transitional inequality, the United States must and will reach a stage of maturity where action along this line is no longer necessary.").

[26] U.S. Const. amend. XIV, § 1.

the strongest nation will be one in which each and every human being is freed from the yoke of identification and discrimination based on race. Only through this recognition of our common humanity and irreducible dignity will Americans come to see that each of us is one of us, that we journey together, not apart, along history's all too treacherous trail.

VII

My last principle of unity lies in an appreciation of the importance of process. At times, process falls victim to impatience. It is in the nature of ruling classes to want results, and process just seems to get in the way. Process is a particular nuisance to authoritarian temperaments, a reproach to their theory that the end justifies the means. Why bother with warrants and hearings and procedures and trials? And, say the autocrats, why not just snuff out those opposition views and voices that might lead to something so embarrassing as an open debate? Process means accountability, which is why those who exercise power periodically try to hold it in contempt.

A democracy, of course, lives by process. Our nation is held together not only by common values and traditions, but by a mutual respect for the rules of the game. If process is respected, losers can absorb defeat and hope to be winners tomorrow. Process, properly understood, leaves even losers with power — the ability to form a vocal opposition and the chance to mobilize for the next election. Thus does process promote unity. With process open, the doors in a democracy never slam shut.

There has been a great deal of confusion lately about what process actually means. It definitely does not mean litigation above all else. Too much litigation is an utter distortion of process, because it takes decisions from Congress, from state and local governments, from school systems and business organizations, and plops them into federal court, where they were never meant to be. There is a thin line between courts making sure that others abide by law and hijacking the decisionmaking process from them. It is also one thing to preserve civil liberties in wartime and quite another to distort the constitutional process for waging war and conducting foreign affairs. Process involves not only a respect for rights but also a respect for constitutional structure — a profound tension as we adapt the paradigms of criminal justice to suspects in our struggle against terror.

So the process that promotes unity does not have a love of litigation at its core. Rather, it embodies above all the idea of tolerance for others and their points of view. Process requires that legislative bodies, for example, respect the rights of the minority to offer floor amendments and to participate in conference committees, and that judicial bodies honor the rights of the dissenter in internal deliberation as well as external expression. Unity contemplates not some unattainable ideal of homogenization, but that we as a people afford process — that is to say opportunity — for those whose views and perspectives we may not share. When I hear someone say, "We are a Christian nation," that is not right. We are a nation that respects the expression of all religious faiths, including the faith of our Muslim friends. It is that process, that bedrock opportunity for expression of difference, that promotes unity through diversity, and it is that ideal of process that must animate both courts and country.

CONCLUSION

I end where I began. Law has two historic purposes: the protection of liberty and the preservation of order. It is time to add to those a third: the maintenance of One America. This is not a call for homogeneity or hollow patriotism. It is rather a plea for a legal framework within which the dynamics of diversity can be put to their most productive use.

In every way one can imagine, Americans are more different from one another than ever before. That is no cause for despair. It is simply a recognition that law can help us to acknowledge and appreciate all we have in common. Or it can drive us irretrievably apart.

Some may question why a sense of national unity is so necessary. It is not simply that national identification helps America present a stronger front against its global adversaries. It is not just that national allegiance helps to overcome the impulse of racial and ethnic separatism. What truly matters is that the great national goals of strength, prosperity, freedom, and humanity become impossible without the capacity to summon some sense of America itself.

It has long been assumed that the promotion of unity was purely a political task, and that law and the judiciary were meant to sit on the sidelines. That is no longer true. Promoting mutual respect, if not agreement, among Americans should figure in judicial judgment. A greater commitment to national unity can properly be expressed through the noble medium of the law. Indeed it must be. One America is too important for one entire branch of government to ignore.

MAY

PLEADING THE BELLY: THE GROANING JULIET

By John V. Orth, with the assistance of Joseph L. Hyde

The Provost, in charge of the prison, asks Angelo: *What shall be done, sir, with the groaning Juliet? / She's very near her hour.* And the deputy brusquely replies: *See you the fornicatress be removed: / Let her have needful, but not lavish, means.* Pregnant female criminals condemned to death were entitled to a stay of execution; their plea came to be called "pleading the belly."[1] But there is no mention in *Measure for Measure* of eventually executing Juliet, even though the Duke, when he confirms that this *most offenseful act / Was mutually committed,* tells her that her sin was *of heavier kind than his* — another example of the play's "unequal justice."

The possibility of pleading the belly to delay execution provided ample scope for ribald comedy. In John Gay's *The Beggar's Opera* (1720) the prison-keeper Lockit and the petty criminal Filch discuss the practicalities:

> *Lockit*: Why, boy, thou lookest as if thou wert half starved; like a shotten herring.
>
> *Filch*: One had need to have the constitution of a horse to go

---

[1] See James Oldham, On Pleading the Belly, 6 *Criminal Justice History* 1 (1985).

through the business. Since the favourite child-getter was disabled by a mishap, I have picked up a little money by helping the ladies to a pregnancy against their being called down to sentence. But if a man cannot get an honest livelihood any easier way, I am sure 'tis what I can't undertake for another Session.

Lockit: Truly, if that great man should tip off, 'twould be an irreparable loss. The vigour and prowess of a knight-errant never saved half the ladies in distress that he hath done.[2]

continued on page 341 . . .

STATE V. JOSE DEJESUS

947 A.2d 873, 875-76 (R.I. May 29, 2008)

Francis X. Flaherty, Associate Justice

"Who knows himself a braggart, Let him fear this[,] for it will come to pass[,] That every braggart shall be found an ass." (William Shakespeare, *All's Well that Ends Well*, act 4, sc. 3.) The defendant Jose DeJesus appeals the judgments of conviction for murder (count 1), first-degree robbery (count 2), discharging a firearm during the commission of a crime of violence with death resulting (count 3), carrying a pistol without a license (count 4), and possessing a firearm after a previous conviction for a crime of violence (count 5).

On April 11, 2003, Mauricio Flores, the operator of a small family business in the Mount Pleasant section of Providence, was shot in the face during the robbery of his store, the Flores Market. The robber escaped with a few hundred dollars. Mauricio's wife, Teresa Flores, also was working in the store at the time of the robbery; she made a hysterical 9-1-1 call to seek help for her mortally wounded husband. Tragically, Mauricio died from his wounds one hundred seven days later.

Law enforcement's attention eventually focused on defendant . . . While defendant was incarcerated on unrelated charges, Thomas Viera, DeJesus' cellmate, acted as an informant for the police and recorded defendant boasting as he described the gruesome details of the crime. The defendant's braggadocio proved to be instrumental in his downfall.

For the reasons stated in this opinion, we affirm the judgments of conviction.

---

[2] John Gay, *The Beggar's Opera* 3.3 (1728).

❧ MAY ❧

SUN	MON	TUES	WED	THUR	FRI	SAT
31					1	2
3	4	5	6	7	8	9
10	11	12	13	14	15	16
17	18	19	20	21	22	23
24	25	26	27	28	29	30

THE LIFE OF KING HENRY THE FIFTH
ACT 4, SCENE 3

William Shakespeare

WESTMORELAND
    O that we now had here
    But one ten thousand of those men in England
    That do no work to-day!

HENRY
    What's he that wishes so?
    My cousin Westmoreland? No, my fair cousin:
    If we are mark'd to die, we are enow
    To do our country loss; and if to live,
    The fewer men, the greater share of honour.
    God's will! I pray thee, wish not one man more.
    By Jove, I am not covetous for gold,
    Nor care I who doth feed upon my cost;

It yearns me not if men my garments wear;
Such outward things dwell not in my desires:
But if it be a sin to covet honour,
I am the most offending soul alive.
No, faith, my coz, wish not a man from England:
God's peace! I would not lose so great an honour
As one man more, methinks, would share from me
For the best hope I have. O, do not wish one more!
Rather proclaim it, Westmoreland, through my host,
That he which hath no stomach to this fight,
Let him depart; his passport shall be made
And crowns for convoy put into his purse:
We would not die in that man's company
That fears his fellowship to die with us.
This day is called the feast of Crispian:
He that outlives this day, and comes safe home,
Will stand a tip-toe when the day is named,
And rouse him at the name of Crispian.
He that shall live this day, and see old age,
Will yearly on the vigil feast his neighbours,
And say 'To-morrow is Saint Crispian:'
Then will he strip his sleeve and show his scars,
And say 'These wounds I had on Crispin's day.'
Old men forget: yet all shall be forgot,
But he'll remember with advantages
What feats he did that day: then shall our names.
Familiar in his mouth as household words
Harry the king, Bedford and Exeter,
Warwick and Talbot, Salisbury and Gloucester,
Be in their flowing cups freshly remember'd.
This story shall the good man teach his son;
And Crispin Crispian shall ne'er go by,
From this day to the ending of the world,
But we in it shall be remember'd;
We few, we happy few, we band of brothers;
For he to-day that sheds his blood with me
Shall be my brother; be he ne'er so vile,
This day shall gentle his condition:
And gentlemen in England now a-bed
Shall think themselves accursed they were not here,
And hold their manhoods cheap whiles any speaks
That fought with us upon Saint Crispin's day.

THE JUSTICE, THE GOVERNOR, AND THE DICTATOR

from

IN RECKLESS HANDS:
SKINNER V. OKLAHOMA AND THE NEAR-TRIUMPH
OF AMERICAN EUGENICS

Victoria F. Nourse[†]

[E]ugenics is as large as man's capacity to hope and dream, as deep as his capacity to penetrate and control the laws of his own nature, and as wide as his capacity to organize his social efforts to ever more and more fruitful ends.

—*Albert E. Wiggam, popular science writer, 1927*[1]

The year is 1932, the third year of the Depression, a hungry year, a year of labor violence and kidnappings and odd spontaneous eruptions of the never-employed. The place is the Vinita, Oklahoma, asylum for the insane and feebleminded. Pajama-clad bodies are huddling "in little knots" on the exercising porch, jittery and muttering, whispering to avoid the attendants' ears. Some, the more courageous ones, asked for copies of the law that frightened them. One trusted patient, a reporter who committed himself to Vinita to cure his alcoholism, held a copy of the statute close, worried that he would be mobbed. The patients were searching for a law decreeing that they should never have children — that all imbeciles, epileptics, insane or feebleminded persons were to be sterilized, in the name

---

[†] Victoria F. Nourse is the L.Q.C. Lamar Professor of Law at the Emory University School of Law. Copyright © 2008 by Victoria F. Nourse. This excerpt of *In Reckless Hands: Skinner v. Oklahoma and the Near-Triumph of American Eugenics* is reprinted with permission of the publisher, W.W. Norton & Company, Inc., and of the author.
[1] Albert E. Wiggam, The Next Age of Man 399 (1927).

of eugenics.[2]

The doctors at the Vinita asylum told patients that it was for the best; they said that mothers could go back to their children and families would be reunited. It was cruel to keep people in a hospital for their entire lives when they could go home, safely. Sterilization, the doctors urged, was compassionate, not cruel. Some patients said they would do anything if they could go home. Some wanted to die: "If they do that to me, they might as well kill me . . . If they don't I'll kill myself anyhow . . . I won't give a damn what becomes of me." Others sought revenge: "I'll kill the man who orders it done if it takes the rest of my life." One patient bemoaned the fact that "[n]one of us can go into court and fight it. Most of us haven't a dime." Another added: "We can not use a telephone . . . [or] send out a telegram without special permission . . . We are hedged in; practically buried."[3]

The men and women inside the Vinita asylum never challenged the statute that frightened them. Men more dangerous and familiar with law, men in Oklahoma's McAlester prison, would battle the law and the science of eugenics, in a case that would become known as *Skinner v. Oklahoma*.

•   •   •   •

On December 22, 1933, an odd troika of men — a justice, a governor and a dictator — appeared in the largest-circulation paper in New York City, the tabloid *New York Daily News*. Oliver Wendell Holmes, Jr., the most famous justice of the United States Supreme Court, was painted in his library, looking distinguished and characteristically dapper, with a vested suit, handlebar mustache, pocket watch, and book in hand. Above him was a portrait of Alfalfa Bill Murray, the populist governor of Oklahoma, collar points askew but, with his spectacles, appearing seriously engaged. Beside them was the dictator who made it a tabloid affair. Their appearance together reflected a shared knowledge and approval of eugenics and sterilization.[4]

Although hardly a household name today, Alfalfa Bill Murray was one of the more famous governors in America at the time. He was a colorful character, a politician likened to the wild "genius" of the state he had helped to create. Murray was beloved for his straight talk, his hobo's look,

---

[2] Behind the Door of Delusion by "Inmate Ward 8" [Vinita Memoir] 125-126, 134 (William W. Savage, Jr. & James H. Lazalier eds., 1994, 1932).

[3] Id. at 125-26, 128, 133-134.

[4] Julia McCarthy, *Sterilization — How it Works*, NYDN at 31 (Dec. 22, 1933).

his long wrinkled brow and tousled mop of hair. When local newspapers ridiculed Murray for wearing trousers that didn't cover his ankles, letting his underwear show, and living in a house with dirt floors and outdoor plumbing, Murray embraced the charges, knowing that many of his supporters, poor farmers, had more to worry about than the length of his rumpled linen suit.[5]

In 1933, the long night of the Depression had already fallen. Murray campaigned for the governorship by blasting Wall Street and big business, carrying along a pound of cheese and a box of crackers as a symbol of both his and the people's poverty. When he won, he pledged, "by the Eternal God," that he would protect the poor and unemployed, telling Oklahomans that as long as he could utter a breath, he would care for the "farmer without seeds to plant" and the "starving children" of the working man. Murray promised to be the governor not only of the "better element," but of "Oklahoma Indians, niggers, and po' white folks." By 1932, his righteous pioneer politics would land him on the cover of *Time* magazine, and helped launch his "bread, butter, bacon and beans" bid for the presidency.[6]

Once in the governor's office, Alfalfa Bill thrilled the national press with the image of the ornery self-made Westerner. They loved his campaign song, "Hoover Made A Soup Houn' Outa Me," his bewhiskered face, his appeal to down-and-out farmers, his story about being born in a "cotton patch," and his prairie jargon topped off with references to Aristotle. There were good reasons to admire him. Murray's definition of a politician was above reproach: a man "too honest to be bought; too wise to be deceived; too brave to be intimidated." And the times were right for his populist message; as the news magazines put it, Murray was the "political darling of really poor men everywhere." Murray was choked with emotion when, in 1931, he screamed at the state Senate for blocking his tax proposals: "With men and women under the very shadow of the capitol begging for clothing and food, you with big salaries in your fine hotels cannot understand the danger."[7]

Governor Murray was full of contradictions. He was an avid constitutionalist, a reader who clung to a library of five thousand volumes even in his leanest years. And yet he would become known less for his learning

---

[5] RD at 49 (Mar. 1932); Time at cover, 15-16 (Feb. 29, 1932); NYT at 12 (July 28, 1934); Keith L. Bryant, Jr., Alfalfa Bill Murray 184 (1968); James R. Scales & Danney Goble, Oklahoma Politics: A History 170 (1982).

[6] *See* Time at cover, 14-16 (Feb. 29, 1932); HW at 9 (Oct. 31, 1931); Oklahoma's Governors, 1929-1955 54 (LeRoy H. Fischer ed., 1983); Bryant, *supra* note 5, at 190.

[7] Time at 14-16 (Feb. 29, 1932); HW at 5 (Feb. 7, 1931); Bryant, *supra* note 5, at 215.

than for his militarism. Murray would declare martial law no less than thirty-four times during his tenure as governor, whether to regulate the price of oil, to enforce the color line in Oklahoma City, or to police the sale of football tickets at the University of Oklahoma. No wonder newspapers said, in the early days of the Depression, that, like Huey Long, Murray was becoming one of the nation's more notorious "strong men."[8]

In 1933, Governor Murray had been supporting Oklahoma's sterilization law for two years. The law he signed in 1931 sought to sterilize persons "afflicted with hereditary forms of insanity" as well as "idiocy, imbecility, feeblemindedness, or epilepsy," whether those persons were housed in asylums or in any institution supported by public funds, a term broad enough to cover the state's prisons. Murray hoped that the law would not only reduce the number of inmates in Oklahoma's asylums, but also frighten criminals out of the state. In this, Murray was no pioneer, nor was he uneducated. Many of America's most respected geneticists, biologists, zoologists, and social scientists held out the hope that crime, mental illness, and even poverty might be traced to genes. As Edwin Grant Conklin, a Princeton biologist, explained: "All modern geneticists approve the segregation or sterilization of persons who are known to have serious hereditary defects." By 1928, over 375 American universities and colleges taught courses in eugenics, as many as 20,000 students took these courses, and 70 percent of high school biology textbooks endorsed eugenics in some form. America was not alone; eugenics was a worldwide phenomenon, stretching from Canada to Denmark and Sweden and beyond.[9]

By 1933, sterilization laws spanned the nation from California to Vermont, some decades old; twenty-seven of the forty-eight states had sterilization laws. Not surprisingly, there were those in Oklahoma who feared that the state was behind the times. Although Murray's attempt to use the law against criminals appeared novel, habitual offenders had been the subject of the earliest sterilization laws, reaching back to the first decade of

---

[8] RD, *supra* note 5, at 49, 51-52 (Mar. 1932); NYT at E6 (Dec. 10, 1933); Time at 15 (Aug. 3, 1931); Time at 9 (Aug. 17, 1931); Time at 9-10 (Aug. 31, 1931); Oklahoma's Governors, *supra* note 6, at 63; Scales and Goble, *supra* note 5, at 167.

[9] 1931 Okla. Sess. Laws ch. 26, sec. 1, at 80; Time at 14 (May 4, 1931); TDW at 13 (Apr. 23, 1931); LD at 20 (May 23, 1931); Edwin G. Conklin, *The Purposive Improvement of the Human Race*, in Human Biology and Racial Welfare 577 (Edmund V. Cowdry ed., 1930); Steven Selden, Inheriting Shame: The Story of Eugenics and Racism in America 48-49, 64 (1999); The Wellborn Science: Eugenics in Germany, France, Brazil, and Russia (Mark B. Adams ed., 1990); Eugenics and the Welfare State: Sterilization Policy in Denmark, Sweden, Norway and Finland (Gunnar Broberg & Nils Roll-Hansen eds., 2005).

the century.[10] In Oklahoma, newspapers proudly announced that sterilization was a "terrific blow in the protection of society," and a "very advanced step, sanctioned by many of the leading medical authorities and criminologists of the country." Even the critics held out hope for progress, fearing the remedy drastic yet lauding Oklahoma's policy as a "pioneering movement in social science."[11]

Eugenics was controversial for some; sterilization laws were loudly opposed by the Catholic Church, for example. But there was also a long history, by 1933, of politicians on both the right and left who supported these laws. There were nativists like Madison Grant, whose bestselling book *The Passing of the Great Race* extolled the Nordic race and fretted about democracy's tendency to yield "lower types." There were also reformers like Margaret Sanger, who saw in eugenics the hope that law could provide release from suffering. The great progressive president Theodore Roosevelt preached the virtues of Anglo-Saxon blood and warned of the failure of the better classes to breed at the same rate as their inferiors, a phenomenon he said could lead to "race death." By the 1930's, eugenics attracted a large and diverse political following, from Junior Leagues and school principals and the Kiwanis to prohibitionists and birth control advocates and anti-miscegenationsists.[12]

Like many progressives, Murray would defend eugenics as a measure to prevent suffering — as prevention of everything from crime to birth defects. "Sterilization is not a punishment but a protection," he explained. "By preventing reproduction, one of the basic causes [of weak minds] can be cured." Murray's favorite story about sterilization appealed neither to nature nor to genetics, but to the fears of every parent. "The most honorable lawyer I ever knew, able and upright, with whom I once practiced,

---

[10] McCarthy, *supra* note 4. Laughlin, at 15-34, enumerates many pre-1922 sterilization laws which included habitual criminals and those convicted of rape and perversity (Indiana, Washington, California, Nevada, Iowa, New Jersey, New York, North Dakota, Kansas, Wisconsin, Nebraska). Landman, at 63-87, demonstrates that post-1922 laws did the same (North Dakota, Michigan, Nebraska, Oregon, Idaho, and Utah). This is true despite the fact that, at the time, it was often said that these laws were inactive.

[11] HW at 6 (Apr. 25, 1931); HW at 14 (Apr. 18, 1931); LD at 20 (May 23, 1931).

[12] Madison Grant, The Passing of the Great Race 5 (1921); Margaret Sanger, The Pivot of Civilization ch.4 (1922); Margaret Sanger, Motherhood in Bondage 100-01 (1928); Paul at 102-3 (quoting Roosevelt); Larson, at 73-74, 132-33 (groups); LAT at A6 (May 1, 1934); NYT at 7 (Dec. 29, 1934); ON at 2 (Nov. 4, 1934) (Kiwanis); W.A. Plecker, *Virginia's Effort to Preserve Racial Integrity*, in A Decade of Progress in Eugenics 105-12 (1934); Bartlett C. Jones, Prohibition and Eugenics: 1920-1933, 18 J. Hist. Med. 158, 160 (Apr. 1963). On Catholic opposition, Syracuse Herald at 2 (Dec. 24, 1933); ON at 2 (Oct. 10, 1934).

has two sons, and they are both in the Institution at Enid, because he, at sixteen years of age, contracted syphilis. Infection was prevented but it did not purify the blood. I am sure [that] he had rather been sterilized."[13] In this, Murray echoed those who claimed that, far from being cruel, sterilization was compassionate: "If you loved your children, surely you would want to spare them the suffering . . . If you were blind, congenitally deaf, epileptic, or insane, would you conceivably want to have children badly enough to run the risk of passing on these defects to them?" Some went even further, invoking the language of rights. Harry Laughlin, a tireless promoter of sterilization laws, declared that the state had the "inherent right" to set up its biological standards, as a matter of self-protection. The zoologist Michael Guyer went further, dubbing the right to a eugenic birth the "right of rights."[14]

Although such pronouncements sound outrageous today, at the time eugenics was a good deal more banal than we imagine. Like all sciences, eugenics was proud and insistent, but its subject was close to home. "What's bred in the bone," "blood will tell," "chip off the old block" — were the familiar sayings that people used to explain their lives and families. These were also the phrases that the apostles of eugenics used to popularize the creed that its founder, Francis Galton, claimed should become a scientific religion. When critics suggested that there might be something terribly dangerous about it all, supporters simply asked: Who could deny that "it was better to be healthy than sick, vigorous than weak, well fitted than ill fitted"?[15]

In the early 1930s, eugenics appeared frequently in the anodyne language of health. Good marriages were termed eugenic, there were eugenic babies, eugenic theories of child-raising, and even eugenic housing. Eugenicists urged mothers to fill out baby books (to trace the family pedigree) and divorce lawyers urged couples to separate based on eugenic

---

[13] Time at 14 (May 4, 1931); William Murray, 3 Memoirs of Governor Murray and True History of Oklahoma 639 (1945).

[14] Leon Whitney, The Case for Sterilization 53-54 (1934); Harry Laughlin, *Further Studies on the Historical and Legal Development of Eugenical Sterilization in the United States* at 96, GP, 11.7 (1936); Michael F. Guyer, Being Well-Born, preface (2d ed. 1927) ("right of rights"); Fred Hogue, *Social Eugenics*, LAT at I23 (Apr. 10, 1938) ("just what are the rights that would be infringed upon. It would be the right to function as a carrier of venereal diseases or the right of the feebleminded to reproduce their kind.").

[15] Editorial, *Blood Will Tell*, Sat. Even. Post at 30 (Mar. 21, 1925); Guyer, supra note 14, at 1; Francis Galton, *Eugenics: Its Definition, Scope, and Aims*, Nature at 82 (May 26, 1904) ("it must be introduced into the national conscience, like a new religion"); Francis Galton, *Studies in Eugenics*, 11 Am. J. of Sociology 11, 20, 24 (1905).

reasoning (a fear that their progeny would be unfit). Housing was eugenic if children flourished, marriages were eugenic if their progeny were healthy, and child-raising was eugenic if it focused on health rather than on the superficial qualities of beauty or success. Eugenics inspired everything from baby contests to poetry to art.[16]

The Depression lent a new sense of urgency to questions of public health, as portraits of destitute and sick children began to appear on the front pages of the newspapers.[17] Eugenics had always thrived on a sense of doom, that the germ plasm (an early term for the gene) was degenerating, that the numbers of insane or impoverished people were increasing exponentially. By the 1930s, this seemed less theoretical, less a question of future population than of everyday life. Any day now, the tent-city rabble might march, the new governor might turn out to be a Red, the labor unions might beat the living daylights out of businessmen, the color line might be broken, marching farmers might occupy the statehouse.

To some, it seemed almost as if the world hung on the edge of a moral abyss. As one Oklahoma editorialist put it: "The old code that lifted men, in spite of their savage impulses, to honor, nobility and decency," was dead; "standing as we do between two worlds, one that is dying and another not yet born, a new code of behavior, a new ethic [has] not been put in its place."[18] By the 1930s, degeneration was no longer merely a theoretical preoccupation; it was a daily worry about whether democracy or life had spent itself, whether the world was spiraling into self-destruction. In a day of dust and drought and depression, the degeneration of the race might well have felt too palpable to be dismissed as the obsession of a few.

If there were doubts about sterilization, the Depression removed them. There wasn't any money left. On January 15, 1933, ten thousand farmers threatened to march on the Oklahoma capital to force relief. Meanwhile, the heads of Oklahoma's asylums and prisons had warned Governor Murray that they were bursting at the seams, with men lining the walls in cots, constantly threatening riot or escape. At the asylums, it was thought that sterilization would allow the release of borderline cases

---

[16] LAT at II, 1 (Mar. 9, 1915) (eugenic babies); *Over Thousand Babies in Eugenic Congress*, LAT at II, 7 (Mar. 7, 1915) ("eugenic congress" of babies); Fred Hogue, Social Eugenics, LAT at 31 (Jan. 5, 1936) (housing); id. at 30 (Mar. 22, 1936); Paul Popenoe & Roswell Johnson, Applied Eugenics 200-01 (1920) (marriage and divorce); Paul A. Lombardo, *Eugenic Sterilization in Virginia: Aubrey Strode and the Case of Buck v. Bell* 114 (Ph.D. diss. 1982) (poetry); Popular Eugenics: National Efficiency and American Mass Culture in the 1930s (Susan Currell & Christina Cogdell eds., 2006) (art).

[17] Frances Corry, ON at 1A (Nov. 5, 1933).

[18] Edith Johnson, DO at 8 (Feb. 3, 1933).

dangerous only because of their potential to propagate. As for the prisons, it was hoped that sterilization would frighten men so much that they would leave the territory. In a day when California deported its "indigent" poor on trains to their "native" states, and Governor Murray issued banishment paroles, Oklahoma hoped to prevent criminals from even entering the state.[19]

• • • •

If Oklahoma's sterilization law made Alfalfa Bill rather obvious pictorial fodder for the *New York Daily News,* there is still the puzzle of why, in late December 1933, his picture was situated above (of all places) that of Oliver Wendell Holmes, Jr., one of the most revered legal minds in the country. Lawyers are familiar with the answer: Governor Murray could not have hoped to do what he was doing without support from the Constitution. And there was no single human being in the United States more important in making sterilization the constitutional law of the land than Holmes.

Before World War I, during the burst of intellectual enthusiasm for eugenics, at least twelve states had passed laws calling for sterilization. By 1924, over thirty bills had been passed. Outside California, very few of these laws were implemented in any significant way. They were not implemented because of legal doubts; doctors feared that, in performing the operation, they could be found to have committed a crime (the ancient crime of mayhem, defined as the intentional destruction of body parts). The result was that very few sterilizations were actually performed before the late 1920s. In many states, the law was window-dressing, a "dead letter" (as the eugenicists themselves put it).[20]

All that would change with Justice Holmes's opinion in the Supreme Court's 1927 decision in *Buck v. Bell.*[21] Carrie Buck's case would become one of the most infamous of the twentieth century. The eighteen-year-old girl had been sent to a home for the feeble-minded, the same one in which her mother, Emma, resided. Carrie had had a child out of wedlock and the

---

[19] ON at 1, 7 (Feb. 15, 1933) (farmers); TDW at 12 (May 24, 1931) (California deports to other states); DO at 4A (Jan. 1, 1933) (banishment paroles); TDW at 4 (Jan. 2, 1933) (overcrowding); HW at 16 (Jan. 10, 1931) (asylums).

[20] Phillip Reilly, The Surgical Solution 39 (1991) (sixteen states passed laws between 1907 and 1913, but four vetoed); Landman at 290-293 (bills, App. B); *id.* at 252 (mayhem); Paul Popenoe, *Eugenical Sterilization: A Review,* 14 J. of Heredity 308, 309 (1923) ("dead letter").

[21] *Buck v. Bell,* 274 U.S. 200 (1927).

state of Virginia sought to sterilize her on the theory that her offspring, then only seven months old, represented the third generation of degeneracy in the family. Decades later, researchers would find evidence that Carrie had been rather successful at classwork (she had been taken out of school and put to work by her foster parents while only in the sixth grade). They would also find that Carrie Buck's child was of normal intelligence and that Carrie, along with many others, had been institutionalized largely based on the idea that she was immoral, loose, given to improper affections. Only later would the travesty of Carrie's case be discovered: Carrie Buck's daughter was the product of rape and Carrie was institutionalized to avoid bringing shame to her foster family. [22]

In the commitment papers, Carrie's foster family claimed that she was feebleminded, epileptic, or both. At her trial, Carrie was described as "incapable of self-support and restraint." Though she was eighteen when tested, Carrie scored at the level of a nine-year-old on the revised Stanford-Binet intelligence test. [23] The term "feebleminded" was no vague epithet at the time but a quasi-medical term encompassing persons we might today call insane, others we might call mentally disabled, and many who were no different from you or me. In 1927, however, the world of the "subnormal" — of the "feebleminded" — was divided among three technical classes: idiots, imbeciles, and morons. Idiots had a mental age of one or two, imbeciles between three and seven, and morons between eight and twelve. These terms were widely used in the field of psychology and psychiatry, not to mention sociology and social work. To apply them required the emerging discipline of intelligence testing. [24]

The testing vogue began after World War I, when one million intelligence exams were administered to men in the Army. A standard early version asked questions like the following: "The *Knight* engine is used in the Packard, Lozier, Stearns, or Pierce Arrow? The Wyandotte is a kind of horse, fowl, cattle, or granite? *Isaac Pittman* was most famous in physics, shorthand, railroading, or electricity? *Bud Fisher* is famous as an actor, author, baseball player, or comic artist? *Salsify* is a kind of snake, fish, lizard,

---

[22] Kevles at 110; Paul A. Lombardo, *Three Generations, No Imbeciles: New Light on Buck v. Bell*, 60 N.Y.U. L. Rev. 30, 52-53, 61 (1985); *id.* at 54 (based on Lombardo's interview with Buck, Carrie was raped by the nephew of her foster mother, Mrs. Dobbs). J. David Smith & K. Ray Nelson, The Sterilization of Carrie Buck 1, 3-6 (1989).

[23] Lombardo, *supra* note 22, at 54 (epileptic claim); *id.* at 32 n. 10 (nine-year-old on the Stanford-Binet); Lombardo, *supra* note 16, at 203 (quoting Harry Laughlin) (incapable of "self-support and restraint," "a record of immorality, prostitution and untruthfulness").

[24] *See* Henry H. Goddard, Feeble-Mindedness: Its Causes and Consequences (1920); Paul at 59 (tiered system).

or vegetable? *Rosa Bonheur* is famous as a poet, painter, composer, or sculptor? *Cheviot* is the name of a fabric, drink, dance, or food?"[*]

Not surprisingly, America's fighting men turned out to be less intelligent than they, or anyone else, imagined. It was reported widely that the average intelligence of American army recruits was not much more than a moron, hovering around the fourteen-year-old level. And, if that were true, "nearly half of the white draft (47.3 percent)" was "feebleminded." Despite the obvious absurdity of this result, the survey inspired enormous respect, and a great deal of fear, for it fit with burgeoning worries about population decline — "degeneration," they often called it. This was not simply a matter of a few people in an asylum, a few Carrie Bucks, but the fate of the nation, a nation apparently slouching toward stupidity.[25]

To the public, the scientific glue holding these claims together was the idea of feeblemindedness as fixed and permanent, an inherited trait of great danger. The feebleminded immigrant was routinely blamed for the waves of crime reported after World War I. The feebleminded would even be blamed for flooding the labor market and causing the Depression. If, as the army tests had seemed to show, the average intelligence of Americans approached that of the feebleminded, was it any surprise that the poor were starving? How was a nation of morons to sustain a market economy, in this fast and sophisticated age of the machine gun and motorcar? As one of America's leading scientific eugenicists put it in 1932: "in this world . . . of the reign of terror of the criminal, of the tragedy of unemployment, eugenics ceases to be the cult of the few pioneers . . . it is forced on our attention." It was not so far from bodily contagion to the body politic.[26]

Curiously, even those who claimed to be the inventors of this science of intelligence testing recognized that what they were talking about was a

---

[*] The answers are Knight Engine: Stearns; Wyandotte: fowl; shorthand; Bud Fisher: comic artist; salsify: vegetable; Rosa Bonheur: painter; Cheviot: fabric. Paul at 66 (reprinting facsimile test). The test is taken from *Psychological Examining in the United States Army*, 15 Memoirs of the Nat'l Acad. of Sciences (Robert M. Yerkes ed., 1921) (examination Alpha, Test 8: Information, Forms 8 & 9).

[25] Paul at 67 ("half of the white draft"); Daniel Kevles, *Testing the Army's Intelligence: Psychologists and the Military in World War I*, 55 J. of Am. Hist. 565-81 (1968).

[26] When the psychologist and eugenicist Goddard administered intelligence tests to immigrants at Ellis Island, he found that 40 percent of recent immigrants were feebleminded. The foreign-born were at the time often charged with causing crime. Paul at 108 (Goddard); *id.* at 99 (crime and foreign-born); Goddard, *supra* note 24, at 571-572; 3 Murray, *supra* note 13, at 639 (1945) (feebleminded causing Depression); *Eugenics As the Cure for All the Race's Ills*, 114 LD 22, 23 (Sept. 10, 1932) ("forced our attention").

moral and social order. The psychologist Henry Goddard, who did more than anyone in the early part of the century to promote the idea of feeblemindedness, explained that the feebleminded differed from the dull normal person because they could not tell right from wrong. Carl Brigham, the psychologist who helped design the army tests, explained that "the diagnosis is . . . in the last analysis, a social diagnosis." Even a person who passed the intelligence test might be determined to be feebleminded, if judged to be "incapable of performing [his or her] duties as a member of society." "[S]ocial inadequacy," sometimes termed "social inefficiency," made at least some of these people "weak-minded."[27]

Eugenics reveled in the appearance of the feebleminded. One of the most well-known "feebleminded" persons in the United States, Deborah Kallikak (whose life was made famous by Goddard), was astonishing to those who studied her because of her beauty, sweet demeanor, and her ability to do a variety of complex tasks despite her very low scores on intelligence tests. In the end, the judgment was that Kallikak had to be feebleminded because she was "socially inadequate." That judgment, in turn, was based in part on the fact that she had the "unmistakable look of the feeble-minded," that a "glance sufficed to establish" low mentality. As eugenics popularizer Leon Whitney would put it in his book on sterilization: "We can visit the institutions where some of them are segregated, and see for ourselves what they look like; decide whether they seem good social animals." Goddard was so convinced of the "look" that, as Stephen Jay Gould would ultimately unearth, he doctored the pictures in his books to make the "unfit" appear sinister.[28]

It was the "look" that would in the end spell the greatest difficulty in Carrie Buck's case. Experts insisted that Carrie was feebleminded. Part of the proof lay in Carrie's mother, who was also institutionalized as feebleminded based on a "record during life of immorality, prostitution, and untruthfulness." The other evidence was Carrie's seven-month-old child,

---

[27] Paul at 59 (Brigham quotation, right and wrong per Goddard); Heredity and Eugenics: A course of lectures 280-281 (William E. Castle et al. eds., 1912) (Davenport lecture) (feeblemindedness is a "lumber room" that includes the inability to "appreciate moral ideas" and inability to "control the appetites and passions"); *Feeblemindedness*, 6 J. of Heredity 32, 32 (1915) ("incapable of performing duties"); John Lewis Gillin, Criminology and Penology 177 (1926) (feebleminded as no different from children); on the equation of social inadequacy and feeblemindedness, *The Unempoyables*, Eugenical News 128 (Sept.-Oct. 1934); Lombardo, *supra* note 16, at 163 ("socially inadequate classes").

[28] Henry H. Goddard, The Kallikak Family 77 (1931 edition, reprinted 1973, first edition 1912) ("unmistakable look of the feeble-minded"); *id.* at 78 ("glance suffered to establish"); Stephen Jay Gould, The Mismeasure of Man 171 (1981); Whitney, *supra* note 14, at 110.

Vivian. A social worker, influenced by those who ran the asylum, concluded that "[t]here is a look about [the child] that is not quite normal, but just what it is, I can't tell." The baby was said not to be developing properly in her foster family — the same one that had thrown Carrie out. As one witness summed up the three generations: "These people belong to the shiftless, ignorant, and worthless class of anti-social whites of the South."[29]

Carrie Buck's case was pursued by Virginia officials with the Constitution in mind. In 1917, Dr. Priddy, the head of the hospital where Carrie was institutionalized, had a legal problem. He was an enthusiastic advocate of sterilization, so enthusiastic that he had gone ahead and sterilized the wife and child of a local workingman and was promptly sued. Although Priddy won the case, he was warned by the court not to engage in any more sterilization operations without more precise legislative authority. By 1924, Priddy and others had convinced the Virginia legislature to pass a law providing for the sterilization of inmates within the asylum. Even those who advocated the law had "grave doubt[s]" about whether it would withstand constitutional scrutiny.[30]

Carrie's best friend in this matter was less her lawyer (a friend of Dr. Priddy and a founding member of the institution that sought to sterilize her) than the law itself.[31] At the time, existing legal precedents were clearly in Carrie's favor. Before World War I, there had already been several constitutional challenges to sterilization laws in state courts; six of seven challenges had been successful.[32] There were difficulties, of course. There was a great deal of confusion among lawyers about why sterilization laws were unconstitutional. Some courts found that the laws violated

---

[29] Paul A. Lombardo, *Medicine, Eugenics, and the Supreme Court: From Coercive Sterilization to Reproductive Freedom,* 13 Contemp. Health L. & Pol. 1, 9 (1996); Lombardo, *supra* note 16, at 189 ("a look about it"); Lombardo, *supra* note 22, at 51 ("shiftless, ignorant").

[30] Lombardo, *supra* note 22, at 40-45 ("Priddy suit"); A.S. Priddy to Harry Laughlin, in Smith & Nelson, *supra* note 22, at 56 ("grave doubt"); Lombardo, *supra* note 16, at 143, 154.

[31] Lombardo, *supra* note 22, at 35; *id.* at 33 (collusive suit); *id.* at 56-58.

[32] Prior to 1922, only one of seven challenges upheld a sterilization law: (1) *Smith v. Board of Examiners,* 88 A. 963 (N.J. 1913); (2) *Davis v. Berry,* 216 F. 413 (S.D. Iowa 1914) *found moot,* 242 U.S. 468 (1917); (3) *Haynes v. Lapeer,* 166 N.W. 938 (Mich. 1918); (4) *Osborn v. Thomson,* 169 N.Y.S. 638 (N.Y. Misc. 1918), *aff'd,* 171 N.Y.S. 1094 (N.Y. App. Div. 1918); (5) *Mickle v. Henrichs,* 262 F. 687 (D. Nev. 1918); (6) *Williams v. Smith,* 131 N.E. 2 (Ind. 1921); but *see* (7) *State v. Feilen,* 126 P. 75 (Wa. 1912) which upheld a sterilization law. *See also* the 1921 decision in *State Bd. of Eugenics v. Cline* (Or. Cir. Ct. Marion Co. Dec. 13, 1921) (unreported opinion) in Laughlin at 287-89 ("the 1917 Statute . . . clearly violates the provisions of the state and federal constitution prohibiting class legislation.").

equal protection; others focused on cruel and unusual punishment; still others on procedural due process or bill of attainder (a constitutional term for a legislative, as opposed to judicial, punishment). And yet high and low courts across the country, in New York and Nevada, Iowa and Oregon, New Jersey and Indiana, had struck down sterilization laws. Some of these courts would later reverse themselves,[33] but as Carrie Buck's case wound its way to the Supreme Court, no lawyer reviewing the legal precedents could have concluded but that the law favored her.

It was not the pain of the operation that was relevant, one federal court urged, but its legacy; sterilization was as degrading and humiliating as castration, it was "mental torture." It was a "brand of infamy," worn for life, like branding cheeks or cutting ears. Experts testified that sterilization would tend to "create a class of people by themselves who would feel that they were . . . different from normal humanity." It was "beyond . . . comprehension," said one judge, to believe the rosy predictions of the eugenicists that sterilization was an "awakening note to a new era." Legislatures were known, under the pressure of extraordinary crimes, to adopt "strange methods of repression." This, said one court, "belongs to the Dark Ages."[34]

Almost none of this skepticism was expressed in terms familiar today; none of the cases striking down sterilization laws in the pre-*Buck* era relied upon natural or fundamental rights — much less on what today's lawyers would call "the right to procreate" — as a prominent part of their rationale. Courts were far more likely to rely upon the unusual nature of the punishment or problems of "class legislation." Today, the term "class legislation" is largely unknown to lawyers, but at the time it was not only a popular expression that could be found in newspapers but also a particular form of constitutional equality argument.[35] For example, New Jersey's

---

[33] When Buck's case reached the Supreme Court, six courts had struck down these laws (Iowa, Indiana, New York, New Jersey, Nevada, Oregon) and two had upheld them (Michigan, Washington). *Smith v. Command*, 204 N.W. 140, 145 (Mich. 1925); *In re Salloum*, 210 N.W. 498 (Mich. 1926); *State v. Feilen*, 126 P. 75 (Wa. 1912).

[34] *Davis*, *supra* note 32, at 416-17 (humiliation and degradation, "Dark Ages," "mental torture"); *Mickle*, *supra* note 32, at 691 ("brand of infamy," strange methods of repression"); *Osborn*, *supra* note 32, at 640, 645 ("class of people," "beyond . . . comprehension").

[35] Of the six reported cases to strike down sterilization laws in the pre-*Buck* period (*Smith, Davis, Hayes, Osborn, Mickle*, and *Williams*, all *supra* note 32), not a single one refers to the right to procreate or to the notion of a fundamental right. *Davis* refers to marriage as a "civil right" but strikes down the law as cruel and unusual punishment and a bill of attainder. The only pre-*Buck* court to refer to natural or fundamental rights is *Smith MI*, *supra* note 33, which *rejects* the argument. The most consistent rationale was equal protection;

highest court wondered aloud whether the law might be used by majorities simply to pick on the poor, or other disfavored classes: "[T]he feebleminded and epileptics are not the only persons in the community whose elimination as undesirable citizens would, or might in the judgment of the legislature, be a distinct benefit to society. . . . There are other things besides physical or mental diseases that may render persons undesirable citizens . . . in the opinion of a majority of a prevailing legislature." As if to make the case even clearer, the court imagined the possibility that sterilization might be based on "[r]acial differences," and this risk was greatest in communities (presumably the South) where the racial "question is unfortunately a permanent and paramount issue."[36]

By 1927, then, when Carrie Buck's case reached the United States Supreme Court, a lopsided majority of courts had found these laws unconstitutional as both dangerous and degrading. They might have even smelled the whiff of racism that clung to sterilization; even if the statutes did not point to particular ethnicities or races, as the New Jersey Supreme Court had said, there were many attributes that could render persons undesirable in the eyes of a legislative majority, and the most obvious, in a world agitated over immigration and lynching, was race. Even Carrie Buck's counsel mentioned that there was always the danger that, in the name of science, new "classes" and even "races" might be added to the scope of the statute.[37]

These arguments were ignored in Justice Holmes's peremptory five-paragraph opinion. Although Carrie's lawyer claimed she had a right of "bodily integrity," Holmes never used those terms, dismissing Carrie's claim of right as obviously untenable because too strong. It "seems to be contended that in no circumstances could such an order be justified,"

---

see *Smith NJ, Osborn, Haynes*, and the unpublished *Cline, supra* note 32. See also governor's and attorney general's messages vetoing laws during this period. Laughlin at 38-39 (Pa: violates equal protections); *id.* at 45 (Vt: "inexcusable discrimination"); *id.* at 50 (Id: class legislation).

[36] *Smith NJ, supra* note 32, at 966 ("not the only persons," "racial differences," "permanent and paramount"); *Osborn, supra* note 32, at 643-44 (following *Smith NJ*); *Haynes, supra* note 32, at 940-941 (Mich. 1918) (following *Smith NJ*). Laughlin at 265, 267, 280-81 (briefs referring to class legislation); *Sterilization Studies of the Committee on Cacogenic Control*, 9 J. Crim. L. & Criminology 596, 597 (1919) (class legislation); Stephen A. Siegel, *Justice Holmes, Buck v. Bell, and the History of Equal Protection*, 90 Minn. L. Rev. 106, 115-16 (2005) ("In most cases, equal protection was either the sole ground or among the prominent grounds of decision . . . The courts never relied on substantive due process.").

[37] *Buck v. Bell*, 274 U.S. 200, 202 (1927) (counsel: "new classes . . . even races may be brought within the scope of such regulation"). The racial fear may explain Holmes's description of Buck as a "white woman." *Id.* at 205.

Holmes wrote, as if to resolve the claim by declaring it absurd. The great bulk of the brief decision extolled the community's interest in sterilization and the dangers of the unfit. There were references to war, patriotism and sacrifice: ". . . the public welfare may call upon the best citizens for their lives. It would be strange if it could not call upon those who already sap the strength of the State for these lesser sacrifices." There was talk of a society "swamped with incompetence." There was even a call to prevent starvation: "It is better for all the world, if instead of waiting to execute degenerate offspring for crime, or to let them starve for their imbecility, society can prevent those who are manifestly unfit from continuing their kind."[38]

In this, Holmes was evoking ideas deeply embedded in his and the nation's past. He had experienced the horror of the Civil War, and it haunted him for much of his life. Like many eugenicists, Holmes was disgusted at the waste of the war, yet perfectly willing to accept that nature might "starve" the imbecile. Although eugenicists detested man-made extermination, they were quite willing to accept the death handed out by nature. As Herbert Spencer, one of the eugenicists' favorite philosophers, had decreed, "If they are sufficiently complete to live, they *do* live, and it is well they should live. If they are not sufficiently complete to live, they die, and it is best they should die."[39] This was viewed not as cruelty, but compassion.

Justice Holmes later wrote that, in deciding *Buck* as he did, he was "getting near the first principle of real reform." The Court's opinion struck a resounding note in favor of the legislative will to sterilize. All the proper procedures had been accorded Carrie Buck, wrote Holmes: "There can be no doubt that so far as procedure is concerned the rights of the patient are most carefully considered"; the asylum had been "in scrupulous compliance with the statute and . . . there is no doubt that in that respect the plaintiff . . . has had due process of law." The state's power to vacci-

---

[38] Brief for Plaintiff, *Buck v. Bell*, No. 292 at 6-7 (U.S. Oct. Term 1926) (invoking the "inherent right to go through life with full bodily integrity, possessed of all those powers and faculties with which God has endowed them"). Buck's lawyer, Whitehead, specifically denied the possibility of a right to procreate. See *id.* at 13 ("We concede that the State has the right to segregate the feeble-minded and thereby deprive them of the 'power to procreate.'"). In rejected bodily integrity, Homes wrote: "It seems to be contended that in no circumstances could such an order be justified." *Buck v. Bell*, 274 U.S. at 207.

[39] *East* at 248-49 (waste of war); Richard Hofstadter, Social Darwinism in American Thought 41 (1944) (quoting Spencer).

nate was "broad enough to cover cutting the Fallopian tubes."[40] Rejecting the most prevalent judicial argument against sterilization, Holmes declared equal protection irrelevant. He dismissed it as the "usual last resort" of constitutional arguments to point out "shortcomings of this sort" (because the claims were so common at the time and because they failed more often than they succeeded). It was for the legislature to decide to whom sterilization should apply; so long as the law indicated a public policy and sought to apply it to all similarly situated, the fact that the statute was underinclusive — that it did not include all diseased or feebleminded persons but only applied within the asylum — posed no constitutional inequality. "Three generations of imbeciles [were] enough." Only Justice Butler, the Court's sole Catholic member, expressed his dissent, and then without opinion.[41]

The *Buck* opinion would become one of Justice Holmes' most flagrant embarrassments. At the time, however, it was precisely because Holmes wrote the opinion in *Buck v. Bell* that it was thought likely to influence legal and popular opinion to embrace sterilization as a progressive cause. Holmes was known for the "realism, humanity and progress" of his opinions; as one commentator put it, "[p]ages would be needed even to list his civilizing, liberalizing decisions." Holmes was the Supreme Court's champion of judicial deference to popular majorities and state legislatures, in large part because of his stand affirming labor legislation. If deference to legislative will was the measure of progress and humanity, then the opinion in *Buck v. Bell* amounted to exactly that: it deferred to sterilization laws on the books across the nation. As the legal historian Lawrence Friedman has put it, "To Holmes, and so many of his contemporaries, the decision was progressive." Legal doubts, lingering for almost two decades, appeared finally to have been put to rest.[42]

The first wave of largely symbolic sterilization statutes was now followed by a second wave, more effective than the last. Two years after *Buck*

[40] Stephen Jay Gould, The Flamingo's Smile 312-13 (1985) (quoting Holmes); *Buck v. Bell*, 274 U.S. 200, 207 (1927); Albert W. Alschuler, Law Without Values: The Life, Work, and Legacy of Justice Holmes 27-28 (2000).

[41] 274 U.S. 200, 207 (1927) ("imbeciles"); *id.* at 208 ("usual last resort," "shortcomings"); WP at M4 (Feb. 12, 1928) (Butler Catholic).

[42] Jacob Aronoff, *The Constitutionality of Asexualization Legislation in the United States*, 1 St. John's L. Rev. 146, 152 (1926-27) (Holmes likely to influence on opinion on humanity of sterilization); J. H. Landman, *The History of Human Sterilization in the United States — Theory, Statute, Adjudication*, 63 U.S. L. Rev. 48, 50 (1929) ("realism, humanity and progress"); LD at 36, 37 (Jan. 23, 1932) ("Pages would be needed"); Lawrence Friedman, American Law in the Twentieth Century 110 (2002) ("progressive").

was decided, twelve states had passed new sterilization legislation; within four years, twenty-two states had introduced new sterilization bills in their legislatures. In 1932, Jacob Landman, student of eugenic legislation, would explain that "*Buck vs. Bell* now definitely committed the United States to a policy of human sterilization for good or for bad as a means of coping with the socially undesirable in our midst." In the years to follow, the "average number of operations performed under compulsory sterilization statutes in the United States jumped tenfold" (before 1920, the average number per year was approximately 200; during the 1930s, the average per year was over 2,000).[43] After *Buck,* there would be a series of constitutional challenges in the states,[44] challenges rebuffed or evaded — until a case called *Skinner v. Oklahoma.*

• • • •

The immediate cause for our troika's appearance in the *New York Daily News* in December 1933 was neither Governor Murray nor Justice Holmes. Today, it is the third portrait that catches the eye, the grandiose pose, the uniform, the mustache. The world's greatest experiment in eugenics was about to begin. The sheer scope of the proposal was stunning: 1,800 hereditary health courts were to be created and 400,000 people sterilized. This dwarfed the American experience; in the ten-year period from 1907 until 1917, there were only 1,422 sterilization operations performed in the United States. Even at its height, the average number of operations per year in America hovered between 2,000 and 3,000.[45]

When the German sterilization law was first proposed, the press emphasized the analogy to American laws. In 1933, the *New York Times*'s editorial page explained that the Nazi program, upon examination, turned out to be little different from those advocated in "every civilized country."

---

[43] Landman at 113 (*"Buck v. Bell* has now definitely committed"); *id.* at 105 (eighteen states new bills, four more passed laws); *id.* at App. B (listing laws passed after 1927); Larson at 28 (citing Robitscher) (number of operations jumped).

[44] The cases arising after *Buck* deferred to Justice Holmes' opinion, although some state procedures were deemed insufficient. *See, e.g., State v. Schaffer*, 270 P. 604 (Kan. 1928) (upholding law); *Davis v. Walton*, 276 P. 921 (Utah 1929) (upholding law, but insufficient evidence to apply); *State v. Troutman*, 299 P. 668 (Ida. 1931) (upholding Idaho law); *In re Main*, 19 P.2d 153 (Okla. 1933) (upholding law); *In re Clayton*, 234 N.W. 630 (Neb. 1931); *Brewer v. Valk*, 167 S.E. 638 (N.C. 1933) (insufficient procedure); *In re Opinion of Justices*, 162 So. 123 (Ala. 1935) (same); *Garcia v. State*, 97 P.2d 264 (Cal. App. 1939).

[45] CDT at 1 (Dec. 21, 1933) (400,000 in Germany); CDT at 10 (Jan. 1, 1934) (same); Reilly, *supra* note 20, at 40 (1,422 in U.S.); Jonas Robitscher, Eugenic Sterilization App. 2 (1973) (2-3,000 in U.S.).

Although noting that the Germans would be disappointed if they believed that sterilization was a cure-all, the editorial nevertheless continued: "Germany is by no means the first to enact laws to permit or compel sterilization of hereditary mental defectives. Some 15,000 unfortunates [since 1907] have thus far been harmlessly and humanely operated upon in the United States to prevent them from propagating their own kind."[46] It was precisely the analogy between German and American laws that revived the American sterilization debate. National news magazines like *Time* and *News-Week* and *Literary Digest* ran stories on sterilization, as did papers across the country, in Chicago and Los Angeles and New York. By 1934, *Scientific American* had issued a four-part series on sterilization and the German program. Hollywood types even made a movie about the dangers of sterilization, promoting it newsreel style: "News Flash! Germany! Hitler Decrees All Unfit to Be Sterilized! 27 States Put Sterilization Laws into Practice / The Topic that's on Everyone's Tongue!"[47]

It had only been a year since Hitler took power; in a brief six months, he had acquired complete dominance over the German government. America hoped to look the other way but, by the middle of 1933, few resisted the notion that Hitler was the greatest autocrat of the civilized world. From the beginning, there were claims that Hitler's invective was ludicrous and vain, that the Nazis' assaults on religion and voting and free speech and minorities — obvious even in 1933 — would crumble his regime. Mainstream publications like *Time* ridiculed the new dictator and his followers as violent buffoons, fond of clownish pageantry. Yet some saw this situation in a different light: that the "strong man" was an inevitable need in a new, complex world; that democracy had spent itself and Hitler had proven it; or, at the very least, that it was time to "understand" the regime rather than to "scold it."[48]

---

[46] Editorial, NYT at 16 (Aug. 8, 1933) ("Some 15,000 unfortunates"); NYHT at 11 (Dec. 21, 1933).

[47] McCarthy, *supra* note 4; LD at 17 (Jan. 13, 1934); NW at 12 (Aug. 5, 1933); NW at 11 (Dec. 30, 1933); NYHT at 1 (Dec. 24, 1933); LAT at 3 (Dec. 21, 1933); LAT at 2 (Jan. 1, 1934); CDT at 5 (Jan. 5, 1934); Whitney, *supra* note 14, at 7; J.H. Landman, *Race Betterment by Human Sterilization*, SA at 292-95 (June 1934); E.S. Gosney, *Eugenic Sterilization: Human Betterment Demands It*, SA at 18-19, 52-53 (July 1934); C. Thomalla, *The Sterilization Law in Germany*, SA at 126-27 (Sept. 1934); Ignatius W. Cox, *The Folly of Human Sterilization*, SA at 188-90 (Oct. 1934). The quotation is taken from a trailer for *Tomorrow's Children*, a melodramatic film about a girl who escapes sterilization when it is discovered that she was adopted. *See* NYT at 16 (May 18, 1938).

[48] *See* P.W. Wilson, *The World Watches Germany*, RR at 22 (Dec. 1933) ("understand," "scold"); *id.* at 24 (Dec. 1933) (decrying Nazi "crushing of minorities," suppressing

In some ways, there were strong resemblances between Germany and America of the early 1930s: the crippling unemployment, the parade of political and private violence, and the humiliations of national and personal failure. The fear of degeneracy and the inability of the people to govern themselves had soured many average Germans on parliamentary democracy. It had also soured thousands of Americans, who were beginning to turn to the strong men of the 1930s. This was the day of Huey Long and Alfalfa Bill, of the radio priest Father Coughlin and the Hitler-following Khaki Shirts, a day of leaders who were not afraid to go directly to the people, to issue incendiary warnings, or to call out the National Guard. Even those who favored Roosevelt's experiments thought that there might be something vaguely Fascist about the New Deal.[49]

Reports from Germany were often enthusiastic about the dictator's great successes. Visitors from Oklahoma reported the German people's enthusiasm for the godlike dictator who got things done. Pointed contrasts were made to America, where Dillingers and Barrows and other public enemies robbed and killed their way across the Midwest in 1933 and 1934. As one Oklahoma visitor exclaimed, "crime practically has been done away with under Hitler . . . for the first time since the war [I] felt safe." And the German people were not complaining, despite the closed elections, the attacks on Communists and Catholics, the Nazi dominance of the press. Exhausted by the endless parliamentary wrangling of the Weimar period, the German public embraced Hitler as the last chance for a bit of order.[50]

In a world where some still held out hope for the great German dictator, it is not surprising that there were those who praised the Nazi sterilization program for its ambition and resolve. Leading American eugenicists gave their initial approval to the plan. Leon Whitney, former executive secretary of the American Eugenics Society, told the press, "This action of Hitler's certainly stamps him as one of the greatest statesmen and social planners in the world, because it requires real statesmanship to plan long-time social programs such as he has by this action." The German compulsory sterilization law shared much with its American predecessors. Like most American laws, the German law applied to those deemed insane,

---

speech); Roger Shaw, *Visiting the Third Reich*, RR at 37 (Jan. 1934) (ridiculing Hitler's 1933 elections); Edith Johnson, DO at 12 (Dec. 8, 1933); *id.* at 8, (Nov. 24, 1934).

[49] Alan Brinkley, Voices of Protest: Huey Long, Father Coughlin, and the Great Depression (1982); RR at 48 (Oct. 1934) (NRA Fascist).

[50] Shaw, *supra* note 48, at 37 ("gets things done"); TDW at 18 (Jan. 12, 1935) ("crime . . . done away with").

feebleminded, or epileptic. As in America, sex offenders were covered, but in Germany the penalty was harsher: castration. Unlike American laws, however, the German law required doctors to report for sterilization anyone they encountered who fell under the law, including not only the feebleminded but also those with severe physical deformities, hereditary deafness, blindness, and habitual alcoholism. In response to religious opposition to sterilization, the German law offered an exemption for those who chose to commit themselves to an asylum during their entire reproductive lives.[51]

Just months after the announcement of the Nazis' proposal, the shadow of race already darkened reports of the program. Hitlerian enthusiasm for the Nordic type was hardly a secret at the time (*Mein Kampf* had been published in 1925), even if the new German state's attacks on the Jewish "race" did not necessarily stand out from its harangues against Communists or Catholics.[52] The science page of the *New York Times* raised the question of Aryanism directly. Waldemar Kaempffert, the science editor, was so enthusiastic about eugenics, he thought it raised questions more important than "the machine" (referring to the automobile). But he was quite direct when it came to the Nazis: when one considers "how the Germans have twisted the meaning of the word Aryan, out of all semblance . . . the skeptical naturally wonder." Given "Germany's present reign of political terror, geneticists wonder whether a law which has much to commend it will be enforced with strict scientific impartiality." Presci-

---

[51] McCarthy, *supra* note 4, at 31 (quoting Leon Whitney, Hitler "greatest statesmen"); LAT at 2 (Jan. 1, 1934) (application to criminals); Richard F. Wetzell, Inventing the Criminal: A History of German Criminology 1880-1945 256-57 (2000) (coverage of law to specific categories of diseases and persons), *id.* at 258 (castration of sex offenders). The original Nazi law did not include criminals but "it emerged that Hitler himself was eager to see 'habitual criminals' sterilized." *Id.* at 257. That aim was fulfilled "when the Ministry of Justice issued a circular requesting that all courts, prosecutors, and prison officials report criminals who might suffer from a 'genetic disease' . . . for a sterilization hearing." *Id.* at 258-59; *Nazi Decree Revives Sterilization Debate*, LD at 17 (Jan. 13, 1934) (physician must refer); NYT at 19 (Jan. 9, 1934) (voluntary confinement as alternative).

[52] As early as 1931, the Nazis were reported to seek "Nordic dominance," to "sterlize some races," and ban miscegenation. NYT at 1 (Dec. 8, 1931). Hitlerian Nordicism was the topic of Dorothy Thompson's popular work I Saw Hitler (1932); NYT at BR5 (Mar. 5, 1932) (review of Thompson's book); NYT at E1 (Oct. 9, 1932); NW at 13 (Apr. 15, 1933) ("Hundreds of Jews have been beaten or tortured"); NW at 14 (May 20, 1933) ("Holocaust: Down Unter Den Linden" marched 5,000 young men burning books; Goebbels says "Jewish intellectualism is dead"); *id.* at 15 (65,000 protesting German anti-Semitic policies); NW at 12 (June 3, 1933) ("ruthless persecution of the Jews"); NW at 10 (Sept. 9, 1933) (Jewry as "a ferment of decomposition").

ently, Kaempffert asked, "What is to stop the governor of a concentration camp from recommending sterilization for a malformed Communist or member of the Catholic Centre?"[53]

Fears of abuse mounted as news of the extent of the program began to find its way west. In January 1934, it was reported that Germany's sterilization law would apply to children as young as ten. Two weeks later, the Germans ordered a census of incurables and demanded that the German criminal courts be scoured for "hereditary defectives" (despite the fact that the original Nazi statute did not cover habitual criminals). Doctors who failed to report a defective individual were to be fined heavily. In February, it was reported that eugenics authorities were insisting on the immediate sterilization of the "Negroid children in the Rhineland and the Ruhr," the legacy of "invading French colonial troops" during World War I.[54]

If Hitler's program raised fears of racism, it was a racism different from today's. In 1934, race was a slippery term: it referred easily to what we would today call a religion — as in "the Jewish race" — or ethnicity, as in "the Italian race" or "the Irish Race."[55] It was not unusual for eugenicists to talk of the feebleminded races or of a race of criminals, on the theory that these groups had a common heredity. For many eugenicists, race and genetics were synonymous; both depended upon inheritance. The prominent zoologist S. J. Holmes would boast that geneticists had the knowledge to "breed an albino race, a deaf race, a feeble-minded race, an insane race, a race of dwarfs, a race with hook-like extremities instead of hands, a race of superior intellectual ability, or a race of high artistic talent."[56]

---

[53] Waldemar Kaempffert, The Week in Science, NYT at XX7 (Oct. 22, 1933); see also NYT at 2 (Aug. 12, 1933) (Nature magazine feared abuse by Germans).

[54] NYT at 10 (Jan. 5, 1934); NYT at 10 (Jan. 4, 1934). The fine for doctors was 150 marks, close to half the monthly salary of the average official, NYT at E3 (Jan. 14, 1934); NYT at 4 (Feb. 8, 1934) ("Negroid children").

[55] Gary Gerstle, American Crucible: Race and Nation in the Twentieth Century 161 (2001) ("in the 1930s and 1940s, many spoke of the Jewish and Italian races as being something other (and lower) than the white race"); Matthew Frye Jacobson, Whiteness of a Different Color: European Immigrants and the Alchemy of Race (1999). On Supreme Court usage, Hill v. Texas, 316 U.S. 400, 402 (1942) ("white race," "colored race"); Stewart v. Keyes, 295 U.S. 403, 415 (1935) (equating "Indians" with a "race"); Morrison v. California, 291 U.S. 82, 85 (1934) ("Japanese race"); Nagle v. Loi Hoa, 275 U.S. 475, 478 (1928) ("Chinese race"); Gong Lum v. Rice, 275 U.S. 78, 80 (1927) ("Caucasian race"); id. at 82, 83 ("colored races"); United States v. Thind, 261 U.S. 204, 215 (1923) ("white races"); Juan Perea et al., Race and Races: Cases and Resources for a Diverse America (2000).

[56] S. J. Holmes, The Trend of the Race 8 (1921) ("breed an albino race"); see, e.g., Stanley Powell Davies, Social Control of the Mentally Deficient 82 (1930) ("feebleminded race");

There was nothing particularly German about this idea of race; the racism of eugenics, whether abroad or in America, was primarily directed against those we no longer see as races. When Madison Grant, a well-known eugenics popularizer, wrote in a bestselling book that inferior races were "moral perverts, mental defectives, and hereditary cripples," he was referring to southern and eastern European immigrants who had flooded the country after World War I. Grant insisted that, when the Nordic races bred with the lesser immigrant races, it sapped the "native American aristocracy" of its vigor and health, reducing it to a lower, more primitive type. This same calculus led the eugenicist Lothrop Stoddard to write that the "basic factor" in human affairs was "not politics, but race": as Grant put it, race was "everything." Stoddard railed against miscegenation; America, he wrote, was a sitting duck for those who would "pacific[ally] penetrat[e]" it — those who by immigration would fester within, tainting American blood. For both Stoddard and Grant, America was, quite literally, being raped by the feebleminded and "criminalistic" races (races we would today call immigrants). Grant's solution was artificial selection, that is, sterilization:

> A rigid system of selection through the elimination of those who are weak or unfit — in other words, social failures — would solve the whole question . . . [and] get rid of the undesirables who crowd our jails, hospitals and insane asylums. . . . [T]he state through sterilization must see to it that his line stops with him. . . . This is a practical, merciful and inevitable solution of the whole problem and can be applied to an ever widening circle of social discards, beginning always with the criminal, the diseased and the insane and extending gradually to types which may be called weaklings rather than defectives and perhaps ultimately to worthless race types.[][57]

Grant's book was not only widely popular, it was reviewed favorably in scientific journals. After all, its claims were not terribly different from those of some scientists of the day. As one text of genetics lectures put it:

E. Wake Cook, Betterment: Individual, Social, and Industrial 8 (1906) ("race of criminals").

[57] Grant, *supra* note 18, at 5, 50-51 ("native American aristocracy," "rigid system of selection"); *id.* at 18 ("primitive," "lower type"); Paul at 104 (quoting Grant on "moral perverts, mental defectives, and hereditary cripples"); Lothrop Stoddard, The Revolt Against Civilization 5 (1923) ("pacific penetration"); Lothrop Stoddard, The Rising Tide of Colour 5 (1920, 1981 reprint) ("not politics, but race"); *id.* at 169 (quoting Grant that race is "everything").

"from one thousand Roumanians today in Boston, at the present rate of breeding, will come a hundred thousand two hundred years hence to govern the fifty descendants of Harvard's sons!"[58] As in most matters of American racism, African-Americans suffered the worst slurs. The zoologist Holmes would write, with apparent approval, that "Negros" were "becoming bleached," and that, if they were ever destined to be "absorbed" into white culture, they would "be considerably bleached before they [were] assimilated." The logic of this position depended, as the eugenics popularizers Paul Popenoe and Roswell Johnson would insist, on the fact that the "Negro race must be placed very near zero on the scale" of racial value.[59]

It is not surprising, then, that, when criticized for their eugenics program, Nazi Party officials turned the tables: how could the German program be so terrible when it mirrored the laws of many American states, laws that criminalized racial intermixing and sterilized the unfit? Statements defending the German program seemed to be written so that "the good example" set by the United States was always in the first few paragraphs. The articles used terms that would not have sounded strange to Governor Murray or Justice Holmes, or to a variety of eugenicists. Dr. Arthur Guett, counselor to the Reich Ministry of the Interior, talked of the "imminent" danger of race degeneration: the "unfit" had been kept alive by social "counter selection," allowing them to poison the bloodstream by outbreeding "the healthy and ambitious." When all was said and done, as in America, Nazi propagandists invoked the economy, claiming that hereditary defects, antisocial persons, and criminals cost Germany one billion marks a year.[60]

In the face of news of the German program, many American commentators remained agnostic, embracing eugenics while worrying about possible abuse. Others found in the German program an "outstanding accomplishment" and "a keynote in social welfare," a confirmation and encouragement for what they believed to be compassion. In January 1934, the *Oklahoma News* would compare Oklahoma's law with the new German

---

[58] Paul at 104 (Grant's favorable reviews); W.E. Castle, Genetics and Eugenics: A Text-Book 290 (1921) (immigrants pose threat to democracy); Heredity and Eugenics, *supra* note 28, at 309 ("from one thousand").

[59] S. J. Holmes, Human Genetics and Its Social Import 357 (1936) ("becoming bleached"); Popenoe & Johnson, *supra* note 16, at 284 (1924) ("placed very near zero"). On the feebleminded "passing," Paul at 68.

[60] NYT at 6, (Jan. 22, 1934) ("good example"); Thomalla, *supra* note 47, at 126 (referring to American laws in defense of German law); NYT at E3 (Jan. 14, 1934) (one billion marks).

program: "Coincident with a more far-reaching program in Germany, Oklahoma today began preparations for sterilizing several hundreds, or thousands of insane and habitual criminals." We are "deliberately and knowingly breeding menaces to future society," insisted the editorial. In such a world, "we can't see that it is wrong for the state to tell an inflicted [sic] man or woman that he or she may not produce a child which is likely to bring suffering to all, including the child itself."[61]

When we are planning for posterity, we ought to remember that virtue is not hereditary.

Thomas Paine (1776)

---

[61] See McCarthy, *supra* note 4, at 31 (Jewish leaders to not object to sterilization but fear abuse); Editorial, *New German Administration Adopts Sterilization Law to Build Up Race*, GP 22.2 (Aug. 1, 1933) ("outstanding accomplishment," "keynote in social welfare"); Editorial, ON at 6 (Jan. 2, 1934).

SHAKESPEARE'S LEGAL ACQUIREMENTS

(continued from page 295)

John Lord Campbell

ALL'S WELL THAT ENDS WELL

In this play we meet with proof that Shakespeare had an accurate knowledge of the law of England respecting the incidents of military tenure, or *tenure in chivalry*, by which the greatest part of the land in this kingdom was held till the reign of Charles II. The incidents of that tenure here dwelt upon are "*wardship of minors*" and "the right of the guardian to dispose of the minor in *marriage* at his pleasure." The scene lies in France, and, strictly-speaking, the law of that country ought to prevail in settling such questions; but Dr. Johnson, in his notes on 'All's Well that Ends Well,' justly intimates his opinion that it is of no great use to inquire whether the law upon these subjects was the same in France as in England, "for Shakespeare gives to all nations the manners of England."

According to the plot on which this play is constructed, the French King laboured under a malady which his physicians had declared incurable; and Helena, the daughter of a deceased physician of great eminence, knew of a cure for it. She was in love with Bertram, Count of Rousillon, still a minor, who held large possessions as tenant *in capite* under the crown, and was in ward to the King. Helena undertook the cure, making this condition:—

> *Hel.* Then shalt thou give me with thy kingly hand
> What husband in thy power I will command.

Adding, however:—

> Exempted be from me the arrogance
> To choose from forth the royal blood of France . . .
> But such a one, thy vassal, whom I know
> Is free for me to ask, thee to bestow.

> (Act II. Sc. 1.)

She effects the cure, and the King, showing her all the noble unmarried youths whom he then held as wards, says to her—

> Fair maid, send forth thine eye: this youthful parcel
> Of noble bachelors stand at my bestowing . . .
>   thy frank election make:
> Thou hast power to choose, and they none to forsake.

> (Act II. Sc. 3.)

Helena, after excusing herself to several of the others, comes to Bertram, and, covered with blushes, declares her election:—

> *Hel.* I dare not say I take you; but I give
> Me and my service, ever whilst I live,
> Into your guiding power.— This is the man.
> *King.* Why then, young Bertram, take her: she's thy wife.

Bertram at first strenuously refuses, saying—

> In such a business give me leave to use
> The help of mine own eyes.

But the King, after much discussion, thus addresses him:—

> It is in us to plant thine honour where
> We please to have it grow. Check thy contempt.
> Obey our will, which travails in thy good. . . .
>   Take her by the hand,
> And tell her she is thine. . . .
> *Bert.* I take her hand.

(Act II, Sc. 3.)

The ceremony of marriage was immediately performed, and no penalty or forfeiture was incurred. But the law not extending to a compulsion upon the ward to live with the wife thus forced upon him, Bertram escapes from the church door, and abandoning his wife, makes off for the wars in Italy, where he unconsciously embraced the deserted Helena.

For the cure of the King by the physician's daughter, and her being deserted by her husband, Shakespeare is indebted to Boccaccio; but the wardship of Bertram, and the obligation of the ward to take the wife provided for him by his guardian, Shakespeare drew from his own knowledge of the common law of England, which, though now obsolete, was in full force in the reign of Elizabeth, and was to be found in Littleton.* The adventure of Parolles's drum and the other comic parts of the drama are quite original, and these he drew from his own inexhaustible fancy.

THE WINTER'S TALE

In this play, Act I. Sc. 2, there is an allusion to a piece of English law procedure, which, although it might have been enforced till very recently,

---

* However, according to Littleton, it is doubtful whether Bertram, without being liable to any penalty or forfeiture, might not have refused to marry Helena,— on the ground that she was not of noble descent. The lord could not "disparage" the ward by a *mésalliance*.— Co. Litt. 80a.

could hardly be known to any except lawyers, or those who had them-selves actually been in prison on a criminal charge,— that, whether guilty or innocent, the prisoner was liable to pay a fee on his liberation. Hermione, trying to persuade Polixenes, King of Bohemia, to prolong his stay at the court of Leontes in Sicily, says to him—

> You put me off with limber vows; but I,
> Though you would seek t' unsphere the stars with oaths,
> Should yet say, "Sir, no going." . . .
> Force me to keep you *as a prisoner*,
> Not like a guest; *so you shall pay your fees*
> *When you depart*, and save your thanks.

I remember when the Clerk of Assize and the Clerk of the Peace were entitled to exact their fee from all acquitted prisoners, and were supposed in strictness to have a *lien* on their persons for it. I believe there is now no tribunal in England where the practice remains, excepting the two Houses of Parliament; but the Lord Chancellor and the Speaker of the House of Commons still say to prisoners about to be liberated from the custody of the Black Rod or the Serjeant-at-Arms, "You are discharged, *paying your fees.*"

***

When the trial of Queen Hermione for high treason comes off in Act III. Sc. 2, although the indictment is not altogether according to English legal form, and might be held insufficient on a writ of error, we lawyers cannot but wonder at seeing it so near perfection in charging the treason, and alleging the overt act committed by her "contrary to the faith and allegiance of a true subject."

It is likewise remarkable that Cleomenes and Dion, the messengers who brought back the response from the oracle of Delphi, to be given in evidence, are sworn to the genuineness of the document they produce almost in the very words now used by the Lord Chancellor when an offi-cer presents at the bar of the House of Lords the copy of a record of a court of justice:—

> You here shall swear . . .
> That you, Cleomenes and Dion, have
> Been both at Delphos; and from thence have brought
> The seal'd-up oracle, by the hand delivered
> Of great Apollo's priest; and that since then
> You have not dar'd to break the holy seal,
> Nor read the secrets in 't.

continued on page 385 . . .

JUNE

LAWS NOT MEN:
"NOT UNDER MAN BUT UNDER GOD AND THE LAW"

By John V. Orth, with the assistance of Joseph L. Hyde

Angelo's first and second responses to Isabella's plea for her brother's life is to deny personal responsibility: *It is the law, not I, condemns your brother . . . I, now the voice of the recorded law, / Pronounce a sentence on thy brother's life.* In traditional legal theory, the personality of the judge is submerged in the judicial office. Personal preferences are supposed to yield to the impersonal force embodied in the law. Indeed, the law is endowed with a sort of life of its own. Sir Edward Coke, Shakespeare's great contemporary, insisted that "reason is the life of the law,"[1] and reminded King James a few years after the premiere of *Measure for Measure* that Englishmen were *"non sub homine, sed sub Deo et lege"* (not under man but under God and the law).[2] The notion is implicit in the American commit-

---

[1] *Coke on Littleton* § 138, p. 97b. See also Oliver Wendell Holmes' famous rejoinder that "the life of the law has not been logic: it has been experience." *The Common Law* 1 (1881).

[2] 12 Co. Rep. 65, 77 Eng. Rep. 1342 (quoting medieval Latin treatise attributed to Henry

341

ment to "a government of laws and not of men."[3]

Yet distinguished American judges have also seen Angelo's response as a sign of personal weakness. Judge Richard Posner described "the conception of law as something existing apart from man" as "a conception that is congenial to people who lack warmth in human relationships," and connected Angelo's legalism "with his being a natural underling, as well as with his effort to transcend his body and become all spirit." Legalism, according to Posner, is "associated with immature, weak, and father-fixated personalities."[4] And Judge John Noonan wrote in a dissenting opinion that a judge who denied responsibility for an official act must have felt "conflict and embarrassment," "tension and turmoil."[5]

continued on page 393 . . .

--------◆--------

RADMIN V. TRANSUNION
2008 WL 2625351 (D. N.J. June 27, 2008)

Jose L. Linares, District Judge

In the face of absent arguments, this Court cannot, like Hamlet, "eat the air, promise-crammed": litigants must provide more meat on an issue than a mere description of the general legal theory, such as subject matter jurisdiction, leaving the court to divine its application to the case. William Shakespeare, *Hamlet*, act 3, sc. 2.

---

de Bracton). See 2 *Bracton on the Laws and Customs of England* 33 (Samuel E. Thorne ed. 1968). The words are inscribed over the main portal to Langdell Hall at the Harvard Law School. Arthur E. Sutherland, *The Law at Harvard: A History of Ideas and Men, 1817-1967*, caption to photograph facing p. 243 (1967).

[3] See Mass. Const. Decl. Rts. 30 (separation of powers is essential, "to the end it may be a government of laws and not of men"). President Franklin Roosevelt invoked the concept when he tried to rally Americans to support his Court Packing Plan: "We want a Supreme Court which will do justice under the Constitution — not over it. In our courts we want a government of laws and not of men." *Public Papers and Addresses of Franklin D. Roosevelt, 1937*, at 122 (Samuel I. Rosenman ed. 1941).

[4] Richard A. Posner, *Law and Literature: A Misunderstood Relation* 105, 109 (1988).

[5] U.S. v. Chischilly, 30 F.3d 1144, 1163-64 (9th Cir. 1994) (Noonan, J., dissenting) ("Angelo's words to Isabella in *Measure for Measure* are classic in denying responsibility for what has to be the act of the judge, however much that act is in conformity with law.").

❧ JUNE ❧

SUN	MON	TUES	WED	THUR	FRI	SAT
	1	2	3	4	5	6
7	8	9	10	11	12	13
14	15	16	17	18	19	20
21	22	23	24	25	26	27
28	29	30				

MR. SUNSTEIN'S NEIGHBORHOOD

WON'T YOU BE OUR CO-AUTHOR?

Paul H. Edelman & Tracey E. George†

In *Six Degrees of Cass Sunstein: Collaboration Networks in Legal Scholarship*[1] we began the study of the collaboration network in legal academia. We concluded that the central figure in the network was Professor Cass Sunstein of Harvard Law School[2] and proceeded to catalogue all of his myriad co-authors (so-called Sunstein 1's) and their co-authors (Sunstein 2's). In this small note we update that catalogue as of August 2008 and take the opportunity to reflect on this project and its methodology.

Collaboration networks, which map connections based on pairs of people working together, are one example of the application of network theory to human behavior. Network theory has been applied to any number of human institutions to study links between blogs, judges' citations of other judges, social acquaintances, and so on. The number and patterns of connections can reveal various aspects of the human activity under consideration. Thus, the fact that any single person may be introduced to another person through five or fewer acquaintances may reveal that the world is a smaller place than we otherwise imagined.

A collaboration network seeks to examine the interconnectedness of an occupation, field, or industry such as movies, as in the *Six Degrees of Kevin Bacon* game, or mathematics as in the almost as famous Erdős number. Such networks may tell us something about an individual in the network. For example, the closer a person is to a central figure in an industry – the fewer the degrees of separation between an actor and Bacon or the lower a

---

† Edelman is Professor of Law and Professor of Mathematics and George is Professor of Law and Professor of Political Science at Vanderbilt University. We thank Yun Chen for valuable research assistance on this project.

[1] 11 Green Bag 2d 19 (2007); *see also* Paul H. Edelman & Tracey E. George, *Sunstein 1s and 2s, in* THE GREEN BAG ALMANAC AND READER 473 (Ross Davies ed., 2008).

[2] Sunstein, who is the most cited legal scholar and one of the most prolific, joined Harvard as the Felix Frankfurter Professor of Law in 2008. www.law.harvard.edu/faculty/directory/index.html?id=552. At the time of our first article Sunstein was at the University of Chicago Law School. This raises a number of interesting questions about the effect of collaboration on faculty mobility, but such a study will have to be postponed for a later time.

scholar's Erdős number – arguably the more central that person is to the discipline. A collaboration network may also tell us about the industry itself: The lower the average degrees of separation between people in the industry, the more tightly connected the field.

At the time of our first paper, Sunstein — the legal academy's Erdős — had co-authored with 73 different people. Those 73 people had 837 co-authors who had not themselves co-authored with Sunstein. As of August 2008, those numbers have risen to 96 (Table 1) and 1632 (Table 2) respectively. The relevant tables are appended to this article. What explains this dramatic increase? We can imagine three possible explanations that we'll consider in turn.

First, the publication of any network revealing a central figure will create an incentive to work with that person or at least to work with someone who has worked with the central figure. Simply put: Our article explains the dramatic increase. Skeptical? Well, consider that someone auctioned on Ebay the opportunity to be an Erdős 3 – the seller was an Erdős 2 who was willing to give a co-author credit for a fee. Our own experience lends some credence to this theory as well. After posting the original article we received quite a number of e-mails from Sunstein 1's and 2's who mistakenly had been omitted from the original listing. All that being said, we too have doubts that this explanation is compelling, leading us to the next possible explanation.

An alternative – or additional – factor could be that the numbers reflect an outlier publication – one with an unusually large number of co-authors -- that has skewed the results. Collaboration networks define collaboration as working together in the same capacity whether as actors in a movie (Bacon) or co-authors on a published work (Erdős). We define collaboration in our study as being a co-author on any published scholarly work. This requires defining co-authorship and scholarship. To be a co-author, an individual must be listed in the "by" line. Thus, contributors identified in an acknowledgement footnote – even those who offered significant input – are not included.[3] We also did not include editors of work published in an edited collection because editors typically are not engaged in the collaborative process in the same way.

We admit that individuals not listed as co-authors often are working closely with authors without this credit. However, we chose – as other

---

[3] It is worth noting that the editors of this fine publication are quite explicit on this subject: "Colleagues who make substantial contributions should share the byline. Colleagues who are helpful in small ways should be recognized in something printed by Hallmark, not the *Green Bag*." www.greenbag.org/submissions.php. We know of no other publication that is as specific in its rules for allocating credit.

studies have chosen – to emphasize a comparable role in the creative process. But, not all listed co-authors are actually co-creators. Co-authorship status may be assigned to individuals who were not closely involved in a work because the other authors wanted to grant some credit to a person, such as a graduate student, who provided meaningful assistance to one or all co-authors, or had to give credit to someone who was initially committed to the project but failed ultimately to participate. Of course, we can't know whether listed co-authors were meaningfully involved in the work without being part of that process ourselves. And we need an efficient, relatively effective measure of true collaboration. While a large number of co-authors on a paper might make one suspicious about whether all of them were truly involved, a small number might just as easily underestimate the contribution of an uncredited individual. At the end of the day, we stand by our co-authoring criterion as being the best possible compromise.

A final possible explanation is that there is an underlying intellectual trend that isn't visible to us given the structure of our data. We began collecting data last year, and our data is not organized by year. Thus, we don't know whether this increase is consistent with the rate of increase in recent years. There are reasons to imagine this might be the case. Law has become increasingly interdisciplinary over the past decade, and Sunstein has been a leader in collaboration with scholars in other fields including psychology and economics. While the rate of co-authorship in law appears to have stagnated, social science articles are more likely to be authored by multiple individuals. Thus, as Sunstein writes with more psychologists and economists, the resulting work is more likely to be authored by more than two people. And, those social scientists also will be one of several co-authors on their own work.

We sought to evaluate these alternative explanations by focusing on the new Sunstein 1's. There is little doubt that a single article is responsible for much of the increase in Sunstein 1's. Sunstein co-wrote an article with 24 people and 20 of them were first-time co-authors.[4] If Sunstein worked in high energy physics, this would not be so unusual,[5] but for a legal academic such an article is highly unusual.

---

[4] Kenneth Arrow, et. al., *The Promise of Prediction Markets*, 320 Science 877 (2008).

[5] Opening the current issue of Physical Review Letters one finds the article: "S. Leoni, G. Benzoni, N. Blasi, A. Bracco, S. Brambilla, F. Camera, A. Corsi, F. C. L. Crespi, P. Mason, B. Million, D. Montanari, M. Pignanelli, E. Vigezzi, O. Wieland, M. Matsuo, Y. R. Shimizu, D. Curien, G. Duchêne, J. Robin, P. Bednarczyk, M. Castoldi, B. Herskind, M. Kmiecik, A. Maj, W. Meczynski, J. Styczen, M. Zieblinski, K. Zuber, and A. Zucchiatti, *Probing the Order-to-Chaos Region in Superdeformed* ^{151}Tb

More than unusual, this article is highly problematic for our methodology. Our study is predicated on the assumption that a joint publication is evidence of a collaborative relationship. Should we believe that the article in question represents a collaborative effort on the part of the authors or merely a joint assertion of their individual positions? Our instinct is that the latter is more likely than the former. On the other hand, it is almost certain that in the writing of the article there was some level of collaboration. Is an exercise in joint writing, even if the ideas themselves are not jointly conceived or developed, sufficient to be called "collaboration?"

A similar issue arose in our first paper, although we did not mention it at the time since the effect was less noticeable. In 1995 the Yale Law Journal published a comment titled *An Open Letter to Congressman Gingrich* that was signed by 17 law professors.[6] It fit the criteria for inclusion that we had set out, and so we included it in our study. Nevertheless we had qualms at the time that the article had more of the qualities of an amicus brief than those of a scholarly publication.

While we find the inclusion of these articles problematic, it is hard to know how to respond. In order to do an empirical study of this sort, objective criteria for inclusion must be specified and the results tolerated. There are too many papers to consider each one separately using a "totality of the circumstances" standard.[7] Publication in the Yale Law Journal should count for something and disqualifying articles with more than some fixed number of authors would bias the study in a different direction. Thus, we have opted to retain our original coding methodology – which mirrors that used in other collaboration and related network studies – and acknowledge the inherent limits posed by this method.

Although the number of academics within two degrees of Sunstein has increased substantially, neither of us made it to either list. Maybe next year?

---

and [196]*Pb Nuclei with Continuum* Υ *Transitions*, 101 Phys. Rev. Lett. 142502 (2008)."
[6] Bruce Ackerman, et. al., *An Open Letter to Congressman Gingrich*, 104 Yale L. J. 1539 (1995).
[7] Voting Rights Act, 42 USC §1973 et seq. (2000), at § 2(b).

TABLE 1. ALL SUNSTEIN 1 AUTHORS (AUGUST 2008)[8]

Ackerman, Bruce *Yale Law School*	Adler, Matthew D. *Univ. of Pennsylvania Law School*
Amar, Akhil Reed *Yale Law School*	Arrow, Kenneth J. *Stanford Univ. Dept. of Economics*
Ashley, Kevin D. *Univ. of Pittsburgh School of Law*	Baird, Douglas G. *Univ. of Chicago Law School*
Balkin, Jack M. *Yale Law School*	Barnett, Randy E. *Georgetown Univ. Law Center*
Bell, Anthony *Univ. of Chicago Dept. of Pediatrics*	Benartzi, Shlomo *UCLA School of Management*
Bloch, Susan Low *Georgetown Univ. Law Center*	Bobbitt, Philip *Univ. of Texas Law School*
Branting, L. Karl *BAE Systems, Inc.*	Breyer, Stephen G. *U.S. Supreme Court*
Cortes, Ernesto Jr. *Industrial Areas Foundation*	Dam, Kenneth *Univ. of Chicago Law School*
Elliott, E. Donald *Willkie Farr & Gallagher LLP*	Ellman, Lisa Michelle *Mayer, Brown, Rowe & Maw LLP*
Epstein, Richard A. *Univ. of Chicago Law School*	Fallon, Richard *Harvard Law School*
Forsythe, Robert E. *Univ. of S. Florida College of Business*	Frank, Robert H. *Cornell Univ. School of Management*
Glaeser, Edward L. *Harvard Univ. Dept. of Economics*	Goldsmith, Jack L. *Harvard Law School*
Gorham, Michael *IIT School of Business*	Hahn, Robert W. *AEI-Brookings Joint Ctr for Reg. Studies*
Hanson, Robin D. *George Mason Dept. of Economics*	Hastie, Reid *Univ. of Chicago School of Business*
Holmes, Stephen *NYU School of Law*	Houston, Christopher E. *Ropes & Gray LLP*

---

[8] Author information for Sunstein 1s reflects institutional affiliation in spring 2008, if available. If we were unable to locate the author, we report the institution affiliation, if any, listed in the publication.

TABLE 1. ALL SUNSTEIN 1 AUTHORS (AUGUST 2008)[8]

Hsiung, Wayne H. *Northwestern Univ. School of Law*	Jolls, Christine M. *Yale Law School*
Kahn, Paul *Yale Law School*	Kahneman, Daniel J. *Princeton Univ. Sch. of Pub. & Int'l Aff.*
Karlan, Pamela S. *Stanford Law School*	King, Robert E. *S. Orange Cty Community College Dist.*
Kuran, Timur *USC Dept of Economics*	Kurland, Philip *Univ. of Chicago Law School (dec.)*
Laycock, Douglas *Univ. of Texas Law School*	Ledyard, John O. *Cal Tech Dept. of Economics*
Leslie, Jeff *Univ. of Chicago Law School*	Lessig, Lawrence *Stanford Law School*
Levinson, Sanford V. *Univ. of Texas Law School*	Levmore, Saul *Univ. of Chicago Law School*
Litan, Robert E. *Kauffman Foundation*	Margolis, Howard *Univ. of Chicago School of Public Policy*
Meadow, William L. *Univ. of Chicago School of Medicine*	Meares, Tracey L. *Yale Law School*
Meltzer, Bernard D. *Univ. of Chicago Law School (deceased)*	Michelman, Frank I. *Harvard Law School*
Miles, Thomas J. *Univ. of Chicago Law School*	Milgrom, Paul R. *Stanford Univ. Dept. of Economics*
Miller, Ellen S. *Sunlight Foundation*	Murphy, Kevin M. *Univ. of Chicago School of Business*
Nelson, Forrest D. *Univ. of Iowa Dept. of Economics*	Neumann, George R. *Univ. of Iowa Dept. of Economics*
Nussbaum, Martha Craven *Univ. of Chicago Law School*	O'Neill, Catherine A. *Seattle Univ. School of Law*
Ottaviani, Marco *Northwestern Univ. Grad. Sch. of Mgmt*	Payne, John W. *Duke Univ. School of Business*
Perry, Michael J. *Emory Law School*	Pildes, Richard H. *NYU School of Law*
Posner, Eric A. *Univ. of Chicago Law School*	Post, Robert *Yale Law School*

TABLE 1. ALL SUNSTEIN 1 AUTHORS (AUGUST 2008)[8]

Rapoport, Miles S. *Demos*	Ritov, Ilana *Hebrew Univ. School of Education*
Rosen, Sherwin *Univ. of Chicago Dept. of Econ. (dec.)*	Rowell, Kristen Arden *Perkins Coie LLP*
Rubenfeld, Jed *Yale Law School*	Sawicki, Andres *Judicial Law Clerk, USCA 2nd Circuit*
Schelling, Thomas C. *Univ. of Maryland School of Public Policy*	Schkade, David A. *UCSD School of Management*
Seidman, Louis Michael *Georgetown Univ. Law Center*	Shiller, Robert J. *Yale Univ. Department of Economics*
Smith, Vernon L. *Chapman Univ. School of Law*	Snowberg, Erik *Stanford Univ. Graduate Sch. of Business*
Spitzer, Matthew L. *USC School of Law*	Stewart, Richard B. *NYU School of Law*
Stone, Geoffrey R. *Univ. of Chicago Law School*	Strauss, David A. *Univ. of Chicago Law School*
Strauss, Peter L. *Columbia Univ. Law School*	Sullivan, Kathleen M. *Stanford Law School*
Tetlock, Paul C. *Yale Univ. School of Management*	Tetlock, Philip E. *UC-Berkeley School of Business*
Thaler, Richard H. *Univ. of Chicago School of Business*	Tushnet, Mark V. *Harvard Law School*
Ullmann-Margalit, Edna *Hebrew Univ. School of Education*	Utkus, Stephen P. *Vanguard Center for Retirement Research*
Varian, Hal R. *UC-Berkeley School of Information*	Vermeule, Adrian *Harvard Law School*
Viscusi, W. Kip *Vanderbilt Law School*	Waldron, Jeremy *NYU School of Law*
Weisbach, David A. *Univ. of Chicago Law School*	Wellington, Harry *New York Law School*
Wolfers, Justin *Univ. of Pennsylvania School of Business*	Zitzewitz, Eric W. *Dartmouth Dept. of Economics*

TABLE 2. ALL SUNSTEIN 2 AUTHORS (AUGUST 2008)

Abram, Thomas G.	Axtell, Robert	Berg, Joyce E.
Abreu, Dilip	Ayres, Ian	Berg, Thomas C.
Abt, Clark C.	Azabou, Mongi	Berger, James E.
Ackerman, John	Azar, Ofer H.	Bergin, Tom
Ackerman, Susan Rose	Babcock, Linda	Bergkamp, Lucas
Acquisti, Alessandro	Backerman, Steven	Bergmann, Ralph
Acs, Zoltan J.	Baer, Arthur A.	Bergstrom, Theodore C.
Adamowicz, Wiktor	Baer, Susanne	Berkman, Richard
Adams, Charles	Baily, Martin Neil	Berkowitz, Bruce
Adda, Jerome	Baize, Harold R., Jr.	Bernanke, Ben
Ades, Alberto F.	Baker, Lynn A.	Berndt, Ernst R.
Adler, Barry	Baker, Tom	Bernstein, Donald S.
Agee, Bobby	Baker-Brown, Gloria	Bernstein, Peter L.
Aha, David W.	Ballard, Elizabeth J.	Bernzweig, Jane
Aharon, I.	Ballbach, John Daniel	Berry, Christopher R.
Akerlof, George A.	Baltussen, Guido	Berry, Donald
Albright, James	Bankman, Joseph	Berry, Jane M.
Aldrich, John Herbert	Banks, Jeffrey S.	Besen, Stanley
Aldy, Joseph E.	Barankin, E. W.	Bettman, James R.
Aleinikoff, T. Alexander	Barberis, Nicholas	Bierer, Michael F.
Alesina, Alberto F.	Bar-Gill, Oren	Bilder, Richard B.
Aleven, Vincent	Baron, Jonathan	Binder, Denis
Allen, R. Michael	Barr, Michael S.	Bishop, Richard C.
Alstott, Anne	Barrett, Christopher	Blackmon, Glenn
Althoff, Klaus-Dieter	Barry, Norman	Blackwell, D.
Amar, Vikram Reed	Bart, Susan T.	Blair, Irene V.
Amir, Eli	Barth, James R.	Blair, Margaret
Anderson, Elizabeth S.	Bateman, Ian	Blanchard, Olivier J.
Anderson, John	Bates, Robert	Blitzstein, David
Anderson, Philip W.	Bator, Francis M.	Block, H. D.
Anderson, Soren	Baumol, William J.	Bloom, Jeremy
Anderson, Terry L.	Baxter, William F.	Bluck, Susan
Andreoni, James	Bazerman, Max H.	Blume, Andreas
Ansolabehere, Stephen	Beatty, Jackson	Blume, Lawrence
Antonanzas, Anton	Bebchuk, Lucian Arye	Boettger, Richard
Antonanzas, Fernando	Becker, Edward R.	Bollag, Burton
Appelbaum, Paul S.	Becker, Gary S.	Bollinger, Lee C.
Appiah, K. Anthony	Becker, Mary	Boltuck, Richard
Argote, Linda	Becker, William	Bonabeau, Eric
Ariely, Dan	Beckmann, Martin J.	Bond, Christopher S.
Arkes, Hal R.	Behbinder, Eckard	Bond, Stephen R.
Arlen, Jennifer H.	Belkin, Aaron	Bonner, Sarah E.
Armor, David	Bell, Jason	Bonnie, Richard J.
Asher, Thomas	Bell, Nancy	Booth, Shawn
Athanasoulis, Stefano G.	Bellman, Steve	Borick, Matthew
Athey, Susan	Belsky, Eric	Born, Patricia
Aultman, Chris	Beltratti, Andrea E.	Borzekowski, Ron
Austin, John	Ben-Ishai, R.	Bose, Subir
Ausubel, Lawrence M.	Benkler, Yochai	Boskin, Michael J.
Avery, Christopher	Bensoussan, Alain	Bosworth, Barry
Avni-Babad, Dinah	Benston, George	Boudreaux, Donald J.

Bove, Timothy
Bowles, Samuel
Bowlus, Audra J.
Boycko, Maxim
Boyd, Roy
Bradley, Curtis A.
Bradlow, Eric
Brady, Henry E.
Brainard, Lael
Brana, Francisco J.
Bratton, W. Kenneth
Brauer, Jurgen
Braunstein, Myron L.
Breger, Marshall J.
Breiter, H.C.
Brennan, Donald G.
Breslauer, George W.
Bresnahan, Timothy F.
Brest, Paul
Brilmayer, Lea
Brinkley, Alan
Bris, Arturo
Brock, Timothy C.
Brodsky, Steve
Brody, Richard A.
Bromage, Robert C.
Bromwich, Michael
Bronfman, Corinne M.
Brookshire, David S.
Broos, Patrick
Brown, Thomas P.
Brucato, Jr., P.F.
Brumbaugh, Jr., R. Dan
Bruninghaus, Stefanie
Brunschwig, Jacques
Bryan, Angela
Buccola, Steven
Buchman, Thomas A.
Bulfin, Robert L.
Bunzel, Henning
Burdett, Ken
Burkell, Jacquelyn
Burkholder, Steve
Burnett, Jason K.
Burnham, Terence
Burtless, Gary
Busemeyer, Jerome
Butler, Judith
Bybee, Jay S.
Cagan, Phillip
Caginalp, Gunduz
Cain, Becky
Cain, Louis
Calabresi, Guido

Calabresi, Steven G.
Calfee, John E.
Califa, Antonio J.
Callaway, Charles B.
Calomiris, Charles
Camerer, Colin
Campbell, Bradley M.
Campbell, John Y.
Campbell, Joseph
Cane, Peter
Canina, Linda
Cantu, Norma
Capan, D.T.
Caplan, Marc
Caprio, Gerard
Capron, William M.
Carlin, Alan
Carlton, Dennis W.
Carmines, Edward G.
Carroll, John S.
Carron, Andrew S.
Carvalho, Irineu
Case, Karl E.
Cass, Glen
Cass, Ronald A.
Cate, Fred H.
Cavallo, Gerald
Cavanagh, Sheila M.
Cavanaugh, Lisa A.
Cecot, Caroline
Chajczyk, D.
Chaloupka, Frank J.
Chan, Yee-Ho I.
Chang, Sheldon
Chang, Shi-jie
Charney, Robert
Charnley, Gail
Chatterji, Manas
Cheeseman, Peter
Chemerinsky, Erwin
Chen, Jingqiu
Chenery, Hollis B.
Chesney, Robert
Chesson, Harrell W.
Chichilnisky, Graciela
Chinnis, Jr., James O.
Choi, Albert H.
Choi, Stephen J.
Choper, Jesse H.
Chopra, Navin
Chorvat, Terrence R.
Christensen, Bent J.
Clark, Karen
Claybrook, Joan

Clesse, Armand
Coglianese, Cary
Cohen, Daniel
Cohen, Joshua
Cohen, Linda R.
Cohen, Marvin S.
Cole, William R.
Collins, Ronald K.L.
Colombatto, Enrico
Colvin, Mary K.
Connaughton, James L.
Conover, C.J.
Conquist, Henrik
Conway, Lucien Gideon III
Cook, Philip J.
Cope, David
Coppinger, V.
Corfman, Kim
Coricelli, Georgio
Corkran, Kelsi Brown
Corley, Dan
Cosmides, Leda
Costa-i-Font, Joan
Cottle, Richard W.
Coupey, Eloise
Courant, Paul
Coursey, Don L.
Cowen, Tyler
Cowgill, Bo
Cox, Adam B.
Cox, James C.
Cox, James D.
Cramton, Peter
Crandall, Robert W.
Crandall, Ronald M.
Crawford, Colin
Crawford, Vincent
Cremers, Martijn
Creyer, Elizabeth H.
Crider, A.
Crocker, Jennifer
Crockett, Sean
Cropper, Maureen L.
Crosby, Faye
Crosby, Travis
Crum, Roy L.
Cuccias, Matthew J.
Cummings, Ronald G
Cummins, Jason G.
Cutler, David M.
Cutler, Lloyd N.
Daalder, Ivo H.
Daily, Gretchen
Dale, A.

Damiano, Peter
Danovitch, Gabriel M.
Dasgupta, Partha
Daughety, Andrew F.
Davidson, Cliff
Davidson, Ralph K.
Davis, Steven J.
Dawes, Robyn M.
Dawson, John P.
Day, Richard Hollis
Day, Robert
De Bondt, Werner F.M.
de Figueiredo, Miguel F.P.
de la Garza, Rodolfo
De Soto, Hernando
de Sousa e Brito, Clara Sattler
Deakin, Simon
Debreu, Gerard
Deere, Donald
Dejong, Douglas V.
Del Rossi, Alison
Delgado, Mauricio R.
DeMuth, Christopher
Deng, Gang
Denton, Michael
Destler, I. M. (Mac)
Desvousges, William H.
Deutch, John M.
Devereux, Michael P.
Devine, Terry
deVries, Brian
DeWitt, Diane
Diascro, Matthew N.
Dickens, William T.
Dickhaut, John
Diederich, Adele
Diener, Ed
Dietrich, J. Richard
Dikens, William T.
Dinar, Ariel
Dinkin, Samuel H.
Dionne, E. J.
DiPasquale, Denise
Djankov, Simeon
Dockins, P. Christen
Dolan, Paul
Donnelly, David
Donoghue, Kristen A.
Donohue, John J. III
Dorf, Michael C.
Dorfman, Howard L.
Douglas, H. Eugene
Dowlatabadi, Hadi
Doyle, Michael W.

Dreben, Elizabeth K.
Dreyfus, Mark
Drogosz, Kayla Meltzer
Drory, Amos
Dubin, Jeff
Dubinsky, Paul
Dudek, Daniel J.
Dudley, Patrick M.
Dumais, Guy
Durbin, David
Durham, Yvonne
Durlauf, Steven N.
Eads, George C.
Eaves, B. Curtis
Eberly, Janice
Edell, Julie A.
Edley, Jr., Christopher
Eggleston, Karen
Ehrlich, Isaac
Ehrlich, Paul
Eisenberg, Theodore
Eizenstat, Stuart
Elam, Joyce
Eli, Michael Bar
Ellickson, Robert
Ellison, Glenn
Elms, Laurel
Elson, Sara Beth
Emerson, Michael
Encaoua, David
Engelbrecht Wiggans, Richard
Enthoven, Alain C.
Erev, Rapporteur Ido
Ericsson, K. Anders
Eskridge, William N.
Esposito, Joseph J.
Esptein, David
Estanol, Albert Banal
Estlund, David M.
Estrich, Susan R.
Evans, William
Fagan, Jeffrey
Fair, Ray C.
Fan, Elliott T.
Faralli, Carla
Farina, Cynthia R.
Farmer, J. Doyne
Faro, David
Farrell, Joseph
Faulhaber, Gerald R.
Fauth, Gary
Feather, Timothy D.
Feinberg, Kenneth R.
Feld, Peter

Feld, Scott L.
Feldman, Jack
Feltus, William
Feng, Qi
Fernandez, Irma-Becerra
Fernandez, Jorge
Ferrara, Alessandro
Fershtman, Chaim
Fessler, Daniel M.T.
Feustel, Bruce
Fiechter, Jonathan
Field, Martha A.
Fienberg, Stephen E.
Fikentscher, Wolfgang
Fine, Janice
Fink, Howard P.
Finkelstein, Claire
Finney, Hal
Finnis, John
Fiorito, Jack
Fischer, Gregory W.
Fischer, Oliver
Fischer, Stanley
Fishback, Bowman
Fisher, Anthony C.
Fishkin, James
Fiske, Alan Page
Fiske, Susan T.
Fitzsimmons, Stephen J.
Flach, Stephen
Flanders, Chad
Fleischmann, Andrew M.
Fleming, Lee
Fletcher, Joseph F.
Flom, Merton C.
Flyer, Fredrick
Fontana, David
Forrest, Anne
Foster, Vivien
Fox, Craig R.
Fox, Eleanor
Foxhall, Lesley C.
Frain, Laura
Franciosi, Robert
Frederick, Shane
Fredrickson, Barbara L.
Freed, Mayer G.
Freeman, Jody
Freeman, Richard T.
Fried, Charles
Friedland, Nehemia
Friedman, Benjamin M.
Friedman, David
Friedman, Lawrence

Friend, Irwin
Fries, Erin
Froot, Kenneth A.
Fryer, Jr., Roland G.
Fuchita, Yasayuki
Fudenberg, Drew
Fullerton, Don
Furchtgott-Roth, Harold
Gaba, Anil
Gaines, Brian J.
Gale, William
Galebach, Brian
Gallant, Jack L.
Garcia Swartz, Daniel D.
Garrett, Elizabeth
Gaspar, Jess
Gaston, Robert S.
Gates, Susan
Gati, Itamar
Gauna, Eileen
Gayer, Ted
Geanakoplos, John
Gelband, Hellen
genannt Döhmann, Indra
  Spiecker
Gentry, William M.
Gentzkow, Matthew
Gerhardt, Michael J.
Gersen, Jacob
Gertner, Robert
Gessford, John
Getman, Karen
Ghiselli, Edwin E.
Ghosh, Prodipto
Gibbard, Allan
Gibbs, Brian J.
Gigone, Daniel
Gillis, Floyd E.
Gilovich, Thomas
Ginsburg, Ruth Bader
Girshick, M. A.
Gitenstein, Mark
Gitlin, Todd
Gjerstad, Steven
Glaser, James M.
Gleason, Abbott
Glendon, Spencer
Glewwe, Paul
Glosten, Larry
Glover, Jonathan
Goetz, Stephan J.
Goldberg, Julie H.
Goldberg, Victor P.
Goldfeld, Stephen M.

Goldgeier, James M.
Goldin, Claudia Dale
Goldman, John T.
Goldstein, Thomas C.
Golove, David
Goodman, Paul S.
Gordon, Roger H.
Gorham, William
Gotfryd, William T.
Gottlieb, Joshua D.
Gould, William
Goulder, Lawrence
Grabowski, Henry
Grafman, Jordan
Graham, Carol
Graham, John D.
Gramm, Wendy L.
Grant, Paul
Green, Donald Philip
Green, Melanie C.
Green, Philip
Greenberg, Karen J.
Greene, William
Gregory, C.
Greif, Avner
Greve, Michael S.
Grey, Thomas C.
Griffin, Dale W.
Griffith, Rachel
Griliches, Zvi
Grimmelman, James
Grofman, Bernard
Gross, Leo
Grossman, Michael
Grossman, Sanford J.
Groves, Theodore
Grullon, Gustavo
Grundfest, Joseph A.
Guasch, J. Luis
Gürkaynak, Refet S.
Guinier, Lani
Gulati, G. Mitu
Gulbranson, Christine A.
Gunnthorsdottir, Anna
Gunter, David
Gunther, Gerald
Gurman, Jesse
Guttentag, Jack
Guttieri, Karen
Gyourko, Joseph
Haass, Richard N.
Hagan, John
Hagel, III, John
Hagen, Michael G.

Hahn, F. H.
Haig, Susan White
Hair, Penda D.
Hakes, Jahn K.
Hakim, Peter
Hall, Robert E.
Halperin, Morton H.
Hamilton, James T.
Hammerle, Oliver
Hammond, III, John S.
Hammond, Kenneth R.
Hanemann, Michael
Hanley, Dena E.
Hannum, Kristen A.
Hansmann, Henry
Hanson, James A.
Hanushek, Eric A.
Hao, Li
Harbord, David
Harcourt, Bernard E.
Harrington, Jr., Joseph E.
Harrington, Scott
Harris, Theodore E.
Harrison, Glenn W.
Hart, Warren
Harvey, Lewis O.
Harvey, William Burnett
Harwood, Alison
Hassler, William T.
Hastings, John
Hatfield, John William
Hauerwas, Stanley
Hausman, Leonard
Hawkins, David
Hawkins, Scott A.
Hazlett, Thomas W.
Heal, Geoffrey
Heaton, Paul S.
Heffetz, Ori
Heinzelman, Susan Sage
Heinzerling, Lisa
Hekeler, Richard W.
Helft, Paul R.
Hemelrijk, Charlotte K.
Henderson, Dale W.
Henderson, M. Todd
Henderson, Stanley D.
Henik, Avishai
Henik, Erika
Hermann, Douglas J.
Herring, Richard J.
Herrmann, Richard K.
Hersch, Joni
Hershey, J.C.

Hertwig, Ralph
Hesse, Carla
Hester, Gordon L.
Higgins, Tracy
Hines, Jr., James R.
Hinich, Melvin J.
Hipps, Robert
Hird, John
Hirsch, Alan
Hirshleifer, Jack
Ho, Katty
Hoch, Stephen J.
Hoffenberg, Marvin
Hoffman, Elizabeth
Hoffmann, Stanley
Holbrook, Morris
Holmstrom, Bengt
Holt, Charles A.
Honkapohja, Seppo
Hopkins, Thomas D.
Horowitz, Alan B.
Horowitz, Joel L.
Houser, Daniel
Hout, Michael
Howard, Matthew
Howe, Amy
Howitt, Richard E.
Howrey, Philip
Hsee, Christopher K.
Huang, Ming
Huang, Peter H.
Huber, Joel
Huber, Peter W.
Hughes, James
Huntington, Samuel P.
Hurwicz, Leonid
Husbands, Jo L.
Hutchens, Robert M.
Hutchinson, Dennis J.
Hutson, John D.
Hyman, David A.
Hynes, Richard M.
Ilieva, Vladmiria A.
Imbrecht, Charles R.
Inderst, Roman
Ingram, Beth
Intriligator, Michael D.
Irwin, Julie R.
Isaac, R. Mark
Ishikida, Takashi
Issacharoff, Samuel
Jackson, Howell
Jackson, Thomas H.
Jackson, Vicki C.

Jacobs, Ann L.
Jacobsen, Richard T.
Jacowitz, Karen E.
James, Bryan
James, Mark
Jarman, M. Casey
Jarvenpaa, Sirkka L.
Jefferis, Eric S.
Jeffries, Jr., John C.
Jensen, P.
Jensen, Shane T.
Jeon, Bang Nam
Jervis, Robert
Jezer, Marty
Jhangiani, R.
Johnson, Eric J.
Johnson, Joseph M.
Johnson, Selmer M.
Johnson, Simon
Johnson, Suzanne Nora
Jonathan Haidt, Rapporteur
Jones, Donald R.
Jones, William M.
Judd, Charles M.
Juhn, Chinhui
Jung, Chulho
Jung, Jeeman
Kafry, Ditsa
Kahan, Dan M.
Kahin, Brian
Kahn, Alfred E.
Kahn, Barbara E.
Kahn, Jeffrey P.
Kahn, Matthew E.
Kallal, Hedi D.
Kalt, Brian
Kalt, Joseph P.
Kalven, Harry Jr.
Kameda, Tatsuya
Kaminski, Robert J.
Kamisar, Yale
Kamlet, Mark S.
Kanda, Hideki
Kane, Rosalie A.
Kanefsky, Bob
Kaplow, Louis
Karasik, Anna D.
Karlawish, Jason H.
Karlin, Samuel
Kartik, Navin
Kass, Leon
Kaswan, Alice
Kates, Jr., Don B.
Katona, George

Katyal, Neal
Katz, Eddan
Katz, Joel
Katz, Lawrence F.
Katz, Michael L.
Katz, Wilber G.
Katzen, Sally
Kaufman, George G.
Kautsky, Nils
Kawagishi, Norikazu
Kearl, James R.
Keeney, Ralph L.
Kehler, Randy
Kehoe, Timothy J.
Keidar-Levin, Yael
Keinan, Giora
Kendrick, Ann
Kennedy, Duncan
Kennedy, Maureen
Kerr, William R.
Kerwin, Jeffrey
Kessler, Daniel P.
Ketcham, Jon
Khadilkar, Jayant
Kiefer, Nicholas M.
Kihlstrom, John F.
Kilbourne, Lynda M.
Kim, Jae I.
Kimbrough, Erik
King, Desmond S.
King, Ronald R.
Kingsbury, Benedict
Klein, Benjamin
Kleinmuntz, Don N.
Klemm, Alexander
Klepper, Steven
Kletzer, Lori G.
Klingman, Darwin
Knetsch, Jack L.
Knez, Mark
Knez, Peter
Kniesner, Thomas J.
Knight, Kathleen
Knopman, David
Koehn, Mark R.
Kogut, Tehila
Koh, Harold
Kohlhase, Janet E.
Kohli, Aarti
Kolko, Jed
Kolp, Paul
Kon-Ya, Fumiko
Koopmans, Tjalling C.
Kop, Yaakov

Kopp, Raymond J.
Kordana, Kevin A.
Korobov, Vladimir
Kosec, Katrina
Kovner, Mark
Kozlovski, Nimrod
Kraft, Richard
Kramer, Larry
Krasner, Stephen D.
Krattenmaker, Thomas G.
Kraus, Susan
Krause, Lawrence B.
Kreag, John
Kreimer, Seth F.
Kremer, Michael
Kreps, David
Krier, James E.
Krimgold, Frederick
Krisch, Nico
Kristel, Orie
Krosnick, Jon
Kroszner, Randy
Krueger, Alan B.
Kruse, Jamie Brown
Krutilla, Kerry
Kubovy, Michael
Kuhlik, Bruce
Kujal, Praveen
Kuklinski, James H.
Kumar, Alok
Kumar, Anjali
Kumar, Purohit A.
Kun, Veronica
Kunreuther, Howard
Kurz, Mordecai
Kurzban, Robert
Laibson, David I.
Lakonishok, Josef
Laland, Kevin N.
Lally, James F.
LaLonde, Robert J.
LaMaster, Shawn
Lamont, Owen A.
Landes, David S.
Landes, William M.
Landsberg, Hans H.
Landsman, R.
Lanir, Zvi
Lanot, Gauthier
Lantos, John D.
LaPorta, Rafael
Lasky, Jeffrey
Laughhunn, Dan J.
Lave, Lester B.

Law, David S.
Lawrence, Gordon R.
Lawrence, Robert Z.
Layburn, Erin M.
Layne-Farrar, Anne
Layton, David
Lazarus, Simon
Lazear, Edward P.
Lebow, Richard Ned.
LeClerc, France
Lee, Charles M.C.
Lee, Grace
Lehmann, Donald
Lehr, William
Leiden, Warren R.
Leigh, Andrew
Lemley, Mark A.
Lempert, Richard O.
Lenton, Alison P.
Lentz, Rasmus
Leonard, Paul
LePore, Michael
Lerner, Andres V.
Lerner, Jennifer S.
Lester, James C.
Letiche, John
Lettow, Renee
Levhari, David
Levi, Ariel
Levin, Simon
Levine, Robert A.
Levinson, Daryl J.
Levitt, Steven D.
Lewis, Tracy R.
Ley, Eduardo
Lichtman, Douglas
Liebman, Lance
Lien, Donald D.
Lin, Herbert S.
Lin, Kathy
Lincoln, Edward J.
Lind, Robert C.
Lindsay, Donald G.
Lock, Reinier
Lockwood, Jeffrey A.
Loewenstein, George
Loftus, Elizabeth F.
Logue, Kyle D.
Lopez de Silanes, Florencio
Lotan, Michael
Lovallo, Dan
Low, David S.
Low, Peter W.
Lowman, Christopher

Lozon, Marie
Lubchenco, Jane
Lucas, J. Robert
Luce, Mary Frances
Ludwig, Jens
Luke, Marcie
Luke, Margaret
Lukens, Leslie
Lundberg, Shelly J.
Lundholm, Russell J.
Lutter, Randall W.
Luttmer, Erzo F.P.
Lyman, Peter
Lynch, Jr., John G.
Lyubomirsky, Sonja
Mac Lane, Saunders
MacAvoy, Paul W.
MacCoun, Robert
MacCrisken, Jack
MacKie-Mason, Jeffrey K.
MacLean, Douglas
Macskassy, Sofus
Maddala, G. S.
Mader, Elizabeth A.
Magat, Wesley A.
Maier, Norbert
Mailloux, Steven
Malani, Anup
Maler, Karl-Goran
Males, Eric
Malik, Rohit
Manes, R. P.
Mank, Bradford C.
Mankiw, N. Gregory
Mann, Thomas E.
Mannering, Fred
Manning, John F.
Manning, Willard G.
Mannino, Michael V.
Manstead, Antony S. R.
Marcus, Jonathan
Marcus, Maeva
Mare, David C.
Margalit, Avishai
Markey, Edward J.
Markman, Keith D.
Marschak, Jacob
Marschak, Thomas
Marshall, William P.
Martin, Francisco Forrest
Martinez, Maria A.
Martorana, Paul
Massa, Massimo
Massey, Cade

Masson, Paul
Mastrangelo, Erin
Matas, Arthur J.
May, Carol A.
May, Ernest R.
Mayer, Colin
Mayers, David
Mazur, James E.
Mazzocco, Philip
McCabe, Kevin A.
McCaffery, Edward J.
McChesney, Robert W.
McCloskey, Robert G.
McCrary, Peyton
Mcculloch, J. Huston
McFadden, Daniel
McGartland, Albert M.
McGlyn, Michele B.
McGowan, Francis
McGrath, Paul
McGraw, A. Peter
McGuire, Charles B.
McManus, Maurice
McRae, Gregory
Medin, Douglas L.
Medvec, Victoria Husted.
Melino, Angelo
Mellers, Barbara A.
Mellinkoff, Sherman M.
Mellor, III, William H.
Meltzer, Daniel J.
Mendez, David
Menkel-Meadow, Carrie
Meyer, Bruce D.
Meyer, John Robert
Meyer, Margaret
Michaely, Roni
Micheletti, Patrick M.
Michelitsch, Roland
Milford, Jana
Miller, D.T.
Miller, James C.
Miller, Ross M.
Millian, John C.
Mills, Edwin S.
Minhas, B. S.
Miron, Jeffrey A.
Mitchell, Bridger
Mitchell, Gregory
Mitchell, Lesa
Mitchell, Olivia S.
Mnookin, Robert H.
Modigliani, Franco
Moglen, Eben

Momany, Elizabeth
Monan, J. Donald
Moore, David H.
Moore, Don A.
Moore, Michael J.
Morales, Luis
Moran, Simone
Morgan, Sean
Morley, Matt T.
Morrall, John
Morrill, Calvin
Morrison, Edward R.
Mortensen, Dale T.
Moscarini, Giuseppe
Mote, John
Mott, Bradford W.
Mottola, Gary R.
Moulin, Sylvie
Moyle, Petrea R.
Muething, Mary Beth
Mullainthan, Sendhil
Mulligan, Elizabeth J.
Munro, Alistair
Murphy, James J.
Muth, Richard F.
Myers, Bill
Nabli, Mustapha
Nader, Ralph
Nadiri, M. Ishaq
Nagel, Robert
Nalebuff, Barry
Narayan, Sanjay A.
Nasmith, Moneen S.
Neal, Derek A.
Nelkin, Dorothy
Nelson, Jon P.
Nerlove, Marc
Neumann, Manfred J. M.
Neumann, Peter
Neustadt, Richard N.
Newhouse, Joseph P.
Newman, Daniel G.
Ng, Yew-Kwang
Nickerson, C.
Niemi, Richard G.
Ninio, Anat
Niskanen, William
Nivola, Pietro S.
Noll, Roger G.
Norberg, Karen
Nordhaus, William D.
Norman, Joel
North, Douglass
Northrup, David A.

Nou, Jennifer
Noveck, Beth
Novemsky, Nathan
Novotny, Thomas E.
Nugent, Jeffrey
Nussim, Jacob
Nutter, Frank
Nye, Jr., Joseph S.
O'Halloran, Sharyn
O'Connell, Jeffrey
O'Connor, Charles
Ogletree, Jr., Charles J.
O'Hanlon, Michael E.
O'Keefe, Mary
Olkin, Ingram
Olmstead, Sheila M.
Olson, Lawrence
Olson, Mark
Olyan, Saul
Onken, James
Onuska, Linda
Oprea, Ryan
Ordeshook, Peter C.
Ordonez, Lisa D.
Orosel, Gerhard
Orszag, Jonathan
Orszag, Peter R.
Ortiz, Daniel R.
Oster, Sharon
Ostrowski, Michele
Owen, Geoffrey
Owens, Pamela D.
Palfrey, Thomas R.
Palmer, Karen
Panchamukhi, Vadiraj
  Raghawendracharya
Panosian, Claire
Papa, Anthony
Papachristos, Andrew V.
Papadopoulos, Ioannis S.
Parisi, Francesco
Park, Bernadette
Parker, Jonathan A.
Parker, Noel Geoffrey
Passell, Peter
Patelli, Paolo
Patusky, Christopher
Paul, Jeffrey
Paul, Jonathan
Paul, Louis C.
Paulson, Anna L.
Pearce, David
Peavler, W. Scott
Pedersen, Peder

Peleg, Ehud
Peller, Gary
Peltman, Sam
Peng, Kaiping
Penniman, Nick
Pennington, Nancy
Pennock, David M.
Penoncello, Steven G.
Penrod, Steven
Perlman, Mark
Perron, Pierre
Pesotchinsky, Leon
Petajisto, Antti
Peterson, Randall S.
Phelps, Elizabeth A.
Philipson, Tomas
Phillips, Nancy V.
Piazza, Thomas
Picker, Randal C.
Piehl, Anne Morrison
Pierce, Brooks
Pierce, Richard J.
Pines, David
Pinkerton, James
Pitofsky, Robert
Pitt, Harvey L.
Plache, Lacey L.
Plesko, George
Plott, Charles R.
Polgreen, Philip L.
Polgreen, Philip M.
Polifroni, Mark
Polinsky, A. Mitchell
Polk, Charles
Pollack, Irwin
Pollock, Alex
Polsby, Daniel D.
Polsby, Nelson W.
Pomerleano, Michael
Ponzetto, Giacomo A.M.
Pope, Clayne L.
Porter, Bruce W.
Porter, David P.
Portillo, Fabiola
Portney, Paul R.
Porzig, Marisa A.
Posner, Richard A.
Post, Thierry
Poterba, James M.
Pound, John
Powell, Walter W.
Prat, Andrea
Pratt, John W.
Prescott, J. J.

Price, Joseph
Prieger, James E.
Priest, George L.
Prior, Markus
Probst, Katherine N.
Putnam, Hilary
Puto, Christopher
Qian, Yingyi
Quigley, John M.
Quillen, Carol
Quirk, James P.
Rabin, Matthew
Rachlinski, Jeffrey J.
Racicot, Marc
Radner, Roy
Ragsdale, E.K. Easton
Raiffa, Howard
Rakoff, Todd D.
Ramirez, Carmenza
Randolph, A. Raymond
Rappaport, Jordan
Rasinski, Kenneth A.
Rasmussen, Douglas
Rasmussen, Robert K.
Rassenti, Stephen J.
Ratain, Mark J.
Ratner, Rebecca K.
Rawson, Katherine A.
Raynaud, Hervé
Rea, Jr., Samuel A.
Rechtschaffen, Clifford
Redelmeier, Donald A.
Reder, Melvin W.
Reed, Ronald O.
Reed, Terryann
Reedy, E. J.
Regan, Dennis T.
Rehbinder, Eckard
Rehder, Bob
Reich, Darcy A.
Reiman, Jeffrey
Reimshisel, Tyler
Reiners, William A.
Reinhardt, Uwe E.
Reis, Ricardo
Ren, Yaya
Renda, Andrea
Renshon, Jonathan
Rescober, Phillip
Resnick, Paul
Restinas, Nicolas P.
Rettinger, David A.
Reuter, Jonathan
Reuter, Peter

Revelle, William
Revesz, Richard L.
Reynolds, Morgan
Reynolds, Stanley S.
Rice, Donald
Richards, Kenneth R.
Riddell, W. Craig
Riepe, Mark W.
Rietz, Thomas
Rigdon, Mary L.
Rigotti, Nancy A.
Riis, Jason
Rissland, Edwina L.
Rissman, Ellen R.
Rivlin, Alice M.
Roberson, Bruce
Roberts, John
Roberts, Marc J.
Robin, Jean-Marc
Robinson, Georgene
Robinson, Lori B.
Roehl, Richard
Rogin, Michael
Romer, Paul M.
Roopnarine, Anil
Rorty, Amelie O.
Rose, Carol
Rosen, Allison
Rosen, Amy
Rosenblum, Nancy
Rosenfeld, Michel
Rosenfield, Andrew M.
Rosenkranz, E. Joshua
Rosenthal, Stuart S.
Rosett, Richard N.
Ross, Lee
Roth, Alvin E.
Roth, D.
Rothschild, David
Rovira, Joan
Rowe, Davis M.
Rowe, Thomas D.
Rowland, Steven R.
Rozin, Paul
Rubin, Paul H.
Rucker, Derek D.
Rudinsky, Brian
Russell, Milton
Russell, Peter H.
Russell, Thomas
Rustow, Dankwart A.
Rutherglen, George
Rutstrom, E. Elizabeth
Rutten, Andrew R.

Ryan, Carey S.
Ryan, Lee
Ryoo, Jaewoo
Saar-Tsechansky, Maytal
Sacerdote, Bruce I.
Saiz, Albert
Saks, Michael J.
Saks, Raven E.
Salop, Steven C.
Samida, Dexter
Samuelson, Pamela
Samwick, Andrew A.
Sanchirico, Chris William
Sanderson, Allen
Sandholm, William H.
Sands, Phillppe
Sanfey, Alan G.
Santomero, Anthony M.
Saposnik, R.
Sarin, Rakesh
Savin, N. Eugene
Sawyer, James W.
Scarf, Herbert
Scharff, Robert L.
Schatzberg, Jeffrey
Schauer, Frederick
Schein, Galit
Scheinkman, Jose A.
Schell, Scott
Scheppele, Kim Lane
Scherer, Frederic M.
Scherer, Klaus R.
Schild, E.O.
Schmalensee, Richard
Schmandt, Alexander
Schmidt, Christian
Schnably, Stephen J.
Schneider, Lynne
Schneider, Ryan
Schneider, Stephen H.
Schnitzler, Mark A.
Schoenbaum, Thomas J.
Schoenholtz, Kermit L.
Schofield, Malcolm
Schramm, Carl Jude
Schrefler, Lorna
Schreiber, Charles A.
Schroeder, Colin
Schuck, Peter H.
Schultze, Charles L.
Schulze, William D.
Schwartz, Alan
Schwartz, Joseph E.
Schwartz, Michael A.

Schwarz, Michael J.
Schwarz, Norbert
Scitovsky, Tibor
Scott, Amanda L.
Scott, Ben
Scott, Kenneth
Scruton, Roger
Seabright, Paul
Seeley, Thomas D.
Segal, Ilya R.
Self, Matthew
Selten, Reinhard
Sen, Amartya
Servan-Schreiber, Emile
Sethi, Suresh
Shachat, Keith
Shafir, Eldar
Shannon, Chris
Shapiro, Carl
Shapiro, David L.
Shapiro, Jesse M.
Shapiro, Robert J.
Sharff, Robert
Shavell, Steven M.
Shaviro, Daniel
Shefrin, Hersch M.
Sheldon, Kennon M.
Shenker, Scott
Shepherd, Roger
Sheshinski, Eytan
Shiffrin, Steven
Shiv, Baba
Shizgal, Peter
Shleifer, Andrei
Shultz, George P.
Sider, Hal S.
Siegel, Jeremy J.
Siegel, Neil S.
Siegel, Reva B.
Siegler, Mark
Sifry, Micah L.
Sihvola, Juha
Silberman, R. Gaull
Simkin, David
Simmons, Emily
Simon, Jonathan S.
Simonson, Itamar
Singer, Hal J.
Singh, Jaideep
Singh, Ramadhar
Skidelsky, Robert
Skitka, Linda J.
Skogan, Wesley
Sloan, F.A.

Slovic, Paul
Smith, Jr., Turner T.
Smith, David
Smith, Dixon B.
Smith, Lones
Smith, Loren A.
Smith, V. Kerry
Snell, Jackie
Sniderman, Paul M.
Snyder, Jr., James M.
Sobel, Milton
Sohn, Michael
Solimine, Michael E.
Solow, Robert M.
Soneji, Samir
Song, Michael
Sørensen, Peter Norman
Sorenson, Olav
Soutter, Christine L.
Sparrow, Bartholomew H.
Spellman, Barbara A.
Spiller, Pablo
Spitzer, Adelbert L.
Sprinkle, Geoffrey B.
Squintani, Francesco
Srinagesh, Padmanabhan
St. Amour, Lynn
Staelin, Richard
Staiger, Robert W.
Starmer, Chris
Starr, Paul
Starrett, David
Stasser, Garold
Staten, Michael E.
Stavins, Robert N.
Steiker, Jordan
Steil, Benn
Steinberg, James B.
Steinzor, Rena I.
Stern, Paul C.
Stevenson, Betsey
Still, Edward
Stokey, Nancy
Stone, Arthur A.
Stone, Dan N.
Stone, Nancy Spector
Stoto, Michael A.
Strange, William C.
Stratton, Jessie
Streufert, Siegfried
Strömberg, David
Stuntz, William
Stutz, John
Suchanek, Gerry L.

Suchman, Peter O.
Suedfeld, Peter
Suen, Wing
Sugden, Robert
Sukhtankar, Sandip
Sullivan, Teresa A.
Sundararajan, Vasudevan
Suppes, Patrick
Suzumura, Kotaro
Swait, Joffre
Swede, Southworth Wells
Swire, Peter P.
Sykes, Alan O.
Szidarovszky, Ferenc
Tadmor, Carmit T.
Takezawa, Masanori
Talley, Eric L.
Tamura, Robert
Tang, Fang-Fang
Tanlu, Lloyd
Tanz, Robert R.
Tao, Yi
Tardiff, Timothy J.
Tarricone, Jason
Taubman, Paul
Taylor, Jr., Stuart
Taylor, Will
Taylor, William E.
Teitel, Ruti
Tenney, Elizabeth R.
Thomas, Oliver S.
Thompson, Grant P.
Thompson, Leigh
Thomson, William
Thum, Marcel
Tietz, Reinhard
Tilly, Charles
Titus, J.
Tobin, James
Tobio, Kristina
Topel, Robert H.
Topping, M.
Townsend, Joy
Trebilcock, Michael J.
Treisman, Anne
Treverton, Gregory
Triantis, George G.
Tribe, Lawrence H.
Trouard, Theodore
Tsutsui, Shunichi
Tsutsui, Yoshiro
Tulving, Endel
Tursky, Bernard
Tversky, Amos

Tyler, Anthony
Tyler, Tom
Ujhelyi, Gergely
Ulvila, Jacob W.
Unger, Rebecca
Utgoff, Kathy
Uzawa, Hirofumi
Valcarce, E.M.
van Alstyne, William W.
van Boening, Mark
van Dissell, Bart
van Parijs, Philippe
van Wallendael, Lori R.
van Wincoop, Eric
Vannoni, Michael G.
Varey, Carol A.
Varian, Chris
Veldkamp, Laura
Verchick, Robert R.M.
Verkuil, Paul R.
Vernon, John M.
Vesterlund, Lise
Vigdor, William R.
Vigdor, Jacob L.
Vishny, Robert W.
Visser, Penny S.
von Bertrab, Herman
von Furstenberg, George M.
Waelbroeck, Susan E.
Wagenhofer, Alfred
Wagman, Shlomit
Wakker, Peter P.
Walker, Brian
Walker, James M.
Wallenberg, Fredrik
Waller, William S.
Wallison, Peter J.
Wallskog, Peter
Wallsten, Scott J.
Walsh, Charles J.
Wang, Hongyan
Ward, Bryce Adam
Warner, Kenneth E.
Warren, Nicholas
Wasserman, David
Wasserstrom, Silas J.
Waverman, Leonard
Wax, Amy
Weber, Renee
Weber, Robert J.
Weber, Rosina
Weber, Steven
Weg, Eythan
Wei, Yulan

Weil, David N.
Weiler, Paul C.
Weinberg, Marca
Weingast, Barry R.
Weisberg, Robert
Weisfeld, Alix
Weiss, Allan N.
Weiss, Laurence
Weiss, Sara L.
Weiss, Yoram
Welch, Finis
Weld, William Charles
Wellford, Charissa P.
Wendt, Paul F.
Wenson, Curt
Werning, Ivan
West, Patricia M.
Westergaard-Nielsen, Niels
Westphal, Larry E.
Wewatz, Axel
Weynouth, F.W.
Whetten-Goldstein, Kathryn
Whitehead, G. Marc
Widawsky, Daniel
Wiener, Jonathan B.
Wilcox, Nathanial
Wiley, Jay W.
Williams, Arlington W.
Williams, Melissa S.
Williamson, Edwin D.
Williamson, J. Peter
Williamson, Jeffrey G.
Willis, Robert J.
Wilson, Bart J.
Wilson, James Q.
Wilson, Richard J.
Wilson, Robert
Winship, Christopher
Winston, Clifford M.
Winter, Ralph K.
Wittenbrink, Bernd
Wolak, Frank A.
Wolfers, Rohan
Wolman, R.
Womack, Kent
Woock, Christopher
Wood, Geoffrey
Woodard, Calvin
Woroch, Glenn
Wright, Jack
Wright, P.
Wu, David
Wu, Timothy
Wurtz, Allan

Mark Snyderman, a friend who clerked with [Lawrence] Lessig on the Supreme Court and is now a labor lawyer for Coca-Cola Co., witnessed what was perhaps Lessig's first demonstration of the power of computer code over the legal system, when as a clerk he was enlisted to help show Justices Scalia and O'Connor the difference between composing a decision on the court's ancient mainframe system compared to a personal computer. Both he and Snyderman were at computers — Snyderman using a terminal connected to the mainframe, Lessig using a PC. "We had identical documents on both computers," Snyderman recalled. "Larry said, 'Now imagine you're writing something and there's a word you've written and you think there's got to be a better word that works here. What do you do under the old system?'" Snyderman's response at the time was to stand up, go to a shelf and get a thesaurus. "'What do you do under the new system?' Larry hit the thesaurus key. Scalia went wild. That's it, he was completely sold."

The New York Times (1997)

JUDGE HENRY FRIENDLY

AND THE MIRROR OF CONSTITUTIONAL LAW

Michael Boudin[†]

My thanks to Dean Revesz, who heads this great law school, to Norman Dorsen — a friend for almost a half century — and to all of you for coming.

Henry Friendly served as a judge on the U.S. Court of Appeals for the Second Circuit from 1959 until his death in 1986. During that period, he wrote almost one thousand opinions,[1] several books,[2] thirty or so full-scale articles,[3] and many tributes and book reviews.[4] The power and quality of his work made him the most admired legal scholar and craftsman

---

[†] Copyright © 2007 by Michael Boudin, Chief Judge, U.S. Court of Appeals for the First Circuit. Appreciation is expressed to David Elsberg, who did preliminary research many years ago; to two sets of clerks who assisted me in different years: Felicia Ellsworth, Stephen Shackelford, Jr., and David Han, and Abby Wright, Matthew Price, and Joshua Kaul; and to two friends who read an early draft of this lecture: Judge Richard Posner and Professor Benjamin Friedman. This article originally appeared at 82 N.Y.U. L. Rev. 975 (2007), and is adapted from his Madison Lecture at the New York University School of Law.

[1] Professor Barnett identified 813 majority opinions for the circuit court. Stephen R. Barnett, *Henry Jacob Friendly*, in YALE BIOGRAPHICAL DICTIONARY OF AMERICAN LAW (Roger K. Newman ed., forthcoming 2008). In addition to these opinions, Judge Friendly wrote majority opinions for three-judge district courts and for the railroad reorganization court whose work he described in his tribute to Judge Wisdom. Henry J. Friendly, *From a Fellow Worker on the Railroads*, 60 TUL. L. REV. 244, 246-54 (1985). A complete count of Friendly's opinions would also include his concurrences and dissents.

[2] Friendly's books include HENRY J. FRIENDLY, FEDERAL JURISDICTION: A GENERAL VIEW (1973); his bound Holmes Lectures at Harvard, THE FEDERAL ADMINISTRATIVE AGENCIES: THE NEED FOR BETTER DEFINITION OF STANDARDS (1962) [hereinafter FRIENDLY, THE FEDERAL ADMINISTRATIVE AGENCIES] and at Dartmouth, THE DARTMOUTH COLLEGE CASE AND THE PUBLIC-PRIVATE PENUMBRA (1969) [hereinafter FRIENDLY, THE DARTMOUTH COLLEGE CASE]; and a collection of essays, articles, and lectures entitled BENCHMARKS (1967) [hereinafter FRIENDLY, BENCHMARKS].

[3] *See infra* notes 24-32 and accompanying text.

[4] *See infra* note 35 and accompanying text.

then sitting on the federal circuit courts, dominating his era as Learned Hand had dominated the 1930s through the 1950s.

A number of Friendly's articles and a share of his opinions concern constitutional law, broadly taken to include not just issues of "rights" but also such matters as jurisdiction, federal common law, and the state action doctrine. Yet my subject today is not legal doctrine, but rather what Friendly's articles and opinions on the subject tell us about him and about appellate judging. Friendly's work in constitutional law is a mirror in which we may hope to catch his reflection and measure his greatness.

Friendly's education and his career in practice bore directly on his judging. He was born in 1903 and grew up in Elmira, New York, then a modest-sized community.[5] From the Elmira public schools, he entered Harvard College in 1919.[6] There, he studied history; it was, as Paul Freund has noted, a period in which Harvard was uncommonly rich in great teachers of the subject.[7] Charles McIlwain was of foremost importance to Friendly, whose special interest was medieval English history.[8] Graduating summa cum laude in 1923,[9] Friendly pondered an academic career as a historian.

Instead, Felix Frankfurter lured Friendly to law school, urging that he should try it for a year before making up his mind between law and history.[10] At Harvard Law School, which he entered in 1924 after a year abroad on a traveling fellowship,[11] Friendly became a legend. When the class was challenged by its professor to identify the language in which the old English cases were reported, Friendly answered correctly that the language was Law French and then offered to translate the example provided to him. Friendly was president of the *Harvard Law Review* and ranked first in his class. Again, he graduated with a rare summa degree and an

---

[5] LEO GOTTLIEB, CLEARY, GOTTLIEB, STEEN & HAMILTON: THE FIRST THIRTY YEARS 32 (1983).

[6] *Id.*

[7] Professor Freund refers, as examples, to McIlwain, Merk, and Langer — he could easily have added Turner — in comparing Hand's experience as a philosophy student with James, Royce, and Santayana in Harvard's golden age of philosophy. Paul A. Freund, Remarks at the Unveiling of the Bust of Judge Henry J. Friendly 5 (Mar. 27, 1989).

[8] Friendly described McIlwain as the one who, more than anyone else, brought F.W. Maitland and his approach to America. Henry J. Friendly, *Mr. Justice Frankfurter*, 51 VA. L. REV. 552, 552 (1965). Maitland's contributions, as a historian of the common law, are so various and remarkable as to defy brief summary. For a general appraisal of Maitland's works, see generally G.R. ELTON, F.W. MAITLAND (1985).

[9] GOTTLIEB, *supra* note 5, at 32.

[10] Friendly, *supra* note 8, at 552.

[11] GOTTLIEB, *supra* note 5, at 32.

astonishing average of 86[12] — approximately an A double plus.

Among his teachers at the Law School was Thomas Reed Powell, an early but subtle exponent of realism in constitutional law.[13] It was Powell who wrote that although law is to some extent "judicial whim or fiat[,] . . . [t]hose who see law as *only* this or *only* that see but narrowly."[14] And the spirit of James Bradley Thayer still hovered over the school with its message of judicial self-restraint in constitutional interpretation.[15] Thayer's view was one that Holmes and Hand championed on the bench. Yet the breadth of views within the faculty was remarkable, as able formalists like Samuel Williston and Joseph Beale contended with new tendencies of thought represented by professors such as Roscoe Pound, Felix Frankfurter, and Zechariah Chafee.

From Harvard Law School, Friendly went on to a clerkship with Justice Brandeis, surely at Frankfurter's recommendation.[16] Brandeis was himself a brilliant outsider who succeeded, as Friendly did thereafter, first at Harvard Law School, then in his law practice, and finally as a great judge. But Friendly, while mildly reformist in politics, had far less of a policy agenda than did Brandeis, whose law practice had mixed business representation with legal good works.[17] Nor did Friendly share Brandeis's crusading zeal.

At the end of the clerkship, Friendly faced a fork in the road: to teach law at Harvard or to enter law practice. Although Frankfurter urged him to return to Cambridge,[18] Friendly chose to practice in New York with

---

[12] *Id.*

[13] For four descriptive tributes to Powell, see generally Felix Frankfurter, *Thomas Reed Powell*, 69 HARV. L. REV. 797 (1956); Paul A. Freund, *Thomas Reed Powell*, 69 HARV. L. REV. 800 (1956); Erwin N. Griswold, *Thomas Reed Powell*, 69 HARV. L. REV. 793 (1956); Henry M. Hart, Jr., *Thomas Reed Powell*, 69 HARV. L. REV. 804 (1956).

[14] Thomas Reed Powell, *My Philosophy of Law*, in MY PHILOSOPHY OF LAW: CREDOS OF SIXTEEN AMERICAN SCHOLARS 269, 280 (Julius Rosenthal Found. ed., 1941); *see also* Freund, *supra* note 7.

[15] *See* James B. Thayer, *The Origin and Scope of the American Doctrine of Constitutional Law*, 7 HARV. L. REV. 129, 136-38, 150-52 (1893). *See generally* Jay Hook, *A Brief Life of James Bradley Thayer*, 88 NW. U. L. REV. 1 (1993). For a broader picture of Thayer's work and influence, *see generally One Hundred Years of Judicial Review: The Thayer Centennial Symposium*, 88 NW. U. L. REV. 1 (1993).

[16] *See* Henry J. Friendly, *Mr. Justice Brandeis: The Quest for Reason*, 108 U. PA. L. REV. 985, 992 (1960).

[17] *See generally* ALPHEUS THOMAS MASON, BRANDEIS: A FREE MAN'S LIFE 4 (1946).

[18] Professor Freund quotes Frankfurter's letter to Friendly: "Your fullest fruition would be not at the bar but in this school . . . . Such powers as you have call for their fulfillment as much as Kreisler's gifts call for playing the violin." Freund, *supra* note 7.

Root, Clark, Buckner & Ballantine. Thirty years later, Friendly chided one of his own law clerks for making the same choice. To the clerk's obvious response that Friendly was the natural scholar, Friendly replied that law teaching was a lot less interesting in the 1920s: The common law subjects, he said, had been worked through, and the explosion of New Deal legislation, the rise of the agencies, and much else was hidden around the corner.

The presiding litigator at Root Clark in 1928 was Emory Buckner, who recruited his young lawyers not just from the regular cadre of conventional Ivy Leaguers but also from among Jewish students, like Friendly, and those whose law training had been obtained in England, like Hugh Cox and John Harlan.[19] Friendly's law practice came to combine administrative law, common-carrier regulation, and appellate practice. In 1946, he and others broke away from Root Clark and, with Hugh Cox returning to private practice after his work for the government, formed the Cleary Gottlieb firm — initially Cleary, Gottlieb, Friendly & Cox. In the same year, Friendly became the general counsel of his longtime client, Pan American World Airways, and thereafter held two full-time jobs.[20]

When Henry Friendly came to the bench in 1959, it was a "merit" selection. Hand had written a letter to President Eisenhower — a rare intervention for Hand — urging Friendly's appointment.[21] Friendly himself told a law clerk that the Republican politician who gave Friendly final clearance had said with dismay that he was tired of being sent candidates like Friendly who had done nothing for the party. A *New York Times* editorial referred glowingly to Friendly's "outstanding qualifications."[22]

The appointment was a salvation for a man who (as he later confided to a law clerk) had been rapidly tiring of large law firm practice. The judgeship opened not only a new perspective on law, which Friendly described in an early essay,[23] but also other opportunities. He joined the Council of the American Law Institute in 1961 and became active in its work; he was already a member of the Council on Foreign Relations and often attended its meetings. In addition, he began the career of extracur-

---

[19] MARTIN MAYER, EMORY BUCKNER 141-44 (1968).
[20] Leo Gottlieb, *Honorable Henry J. Friendly (1903-1986)*, 28 CLEARGOLAW NEWS 155, 158 (1986).
[21] GERALD GUNTHER, LEARNED HAND: THE MAN AND THE JUDGE 650 (1994). Hand's letter spoke of Friendly's "unblemished reputation," "high scholarship," "balanced wisdom," and "wide outlook." *Id.* Later, Hand wrote that "Friendly is realizing all our hopes." *Id.* at 652.
[22] Editorial, *Mr. Friendly for the Bench*, N.Y. TIMES, Mar. 11, 1959, at 34.
[23] Henry J. Friendly, *Reactions of a Lawyer — Newly Become Judge*, 71 YALE L.J. 218, 219-22 (1961).

ricular legal scholarship that dovetailed with his judicial work and much magnified his influence as a judge.

From 1959 onward, Friendly produced a set of major articles of extraordinary quality, as well as books, shorter articles, book reviews, and tributes.[24] Among the articles — to mention only constitutional subjects — are his Cardozo Lecture on *Erie v. Tompkins*[25] at the New York City Bar Association,[26] his Holmes Lectures at Harvard on administrative law,[27] another Holmes Lecture at Dartmouth on the public-private distinction in constitutional law,[28] and important articles on the Fifth Amendment,[29] the right to hearings,[30] criminal procedure,[31] and habeas corpus.[32]

Friendly's natural gifts — the mainspring of his achievements — began with the raw power of his mind. In the summer of 1959, while awaiting his Senate confirmation hearing, Friendly absorbed for the first time Hart and Wechsler's famous (and famously intricate) casebook, *The Federal Courts and the Federal System*,[33] saying afterwards: "The book, while not exactly summer reading, proved to be the most stimulating and exciting law book I had encountered since Wigmore's *Evidence*."[34] The invited mental picture of the young law student plowing steadily through the five volumes of Wigmore's 1923 edition may not be wholly imaginary.

Nor did Friendly forget very much of what he read. He could say to a clerk, "I think the passage to support this proposition is in such and such decision, in volume 274 U.S., somewhere near the end of the opinion." His essays, even his book reviews, glimmer with aphorisms and quotations, especially to works of legal history and philosophy, that were stored in his head. An early book review of Mark de Wolfe Howe's biography of

---

[24] FRIENDLY, BENCHMARKS, *supra* note 2, contains many but by no means all of the lectures, articles, and tributes.

[25] 304 U.S. 64 (1938).

[26] Henry J. Friendly, *In Praise of Erie — And of the New Federal Common Law*, 39 N.Y.U. L. REV. 383 (1964).

[27] FRIENDLY, THE FEDERAL ADMINISTRATIVE AGENCIES, *supra* note 2.

[28] FRIENDLY, THE DARTMOUTH COLLEGE CASE, *supra* note 2.

[29] Henry J. Friendly, *The Fifth Amendment Tomorrow: The Case for Constitutional Change*, 37 U. CIN. L. REV. 671 (1968).

[30] Henry J. Friendly, *"Some Kind of Hearing,"* 123 U. PA. L. REV. 1267 (1975).

[31] Henry J. Friendly, *The Bill of Rights as a Code of Criminal Procedure*, 53 CAL. L. REV. 929 (1965).

[32] Henry J. Friendly, *Is Innocence Irrelevant? Collateral Attacks on Criminal Judgments*, 38 U. CHI. L. REV. 142 (1970).

[33] HENRY M. HART & HERBERT WECHSLER, THE FEDERAL COURTS AND THE FEDERAL SYSTEM (1953).

[34] Henry J. Friendly, *In Praise of Herbert Wechsler*, 78 COLUM. L. REV. 974, 974 (1978).

Justice Holmes shows Friendly's intimidating command of legal history and jurisprudence.[35]

Writing ability was another gift: The connection between quality of writing and influence as an appellate judge cannot be overstated. Friendly wrote his own opinions from scratch and so maintained a distinctive voice. Although without the poetic magic of Holmes or the King James resonances of Hand or Jackson, Friendly had a command of metaphor, a stock of literary and operatic references, a deft use of sarcasm, and a crisp way of summing up a matter. Consider this classic first line in an opinion: "Our principal task, in this diversity of citizenship case, is to determine what the New York courts would think the California courts would think on an issue about which neither has thought."[36]

To watch Friendly crafting an opinion was to feel sorry for the Learned Hand depicted in Gerald Gunther's magnificent biography.[37] Hand prepared meticulously even to the point of modeling or diagramming ship collisions on his desk, often wrote draft after draft, and visibly agonized in hard cases.[38] Friendly, writing on a pad with briefs and law books stacked around him, normally produced a single draft — often over a period no longer than a weekend. It was then typed, edited by the judge in a single session with a law clerk who had read the cases cited in the opinion, and dispatched for a final retyping and circulation to his colleagues.

This disciplined energy probably owed something to the demands of law practice and, without it, Friendly could not have led the double life of a judge and a scholar. If nothing else, a successful lawyer is an overworked and therefore usually efficient lawyer. The reflective tone of Hand's opin-

---

[35] Henry J. Friendly, *A Shattering Book from Beacon Hill*, N.Y. TIMES, Aug. 11, 1963, § 7 (Book Review), at 6 (reviewing MARK DEWOLFE HOWE, JUSTICE OLIVER WENDELL HOLMES, VOL. II: THE PROVING YEARS, 1870-1882 (1963) and OLIVER WENDELL HOLMES, THE COMMON LAW (Mark DeWolfe Howe ed., 1963)). In the course of this review, Friendly referred to, among others, Immanuel Kant, J.G. Heineccius, Sir Frederick Pollock, Justice Cardozo, Justice Stone, John Austin, James Bradley Thayer, John Chipman Gray, William James, Charles Darwin, Sir Henry Maine, Friedrich Carl von Savigny, and F.W. Maitland.

[36] Nolan v. Transocean Air Lines, 276 F.2d 280, 281 (2d Cir. 1960). Or consider another Friendly classic: "We cannot subscribe to plaintiffs' view that the Eighth Commandment 'Thou shalt not steal' is part of the law of nations." IIT v. Vencap Ltd., 519 F.2d 1001, 1015 (2d Cir. 1975). In *IIT*, Friendly also described the Alien Tort Claims Act, 28 U.S.C. § 1350 (1970), as "a kind of legal Lohengrin." 519 F.2d at 1015.

[37] GUNTHER, *supra* note 21.

[38] *See id.* at 306-10.

ions, such as his brilliant soliloquy on the Sherman Act,[39] is less common with Friendly; Friendly's thinking was deep but swift, and his sometimes cryptic sentences mirror the train of his actual thinking as words flowed from his mind through his pen. Consider this dense gem from an opinion discussing a hearsay exception:

> True, inclusion of a past event motivating the plan adds the hazards of defective perception and memory to that of prevarication; but this does not demand exclusion or even excision, at least when, as here, the event is recent, is within the personal knowledge of the declarant and is so integrally included in the declaration of design as to make it unlikely in the last degree that the latter would be true and the former false.[40]

These gifts were merely the ingredients. What mattered most about Friendly as a judge was the pattern of thinking that his opinions and other writing revealed. Out of a number of Friendly's characteristics, let us dwell briefly on four: his intense respect for precedent and the other constraints of the craft; his immense practicality; his intellectual seriousness and integrity; and his essential moderation.

In the common law tradition, judges — especially appellate judges — occupy a curious position. In the course of deciding cases, often the judge is not just applying law but making law in miniature. Yet, in principle, such lawmaking is not free-form legislative action: It is constrained lawmaking. There is room to create and alter, but it is limited room. As Willard Hurst once wrote: "[T]he wisdom of the great judge consists in a grasp both of the potentialities and the limitations of the kind of power that he wields."[41] And the integrity of the process — indeed, the legitimacy of the judge's action — depends upon respecting the constraints and acting within the boundaries they set.

The constraints are the familiar stuff of first-year law school: the language of statutes and constitutions, history and precedent, public and legislative policy, stare decisis, canons of construction and legal maxims, neutral principles, and all the rest. Still, these are elastic constraints whose force varies from one case to another. Nor is it easy to weigh one hard-to-measure variable against another of a different kind. And the formal constraints may vie with practical considerations.

Friendly was a master of the formal constraints and, what is more im-

---

[39] United States v. Aluminum Co. of Am., 148 F.2d 416, 427-30 (2d Cir. 1945).
[40] United States v. Annunziato, 293 F.2d 373, 378 (2d Cir. 1961).
[41] Willard Hurst, *Who Is the "Great" Appellate Judge?*, 24 IND. L.J. 394, 399 (1949).

portant, he took them very seriously, perhaps more seriously than our own jaded age allows. True, the ability to operate inventively within the constraints is one of the marks of great and creative judges. To take this as saying that clever judges can get around the rules is a mistranslation. Rather, a judge like Friendly can justify an improving change while at the same time shaping and limiting the change to maintain continuity, to minimize disruption, and to mark its limits in the interest of a new stability.

To Friendly, precedent was a constraint as central as any. Recall that Friendly was trained at Harvard College as a historian. Decided cases are themselves history comprised of the real-world events, the litigation, and the rules thus generated. Precedents, and the wisdom encoded in them, are one of the central motivating forces of the common law but also one of the great constraints. Law, said Hand, "is the precipitate of a long past of active controversy."[42]

Friendly's most dramatic excursion into precedent and large-scale history is his tour de force Cardozo Lecture at the New York City Bar Association, titled *In Praise of* Erie — *and of the New Federal Common Law*.[43] The lessons of this lecture were that *Erie*[44] had been correctly decided, that Brandeis had been correct to declare *Swift v. Tyson*[45] at odds with the Constitution, and that by obliterating *Swift*'s "spurious uniformity" the decision opened the way "for the truly uniform federal common law on issues of national concern."[46] What was extraordinary about the lecture was the conceptual basis of this assessment, which displays (among other virtues) Friendly's use of history at every level.

He begins with a terse recounting of the scholarly backlash against the reasoning of the *Erie* decision. Then, with a study of precedent and constitutional history, he demolishes two of the less ambitious lines of reasoning that *Erie*'s critics proposed to substitute for that of Brandeis: namely, a withering-away approach to *Swift*[47] and a broad construction of section 34

---

[42] Learned Hand, *Mr. Justice Holmes at Eighty-five, in* THE SPIRIT OF LIBERTY 24, 24 (Irving Dilliard ed., 1952).

[43] Friendly, *supra* note 26.

[44] Erie R.R. v. Tompkins, 304 U.S. 64 (1938).

[45] 41 U.S. 1 (1842).

[46] Friendly, *supra* note 26, at 384.

[47] Judge Clark had criticized Brandeis's supposed failure to realize that *Swift*'s doctrine, "already tending toward decay and death, did not need the sledge-hammer blows" of Erie. Charles E. Clark, *State Law in the Federal Courts: The Brooding Omnipresence of Erie v. Tompkins*, 55 YALE L.J. 267, 295 (1946).

of the Judiciary Act of 1789.[48] The withering-away approach Friendly shows to be medicine worse than the disease;[49] the expansion of section 34, Friendly refutes — in a neat move of confession and avoidance — by assuming the accuracy of Charles Warren's account of the statute's original intent but showing that Story's reading of the statute was too settled to disturb.[50]

This leads him to consider the constitutional rightness of *Swift v. Tyson*, constitutional errors being more open to correction by the Court despite their age than statutes, where errors of interpretation can always be repaired by Congress. Friendly embarks on a demonstration of the soundness of *Erie* as constitutional law, grappling with section 34, pertinent case law, and the implications of the "necessary and proper" clause.[51] The conclusion, temperate but forceful, is vintage Friendly and gives one some sense of the powerful generalizations to which his elegant and detailed analysis led him:

> A great constitutional decision is not often compelled in the sense that a contrary one would lie beyond the area of rationality. I shall not insist that *Erie* was the rare exception. But it provided a far better fit with the scheme of the Constitution as that had developed over the years than do the assertions that the "necessary and proper" clause empowers Congress to establish substantive law for the federal courts in fields otherwise reserved to the states, or that federal courts themselves may do so — thereby not merely permitting but insuring unequal justice under law.[52]

This lecture was on a grand scale; but many of Friendly's opinions, constitutional and otherwise, contain remarkable essays that trace, summarize, and explain the evolution of precedent on the subject in question. A memorable example is his treatment of the "arising under" test for federal jurisdiction in *T.B. Harms Co. v. Eliscu*,[53] neatly distinguishing between the phrase's use in the Constitution and the narrower reading given to the same phrase in the statute and offering this gracious gloss on Holmes's

---

[48] Ch. 20, § 34, 1 Stat. 73, 92 (codified as amended at 28 U.S.C. § 1652 (2000)). This view, reading the Judiciary Act to bind federal courts to respect state common law as well as statutory law, had been endorsed by Justice Reed in his *Erie* concurrence. 304 U.S. at 91 (Reed, J., concurring).

[49] Friendly, *supra* note 26, at 386-88.

[50] *Id.* at 388-91.

[51] *Id.* at 392-98.

[52] *Id.* at 398.

[53] 339 F.2d 823 (2d Cir. 1964).

own incomplete "cause of action" test: "It has come to be realized that Mr. Justice Holmes' formula is more useful for inclusion than for the exclusion for which it was intended."[54]

Precedent is only one of the constraints with which Friendly dealt masterfully. Others of particular importance to him were statutory language and institutional competence, and on both subjects he wrote thoughtful articles.[55] Needless to say, Friendly learned much else from his training as a historian, including a commitment to factual accuracy and the need to underpin generalizations, surely reinforced by his work with Brandeis. But we must pass on to another subject: practical judgment.

Ordinarily, a judge faced with a legal problem starts with the directions or clues provided by language, historical context, precedent, and the underlying policies imputed to the constitutional provision or statute involved or derived from prior common law decisions. If these were enough, judging would be a self-contained, if still demanding, discipline. In truth, more worldly considerations bear upon decision: They range from broad-canvas judgments of social problems, institutions, and tolerable rates of change, to more specific mental pictures as to what goes on in police stations, union meetings, or households, and as to what remedies will fix an existing problem.

Friendly brought to his task something more than the ordinary, though invaluable, experience of a practicing lawyer who had spent three decades addressing real-world problems. His work for Pan American had exposed him not only to federal regulation and administrative practice but also to international issues and war-related matters and a certain amount of work with Congress and state legislatures. He once remarked to a law clerk that Justice Brandeis, always enthusiastic about local governance, might have been shocked by some of what Friendly had encountered in state legislatures.

Whatever the sources of his insights, Friendly rivaled Justice Jackson in giving readers the sense that his decisions were grounded in reality. An illustration is provided by a pair of Friendly's articles. The first is *The Bill*

---

[54] *Id.* at 825.
[55] On competence, see Henry J. Friendly, *The Gap in Lawmaking — Judges Who Can't and Legislators Who Won't*, 63 COLUM. L. REV. 787 (1963) [hereinafter Friendly, *The Gap in Lawmaking*], and Friendly's Harvard Holmes Lectures, FRIENDLY, THE FEDERAL ADMINISTRATIVE AGENCIES, *supra* note 2. On statutory language, see Henry J. Friendly, *Mr. Justice Frankfurter and the Reading of Statutes*, in FELIX FRANKFURTER: THE JUDGE 30 (Wallace Mendelson ed., 1964).

of Rights as a Code of Criminal Procedure,[56] which challenged (among much else) the Warren Court's selective incorporation doctrine, the mechanical application of provisions of the first eight amendments — by their terms applicable only to the federal government — to the states as well.[57] Friendly's concern was in part the inflexibility of the federal regime thereby imposed on the states and in part the questionable basis and reach of a number of the Warren Court's decisions interpreting specific Bill of Rights provisions.[58]

But what animates the article is Friendly's larger concern with the Supreme Court's seeming indifference to any countervailing interests and its unwillingness to place any limits on its newly expanded rights and remedies. As Friendly observed, "Maximizing protection to persons suspected of crime was hardly [the Framers'] sole objective; the famous words of the Preamble speak of establishing justice, insuring domestic tranquillity, and promoting the general welfare."[59] He continued in even more practical terms, speaking of the line of precedent that would culminate in the *Miranda*[60] decision:

> Kidnapping raises the issue still more poignantly. If such a tragedy were to strike at the family of a writer who is enthused about extending the assistance of counsel clause to the station house, would he really believe the fundamental liberties of the suspect demanded the summoning of a lawyer, or at least a clear warning as to the right immediately to consult one, before the police began questioning in an effort to retrieve his child?[61]

The companion piece, *Is Innocence Irrelevant?*,[62] had a different target. The Warren Court was in the midst of a campaign to expand habeas cor-

---

[56] Friendly, *supra* note 31.

[57] *Id.* at 933-38 ("Whatever one's views about the historical support for Mr. Justice Black's wholesale incorporation theory, it appears undisputed that the selective incorporation theory has none.").

[58] *See, e.g.,* Griffin v. California, 380 U.S. 609 (1965) (incorporating Fifth Amendment protection against commentary by prosecutor on silence of accused); Escobedo v. Illinois, 378 U.S. 478 (1964) (incorporating qualified Sixth Amendment guarantee of consultation with counsel); Mapp v. Ohio, 367 U.S. 643 (1961) (incorporating exclusionary rule for Fourth Amendment violations). Friendly discusses these opinions in Friendly, *supra* note 31, at 940-43, 951-53.

[59] Friendly, *supra* note 31, at 948.

[60] Miranda v. Arizona, 384 U.S. 436, 444 (1966) (holding that evidence obtained as a result of interrogation is inadmissible unless prosecution demonstrates that prescribed warnings were given).

[61] Friendly, *supra* note 31, at 949.

[62] Friendly, *supra* note 32.

pus for state prisoners.[63] This took the form of extending the writ from its historic function of testing the authority of a jailer into a device for de novo review by lower federal courts of anything in a state court criminal case to which the label of constitutional error could be attached. And, as the Supreme Court was rapidly cultivating the garden of new rights so labeled, the effect was a revolution, only partly completed at the time that Friendly wrote.

The title of Friendly's habeas lecture raised the question whether the Warren Court had lost sight of the central objectives of criminal law: to convict the guilty so as to deter crime and to protect the public while taking all reasonable precautions to avoid conviction of innocent defendants. Many of the Warren Court's substantive rulings were concerned with neither of these goals but with other objectives: for example, with excluding illegally seized but often reliable evidence,[64] and with giving the poor the same opportunities to thwart police interrogation as were enjoyed by the rich.[65]

Friendly thought it unsound that federal courts should spend their time undoing state court convictions of defendants whose trials had provided them with basic fairness and who made not the slightest pretense of actual innocence. Friendly's own remedy was that habeas should be restricted to cases of fundamental unfairness or, absent that, error coupled with some showing of potential innocence.[66] In time, the pendulum did swing back, although along a somewhat different axis.[67]

Friendly's concern with the real world was not limited to such large is-

---

[63] *See, e.g.*, Fay v. Noia, 372 U.S. 391, 426-27, 435 (1963) (limiting federal habeas statute's exhaustion requirement to "state remedies still open to the habeas applicant at the time he files his application in federal court"); Townsend v. Sain, 372 U.S. 293, 312-13 (1963) ("Where the facts are in dispute, the federal court in habeas corpus must hold an evidentiary hearing if the habeas applicant did not receive a full and fair evidentiary hearing in a state court . . . .").

[64] Mapp v. Ohio, 367 U.S. 643, 648-49 (1961).

[65] *Miranda*, 384 U.S. at 472-73.

[66] Friendly, *supra* note 32, at 160.

[67] *See, e.g.*, Antiterrorism and Effective Death Penalty Act of 1996, Pub. L. No. 104-132, §§ 101-107, 110 Stat. 1214, 1217-26 (codified at 28 U.S.C. §§ 2244, 2253-55, 2261-66 (2000)) (establishing limits to habeas review); Teague v. Lane, 489 U.S. 288, 310 (1989) (generally denying application of new constitutional rulings to cases on habeas review); Wainwright v. Sykes, 433 U.S. 72, 90-91 (1977) (adopting cause-and-prejudice test for unpreserved claims of unconstitutional admissions of evidence); Stone v. Powell, 428 U.S. 465, 494-96 (1976) (holding that where state has provided full and fair opportunity to present Fourth Amendment claim, state prisoner cannot obtain habeas relief for admission of evidence obtained by unconstitutional search or seizure).

sues. Many of his decisions remind one of Jackson's arresting injections of common sense into his opinions.[68] For example, in explaining the rule allowing inconsistent jury verdicts in criminal cases, Friendly added that "[t]he vogue for repetitious multiple count indictments may well produce an increase in seemingly inconsistent jury verdicts, where in fact the jury is using its power to prevent the punishment from getting too far out of line with the crime."[69]

Similarly, in Friendly's article *"Some Kind of Hearing,"*[70] there is a passage in which he suggests differentiating between license denial and license revocation, adding that even the Magna Carta drew the distinction;[71] and, more broadly, he urges that some consequences in some contexts do not justify the cost of hearings and that the extent of a hearing should vary with need and cost.[72] He put these recipes into effect in his own management as chief judge of the special railroad court, whose achievements included assigning (within a relatively brief period) a dollar value to the entire northeastern railroad system, which was being taken over by the government.[73]

A story exists that the prospect of a district court judgeship had once been presented to Friendly and that, to inform himself, he spent some hours watching proceedings in the federal district court in Manhattan, concluding that the job was not for him. Yet when he took over the railroad court, he and his two colleagues managed the litigation, narrowing the legal issues in a series of opinions; and, without the use of special masters, they superintended the mammoth discovery of facts pertinent to the valuation puzzle. After four years of discovery, in a matter that could have lasted decades, a set of opinions on major issues precipitated settlements for all of the railroads but one (whose claim was then swiftly resolved on

---

[68] Especially memorable is Jackson's summing up of certain rules governing impeachment as "archaic, paradoxical and full of compromises and compensations," but then concluding, "[t]o pull one misshapen stone out of the grotesque structure is more likely simply to upset its present balance between adverse interests than to establish a rational edifice." Michelson v. United States, 335 U.S. 469, 486 (1948).

[69] United States v. Maybury, 274 F.2d 899, 902 (2d Cir. 1960). For another example of Friendly's practicality, see his treatment of interlocutory appeals in *Parkinson v. April Industries, Inc.*, 520 F.2d 650, 659-60 (2d Cir. 1975) (Friendly, J., concurring).

[70] Friendly, *supra* note 30.

[71] *Id.* at 1295-96.

[72] *Id.* at 1275-76.

[73] *See* Friendly, *supra* note 1, at 244, 247, 253-54 (discussing work of special railroad court).

the merits).[74]

This brings us to a third element in Friendly's work: a combination of rigor, candor, and depth. Even the many admirers of the Warren Court must admit that its decisions in the 1960s and 1970s are not always models of serious reflection. Fiercer critics have pointed to doubtful assumptions of fact, rhetorical overstatement, law-office history, a wrenching of constitutional phrases from historical context, and an unwillingness to address contrary arguments or to acknowledge limits on the generalizations abundantly produced.[75]

"Conventional notions of finality of litigation," said Justice Brennan in a habeas case, "have no place where life or liberty is at stake and infringement of constitutional rights is alleged."[76] "Why do they have *no* place?" asked Friendly in his article on habeas, going on to point out the implications and weaknesses of Brennan's rhetoric.[77] In his *Bill of Rights* lecture, Friendly compared a sonorous pronouncement of Chief Justice Taft in defense of property rights with an almost identically phrased one by Justice Goldberg in a civil liberties case.[78]

By contrast, Friendly's own opinions sought to grapple with the underlying dilemmas in cases: to reveal the tensions between policies and the confusions in the precedents and to acknowledge that one goal often comes at the price of another. None of this made him doubt the capacity of reason to resolve an issue — he almost never showed Hand's unease[79] — nor was Friendly hesitant about coming to conclusions and laying down rules. After all, for decades as a lawyer he had made decisions or given advice on which others would act. And he had the skilled craftsman's confidence that the process of legal thinking would lead him in the right direction.

In this belief, Friendly in part reflected the outlook of the legal process movement that came to dominate Harvard Law School from World War

---

[74] *Id.* at 253-54.

[75] *See, e.g.*, ALEXANDER M. BICKEL, THE SUPREME COURT AND THE IDEA OF PROGRESS 45-101 (1978); PHILIP B. KURLAND, POLITICS, THE CONSTITUTION, AND THE WARREN COURT 101-06 (1970); Alfred H. Kelly, *Clio and the Court: An Illicit Love Affair*, 1965 SUP. CT. REV. 119, 135-42.

[76] Sanders v. United States, 373 U.S. 1, 8 (1963).

[77] Friendly, *supra* note 32, at 149.

[78] *See* Friendly, *supra* note 31, at 955 & n.141 (noting similarity of language used in Pointer v. Texas, 380 U.S. 400, 413 (1965) (Goldberg, J., concurring), and Truax v. Corrigan, 257 U.S. 312, 338 (1921) (Taft, C.J.)).

[79] *See supra* note 38 and accompanying text (comparing writing styles of Friendly and Hand).

II through the mid-1960s. Once again, the protean Thomas Reed Powell was a forerunner. Powell, who knew and admired John Dewey, had leanings both toward pragmatism and toward the weight that Thayer placed on self-restraint and stare decisis. But Powell, perhaps above all else, was concerned with the integrity of the process of judging. The minimum, Powell thought, was (in the words of a scholar):

> internal coherence, consistency with professed criteria, and fair treatment of the existing precedents, whether favorable or not. The most vital ingredient, however, was "intellectual rectitude"; judges must "support their judgments with that degree of candor" that will provide "adequate disclosure of the real steps by which they have reached where they are."[80]

The emphasis on these values came to represent a school of legal thought to which many figures contributed. The canonical text is Hart and Sacks's *The Legal Process*, and the hallmark phrase is "reasoned elaboration."[81] Of this technique Friendly was a master, and he was greatly admired by the Harvard Law School faculty of the 1960s. But Friendly was an exemplar and not a product of such thinking; as already noted, his own legal education had covered a period of greater ferment,[82] and it was probably the richer for it.

But why should rigor in reasoning and candor in expression matter in judicial opinions? Especially in constitutional law, as it has developed in this country, analysis can take one only so far — for example, in resolving matters for which the framers used general language but (so far as we can tell) gave no precise thought. In such instances an instinct for judicial statesmanship matters more than technical excellence. Even candor perhaps can occasionally be unwise: Would it have been better in *Brown v. Board of Education*[83] for the Court to have dwelled on the weight of precedent, or might this have been the wrong occasion to sound an uncertain

---

[80] John Braeman, *Thomas Reed Powell on the Roosevelt Court*, 5 CONST. COMMENT. 143, 150 (1988) (quoting Thomas Reed Powell, *Some Aspects of American Constitutional Law*, 53 HARV. L. REV. 529, 549-50, 552 (1940)).

[81] HENRY M. HART, JR. & ALBERT M. SACKS, THE LEGAL PROCESS: BASIC PROBLEMS IN THE MAKING AND APPLICATION OF LAW (tent. ed. 1958) was finally published in 1994 in an edition edited by William Eskridge and Philip Frickey whose introductory essay recounts the history of the movement. William N. Eskridge, Jr. & Philip P. Frickey, *An Historical and Critical Introduction to* The Legal Process, *in* HART & SACKS, *supra*, at li (William N. Eskridge, Jr. & Philip P. Frickey eds., 1994); *see also* Braeman, *supra* note 80, at 150 (describing Powell as intellectual father of "reasoned elaboration" school).

[82] *See supra* text accompanying notes 13-15.

[83] 347 U.S. 483 (1954).

trumpet?

Yet a sound decision, even if its origins lie (as they often do) in the instinct of the experienced judge, is usually confirmed and fine-tuned by good reasoning. Hand, it appears, sometimes wrote a decision both ways to see which one worked best. So, too, good reasoning tends to check bad results, overexpansive holdings, or unnecessary dicta. Thus, a judge may report back to colleagues that the tentative conclusion reached at *semble* after the oral argument "just would not write." To rest on rhetoric instead of analysis leads not merely to poor thinking but also to results that are poorer than they need be.

For example, if the exclusionary rule for illegally seized evidence in state courts had been developed thoughtfully, *Mapp v. Ohio*[84] would have been a better opinion and more widely accepted. As Friendly suggested,[85] the rule might well have directed the exclusion of evidence where it was seized in patent violation of the Fourth Amendment but not (in Cardozo's phrase) where the constable had merely blundered.[86] The deterrent value of exclusion is minimal for inadvertent fumbles, and the evidence remains reliable albeit wrongly seized. The Supreme Court has been inching in this direction.[87] How much better to have struck the balance at the outset.

Nowhere is the rigor of Friendly's thinking more in evidence than in his Dartmouth Holmes Lecture devoted to the so-called state action doctrine.[88] This is the label for a set of Supreme Court decisions determining when action is so governmental as to bring into play constitutional constraints that apply only to official (as opposed to private) conduct. Lowering the threshold could bring vast areas of previously private conduct within the Constitution and so within the reach of the federal courts.

At the time Friendly spoke, it was unclear whether the balance was going to tip in the direction of a major enlargement of this sphere, for example, by treating at least some corporations as state actors, so as to expand the kinds of activities treated as inherently governmental, or by extending the state action label to the state toleration of private discrimination. His lecture treats with exquisite subtlety the case law, the possibilities for line

---

[84] 367 U.S. 643 (1961).

[85] *See supra* notes 66-67 and accompanying text.

[86] People v. Defore, 150 N.E. 585, 587 (N.Y. 1926).

[87] *See* United States v. Leon, 468 U.S. 897, 926 (1984) (holding that exclusionary rule does not apply when officers rely in good faith on invalid warrant); Stone v. Powell, 428 U.S. 465, 482 (1976) (denying federal habeas relief for introduction of unconstitutional evidence at trial).

[88] FRIENDLY, THE DARTMOUTH COLLEGE CASE, *supra* note 2.

drawing, and the dangers of a promiscuous enlargement of the state action category.

Friendly saw that his own vision was more likely to prevail if the Supreme Court did not attempt to lay down the abstract doctrines that it had so favored in the criminal area but rather confined itself to results:

> Today's activist Court has thus far been treading rather cautiously in the area we have been discussing. . . . The lack of satisfactory theoretical explication may have been an advantage rather than the ground for criticism it seemed at first to be; on the whole it may be better that the Court should plot a few reference points, even on what may be largely an intuitive basis, which can be erased if they prove unwise, before it attempts to project a curve to which all future determinations must conform.[89]

There may be some irony in having Friendly, himself a master of synthesis and the projection of doctrine, recommend that the Supreme Court concentrate on results rather than reasoning. But he was nothing if not practical and, as with criminal law, he trusted the Court's intuitive judgment more than its explanations. He had one more practical lesson in mind, warning that legislative action to resolve unrighted wrongs was the key: "[W]e can learn a lesson from the consequences of the long legislative default in the reform of criminal procedure if we only will."[90]

This Dartmouth Holmes Lecture, like much of his academic writings, showed a continuing interplay between Friendly's scholarship and his judicial writing.[91] An issue addressed in an opinion might spark further reflections in a talk or book review; a synthesis developed in a lecture could provide context for an opinion. With ease, Friendly bridged the gap, which has sadly grown wider since his time, between the twin worlds of legal scholarship and the law in action.

The same lecture, along with much else that he wrote, illustrates the final facet of Friendly's approach to constitutional issues on which we have time to dwell: temperance. Most of Friendly's writings on constitutional

---

[89] *Id.* at 31 (citations omitted).

[90] *Id.*

[91] For example, Friendly also addressed state action issues in cases. *See* Jackson v. Statler Found., 496 F.2d 623, 636-41 (2d Cir. 1974) (Friendly, J., dissenting from denial of reconsideration en banc) ("A holding that an otherwise private institution has become an arm of the state . . . can have far more serious consequences than a determination that the state has impermissibly fostered private discrimination."); Powe v. Miles, 407 F.2d 73, 82 (2d Cir. 1968) (Friendly, J.) (holding that limits on protests by administrators of state college qualify as state action).

law aim at intermediate solutions: *Swift* was wrong but federal common law — a much narrower and better-justified variation on *Swift* — is right; the exclusionary rule is justifiable (perhaps) but not for reasonable violations of officers committed in good faith; habeas should go beyond jurisdictional error but with marked qualifications such as a threshold showing of potential innocence; the state action label should be applied beyond the classic case of the purely government actor but with great discretion.

This is what Paul Freund, speaking of Lewis Powell, called "the gift of moderation"[92] and, quoting Thomas Fuller, the "silken string running through the pearl-chain of all virtues."[93] So, too, the *Book of Common Prayer*, in a passage that might have been written for judges, lauds "the happy mean between too much stiffness in refusing, and too much easiness in admitting variations in things once advisedly established."[94] As Friendly himself said in the Dartmouth Holmes Lecture — the phrase was addressed to a particular issue but could have been a motto — "I prefer the midway course, with all its difficulties."[95]

The argument for temperance in making new constitutional law is familiar. A statutory interpretation, a reading of an agency rule, and a new direction in common law: all these can be overturned by legislation. A constitutional ruling, with limited exceptions,[96] tends to be final — regardless of what Congress or anyone else thinks about it — unless or until the Court changes its mind. It is therefore easy to argue for a presumption against interference. Hand said that a law that gets enacted is likely to be "not wholly unreasonable";[97] for federal enactments, it is probably constitutional as well.

Yet little in Friendly's writings or decisions shows a mechanical hostility to judicial intervention. Friendly knew that much of constitutional law was open ended and that choices were available to judges. And unlike Holmes, he was not a skeptic about betterment. On the contrary, his

---

[92] Paul A. Freund, *Justice Powell — the Meaning of Moderation*, 68 VA. L. REV. 169, 169 (1982).

[93] *Id.* at 170 (quoting 2 THOMAS FULLER, THE HOLY STATE AND THE PROFANE STATE 205 (Maximilian Graff Walten ed., AMS Press, Inc. 1966) (1642).

[94] *Preface* to THE BOOK OF COMMON PRAYER, at v, v (1928) (1789).

[95] FRIENDLY, THE DARTMOUTH COLLEGE CASE, *supra* note 2, at 23 (advocating against all-or-nothing approach to Fourteenth Amendment state action restrictions on charitable institutions).

[96] Although constitutional amendments and jurisdiction-stripping statutes are sometimes employed, the principal means of undoing mistaken constitutional decisions is the appointing of new Justices, an alternative with the disadvantages of uncertainty and delay.

[97] Hand, *supra* note 42, at 28.

pragmatic impulse was strong. Speaking in praise of Frankfurter, he said: "[T]o [Frankfurter], as to Brandeis, law was pre-eminently an aspect of public affairs, an instrument for maximizing the goodness of life for all."[98] These were two of the men that Friendly most admired. Consider, as well, the following passage from the introduction to Friendly's *Bill of Rights* lecture:

> [T]here are few brighter pages in the history of the Supreme Court than its efforts over the past forty years to improve the administration of criminal justice. How can any lawyer not be proud of the decisions condemning convictions obtained by mob rule, testimony known to the prosecutor to be perjured, coerced confessions, or trial by newspaper? . . . [Or] insistence that persons charged with serious crime shall receive the assistance of counsel at their pleas and trials[?] . . . [T]he fingers of one hand would outnumber the instances where I disagree with decisions, as distinguished from opinions, in this area.[99]

But while Friendly believed that law was an instrument for social change, he also believed that, as Thayer had taught, legislators must take the lead in altering the law, and that courts should be slow to interfere with considered legislative judgments and cautious when they do so. This view reinforced his respect for the craft's constraints — which temper the pace and extent of intervention and changes in the law by judges. He was thus often counted as a conservative judge, but this label — so far as it implies conservative political values — is misleading.

Friendly's judicial career coincided with the Warren Court era — certainly the most liberal federal judiciary in American history — and against that backdrop his generally moderate views appear conservative. Critics of the Warren Court were free to seize on Friendly's pointed criticisms for their own ends, ignoring the fact that many were directed only to the breadth of the opinions and the weaknesses of analysis. They also ignored the truth that Friendly was often for reform but discriminated as to when it was within the province of judges.

One clue lies in Friendly's ever-present concern with relative competence. Judges are good at working out what kind of hearing the Constitution ought to — and therefore will — provide in diverse circumstances. Procedural rights in criminal cases are, and should be, a specialty of

---

[98] Henry J. Friendly, Mr. Justice Frankfurter, Remarks at a Memorial Meeting of the Bar of the Supreme Court of the United States (Oct. 25, 1965), *in* FRIENDLY, BENCHMARKS, *supra* note 2, at 320.

[99] Friendly, *supra* note 31, at 931.

judges. But the bench, he thought, is perhaps less well-equipped to decide when to innovate where divisive issues of social policy are at stake or where a solution requires the kind of information or line drawing in which Congress has the advantage.

Friendly's article subtitled *Judges Who Can't and Legislators Who Won't*[100] speaks directly to this subject. It is a thoughtful explanation — with roots in Thayer and Brandeis — of why legislatures, having superior information and a greater choice in solutions, are usually better than courts at solving large social problems. But, of course, the larger context is the ability of legislatures to reflect public preferences and the doubtful charter of judges to act as what Hand called "Platonic Guardians."[101] Elected officials, after all, can easily be replaced.

Friendly would readily have joined in *Brown v. Board of Education*,[102] sharing none of the doubts Hand expressed in his own Holmes Lecture.[103] Indeed, speaking of *Shelley v. Kraemer*,[104] Friendly later wrote: "[M]ost people would say of it, as Paul Freund is reputed to have said of *Brown v. Board of Education*, 'can you imagine it having been decided in the other way?'"[105] Whatever the claims of stare decisis, the Equal Protection Clause spoke directly to racial discrimination. Similarly, Friendly's notion of using the First Amendment against McCarthyesque abuses was more aggressive than the Warren Court's procedural tactics.[106] But, again, the language of the First Amendment and its historical concern with protecting political speech gave some warrant for what he proposed.

It is not surprising that Friendly, according to Judge Randolph's re-

---

[100] Friendly, *The Gap in Lawmaking, supra* note 55, at 791-92 (discussing legislative superiority to courts in fact gathering, generality, pragmatism, transformation, prospectivity, and legitimacy); *see also* FRIENDLY, THE DARTMOUTH COLLEGE CASE, *supra* note 2, at 17-19 (same).

[101] LEARNED HAND, THE BILL OF RIGHTS 73 (1958).

[102] *See* Henry J. Friendly, *The Public-Private Penumbra — Fourteen Years Later*, 130 U. PA. L. REV. 1289, 1292 (1982) [hereinafter Friendly, *The Public-Private Penumbra*] ("The equal protection clause does not allow a state or a city to institutionalize Jim Crow."); Henry J. Friendly, *The Courts and Social Policy: Substance and Procedure*, 33 U. MIAMI L. REV. 22, 29 (1978) (arguing that psychological data in *Brown v. Board of Education*, 347 U.S. 483, 494-95 & n.11 (1954), were unnecessary in light of unconstitutionality of racial discrimination).

[103] Hand, *supra* note 42, at 54-55 (arguing that *Brown* and *Bolling v. Sharpe*, 347 U.S. 497 (1954), were reappraisals of legislative decisions and expressing concern that there was no principle to "explain when the Court will assume the role of a third legislative chamber").

[104] 334 U.S. 1 (1948).

[105] Friendly, *The Public-Private Penumbra, supra* note 102, at 1292.

[106] *See* Friendly, *supra* note 29, at 696-97.

port, faced the abortion issue later resolved in *Roe v. Wade*[107] and tentatively came out the other way before the case was mooted by New York's repeal of the challenged statute.[108] Friendly's draft opinion makes the familiar arguments: for example, that the extension sought by the plaintiffs would imperil a good many other statutes not yet brought into question, such as those punishing attempted suicide, sodomy, bestiality, and perhaps drug use.[109] Friendly said that the Constitution did not enact "Mill's views on the proper limits of law-making."[110]

One closing observation in the opinion is of special interest, however, and is underscored by Friendly's own dislike of the New York anti-abortion statute, which is clearly expressed in the opinion. The opinion concludes with one of his signature multipart sentences:

> The contest on this, as on other issues where there is determined opposition, must be fought out through the democratic process, not by utilizing the courts as a way of overcoming the opposition of what plaintiffs assume but we cannot know to be a minority and thus clearing the decks, thereby enabl[ing] legislators to evade their proper responsibilities.[111]

No one can prove that a judge should take Friendly's temperate approach to changing settled rules of constitutional law. Self-restraint was Holmes's view of a judge's role, but it was not John Marshall's or Hugo Black's or Roger Traynor's. As it happens, Friendly had a grudging respect for Black, fighting successfully to get him an honorary degree from Harvard, and his tribute to Traynor, a liberal judge, was titled, *Ablest Judge of His Generation*.[112] What mattered most to Friendly was that Black and Traynor, although different from one another, each had a commitment to law.

What should be said in closing about Friendly's influence? In contrast to almost all other lower court judges, whose views rarely outlive them, Friendly did have an effect on the legal landscape in a few areas: for example, in crafting the template for the modern view of federal common law and in calling for a saner balance in criminal law between the interests of

---

[107] 410 U.S. 113 (1973).

[108] A. Raymond Randolph, *Before* Roe v. Wade: *Judge Friendly's Draft Abortion Opinion*, 29 HARV. J.L. & PUB. POL'Y 1035, 1037, 1040 (2006).

[109] *Id.* at 1038.

[110] *Id.* at 1039.

[111] *Id.* at 1061.

[112] 71 CAL. L. REV. 1039 (1983). Friendly put Hand to one side, noting that Hand had begun his work many years before Traynor and ended it earlier. *Id.* at 1039 n.1.

defendants and the needs of society. So also, Friendly's skeptical view in his Dartmouth College Holmes Lecture toward expansion of the state action doctrine[113] has largely prevailed, with only small back-and-forth shifts in where the line is drawn.[114]

Still, these results owe more to a shift in the tidal current than to any individual's views. And Friendly did not bequeath to us an explicit philosophy of law or, in contrast to Holmes and Cardozo, express much interest in the subject. His own attitude was a composite of the influences already described: his training as a historian and respect for precedent, a dose of legal realism, a pragmatic interest in outcomes, a respect for legal process, an insistence on relative competence, a sense of what is practical, and a concern with judicial overreaching.

Friendly tended to decide cases from the inside out; he knew, as the critic Louis Menand observed in his study of Holmes and his circle, that "a case comes to court as a unique fact situation" and enters a "vortex of discursive imperatives," an "unpredictable weather pattern" of diverse pressures to conform to precedent, to do justice, to achieve a socially useful result, and so on.[115] A judge's first take is often an intuitive response to these pressures. The obligation remains to test this first approximation against reasoning and to articulate an explanation. Judging is about exercising judgment, for which no mechanical formula has yet been found adequate.

Friendly's influence on the law, including constitutional law, is primarily of a different kind. He provides a model — of ability, of scholarship, of integrity in analysis, of practicality, and of balanced judgment — for others who labor in the same workshop. Even after years in the profession, one learns in reading a Friendly opinion what can be wrought out of such virtues, coupled with immense hard work, and what great judging can be.

Grant Gilmore once wrote that "the opinions of our better judges set a model for rational and humane discourse which the rest of us can only

---

[113] FRIENDLY, THE DARTMOUTH COLLEGE CASE, *supra* note 2, at 11-12.
[114] *Compare, e.g.*, Am. Mfrs. Mut. Ins. Co. v. Sullivan, 526 U.S. 40, 43-44 (1999) (holding that insurers acting pursuant to state workers' compensation scheme are not state actors), *with* Brentwood Acad. v. Tenn. Secondary Sch. Ass'n, 531 U.S. 288, 291 (2001) (holding that regulation of public school athletics by nonprofit interscholastic association constitutes state action), *and* Lebron v. Nat'l R.R. Passenger Corp., 513 U.S. 374, 400 (1995) (holding that government-created and -controlled corporations are part of government for First Amendment purposes).
[115] LOUIS MENAND, THE METAPHYSICAL CLUB 339 (2001).

envy."[116] No one on the federal circuit courts ever did this better than Henry Friendly and Learned Hand. No one ever will.

Of course I am not saying that we must consecrate the mere blunders of those who went before us, and stumble every time we come to the place where they have stumbled. A palpable mistake, violating justice, reason, and law, must be corrected, no matter by whom it may have been made. There are cases in our books which bear such marks of haste and inattention, that they demand reconsideration. There are some which must be disregarded, because they cannot be reconciled with others. There are old decisions of which the authority has become obsolete, by a total alteration in the circumstances of the country and the progress of opinion. *Tempora mutantur.* We change with the change of the times, as necessarily as we move with the motion of the earth. But in ordinary cases, to set up our mere notions above the principles which the country has been acting upon as settled and established, is to make ourselves not the ministers and agents of the law, but the masters of the law and the tyrants of the people.

Jeremiah S. Black (1853)

---

[116] GRANT GILMORE, THE AGES OF AMERICAN LAW 16 (1977).

Shakespeare's Legal Acquirements

(continued from page 340)

John Lord Campbell

King John

In Shakespeare's dramas founded upon English history, more *legalisms* might have been expected; but I have met with fewer than in those which are taken from the annals of foreign nations, or which, without depending on locality, "hold the mirror up to nature." This paucity of reference to law or to law proceedings may, perhaps, in part be accounted for by the fact that, in these "Histories," as they are called, our great dramatist is known to have worked upon foundations already laid by other men who had no technical knowledge, and in several instances he appears only to have introduced additions and improvements into stock pieces to revive their popularity. Yet we find in several of the "Histories," Shakespeare's fondness for law terms; and it is still remarkable, that whenever he indulges this propensity he uniformly lays down good law.

Thus in the controversy, in the opening scene of 'King John,' between Robert and Philip Faulconbridge, as to which of them was to be considered the true heir of the deceased Sir Robert, the King, in giving judgment, lays down the law of legitimacy most perspicuously and soundly,—thus addressing Robert, the plaintiff:—

> "Sirrah, your brother is legitimate:
> Your father's wife did after wedlock bear him;
> And if she did play false, the fraud was hers,
> Which fault lies on the hazards of all husbands
> That marry wives. Tell me, how if my brother,
> Who, as you say, took pains to get this son,
> Had of your father claim'd this son for his?
> In sooth, good friend, your father might have kept
> This calf, bred from his cow, from all the world:
> In sooth, he might: then, if he were my brother's,
> My brother might not claim him, nor your father,
> Being none of his, refuse him. This concludes—
> My mother's son did get your father's heir;
> Your father's heir must have your father's land."

This is the true doctrine, "*Pater est quem nuptiæ demonstrant.*"

It was likewise properly ruled that the father's will, in favour of his son Robert, had no power to dispossess the right heir. Philip might have recovered the land, if he had not preferred the offer made to him by his grandmother, Elinor, the Queen Dowager, of taking the name of Plantagenet, and being dubbed Sir Richard.

———

In Act II. Sc. 1, we encounter a metaphor which is purely legal, yet might come naturally from an attorney's clerk, who had often been an attesting witness to the execution of deeds. The Duke of Austria, having entered into an engagement to support Arthur against his unnatural uncle, till the young prince should be put in possession of the dominions in France to which he was entitled as the true heir of the Plantagenets, and should be crowned King of England, says, kissing the boy to render the covenant more binding,

> "Upon thy cheek I lay this zealous kiss,
> *As seal to this indenture of my love.*"

———

In a subsequent part of this play, the true ancient doctrine of "the supremacy of the crown" is laid down with great spirit and force: and Shakespeare clearly shows that, whatever his opinion might have been on speculative dogmas in controversy between the Reformers and the Romanists, he spurned the ultramontane pretensions of the Pope, which some of our Roman Catholic fellow subjects are now too much disposed to countenance, although they were stoutly resisted before the Reformation by our ancestors, who were good Catholics. King John declares, Act III. Sc. 1,

> "No Italian priest
> Shall tithe or toll in our dominions;
> But as we under heaven are supreme head,
> So, under heaven, that great supremacy,
> Where we do reign, we will alone uphold,
> Without th' assistance of a mortal hand.
> So tell the Pope; all reverence set apart
> To him and his usurp'd authority.
>
> *King Philip.* Brother of England, you blaspheme in this.
>
> *King John.* Though you and all the kings of Christendom
> Are led so grossly by this meddling priest,
> Dreading the curse that money may buy out,
> And by the merit of vile gold, dross, dust,
> Purchase corrupted pardon of a man,
> Who in that sale sells pardon from himself,—
> Though you and all the rest, so grossly led,
> This juggling witchcraft with revenue cherish,

> Yet I alone, alone do me oppose
> Against the Pope, and count his friends my foes."

At the same time, it is clear, from Shakespeare's portraiture of Friar Lawrence and other Roman Catholic ecclesiastics, who do honour to their church, that he was no bigot, and that he regarded with veneration all who seek to imitate the meek example of the divine founder of the Christian religion.

KING HENRY THE FOURTH, PART I

In Act III. Sc. 1, we have the partition of England and Wales between Mortimer, Glendower, and Hotspur, and the business is conducted in as clerk-like, attorney-like fashion, as if it had been the partition of a manor between joint tenants, tenants in common, or co-parceners.

> *Glend.* Come, here's the map: shall we divide our right,
> According to our three-fold order ta'en?
>
> *Mort.* The archdeacon hath divided it
> Into three limits very equally.
> England, from Trent and Severn hitherto,
> By south and east is to my part assign'd:
> And westward, Wales, beyond the Severn shore:
> And all the fertile land within that bound,
> To Owen Glendower:— and, dear Coz, to you,
> The remnant northward, lying off from Trent;
> *And our indentures tripartite are drawn,*
> *Which being sealed interchangeably,*
> (A business that this night may execute,)
> To-morrow, cousin Percy, you and I,
> And my good Lord of Worcester, will set forth.

It may well be imagined, that in composing this speech Shakespeare was recollecting how he had seen a deed of partition tripartite drawn and executed in his master's office at Stratford.

Afterwards, in the same scene, he represents that the unlearned Hotspur, who had such an antipathy to "metre ballad-mongers" and "mincing poetry," fully understood this conveyancing proceeding, and makes him ask impatiently,

> "Are *the indentures drawn?* shall we be gone?"

Shakespeare may have been taught that "livery of seisin" was not necessary to a deed of partition, or he would probably have directed this ceremony to complete the title.

So fond was he of law terms, that afterwards, when Henry IV. is made to lecture the Prince of Wales on his irregularities, and to liken him to Richard II., who, by such improper conduct, lost the crown, he uses the forced and harsh figure, that Richard

"Enfeoffed himself to popularity"

(Act III. Sc. 2).

I copy Malone's note of explanation on this line:— "Gave himself up absolutely to popularity. A feoffment was the ancient mode of conveyance, by which all lands in England were granted in fee-simple for several ages, till the conveyance of lease and release was invented by Serjeant Moor about the year 1630. Every deed of feoffment was accompanied with livery of seisin, that is, with the delivery of corporal possession of the land or tenement granted in fee."

To "sue out livery" is another law term used in this play (Act IV. Sc. 3),— a proceeding to be taken by a ward of the crown, on coming of age, to obtain possession of his lands, which the king had held as guardian in chivalry during his minority. Hotspur, in giving a description of Henry the Fourth's beggarly and suppliant condition when he landed at Ravenspurg, till assisted by the Percys, says,

> "And when he was not six-and-twenty strong,
> Sick in the world's regard, wretched and low,
> A poor unminded outlaw, sneaking home,
> My father gave him welcome to the shore:
> And when he heard him swear, and vow to God,
> He came but to be Duke of Lancaster,
> To *sue his livery*, and beg his peace,
> With tears of innocency and terms of zeal,
> My father, in kind heart and pity mov'd,
> Swore him assistance."

KING HENRY THE FOURTH, PART II

Arguments have been drawn from this drama against Shakespeare's supposed great legal acquirements. It has been objected to the very amusing interview, in Act I. Sc. 2, between Falstaff and the Lord Chief Justice, that if Shakespeare had been much of a lawyer, he would have known that this great magistrate could not examine offenders in the manner supposed, and could only take notice of offences when they were regularly prosecuted before him in the Court of King's Bench, or at the assizes. But although such is the practice in our days, so recently as the beginning of the eighteenth century that illustrious Judge, Lord Chief Justice Holt, acted as a police magistrate, quelling riots, taking depositions against parties accused, and, where a primâ facie case was made out against them, committing them for trial. Lord Chief Justice Coke actually assisted in taking the Earl and Countess of Somerset into custody when charged with the murder of Sir Thomas Overbury, and examined not less than three hundred witnesses against them, — writing the depositions with his own hand. It was quite in course that those charged with the robbery at Gadshill should be "had up" before Lord Chief Justice Gascoigne, and that he should take notice of any of them who, having disobeyed a summons to appear before him, happened to come casually into his presence.

His Lordship is here attended by the tip-staff (or orderly), who, down to the present day, follows the Chief Justice, like his shadow, wherever he officially appears. On this occasion the Chief Justice meeting Sir John, naturally taxes him with having refused to obey the summons served upon him to attend at his Lordship's chambers, that he might answer the information laid against him; and Sir John tries to excuse himself by saying that he was then advised by his "counsel learned in the laws," that, as he was marching to Shrewsbury by the king's orders, he was not bound to come.

Again, it is objected that a Chief Justice could not be supposed, by any person acquainted with his station and functions, to use such vulgar language as that put into the mouth of Sir William Gascoigne when Falstaff will not listen to him, and that this rather smacks of the butcher's shop in which it is alleged that young Shakespeare employed himself in killing calves.

> Ch. Just. To punish yon by the *heels* would amend the attention of
> your *ears*; and I care not if I do become your physician.

But to "lay by the heels" was the technical expression for committing to prison, and I could produce from the Reports various instances of its being so used by distinguished judges from the bench. I will content myself with one. A petition being heard in the Court of Chancery, before Lord Chancellor Jeffreys, against a great City attorney who had given him many briefs at the bar, an affidavit was read, swearing that when the attorney was threatened with being brought before my Lord Chancellor, he exclaimed — "My Lord Chancellor! I made him!" *Lord Chancellor Jeffreys*: "Then will I lay *my maker by the heels*." A warrant of commitment was instantly signed and sealed by the Lord Chancellor, and the poor attorney was sent off to the Fleet.

I must confess that I am rather mortified by the advantage given to the fat knight over my predecessor in this encounter of their wits. Sir John professes to treat the Chief Justice with profound reverence, interlarding his sentences plentifully with *your Lordship* — "God give your *Lordship* good time of day: I am glad to see your *Lordship* abroad: I heard say your *Lordship* was sick: I hope your *Lordship* goes abroad by advice. Your *Lordship*, though not clean past your youth, hath yet some smack of age in you, some relish of the saltness of time; and I most humbly beseech your *Lordship* to have a reverend care of your health." Yet Falstaff's object is to turn the Lord Chief Justice into ridicule, and I am sorry to say that he splendidly succeeds,— insomuch that after the party accused of felony has vaingloriously asserted that he himself had done great service to the state, and that his name was terrible to the enemy, the Chief Justice, instead of committing him to Newgate to answer for the robbery at Gadshill, is contented with admonishing him *to be honest*, and dismisses him with a blessing;— upon which Sir John is emboldened to ask the Chief Justice for the loan of a thousand pounds. To lower the law still further, my Lord Chief Justice is made to break off the conversation, in which Falstaff's wit is so sparkling, with a very bad pun.

> *Ch. Just.* Not a penny, not a penny: you are impatient to bear crosses.*

The same superiority is preserved in the subsequent scene (Act II. Sc. 1), where Falstaff being arrested on mesne process for debt at the suit of Dame Quickly, he gains his discharge, with the consent of the Chief Justice, by saying to his Lordship — "My Lord, this is a poor mad soul; and she says, up and down the town, that her eldest son is like you:" and by insisting that although he owed the money, he was privileged from arrest for debt, "being upon hasty employment in the king's affairs."

In Act V. Sc. I, Falstaff, having long made Justice Shallow his butt during a visit to him in Gloucestershire, looks forward with great delight to the fun of recapitulating at the Boar's Head, East Cheap, Shallow's absurdities; and, meaning to intimate that this would afford him opportunities of amusing the Prince of Wales for a twelvemonth, he says—

> "I will devise matter enough out of this Shallow to keep Prince Henry in continual laughter the wearing out of six fashions (which

---

* So bad is this pun that perhaps it may not be useless to remind you that the *penny* and all the royal coins then had impressed upon them the sign of the cross.

is four terms, or *two actions*), and he shall laugh without inter-vallums."

Dr. Johnson thus annotates on the *"two actions:"* — "There is something humorous in making a spendthrift compute time by the operation of an action for debt." The critic supposes, therefore, that in Shakespeare's time final judgment was obtained in an action of debt in the second term after the writ commencing it was sued out; and as there are four terms in the legal year,— Michaelmas Term, Hilary Term, Easter Term, and Trinity Term — this is a legal circumlocution for a *twelve-month*. It would seem that the author who dealt in such phraseology must have been early initiated in the mysteries of *terms* and *actions*.

Shakespeare has likewise been blamed for an extravagant perversion of law in the promises and threats which Falstaff throws out on hearing that Henry IV. was dead, and that Prince Hal reigned in his stead.

> *Fal.* Master Robert Shallow, choose what office thou wilt in the land, 'tis thine.— Pistol, I will double charge thee with dignities. . . . Master Shallow, my Lord Shallow, be what thou wilt, I am Fortune's steward. . . . Come, Pistol, utter more to me; and withal devise something to do thyself good.— Boot, boot, master Shallow: I know the young King is sick for me. Let us take any man's horses; the laws of England are at my commandment. Happy are they which have been my friends, *and woe unto my Lord Chief Justice!*
> —Act V, Sc. 4.

But Falstaff may not unreasonably be supposed to have believed that he could do all this, even if he were strictly kept to the literal meaning of his words. In the natural and usual course of things he was to become (as it was then called) "favourite" (or, as we call it, *Prime Minister*) to the new king, and to have all the power and patronage of the crown in his hands. Then, why might not Ancient Pistol, who had seen service, have been made *War Minister*? And if Justice Shallow had been pitchforked into the House of Peers, he might have turned out a distinguished *Law Lord.*— By taking "any man's horses" was not meant *stealing them*, but *pressing* them for the king's service, or appropriating them at a nominal price, which the law would then have justified under the king's prerogative of *preemption*. Sir W. Gascoigne was continued as Lord Chief Justice in the new reign; but, according to law and custom, he was removable, and he no doubt expected to be removed, from his office.

Therefore, if Lord Eldon could be supposed to have written the play, I do not see how he would be chargeable with having forgotten any of his law while writing it.

It is remarkable that while Falstaff and his companions, in Act V. Sc. 5, are standing in Palace Yard to see the new king returning from his coronation in Westminster Abbey, Pistol is made to utter an expression used, when the record was in Latin, by special pleaders in introducing a special traverse or negation of a positive material allegation of the opposite side, and so framing an issue of fact for the determination of the jury;— *absque hoc*, "without this that;" — then repeating the allegation to be negatived. But there is often much difficulty in explaining or accounting for the phraseology of Ancient Pistol, who appears "to have been at a great feast of languages and stolen the scraps;" — so that if, when "double charged with dignities," he had been called upon to speak in debate as a leading member of the government, his appointment might have been carped at.

continued on page 401 . . .

JULY

THE MARRIAGE CONTRACTS:
A TRUE CONTRACT / A PRE-CONTRACT

By John V. Orth, with the assistance of Joseph L. Hyde

Much ink has been spilled by Shakespeare scholars over the marriage contracts in *Measure for Measure*.[1] In protesting the charge of fornication, Claudio insists that *upon a true contract / I got possession of Julietta's bed. / . . . she is fast my wife / Save that we do the denunciation lack / Of outward order*, while the Duke in his guise as a friar urges Mariana to substitute for Isabella in the *repair i'th' dark* and insists on its morality (if not its legality): *He is your husband on a pre-contract; / To bring you thus together, 'tis no sin.* A *true contract* and a *pre-contract* — are these different? And how can they be reconciled with the Duke's orders at the play's conclusion — to Angelo:

---

[1] See, e.g., S. Nagarajan, *Measure for Measure* and Elizabethan Betrothals, 14 Shakespeare Quarterly 115 (1963); Karl P. Wentersdorf, The Marriage Contracts in *Measure for Measure*, 32 Shakespeare Survey 129 (1979); Margaret Scott, 'Our City's Institutions': Some Further Reflections on The Marriage Contracts in *Measure for Measure*, 49 English Literary Hist. 790 (1982). See also C.M.A. McCauliff, The Bawd and the Bard: Mercy Tempers Strict Statutory Application in Shakespeare's *Measure for Measure*, 43 Cath. Law. 81 (2004).

Go take her hence, and marry her instantly, and to Claudio: *She that you wronged, look you restore.*

The answer, or at least part of it, lies in the peculiar way the medieval Church defined a valid marriage, distinguishing words of future consent (*verba de futuro*) from words of present consent (*verba de presenti*). Angelo and Mariana had made a public declaration of their future consent, which created an indissoluble union when followed by sexual relations.[2] So they were not validly married until they consummated their union, as Mariana clearly understands: *I am affianced this man's wife as strongly / As words could make up vows: and, my good lord, / But Tuesday night last gone in's garden-house / He knew me as a wife.* The act of consummation is objective: Angelo's intercourse with Mariana is all that is required, even though *i'th' dark* he thought he was having sexual intercourse with Isabella. By contrast, the pledge of matrimony between Claudio and Juliet was in the present tense and became binding (*a true contract*) in *Julietta's bed,* but was kept secret by the couple.

Secrecy posed problems for secular law which attached significant consequences, particularly concerning property, to the status of marriage. In 1563 Catholic canon law was reformed to require that the exchange of vows be made in the presence of a priest and at least two witnesses.[3] The law of Vienna seems also to have required publicity (*the denunciation of outward order*); without it both couples were apparently guilty of legal fornication, which is why the Duke forthwith ordered them to marry.

continued on page 419 . . .

UNITED STATES V. THOMAS
566 F.Supp.2d 830, 831 (N.D.Ill. July 17, 2008)

Milton I. Shadur, Senior District Judge

[T]his Court sees no need "to gild refined gold, to paint the lily, to throw a perfume on the violet." (William Shakespeare, *King John,* act 4, sc. 2, lines 11-12.) It finds both the reasoning and the result of Judge Kennelly's *Witherspoon* opinion fully persuasive — and because that opinion is (perhaps inexplicably) not available on either Westlaw or LEXIS, this opinion attaches and adopts the Kennelly opinion in its entirety.

---

[2] See R.H. Helmholz, *Marriage Litigation in Medieval England* 26 (1974).
[3] See James Brundage, *Law, Sex, and Christian Society in Medieval Europe* 564 (1987). For the current codification, see *Code of Canon Law: Latin-English Edition* can. 1108, p. 403 (1983).

❧ JULY ❧

SUN	MON	TUES	WED	THUR	FRI	SAT
			1	2	3	4
5	6	7	8	9	10	11
12	13	14	15	16	17	18
19	20	21	22	23	24	25
26	27	28	29	30	31	

DID THE FOUNDERS KNOW BRUTUS?

There is a tide in the affairs of men,
Which, taken at the flood, leads on to fortune:
Omitted, all the voyage of their life
Is bound in shallows and in miseries.
On such a full sea are we now afloat;
And we must take the current when it serves,
Or lose our ventures.

> Brutus to Cassius
> Julius Caesar, Act. IV, Sc. 3, ll. 218-224 (1599)

It is now perhaps the most critical Moment that America ever saw. There is a Tide in the affairs of Men — and Consequences of infinite Moment depend upon the Colonies assuming Government at this Time.

> John Adams to William Heath
> April 15, 1776

[T]he Government taken up ought to be the best, whither it be for this, that, or another term of years. This I take to be the time & thing meant by Shakespeare when he says "There is a Tide in the Affairs of Men which taken at the Flood leads on to fortune- That omitted, we are ever after bound in Shallows" &c. Let us therefore, quitting every other consideration heartily unit[e] in leading our countrymen to embrace the present flowing tide, which promises fair to waft us into the harbor of safety, happiness, liberty and virtue.

> Richard Henry Lee to Patrick Henry
> April 20, 1776*

---

* There are plenty more. Among the *Green Bag*'s favorites:

I recollect however that Shakespeare tells us, there is a Tide in human Affairs, an Opportunity which wise Men carefully watch for and improve, and I will never forget because it exactly coincides with my religious opinion and I think it warranted by holy Writ, that "God helps those who help themselves."

Samuel Adams to Richard Henry Lee, July 15, 1777.

PENNSYLVANIA V. DUNLAP

John G. Roberts, Jr.[†]

North Philly, May 4, 2001. Officer Sean Devlin, Narcotics Strike Force, was working the morning shift. Undercover surveillance. The neighborhood? Tough as a three-dollar steak. Devlin knew. Five years on the beat, nine months with the Strike Force. He'd made fifteen, twenty drug busts in the neighborhood.

Devlin spotted him: a lone man on the corner. Another approached. Quick exchange of words. Cash handed over; small objects handed back. Each man then quickly on his own way. Devlin knew the guy wasn't buying bus tokens. He radioed a description and Officer Stein picked up the buyer. Sure enough: three bags of crack in the guy's pocket. Head downtown and book him. Just another day at the office.

• • • •

That was not good enough for the Pennsylvania Supreme Court, which held in a divided decision that the police lacked probable cause to arrest the defendant. The Court concluded that a "single, isolated transaction" in a high-crime area was insufficient to justify the arrest, given that the officer did not actually see the drugs, there was no tip from an informant, and the defendant did not attempt to flee. 941 A.2d 671, 679 (2007). I disagree with that conclusion, and dissent from the denial of certiorari. A drug purchase was not the only possible explanation for the defendant's conduct, but it was certainly likely enough to give rise to probable cause.

The probable-cause standard is a "nontechnical conception that deals with the factual and practical considerations of everyday life on which reasonable and prudent men, not legal technicians, act." *Maryland v. Pringle*, 540 U.S. 366, 370 (2003) (internal quotation marks omitted). What is required is simply "a reasonable ground for belief of guilt," *id.*, at 371

[†] Chief Justice of the United States, joined by Justice Anthony M. Kennedy, dissenting from the denial of a petition for a writ of certiorari. This opinion is reported at 129 S. Ct. 448 (2008).

(same) — a "probability, and not a prima facie showing, of criminal activity," *Illinois v. Gates*, 462 U.S. 213, 235 (1983) (same). "[A] police officer may draw inferences based on his own experience in deciding whether probable cause exists," *Ornelas v. United States*, 517 U.S. 690, 700 (1996), including inferences "that might well elude an untrained person," *United States v. Cortez*, 449 U.S. 411, 418 (1981).

On the facts of this case, I think the police clearly had probable cause to arrest the defendant. An officer with drug interdiction experience in the neighborhood saw two men on a street corner — with no apparent familiarity or prior interaction — make a quick hand-to-hand exchange of cash for "'small objects.'" 941 A.2d, at 673. This exchange took place in a high-crime neighborhood known for drug activity, far from any legitimate businesses. Perhaps it is possible to imagine innocent explanations for this conduct, but I cannot come up with any remotely as likely as the drug transaction Devlin believed he had witnessed. In any event, an officer is not required to eliminate all innocent explanations for a suspicious set of facts to have probable cause to make an arrest. As we explained in *Gates*, "[i]n making a determination of probable cause the relevant inquiry is not whether particular conduct is 'innocent' or 'guilty,' but the degree of suspicion that attaches to particular types of noncriminal acts." 462 U.S., at 244, n.13.

The Pennsylvania Supreme Court emphasized that the police did not actually see any drugs. 941 A.2d, at 679. But Officer Devlin and his partner were conducting undercover surveillance. From a distance, it would be difficult to have a clear view of the small objects that changed hands. As the Commonwealth explains in its petition for certiorari, the "classic" drug transaction is a hand-to-hand exchange, on the street, of cash for small objects. Pet. for Cert. 5-8. The Pennsylvania Supreme Court's decision will make it more difficult for the police to conduct drug interdiction in high-crime areas, unless they employ the riskier practice of having undercover officers actually make a purchase or sale of drugs.

The Pennsylvania Court also noted that the defendant did not flee. 941 A.2d, at 671. Flight is hardly a prerequisite to a finding of probable cause. A defendant may well decide that the odds of escape do not justify adding another charge to that of drug possession. And of course there is no suggestion in the record that the defendant had any chance to flee — he was caught redhanded.

Aside from its importance for law enforcement, this question has divided state courts, a traditional ground warranting review on certiorari. S. Ct. Rule 10(b). The New Jersey Supreme Court has held that an "experienced narcotics officer" had probable cause to make an arrest when — in a vacant lot in a high-drug neighborhood — he "saw defendant and his companion give money to [a] third person in exchange for small unknown objects." *State v. Moore*, 181 N.J. 40, 46-47, 853 A.2d 903, 907 (2004). The Rhode Island Supreme Court reached the same conclusion in a case where the defendants — through their car windows — exchanged cash for a small "bag of suspected narcotics." *State v. Castro*, 891 A.2d 848, 851-854 (2006). In contrast, the Colorado Supreme Court held that a hand-to-hand exchange of unknown objects did not give the police probable cause to make an arrest, even where one of the men was a known drug dealer. *People v. Ratcliff*, 778 P.2d 1371, 1377-1378 (1989). All these cases have unique factual wrinkles, as any probable-cause case would, but the core fact pattern is the same: experienced police officers observing hand-to-hand exchanges of cash for small, unknown objects in high-crime neighborhoods.

The Pennsylvania Supreme Court speculated that such an exchange could have been perfectly innocent. But as Judge Friendly has pointed out, "[j]udges are not required to exhibit a naiveté from which ordinary citizens are free." *United States v. Stanchich*, 550 F.2d 1294, 1300 (CA2 1977). Based not only on common sense but also his experience as a narcotics officer and his previous work in the neighborhood, Officer Devlin concluded that what happened on that street corner was probably a drug transaction. That is by far the *most* reasonable conclusion, even though our cases only require it to be *a* reasonable conclusion.

I would grant certiorari and reverse the judgment of the Pennsylvania Supreme Court.

--*≡◎≡*--

We go up dark stairways to get a gun punk with a skinful of hop and sometimes we don't get all the way up, and our wives wait dinner that night and all the other nights. We don't come home any more. And nights we do come home, we come home so goddam tired we can't eat or sleep or even read the lies the papers print about us. . . . Nothing we do is right, not ever. Not once. If we get a confession, we beat it out of the guy, they say, and some shyster calls us Gestapo in court and sneers at us when we muddle our grammar.

Christy French (1949)

Troilus and Cressida.

Shakespeare's Legal Acquirements

(continued from page 392)

John Lord Campbell

King Henry the Sixth, Part II

In the speeches of Jack Cade and his coadjutors in this play we find a familiarity with the law and its proceedings which strongly indicates that the author must have had some professional practice or education as a lawyer. The second scene in Act IV. may be taken as an example.

> *Dick.* The first thing we do, *let's kill all the lawyers.*
> *Cade.* Nay, that I mean to do. Is not this a lamentable thing, that the skin of an innocent lamb should be made parchment?— that parchment, being scribbled o'er, should undo a man? Some say the bee stings; but I say 'tis the bee's wax, for I did but seal once to a thing, and I was never mine own man since.

The Clerk of Chatham is then brought in, who could "make obligations and write court hand," and who, instead of "making his mark like an honest plain-dealing man," had been "so well brought up that he could write his name." Therefore he was sentenced to be hanged with his pen and ink-horn about his neck.

Surely Shakespeare must have been employed to write *deeds* on *parchment* in *court hand*, and to apply the *wax* to them in the form of *seals*: one does not understand how he should, on any other theory of his bringing up, have been acquainted with these details.

Again, the indictment on which Lord Say was arraigned, in Act IV. Sc. 7, seems drawn by no inexperienced hand:—

> "Thou hast most traitorously corrupted the youth of the realm in erecting a grammar-school: and whereas, before, our forefathers had no other books but the score and the tally, thou hast caused printing to be used; and *contrary to the king, his crown and dignity,* thou hast built a paper-mill. It will be proved to thy face that thou hast men about thee that usually talk of a noun and a verb, and *such abominable words as no Christian ear can endure to hear.* Thou hast appointed justices of peace, to call poor men before them about matters they were not able to answer. Moreover thou hast put them in prison; and because they could not read, thou hast

---

* *"Inter Christianos non nominand."*

hanged them, when indeed only for that cause they have been most worthy to live."

How acquired I know not, but it is quite certain that the drawer of this indictment must have had some acquaintance with 'The Crown Circuit Companion,' and must have had a full and accurate knowledge of that rather obscure and intricate subject— "Felony and Benefit of Clergy."

Cade's proclamation, which follows, deals with still more recondite heads of jurisprudence. Announcing his policy when he should mount the throne, he says:—

> "The proudest peer in the realm shall not wear a head on his shoulders unless he pay me tribute: there shall not a maid be married but she shall pay me her maidenhead ere they have it. Men shall hold of me *in capite;* and we charge and command that their wives be as *free as heart can wish, or tongue can tell.*"

He thus declares a great forthcoming change in the tenure of land and in the liability to taxation: he is to have a poll-tax like that which had raised the rebellion; but, instead of coming down to the daughters of blacksmiths who had reached the age of fifteen, it was to be confined to the nobility. Then he is to legislate on the *mercheta mulierum.* According to Blackstone and other high authorities this never had been known in England; although, till the reign of Malcolm III., it certainly appears to have been established in Scotland; but Cade intimates his determination to adopt it—with this alteration, that instead of conferring the privilege on every lord of a manor, to be exercised within the manor, he is to assume it exclusively for himself all over the realm, as belonging to his prerogative royal.

He proceeds to announce his intention to abolish tenure in *free soccage,* and that all *men* should hold of him *in capite,* concluding with a licentious jest, that although his subjects should no longer hold in free soccage, "their wives should be as free as heart can wish, or tongue can tell." Strange to say, this phrase, or one almost identically the same, "as free as tongue can speak or heart can think," is feudal, and was known to the ancient law of England. In the tenth year of King Henry VII., that very distinguished judge, Lord Hussey, who was Chief Justice of England during four reigns, in a considered judgment delivered the opinion of the whole Court of King's Bench as to the construction to be put upon the words, "as free as tongue can speak or heart can think." See YEAR BOOK, *Hil. Term,* 10 *Hen. VII.,* fol. 13, pl. 6.

TROILUS AND CRESSIDA

In this play the author shows his insatiable desire to illustrate his descriptions of *kissing* by his recollection of the forms used in executing deeds. When Pandarus (Act III. Sc. 2) has brought Troilus and Cressida together in the Orchard to gratify their warm inclinations, he advises Troilus to give Cressida *"a kiss in fee-farm,"* which Malone explains to be "a kiss of a duration that has no bounds,— a fee-farm being a grant of lands in fee, that is for ever, reserving a rent certain."

The advice of Pandarus to the lovers being taken, he exclaims—

> "What! billing again? Here's— *In witness the parties interchangeably*
> —"

the exact form of the *testatum* clause in an indenture— "In witness whereof the parties interchangeably have hereto set their hands and seals."

To avoid a return to this figure of speech I may here mention other instances in which Shakespeare introduces it. In 'Measure for Measure,' Act IV. Sc. 1—

> "But my kisses bring again
> *Seals* of love, but *seal'd* in vain:"

and in his poem of "Venus and Adonis"—

> "Pure lips, *sweet seals* in my soft lips imprinted,
> What bargains may I make, still to be *sealing?*"

KING LEAR

In Act I. Sc. 4 the Fool makes a lengthy rhyming speech, containing a great many trite but useful moral maxims, such as—

> Have more than thou showest,
> Speak less than thou knowest, &c.,

which the testy old King found rather flat and tiresome.

> *Lear.* This is nothing, fool.
> *Fool.* Then, 'tis *like the breath of an unfeed lawyer:* you gave me nothing for it.

This seems to show that Shakespeare had frequently been present at trials in courts of justice, and now speaks from his own recollection. There is no trace of such a proverbial saying as "like the breath of an unfeed lawyer," — while all the world knows the proverb, "Whosoever is his own counsel has a fool for his client."

How unfeed lawyers may have comported themselves in Shake-speare's time I know not; but I am bound to say, in vindication of "my order," that in my time there has been no ground for the Fool's sarcasm upon the bar. The two occasions when "the breath of an unfeed lawyer" attracts notice in this generation are when he pleads for a party suing *in formâ pauperis*, or when he defends a person prosecuted by the crown for high treason. It is contrary to etiquette to take a fee in the one case as well as in the other; and on all such occasions counsel, from a regard to their own credit, as well as from conscientious motives, uniformly exert themselves with extraordinary zeal, and put forth all their learning and elo-quence.

I confess that there is some foundation for the saying that "a lawyer's opinion which costs nothing is worth nothing;" but this can only apply to opinions given off-hand, in the course of common conversation, — where there is no time for deliberation, where there is a desire to say what will be agreeable, and where no responsibility is incurred.

In Act II. Sc. 1, there is a remarkable example of Shakespeare's use of technical legal phraseology. Edmund, the wicked illegitimate son of the Earl of Gloster, having succeeded in deluding his father into the belief that Edgar, the legitimate son, had attempted to commit parricide, and had been prevented from accomplishing the crime by Edmund's tender solici-tude for the Earl's safety, the Earl is thus made to express a determination that he would disinherit Edgar (who was supposed to have fled from jus-tice), and that he would leave all his possessions to Edmund: —

> *Glo.* Strong and fasten'd villain!
> . . .
> All ports I'll bar; the villain shall not 'scape.
> * * *
> Besides, his picture
> I will send far and near, that all the kingdom
> May have due note of him;[†] and of my land,
> Loyal and natural boy, I'll work the means
> *To make thee capable.*

In forensic discussions respecting legitimacy, the question is put, whether the individual whose *status* is to be determined is "capable," *i.e.* capable of inheriting; but it is only a lawyer who would express the idea of legitimising a natural son by simply saying —

[†] One would suppose that photography, by which this mode of catching criminals is now practised, had been invented in the reign of King Lear.

> I'll work the means
> To make him capable.

Again, in Act III. Sc. 5, we find Edmund trying to incense the Duke of Cornwall against his father for having taken part with Lear when so cruelly treated by Goneril and Regan. The two daughters had become the reigning sovereigns, to whom Edmund professed to owe allegiance. Cornwall having created Edmund Earl of Gloster says to him—

> "Seek out where thy father is, that he may ready for our apprehension."

On which Edmund observes aside:

> "If I find him *comforting* the King, it will stuff suspicion more fully."

Upon this Dr. Johnson has the following note:— "He uses the word [comforting] in the juridical sense, for supporting, helping."

The indictment against an accessory after the fact, for treason, charges that the accessory "comforted" the principal traitor after knowledge of the treason.

In Act III. Sc. 6, the imaginary trial of the two unnatural daughters is conducted in a manner showing a perfect familiarity with criminal procedure.

Lear places the two Judges on the bench, viz., Mad Tom and the Fool. He properly addresses the former as "the robed man of justice," but, although both were "of the commission," I do not quite understand why the latter is called his "yokefellow of equity," unless this might be supposed to be a special commission, like that which sat on Mary, Queen of Scots, including Lord Chancellor Audley.

Lear causes Goneril to be arraigned first, and then proceeds as a witness to give evidence against her, to prove an overt act of high treason:

> "I here take my oath before this honourable assembly, she kicked the poor king, her father."

But the trial could not be carried on with perfect regularity on account of Lear's madness, and, without waiting for a verdict, he himself sentences Regan to be anatomized:—

> "Then, let them anatomize Regan; see what breeds about her heart."

continued on page 443 . . .

TO ERR IS HUMAN, TO MOO BOVINE

THE ROSE OF ABERLONE STORY

Norman Otto Stockmeyer[†]

More than a century ago, T.C. Sherwood of Plymouth entered into a contract to purchase a cow from Hiram Walker of Detroit. Because it was thought that the cow was barren, it was sold for beef. The price amounted to eighty dollars. Later, when Walker tried to back out of the deal, Sherwood sued him.

The resulting opinion, *Sherwood v. Walker*, 66 Mich. 568, 33 N.W. 919 (1887), handed down by the Supreme Court of Michigan in 1887, became a legal classic and is still studied by law students across the country. Indeed, in 1985 American Heritage magazine picked *Sherwood v. Walker* as one of its "Five Classic Cases" that every law student must know. Additionally, in Sherwood's hometown, the State Bar of Michigan dedicated a Legal Milestone historical marker that, according to the Michigan Bar Journal for August 1993, recognizes the case as "one of the most celebrated contracts cases in American history."

What could possibly be of such lasting importance about a dispute between two farmers over a barren cow?

For one thing, nothing about the case is quite as it appears. Neither the buyer nor the seller were farmers; rather, they were prosperous business men who could afford to pursue their dispute throughout Michigan's

---

[†] Norman Otto Stockmeyer is an emeritus professor at Thomas M. Cooley Law School. He is a graduate of Oberlin College and the University of Michigan Law School. This is his fourth article for the Thomas M. Cooley Law Review. Readers seeking more complete source citations may email the author at stockmen@cooley.edu. The author thanks Texas Wesleyan University Law professor Franklin G. Snyder for sharing his research into cattle registry records relating to Rose and her offspring. This article originally appeared at 24 Thomas M. Cooley L. Rev. 491 (2007). Copyright © 2007. Reprinted by permission of the author and the publisher.

court system. More importantly, the cow turned out not to be barren after all, a mistake that formed the basis of the court's decision. And although Walker won the lawsuit, Sherwood ended up with the cow.

Here is the curious story behind the "Case of the Barren Cow," the parties to the lawsuit, its surprising aftermath, and its continuing importance.

THE LAWSUIT

The story begins in May of 1886 when Sherwood approached Walker about buying some of his stock of purebred Angus cattle. Sherwood did not find any to his liking on one farm, so Walker suggested that Sherwood look at a few head of cattle on another farm, Walker's Greenfield farm, which was located some eight miles northwest of downtown Detroit in what was then Greenfield Township and now part of Detroit.

Walker told Sherwood that the cows on that farm were probably barren and, therefore, could not breed. Sherwood picked out a cow with the fancy name of "Rose 2d of Aberlone." The parties agreed on a price of 5 cents a pound, and Walker confirmed the sale in writing.

When Sherwood later returned to the Greenfield farm to take delivery of the cow, Walker refused to take Sherwood's money or to deliver the cow. By then, Walker suspected that Rose was expecting a calf, and if so, she was worth as much as $1,000.

Walker offered Sherwood a different cow instead, "Lucy 8th." Sherwood refused. Instead, in July, Sherwood sued Walker, in Justice of the Peace court, to obtain possession of Rose under a writ of replevin, and he won.

Walker appealed to Wayne County Circuit Court. However, following a full jury trial that December, Sherwood won the case again. Meanwhile, Rose delivered a calf in October, therefore proving that she was on the way to motherhood when the contract was made. (The gestation period for a cow is nine months.)

Determined not to lose his cow, Walker appealed again, this time to the Michigan Supreme Court. His lawyers raised twenty-five assignments of error. Sherwood's lawyer responded that because of the contract, title to the cow had passed to Sherwood, and it was Walker's turn to deliver.

The Michigan Supreme Court overruled the lower courts. It held that if both parties believed that the cow was barren and useless for breeding purposes — when, in fact, she was capable of breeding — then the seller could avoid the contract. Why? Because the contract would have then been based on a mutual mistake.

The bronze letters on the Legal Milestone plaque summarize the decision this way: "Because a mutual mistake affecting the substance of the transaction had been made, Hiram Walker had a right to rescind the contract, and keep the cow."

Central to the Supreme Court's decision was its belief that the parties' mistake went to the very essence of the contract, the "root of the matter." To those nineteenth-century jurists, a barren cow was a substantially different creature than a breeding one; as different, the Court said, as "an ox and a cow." Thus, the animal as contracted for, a barren cow, did not exist. ·

(One may assume that the litigation delighted the lawyers. The case could well have served as the inspiration for "The Lawsuit," a lithograph from the 1800s that depicts a plaintiff and a defendant tugging at opposite ends of a cow while a lawyer milks it.)

THE PARTIES

Theodore Clark Sherwood

Theodore Clark Sherwood (1839-1910) was age forty-seven at the time of the controversy. He owned an eighty-acre farm on Ann Arbor Road at Sheldon Road, just south of the village of Plymouth. There he raised the best breeds of livestock; his farm was one of the finest in the county. But Sherwood made his living as a banker. A refined individual and prominent member of the Plymouth community, it has been said that he always appeared in public wearing a tall silk hat.

Sherwood was born in Geneva, New York, in 1839, and he moved with his parents to the Detroit area in 1854. After stints as a schoolteacher in a district near Detroit and as a railroad cashier in Kalamazoo, he began his banking career working for the First National Bank of Battle Creek, thereafter the First National Bank of Plymouth, and the Grand Rapids National Bank. He returned to Plymouth in 1884 to become president of the newly organized Plymouth National Bank.

Two years after the Supreme Court's Sherwood decision, Governor Cyrus Luce appointed Sherwood to be Michigan's first State Commissioner of Banking, a position he held from 1889 to 1896. He had the task of organizing the new state banking department and drawing up rules and regulations for banking institutions. According to his first annual report, published in the New York Times for January 29, 1890, Commissioner Sherwood had oversight responsibility for 90 state-chartered banks with assets of $47 million.

As Banking Commissioner Sherwood was credited with helping Michigan's banks through the financial panic of 1893 and the business depression that followed. A contemporary account said, "he is considered by business men of Michigan as one of the ablest financiers and one of the best informed men on financial questions in the state."

After his service as Banking Commissioner, Sherwood was president of Peninsular Savings Bank of Detroit for two years before retiring in 1898. He died October 1, 1910, at the age of seventy-one. He is buried in Plymouth's Riverside Cemetery, located on Plymouth Road west of Haggerty Road. An obituary referred to him as "a man of fine culture and pleasant address" and "the father of the state banking laws."

Coincidently, the cemetery is directly behind the 35th District Courthouse. District Courts replaced the old Justice of the Peace court system, in which Sherwood began his famous lawsuit. A former Contracts student of mine, 35th District Court Judge Ronald Lowe, has installed a display commemorating *Sherwood v. Walker*. It is located on the third floor of the courthouse and is open to the public.

Sherwood's Plymouth National Bank went through several consolidations before merging with the National Bank of Detroit. It subsequently became First Chicago NBD Corp, and then Bank One, which in 2004 was acquired by JPMorgan Chase. A toy store is now located on the site the bank once occupied at the corner of Main Street and Penniman Street in downtown Plymouth. The State Bar of Michigan's Legal Milestone marker stands across the street in Kellogg Park.

An indication of his banker's frugality may be gleaned from Sherwood's instruction not to water Rose on the morning she originally was to be weighed and handed over. Why pay 5 cents a pound for water?

Hiram Walker

Hiram Walker (1816-1898), then age seventy, seemingly was of a more generous nature. Even though Rose was being sold for a small fraction of what he had paid for her, Walker instructed his farm manager to throw in a free halter. (Of course, that was before he discovered that Rose might be worth ten times the sale price.) Walker could well afford to be generous, as he was at the time one of Detroit's most successful industrialists.

(Much of the information that follows comes from a collection of columns from the Walkerville Times, republished in 2006 in the second edition of Best of the Times.)

Walker was born on the 4th of July, 1816, in East Douglas, Massachusetts, near Boston. At age twenty-two, he headed west to Detroit to seek his fortune. His first ventures were not successful. His Detroit grocery store failed, and a tannery in which he was a partner burned down. But he had more luck as a grain merchant, buying and selling grain, and distilling some of it into whisky.

Attracted by lax liquor laws and cheap land across the Detroit River in Ontario, Canada, in 1856 Walker purchased 468 acres of land 1½ miles upstream from Windsor for $40,000, and he went into the liquor business in a big way. An innovative merchandiser, he was among the first distillers to brand his barrels, the first to sell whisky in individual glass bottles, the first to employ whisky "runners" to promote his product, and the first to advertise with billboards and electric signs.

Walker was an innovator in other ways. He built the town of Walkerville to house his workers. By 1895, it had a population of 600. He used leftover mash to feed herds of cows, which led to a large dairy operation. He constructed Canada's first concrete road between his distillery and cattle barn. The first electric streetcar in Canada ran from Walkerville to Windsor, powered by current from Walker's plant. His Walkerville Wagon Works later became Ford of Canada. Indeed, he has been called "the Henry Ford of Canada."

Hiram Walker's Canadian whiskey — "lighter than Scotch and smoother than bourbon" — achieved great success. By the time of his dispute with Sherwood, Walker's "Club Whisky" was being marketed throughout Canada and the United States.

In 1891, a new U.S. law required that product labels identify the country of origin. Walker boldly added "Canadian" to his product's name. "Canadian Club" eventually became one of the most recognized brand names in the world.

The Canadian Club Brand Center in historic Walkerville (now part of Windsor) offers tours of Hiram Walker & Sons' magnificent main office building, built in 1894. Located on the banks of the Detroit River, it is five minutes east of the Detroit-Windsor Tunnel on Riverside Drive. Yes, there is a tasting room. Legions of law students have made pilgrimages to the site.

The most imposing residence in Walkerville is Willistead Manor. Noted architect Albert Kahn designed it for Edward Chandler Walker, Hiram's eldest son. Tours of the thirty-six-room mansion are available.

An article in the March 1995 Michigan Living magazine suggests that a day tour of Walkerville also might include the Town Hall, designed by Albert Kahn in 1904, and the Crown Inn on Devonshire, the town's earliest hotel. Do not overlook Kildare House, on the corner of Kildare and Wyandotte, built in 1885 for a Walker employee, which, fittingly, has been turned into a neighborhood pub. A virtual tour of historic Walkerville can be accessed at www.walkervilletimes.com/virtual-tour/virtual_tour.htm.

Except for a few early years in Walkerville, Hiram Walker continued to live in Detroit. He commuted to work by horse and buggy from his home at the corner of Shelby and Fort Streets, on the site now occupied by the Federal Reserve Bank Building, to a dock off Atwater Street, then by ferry across the mile-wide Detroit River to a dock he built at Walkervile.

Walker never gave up his U.S. citizenship, but considered himself neither a Canadian nor an American, but rather (recalling his date of birth) a "Yankee."

Hiram Walker died in 1899 at his home in Detroit. He was 84. He is buried in Elmwood Cemetery on Detroit's near east side. His three surviving sons inherited the business. Hiram Walker & Sons was sold in 1926 for $14 million, not a bad return on Hiram's initial $40,000 investment.

A glimpse into why a man of such means would take a fight over a single cow all the way to Michigan's highest court is provided by this reflection at his seventy-fo[u]rth birthday in 1890: "The young men of the present do not know the value of money. I had hardly the time, as a young man, to go fishing, for I was always working. My habit, in my younger days, of saving the pennies, has placed me where I am today."

Walker could pinch pennies until they squealed — or in Rose's case, mooed.

Rose

Rose (1881-?) was not what one would think from reading the opinion in *Sherwood v. Walker*. First, her name was not Rose 2d of Aberlone. There was little reason to think that she was barren. And despite the ruling in favor of Walker, she ended up in Sherwood's possession. (All of this has been uncovered by the careful detective work of Texas Wesleyan University law professor Franklin G. Snyder, who has poured over cattle registry records of the period.)

She is called Rose 2d of Aberlone in the contract and in court papers, but her name was Rose 2d of Aberlour, not Aberlone. She was foaled at the Mains of Aberlour, near the River Spey, in Scotland. The purity of the river's water, and the proximity to grain, led the distilling industry to flourish in that region. More than half of Scotland's whisky comes from within twenty miles of Aberlour.

Rose was born on January 8, 1881, and subsequently registered with the American Angus breeders as number 2782. Her sire was Souter Johnny, named for a character in Burns's "Tam O'Shanter," and her dam was Delilah of Burnside.

Although no photo of Rose is known to exist, an engraving was made of her sister, Elaine of Aberlour. Rose herself became a "cover girl," being depicted on the cover of the Student Lawyer Journal for April 1965, wearing the halter.

We do not know when or where Hiram Walker purchased Rose, but given his interest in whisky distilling and breeding Angus cattle, it is entirely possible that he bought her while visiting Scotland. Records show that Walker paid $850 for Rose, so parting with her for $80 can only be explained by his belief that she was unable to breed.

But was that belief justified? Here is perhaps the biggest surprise: Rose had given birth to a calf in 1883, registered to Walker as the breeder. She did not calve in 1884 or 1885, but she had proven her breeding potential.

Moreover, the court record lists four other Angus cattle for sale at the Greenfield farm in the spring of 1886. One, Waterside Standard, was a bull. Clearly, Rose's delicate condition that May was not wholly unexplainable.

The Aftermath

Professor Snyder has also discovered another surprising fact: that after the case was decided, Sherwood bought Rose from Walker for an undisclosed amount. Her subsequent offspring list "T.C. Sherwood" as breeder. So, despite protracted litigation over the right to her possession, to Walker it was never about Rose, just her price.

At the unveiling of the Legal Milestone, one speaker was quoted in the Plymouth Observer as saying, "Plymouth never got to be the hometown of Rose of Aberlone, but (the city) got the plaque — What a perfect way to make amends." As we now know, however, Rose did get to graze on Sherwood's farm after all.

(Writing in the June 1998 Michigan Bar Journal, another former student, Michael Ellis, reported that the unveiling was accompanied by presentations pregnant with puns. "People were 'udderly' pleased, not 'cowed' by the experience, and 'milked' it for all it was worth." But let us moove on before the editors start beefing and apply a cleaver to this paragraph.)

Being the most sympathetic character in the case, Rose has become much celebrated in verse. The most widely published poem is that of UCLA law professor Brainerd Currie, which first appeared in the Harvard Law School Record in 1954 and has been reprinted several times in other legal publications. The 350-line epic concludes with a scene that genera-tions of law students can recall — perhaps more fondly now than at the time:

> Tis the middle of the night before the exam,
> And there's nothing to eat but a cold bit of ham . . . .
> Mark how the eager students cram.
> A dismal specter haunts this wake-
> The law of mutual mistake;
> And even the reluctant drone
> Must cope with Rose of Aberlone.
> She rules the cases, she stalks the page
> Even in this atomic age . . .
> In many a hypothetical
> With characters alphabetical,
> In many a subtle and sly disguise
> There lurks the ghost of her sad brown eyes.
> That she will turn up in some set of facts is
> Almost as certain as death and taxes:
> For students of law must still atone
> For the shame of Rose of Aberlone.
> (Harvard Law School Record, Thursday, March 4, 1954)

Sherwood v. Walker became "the single most loved law case at Harvard" due to Currie's poem and the delight that Professor John P. Dawson, a native Detroiter, took in teaching the case to generations of Harvard law students. But law students at the University of Iowa (who might know a thing or two about cows) were not impressed with Currie's poem, ac-cording to this response:

> My Wild Iowa Rose
> (Anonymous)
> Unlike another, my rhyme is terse:
> Your name, Oh Rose is under curse.
> I can think of nothing worse
> Than to suffer through the Harvard verse . . . .
> (Journal of Legal Education, 1982)

Other tributes to Rose's fertility include these two limericks, the first by Indiana University law professor Douglass G. Boshkoff, the other by an unknown author:

We've all heard the story of Rose
Whose failure to bear was a pose.
"For the stew pot, I'm not,"
Said Rose, like a shot.
And she wasn't, as everyone knows."
(Northwestern University Law Review, 1996)

-and-

For this beef-cow who carried a calf,
The 80-buck price was a gaffe.
The injustice moves us
And so, it behooves us
To say: Here's a cow-and-a-half.

Then there are these lyrics, by Professor Snyder, to the tune of Bob Dylan's *Just Like a Woman*:

JUST LIKE A HEIFER
Now Sherwood needed a cow.
It's not clear if for breeding, or for chow.
He went to Walker's farm,
Thought there would be no harm-
But there he fell under Rose's fatal charm
And he knew-
She's the one.
CHORUS
She moos, just like a heifer
(Yes she does)
And she chews grass just like a heifer
(Yes she does)
And she woos bulls just like a heifer-
But she's priced just like a side of beef.
(Contracts Prof Blog, May 15, 2006)

My favorite tribute to the case, which summarizes it fairly well in far fewer words, was handed to me after class one day by a student, James Marchant:

To err is human,
To moo, bovine.

CONTINUING IMPORTANCE

Sherwood v. Walker has been cited as legal authority in more than fifty court decisions, from New York to California. Judges have called it "celebrated," "classic," "leading," and "seminal," as well as a "paradigm case" "revered by teachers of contract law."

James J. White, a distinguished professor of Contracts at the University of Michigan, recalled recently in exquisite detail how his Contracts professor dealt with the "barren cow" case nearly fifty years earlier:

> I can still remember the Monday morning when we took up the doctrine of mistake in Contracts class. After we had the normal Socratic discourse about the cases, Bob [U-M law professor Robert J. Harris] set out his theory about how the cases should be put together . . . . Being good obsessive, compulsive law students who yearn for certainty, we eagerly wrote down his interpretation of these cases. . . .
>
> On Tuesday Bob commenced the class by saying, ... "Yesterday I told you that the cow case was correctly decided; now I think it was not. Today I believe the buyer not the seller should have won." You could smell the hostility in the air that day. If any of us had had a gun, we would have killed him. Our learning-so carefully put down on Monday — was worthless and, worse, we feared Bob might disavow Tuesday's analysis on Wednesday. (Law Quadrangle Notes, Fall 2005.)

Eventually White and his colleagues came to love and respect their Contracts professor for showing them "the uncertainly and ambiguity inherent in contract law." In that sense, *Sherwood v. Walker*, whether correctly decided or not, remains a great teaching vehicle.

Last fall I learned from a former Contracts student, Stephen M. Rice, that he had entered upon a career at Liberty University School of Law teaching Contracts. Perhaps his classroom discussion of *Sherwood v. Walker* will be influenced by recollections of our class back in 1992.

As suggested by Professor Harris's change of mind, respect for the decision in Rose's case has not been universal. First, there was a dissent in the case itself. Justice Thomas R. Sherwood (another coincidence?) agreed with the majority opinion on mutual mistake as a basis for rescission. But he doubted that the buyer shared the seller's belief in Rose's infertility. In the dissent's view, the buyer thought that Rose "could be made to breed" and that "there is no pretense that (Sherwood) bought the cow for beef."

University of Michigan law professor George Palmer in his 1962 book, *Mistake and Unjust Enrichment*, sided with the dissent: "I find it most difficult to accept the statement of the majority of the court that the buyer, Sherwood, shared the mistake . . . . The whole sense of the matter suggested that . . . he thought there was a chance that Rose 2d would breed."

Today's students often harbor the same suspicions. One Contracts student, Donna Shackelford, was so worked up over the decision that she wrote me a long note saying that the author of the majority opinion, Justice Allen B. Morse, must never have owned cattle. "All breeders know that there is always a chance that if a cow is left with a bull (as Rose was) it could produce a calf. . . . Plaintiff could not have wanted the cow for meat . . . because you don't buy a cow for meat-you buy a steer. And you certainly don't spend your time shopping around in herds to pick one out-the first plump one will do."

(Ah, the "plumpness" factor. Did Sherwood pick Rose over the other cows on the Greenfield farm because she was showing a little something extra? And if so, was Sherwood thinking "beef on the hoof" or "baby on board?")

According to the Michigan Supreme Court Historical Society's website, www.micourthistory.org/resources, Justice Morse attended Michigan Agricultural College, so he would have known something about cows. But Justice Sherwood was actually raised on a farm. In another of the case's coincidences, after his service on the court Justice Morse was named Ambassador to Scotland, Rose's birthplace.

A more veiled criticism of *Sherwood v. Walker* came from the distinguished Federal judge Irving R. Kaufman. He declared in the 1969 case of *H. Kook & Co. v. Scheinman, Hochstin & Trotta*, that the opinion brought "a flood of nostalgia" but did not "furnish a flood of light" on the case before him.

WHAT ABOUT THE LENAWEE CASE?

At one point the Michigan Supreme Court, sharing Judge Kaufman's difficulty in applying *Sherwood v. Walker*, tried to disown Rose. The 1982 case was *Lenawee County Board of Health v. Messerly*. 417 Mich. 17, 331 N.W.2d 203 (1982). It involved the sale of a three-unit apartment building located on a 600-square-foot tract of land for $25,500. Unknown to either party, a previous owner had installed the septic tank without a permit.

Within a week of the purchase, the buyers (Mr. and Mrs. Pickles) discovered raw sewage seeping out of the ground. The lot size was too small to support a legal septic system, rendering the property uninhabitable and virtually without value. The buyers sought to rescind their purchase based on mutual mistake. The issue was whether the parties' mistake went to the essence of the property — in one sense it surely did — or merely its value.

The learned justice who wrote the Supreme Court's decision, the

Honorable James L. Ryan, expressed the view that *Sherwood v. Walker*'s essence/value distinction was "inexact and confusing" and "an impediment to a clear and helpful analysis." Its holding was therefore to be limited to its facts (and thus of no legal precedent in non-cow cases).

But wait! What tipped the scales in *Lenawee* was an "as is" clause in the contract. Legally, the court said, that placed the risk of any unknown defect on the buyers. So, despite the mutual mistake, the buyers could not back out.

When *Lenawee* came out, some scholars thought Rose's days were numbered. Law professor Michelle Oberman at Santa Clara University, writing in the *Arizona Law Review* in 2005, pronounced *Sherwood* to be essentially "dead law." And a limerick celebrating *Lenawee* by Valparaiso University law professor Jeremy Telman began making the rounds:

> The sewage leak, that was no trickle.
> Now the property ain't worth a nickel.
> When "as is" you take,
> You eat your mistake,
> So bon appetite, Mr. Pickles.
> (*Contracts Prof Blog*, November 13, 2006)

Yet, in the twenty-five years since it was decided, *Lenawee* has failed to supplant *Sherwood v. Walker*. In the 2008 edition of Professor Dawson's popular law school casebook (carried on by others since his death in 1985), *Sherwood* is still reprinted in full, replete with a photo of Hiram Walker and an unidentified Angus cow. A relatively brief comment on *Lenawee* follows it.

I have examined 28 Contracts casebooks currently available. Thirteen reprint *Sherwood* and another 10 mention it, for a total of 23 (82%). Eleven reprint *Lenawee* and seven more mention it, for a total of 18 (64%). So, Rose holds the lead in law-school casebook coverage. (Six casebooks reprint both cases. Only two ignore both.)

The monumental encyclopedia of contract law *Williston on Contracts* continues to pay tribute to Rose. Volume twenty-seven of the fourth edition, which was published in 2003, devotes fully five pages to a discussion of *Sherwood v. Walker*. *Lenawee* rates a single citation — under the heading "Septic and sewer" cases.

Perhaps most telling of all, in a 2006 mutual-mistake case, *Ford Motor Co. v. Woodhaven*, a unanimous Michigan Supreme Court discussed *Sherwood* at length, ignored *Lenawee* completely, and announced that Rose's case was still viable: "Our review of our precedents involving the law of mistake indicates that the peculiar and appropriate meaning that the term 'mutual mistake' has acquired in our law has not changed since *Sherwood*."

So it has come to pass that the septic-tank case, rather than the barren-cow case, has become limited to its facts. And thank goodness. What law professor would not prefer to spend class-time discussing a frolicsome cow, rather than a leaking sewer system?

In addition to Rose's case, today's Contracts professors have several other mistaken-animal cases to choose from. There is the 1951 Appellate Division of the Supreme Court of New York case, *Backus v. MacLaury*, involving a bull costing $5,000 that turned out to be sterile. In the 1976 United States District Court in Kentucky case, *Keck v. Wacher*, a buyer who paid $117,000 for a horse, which turned out to be "slipped" and worth just $40,000, obtained rescission of the sale. A German court in 2006 ordered Viagra to be administered to a stallion after his new owner claimed he was impotent and refused to pay to full contract price. It worked, and the court ordered the buyer to pay the full price.

But those cases are merely variations on Rose's theme of shame and redemption.

CONCLUSION

Many erroneous beliefs and eerie coincidences surround this historic case. Nevertheless, it remains one of the great contributions to contracts jurisprudence and law-school lore.

Michigan Governor John Engler, another former student, issued a proclamation of tribute to Rose's case in 1993. In it, he rightly asserted that its significance transcends the misguided individuals involved in it: "The details of this case are less important than the ruling, which remains as sound today as it was over a century ago. The principals are gone but the principle will never die."

Joe Manchester's contract with James Thurber's widow, giving him the go-ahead on a musicalizatioin [sic] of "Walter Mitty," runs 24 pages, 2½ pages longer than the Thurber classic.

The Washington Post (1964)

AUGUST

A Rogues' Gallery:
ALL GREAT DOERS IN OUR TRADE

By John V. Orth, with the assistance of Joseph L. Hyde

Measure for Measure takes us on a tour of the underside of Viennese society. When in disguise, Duke Vincentio encounters Lucio, one of the dissolute gentlemen of the city, and the tapsters and bawds who serve them. In
the prison, he meets not only the well-born Claudio, sentenced to death
for fornication, but also the unregenerate murderer Barnardine, *insensible
of mortality, and desperately mortal.* Incongruously for an inland city such as
Vienna (but not for a great port like London), there is also the pirate
Ragozine, whose convenient death and resemblance to Claudio provides
the severed head that convinces Angelo his order has been carried out.

But it is Pompey Bum (alias Thomas Tapster and Hannibal), the
clownish tapster, bawd, and picklock, who serves as guide through this
underworld. In prison and apprenticed to Abhorson the executioner,
Pompey feels himself right at home, *as well acquainted here as I was in our
house of profession.* Among the prisoners recognized by Pompey, there are
*Master Starve-lackey, the rapier and dagger man, and young Drop-heir that
killed lusty Pudding . . . , and wild Half-can that stabbed Potts.* Violence in

taverns and brothels is endemic, but Shakespeare's London was convulsed by upper class violence as well. In fact, affrays between Englishmen and Scotsmen were so prevalent at the court of King James I when *Measure for Measure* was first performed that parliament enacted the Statute of Stabbing, raising a conclusive presumption of malice aforethought if the victim had not first drawn a weapon or struck his assailant and died of his wound within six months.[1]

Along with the *rapier and dagger men*, there are the usual assortment of petty thieves and brawlers. There, too, is *young Master Rash; he's in for a commodity of brown paper and old ginger.* The reference is to a scam to evade the usury laws, comparable to some of the practices of modern "predatory lenders." Goods were first sold on credit to a needy person, who immediately re-sold them at a (usually steep) discount, generally to the usurer himself; the borrower ended up with cash in hand and a debt for the (much) larger amount.[2] So common was the practice that the *Oxford English Dictionary* includes in its comprehensive definition of "commodity" the note that "an accommodation of this kind, designed to evade the usury laws, in which the goods were trumpery, was known as *a commodity of brown paper*, or the like."[3]

continued on page 447 . . .

R&R CAPITAL V. BUCK & DOE RUN VALLEY FARMS
2008 WL 3846318 (Del. Ch. August 19, 2008) (Not Reported in A.2d)

William B. Chandler III, Chancellor

For Shakespeare, it may have been the play, but for a Delaware limited liability company, the contract's the thing. *Compare* William Shakespeare, *Hamlet*, act 1, sc. 2, ln. 604 ("the play's the thing"), *with Travel-Centers of Am., LLC v. Brog*, C.A. No. 3516-CC, 2008 WL 1746987, at *1 (Del. Ch. Apr. 3, 2008) ("Limited Liability Companies are creatures of contract").

---

[1] 1 Jac. 1, c. 8 (1604). See 4 William Holdsworth, *History of English Law* 501 (3d ed. 1945); 9 Id. 142 (3d ed. 1944).

[2] See Isaac D'Israeli, *Curiosities of Literature* 230 (12th ed. 1841). The author was the father of British Prime Minister Benjamin Disraeli, who altered the spelling of his family name. See 1 William Flavelle Monypenny, *The Life of Benjamin Disraeli* 41 (1910).

[3] 3 *Oxford English Dictionary* 564 (2d ed. 1989) (citing D'Israeli).

❧ AUGUST ❧

SUN	MON	TUES	WED	THUR	FRI	SAT
30	31					1
2	3	4	5	6	7	8
9	10	11	12	13	14	15
16	17	18	19	20	21	22
23	24	25	26	27	28	29

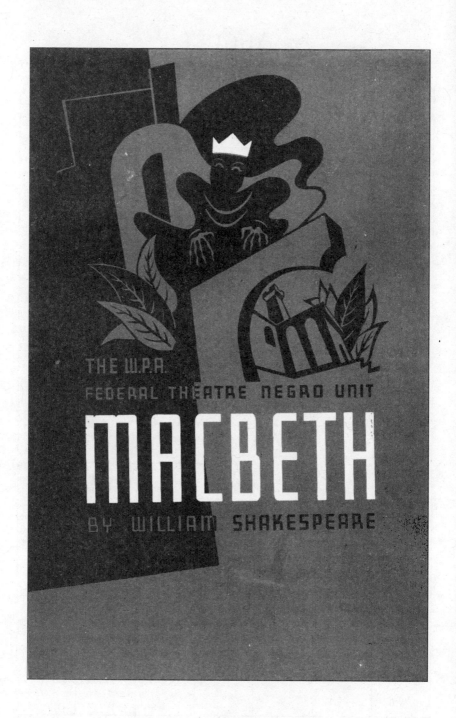

THE W.P.A.
FEDERAL THEATRE NEGRO UNIT

MACBETH

BY WILLIAM SHAKESPEARE

BLACK-LETTER LAW

from

THE DAY FREEDOM DIED: THE COLFAX MASSACRE, THE
SUPREME COURT, AND THE BETRAYAL OF RECONSTRUCTION

Charles Lane[†]

*Editor's note: For the convenience of the reader, all footnotes and endnotes have
been converted to footnotes in the version printed here. For the full versions of the
short cites in footnotes, please see the notes section of the book itself. In the author's
note at the beginning of the book, Lane explains that*

> Terms such as *Negro* and *colored*, as well as *mulatto*, are used
> throughout most of this book. I understand that these words are
> obsolete and that readers may find them repellent. No offense is
> intended; rather, I employed them because I could see no alterna-
> tive. Practically all Americans — regardless of their race or their
> views about race — employed them during the period covered by
> this narrative. They pervaded the speech and writing of the times.
> I felt it would have been anachronistic and, in a sense, untrue to
> the story to use the preferable, modern term, *African-American.*

On the evening of April 22, 1873, the leading colored men and women of
New Orleans crowded the St. James African Methodist Episcopal Church
on Roman Street, in a quiet residential section north of the French Quarter. Founded by free people of color in 1844, St. James became an abolitionist stronghold in a city decidedly unfriendly to that cause. By 1851, the
congregation had erected its small but opulent Victorian Gothic chapel,
set back from the unpaved street, with white walls and soaring white stee-

---

[†] Charles Lane is an editorial writer for *The Washington Post. Chapter Six: Black Letter Law,
from* THE DAY FREEDOM DIED: THE COLFAX MASSACRE, THE SUPREME COURT, AND THE
BETRAYAL OF RECONSTRUCTION by Charles Lane. Copyright © 2008 by Charles Lane.
Reprinted by permission of Henry Holt and Company, LLC, and by permission of the
author.

ples. St. James was an architectural pearl, emblematic of the free people of color's prosperity and solidarity. It was the logical place for New Orleanians of African descent to gather and express their grief, and their fury, at the horror in Colfax — and to consider what, if anything, they might do about it.[1]

Thomas Morris Chester addressed the assembly. The Pennsylvania-born son of an escaped slave mother and a free black father, Chester had been an active abolitionist before the war — an advocate of colonization in Liberia, where he lived for several years. He spent part of the Civil War in England, lecturing on the evils of slavery, and then worked as a war correspondent in Virginia for the *Philadelphia Press*. After the war, he found his way to New Orleans, became a lawyer, and dabbled in Republican politics. He later became a general in the state militia.[2]

Powerfully built, with a pair of intense dark eyes set off by a high forehead and a thick, curly beard, Chester offered his audience the first public narrative of the massacre from an authoritative member of their own race. It was a rhetorical tour de force that took his listeners from the peaceful occupation of the courthouse to the gunning down of fleeing black men — many of whom, he said, were "on fire to the waist."[3]

Chester's account was far from precisely accurate: he claimed that a white man had torched the courthouse roof and that Christopher Columbus Nash had personally blocked the door of the burning building. As a moral statement, though, Chester's oration rang true. "On Easter Sunday," he thundered, "when the Christian world was chanting anthems in commemoration of the resurrection of the world's Redeemer, when from every sanctuary the gospel of love and peace was proclaimed, it was then that angels veiled their faces, and devils howled at the bloody and revolting scenes that were enacted on the banks of the Red River."

---

[1] Photographs of St. James AME are at John and Kathleen DeMajo, "Historic New Orleans Churches," http://www.neworleanschurches.com/stjamesamc/stjamesamc.htm (accessed August 11, 2007); *The African Methodist Episcopal Church: One Hundred Eighty-Eight Years of Progress — Our Beginning*, pamphlet provided to the author by Dr. Dennis C. Dickerson, executive director, Research and Scholarship, African Methodist Episcopal Church, Nashville, TN.

[2] The African American Registry, http://www.aaregistry.com/african_american_history/660/Lawyer_and_politician_Thomas_Chester (accessed August 11, 2007); Harrisburg, PA, http://www.harrisburgcitycalendar.org/pressReleases/prArchives/2004/10/chesterBackground.pdf; George F. Nagle, "Chester Tombstone Dedication," *Harrisburg Patriot News*, September 21, 2002.

[3] All quotations of Chester's speech are from "The St. James Chapel: The Colored Men in Council," *NOR*, April 23, 1873.

Yet Chester had no new ideas for how his community could deal with the outrage. He ended up advocating trust in powerful whites. "We appeal to the government which made us free men and citizens, and especially to the administration of President Grant, which we assisted in placing in power, to protect us in our liberties and lives from the wrath of our Democratic neighbors," he concluded. The assembly voted to endorse and publish Chester's statement, then filed out of the little church and into the night.

• • • •

The colored people of New Orleans were fortunate in one thing: of all the white men in the city who might be receptive to their pleas, the most receptive was the U.S. attorney assigned to prosecute the massacre. What distinguished James Roswell Beckwith from the vast majority of whites in Louisiana — and most whites in the country as a whole, probably — was his belief that men and women of African descent were human beings. There was nothing political or expedient about Beckwith's attachment to this idea, which he had probably absorbed as a youth in Cazenovia. It was just a part of who he was. "I know if I had been there," in the Grant Parish courthouse, he said, "I should have hurt just as many [whites] as I could and just as fast as I could, under the law of self-preservation."[4] When black people were killed in cold blood, Beckwith believed, they had a right to swift and equal justice.

The U.S. attorney pored over the Colfax Massacre file in his barracks-like office at the Custom House, growing more and more committed. He assigned all of his office's other work to his deputy and devoted his own time exclusively to the Grant Parish case. "It has never been my portion," Beckwith wrote Attorney General George H. Williams, "to be connected with the prosecution of a crime so revolting and horrible in the details of its perpetration and so burdened with atrocity and barbarity. Protection from repetition in the future demands prompt and severe punishment of the guilty."[5]

His investigation moved swiftly. On May 9, Beckwith convened a new grand jury, most of whose members were men of color, and began laying out the evidence — more than enough, Beckwith felt, to warrant indictments. There was DeKlyne and Wright's account, now buttressed by firsthand testimony from Levi Allen, who had emerged unhurt from hid-

---

[4] Beckwith Testimony I, 420.
[5] Beckwith to Williams, June 11, 1873, DOJ Letters from LA.

ing in Colfax and accompanied the deputy U.S. marshals back to New Orleans. Beckwith had statements from the Grant Parish Republicans — William Ward, Eli Flowers, and Robert Register — who had come to the Crescent City before April 13. John J. Hoffman had found Negro survivors of the massacre who would be willing to testify. And Hoffman had identified twenty-three additional potential witnesses, whites from Catahoula Parish who had seen and heard the Catahoula Klansmen organizing their ride to Colfax.[6]

Hoffman himself was Beckwith's star witness before the grand jury. In a closed session on June 11, the Secret Service agent revealed the grim details he had gathered working undercover among perpetrators of the massacre. He produced dozens of their names. He described not only the extent of the killing but also its racially tinged sadism. The agent noted that the whites had mocked and taunted their black prisoners, calling them "beeves" before gunning them down. He confirmed that the killers slashed with their knives at some victims who had not been immediately dispatched by bullets. Hoffman reported the drunken boasts of men like Paul Hooe, who had come to the slaughter with the Rapides Parish contingent. Intriguingly, Hoffman revealed that Judge Thomas C. Manning of Alexandria had helped organize the white forces. Manning's plea to Governor Kellogg not to send troops in the week before Easter Sunday was apparently a deliberate deception, part of a plan to buy time for the assault on the courthouse.[7]

Of all James Beckwith's radical notions, his most audacious was that a white man should face the same "severe punishment" for murdering a black man that a black man would surely face if the roles were reversed. In Louisiana in 1873, that penalty would be death. Beckwith was determined to seek capital punishment for the authors of the Colfax Massacre — and, in a state where black people had been routinely whipped and shot by whites for generations, with total impunity, that was unheard of. The fact that he hoped to send white men to the gallows based on the testimony of black witnesses was utterly revolutionary.

---

[6] Secret Service Report II. Indictment, *United States v. Columbus C. Nash* [sic] *et al.*, Supreme Court of the United States, Transcript, *United States v. Cruikshank*, no. 339 (hereafter cited as Supreme Court Transcript), 5. The grand jury that returned the indictment was impaneled on May 9, 1873; it was actually the second grand jury to look at the case. Beckwith called in an already-existing grand jury immediately after the massacre, and it concluded that what its foreman called "a most unparalleled act of barbarity" had been committed. But it did not return an indictment because its term expired in late April, before it could identify the culprits by name. *Rapides Gazette*, May 10, 1873.

[7] Hoffman grand jury testimony, derived from Secret Service Reports I and II.

But if Beckwith was going to have any chance of pulling that off, he would have to be careful, very careful. He must be a lawyer — "the noblest work of science." He could not indulge his emotions. Unlike Thomas Morris Chester, he did not have the luxury of rhetorical excess. He could not allow himself to focus exclusively on the horrific facts of the case; he also had to face the technical legal questions it posed.

The most pressing of these was: what crime, exactly, could he charge? Men had been murdered in Colfax; there was no disputing it. Ordinarily, however, prosecuting murder was not the U.S. attorney's job. State governments had the primary responsibility to investigate and punish criminal offenses, except where some provision of the Constitution provided clear authority for federal action.

The Enforcement Act, adopted on May 31, 1870 (and the subsequent amendments toughening it), marked a bold departure. The legislation assumed that the Fourteenth and Fifteenth amendments to the Constitution made people of color American citizens and recognized their civil rights, among which was the right to vote on equal terms with whites. It also assumed that the post-Civil War amendments empowered Congress to criminalize acts by private individuals or groups — such as the Ku Klux Klan — that interfered with the exercise of those rights. The new phenomenon of racist terrorism against an emancipated Negro population, which the Southern states were either unwilling or unable to stop, had created an exception to the usual rule.[8]

Ambitious and noble as they were, the post-Civil War amendments and the Enforcement Act were, like all legal texts, open to interpretation. Beckwith was too good a lawyer not to recognize this. But to him, the fundamental issue in the Colfax case was nothing less than the true meaning of the Civil War.

•　•　•　•

---

[8] Section 6 of the Enforcement Act made it a federal crime, punishable by ten years in jail, for "two or more persons [to] band or conspire together, or go in disguise upon the public highway, or upon the premises of another, with intent to violate any provisions of this act, or to injure, oppress, threaten, or intimidate any citizen with intent to prevent or hinder his free exercise and enjoyment of any right or privilege granted or secured to him by the constitution or laws of the United States, or because of his having exercised the same."

Section 7 provided that if any common-law crime were committed in furtherance of such a conspiracy — that is, if Klansmen committed assault, robbery, or burglary in the process of violating civil rights — the perpetrator would face the penalty for that offense set by the state where the crime occurred. This made it possible to sentence Klansmen to death when their conspiracies resulted in murder. It was Beckwith's legal avenue to capital punishment.

At the war's end, the federal courts consisted of little more than the Supreme Court in Washington and forty-six district judges spread out over thirty-six states. The Supreme Court both ruled on appeals and helped district judges conduct trials: each justice was assigned to one of nine geographically defined "circuits" and spent months each year "riding circuit," dealing mostly with the arcana of admiralty law or interstate commerce.

The Civil Rights Act of 1866 flooded the federal courts with new business as the freedmen sued to protect their rights as citizens. In late 1869, Congress authorized President Grant to appoint nine new circuit judges to help with the workload. These new judges were not limited to hearing appeals, as today's circuit courts are; rather, they sat on trials, including jury trials of both civil and criminal cases. In time, this came to include many Enforcement Act trials. The Republican-controlled Congress also created the circuit judgeships so that Grant could fill them with Republicans to counter the conservatism of Southern district judges, some of whom had been appointed by Andrew Johnson.[9]

The new judges soon faced constitutional questions related to the Enforcement Act and its use against the Ku Klux Klan. In October 1870, Klansmen burst in on a Republican campaign meeting in Eutaw, Alabama, revolvers blazing and whips flaying. They killed four men of color and wounded fifty-four others. In prosecuting the case, *United States v. Hall*, the U.S. attorney in Alabama, John P. Southworth, became one of the first Justice Department officials to attempt a practical definition of the rights protected by the Enforcement Act. Southworth's indictment assumed a broad interpretation of the post-Civil War amendments: that the "privileges or immunities" of citizenship protected in the Fourteenth Amendment included the rights enumerated in the Bill of Rights. Accordingly, Southworth reasoned, the "rights and privileges" covered by the Enforcement Act must also be those in the Bill of Rights. In two separate counts, Southworth's indictment charged the Klansmen with conspiring to violate two of the Republicans' First Amendment rights: freedom of speech and freedom of assembly.[10]

Southworth's approach matched the expectations and constitutional principles of many members of the Republican Congress that had drafted the Fourteenth Amendment.[11] But the Klansmen's defense lawyers denied that it was correct. They argued that the Bill of Rights was mainly in-

---

[9] Kaczorowski, 38-61.

[10] Foner, 427; *United States v. Hall*, 26 F. Cas. 79 (C.C.S.D. Ala., 1871).

[11] Richard L. Aynes, "On Misreading John Bingham and the Fourteenth Amendment," *Yale Law Journal* 103 (Fall 1993), 57-104.

tended as a limitation on Congress's power. The First Amendment said that "Congress shall make no law" abridging freedom of speech or assembly. It did not say anything about states — which therefore remained free to define the rights of their citizens within their boundaries. The great chief justice John Marshall had said as much in the seminal 1833 case of *Barron v. Baltimore*. And nothing in the Fourteenth Amendment overturned that basic understanding. Furthermore, the defense argued, the prosecution did not allege that the *state* had done anything wrong in this case. Alabama had not passed or enforced a law that discriminated against the freedmen. Instead, the colored men killed at Eutaw were victims of violent crimes by private individuals. And fighting crime was the state's job. [12]

If accepted by the court and applied across the Fifth Circuit, which included not only Alabama but Florida, Georgia, Mississippi, Louisiana, and Texas, the defense arguments would have crippled federal protection of freedmen in that vast segment of the former Confederacy. Still, the defense's narrow construction of the Enforcement Act was hardly farfetched — especially in a constitutional culture inherently suspicious of federal power and still largely defined by pre-Civil War concepts and traditions. *Barron v. Baltimore* was a powerful precedent, one of the great constitutional rulings of the age.

William Burnham Woods, the Grant-appointed circuit judge for the Fifth Circuit — and a former Union army officer — presided over the case. He accepted Southworth's view of citizenship and federal power. "By the original constitution," Woods conceded, "citizenship in the United States was a consequence of citizenship in a state," but thanks to the Fourteenth Amendment, "this order of things is reversed." U.S. citizenship was primary, and its fundamental attributes — the "privileges or immunities" of citizens — were, indeed, defined by the Bill of Rights, Woods ruled. [13] Congress could criminalize conspiracies that prevented people from speaking or assembling freely.

Furthermore, no "state action" was required to trigger the exercise of federal power, as the defense had contended. Woods ruled that "denying the equal protection of the laws includes the omission to protect, as well as the omission to pass laws for protection." The federal government thus had the power to protect freedmen not only from discriminatory state legislation, but also from "state inaction, or incompetency." In other

---

[12] The defense lawyers' arguments were summarized in Woods's opinion, *United States v. Hall*, 26 F. Cas. 79 (C.C.S.D. Ala., 1871).
[13] All quotations of Woods's opinion are from *United States v. Hall*, 26 F. Cas. 79 (C.C.S.D. Ala., 1871).

words, the federal government could fill the power vacuum that the Klan was trying, with alarming success, to create through murder and intimidation of Republican state and local officials across the South. According to Woods, the Fourteenth Amendment was a shield against anarchy as well as tyranny.

Woods's opinion, issued in May 1871, helped federal prosecutors combat the Klan in Alabama, Georgia, and Mississippi. Then the action moved the Fourth Circuit (encompassing the Carolinas, Maryland, Virginia, and West Virginia). In the late fall of 1871, mass Ku Klux Klan trials opened at Columbia, South Carolina.

One of the first cases was *United States v. Crosby*. On the night of February 1, 1871, a mob of Klansmen led by Allen Crosby arrived at the York County, South Carolina, home of Amzi Rainey, a mulatto freedman. Klansmen burst into Rainey's house, beat his wife unconscious as she clung to her young child, raped one of his daughters, and shot another in the head — miraculously, the latter was not seriously wounded. They dragged Rainey out of the house, clubbing him on the head, neck, and shoulders, shouting that they were going to kill him. Finally, they let him run for his life when he swore never to vote Republican again.[14] Then they moved on to whip and intimidate other Negroes in the neighborhood.

U.S. attorney Daniel T. Corbin proceeded under a theory much like the one that Southworth, his Alabama counterpart, had adopted: that the Fourteenth Amendment had nationalized citizenship, and that the rights of citizens were defined by the Bill of Rights. He indicted Crosby and other Klansmen on charges including two counts of conspiring to deprive Rainey of his constitutionally guaranteed privileges and immunities, and one count of violating his right against unreasonable searches and seizures, protected by the Fourth Amendment of the Bill of Rights. The main difference between *Crosby* and *Hall* was that Corbin also alleged a conspiracy to violate both Rainey's individual right to vote and that of Negroes in the community generally. The right to vote, Corbin argued, was not part of the Bill of Rights but had been established by the Fifteenth Amendment.

Wade Hampton, a leading South Carolina Democrat, raised ten thousand dollars to assemble a crack team of defense lawyers: former U.S. senator Reverdy Johnson of Maryland, a lion of the Supreme Court bar who had argued, and won, the 1857 *Dred Scott* case on behalf of Scott's master; and Henry Stanbery, who had served as attorney general under Andrew Johnson. They immediately filed a motion challenging the entire

---

[14] Kaczorowski, 99.

constitutional and legal basis of the indictment against Crosby and the other Klansmen, employing the same arguments that the defense in *Hall* had articulated — buttressed by their greater rhetorical skill, political clout, and personal prestige.[15]

Presiding over the case was Hugh Lennox Bond, the new circuit judge for the Fourth Circuit. Bond was a Methodist, a die-hard Union man, and a Republican, who led the Association for the Moral and Educational Improvement of the Colored People in Baltimore.[16] Bond knew Reverdy Johnson, his fellow Marylander. He knew that he and Stanbery were using this case to get the Enforcement Act before the Supreme Court, where they thought — accurately, Bond feared — that the justices would strike it down. Under the legal procedures of the time, Johnson and Stanbery's Klan clients would have no right to appeal to the high court if they were convicted. But they could get the case there if Bond and George Seabrook Bryan, the conservative district judge who shared the two-man bench with him, disagreed on the defense motion.

In his heart, Bond likely favored a sweeping affirmation of the Enforcement Act based on a broad theory of national citizenship. But Bryan would never agree to that. If Bond insisted on it, he would provoke a split — and give Johnson and Stanbery their Supreme Court case. The Klan trials would be paralyzed until the Supreme Court acted. So, instead, Bond struck down most of the indictment. He rejected U.S. attorney Corbin's argument that the Fourteenth Amendment incorporated the Bill of Rights, as well as his claim that the Fifteenth Amendment created a constitutionally protected right to vote.

Yet Bond did uphold two counts of the indictment that charged Allen Crosby with conspiring to prevent black voters generally, and Amzi Rainey specifically, from voting. He found authority for these counts not in the Fifteenth Amendment, or any other post-Civil War law, but rather in Congress's inherent power to protect federal elections. That power, he said, had always existed. "It is a power necessary to the existence of Congress," Bond explained.[17] Bryan had to agree. Bond's clever, pragmatic

---

[15] Lou Falkner Williams, *The Great South Carolina Ku Klux Klan Trials, 1871-1872* (Athens, GA: University of Georgia Press, 1996), 61-75.

[16] Richard Paul Fuke, "Hugh Lennox Bond and Radical Republican Ideology," *Journal of Southern History* 45, no. 4 (November 1979), 569-86.

[17] "Opinion of the Court," December 7, 1871, U.S. Circuit Court, *Proceedings in the Ku Klux Trials at Columbia, S.C., November Term 1871* (Columbia, SC: Republican Printing, 1872), 89-92. Bond privately expressed "disgust" with Bryan; he felt that the judge was siding with the defense in the Klan cases because South Carolina Democrats had promised him the governorship. Kaczorowski, 53-54.

ruling preserved a narrow but sufficient basis for federal prosecution of Klansmen in the Fourth Circuit. Cases proceeded to trial and, most of the time, to guilty pleas or convictions.

As President Grant's second term began in March 1873, then, the Supreme Court had not addressed the constitutionality of the Enforcement Act. The prevailing law on the issue was still defined, albeit not uniformly, in the lower courts — by judges such as Woods and Bond. And their rulings had, for the most part, preserved federal authority to use the statutes against white terrorists.[18]

But the Supreme Court would not remain uninvolved in the momentous debate over the post-Civil War amendments. On the morning of April 14, 1873, as Benjamin Brim lay in the weeds of Colfax, soaked in his own blood, the Supreme Court announced a ruling that would redefine the Fourteenth Amendment's scope and meaning — and complicate James Beckwith's prosecution of the Colfax Massacre.

• • • •

The Court's decision concerned a group of consolidated lawsuits from Louisiana known as *The Slaughterhouse Cases*, which began because Henry Clay Warmoth kept his promise to modernize Louisiana.[19] For decades, butchers in New Orleans had routinely herded steers, sheep, and pigs through the streets and, after they killed and gutted them, dumped the offal in the Mississippi — just upriver from intake pipes that supplied the city's drinking water. And for decades, people in New Orleans had been complaining about it. Finally, in March 1869, Warmoth signed a new law creating a central abattoir under the exclusive control of a state-chartered corporation. The slaughterhouse would be located across the Mississippi from the city and downstream from its water intake pipe. As of June 1, 1869, all butchers would have to slaughter their animals at this location, under the watchful eye of a state inspector.

The slaughterhouse law was a sensible measure, similar to laws in New York, San Francisco, and Boston, as well as several European cities. But New Orleans's Democratic press and politicians furiously attacked it. The

---

[18] Kaczorowski, 106-7.

[19] The following account of *The Slaughterhouse Cases* is derived from Labbé and Lurie, *The Slaughterhouse Cases*; Michael A. Ross, "Justice Miller's Reconstruction: The Slaughter-House Cases, Health Codes, and Civil Rights in New Orleans, 1861-1873," *Journal of Southern History* 64, no. 4 (November 1998), 649-76; Michael A. Ross, *Justice of Shattered Dreams: Samuel Freeman Miller and the Supreme Court during the Civil War Era* (Baton Rouge: LSU Press, 2003), 189-211.

legislation, Democrats claimed, was a corrupt insider deal, an "odious monopoly" that would enrich Warmoth and his cronies by oppressing humble butchers, white men who traced their ancestry to the French region of Gascony. The *Daily Picayune* called the law "an outrageous bartering away of birthrights."

The Democrats' true objections were political and racial. Partly, they were angry that the new slaughterhouse would be open to all butchers, regardless of race. Mostly, however, they were simply determined to obstruct any legislation adopted by the biracial Republican-majority legislature, whose acts were, in the words of the *New Orleans Bee*, "of no more binding force than if they bore the stamp and seal of a Haytian [*sic*] Congress of human apes instead of the once honored seal of the state."

John Archibald Campbell led the legal assault on the slaughterhouse law. Before the Civil War, Campbell, born in Georgia, had been an associate justice of the U.S. Supreme Court. In 1857, he was part of the six-justice majority in *Dred Scott*. When hostilities broke out, though, he resigned and became the Confederacy's assistant secretary of war. After the war, Campbell settled in New Orleans, nursing a deep resentment of Reconstruction and an even deeper loathing for people of color. "We have Africans in place all around us," he wrote to his daughter. "They are jurors, post office clerks, custom house officers and day by day they barter away their obligations and duties." He once mused that white "insurrection" would be preferable to Reconstruction.

Filing his cases before the most conservative judges he could find, Campbell launched a series of lawsuits whose main purpose was to harass Warmoth's government. The Louisiana Supreme Court, dominated by Warmoth appointees, generally overturned Campbell's lower-court victories, but the costs to the state — in time, dollars, and loud, hostile coverage in the New Orleans Democratic press — were substantial.[20]

Campbell's legal arguments were as creative as they were insistent. Representing the butchers, Campbell portrayed the slaughterhouse law as a modern-day version of royally ordained trade monopolies in medieval England. It violated the butchers' "right to exercise their trade," he asserted, which made it both a form of involuntary servitude banned by the Thirteenth Amendment and an abridgement of the "privileges or immunities" of citizenship protected by the Fourteenth Amendment.

---

[20] Michael A. Ross, "Obstructing Reconstruction: John Archibald Campbell and the Legal Campaign Against Louisiana's Republican Government, 1868-1873," *Civil War History* 49, no. 3 (September2003), 235-53.

Campbell, like most of white Louisiana, supported the Black Codes and bitterly opposed the Fourteenth Amendment. Now, however, he claimed that the Thirteenth Amendment protected white butchers as well as black freedmen, and that the Fourteenth "secures to all protection from state legislation that involves the rights of property, the most valuable of which is to labor freely in an honest avocation [sic]."

The Louisiana Supreme Court made short work of Campbell's case, as usual. But since it raised constitutional questions, Campbell had a basis for an appeal to the U.S. Supreme Court. There, he repeated the arguments he had made in the Louisiana courts, and embellished them.[21] His brief called the carpetbaggers the "foulest off-spring of the war." In an obvious allusion to the (unproven) charges that the slaughterhouse law was a product of corruption, he added that "the misfortune is that the issue of the bonds and shares in the companies find their way in large parcels among those whose official duty it is to protect the public honor and credit." Referring to Negro suffrage, Campbell wrote that "whatever ambition, avarice, usurpation, servility, licentiousness, or pusillanimity needs a shelter will find it under its protecting influence." Meanwhile, he noted, "a large portion of the dominant population had been disfranchised."

Justice Samuel Freeman Miller wasn't having any of this.[22] Miller was fifty-seven years old and hailed from Kentucky, a former slave state. He turned against the peculiar institution as a child, when he saw his colored nursemaid whipped for some supposed transgression. After leaving his first career — medicine — to practice law, Miller joined the movement to amend Kentucky's state constitution to provide for gradual abolition. In 1850, after it became clear that proslavery forces would win, he left for the free soil of Keokuk, Iowa. There, he manumitted the last of his own slaves and became a prominent Republican member of the bar. Abraham Lincoln appointed him to the Supreme Court in 1862.

As a physician, Miller had studied cholera and was one of the first Americans to argue that the illness was caused by contaminated water. He also did not much care for John Campbell, disdaining both Campbell's support for the South during the war and his subsequent efforts against Reconstruction. "I have never seen nor heard of any action of Judge Campbell's since the rebellion that was aimed at healing the breach he

---

[21] All quotations and paraphrases of Campbell's brief are from *The Slaughterhouse Cases*, 83 U.S. 36, 45-57.

[22] Miller's biography, especially his early years as a country doctor and lawyer, is explored in Charles Fairman, *Mr. Justice Miller and the Supreme Court, 1862-1890* (Cambridge, MA: Harvard University Press, 1939), 1-17; Ross, *Justice of Shattered Dreams*, 1-64.

contributed so much to make," he wrote privately. "He has made himself an active leader of the New Orleans democracy. Writing their pronunciamientos, arguing their cases in our Court, and showing all the evidences of a discontented and embittered old man, filled with the disappointments of an unsuccessful partisan politician."[23]

On the Supreme Court, Miller struggled for five votes to uphold Louisiana's law. The justices first heard oral arguments in The Slaughterhouse Cases in January 1872. Only eight members of the Court were present, because Justice Samuel Nelson was ill. The justices divided four to four; the Court ordered reargument in February 1873. By this time, Nelson had resigned and Justice Ward Hunt had replaced him, so the Court was at full strength. Hunt gave Miller a fifth vote for his opinion.

On April 14, 1873, Miller read it to a near-empty courtroom. He began by reminding those present that this would be the Court's first authoritative interpretation of the post-Civil War amendments — a matter of "far-reaching" importance. And then he proceeded to shred John Archibald Campbell's case.[24]

Louisiana's slaughterhouse law was an exercise of the state's traditional power to protect public health and safety, Miller said, and Campbell's claim that it subjected the butchers to "involuntary servitude" was basically preposterous. The purpose of the Thirteenth Amendment was to abolish "the institution of African slavery, as it existed in about half the States of the Union," he wrote, "and its obvious purpose" was to forbid slavery's reemergence. These self-evident points were "all that we deem necessary to say on the application of that article to the statute of Louisiana, now under consideration," Miller concluded.

The question of the Fourteenth Amendment was more complicated, Miller conceded. But as he had done with the Thirteenth Amendment, the justice analyzed the Fourteenth in light of its purposes. It had been adopted, he said, to counter the Black Codes in ex-Confederate states. Its framers felt "something more was necessary in the way of constitutional protection to the unfortunate race who had suffered so much," Miller pointed out. The amendment was not, in short, designed to protect white butchers from inconvenient but defensible state public-health regulations.

Miller still had to address Campbell's broad argument: that the plain language of the Fourteenth Amendment, whatever its framers' intentions, had the effect of nationalizing citizenship — black and white — and put-

---

[23] Ross, *Justice of Shattered Dreams*, 200.
[24] All quotations of Miller's opinion are from *The Slaughterhouse Cases*, 83 U.S. 36, 57-83.

ting the states "under the oversight and restraining and enforcing hand of Congress," such that "every member of the empire shall understand and appreciate the fact that his privileges and immunities cannot be abridged by State authority." Campbell's sweeping definition of privileges and immunities encompassed not just the Bill of Rights but "the personal and civil rights which usage, tradition, the habits of society, written law, and the common sentiments of people have recognized as forming the basis of the institutions of the country."

This was tricky. Miller sensed, correctly, that Campbell's true agenda was to turn every grievance of the South's former ruling class into a federal court case against the Reconstruction governments. Yet the justice knew that many of the Fourteenth Amendment's own authors saw it as both expanding the content of citizenship and strengthening federal power vis-á-vis the states.

Miller tried to find a middle ground. Though it imposed "additional limitations on the States," and conferred "additional power on . . . the Nation," he wrote, the Fourteenth Amendment was not meant to overthrow federalism, as Campbell insincerely contended. "Under the pressure of all the excited feeling growing out of the war," he declared, "our statesmen have still believed that the existence of the State with powers for domestic and local government, including the regulation of civil rights — the rights of person and of property — was essential to the perfect working of our complex form of government." U.S. citizenship and citizenship in a state were still two different things, each with its own corresponding privileges and immunities, the justice said.

Miller might easily have ended his opinion there, having shown that the Louisiana law was within the state's power and did not abridge the privileges and immunities of American citizenship — whatever they might be. But he felt compelled to rebut Campbell's expansive notion of citizenship in detail, by offering examples of the true privileges and immunities of national citizenship.

And this was the part of his ruling that would ultimately entangle Beckwith. Prosecutors in Enforcement Act cases had based their charges against the Klan on a broad notion of privileges and immunities that encompassed the Bill of Rights. But in the context of this very different case, Miller defined the phrase to include only "those rights which depended on the Federal government for their existence or protection" — meaning those which could not have existed but for creation of a federal government by the states' ratification of the Constitution in 1789. For Miller, this included the right to seek a writ of habeas corpus, to travel freely from state to state and through American ports, or the right to come to Washington to assert a financial claim on the federal government.

Only these relatively arcane privileges and immunities "are placed by [the Fourteenth Amendment] under the protection of the Federal Constitution," Miller said. Everything else — including the rights spelled out in the Bill of Rights — "must rest for their security and protection where they have heretofore rested": on the states. Any other interpretation, he declared, "would constitute this court a perpetual censor upon all legislation of the States, on the civil rights of their own citizens."

Writing at a moment when it was widely believed that Grant's crackdown on the Ku Klux Klan had slain the dragon of white terrorism, Miller was not thinking about the impact of his ruling on the Enforcement Act. He undoubtedly thought he was striking a blow for the legitimacy of the post-Civil War Republican governments of the South, inasmuch as he was instructing recalcitrant Southern whites to live under the laws made by legislatures chosen through universal suffrage. His sympathy for the freedmen permeated his opinion, which noted that, during the war, colored soldiers in the "armies of freedom" had "proved themselves men." He quite plausibly thought both white and black citizens could vindicate their rights under state law at a time when Louisiana's constitution — drafted by a mixed-race convention under the watchful eye of a Republican Congress — was arguably more progressive than the U.S. Constitution. The Republican lawyer who represented the state in *Slaughterhouse* had urged just such a view on the Court.[25]

But Miller went too far. In destroying Campbell's extreme and self-serving view, Miller substituted a definition of privileges and immunities so cramped that it emptied the clause of practical meaning. It was fine for him to say that it protected access to the ports, but the Klan had not killed any colored men in the South for exercising that right. As one of the four dissenting justices complained, Miller's view could make the Fourteenth

---

[25] Because of their restrictive impact on civil rights, *The Slaughterhouse Cases* rank with *Dred Scott* among the Supreme Court's most criticized rulings. See, for example, Charles L. Black, Jr., *A New Birth of Freedom* (New Haven, CT: Yale University Press, 1997), 41-85, in which Black mocks Miller for "blow[ing] a kiss at the recently freed slaves." Yet for many years, historians and constitutional lawyers either failed to account for, or ignored, the fact that this "regressive" ruling was written by a staunchly antislavery member of the Court and supported by its most progressive members — while the lawsuit was brought by a deeply racist, ex-Confederate lawyer with an obvious anti-Reconstruction agenda. Scholars such as Michael A. Ross, Jonathan Lurie, and Ronald M. Labbé have found the solution to this riddle: the ruling was, in Miller's mind, a progressive (or at least moderate) pro-Reconstruction, pro-public health decision.

Amendment "a vain and idle enactment, which accomplished nothing, and most unnecessarily excited Congress and the people on its passage."[26]

Clever Democratic lawyers in New Orleans quickly recognized Miller's opinion as a potential silver lining for them in Campbell's defeat. Yes, the perfidious slaughterhouse monopoly had been upheld; that was a shame and a disgrace. But the Enforcement Act might have been dealt a serious blow.[27] Miller had not only emptied out the Fourteenth Amendment's "privileges or immunities" clause, he had declared the primacy of state citizenship over national citizenship. This was the opposite of the position William B. Woods had articulated just two years earlier in *United States v. Hall*.

Beckwith, too, spotted the issue. Less than two days after he found out about the massacre at Colfax, he sent a telegram to Attorney General George H. Williams, asking for an official copy of Miller's *Slaughterhouse* opinion. The decision had been reported in the New Orleans press. But Beckwith wanted to be absolutely sure of what it said. He was concerned, he wrote Williams, because the decision "is believed here to limit the criminal jurisdiction of federal courts under recent acts."[28]

. . . .

And *Slaughterhouse* was not James Beckwith's only headache-inducing obstacle. In one crucial respect, the Colfax case was quite unlike the South Carolina or Alabama Klan prosecutions. Those cases centered on incidents in which blacks had been attacked by surprise while in their homes or attending clearly peaceful political gatherings. It was hard enough to wedge these incidents into the legal paradigm of the Enforcement Act, which required federal prosecutors to frame their cases in the artificial language of violated civil rights — rather than murder, rape, or assault. In the Colfax case, the defense team could depict the killing as the unfortunate, but hardly unprovoked, consequence of an armed clash. In fact, they would probably portray it as R.G. Hill, the steamboat passenger, had in his letter to the *New Orleans Times*: a wild Negro "riot" stymied in the nick of time by Grant Parish's rightful officeholders.

Even if the jury did not accept that interpretation, the difficult fact was that there had been a fight — albeit a brief and highly unequal one — between the whites and the blacks. The victims were genuine, but not necessarily as innocent as Beckwith might have preferred. The Colfax Massacre

---

[26] *The Slaughterhouse Cases*, 83 U.S. 36, 96 (dissenting opinion of Justice Stephen J. Field).

[27] Robert H. Marr, Letter to the Editor, *NODP*, May 24, 1873.

[28] Beckwith to Williams, Telegram, April 18, 1873, DOJ Letters from LA.

was most properly categorized as a war crime, but political and legal realities did not permit dealing with it in those terms. No one wanted to consider the possibility that a new war was under way in the Deep South, much less that the old one had never really ended. Beckwith had no choice but to work within the legal framework of the Enforcement Act.

Beckwith's solution was to focus his case on two of the most sympathetic black victims.[29] The first was Levi Nelson. Nelson had quit the fight early, been taken prisoner as he fled, and then obeyed an order to put out the fire at the warehouse. Bill Cruikshank marched him out at night with the other defenseless prisoners and tried to kill him, and another man, with a single bullet. No matter what the provocation, shooting prisoners was an outrage, and who better to make that point to the jury than a surviving eyewitness?

The second victim was Alexander Tillman. Tillman, of course, was dead, so he could not testify. But unlike others killed in the massacre, there was no doubt about who he was; he had been positively identified by DeKlyne and Wright. Like Nelson, he had tried to surrender when the whites torched the courthouse, but they shot him, rode him down in the fields, and then savagely finished him off. The wounds in his body, and its position — hundreds of feet from the courthouse — proved that he had been slaughtered when he was fleeing and posed no threat to anyone. Tillman's well-known political activities would make it easier to charge that he had been singled out for attack because he had exercised rights protected under the Enforcement Act. And, finally, Tillman's murder gave Beckwith a legal basis for seeking the death penalty.

Beckwith's indictment contained thirty-two separate counts, covering 150 handwritten pages. Its structure was complex but logical. The first half — counts 1 through 16 — was based on section 6, the Enforcement Act's anticonspiracy provision. Counts 1 through 8 charged the white perpetrators with "banding together" to "injure, oppress, threaten, or intimidate" both Nelson and Tillman, so as "to prevent or hinder" their "free exercise and enjoyment" of various rights guaranteed by the Constitution or federal law.

In specifying these rights, Beckwith necessarily improvised, doing his best to fit within both the precedents set by Judges Woods and Bond, and Miller's new *Slaughterhouse* opinion. In count 1, Beckwith charged the defendants with banding together to violate the colored man's "right and

---

[29] The following description of Beckwith's indictment is based on: Supreme Court Transcript, 5-57; Beckwith to Williams, October 15, 1874, DOJ Letters from LA.

privilege peaceably to assemble." In count 2, he charged a violation of their "right to keep and bear arms for a lawful purpose." The case for these two counts, which were based on rights protected in the First and Second amendments of the Bill of Rights, respectively, was, indeed, harder to make after *Slaughterhouse*. But the ruling gave him plausible reasons to try. In enumerating the privileges and immunities of citizenship that the federal government *could* still protect, Miller had specifically mentioned "the right to peaceably assemble and petition for redress of grievances." As for the right to bear arms, *Slaughterhouse* had said nothing one way or the other.

Count 3 spoke of the two men's right not to be deprived of life and liberty without due process of law. This resembled a claim Campbell had made on behalf of the butchers in *Slaughterhouse*, only to be rejected by Miller. However, the right to due process was not only in the post-Civil War Fourteenth Amendment but also in the prewar Fifth Amendment. And though he dissected privileges and immunities, Miller had dismissed Campbell's due-process claim briefly, saying only that "under no construction of that provision that we have ever seen, or any that we deem admissible, can the restraint imposed by the State of Louisiana upon the exercise of their trade by the butchers of New Orleans be held to be a deprivation of property within the meaning of that provision." To Beckwith, this must have left open the possibility that the Fourteenth Amendment could protect a due-process right for men who were not resisting paying a fee to slaughter their cattle, but who themselves had been imprisoned, beaten, and killed like animals.

Count 4 cited Tillman and Nelson's right to the same legal protection "for the security of their persons and property . . . that is enjoyed by white citizens." Beckwith derived this from the Civil Rights Act of 1866, which guarantees "all persons" the same right "to make and enforce contracts, to sue, be parties, give evidence, and to the full and equal benefit of all laws and proceedings for the security of persons and property as is enjoyed by white citizens, and shall be subject to like punishment, pains, penalties, taxes, licenses, and exactions of every kind, and to no other." In Beckwith's view, the allegation flowed from the simple and obvious fact that the white mob at Colfax would never have treated the Negroes this way if they had been white men.

Count 5 was more general. It spoke of an enterprise to violate the men's "rights, privileges, immunities and protection as citizens of the state of Louisiana and the United States . . . on account of their race and color and for the reason that they, being such citizens, were persons of African descent and race and persons of color and not white citizens." Count 6 charged the men with banding together to punish Nelson and Tillman because they had voted on Election Day, November 4, 1872, at which both state and federal offices had been contested. Count 7 charged them with combining to prevent the Negroes from voting in any future elections. These two counts could have been valid either under the theory that the Fifteenth Amendment created a right to vote or under Judge Bond's ruling in *United States v. Crosby*.

Count 8 charged the violation of "every, each and all and singular of the several rights and privileges granted or secured to them respectively by the constitution and laws of the United States." It was vague, but Beckwith thought that its advantage lay precisely in its generality. It was a catch-all charge that said, essentially, "Whatever rights Levi Nelson and Alexander Tillman may have under the Constitution or federal law, the conspirators violated them."

Counts 9 through 16 were almost identical to counts 1 through 8, the only difference being the substitution of the phrase "combined, conspired and confederated" for "banding together" — in case the defense tried to quibble over that linguistic nicety.

Beckwith based counts 16 through 32 on section 7 of the Enforcement Act — its penalty provision. They repeated the first sixteen counts but added that, in carrying out their unlawful enterprise, the conspirators had murdered Alexander Tillman. If the jury found them guilty on one of these sixteen counts, the defendants would hang.

Beckwith was anticipating every conceivable defense objection — and giving the jury so many different ways to convict that they would take at least one. Given the ambiguous text of the Enforcement Act and the uncertainties created by *Slaughterhouse*, the indictment was a credible effort. In crucial respects, it was similar to indictments used to convict Klansmen in other states. Moreover, as a good real-world practitioner, Beckwith was probably anticipating that William Woods, the Republican author of *United States v. Hall*, would preside over this trial as circuit judge. To be sure, in *Slaughterhouse* — now binding precedent — the Supreme Court had not embraced Woods's broad view of U.S. citizenship. But given Woods's record, Beckwith had every reason to hope he would find a way around that problem.

The grand jury approved the indictment in *United States v. C.C. Nash, et al.* on June 16. In addition to Nash, it named ninety-seven other defendants. They were all "men of evil minds and dispositions," the indictment averred. But everything Beckwith had done so far was easy compared with his next tasks: to organize a manhunt across the pine-cloaked hills and meandering swamps of northwestern Louisiana, locate almost one hundred accused killers, capture them, and bring them to New Orleans to face justice.

Power may justly be compar'd to a great River, while kept within it's due Bounds, is both Beautiful and Useful; but when it overflows, it's Banks, it is then too impetuous to be stemm'd, it bears down all before it, and brings Destruction and Desolation wherever it comes. If then this is the Nature of Power, let us at least do our Duty, and like wise Men (who value Freedom) use our utmost Care to support Liberty, the only Bulwark against lawless Power, which in all Ages has sacrificed to it's wild Lust and boundless Ambition, the Blood of the best Men that ever liv'd.

Andrew Hamilton (1735)

SHAKESPEARE'S LEGAL ACQUIREMENTS

(continued from page 405)

John Lord Campbell

HAMLET

In this tragedy various expressions and allusions crop out, showing the substratum of law in the author's mind,— *e.g.*, the description of the disputed territory which was the cause of the war between Norway and Poland:—

> We go to gain a little patch of ground,
> That hath in it no profit but the name.
> To pay five ducats, five, I would not farm it,
> Nor will it yield to Norway or the Pole
> A ranker rate, *should it be sold in fee.*

(Act IV, Sc. 4.)

Earlier in the play (Act I. Sc. 1) Marcellus inquires what was the cause of the warlike preparations in Denmark—

> And why such daily cast of brazen cannon,
> And foreign mart for implements of war?
> *Why such impress of shipwrights, whose sore task*
> *Does not divide the Sunday from the week*?

Such confidence has there been in Shakespeare's accuracy, that this passage has been quoted, both by text writers and by Judges on the bench, as an authority upon the legality of the *press-gang*, and upon the debated question whether *shipwrights*, as well as *common seamen*, are liable to be pressed into the service of the royal navy.[*]

Hamlet, when mortally wounded in Act V. Sc. 2, represents that Death comes to him in the shape of a sheriff's officer, as it were to take him into custody under a *capias ad satisfaciendum*:—

> "Had I but time (as this fell serjeant, Death,
> Is strict in his arrest), Oh! I could tell you," &c.

The Grave-diggers' scene, however, is the mine which produces the richest legal ore. The discussion as to whether Ophelia was entitled to Christian burial proves that Shakespeare had read and studied Plowden's

---

[*] See Barrington on the Ancient Statutes, p. 300.

Report of the celebrated case of Hales *v.* Petit, tried in the reign of Philip and Mary, and that he intended to ridicule the counsel who argued and the Judges who decided it.

On the accession of Mary Tudor, Sir James Hales, a puisne Judge of the Common Pleas, was prosecuted for being concerned in the plot which placed the Lady Jane Grey for a few days upon the throne; but, as he had previously expressed a strong opinion that the succession of the right heir ought not to be disturbed, he was pardoned and released from prison. Nevertheless, so frightened was he by the proceedings taken against him that he went out of his mind, and, after attempting suicide by a penknife, he drowned himself by walking into a river. Upon an inquisition before the Coroner, a verdict of *felo de se* was returned. Under this finding his body was to be buried in a cross-road, with a stake thrust through it, and all his goods were forfeited to the crown. It so happened that at the time of his death he was possessed of a lease for years of a large estate in the county of Kent, granted by the Archbishop of Canterbury jointly to him and his wife, the Lady Margaret, who survived him. Upon the supposi-tion that this lease was forfeited, the estate was given by the crown to one Cyriac Petit, who took possession of it,— and Dame Margaret Hales, the widow, brought this action against him to recover it. The only question was whether the forfeiture could be considered as having taken place in the lifetime of Sir James Hales; for, if not, the plaintiff certainly took the estate by survivorship.

Her counsel, Serjeants Southcote and Puttrel, powerfully argued that, the offence of suicide being the killing of a man's self, it could not be com-pleted in his lifetime, for as long as he was alive he had not killed himself, and, the moment that he died, the estate vested in the plaintiff. "The fel-ony of the husband shall not take away her title by survivorship, for in this manner of felony two things are to be considered — first, the cause of the death; secondly, the death-ensuing the cause; and these two make the felony, and without both of them the felony is not consummate. And the cause of the death is the act done in the party's lifetime, which makes the death to follow. And the act which brought on the death here was the throwing himself voluntarily into the water, for this was the cause of his death. And if a man kills himself by a wound which he gives himself with a knife, or if he hangs himself, as the wound or the hanging, which is the act done in the party's lifetime, is the cause of his death, so is the throwing himself into the water here. Forasmuch as he cannot be attainted of his own death, because he is dead before there is any time to attaint him, the finding of his death by the Coroner is by necessity of law equivalent to an attainder in fact coming after his death. He cannot be *felo de se* till the death is fully consummate, and the death precedes the felony and the forfeiture."

Walsh, Serjeant, *contra*, argued that the felony was to be referred back to the act which caused the death. *"The act consists of three parts*: the first is the imagination, which is a reflection or meditation of the mind, whether or not it is convenient for him to destroy himself, and what way it can be done; the second is the resolution, which is a determination of the mind to destroy himself; the third is the perfection, which is the execution of what the mind had resolved to do. And of all the parts, the *doing of the act* is the greatest in the judgment of our law, and it is in effect the whole. Then here the act done by Sir James Hales, which is evil, and the cause of his death, is the throwing himself into the water, and the death is but a sequel thereof."

Lord C.J. Dyer and the whole court gave judgment for the defendant, holding that although Sir James Hales could hardly be said to have killed himself in his lifetime, "the forfeiture shall have relation to *the act done* by Sir James Hales in his lifetime, which was the cause of his death, viz., the throwing himself into the water." Said they, "Sir James Hales was dead, and how came he to his death? by drowning; and who drowned him? Sir James Hales; and when did he drown him? in his lifetime. So that Sir James Hales, being alive, caused Sir James Hales to die; and the act of the living man was the death of the dead man. He therefore committed felony in his lifetime, although there was no possibility of the forfeiture being found in his lifetime, for until his death there was no cause of forfeiture."

The argument of the gravediggers upon Ophelia's case is almost in the words reported by Plowden:—

1 *Clo.* Is she to be buried in Christian burial, that wilfully seeks her own salvation?

2 *Clo.* The crowner hath sate on her, and finds it Christian burial.

1 *Clo.* How can that be, unless she drowned herself in her own defence?

2 *Clo.* Why, 'tis found so.

1 *Clo.* It must be *se offendendo*; it cannot be else. For here lies the point: if I drown myself wittingly, it argues an act; and an act hath three branches; it is to act, to do, and to perform. *Argal* she drowned herself wittingly. . . . Here lies the water; good: here stands the man; good. If the man go to this water and drown himself, it is, will he, nill he, he goes; mark you that: but if the water come to him and drown him, he drowns not himself. *Argal* he that is not guilty of his own death shortens not his own life.

2 *Clo.* But is this law?

1 *Clo.* Ay' marry is't, crowner's quest law.

Hamlet's own speech, on taking in his hand what he supposed might be the skull of a lawyer, abounds with lawyer-like thoughts and words:—

> "Where be his quiddits now, his quillets, his cases, his tenures, and his tricks? Why does he suffer this rude knave now to knock him about the sconce with a dirty shovel, and will not tell him of his action of battery? Humph! This fellow might be in's time a great buyer of land, with his statutes, his recognizances, his fines, his double vouchers, his recoveries: is this the fine of his fines, and the recovery of his recoveries, to have his fine pate full of fine dirt? will his vouchers vouch him no more of his purchases, and double ones too, than the length and breadth of a pair of indentures?"

These terms of art are all used seemingly with a full knowledge of their import; and it would puzzle some practicing barristers with whom I am acquainted to go over the whole *seriatim*, and to define each of them satisfactorily.

MACBETH

In perusing this unrivalled tragedy I am so carried away by the intense interest which it excites, that I fear I may have passed over legal phrases and allusions which I ought to have noticed; but the only passage I find with the *juridical* mark upon it in "Macbeth" is in Act IV. Sc. 1, where, the hero exulting in the assurance from the Weird Sisters that he can receive harm from "none of woman born," he, rather in a lawyer-like manner, resolves to provide an indemnity, if the worst should come to the worst,—

> "But yet I'll make assurance double sure,
> And take a *bond of fate*;"

— without much considering what should be the penalty of the bond, or how he was to enforce the remedy, if the condition should be broken.

He, immediately after, goes on in the same legal jargon to say:—

> "— our high-plac'd Macbeth
> Shall live *the lease* of nature."

But, unluckily for Macbeth, the lease contained no covenants for *title* or *quiet enjoyment*:— there were likewise *forfeitures* to be incurred by the tenant,— with a *clause of re-entry*,— and consequently he was speedily *ousted*.[*]

continued on page 472 . . .

---

[*] The lease frequently presents itself to Shakespeare's mind, as in "Richard III.," Act IV. Sc. 4—

Tell me what state, what dignity, what honour,
Canst thou *demise* to any child of mine?

This is as clear a reference to *leasing*, as if he had said in full, "demise, lease, grant and to farm let."

SEPTEMBER

A JUDGE IN HIS OWN CAUSE: "JUDEX IN PROPRIA CAUSA"

By John V. Orth, with the assistance of Joseph L. Hyde

When at the play's climax the Duke orders Angelo to judge the charge of corruption brought against him, he is inviting the deputy to measure out his own punishment. *Come, cousin Angelo / In this I'll be impartial; be you judge / Of your own cause.* Long before Shakespeare's day, making a man a judge in his own cause had been established as the paradigm case of a violation of due process.[1] Quoting the Digest of Justinian, "*Non debet esse judex in propria causa,*" Sir Edward Coke held it to be "a maxime in law" that even parliament could not violate.[2] Only if Angelo really were other or more than human — *begot between two stock-fishes* as Lucio claims or *Justice* personified as Escalus more politely puts it — could he judge himself.

---

[1] See John V. Orth, *Due Process of Law: A Brief History* 15-32 (2003).
[2] *Coke on Littleton* 141a; Dr. Bonham's Case, 8 Co. Rep. 107a, 118a, 77 Eng. Rep. 638, 652 (C.P. 1610) (Coke, C.J.) (citing Digest 5.1.17). See also D.E.C. Yale, *Judex in Propria Causa: An Historical Excursus,* 33 *Cambridge L. J.* 80 (1974).

So shocking is the Duke's violation of this maxim that early editors of Shakespeare thought there must have been some mistake and corrected the line: *In this* I will be partial; *be you judge / Of your own cause.*[3] But there was no need to amend the text. The Duke knows what he is doing and accuses himself of injustice when he temporarily returns in his disguise as the friar: *The Duke's unjust, / Thus to retort your manifest appeal / And put your trial in the villain's mouth / Which here you come to accuse.*

The judge in his own cause seemed to haunt Shakespeare. Earlier in *The Merchant of Venice* Portia declares that "to offend and judge are distinct offices, / And of opposed natures."[4] It turns up again in *Twelfth Night.* Olivia comforts the wronged Malvolio: "Prithee be content. / This practice hath most shrewdly passed upon thee; / But when we know the grounds and authors of it, / Thou shalt be both the plaintiff and the judge / Of thine own cause."[5] And there is something similar in *Othello.* The Venetian Duke comforts Brabantio, who had accused the Moor of seducing his daughter Desdemona: "Whoe're he be that in this foul proceeding / Hath thus beguiled your daughter of herself, / And you of her, the bloody book of law / You shall yourself read in the bitter letter / After your own sense . . . ."[6]

continued on page 477 . . .

LOWERY V. STATE

192 P.3d 1264, 1274 n.1 (Okla. Crim. App. September 5, 2008)
(concur in part/dissent in part)

Gary L. Lumpkin, Presiding Judge

My colleague's extensive footnotes seeking to justify the deviation I have noted seems to fit William Shakespeare's great line from Hamlet, Act III, Scene II, "The [gentleman] protests too much, methinks".

---

[3] 1 Lewis Theobald, *The Works of Shakespeare* 387-88 (1733). Edmond Malone, whose text is now considered authoritative, admitted that "all the editors" followed Theobald, although he himself reverted to the wording of the First Folio. But Malone also maintained that in Shakespeare's time "im" could be used as an intensive particle, so *impartial* could have been used in the same sense as "partial." 9 *The Plays and Poems of William Shakespeare* 187, n. 7 (Edmond Malone ed. 1821).

[4] 2.9.60-61. Portia herself, of course, goes on to judge (in disguise) a case in which she has a personal interest.

[5] 5.1.341-44.

[6] 1.3.67-69.

❧ SEPTEMBER ❧

SUN	MON	TUES	WED	THUR	FRI	SAT
		1	2	3	4	5
6	7	8	9	10	11	12
13	14	15	16	17	18	19
20	21	22	23	24	25	26
27	28	29	30			

Desdemona and Othello.

QUO VADIS, HABEAS CORPUS?[1]

James Robertson[†]

The poster that advertised this lecture emphasized two decisions of mine that brought down upon me my allotted fifteen minutes of fame, but Professor Steinfeld[2] was quite discreet when he extended the University's invitation last March: he did not ask me to discuss either my opinion in the Guantánamo Bay case[3] or my resignation from the Foreign Intelligence Surveillance (FISA) Court.[4] What he did, instead, was advise me that the very first Mitchell Lecture, given here 56 years ago by Justice Robert H. Jackson, was entitled *Wartime Security and Liberty Under Law*,[5] and suggest that I might wish to speak on a similar subject. I have never said anything to anybody about my resignation from the FISA court, however, at least not publicly, and I don't plan to start now. And it would be improper for me to discuss or comment upon the *Hamdan* case, which is still pending, or, should I say, pending again. And so what I told Professor Steinfeld was that I would talk more abstractly: about that three-vector force diagram of our government that we call checks and balances — about the ambitions of presidents to power, the fecklessness of the legislature, and the limitations upon the judiciary to do anything much about the other two branches. What happened, in other words, to checks and balances? Then,

---

[1] The 2007 James McCormick Mitchell Lecture, University at Buffalo Law School, March 21, 2007.

[†] United States District Judge for the District of Columbia. The helpful comments of Judge Louis F. Oberdorfer and the invaluable assistance of Emily Coward, Jonathan Olin, and Joel Meyer are gratefully acknowledged. This article was originally published at 55 Buff. L. Rev. 1063 (2008). Copyright © 2008 by Buffalo Law Review. Reprinted by permission of the author and the publisher.

[2] Robert J. Steinfeld, Robert and Karen Jones Faculty Scholar and Professor and Chair, Mitchell Lecture Committee, University at Buffalo Law School, The State University of New York.

[3] *Hamdan v. Rumsfeld*, 344 F. Supp.2d 152 (D.D.C. 2004).

[4] *See, e.g.*, Carol D. Leonnig & Dafna Linzer, *Spy Court Judge Quits in Protest*, WASH. POST, Dec. 21, 2005, at A1.

[5] Robert H. Jackson, *Wartime Security and Liberty Under Law*, 1 BUFF. L. REV. 103 (1951).

a few months later, last July, the Supreme Court declared in *Hamdan v. Rumsfeld*[6] that the President had indeed overstepped his powers at Guantánamo, and it challenged Congress to wake up and act. That decision, and what it brought about, gave us all a civics lesson in checks and balances — not the one we had hoped for, perhaps, but a lesson nevertheless, and a lesson as well in the law of unintended consequences. Congress not only authorized the Executive to conduct trials by military commission at Guantánamo Bay, but, *en passant*,[7] it also stripped the federal courts of their statutory jurisdiction to hear habeas corpus petitions or any other actions filed by aliens who are detained as enemy combatants or who are even awaiting a determination of whether or not they are enemy combatants.[8] So much for what I had thought was the fecklessness of the legislature!

One of the consequences of this intense little piece of American legal history has been to reveal how little understood is the writ of habeas corpus, even by Congress (or, perhaps, especially by Congress); and, despite the lofty language of Blackstone and the rhetorical flourishes of Supreme Court opinions about habeas corpus, how much the writ is at risk of becoming a rather impotent legal anachronism. The Great Writ of habeas corpus, "esteemed" by the Supreme Court as "the best and only sufficient defence of personal [liberty],"[9] and considered by Blackstone to be a "second magna carta,"[10] has been reduced in our own time to a procedural quagmire for jailhouse lawyers, and it has been treated by the judiciary, I fear, as something of a nuisance.

The history of the writ that came to our shores with English settlers is interesting for its own sake, but you may be startled by its parallels with what is happening today. As I outline that history — and I can only outline it — I will try to demonstrate that, for three hundred years, habeas corpus has been a reliable barometer for observing changes in the atmosphere of liberty, and also, if you will forgive the mixed metaphor, a voltmeter (or maybe I mean an ammeter) — a device, in any event, for measuring the distribution of power between and among the three branches of our

---

[6] 126 S. Ct. 2749 (2006).

[7] This chess metaphor is apt, if one considers district judges to be pawns who forgot their place.

[8] Military Commissions Act of 2006, Pub. L. No. 109-366, § 7(a), 120 Stat. 2600, 2635-36. Section 7(a) is the jurisdiction-stripping provision.

[9] *Ex parte* Yerger, 75 U.S. (8 Wall.) 85, 95 (1868).

[10] WILLIAM BLACKSTONE, 1 COMMENTARIES *138.

national government.[11] I will also have a few words about the future of habeas — not predictions, but suggestions, or, perhaps, wishes.

I. ENGLISH ORIGINS OF HABEAS CORPUS

Some commentators seem to believe, without having consulted either Google or Wikipedia, that the writ of habeas corpus was mentioned in, and dates to, Magna Carta. It was not, and it does not. Magna Carta, as we all know, was a document King John's barons more or less forced him to sign in a meadow at Runnymede in the year 1215. Known today as the Charter of Freedom, it contained many concessions by the King, promising, among other things, that

> [n]o free man shall be seized or imprisoned, or stripped of his rights or possessions, or outlawed or exiled, or deprived of his standing in any other way, nor will we [the royal we] proceed with force against him, or send others to do so, except by the lawful judgment of his equals or by the law of the land.[12]

The King signed with his fingers crossed behind his back, having no intention of keeping that promise or any of the other fifty or sixty set forth in the document, but Magna Carta outlived him and was the seed from which grew both parliamentary government and the Rule of Law. As the great English historian Trevelyan wrote, Magna Carta's "historical importance lay not only in what the men of 1215 intended by its clauses, but in the effect which it has had on the imagination of their descendants."[13] No, habeas corpus was not present at Runnymede. It is fair to say, however, that, nearly four hundred years later, habeas corpus *gave effect* to Magna Carta.

Other commentators seem to think, without having consulted their Latin dictionaries, that the words "habeas corpus" mean "produce the body."[14] The literal words do not. They mean, "you have the body."[15]

---

[11] Now seems to be an especially appropriate time to consult this barometer. *See generally* FREDERICK A.O. SCHWARZ JR. & AZIZ Z. HUQ, UNCHECKED AND UNBALANCED: PRESIDENTIAL POWER IN A TIME OF TERROR (2007).

[12] British Library Treasures in Full: Magna Carta — English Translation, http://www.bl.uk/treasures/magnacarta/translation.html (last visited Sept. 28, 2007).

[13] GEORGE MACAULAY TREVELYAN, HISTORY OF ENGLAND 172 (1926).

[14] *See, e.g.*, Public Citizen, *Get the FAQs on Habeas Corpus: Frequently Asked Questions*, http://action.citizen.org/content.jsp?content_KEY=2358 (last visited Sept. 24, 2007) ("Habeas Corpus means 'produce the body.'").

[15] This worked better in a lecture hall than it does in a scholarly journal. My own Latin dictionary was actually no help. I relied upon my schoolboy Latin, and I now freely ac-

They were the introductory words of a writ, or formal document, usually under seal, addressed by a judge to a jailer or to someone having custody of a prisoner. Perhaps Professor Bozer or Professor Baumgarten[16] has the full text of an actual writ of habeas corpus from medieval times — I have never been able to find one — but the gist of it was something like this: "You have the body of William. Bring him to me, in three days time, and show me what legal cause you have for detaining him." That at least, was the writ as it had evolved by the late sixteenth century. And evolution is the right concept, not intelligent design: habeas corpus had existed for a couple of hundred years, but as a lower order of writ — a piece of paper compelling someone to move a prisoner from one place to another.[17] It was not until the reign of Elizabeth I that habeas corpus began to be recognizable as what one scholar has called "a palladium against arbitrary government,"[18] and it was another hundred years before it became the Great Writ.

In 1587, Frances Walsingham, a member of Elizabeth's Privy Council, ordered the detention of a man named Hellyard. Treason was afoot — it was Walsingham who, in the same year, perhaps even as part of the same investigation, discovered a plot to kill Elizabeth and learned that Mary Queen of Scots was "acquainted" with it[19] — which was why Mary lost her head. (It is tempting to name modern-day avatars for Walsingham and for a number of other characters in this story, but I will resist the temptation.) Application was made on Hellyard's behalf for a writ of habeas corpus. The question was not whether the writ would issue — that was virtually automatic, and immediate — in those times a judge presented with an affidavit was required to act immediately[20] — but issuance of the writ

---

knowledge that, in some long-forgotten declension of the verb (*habeo, habere*), "habeas" may be a command, as in "have him here."

[16] Alan J. Bozer is an adjunct lecturer, and Mary C. Baumgarten an adjunct instructor, at the University at Buffalo Law School, The State University of New York. They teach L-812 "The Great Writs and Post-Conviction Remedies."

[17] *See* Alan Clarke, *Habeas Corpus: The Historical Debate*, 14 N.Y. L. SCH. J. HUM. RTS. 375, 378 (1998) (noting that the purpose of the original writ of habeas corpus was "'firmly established by 1230' as a procedural writ to bring people . . . before the court").

[18] WILLIAM F. DUKER, A CONSTITUTIONAL HISTORY OF HABEAS CORPUS 40 (1980) ("The fiction that the writ of habeas corpus provided the English subject with a palladium against arbitrary government pressed closer to reality when the courts of common law began to resist what they perceived as interference from the Privy Council.").

[19] *See* TREVELYAN, *supra* note 13, at 352.

[20] *See* Allen E. Shoenberger, *The Not So Great Writ: The European Court of Human Rights Finds Habeas Corpus an Inadequate Remedy: Should American Courts Reexamine the Writ?*, 56 CATHOLIC U. L. REV. 47, 54 (2006) ("Indeed, the court itself, including the lord chancellor, lord

only started the process. The question was, what cause Walsingham would give for Hellyard's detention when he made his return. Walsingham's return said, essentially, "I, Walsingham, am the principal military secretary of Her Majesty's household, and the prisoner was committed at my order." That pomposity was held, by some long forgotten but courageous judge, to be an insufficient reason; Hellyard was ordered released.[21]

I call the judge in *Hellyard's Case*[22] courageous because, in his time, there was really only one branch of government that counted. Judges served at the pleasure of the Crown, and "feckless" did not begin to describe the timidity of Parliament. Forty years later, though, after Elizabeth was gone, and her successor James I was gone, and young King Charles I was on the throne, it was a different story. Almost as soon as Charles was crowned, he involved England in a series of "warlike expeditions" against the France of Cardinal Richelieu and against Spain.[23] "The wars, such as they were," wrote Trevelyan, became a "tale of folly and disaster," and "lowered the prestige of [the] monarchy in England, and brought the Crown into fierce conflict with the House of Commons."[24] By 1628, less than three years after his coronation, Charles had accumulated a stack of grievances in Parliament. He had forced merchants and even noblemen to loan money to the Crown, he had quartered troops among the populace, he had authorized arbitrary arrests, he had people thrown in prison in violation of Magna Carta. Parliament had had enough. It prepared and delivered to Charles a document that came to be known as The Petition of Right.[25] The Petition of Right asked that no one be imprisoned without a showing of cause, that habeas corpus be available in all cases to examine the cause, and, if a writ were returned without cause, that the prisoner be released — even if he had been committed by order of the King himself or by the entire Privy Council.

The King agreed to The Petition of Right in Parliament, but he almost immediately disavowed it. His attorney general said that the petition was not law, and that it was "the duty of the people not to stretch it beyond

---

keeper, any judge, or baron, was potentially liable to the prisoner for five hundred pounds for denial of a required writ of habeas corpus.").

[21] *See* DUKER, *supra* note 18, at 41 (citing *Hellyard's Case*, (1587) 74 Eng. Rep. 455 (C.P.)).

[22] (1587) 74 Eng. Rep. 455 (C.P.).

[23] TREVELYAN, *supra* note 13, at 389.

[24] *Id.*

[25] THE PETITION OF RIGHT (Eng. 1628), *available at* http://www.constitution.org/eng/petright.htm. Its language is flowery and obsequious, but, if you read it, you will have a better understanding of the provenance of the Declaration of Independence.

the words and intention of the king."[26] Call that, perhaps, the first signing statement.[27] And Charles was as bad as his word. A judge released a man on a writ of habeas corpus when it appeared that the man's only crime was insolent behavior before the Privy Council, so the man was recharged in the Court of Star Chamber[28] — the dreaded high court that operated in secret, without indictments, juries, or even witnesses, and without appeals. The Star Chamber was indeed a court, so the judges could do nothing about the new charge, and Parliament had nothing to say about it, because the King had taken Parliament completely out of the picture by the simple expedient of dissolving it.[29] In other words, there were no checks and balances.

Charles ruled for the next eleven years without Parliament and with a submissive judiciary, but of course he became increasingly unpopular. Eventually, he ran out of money and was forced to call Parliament into session. As soon as it assembled, Parliament asserted itself — by enacting the Habeas Corpus Act of 1640.[30] That statute essentially codified The Petition of Right, which Charles had ignored, and it abolished the Court of Star Chamber. It was the tipping point in a long confrontation between King and Parliament that culminated in the English Civil War, the rise of Oliver Cromwell, and the removal of King Charles. (He was not merely removed — he was beheaded.)

Cromwell the executive was no more supportive of habeas corpus than Charles the monarch had been. He, too, dissolved Parliament. Parliament was restored after Cromwell died, and the monarchy was restored, and Charles II became king, but this Charles, too, had his problems. The Great Plague of 1665 and the Great Fire of London in 1666 happened on his watch — they were the seventeenth century's version of Hurricane Katrina. Charles II made war on the Dutch and had his "mission-accomplished" moment when the English captured New Amsterdam,[31] but that was followed by serious setbacks, for which he made a scapegoat

---

[26] Proceedings against William Stroud, (1629) 3 State Trials 235, 281 (K.B.).

[27] *Cf.* Charlie Savage, *Bush Challenges Hundreds of Laws*, BOSTON GLOBE, Apr. 30, 2006, available at http://www.boston.com/news/nation/articles/2006/04/30/bush_challenges_hundreds_of_laws/.

[28] *See* DUKER, *supra* note 18, at 46-47 (citing Chamber's Case, (1679) 79 Eng. Rep. 717 (K.B.) (Privy Council); Chamber's Case, (1630) 79 Eng. Rep. 746 (K.B.) (Star Chamber)).

[29] *See* TREVELYAN, *supra* note 13, at 390.

[30] 16 Car., c.10 (Eng.).

[31] New Amsterdam was later renamed in honor of Charles's brother, the Duke of York. *See, e.g.*, DAVID M. ELLIS ET AL., A SHORT HISTORY OF NEW YORK STATE 28 (1957).

of his closest personal advisor, Edward Hyde, Lord Clarendon, Lord Chancellor of England. Not only did Clarendon give poor advice about the war — he was also impeached in the House of Commons, for sending "divers of his majesty's subjects to be imprisoned against [the] law, in [the] remote islands, garrisons, and other places, thereby to prevent them from the benefit of the law, and to produce precedents for the imprisoning any other of his majesty's subjects in like manner."[32] Interestingly enough, the people he sent to be imprisoned in the remote islands were primarily the religious fundamentalists of their times: the defeated Puritans, the regicides, thought to be "at large, plotting out there."[33]

Charles II was also at odds with Parliament. He dissolved it four times. The 1679 Parliament, however, managed to enact the Habeas Corpus Act of 1679, described as "probably the most famous statute in the annals of English Law."[34] "Habeas Corpus Act" is not the name Parliament gave to the statute. The official name was "An Act for the better secureing the Liberty of the Subject and for Prevention of Imprisonments beyond the Seas."[35] This Act not only established once and for all the right of a subject to petition for habeas corpus, but it also laid out the procedure: it commanded that a return be made and the prisoner produced within three days (ten days, if the prisoner had to be transported more than twenty miles; twenty, if more than 100 miles);[36] a return was to "certify the true causes of [the person's] detainer and imprisonment"; and, unless it appeared from the return that the prisoner was "detained upon a legal process, order or warrant, out of some court that hath jurisdiction of criminal matters," the prisoner was to be discharged — that is, set free.

II. HABEAS CORPUS AT THE FOUNDING

That was the Great Writ. That was the fully evolved writ of habeas corpus, as it was imported, sometimes wholesale, sometimes piecemeal, into

---

[32] DUKER, *supra* note 18, at 53 (citing Proceedings in Parliament against Edward Earl of Clarendon, (1663-1667) 6 State Trials 291, 330).

[33] *This American Life: Habeas Schmabeas* (Chicago Public Radio broadcast Mar. 10, 2006), *available at* http://www.thislife.org/Radio_Episode.aspx? episode=310.

[34] *See* DUKER, *supra* note 18, at 52.

[35] (1679) 31 Car. 2, c.2 (Eng.), *available at* http://www.british-history.ac.uk/report.asp? compid=47484.

[36] Cognoscenti will know that the three-day period for returning the writ has been preserved intact in the federal habeas statute, 28 U.S.C. § 2243 (1971), with an allowance of up to twenty days for good cause.

the laws of all thirteen American colonies.[37] Every member of the Constitutional Convention that convened in Philadelphia 110 years after the Habeas Corpus Act of 1679 knew about it.[38] English history was their history, after all, so they knew that the Great Writ had been forged on the anvil of struggle between King and Parliament over nearly a century.

They also knew that the writ could be, and had been, suspended. Indeed, it was only months after James II was forced into exile by the so-called Glorious Revolution of 1688, and William and Mary had been crowned upon their acceptance of an English Bill of Rights, and a century of turmoil over religion and arbitrary monarchical power had finally come to a peaceful end, that the new king suggested that habeas be suspended for three months — because "several persons about the Town, in Cabals [were conspiring] against the Government, for the interest of King James," because some of these people had been "apprehended and secured," because others might also be apprehended and secured, and because "[i]f these should be set at liberty, 'tis apprehended we shall be wanting to our own safety, the Government, and People."[39] Parliament agreed to one suspension, for three months, but not to another, perhaps accepting the argument of Sir Robert Napier, who said "This Mistress of ours, the *Habeas Corpus* Act, if we part with it twice, it will become quite a common Whore. Let us not remove this Landmark of the Nation, for a curse attends it."[40]

The Founders also knew that the writ of habeas corpus had uses that transcended criminal law and extended to questions of public policy and even morality, as in the celebrated case of James Sommersett, who was a slave.[41] An Englishman named Stewart purchased Sommersett in Virginia and brought him to England. Sommersett escaped, but he did not get away. He was seized by Stewart's agents and chained up in a ship bound for Jamaica, where Stewart, who had no use for an escape-minded slave,

---

[37] *See* DUKER, *supra* note 18, at 95-125.

[38] *See generally* Max Rosenn, *The Great Writ—A Reflection of Societal Change*, 44 OHIO ST. L.J. 337, 337-38 (1983) (describing a published account of English jurors securing their freedom through habeas corpus that received "noteworthy attention in the American colonies").

[39] DUKER, *supra* note 18, at 61 (quoting 9 DEBATES OF THE HOUSE OF COMMONS 129-30 (Anchitell Grey ed., 1763)) (emphasis omitted).

[40] DUKER, *supra* note 18, at 61 (quoting 9 DEBATES OF THE HOUSE OF COMMONS 263 (Anchitell Grey ed., 1763)).

[41] The Case of James Sommersett, (1772) 20 State Trials 1, 79-82 (K.B.); *see* A. LEON HIGGINBOTHAM, JR., IN THE MATTER OF COLOR: RACE AND THE AMERICAN LEGAL PROCESS, THE COLONIAL PERIOD 353 (1978).

was going to sell him. Three English citizens submitted affidavits in support of a petition to Lord Mansfield for a writ of habeas corpus. The captain of the slave ship responded that this was a property matter — that Sommersett had not been manumitted, enfranchised, set free, or discharged. I refer you to Judge Higginbotham's brilliant exegesis of this case[42] and note here only the peroration of Lord Mansfield's judgment:

> The state of slavery is of such a nature, that it is incapable of being introduced on any reasons, moral or political, but only by positive law which preserves its force long after the reason, occasion, and time itself when it was created, is erased from memory. It is so odious that nothing can be suffered to support it, but positive law. Whatever inconveniences, therefore, may follow from the decision, I cannot say that this case is allowed or approved by the law of England; and therefore the black must be discharged.[43]

Understanding the history of habeas corpus, which by then was universally understood to be a privilege of the King's subjects and defined by common law, the Founders included this clause in Article I, Section 9 of the Constitution:

> The Privilege of the Writ of Habeas Corpus shall not be suspended, unless when in Cases of Rebellion or Invasion the public Safety may require it.[44]

Habeas corpus was the only common law writ mentioned in the Constitution. It was also one of the first subjects to which the first Congress turned its attention, in the Judiciary Act of 1789, empowering federal courts, for the purpose of inquiring into the cause of commitment, to "issue writs of . . . habeas corpus, and all other writs not specially provided for by statute, which may be necessary for the exercise of their respective jurisdictions, and agreeable to the principles and usages of law."[45]

III. JEFFERSON AND LINCOLN

There have been many notable developments in the writ of habeas corpus in this country since 1789. The nuance and filigree added by countless court decisions and law review articles is by now far beyond the ability of any ordinary person to absorb. I have time, and you will have patience,

---

[42] HIGGINBOTHAM, *supra* note 41, at 353.
[43] The Case of James Sommersett, (1772) 20 State Trials 1, 82 (K.B.).
[44] U.S. CONST. art. I, § 9, cl. 2.
[45] Act of Sept. 24, 1789, ch. 20, § 14, 1 Stat. 73, 81.

only for two historical events that show clearly how the Great Writ and the liberty interests that it represents are supported by balanced power in government and challenged when power is unbalanced and unchecked.

In 1805, Aaron Burr had completed his term as vice president in Jefferson's first term. He had killed Alexander Hamilton in a duel, he was deeply in debt, he had failed to be elected governor of New York, and he had no law practice left — so he set off on an excellent adventure involving lands in the Ohio River Valley and the Louisiana Purchase.[46] In late 1806 Jefferson became convinced that these adventures were in fact a treasonous conspiracy, and that Burr planned to seize New Orleans, attack Mexico, assume Montezuma's throne, add Louisiana to his empire, and then add the North American states from the Allegheny Mountains west. Jefferson sent a special message to Congress naming Burr as the "arch conspirator" and asserting that his "guilt [was] placed beyond question."[47] Jefferson also asserted that Erick Bollman and Samuel Swartwout were Burr's accomplices.[48] On orders from the president, General James Wilkinson, acting governor of the New Orleans territory, seized Bollman and Swartwout and sent them to Washington for trial. The Supreme Court of the territory issued a writ of habeas corpus. Wilkinson ignored it. Another habeas was issued by the district court in South Carolina when Bollman and Swartwout were landed at Charleston, but that one, too, was ignored. The day the two prisoners arrived in Washington, Jefferson hand-carried information about them to the U.S. Attorney and instructed the prosecutor to go to court immediately and seek a bench warrant charging them with treason.[49] That same afternoon, activated by Jefferson's agents, the Senate passed a bill suspending habeas corpus for three months.[50] George Washington had assured Jefferson that Senators, with their six-year terms of office, would be the saucer that could cool the hot tea of democracy,[51] but this time it was the House that controlled the situation, rejecting the habeas suspension bill by a vote of 113 to 19.[52] Shortly thereafter, Chief Justice Marshall issued an order for the release of Bollman and Swartwout with an opinion, one of first impression, that established the

---

[46] See JEAN EDWARD SMITH, JOHN MARSHALL: DEFINER OF A NATION 352 (1996).

[47] Id. at 353.

[48] Id.

[49] Id. at 354-55.

[50] Id. at 355. Note the attention to precedent: it was for three months that Parliament suspended the writ at the suggestion of William and Mary in 1689.

[51] See NewsHour with Jim Lehrer (PBS television broadcast Nov. 7, 2000) (transcript available at http://www.pbs.org/newshour/bb/politics/july-dec00/hist_11-7.html).

[52] SMITH, supra note 46, at 355.

Supreme Court's power to grant relief on a writ of habeas corpus as an original action.[53] *Ex parte Bollman* has since been understood to hold that the Constitution not only constrains the suspension of habeas corpus, but also guarantees its continuing existence.[54]

The next major habeas event came sixty years later, at the start of the Civil War. I expect that almost everyone in this room is generally aware that Abraham Lincoln suspended habeas corpus. My guess is that many if not most of you also believe that it was really okay — that Lincoln could do no wrong, that he explained himself to Congress, that his acts were ratified, that history presents imperatives, et cetera, et cetera. But the more one knows about this story, the more uncomfortable one becomes with it — at least if one is a judge. Within weeks after his inauguration in March 1861, and within days after the surrender of Ft. Sumter, Lincoln became concerned that troops coming to the defense of Washington from the North might be interdicted by the destruction of railroad bridges between Philadelphia and Washington, and particularly in the vicinity of Baltimore.[55] On April 27, 1861, he gave an order to General Winfield Scott, the Commanding General of the Army of the United States. He wrote:

> If at any point on or in the vicinity of the military line, which is now [or which shall be] used between the City of Philadelphia and the City of Washington . . . you find resistance which renders it necessary to suspend the writ of Habeas Corpus for the public safety, you, personally or through the officer in command at the point where resistance occurs, are authorized to suspend that writ.[56]

A month later, John Merryman was arrested — by military troops, not by civilian law enforcement authorities — and charged with participation in the destruction of railroad bridges after the Baltimore riots in April. His lawyers addressed a petition for habeas corpus to Roger Taney, who was

---

[53] *Ex parte* Bollman, 8 U.S. 75 (1807).
[54] Justice Scalia, dissenting in *INS v. St. Cyr*, 533 U.S. 289, 337 (2001), does not agree: "A straightforward reading of this text discloses that [the habeas clause of the Constitution] does not guarantee any content to (or even the existence of) the writ of habeas corpus, but merely provides that the writ shall not (except in case of rebellion or invasion) be suspended."
[55] *See* DAVID HERBERT DONALD, LINCOLN 298-99 (1995).
[56] Letter from Abraham Lincoln, President, United States, to Winfield Scott, Commanding General, (Apr. 27, 1861), *reprinted in* ABRAHAM LINCOLN: SPEECHES AND WRITINGS 1859-1865, at 237 (1989) [hereinafter SPEECHES AND WRITINGS].

Chief Justice of the United States but who was sitting as a circuit judge. Taney was a Marylander of the Southern persuasion who hated Lincoln. Lincoln was not very fond of Taney either. Taney had written the *Dred Scott* decision,[57] a disgustingly racist opinion finding among other things that the Founders considered black people "so far inferior, that they had no rights which the white man was bound to respect."[58] *Dred Scott* had been the centerpiece of many of Lincoln's speeches that paved his way to the presidency.[59] In his first inaugural address, in fact, just before Taney administered the oath of office to him, Lincoln gave advance notice that he would not let Taney's Court stand in his way. He said:

> [T]he candid citizen must confess that if the policy of the govern-
> ment, upon vital questions, affecting the whole people, is to be
> irrevocably fixed by decisions of the Supreme Court, the instant
> they are made, in ordinary litigation between parties, in personal
> actions, the people will have ceased to be their own rulers, hav-
> ing, to that extent, practically resigned their government, into
> the hands of that eminent tribunal.[60]

For people like me — who think Abraham Lincoln wore a halo, the country lawyer from Illinois who personified devotion to the Rule of Law — that statement is something of a head slap. And so was Lincoln's response to Taney's decision in the *Merryman* case,[61] which was, essentially, to ignore it.[62]

It must be said, in Lincoln's defense, that Taney was as confrontational with his *Merryman* decision as a judge could possibly be. Merryman was arrested on Saturday, his petition was delivered to Taney on Sunday, and Taney first demanded that a return be made on Monday. He relented and

---

[57] Scott v. Sanford, 60 U.S. 393 (1856).

[58] *Id*. at 407.

[59] *See, e.g.*, Abraham Lincoln, Speech at Columbus, Ohio (Sept. 16, 1859), *reprinted in* SPEECHES AND WRITINGS, *supra* note 56, at 49-54; Abraham Lincoln, Address at Cooper Institute (Feb. 27, 1860), *reprinted in* SPEECHES AND WRITINGS, *supra* note 56, at 111.

[60] Abraham Lincoln, President, United States, First Inaugural Address, (Mar. 4, 1861), *reprinted in* SPEECHES AND WRITINGS, *supra* note 52, at 221. Lincoln had been persuaded by William H. Seward to tone this down from his first draft, which said, "the people will have ceased to be their own rulers, having turned their government over to the *despotism of the few life-officers composing the Court*." DOUGLAS L. WILSON, LINCOLN'S SWORD: THE PRESIDENCY AND THE POWER OF WORDS 63 (2006) (emphasis added).

[61] *Ex parte* Merryman, 17 F. Cas. 144 (C.C.D. Md. 1861) (No. 9,487).

[62] Consider, by way of contrast, the penitential response of Andrew Jackson to the contempt citation of a judge whom Jackson had arrested for issuing a writ of habeas corpus at the end of the War of 1812. *Cf.* Caleb Crain, *Bad Precedent: Andrew Jackson's Assault on Habeas Corpus*, THE NEW YORKER, Jan. 29, 2007, at 78.

gave General Cadwalader until Tuesday, but he had already prepared his decision, and, when no return was made on Tuesday, he read it from the bench.[63] He found that the President did not have the power to suspend the writ, or the power to authorize any military officer to do so, and that military officers had no right to arrest anybody not subject to the Articles of War for an offense against the United States. Taney conceded in his opinion that he had no power to enforce his own order. He said he had exercised all the power the Constitution conferred upon him but that "that power has been resisted by a force too strong for me to overcome."[64] He directed the Clerk to transmit a copy of his order under seal to the President and said "[i]t will then remain for that high officer, in fulfillment of his constitutional obligation to 'take care that the laws be faithfully executed,' to determine what measures he will take to cause the civil process of the United States to be respected and enforced."[65] Then, at his own expense, he had his decision printed as handbills and distributed them as widely as he could.

Lincoln's answer was not to answer, except, in a July Fourth message to a special session of Congress, to point out that the Constitution was silent as to which branch of the government had authority to suspend the writ and to assert that, in an emergency, when Congress was not in session, the President had the authority.[66] He went on to ask a famous rhetorical question, whether Taney meant that "all the laws, but one" could go unexecuted, and "the government itself go to pieces, lest that one be violated?"[67] A month later, Congress bailed Lincoln out of the serious trouble he would otherwise be in among historians — legal historians, anyway. On August 6, 1861, it enacted a statute approving, legalizing, and validating all the acts, proclamations, and orders that Lincoln had issued since his inauguration,[68] and in March 1863 it enacted another stat-

---

[63] See WILLIAM H. REHNQUIST, ALL THE LAWS BUT ONE: CIVIL LIBERTIES IN WARTIME 33 (1998); CARL B. SWISHER, THE OLIVER WENDELL HOLMES DEVISE 844-48 (1974).

[64] Ex parte Merryman, 17 F. Cas. at 153.

[65] Id.

[66] Abraham Lincoln, President, United States, Special Message to Congress (July 4, 1861), reprinted in SPEECHES AND WRITINGS, supra note 56, at 252-53.

[67] SPEECHES AND WRITINGS, supra note 56, at 253.

[68] Act of Aug. 6 1861, ch. 63, § 3, 12 Stat. 326. "Scholars assert there is uncertainty as to whether this August 6 Act included the suspension of habeas corpus, although there seems to be no doubt that it included the declaration of martial law." Anne English French, Trials in Times of War: Do the Bush Military Commissions Sacrifice Our Freedoms?, 63 OHIO ST. L.J. 1225, 1232 n.31 (2002) (citing PAUL BREST ET AL., PROCESSES OF CONSTITUTIONAL DECISION MAKING: CASES AND MATERIALS 225 (4th ed. 2000)); see also, David Currie, The

ute unambiguously authorizing the President to suspend habeas "during the present rebellion."[69]

The *Merryman* story is a necessary part of any history of habeas corpus in America, but my purpose for retelling it here is to emphasize the vulnerability of the writ when the delicate constitutional system of checks and balances is upset. There was no effective opposition to what Lincoln did. His Republican party had complete control of both houses of Congress, the Southern senators and representatives having withdrawn.[70] Taney's Supreme Court and all the federal courts were at the historic low point of their influence after *Dred Scott*. Indeed, as one scholar puts it, during the Civil War, "[p]etitioners applied to the President and to military leaders rather than to the courts. So great . . . was the scope of executive power, and so limited the power of the courts, that by the end of the war much of the deference ordinarily accorded to the judiciary was accorded elsewhere . . . ."[71] The President had a clear field on which to act, and act he did, issuing further proclamations suspending the privilege of the writ throughout the country, "authorizing the arbitrary arrest of any person 'guilty of any disloyal practice, affording aid and comfort to Rebels against the authority of the United States,'"[72] and, in one case perhaps better remembered in my town than yours, actually dissolving the District of Columbia court that was the predecessor of my own court, because its judges had defied Lincoln's military officers on a habeas petition.[73]

IV. HABEAS BECOMES A POST-CONVICTION REMEDY

In 1867, a new Congress dominated by northern radical Republicans rejected Andrew Johnson's permissive policies toward the rebel states and

---

Civil War Congress, 73 U. CHI. L. REV. 1131, 1140 (2003) (noting Maine Senator William Pitt Fessenden's assurances that the Act "'avoids all questions with regard to the habeas corpus and other matters, and refers' only to the 'military appropriations' . . . ; 'there is nothing in the world in it except what relates to the Army and Navy volunteers'" (quoting 37 CONG. GLOBE, 37th Cong. 1st Sess. 442 (1861))).

[69] Act of Mar. 3, 1863, 12 Stat. 755, 755.

[70] Republicans held the Senate 32-16 and the House 106-70. DONALD, *supra* note 55, at 304-05.

[71] SWISHER, *supra* note 63, at 901-02.

[72] DONALD, *supra* note 55, at 380.

[73] *See* MATTHEW F. McGUIRE, AN ANECDOTAL HISTORY OF THE UNITED STATES DISTRICT COURT FOR THE DISTRICT OF COLUMBIA 1801-1976, at 44-46 (1977); JEFFREY BRANDON MORRIS, CALMLY TO POISE THE SCALES OF JUSTICE; A HISTORY OF THE COURTS OF THE DISTRICT OF COLUMBIA CIRCUIT 36-37 (2001).

passed Reconstruction Acts that divided the South into military districts.[74] This Reconstruction legislation gave a great deal of new habeas power to federal courts and judges — the power, "in addition to the authority already conferred by law," to issue writs of habeas corpus "in all cases where any person may be restrained of his or her liberty in violation of the [C]onstitution, or of any treaty or law of the United States . . . ."[75] A year later, in *Ex parte McCardle*, the Supreme Court held that the 1867 Act "[brought] within the habeas corpus jurisdiction of every court and of every judge every possible case of privation of liberty contrary to the National Constitution, treaties, or laws. It is impossible to widen this jurisdiction."[76] What federal judges now had was the authority to reach into state and local jails. This, too, was a power play: strong Congress, weak president, defeated and compliant state governments in the rebel South.

It took the courts another fifty years, until about 1920, to begin exercising these broader powers, but, beginning around 1920, habeas began its transition into what it mostly is today — a legal tool for bringing post-conviction, collateral challenges in criminal cases. By 1945, except for the great World War II cases — *Quirin*,[77] *Yamashita*,[78] *Eisentrager*,[79] *Endo*[80] — habeas had become a vehicle for challenging convictions "on facts dehors the record"[81]: "mob domination of trial[s]," "knowing use of perjured testimony by [the] prosecution," "[absence of] intelligent waiver[s] of counsel[]," "coerced plea[s] of guilty," "[absence of] intelligent waiver[s] of jury trial," and "denial[s] of right to consult with counsel."[82]

After World War II, habeas continued to develop along those lines, and its development is hard to explain in terms of checks and balances. Certainly there were disturbances in the power grid during that period — Truman's seizure of the steel mills, the Warren Court's orders to desegregate public schools, Johnson's war in Vietnam, Nixon's legal problems and Clinton's impeachment — but these disturbances created little demand for a check against unlawful or unexplained executive detention. For fifty years, habeas was largely the province of the judiciary, which, left

---

[74] *See* John Harrison, *The Lawfulness of the Reconstruction Amendments*, 68 U. CHI. L. REV. 375, 405-08 (2001).

[75] Habeas Corpus Act of 1867, ch. 28, 14 Stat. 385, 385.

[76] *Ex parte* McCardle, 73 U.S. 318, 325-26 (1868).

[77] *Ex parte* Quirin, 317 U.S. 1 (1942).

[78] *In re* Yamashita, 327 U.S. 1 (1946).

[79] Johnson v. Eisentrager, 339 U.S. 763 (1950).

[80] *Ex parte* Endo, 323 U.S. 283 (1944).

[81] United States v. Hayman, 342 U.S. 205, 212 (1951) (emphasis omitted).

[82] *Id.* at 212 n.12 (citations omitted).

to its own devices, both expanded its reach into state judicial proceedings and managed, as judges will, to create a frustrating procedural maze for petitioners. In recent times, instead of providing a judicial check against arbitrary and unlawful executive detention, habeas has devolved into a federal judicial check against state judicial proceedings.

By 1947, the number of habeas filings had expanded to the point where the Judicial Conference of the United States — think of it as the judiciary's College of Cardinals — recommended statutory changes designed to streamline procedures and reduce frivolous or repetitive prisoner filings.[83] One such change, a new provision on finality, now codified as 28 U.S.C. § 2244, would "exclude applications presenting no new grounds,"[84] and allow judges to refuse to entertain repetitive or "nuisance" habeas applications. Another was a new way for federal prisoners to bring post-trial challenges to their sentences, or to the constitutional or jurisdictional bases of their convictions. This procedure, now 28 U.S.C. § 2255, was a kind of quasi-habeas. A motion under § 2255 would be filed, not where the prisoner's custodian was, as habeas petitions had to be, but in the court that had imposed the sentence. There was no automatic requirement for the government to make a return, and no requirement that the prisoner be produced. A § 2255 motion could be, in practice almost always was, and still is, handled entirely on paper.

Apparently nobody told the Supreme Court about this effort to shrink the habeas caseload. *Brown v. Allen*,[85] decided in 1953, just before Earl Warren's arrival as Chief Justice, removed any lingering doubt that the federal courts were empowered to test the constitutionality of state court convictions. That decision was followed by landmark decisions of the Warren Court that dramatically expanded the scope of constitutional protections for criminal defendants,[86] and the flood gates of prisoner habeas litigation opened wide. Between the early 1950s and the late 1980s, when the "abuse" question came to a head again, the number of habeas petitions

---

[83] *See* REPORT OF THE JUDICIAL CONFERENCE OF SENIOR CIRCUIT JUDGES OF THE UNITED STATES (1947).

[84] George F. Longsdorf, *The Federal Habeas Corpus Acts Original and Amended*, 13 F.R.D. 407, 418 (1953).

[85] 344 U.S. 443 (1953).

[86] *See, e.g.*, Benton v. Maryland, 395 U.S. 284 (1969); Terry v. Ohio, 392 U.S. 1 (1968); Duncan v. Louisiana, 391 U.S. 145 (1968); Washington v. Texas, 388 U.S. 14 (1967); Klopfer v. North Carolina, 386 U.S. 213 (1967); Miranda v. Arizona, 384 U.S. 436 (1966); Pointer v. Texas, 380 U.S. 400 (1965); Malloy v. Hogan, 378 U.S. 1 (1964); Massiah v. United States, 377 U.S. 201 (1964); Gideon v. Wainwright, 372 U.S. 335 (1963); Mapp v. Ohio, 367 U.S. 643 (1961).

filed in federal courts grew geometrically, if not logarithmically, from fewer than 1,000 per year to more than 20,000.[87]

In 1995, in order to "curb the abuse of the habeas corpus process, and particularly to address the problem of delay and repetitive litigation in capital cases,"[88] Congress.enacted the Antiterrorism and Effective Death Penalty Act (AEDPA).[89] The federal courts, obsessing, as judges will do, about caseloads and statistics,[90] essentially asked for the AEDPA, after receiving another report from the Judicial Conference, this one chaired by Justice Louis Powell.[91] The AEDPA imposed a one-year period of limitation for motions filed under § 2255,[92] and it precluded habeas relief for any claim that had been adjudicated on the merits in state court unless the state court result was contrary to "clearly established federal law, as determined by the Supreme Court."[93] In other words, lower federal courts were to be seen and not heard; we certainly were not to get all creative with the Constitution.[94] Since the AEDPA, writes Professor Shoenberger

---

[87] *Compare* United States v. Hayman, 342 U.S. 205, 212 n.13 ("By 1943, 1944 and 1945 . . . the annual average of filings reached 845 . . . .") *with* ADMIN. OFFICE OF THE U.S. COURTS, JUDICIAL BUSINESS OF THE UNITED STATES COURTS, at table C-2 (2004) (23,344 federal habeas petitions filed), and ADMIN. OFFICE OF THE U.S. COURTS, JUDICIAL BUSINESS OF THE UNITED STATES COURTS, at table C-2 (2005) (24,633 federal habeas petitions filed).

[88] H.R. REP. No. 23, at 8 (1995).

[89] Antiterrorism and Effective Death Penalty Act of 1996, Pub. L. No. 104-132, 110 Stat. 1214 (codified as amended in scattered sections of 28 U.S.C.).

[90] Nobody has written more, or more perceptively, about the development of the judiciary into a cadre of managers, more than adjudicators, than Professor Judith Resnik of Yale. *See, e.g.*, Judith Resnik, *Managerial Judges*, 96 HARV. L. REV. 374 (1982); Judith Resnik, *Whither and Whether Adjudication?*, 86 B.U. L. REV. 1101 (2006).

[91] *See* H.R. REP. No. 23, at 8; JUDICIAL CONFERENCE OF THE UNITED STATES, AD HOC COMMITTEE ON FEDERAL HABEAS CORPUS IN CAPITAL CASES (Lewis F. Powell, Jr., Chairman 1989). Justice Powell was not chosen at random to chair this committee. In his concurring opinion in *Schneckcloth v. Bustamonte*, 412 U.S. 218, 259 (1973) (joined by then-Associate Justice Rehnquist), he had spoken of the "unprecedented extension of habeas corpus far beyond its historic bounds and in disregard of the writ's central purpose . . . ." The early development of what eventually became the AEDPA, and the role of judicial thinking in that development, are authoritatively spelled out in an article in this *Review*, by the University at Buffalo Law School's present dean, R. Nils Olsen, Jr., *Judicial Proposals to Limit the Jurisdictional Scope of Federal Post-Conviction Habeas Corpus Consideration of the Claims of State Prisoners*, 31 BUFF. L. REV. 301 (1982).

[92] 28 U.S.C. § 2255(1)-(4) (2000).

[93] 28 U.S.C. § 2254(d)(1) (2000).

[94] In *Carey v. Musladin*, 127 S. Ct. 649, 654 (2006), the Supreme Court reinforced this directive, stressing that federal courts considering habeas petitions may declare trial court proceedings unconstitutional only if the proceedings under review ignored explicit direction from prior Supreme Court opinions concerning clearly established federal law. After

in a recent *Catholic University Law Review* article, "the ambit of the writ has been greatly limited — some would say to the virtual vanishing point."[95]

V. QUO VADIS?

So here we are, in 2007. We have no jurisdiction of habeas petitions by alien combatants or suspected ones. We have no power to hear post-conviction claims more than a year old. We are instructed not to be creative. Where are you going, habeas corpus? (That, by the way, is the meaning of *"quo vadis."*) The answer, in my view, is nowhere — unless attention is paid to several problems.

One problem, not widely known or understood, perhaps, because habeas is now almost exclusively about collateral review of criminal convictions, and because prisoners have no political constituency, is delay. It takes far too long to move a habeas petition, or a § 2255 application, through the system. The habeas statute continues to pay lip service to the three-day return period imported directly from the 1679 English statute, but in practice habeas and § 2255 petitions linger for months, or even years. Each district judge is required to report semiannually his or her "old motions" in civil cases — those that have been pending undecided for longer than six months.[96] It's a negative incentive — a shaming device — and it has been quite effective in getting judges to move their cases along. Habeas corpus cases and § 2255 applications, however, are not regarded as "motions." They are not reportable, so, if they are sitting on remote corners of our desks gathering dust, there is no public accountability. Transparency does wonders.

Another problem that needs to be addressed is the procedural obstacles that confront prisoners seeking review on the merits of their petitions. I have done no empirical research on this subject, but I can tell you that virtually every habeas petition and § 2255 application on my docket has to be dismissed, or transferred to another court, before I ever get close to the merits: the application was filed too late, or it is a second or successive application, or it was filed in the wrong court, or it seeks application of a Supreme Court decision that has no retroactive application.[97] I

---

the AEDPA, a finding that trial court proceedings were "so inherently prejudicial that they deprive[d] the defendant of a fair trial," absent Supreme Court precedent directly on point, is not enough. *Musladin*, 127 S. Ct. at 651.

[95] Shoenberger, *supra* note 20, at 56.

[96] *See* Civil Justice Reform Act, 28 U.S.C. § 476(a)(1) (2000).

[97] At common law, the refusal of one court to discharge a prisoner was no bar to the filing of second and successive applications to other[] courts, and indeed an important part of the

think my experience is common among district judges. Most post-conviction claims do lack merit, it's true, but I suspect that we expend a lot more energy crafting careful opinions explaining why we cannot reach the merits than we would if we simply ruled on the issues that petitioners ask us to decide.[98]

The third problem, of course, is the jurisdiction-stripping provision of the Military Commissions Act of 2006.[99] I cannot comment outside my own courtroom on the constitutional validity of what Congress did last year. What I can and do say is that, when it silences the judiciary, Congress abdicates its own historic role in the system of checks and balances, and it leaves the way open to abuse of the executive's power to detain. When the House of Representatives refused to suspend the writ for Thomas Jefferson, it left John Marshall free to act. When Congress gave Lincoln carte blanche during the Civil War, there was no space for the courts to act. It takes all three branches to get it right; one cannot sit on the sidelines.

There is no legislative history that explains what Congress did. One Congressman, formerly chair of the House Judiciary Committee, pointed to a lawyer who talked about making trouble for the government,[100] and it may be that Congress was stampeded into thinking that unscrupulous lawyers and activist judges would just gum things up at Guantánamo. If that is what Congress thought, it had faulty intelligence.

The accumulated record demonstrates only professionalism on the part of lawyers and moderation and restraint from the bench. I canvassed my colleagues on their handling of the Guantánamo detainee cases and confirmed my understanding that no judge has ordered the release of any petitioner, and no judge has ordered a change in the conditions of con-

---

history of the writ was its employment by courts to exercise their own jurisdiction and fend off encroachments by other courts. *See* DUKER, *supra* note 18, at 28-41.

[98] For an exhaustive commentary on the ramifications of habeas corpus procedure, see Judith Resnik, *Tiers*, 57 S. CAL. L. REV. 837 (1984).

[99] Military Commissions Act of 2006, Pub. L. No. 109-366, § 7(a), 120 Stat. 2600, 2635 (2006).

[100] 152 CONG. REC. H7522, H7547 (daily ed. Sept. 27, 2006) (statement of Rep. Sensenbrenner). To demonstrate the alleged obstructionism of lawyers at Guantánamo, the Congressman quoted Michael Ratner, of the Center for Constitutional Rights, this way: "The litigation is brutal [for the United States] . . . [y]ou can't run an interrogation . . . with attorneys." Michael Ratner, *Letter to the Editor*, WALL ST. J., Mar. 14, 2007, at A13 (quoting "an article by Onnesha Roychoudhuri in a March 2005 piece for Mother Jones"). What Mr. Ratner actually said was, "Every time an attorney goes down there, it makes it much harder for the U.S. military to do what they are doing. You can't run an *interrogation and torture camp* with attorneys." *Id.* (emphasis added).

finement or the treatment of any Guantánamo detainee. One judge did order, early on, that the government permit access by attorneys to their detainee clients,[101] but the government neither seriously resisted nor appealed that order, and thereafter lawyers were routinely permitted access. The government did resist giving counsel access to the medical records of one detainee who had been force-fed, but it acquiesced in the judge's remedial order.[102] My court agreed, for our own efficiencies and to make life easier for government counsel, that a single judge would deal with administrative matters, such as the appointment of counsel and the treatment of classified documents.[103] Many of us did require the government to prepare and file factual returns — but, of course, that's how habeas corpus works, and we waited much longer for returns than the twenty days the habeas statute allows.

I do not say that the involvement of lawyers and judges made it easy for the government at Guantánamo, but nothing about the justice system we boast about — not habeas corpus, grand juries, public trials, the presumption of innocence, the right to counsel, the confrontation clause, the privilege against self-incrimination, unanimous verdicts — nothing about our system is designed to make it easy or comfortable for the government to lock people up indefinitely without charges.

The extraterritorial reach of habeas corpus presents a difficult set of issues, to be sure. The great World War II decisions established that the writ "acts upon" the custodian, not the prisoner,[104] but just who the custodian is, and where the custodian may be sued, and what rights a petitioner has if the custodian fails to return just cause for detention, remain unclear.[105] Not only are these difficult issues, but no answer fits every case. Nobody would grant a writ of habeas corpus to a combatant on the battlefield, but should the United States government not be required to show cause why it detains a Canadian citizen somewhere in Poland? Dealing with questions like that, case by case, is quintessentially the role of judges, as Anthony Lewis wrote in a recent column: "Judges are not always wise. But in our system they are the ones we trust to weigh acutely

---

[101] *See In re* Guantánamo Bay Detainee Cases, 344 F. Supp.2d 174 (D.D.C. 2004) (setting forth procedures for counsel access to detainees).

[102] *See* Majid Abdulla Al-Joudi v. Bush, 406 F. Supp.2d 13 (D.D.C. 2005).

[103] *See, e.g., In re* Guantánamo Bay Detainee Cases, 344 F. Supp.2d 174 (D.D.C. 2004).

[104] *See, e.g., Ex parte* Endo, 323 U.S. 283, 304-05 (1944).

[105] Compare the majority, concurring, and dissenting opinions in Rumsfeld v. Padilla, 542 U.S. 426 (2004).

conflicting interests."[106] Judges cannot play that role if they have no jurisdiction, however. Nor, as I hope I have shown here, can Congress's own force vector be effective in our tripartite system of government if the judiciary is rendered impotent. It is worth remembering what Chief Justice Marshall wrote, 200 years ago in the *Bollman* case, about "positive law,"[107] by which he meant, not judge-made, common law, but law enacted by the legislature: statutory law. Congress can indeed remove our jurisdiction, but Congress can also establish it, and clarify it.

Congress may soon consider legislation that would "restore" habeas to where it was before the enactment of the Military Commissions Act.[108] My suggestion — my wish — is that Congress do more than that. We seem to be, right now, at one of those moments in history when the vectors of power are changing. At such moments, as I think I have shown, the writ of habeas corpus has been vulnerable, or it has been ascendant. Now is a time when Congress should not only *restore* full habeas corpus jurisdiction to the federal courts, but also *revisit* the history and the fundamental purposes of the Great Writ, and *repair* it. In particular, I suggest that Congress address and consider removing or reducing the procedural barriers that so often frustrate merits review of habeas and § 2255 petitions; insist on the prompt, timely handling of habeas and § 2255 petitions, perhaps by enacting public reporting requirements; and, most importantly, proclaim that the federal writ of habeas corpus shall run to any place in the world where people may be detained or otherwise deprived of their freedom by officers or agents of the American government — so that American justice may be, and may be seen to be, present wherever in the world America shows her flag, projects her power and influence, and trumpets her values of liberty and freedom.

---

[106] Anthony Lewis, *Not all Sources are Equal*, N.Y. TIMES, Mar. 7, 2007, at A21.

[107] *Ex parte Bollman*, 8 U.S. 75, 125-37 (1807). See also the later observation of Justice Miller in *In re Neagle*, 135 U.S. 1, 78 (1989), that the habeas authority of federal courts comes *only* from the habeas statute, or "positive law."

[108] *See, e.g.*, Habeas Corpus Restoration Act of 2007, S. 185, 110th Cong. (2007); Restoring the Constitution Act of 2007, S. 576, H.R. 1415, 110th Cong. (2007).

SHAKESPEARE'S LEGAL ACQUIREMENTS

(continued from page 446)

John Lord Campbell

OTHELLO

In the very first scene of this play there is a striking instance of Shakespeare's proneness to legal phraseology:— where Iago, giving an explanation to Roderigo of the manner in which he had been disappointed in not obtaining the place of Othello's lieutenant, notwithstanding the solicitations in his favour of "three great ones of the city," says—

> "But he, as loving his own pride and purposes,
> Evades them with a bombast circumstance
> Horribly stuff'd with epithets of war,
> And, in conclusion,
> *Nonsuits* my mediators."

"Nonsuiting" is known to the learned to be the most disreputable and mortifying mode of being beaten: it indicates that the action is wholly unfounded on the plaintiff's own showing, or that there is a fatal defect in the manner in which his case has been got up: insomuch that Mr. Chitty, the great special pleader, used to give this advice to young barristers practicing at *nisi prius*:— "Always avoid your attorney when nonsuited, for till he has a little time for reflection, however much you may abuse the Judge, he will think that the nonsuit was all your fault."

———

In the next scene Shakespeare gives us, very distinct proof that he was acquainted with Admiralty law, as well as with the procedure of Westminster Hall. Describing the feat of the Moor in carrying off Desdemona against her father's consent, which might either make or mar his fortune, according as the act might be sanctioned or nullified, Iago observes—

> "Faith, he to-night hath boarded a land carack:
> If it prove *lawful prize*, he's made for ever;" —

the trope indicating that there would be a suit in the High Court of Admiralty to determine the validity of the capture.

———

Then follows, in Act I. Sc. 3, the trial of Othello before the Senate, as if he had been indicted on Stat. 33 Hen. VII. c. 8, for practising "conjuration, witchcraft, enchantment, and sorcery, to provoke to unlawful love." Brabantio, the prosecutor, says—

> "She is abused, stol'n from me, and corrupted
> By spells and medicines bought of mountebanks;
> For Nature so preposterously to err . . .
> Sans witchcraft could not."

The presiding Judge at first seems alarmingly to favour the prosecutor, saying—

> *Duke.* Whoe'er he be that in this foul proceeding
> Hath thus beguil'd your daughter of herself,
> And you of her, the bloody book of law
> You shall yourself read, in the bitter letter,
> After your own sense.

The Moor, although acting as his own counsel, makes a noble and skilful defence, directly meeting the statutable misdemeanour with which he is charged,— and referring pointedly to the very words of the indictment and the Act of Parliament:—

> "I will a round unvarnish'd tale deliver
> Of my whole course of love; *what drugs, what charms,*
> *What conjuration, and what mighty magic*
> (For such proceedings I am charged withal)
> I won his daughter with."

Having fully opened his case, showing that he had used no forbidden arts, and having explained the course which he had lawfully pursued, he says in conclusion:—

> This only is the *witchcraft* I have used:
> Here comes the lady — let her witness it.

He then examines the witness, and is honourably acquitted.

———

Again, the application to Othello to forgive Cassio is made to assume the shape of a juridical proceeding. Thus Desdemona concludes her address to Cassio, assuring him of her zeal as his *Solicitor:*—

> "I'll intermingle every thing he does
> With Cassio's *suit:* Therefore be merry, Cassio;
> For thy *Solicitor* shall rather die
> *Than give thy cause away."* —

(Act III. Sc. 3.)

———

The subsequent part of the same scene shows that Shakespeare was well acquainted with all courts, low as well as high;— where Iago asks—

> Who has a breast so pure
> But some uncleanly apprehensions
> *Keep leets and law-days,* and in session sit
> With meditations lawful?

ANTONY AND CLEOPATRA

In "Julius Caesar" I could not find a single instance of a Roman being made to talk like an English lawyer; but in "Antony and Cleopatra" (Act I. Sc. 4) Lepidus, in trying to palliate the bad qualities and misdeeds of Antony, uses the language of a conveyancer's chambers in Lincoln's Inn:—

> "His faults, in him, seem as the spots of heaven,
> More fiery by night's blackness; *hereditary*
> Rather than *purchas'd.*"

That is to say, they are taken by *descent*, not by *purchase.**

Lay gents (viz., all except lawyers) understand by "purchase" buying for a sum of money, called the price; but lawyers consider that "purchase" is opposed to *descent* — that all things come to the owner either by *descent* or by *purchase*, and that whatever does not come through operation of law by *descent* is *purchased*, although it may be the free gift of a donor. Thus, if land be devised by will to A. in fee, he takes by *purchase*, or to B. for life, remainder to A. and his heirs, B. being a stranger to A., A. takes by *purchase*; but upon the death of A., his eldest son would take by *descent*.

English lawyers sometimes use these terms metaphorically, like *Lepidus*. Thus a Law Lord who has suffered much from hereditary gout, although very temperate in his habits, says, "I take it by *descent*, not by *purchase*." Again, Lord Chancellor Eldon, a very bad shot, having insisted on going out quite alone to shoot, and boasted of the heavy bag of game which he had brought home, Lord Stowell, insinuating that he had filled it with game bought from a poacher, used to say, "My brother takes his game — not by *descent*, but by — *purchase*;" — this being a pendant to

---

* So in "the Second Part of Henry IV.," Act IV. Sc. 4, the King, who had usurped the crown, says to the Prince of Wales—

> For what in me was purchas'd
> Falls upon thee in a more fairer sort.

i.e. I took by *purchase*, you will take by *descent*.

another joke Lord Stowell was fond of — "My brother, the Chancellor, in vacation goes out with his gun to kill — time."

CORIOLANUS

In this drama, in which we should not expect to find any allusion to English juridical proceedings, Shakespeare shows that he must have been present before some tiresome, testy, choleric judges at Stratford, Warwick, or Westminster,— whom he evidently intends to depict and to satirise,— like my distinguished friend *Charles Dickens*, in his famous report of the trial of *Bardel* v. *Pickwick*, before Mr. Justice Starey, for breach of promise of marriage. Menenius (Act II. Sc. 1), in reproaching the two tribunes, Sicinius and Brutus, with their own offences, which they forget while they inveigh against Coriolanus, says—

> "You wear out a good wholesome forenoon in hearing a cause between an orange-wife and a posset-seller and then re-journ the controversy of three pence to a second day of audience. When you are hearing a matter *between party and party*, if you chance to be pinched with the colic, you make faces like mummers, set up the bloody flag against all patience, and in roaring for a — pot dismiss the controversy pleading more entangled by your hearing: all the peace you make in their cause is, calling both the parties knaves.

Shakespeare here mistakes the duties of the *Tribune* for those of the *Prætor;*— but in truth he was recollecting with disgust what he had himself witnessed in his own country. Nowadays all English judges are exemplary for dispatch, patience, and good temper!!!

ROMEO AND JULIET

The first scene of this romantic drama may be studied by a student of the Inns of Court to acquire a knowledge of the law of "assault and battery," and what will amount to a *justification*. Although Sampson exclaims, "My naked weapon is out: quarrel, I will back thee," he adds, "Let us take the law of our sides; let them begin." Then we learn that neither *frowning*, nor *biting the thumb*, nor answering to a question, "Do you bite your thumb at us, Sir?" "I do bite my thumb, Sir,"— would be enough to support the plea of *se defendendo*.*

---

* To show the ignorance and stupidity of Sir Andrew Aguecheek ('Twelfth Night,' Act IV. Sc. 1) in supposing that *son assault demesne* (or that the Plaintiff gave the first blow) is not a good defence to an action of battery, he is made to say, "I'll have an

The scene ends with old Montagu and old Capulet being bound over, in the English fashion, *to keep the peace,*— in the same manner as two Warwickshire clowns, who had been fighting, might have been dealt with at Charlecote before Sir Thomas Lucy.

⸺

The only other scene in this play I have marked to be noticed for the use of law terms is that between Mercutio and Benvolio, in which they keenly dispute which of the two is the more quarrelsome;— at last Benvolio,— not denying that he had quarrelled with a man for coughing in the street, whereby he wakened Benvolio's dog that lay asleep in the sun,— or that he had quarrelled with another for tying his new shoes with old riband,— contents himself with this *tu quoque* answer to Mercutio:

> An I were so apt to quarrel as thou art, any man should buy
> the *fee-simple of my life* for an hour and a quarter.
>
> (Act III. Sc. 1.)

Talking of the *fee-simple of a man's life*, and calculating how many hours' purchase it was worth, is certainly what might not unnaturally be expected from the clerk of a country attorney.[*]

continued on page 488 . . .

---

action of battery against him, if there be any law in Illyria: *though I struck him first, yet it's no matter for that.*"

[*] So in 'All's Well that Ends Well' (Act IV. Sc. 3) Parolles, the bragging cowardly soldier, is made to talk like a conveyancer in Lincoln's Inn:— "He will sell the *fee-simple of his salvation . . .* and *cut the entail from all remainders.*"

OCTOBER

MEASURE FOR MEASURE: "THE GOLDEN METWAND"

By John V. Orth, with the assistance of Joseph L. Hyde

On the return from his apparent absence, the Duke arranges to meet *at the consecrated fount / A league below the city; and from thence, / By cold gradation and well-balanced form, / We shall proceed with Angelo.* The distance (and temperature) are measured by degrees; the scales *well-balanced.* Throughout the play, images of weights and measures appear and reappear. Isabella admits, *We cannot weigh our brother with ourself.* Angelo, who before he succumbs to temptation prides himself on his *gravity,* which he would not change *for an idle plume, / Which the air beats for vain,* is soon taunting Isabella: *Say what you can, my false o'erweighs your true.* And the Duke pretends to disbelieve Isabella because if Angelo were guilty, *he would have weighed thy brother by himself, / And not have cut him off.* Finally dropping his disguise, the Duke truly *proceeds with Angelo* — proceeds to have him properly *scaled,* declaring the measure of justice (and the play's title): *'An Angelo for Claudio, death for death!' / Haste still pays haste, and leisure answers leisure, / Like doth quit like, and MEASURE still FOR MEASURE.* To Angelo, the Duke now appears *like power divine,* measuring him by the divine standard: "With what judgement ye judge, ye shall be judged, and with what measure ye mete, it shall be measured to you againe."[1]

Proper measurement is a legal preoccupation. Land is measured out by metes and bounds, marked off in Shakespeare's day by a "metewand" or "metwand." Sir Edward Coke, England's greatest expert on property law and vigorous opponent of royal absolutism, lectured King James that the law was "the golden metwand and measure to try the causes of the subjects; and which protected His Majesty in safety and peace,"[2] words the King found insulting if not treasonous. There is another maxim, Coke told the House of Commons: "The common law hath admeasured the King's prerogative. It is not I, Edward Coke, that speaks it but the records that speak it."[3] And John Selden, contemporary of Coke and Shakespeare, expressed the common law's fear of discretionary justice by his famous comparison of equity to the length of the Chancellor's foot: "For law we have a measure, know what to trust to: equity is according to the conscience of him that is Chancellor, and as it is larger or narrower, so is equity. 'Tis all one as if they should make the standard for the measure we call a foot, to be the Chancellor's foot."[4]

continued on page 493 . . .

STATE V. CUNNINGHAM
2008 WL 4447694 ¶18 (Ohio App. 2d Dist. October 3, 2008)

James A. Brogan, Judge

Cunningham sought to obtain an intangible "valuable benefit" from H.D. Despite his assertions to the contrary, we are unconvinced that he was seeking to obtain her recantation for its own sake. Rather, we think that he wanted to obtain the valuable benefits that her recantation would bring — benefits such as the ability to deny that he had committed a crime . . . . Shakespeare recognized the importance of individual reputation in 1604:

> Who steals my purse steals trash; 'tis something, nothing;
> Twas mine; 'tis his, and has been slave to thousands;
> But he that filches from me my good name
> Robs me of that which not enriches him,
> And makes me poor indeed. *Othello*, act III.

---

[1] Matt. 7:1-2 (Geneva Bible).

[2] 12 Co. 65, 77 Eng. Rep. 1343.

[3] Quoted in Catherine Drinker Bowen, *The Lion Under the Throne: The Life and Times of Sir Edward Coke* 291 (1956).

[4] *Table Talk of John Selden* 43 (Frederick Pollock ed. 1927) (spelling and punctuation modernized).

❧ OCTOBER ❧

SUN	MON	TUES	WED	THUR	FRI	SAT
				1	2	3
4	5	6	7	8	9	10
11	12	13	14	15	16	17
18	19	20	21	22	23	24
25	26	27	28	29	30	31

SONNET 116

William Shakespeare

Let me not to the marriage of true minds
Admit impediments. Love is not love
Which alters when it alteration finds,
Or bends with the remover to remove.
O no, it is an ever-fixèd mark
That looks on tempests and is never shaken;
It is the star to every wand'ring bark,
Whose worth's unknown, although his height be taken.
Love's not time's fool, though rosy lips and cheeks
Within his bending sickle's compass come.
Love alters not with his brief hours and weeks,
But bears it out ev'n to the edge of doom.
If this be error and upon me proved,
I never writ, nor no man ever loved.

ARIS V. MUKASEY

Robert A. Katzmann[†]

With disturbing frequency, this Court encounters evidence of ineffective representation by attorneys retained by immigrants seeking legal status in this country. We have previously indicated that ineffective assistance of counsel can constitute an "exceptional circumstance" warranting the reopening of a deportation order entered in absentia. *See Twum v. INS*, 411 F.3d 54, 59 n.4 (2d Cir. 2005). We write today to establish what we would have thought self-evident: A lawyer who misadvises his client concerning the date of an immigration hearing and then fails to inform the client of the deportation order entered in absentia (or the ramifications thereof) has provided ineffective assistance. We further clarify that such misadvice may constitute ineffective assistance of counsel even where it is supplied by a paralegal providing scheduling information on behalf of a lawyer.

Petitioner Garfield Livern St. Valentine Aris, a native and citizen of Jamaica, seeks review of a decision of the Board of Immigration Appeals ("BIA") denying his motion to rescind an order of deportation entered in absentia and reopen his deportation proceedings.[2] *In re Garfield Livern St. Valentine Aris*, No. A37 776 177 (BIA Feb. 26, 2007). The Immigration Judge ("IJ"), Sandy Hom, ordered Aris deported on May 3, 1995, following his failure to appear at the hearing scheduled for the previous day. *In re Garfield Livern St. Valentine Aris*, No. A37 776 177 (Immig. Ct. N.Y. City May 3, 1995). For the reasons set forth below, we grant the petition, vacate the denial of petitioner's motion to reopen, and remand the case for further proceedings consistent with this opinion.

[†] Judge of the United States Court of Appeals for the Second Circuit, joined by , joined by Judges Fred I. Parker and Reena Raggi. This opinion is reported at 517 F.3d 595 (2d Cir. 2008). Editor's note: Footnote 1 is not necessary for our purposes, and so we cut it.

[2] Under the current system, what were once known as "deportation" proceedings are now termed "removal" proceedings. Aris's case, however, arose under former § 242 of the Immigration and Nationality Act, which governed deportation proceedings.

BACKGROUND

In 1983, at the age of twelve, Aris entered the United States as a lawful immigrant. Aris's wife, daughter, stepdaughter, and mother all reside in the United States and are citizens of this country. Aris financially supports his wife and stepdaughter. He has no close family members in Jamaica.

On August 21, 1991, Aris was convicted after a guilty plea in the United States District Court, Western District of New York of unlawful possession of cocaine in violation of 21 U.S.C. § 844(a). *United States v. Aris*, No. 91-00150-01(MAT) (W.D.N.Y. Aug. 21, 1991). The district court sentenced him to three years' probation and imposed a $1000 fine and a $25 special assessment.

Sixteen months later, the Immigration and Naturalization Service ("INS") issued an order to show cause charging that Aris was subject to deportation based on the 1991 cocaine conviction pursuant to what was then § 241(a)(2)(B)(i) of the Immigration and Nationality Act ("INA"), 8 U.S.C. § 1251(a)(2)(B)(i) (1992) (current version at INA § 237(a)(2)(B)(i), 8 U.S.C. § 1227(a)(2)(B)(i)). After he received the order to show cause, Aris hired David Scheinfeld of David Scheinfeld & Associates, PLLC to represent him in the immigration proceedings.

On April 15, 1994, accompanied by an associate from the firm, Aris attended a hearing before the IJ. Aris conceded deportability, and the IJ scheduled a hearing for May 2, 1995. In addition, the IJ granted Aris permission to apply for discretionary relief under former § 212(c) of the INA, 8 U.S.C. § 1182(c) (1994) (repealed by the Illegal Immigration Reform and Immigrant Responsibility Act of 1996 ("IIRIRA"), Pub. L. No. 104-208, § 304(b), 110 Stat. 3009-597 (Sept. 30, 1996)), but required that Aris do so by the end of business that day.[3] Counsel failed to file the application for § 212(c) relief, which in and of itself likely constitutes ineffective assistance of counsel in light of the equities of Aris's case.[4] *See Rabiu v. INS*, 41 F.3d 879, 882-84 (2d Cir. 1994).

---

[3] Former § 212(c) of the INA gave the Attorney General discretion to grant a waiver of certain grounds of deportability to a subset of legal permanent residents. Section 212(c) was repealed in 1996 by IIRIRA, but § 212(c) relief remains available to aliens who pleaded guilty to certain crimes prior to the enactment of IIRIRA and who otherwise would have been eligible for that relief. *See INS v. St. Cyr*, 533 U.S. 289, 326 (2001); *see also Blake v. Carbone*, 489 F.3d 88, 93-99 (2d Cir. 2007).

[4] Although the issue is not before us on appeal and we cannot know what a fuller review of the record would yield, Aris would seem to have a compelling case for § 212(c) relief in light of the "social and humane considerations" of his case. *Douglas v. INS*, 28 F.3d 241, 243-44 (2d Cir. 1994) (quoting *Matter of Marin*, 16 I. & N. Dec. 581, 584 (BIA 1978)).

There is no real disagreement about the key facts of this case. On May 2, 1995, having heard nothing from his lawyer, Aris phoned the law firm to check the status of the hearing. Aris spoke to a paralegal at the office who told him something to the effect that the firm calendar did not indicate any hearing scheduled for that day and that no attorneys were available to speak with him. Aris states that he relied on this information and did not appear at the May 2, 1995 hearing.

Evidently, the paralegal subsequently telephoned the immigration court, learned there was in fact a hearing scheduled, and tried to obtain an adjournment. But by the time she reached the court, the determination had been made to deport Aris. No one from the law firm ever contacted Aris to inform him that the paralegal had been mistaken concerning the hearing date or that he had been ordered deported in absentia.

Aris did receive a letter, dated September 25, 1995, informing him that the INS had made arrangements for his deportation. Aris took the letter to a lawyer at the firm, who assured Aris that he would take care of everything.

That lawyer then filed a motion to reopen the deportation proceedings on November 7, 1995. In an affidavit, the lawyer stated that the date of Aris's hearing was not noted on the firm calendar and that the associate who initially represented Aris had subsequently left the firm. This calendar error explained the failure of counsel to appear at the May 2, 1995 hearing. Nowhere in the affidavit or other motion papers, however, did counsel convey that Aris had relied on the erroneous information relayed to him by the paralegal. The IJ promptly denied the motion. Counsel filed an appeal of the IJ's denial of the motion to reopen, which suffered from the same defect, and the BIA dismissed the appeal.

Aris's lawyers persisted in their failure to inform him of the status of the case. For nearly a decade, Aris lived under the mistaken belief that the law firm had resolved his immigration problems. This is apparent from the fact that, in 2004, Aris took initial steps toward applying for United States citizenship.

It was only on June 1, 2005, upon his arrest on the outstanding 1995 deportation order, that Aris learned that the deportation proceedings had not been resolved in his favor and that he had been living in violation of a deportation order. Almost immediately, Aris obtained new counsel who

---

The offense that triggered Aris's deportation proceeding was a relatively minor drug offense. Deporting Aris would separate him from his mother, daughter, step-daughter and wife and deliver him to a country where he has spent virtually no time since emigrating at the age of twelve and has no social or familial connections.

proceeded to file a number of factually erroneous and legally flawed submissions on his behalf. None of these submissions discussed prior counsel's role in Aris's failure to appear at the May 2, 1995 deportation proceeding, and none achieved the desired result. All in all, Aris was detained for nine months. Without Aris's income from the two jobs he had worked, his wife and stepdaughter were unable to pay rent. They were evicted from the family apartment and left with no choice but to move to a homeless shelter.

At year's end, Aris's family, concerned about his representation, sought the assistance of attorneys at Cleary Gottlieb Steen & Hamilton LLP, who agreed to represent him pro bono. New counsel promptly investigated the various errors committed by Aris's prior counsel and filed disciplinary complaints against them with the New York and New Jersey bars. New counsel also collected the necessary documents and moved before the BIA to reopen Aris's deportation proceedings, rescind the order entered in absentia, and remand the case to the immigration court. [5]

Aris's motion alleged ineffective assistance of prior counsel. It finally explained for the first time that Aris failed to appear at the May 2, 1995 hearing because a paralegal at his first lawyer's office wrongly informed him that there was no hearing scheduled for that day.

In a decision dated February 26, 2007, the BIA denied Aris's motion, claiming that it had "already addressed the circumstances of his failure to appear" in a prior ruling. [6] The decision gave no indication that the BIA considered the new information that Aris neglected to appear at the May 2, 1995 hearing in reliance on erroneous advice from a paralegal at the firm representing him. Aris now petitions for review of that decision.

Discussion

We review the BIA's denial of a motion to reopen for abuse of discretion. *See Twum*, 411 F.3d at 58. An abuse of discretion may be found where the

---

[5] The diligence of Aris's counsel at Cleary Gottlieb, including Lewis Liman, Esq. and the advocate before this Court, Tanisha Massie, Esq., is commendable. We thank them for their service and encourage other attorneys to follow in their example.

[6] The BIA also stated that it lacked jurisdiction to hear the motion to reopen because it should have been filed with the IJ in the first instance. Even the government concedes that this rationale is "superfluous and unworthy of this Court's attention." Given the multiple motions previously filed in this case, the instant filing encompassed more than merely a motion to rescind an in absentia order. *Cf. Matter of Gonzalez-Lopez*, 20 I. & N. Dec. 644, 646 (BIA 1993). Indeed, the IJ and BIA explicitly advised Aris that only the BIA had jurisdiction to hear the instant motion.

BIA's decision "provides no rational explanation, inexplicably departs from established policies, is devoid of any reasoning, or contains only summary or conclusory statements; that is to say, where the Board has acted in an arbitrary or capricious manner." *Ke Zhen Zhao v. U.S. Dep't of Justice*, 265 F.3d 83, 93 (2d Cir. 2001) (internal citations omitted).

Under the version of the INA applicable to this case, an alien ordered deported in absentia may reopen the case by filing a motion within 180 days after the order of deportation "if the alien demonstrates that the failure to appear was because of exceptional circumstances." INA § 242B(c)(3)(A), 8 U.S.C. § 1252b(c)(3)(A) (1994) (current version at INA § 240(b)(5)(C), 8 U.S.C. § 1229a(b)(5)(C)). That provision defines exceptional·circumstances as "circumstances (such as serious illness of the alien or death of an immediate relative of the alien, but not including less compelling circumstances) beyond the control of the alien." INA § 242B(f)(2), 8 U.S.C. § 1252b(f)(2) (1994) (amended and renumbered as INA § 240(e)(1), 8 U.S.C. § 1229a(e)(1)). We now join our sister circuits in concluding that, under BIA precedent applicable to the pre-1996 version of the INA as well as its current iteration, a lawyer's inaccurate advice to his client concerning an immigration hearing date can constitute "exceptional circumstances" excusing the alien's failure to appear at a deportation hearing, see *In re Grijalva-Barrera*, 21 I. & N. Dec. 472, 474 (BIA 1996); *Galvez-Vergara v. Gonzales*, 484 F.3d 798, 801-02 (5th Cir. 2007); *Lo v. Ashcroft*, 341 F.3d 934, 937-38 (9th Cir. 2003), and meriting the reopening of an in absentia deportation order, see *Twum*, 411 F.3d at 59 n.4.[7]

The government acknowledges that the "only issue of consequence" in this appeal is whether the advice that Aris received from the first law firm representing him on May 2, 1995 constitutes ineffective assistance of counsel, justifying the reopening of this case.[8] The government does not meaningfully contest Aris's account of his conversation with the paralegal beyond noting some ambiguity in the record concerning whether the paralegal told Aris something akin to, "you do not have a hearing," or rather, "our records indicate that you do not have a hearing scheduled."

---

[7] The deadline for moving to reopen may be equitably tolled until the ineffective assistance of counsel "is, or should have been, discovered by a reasonable person in the situation." *Iavorski v. INS*, 232 F.3d 124, 134 (2d Cir. 2000). The government does not raise a due-diligence challenge to equitable tolling in this case.

[8] The government does not challenge that Aris has satisfied the evidentiary requirements established by the BIA for claims of ineffective assistance of counsel. See *Matter of Lozada*, 19 I. & N. Dec. 637 (BIA 1988).

We conclude that any such ambiguity is immaterial, and we are troubled by the government's unwillingness at oral argument to recognize it as such. Even if the paralegal told Aris only that the firm records did not indicate a scheduled hearing, Aris, an immigrant with limited familiarity with American immigration law, acted reasonably when he relied on this information and concluded that he did not need to appear before the IJ. "One reason that aliens . . . retain legal assistance in the first place is because they assume that an attorney will know how to comply with the procedural details that make immigration proceedings so complicated." *Iturribarria v. INS*, 321 F.3d 889, 901 (9th Cir. 2003).

The BIA's February 26, 2007 opinion, moreover, did not discuss this evidence. The omission is striking in light of BIA precedent that misadvice from counsel concerning a petitioner's need to appear at a hearing constitutes exceptional circumstances warranting the reopening of a removal order entered in absentia. *See In re Grijalva-Barrera*, 21 I. & N. Dec. at 474. Because this evidence had not been presented earlier, neither the IJ nor the BIA had previously considered it. Accordingly, the BIA erred when it rested on its prior decisions in rejecting this claim. In not addressing the petitioner's new evidence of ineffective assistance or providing a rational explanation for its departure from its own precedent concerning when such ineffectiveness constitutes exceptional circumstances, the BIA abused its discretion. *See Douglas v. INS*, 28 F.3d at 243.

The importance of quality representation is especially acute to immigrants, a vulnerable population who come to this country searching for a better life, and who often arrive unfamiliar with our language and culture, in economic deprivation and in fear. In immigration matters, so much is at stake — the right to remain in this country, to reunite a family, or to work. While binding Second Circuit precedent holds that aliens in deportation proceedings have "no specific right to counsel," the Fifth Amendment does require that such proceedings comport with due process of the law. *Jian Yun Zheng v. U.S. Dep't of Justice*, 409 F.3d 43, 46 (2d Cir. 2005). Because the attorney conduct described herein so clearly ran afoul of the standard embodied in *In re Grijalva-Barrera*, 21 I. & N. Dec. 472, we need not pursue the issue of due process. Nevertheless, given the disturbing pattern of ineffectiveness evidenced in the record in this case (and, with alarming frequency, in other immigration cases before us), we reiterate that due process concerns may arise when retained counsel provides representation in an immigration proceeding that falls so far short of professional duties as to "impinge[] upon the fundamental fairness of the hearing." *Saleh v. U.S. Dep't of Justice*, 962 F.2d 234, 241 (2d Cir. 1992).

Members of the bar enjoy a monopoly on legal practice, "a profession-alized system designed in large part around [their] needs." David Luban, *Lawyers and Justice* 286 (1988). And for that reason, among others, lawyers have a duty to render competent services to their clients. *See* Robert W. Gordon, *The Independence of Lawyers*, 68 B.U. L. Rev. 1, 6 (1988) ("These freedoms are usually analyzed as part of a social bargain: they are public privileges awarded in exchange for public benefits."). When lawyers representing immigrants fail to live up to their professional obligations, it is all too often the immigrants they represent who suffer the consequences. *See generally* Robert A. Katzmann, *The Legal Profession and the Unmet Needs of the Immigrant Poor*, 21 Geo. J. Legal Ethics 3, 8 (2008).

We appreciate that, unfortunately, calendar mishaps will from time to time occur. *See, e.g., Pincay v. Andrews*, 389 F.3d 853 (9th Cir. 2004) (en banc). But the failure to communicate such mistakes, once discovered, to the client, and to take all necessary steps to correct them is more than regrettable — it is unacceptable. It is nondisclosure that turns the ineffec-tive assistance of a mere scheduling error into more serious malpractice. *See generally* Lisa G. Lerman, *Lying to Clients*, 138 U. Pa. L. Rev. 659, 725 (1990).

In sum, to the extent there was any uncertainty, we hold today that the logic of *In re Grijalva-Barrera* applies with equal force where the com-munication at issue involves the incorrect — and uncorrected — advice of a paralegal speaking on behalf of an attorney as to the scheduling of an immigration hearing. In addition, *In re Grijalva-Barrera* applies to com-ments, such as the one at issue in the instant case, concerning whether or not a hearing appears on the law firm's official schedule.

Mr. Aris's prior attorneys failed spectacularly to honor their profes-sional obligation to him and to the legal system they were duty-bound to serve. Governmental authorities, whatever their roles, must be attentive to such lapses that so grievously undermine the administration of justice. Accordingly, we remand so Aris may have his § 212(c) application consid-ered on the merits.

CONCLUSION

For the reasons set forth above, we GRANT the petition for review, VACATE the decision of the BIA and REMAND this case for further pro-ceedings consistent with this opinion.

SHAKESPEARE'S LEGAL ACQUIREMENTS

(continued from page 476)

John Lord Campbell

POEMS

With a view to your inquiry respecting the learning of Shakespeare I have now, my dear Mr. Payne Collier, gone through all his plays,— and I can venture to speak of their contents with some confidence, having been long familiar with them. His Poems are by no means so well known to me; for, although I have occasionally looked into them, and I am not blind to their beauties, I must confess that I never could discover in them (like some of his enthusiastic admirers) the same proofs of surpassing genius which render him immortal as a dramatist. But a cursory perusal of them does discover the propensity to legal thoughts and words which might be expected in an attorney's clerk who takes to rhyming.

I shall select a few instances, without unnecessarily adding any comment.

FROM *VENUS AND ADONIS*

"But when the *heart's attorney* once is mute,
The *client* breaks as desperate in the *suit*."

———▲———

"Which purchase if thou make for fear of slips
Set thy *seal-manual* on my *wax-red lips*."

———▲———

"Her *pleading* hath deserved a *greater fee*."

FROM THE *RAPE OF LUCRECE*

"Dim *register* and *notary* of shame."

———▲———

"For me I force not argument a straw,
Since that *my case is past the help of law*."

———▲———

"No rightful *plea* might plead for justice there."

———▲———

"Hath served a *dumb arrest* upon his tongue."

From the Sonnets

"When to the *sessions of sweet silent thought*
I *summon up* remembrance of things past."

"So should that beauty which you *hold in lease*."

"And summer's *lease* hath all too short a date."

"And 'gainst thyself a *lawful plea* commence."

"But be contented; when that fell *arrest*
Without all bail shall carry me away."*

"Of faults concealed, wherein I am *attainted*."

"Which works on *leases* of short numbered hours."

"*Lord of my love*, to whom in *vassalage*
Thy merit hath my duty strongly knit,
To thee I send this written embassage."†

"And I myself am *mortgag'd*."

"Why so large cost, having so *short a lease*?"‡

"So should that beauty, which you *hold in lease*,
Find no *determination*."§

---

* Death is the sheriff's officer, strict in his arrest, and will take no bail.
† This is the beginning of a love-letter, in the language of a vassal doing homage to his liege lord.
‡ Taxing an overcharge in the attorney's bill of costs.
§ The word "determination" is always used by lawyers instead of "end."

Sonnet XLVI

"Mine Eye and Heart are at a mortal war
How to divide the conquest of thy sight;
Mine Eye my Heart thy picture's sight would bar,
My Heart mine Eye the freedom of that right.
My Heart doth plead that thou in him cost lie
(A closet never pierced with crystal eyes),
But the Defendant doth that plea deny,
And says in him thy fair appearance lies.
To 'cide this title is impannelled
A quest of thoughts, all tenants to the Heart;
And by their *verdict* is determined
The clear Eye's moiety, and the dear Heart's part;
   As thus: mine Eyes' due is shine outward part,
   And my Heart's right, shine inward love of heart."

I need not go further than this sonnet, which is so intensely legal in its language and imagery, that without a considerable knowledge of English forensic procedure it cannot be fully understood. A lover being supposed to have made a *conquest* of [*i.e.* to have gained by *purchase*] his mistress, his *Eye* and his *Heart*, holding as *joint-tenants*, have a contest as to how she is to be partitioned between them,— each moiety then to be held in severally. There are regular Pleadings in the suit, the *Heart* being represented as Plaintiff and the *Eye* as Defendant. At last issue is joined on what the one affirms and the other denies. Now a jury [in the nature of an inquest] is to be impannelled to 'cide [decide] and by their verdict to apportion between the litigating parties the subject matter to be divided. The jury fortunately are unanimous, and after due deliberation find for the *Eye* in respect of the lady's outward form, and for the *Heart* in respect of her inward love.

Surely Sonnet XLVI. smells as potently of the attorney's office as any of the stanzas penned by Lord Kenyon while an attorney's clerk in Wales.

continued on page 529 . . .

THE TOP TEN THINGS
I LEARNED FROM

APPRENDI, BLAKELY, BOOKER, RITA, KIMBROUGH AND GALL

Richard G. Kopf[†]

As a district judge, I read with interest, and even tried to follow, the Supreme Court's sentencing opinions in *Apprendi*, *Blakely*, *Booker*, *Rita*, *Kimbrough* and *Gall*. With tongue partly in cheek, here, in descending order, are the top ten things I learned from those missives:

10. Following the Court's approach, always put off to tomorrow what you can do today.

9. You don't need experience in actually sentencing people in order to totally screw up the law of sentencing. It is telling and painfully obvious that not a single Justice ever had to look a federal defendant in the eye while not knowing what law to apply.

8. Footnote 9 in *Blakely* ("The Federal Guidelines are not before us, and we express no opinion on them.") is the biggest practical joke in the history of American law. See lesson One below.

7. The "merits" and "remedial" opinions in *Booker* satisfy George Orwell's definition of "Doublethink." That is, the two opinions, and Justice Ginsburg's swing vote to make both the law, reveal "the power of holding two contradictory beliefs in one's mind simultaneously, and accepting both of them."

[†] United States District Judge, District of Nebraska. This article originally appeared at OSJCL Amici: Views from the Field (January 2008), osjcl.blogspot.com. Copyright © 2008. Reprinted by permission of the author and the publisher.

6. Never impose a sentence that is too harsh or too lenient. To quote Baby Bear, make it "just right" or, perhaps more importantly, to satisfy Justice Breyer, make sure it is just "reasonable."

5. Some sentencing judges used to take the Supreme Court seriously, but that got harder and harder beginning with and following *Apprendi*.

4. In an Ivy League sort of way, it makes sense to address the "crack" question fifteen years after everyone else knew something was terribly wrong. See lesson One below.

3. Justice Scalia's dictum should be rewritten this way: The rule of law is the law of rules except when it isn't.

2. Sentencing judges can be divided into two groups — those who are damn sure they're right and those (like me) who have no clue.

1. There are a lot of really good, hard-working people "in the field" plus tens of thousands of defendants who deserved far better than the seven years of "water boarding" that ensued between *Apprendi* and *Gall*.

We have an America that, in
Bob Dylan's phrase, is busy
being born, not busy dying.

James Earl Carter (1976)

NOVEMBER

MENS REA: BAD INTENT

By John V. Orth, with the assistance of Joseph L. Hyde

At the very beginning of Glanville Williams' treatise on Criminal Law, he quotes Marianna's moving plea to the Duke to pardon Angelo — *His act did not o'ertake his bad intent, / And must be buried but as an intent / That perished by the way. Thoughts are no subjects, / Intents but merely thoughts*[1] — and Chief Justice William Rehnquist used the quotation to illustrate the rule that "in the criminal law, both a culpable *mens rea* and a criminal *actus reus* are generally required for an offense to occur."[2]

One Shakespeare scholar has seen in these lines a poetic translation of the argument made by a serjeant at law in a sixteenth century case: "For the imagination of the mind to do wrong, without an act done, is not pun-

---

[1] Glanville Williams, *Criminal Law* 6 (2d ed. 1961).

[2] U.S. v. Apfelbaum, 445 U.S. 115, 132 n. 13 (1980) (Rehnquist, C.J.). Rehnquist also quoted Shakespeare in a later case, although not from *Measure for Measure*. Milkovich v. Lorain Journal Co., 497 U.S. 1, 12 (1990) (quoting Iago's "good name" speech in *Othello* 3.3.160-66). He could just have easily used the Duke's speech in *Measure for Measure* on the subject of calumny: *No might nor greatness in mortality / Can censure 'scape; back-wounding calumny / The whitest virtue strikes.*

ishable in our law; neither is the resolution to do that wrong, which he does not, punishable, but the doing of the act is the only point which the law regards, for until the act is done it cannot be an offence to the world."[3] Another heard an echo of Sir Edward Coke's speech as Attorney General at the trial of the Earls of Essex and Southampton (the latter was Shakespeare's patron): "By the law the thought or imagination of the death of the Prince is treason; but because the thoughts are only known to God, it is not permitted to be so adjudged, till they appear by discovery either by word or writing, or some outward act."[4] Queen Elizabeth herself, in trying to calm the religious controversies during her reign, avowed that she had no wish to "make a window into men's souls."[5]

continued on page 537 . . .

⊷◦⊷

SOMMERFIELD V. CITY OF CHICAGO

2008 WL 4786509 n.10 (N.D. Ill. November 3, 2008)

Jeffrey N. Cole, Magistrate Judge

As the instant case shows, parties who do not pay heed to Shakespeare's injunction — "Defer no time, delays have dangerous ends." *Henry VI*, Part I (1592) Act III, sc. ii 1.33 — imperil their own interests. The Seventh Circuit is partial to *Twelfth Night*. *Sanders v. Venture Stores, Inc.*, 56 F.3d 771, 775 (7th Cir. 1995) ("'In delay there lies no plenty.'"). No matter. The point is the same.

---

[3] Hales v. Petit, 1 Plow. 253, 259, 75 Eng. Rep. 387, 397 (C.P. 1564) (Serjeant Walsh). See W. Nicholas Knight, *Shakespeare's Hidden Life: Shakespeare at the Law, 1585-1595*, at 231 (1973).

[4] Quoted in Catherine Drinker Bowen, *The Lion and the Throne: The Life and Times of Sir Edward Coke* 145 (1956). Compare Coke's insistence on an "outward act" as an element of the crime of treason with the American constitutional requirement of proof of an "overt Act." U.S. Const. art. III, § 3, cl. 1 ("No Person shall be convicted of Treason unless on the Testimony of two Witnesses to the same overt Act, or on Confession in open Court.").

[5] Quoted in J.B. Black, *Reign of Elizabeth, 1558-1603*, at 23 (2d ed. 1959).

❧ NOVEMBER ❧

SUN	MON	TUES	WED	THUR	FRI	SAT
1	2	3	4	5	6	7
8	9	10	11	12	13	14
15	16	17	18	19	20	21
22	23	24	25	26	27	28
29	30					

LAW & . . .

Law schools have been showing great interest in hiring faculty with terminal degrees in fields other than law. On its website, the Northwestern University School of Law provides a nice snapshot of some of the results of this development (www.law.northwestern.edu/faculty/):

FACULTY RESEARCH & ACHIEVEMENT

Northwestern Law students have access to the most interdisciplinary and highly-credentialed research faculty in the nation. No other law school can boast as high a percentage of PhD-trained faculty members.

The following charts show the comparative percentages of the top 14 law schools (as ranked by *U.S. News and World Report*) and the distribution of Northwestern Law's research faculty with PhDs by discipline. Northwestern Law has the highest percentage (45%) of full-time research faculty with social science PhDs in the nation.

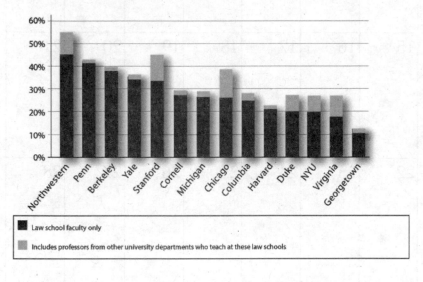

Law school faculty only

Includes professors from other university departments who teach at these law schools

NORTHWESTERN LAW RESEARCH FACULTY PHDS BY DISCIPLINE

Business	1	Psychology	3
Economics	7	Philosophy	1
Political Science	5	History	2
Anthropology	1	Sociology	1
	Math	1	

THE REAL GUANTÁNAMO

from

LAW AND THE LONG WAR: THE FUTURE OF JUSTICE IN THE AGE OF TERROR

Benjamin Wittes[†]

The weirdness of the American naval base at Guantánamo Bay, Cuba, beggars easy description. Large iguanas roam the forty-five-square-mile tract of land as though they own the place. At roughly two thirds the size of Washington D.C., Guantánamo sits on either side of the bay that gave the base its name. Heavily armed Coast Guard speedboats zoom back and forth across the water, passing off-duty personnel lolling about on pontoon boats that motor pacifically in the lagoons off the main channel. Guantánamo is not far off America's shores, barely past Miami — a quick three-hour hop by Gulfstream jet from Andrews Air Force Base near Washington. And despite its being on the land mass of one of this country's most implacable enemies, you don't need a passport to get there. At the same time, it's a world away. The detention facilities there constitute a kind of prison within a prison, a lockup located in an oasis of America wedged between a sea of Cuban communism and the sea itself. And while you may have little sense of leaving the United States when you travel to Guantánamo, in a strange recognition of the facility's foreign status, you do need your passport to get back home.

The very oddities that make Guantánamo such a peculiar place to visit render it operationally — though not optically — ideal as a detention site. At once secure and nearby, Guantánamo operations are not subject to the discontent or objections of the host government. And at least until the

---

† Benjamin Wittes is a Fellow and Research Director in Public Law at the Brookings Institution. *The Real Guantanamo, from* LAW AND THE LONG WAR by Benjamin Wittes. Copyright © 2008 by Benjamin Wittes. Used by permission of The Penguin Press, a division of Penguin Group (USA) Inc., and of the author.

outset of the war on terrorism, successive administrations had assumed as well that the area lay outside the purview of the American courts. At Guantánamo, they reasoned, the government can do as it likes — as long as it can take the political heat. And so, amid the lizards and the blazing heat, the military built a set of detention camps, which have indelibly etched into the public mind images of shackled, hooded prisoners in cages.

The images, however they might dominate public perceptions, bear little relation to Guantánamo's contemporary reality, which is coolly professional. The detention facilities at the base vary a great deal. As of April 2007, when I visited Guantánamo, only Camp 1 still had cells with mesh walls — and the military was then phasing detainees out of there as it completed its new facilities. Camp 4, which houses relatively compliant detainees, looks a lot like a basic prisoner-of-war camp. Dormitory-like barracks open onto a courtyard, of which detainees have the run. Detainees have access to English classes. It's not a resort, by any means, but inmates in many prisons in the United States would surely see it as an improvement were they shipped there. Camps 5 and 6, by contrast, are pretty grim. Built for the less cooperative and more dangerous detainees, they are the equivalent of a modern "supermax" prison. The facilities are clean, and detainees are fed well and have more exercise time than comparable high-security prisoners in the United States. Still, the military keeps them locked down most of the day in individual cells. It candidly admits that how much cooperation a detainee offers in interrogations helps determine in which camp he lives.

Running Guantánamo is a nightmare. Guards face intense stress. Between July 2005 and August 2006, detainees conducted 432 "bodily fluid attacks." Detainees in Camp 4 — the facility for the most compliant detainees — conducted a violent uprising. Suicide attempts and hunger strikes have occurred relatively frequently — often requiring involuntary feeding to keep detainees alive. Maintaining the fewer than four hundred detainees present at that time required almost eleven hundred guards. The tension at Guantánamo is so palpable that one has no trouble imagining how, but for stringent military discipline, a site like this could degrade into anarchic brutality — as Abu Ghraib degraded in the face of command failures.[1]

Detention itself, even under worse conditions and of many more people, does not normally spark the controversy that has attended

---

[1] The information in these paragraphs was either given in briefings by uniformed service members or observed first hand on a site visit to Guantánamo in April 2007.

Guantánamo. America keeps more than two million people under lock and key these days domestically, many of them in prisons that make Guantánamo seem tame. The detainee population in Iraq dwarfs that of Guantánamo by almost two orders of magnitude, and these detainees get *less* legal process — yet they prompt little outcry. Guantánamo differs because detentions there seem to reflect arbitrary government power so close to home yet self-consciously kept offshore in a fashion too clever by half. Detentions there seem somehow punitive, yet the Pentagon has never publicly justified them on an individual basis. Its evidence that the detainees are who it claims mostly remains secret. And many Americans — and a growing international consensus — have come to doubt the very premise that the laws of war permit indefinite detentions of such people without criminal charges supported by proof in court beyond a reasonable doubt using admissible evidence.

Many Americans have come to doubt something else too: the premise that the people detained at Guantánamo warrant incarceration at all. This doubt flows in part from the frankly irresponsible rhetoric the administration used about its captives at the outset of the conflict. Presidential spokesman Ari Fleischer famously called them the "worst of the worst"[2] and Rumsfeld declared them "among the most dangerous, best trained vicious killers on the face of the earth."[3] This kind of talk quite reasonably spawned a cottage industry of doubt and evaluation. A law professor — and habeas lawyer — from Seton Hall University named Mark Denbeaux issued a report in February 2006, which evaluated 517 CSRT summaries of government evidence against detainees. Denbeaux and his coauthor found that 55 percent "of detainees are not determined to have committed any hostile acts against the United States or its coalition allies," that only 8 percent of detainees "were characterized as al Qaeda fighters," and that most detainees were not captured by American forces but by either the Northern Alliance or the Pakistani army.[4] Around the same time, *National Journal* published its own evaluation of the still-sketchy data released from the CSRT process. Far from the "worst of the worst," the magazine con-

---

[2] The transcript of Fleischer's press briefing, given on January 23, 2002, is available at http://www.whitehouse.gov/news/releases/2002/01/20020123-18.html.

[3] The transcript of Rumsfeld's press briefing, given January 27, 2002, en route from Andrews AFB, Maryland to Naval Station Guantánamo Bay, Cuba, is available at http://www.defenselink.mil/transcripts/transcript.aspx?transcriptid=2320.

[4] Mark Denbeaux and Joshua Denbeaux, "Report on Guantánamo Detainees: A Profile of 517 Detainees Through Analysis of Department of Defense Data," February 8, 2006, is available at http://law.shu.edu/news/guantanamo_report_final_2_08_06.pdf.

cluded, "Many [detainees] are not accused of hostilities against the United States or its allies. Most, when captured, were innocent of any terrorist activity, were Taliban foot soldiers at worst, and were often far less than that. And some, perhaps many, are guilty only of being foreigners in Afghanistan or Pakistan at the wrong time."[5] Within a few weeks of the publication of these reports, the *New York Times*, based on CSRT hearing transcripts, had editorialized that "far too many [detainees] seemed to be innocents or lowly foot soldiers simply caught up in the whirlwind after 9/11."[6] A few months later, "far too many" had turned in the eyes of the *Times* editorialists into "hundreds of innocent men . . . jailed at Guantánamo Bay without charges or rudimentary rights."[7] Four short years of the administration's Guantánamo policy had turned the "worst of the worst" into the oppressed of the earth.

This perverse turnabout simply would not have taken place had a strong and open legal architecture guided detention decisions at Guantánamo. Any person at any time can look up the basis for the incarceration of any of the two million people serving time in prisons in the United States. The government charges them in public and subjects its evidence freely to attack at trial. You don't have to go so far as to envision the criminal law as the basis for war-on-terrorism detentions to see how this open application of agreed-upon rules serves to justify criminal convictions over the years and to lessen doubt about the legitimacy of long-term imprisonments. Individual criminal cases provoke debate, sometimes passionate debate, and Americans disagree about numerous policy questions surrounding the criminal justice system at large. But the openness of that system, the fact that it carries out a set of rules we've agreed upon in advance, and the resulting ability of the public to examine each case on its own for compliance with those rules cumulatively ensure that doubts about any given conviction do not erode confidence in the mass of others. By contrast, the review systems the military belatedly set up at Guantánamo lacked all of the elements that would have rendered their judgments credible and durable. The government released no information about the detainees — not even their names — until litigation forced it to make disclosures. The rules it finally did apply, also under pressure from the courts, reflected no sort of consensus as to how to balance fairness and due process against the military's concerns about security and protecting

---

[5] Corine Hegland, "Empty Evidence," *National Journal*, February 3, 2006.
[6] Editorial, "They Came for the Chicken Farmer," *New York Times*, March 8, 2006, A22.
[7] Editorial, "The Real Agenda," *New York Times*, July 16, 2006, section 4, 11.

intelligence sources and methods. And the public consequently could not consider these cases on their individual merits, only as a group.

When the public lacks information about a process to which it has not consented and in which people's long-term liberty is at stake, the government cannot reasonably expect its confidence. Our traditions of public trials and transparency in government action are simply too strong and well entrenched for Americans to tolerate a detention procedure based on trust in executive competence and goodwill to resolve complex disputes over facts and evidence. When the military compounds this basic flaw by releasing information in dribs and drabs and making it painstakingly difficult to figure out what happened to each detainee, when, and why, it breeds suspicion. And the lack of any solid information about the detainees ironically allows each observer to see in them more or less what he or she comes looking for. Those suspicious of the CSRT process had little trouble finding unfairness and arbitrary justice.[8] Journalists came looking for innocent detainees — as is their job — and they found detainees with compelling stories.[9] Some writers seemed to find oppressed innocence everywhere they looked.[10] On the other hand, a team at West Point, looking at the same data the Seton Hall report examined, determined that 73 percent of allegations against detainees described a "demonstrated threat" and 95 percent of allegations described at least a "potential threat."[11]

Over the years, the public data has grown richer. Because the CSRTs and ARBs did not provide a forum in which the government's evidence faced systematic testing, the data still cannot offer a comprehensive portrait of the detainee population at Guantánamo. But the many thousands of declassified pages of analytical memos, allegations, and transcripts related to detainee hearings nonetheless paint a more complicated and interesting portrait of the detainee population that is reflected in most public debate.

---

[8] Mark Denbeaux and Joshua Denbeaux, "No-Hearing Hearings: An Analysis of the Government's Combatant Status Review Tribunals at Guantánamo," November 17, 2006, is available at http://law.shu.edu/news/final_no_hearing_hearings_report.pdf.

[9] See, for example, Neil A. Lewis, "Freedom for Chinese Detainees Hinges on Finding a New Homeland," New York Times, November 8, 2004, A17. See also Carol D. Leonnig, "Panel Ignored Evidence on Detainee," Washington Post, March 27, 2005, Al; Carlotta Gall and Andy Worthington, "Time Runs Out for an Afghan Held by U.S.," New York Times, February 5, 2008, Al.

[10] See, for example, Worthington, The Guantánamo Files.

[11] Joseph Felter and Jarret Brachman, "CTC Report: An Assessment of 516 Combatant Status Review Tribunal (CSRT) Unclassified Summaries," July 25, 2007, is available at http://www.ctc.usma.edu/csrt/CTC-CSRT-Report-072407.pdf.

On one side, the public record now offers, at a minimum, a sketch of the government's CSRT evidence against each detainee — usually just a few sentences of allegations, sometimes significantly more. The government often supplemented these allegations in the annual ARB reviews, the parolelike hearings that followed CSRT judgments. Because the government never carried the burden of supporting its allegations rigorously, its evidence, to whatever extent it has evidence, remains classified, unavailable for the detainee to attack or the public to assess. These records, therefore, do not represent the facts the government could prove but offer a window into what it believes, rightly or wrongly, that its intelligence shows about each detainee.

On the other side, the public record also now generally includes the detainee's side of the story. These data too have limitations. The detainees lacked access to counsel to help them rebut government allegations. Their opportunity to call witnesses was seriously impaired; in fact, in the CSRT process, no detainee managed to call a witness other than those also detained at Guantánamo.[12] They generally lacked the ability to prove their stories true. Nonetheless, in both the CSRT process and during each round of ARB hearings, the military gave each detainee the opportunity to respond to the allegations against him. In the CSRTs, the majority of detainees took that opportunity. The number appearing at their hearings dwindled during the ARBs, but the cumulative impact of these opportunities is that of 572 detainees whose CSRT records the public can access, more than 70 percent made some statement that has been subsequently declassified.

The result is that in most cases, while the public still has nothing quite like the process of testing evidence in an adversarial court proceeding, it does now have some picture of both sides of the story. We can describe in some detail whom the government contends it captured and how those captives describe themselves. We can compare the government's collective portrait with the collective self-portrait of the detainees and examine the areas of congruence and incompatibility of these pictures. We can, in short, figure out how much really stands in dispute concerning this much fought over group of men. And the comparison illuminates a good deal, because it turns out that a lot of information about the detainees is *not* in dispute. Notwithstanding its overblown rhetoric, the government does not deny it has erred in certain cases, and many detainees do not deny their belligerency.

---

[12] Denbeaux and Denbeaux, "No-Hearing Hearings."

Indeed, examining in detail the detainee population brings into stark relief the utter inadequacy of the administration's law-of-war approach to these long-term detentions and the urgent need for a more open and adversarial regime that reflects the will of more than one elected official. The system the military used probably approved the detentions of some innocent men — and the military's tardiness in building any system certainly delayed the release of innocents. But the greatest victim of the administration's failure to forge with Congress a process that separated rigorously and publicly those rightly detained from those wrongly detained was surely the government itself. For in an elaborate game of "heads I win, tails you lose," the government managed to lose in the public arena no matter what the evidence showed. Where CSRTs and ARBs sent detainees home, the government received no credit for this as a substantial check on its power. Where they brought out genuine factual disputes attending particular detentions, they lacked both the procedural rules and the perceived independence to resolve them credibly — the result being that they never served usefully to validate detentions in the public arena. Even, ironically, in the many cases in which no material factual dispute existed between the detainees and the government, the secrecy of the process ensured that the public could not know. This was a needless self-inflicted wound, not only in the public relations arena but also insofar as it invited judicial skepticism and scrutiny. In many cases, a reasonable process would have had the effect not of freeing scary people but of better selling to the world and to the American courts and public the need to keep them locked up and the propriety of doing so.

• • • •

The detainees at Guantánamo came from literally all over the world. More than forty countries saw at least one of their nationals detained there. The lion's share, however, came from only three countries — Afghanistan, Saudi Arabia, and Yemen — which together contributed almost 65 percent of the total population. No other country contributed more than twenty-five detainees. The population at Guantánamo has been in a precipitous decline since even before the CSRT process began. Nearly 800 detainees have passed through Guantánamo at one point or another, yet only 558 detainees were there when the original CSRT process was launched. And of those subjected to ARB review, the military had cleared for release or transfer all but 273 by the time it completed the second round of ARBs in 2007. Actually effectuating these transfers presents enormous logistical headaches — and there has been a years-long lag in some cases between the decision to send detainees home and their actually leaving Guantánamo. But in principle, at least, the military now contends it needs to hold only a rump group of detainees, plus the handful of high-value detainees and the overlapping group it has designated for trial before military commissions. The residual population has continued shrinking over the course of the third round of ARBs, about which the military has not yet made extensive data public. During 2007, the Pentagon repatriated the overwhelming majority of the Saudi nationals — even some it had reason to regard as dangerous — under a program in which the Saudi government has sought to mitigate the risk they pose.[13] In this chapter, I deal almost entirely with data from the CSRTs and the first two rounds of ARBs.

The government's portrait of each detainee starts with a brief summary of evidence given to the detainee as part of the CSRT process. This document, in most cases, contains two categories of allegation. The first is a broad suggestion of some level of association with a group engaged in military hostilities against the United States — overwhelmingly either the Taliban or Al Qaeda or both. The military accused each detainee of being a member, a fighter, or an associate — or sometimes two of these in combination — of these groups. While it isn't quite clear how the military drew lines between these categories, in many instances, it produced a relatively simple top-line allegation. The government, for example, alleged that the detainee population that went through the CSRT process included the following:

- 68 members of Al Qaeda
- 9 Al Qaeda fighters
- 101 people associated with Al Qaeda
- 64 members of the Taliban
- 23 fighters for the Taliban
- 43 people associated with the Taliban[14]

But for many other detainees, the government had a harder time articulating even this highest altitude charge. In some instances, for example, it had understandable difficulty distinguishing between groups that were

---

[13] For information on this program, see Josh White and Robin Wright, "After Guantánamo, 'Reintegration' for Saudis," *Washington Post*, December 10, 2007, A1.

[14] The data reported in this chapter are fleshed out in greater detail in a more technical paper, Benjamin Wittes and Zaahira Wyne, "The Detainee Population of Guantánamo: An Empirical Examination," forthcoming 2008.

tightly intertwined — and therefore had trouble identifying a principal affiliation for individual detainees. The result is that it described 11 detainees as members of *both* Al Qaeda and the Taliban, 109 as affiliates of both groups, and 28 as affiliates of one and fighters for or members of the other.

In other cases, the military struggled to identify the level of attachment a detainee had demonstrated. It labeled four detainees, for example, as either affiliates or members of Al Qaeda and an additional one as either an affiliate or member of the Taliban. In an additional forty-six cases, reflecting an even greater level of ambiguity, it alleged that detainees were tied not to both groups but to *one group or the other*, or, stranger yet, *one group "and/or" the other*. The government accused thirty-nine detainees of being attached to unspecified groups hostile to coalition forces, and in twenty-four cases made no top-line allegations at all.

These troubles with basic classification reflect in some instances the amorphous structure of Al Qaeda and the Taliban. They undoubtedly also sometimes reflect weakness in the government evidence linking detainees to the groups and a certain sloppiness in the military's categorization of and standards for the detainees. Ultimately, the government labeled more than twice as many detainees as associated with the groups than it branded as "members" of them — and it branded almost four times as many detainees "members" as it did "fighters."[15]

Compounding these evidentiary difficulties was the fact that the vast majority of detainees were not captured by American forces. The Pakistani army caught a plurality crossing into their country after the American air attacks in Afghanistan began. The Northern Alliance also caught many detainees. Because a large number of Taliban fighters fled the battlefield in civilian clothing, the circumstances of their belligerency grew murkier than it would have been had they been caught on the battlefield itself. And it grew murkier still because American forces often learned the evidence surrounding their conduct secondhand from forces that lack the professionalism of American military personnel. The fact that U.S. forces offered bounties for Al Qaeda members, though it undoubtedly netted a bunch of genuine operatives, also made this problem worse.[16]

---

[15] The allegations summaries list 345 detainees as associates of Al Qaeda, the Taliban, or other hostile groups. By contrast, they list 156 members and only 41 fighters.

[16] It is unclear how many detainees were sold to U.S. forces for bounty. A number of detainees claim to have been "sold," and the military did offer bounties in some instances. See Nancy Gibbs with Viveca Novak, "Inside 'The Wire'," Time, November 30, 2003, 40; Michelle Faul, "Guantánamo Detainees Say Arabs, Muslims Sold for U.S. Bounties," Asso-

It is a grave mistake, however, to see all this ambiguity as evidence of a general triviality in the government's allegations against the detainees — as the authors of the Seton Hall reports describe it. The military also included a list of more specific allegations against each detainee, and these allegations are, generally speaking, not trivial at all — although many of them are vague, weakly sourced, entirely unsourced, or even stated as possibilities or likelihoods, rather than as certainties. Many detainees, if you take the government's portraits seriously, are committed jihadists. And while their individual stories differ considerably, there are important common threads that make them look like something other than innocent relief workers, laborers, and Koranic instructors — common threads the military could not regard as anything other than extremely dangerous. According to the government's summaries of CSRT and ARB evidence in the nonhigh-value cases, for example:

- At least 179 traveled to Afghanistan for jihad
- At least 234 stayed in Al Qaeda, Taliban, or other guest or safe-houses.
- At least 317 detainees took military or terrorist training in Afghanistan
- At least 151 actually fought for the Taliban, many of them on the front lines against the Northern Alliance
- At least 160 were at Tora Bora
- At least 157 detainees' names or aliases were found on computers, hard drives, or physical lists of Al Qaeda operatives, material seized in raids on Al Qaeda safe houses and facilities
- At least 136 detainees were captured under circumstances — military surrenders, live combat actions, traveling in a large pack of Mujahideen, or in the company of senior Al Qaeda figures, for example — that strongly suggest belligerency
- 34 detainees served on Osama bin Laden's security detail

The government processes also brought out a significant number of mistakes. The thirty-eight detainees found by the CSRTs to be erroneously categorized included a number of Uighurs — ethnic Turkic Central Asians from China who had traveled to Afghanistan to train for insurgent activity against Beijing but who clearly had no beef against the United States. Reflecting the oddity of these cases, however, commissions found other

---

ciated Press, May 31, 2005; Carol J. Williams, "Detainee Lawyers See Stacked Deck," *Los Angeles Times*, November 13, 2007, A14.

Uighurs, whose cases were materially similar, to be enemy combatants.[17] The commissions also seem to have believed certain non-Afghan detainees who claimed to have been in Afghanistan for innocent reasons. These stories, some of which seem a bit implausible in black and white, include a Turk who had stayed with a suspected Al Qaeda operative for two months,[18] a Saudi man whom the Taliban had imprisoned for five years,[19] a Yemeni man who claimed to be at the Afghanistan-Pakistan border doing drug deals,[20] an Uzbek who suggested that "special forces" had sent him from Tajikistan to Afghanistan by helicopter in an effort to get him out of the country,[21] and a Frenchman who lied about his nationality and identity on capture and contended he had traveled from Iran to Afghanistan two months after September 11 "just to visit," carrying ten thousand dollars in cash given him accidentally by a stranger.[22]

The saddest of these cases involve detainees, mostly but not exclusively Afghans, who got rounded up, sometimes in simple error and sometimes in confusion about which groups were really fighting America and its allies. There were some cases of simple mistaken identity. The government identified Shed Abdur Rahman, for example, as a high-ranking Taliban "military judge" who "tortured, maimed, and murdered" other Afghans in Taliban jails. The detainee — who was born in Pakistan — contended that he had "never even hit my own child at home and . . . never hurt anyone." Far from being a military judge, he said, "the only time I have ever been in Afghanistan was for two days to attend a funeral." The CSRT ultimately accepted his claim that he actually worked on a chicken farm.[23] The military claimed that Mohammed Nasim "commanded a squad of Mujahidin fighters for a Kabul commander" and that his name "was referenced in intercepted radio transmissions regarding Northern Alliance troop movement." The detainee, by contrast, said he had "never been a

---

[17] Compare, for example, CSRT hearing for Yusef Abbas, ISN #275, Set 20, 1623-30, to CSRT hearing for Akhdar Qasem Basit, ISN #276, Set 16, 1363-68. Both acknowledge traveling from China and receiving training at the Uighur training camp at Tora Bora on the AK-47 rifle with the intention of fighting the Chinese government. Both acknowledge fleeing when the United States began bombing the region. The CSRTs deemed the former an enemy combatant and the latter no longer an enemy combatant.

[18] CSRT hearing for Salih Uyar, ISN #298, CSRT Set 29, 2015-21.

[19] CSRT Summary of Evidence for Sadik Ahmad Turkistani, ISN #491, 414.

[20] CSRT hearing for Karam Khamis Sayd Khamsan, ISN #586, CSRT Set 26, 1859-65.

[21] CSRT hearing for Zakirjan Asam, ISN #672, CSRT Set 29, 2001-14.

[22] CSRT hearing for Mustaq Ali Patel, ISN #649, CSRT Set 18, 1470-76.

[23] CSRT hearing for Shed Abdur Rahman, ISN #58 1, CSRT Set 3, 272-94, Sets 22-23, 1722-54.

commander. I never saw Kabul. I was always in my area, in my place, in my home farming. I was a farmer." His CSRT believed him, too.[24]

Other cases involved not mistaken identities per se but murky circumstances or the difficulty of distinguishing military from civilian functions in a regime run by a militia. For example, Janut Gul, whose CSRT record also calls him Hammdidullah, avoided conscription into the Taliban by becoming a civilian employee for the national airlines, of which he eventually became a top officer. The CSRTs struggled in many cases with claims by detainees that they performed only civilian functions. While in many instances, tribunals did not buy the distinction, Hammdidullah's tribunal did.[25] Likewise, in the case of Nasibullah Darwaish, whom the government described as a security commander for a Taliban-linked governor of an Afghan province, the detainee acknowledged that he served in that role under the current government of Hamid Karzai, but insisted that the governor he served was "not Taliban and he was nowhere near Taliban" and that "when I accepted the job as district chief of police that made me a lifetime enemy with Taliban."[26] The shifting alliances of Afghan politics left a goodly number of Afghan detainees claiming not that they were not combatants, but that they were not *enemy* combatants. Between the CSRTs and ARBs, the majority of these people have been cleared for removal from Guantánamo.

In general, however, the CSRTs did not free detainees but validated the government's allegations and the detention decisions based upon them. Because the government's top-line allegations are so confused, I have tried to simplify them, grouping the military's core allegations into a few loose categories. These categories are admittedly somewhat impressionistic, and there is a great deal of overlap among them. As such, reasonable minds can argue about which detainees belong in which box — and even how distinct the boxes really are. Moreover, the categories reflect nothing about the strength or quality of evidence against individual detainees, only about the nature of the claims the government has made about them. They are designed to provide a somewhat easier and more vivid picture of the detainee population as seen through the government's summaries of evidence. Taking all government allegations in both the CSRT and ARB processes as true, the population can be described as including:

---

[24] CSRT hearing for Mohammed Nasim, ISN #958, CSRT Set 51, 3572-81.
[25] CSRT hearing for Janat Gul, ISN #953, CSRT Set 29, 2030-47.
[26] CSRT hearing for Nasibuilah Darwaish, ISN #1019, CSRT Set 43, 2837-43.

- 25 members of Al Qaeda's leadership cadre. This category, which comprises 4 percent of the population, ranges from Khalid Sheik Mohammed to the movement's top money men and recruiters, the aides de camp of its chieftains, and the operational heads of and key participants in major Al Qaeda terrorist operations. It also includes some leaders of terrorist groups, like the Indonesian Jemmah Islamiyah, which allied themselves with Al Qaeda but retained some measure of independent identity.

- 182 lower-level Al Qaeda operatives, people who played a variety of roles in moving personnel and money, planning attacks, and carrying them out. This category, which makes up 32 percent of the population, includes Al Qaeda fighters with particularly close ties to the movement leaders — Bin Laden bodyguards and those who have sworn an oath of loyalty to him. It also includes fighters whose training bears some particular indicia of terrorism, as opposed to military combat. And it includes people who worked in Afghanistan and Pakistan for charities that operated as fronts for Al Qaeda, as well as operatives of terrorist groups like the Libyan Islamic Fighting Group, which are affiliated with Al Qaeda but remain to some degree distinct.

- 17 members of the Taliban's leadership cadre, ranging from ministers in the ultra-Islamist government and those who actively provided them high-level aid from outside the government to field commanders who led substantial numbers of soldiers. This group, 3 percent of the population, includes some people who could also reasonably be deemed Al Qaeda operatives, given the intertwined nature of the organizations. It also includes the leadership of native Afghan militias allied with the Taliban against coalition forces.

- 240 foreign fighters of varying levels of commitment and ferocity, from fervent international jihadists to the Gulf Arab youth who migrated to Afghanistan out of a relatively common desire for military "training" or a romantic religious attachment to the "pure" Islam of the Taliban. The government generally classifies these people, who make up a 42 percent plurality of the detainee population, as either Taliban or Al Qaeda, the groups that recruited them, trained them, and for whom they fought — or, in many cases, did not ultimately end up fighting. And there is undoubtedly a great deal of overlap among this group and the others. For present purposes, however, a foreign fighter is a non-Afghan who came to the region to fight or train but whom the government does not allege either to have had extensive access to high-level Al Qaeda operatives or to have planned or trained for terrorism — as opposed to military operations — specifically.

- 93 Taliban fighters and operatives. This group, which makes up 16 percent of the population, includes people who resemble conventional soldiers, as well as people who seem far closer to terrorists but are generally native Afghans whose principal affiliation is with their militia, not with Al Qaeda. It also includes fighters for the Taliban-allied militias, and other native Afghan groups fighting coalition forces in Afghanistan.

- 15 people who fell into none of these categories.

The government, as previously noted, did not disturb CSRT findings that thirty-eight detainees were "no longer enemy combatants," and the military cleared an additional fourteen for outright release in the first round of ARB review. Approximately thirty others had been cleared for release or transfer under procedures that predated the CSRTs but were still present when the military convened the tribunals.[27] These groups — those either cleared or sufficiently unthreatening to be quickly releasable anyway — comprised about 14 percent of the population that went through the CSRTs.

In other words, the government's portrait of the detainee population comprises a motley mixture of highly dangerous characters, buffoons who with varying degrees of plausibility imagined themselves warriors, and a few unlucky people in the wrong place at the wrong time. Particularly after the addition of the high-value detainees in September 2006, the group certainly included some of the "worst of the worst." But it principally comprised a different group: low- and mid-level Al Qaeda and Taliban operatives and the foreign fighters they recruited to man the barricades in Afghanistan. This group, the cannon fodder of international jihad, can pose a real menace both to American soldiers in the field and to American (and non-American) civilians. But unlike the true worst of the worst, who have almost always committed crimes one could try to prosecute, the members of this group may have done little more than train to fight against forces that later became America allies. Unless one is prepared to stretch the law of conspiracy so far as to criminalize association with certain groups, some of these people are almost certainly innocent of criminal activity.

• • • •

---

[27] The military has not identified the list of detainees cleared for release or transfer under pre-CSRT procedures. I have attempted to reconstruct it, though my effort may be either somewhat incomplete or somewhat over inclusive.

The picture looks different when considered from the point of view of the detainees. Most detainees, after all, do not describe themselves as terrorists. They tend, rather, to minimize their involvement. People whom the government labels Al Qaeda operatives call themselves relief workers; people whom the government calls moneymen call themselves businessmen; people whom the government calls jihadist fighters call themselves instructors in the Koran, and some call themselves farmers.

Yet the picture looks a good deal less different than one might think from a public debate that has tended to treat the detainees as a bloc. A substantial percentage of detainees do not seriously contest their status. The Venn diagrams of the government's portrait of the detainees and their collective self-portrait, rather, have a significant zone of overlap.

Start with the fact that of the 534 detainees found to be enemy combatants by the CSRTs, 59 openly admit either membership or significant association with Al Qaeda, the Taliban, or some other armed group the government considers militarily hostile to the United States. An additional 13 acknowledge being Taliban but claim to have been pressed into service. In these cases, the military can justify its detention judgments with reference to the detainees' statements alone. A further group of 64 detainees deny affiliation with Al Qaeda or the Taliban yet admit facts that, under the broad authority the laws of war give armed parties to detain the enemy, offer the government ample legal justification for its decisions. An additional group of 62 detainees admits to some lesser measure of affiliation — like staying in Taliban or Al Qaeda guesthouses or spending time at one of their training camps. In these cases, the detainees' statements alone only partially justify the detentions, but it's not hard to imagine how the classified evidence might push the government over the hump. Together, these groups amount to more than one third of the population the CSRTs deemed enemy combatants. While by no means a majority this is a sizable block of detainees who concede at least something substantial in support of their detentions. The remaining detainees divide almost evenly between those who deny all the material allegations against them and those who make no statements at all. Each of these groups bears a more detailed examination.

Those who admit operating on behalf of the enemy are not necessarily the worst of the detainees — though some of them certainly are. "I helped out Bin Laden," an Afghan named Mohammed Hashim told his CSRT panel. "We were told by the Arabs, who had all the money, that they were planning an attack on the United States with 20 pilots." For five years, he said, "I have been a member of the Taliban," on behalf of whom "I took

part in a lot of battles." Of the government's summary of evidence, he
said, "All of it is true. There are no lies in there."[28] Walid Bin 'Attash
quibbled with details but acknowledged proudly that he had taken part in
the attack on the U.S.S. *Cole* and the East African embassy bombings:

> **Tribunal:** What exactly was his role as the — both the USS *Cole* and
> the — ah — embassy thing?
>
> **Detainee:** Many roles, I participated in the buying or purchasing of
> the explosives. I put together the plan for the operation a year and
> a half prior to the operation. Buying the boat and recruiting the
> members that did the operation. Buying the explosives . . .
>
> **[Tribunal] President:** Where were you, physically, at the time of
> the *Cole* attacks?
>
> **Detainee:** [I] was with Sheik Usama bin Laden in Kandahar.
>
> **President:** And at the time of the embassy attacks?
>
> **Detainee:** I was in Karachi meeting the operator, the guy that basi-
> cally did the operation a few hours before the operation took
> place. . . . I was the link between Usama bin Laden and his deputy
> Sheikh Abu Hafs Al Masri and the cell chief in Nairobi.[29]

Khalid Sheikh Mohammed admitted to a long list of terrorist acts — perhaps more than he actually conducted — and declared: "I will not regret
when I say I'm [an] enemy combatant."[30] Abdul Rahman Al Zahri, whom
the government also accused of advance knowledge of the September 11
attacks, announced at his ARB hearing: "I do pose a threat to the United
States and its allies. I admit to you it is my honor to be an enemy of the
United States. I'm a Muslim jihadist . . ." Al Zahri denied membership in
Al Qaeda but proudly declared that he trained at Al Qaeda camps and met
with Bin Laden many times. "I'm not one of his men and not one of his
individuals. I am one of his sons. I will kill myself for him and will also
give my family and all of my money to him. I praise Mullah Omar. Relating to my relationship with [the] Taliban, it is a Muslim country. My duty
toward them is like any duty of a Muslim person to defend the Taliban and

---

[28] CSRT hearing for Mohammed Hashim, ISN #850, CSRT Set 34, 2442-44.

[29] CSRT hearing for Walid Muhammad Salih Bin 'Attash, ISN #10014. The CSRT hearings
for the high value detainees were released separately from those of the other detainees. Bin
Attash's transcript is available at http://www.defenselink.mill/news/transcript_
ISN10014.pdf.

[30] CSRT hearing for Khalid Sheikh Muhammed, ISN #10024, available at http://www.
defenselink.mil/news/transcript_ISN10024.pdf.

its stay. . . . With the help of God, we will stand Mujahedin and terrorists against Americans."[31]

Most of the admissions are more pedestrian than these. Indeed, while the percentage of people the government describes as Al Qaeda operatives, Al Qaeda leadership, and senior Taliban is significantly higher among this group than among the Guantánamo population at large, it is not dramatically so. For most of the detainees who admit their roles, the frankness of their statements may reflect less the intensity or fervor of their commitment to jihad — which may well not exceed the commitment of many of those who deny everything — than simple honesty or the sense that the government's evidence is strong enough to render any denial fruitless. Many detainees acknowledged openly that they traveled to Afghanistan to train for and participate in the fight against the Northern Alliance.[32] Some dispute fighting American forces specifically or contend they never formally joined the Taliban or Al Qaeda as members. But they admit an affiliation with the other side in the fight. A typical example of this group is Adnan Muhammed Ali Al Saigh, whose CSRT hearing contains the following exchanges:

> **Tribunal President:** What do you have to say about that, are you or are you not with the Taliban?
>
> **Detainee:** I am.
>
> [The next allegation is then read to the tribunal]: *3a1. Detainee stated he answered an Islamic fatwah in Saudi Arabia to fight for the Taliban forces in Afghanistan.*
>
> **Detainee:** That is a religious activity, are you fighting my cause?
>
> . . .
>
> *3b. The Detainee participated in military operations against the coalition.*
>
> **Detainee:** I never participated.
>
> **Personal Representative:** When I spoke with the Detainee, he said he fought with the Taliban against the (forces led by General) Massoud but not against the American allies.
>
> **Detainee:** That's true.
>
> . . .

---

[31] ARB Round II hearing for Abd Al Rahman Al Zahri, ISN #441, ARB II Transcripts, 2285-93.

[32] See, for example, CSRT hearing for Muhsin Muhammad Musheen Moqbill ISN #193 CSRT Set 47, 3210-17; CSRT hearing for Yasim Muhammed Basardah, ISN #252, CSRT Set 44, 2930-38; CSRT hearing for Khalil Rahman Hafez, ISN #301, CSRT Set 11, 1153-54.

Tribunal Member: Did you answer a fatwah from a religious leader in Saudi Arabia to go to Afghanistan?

Detainee: Yes. . . . I went there to fight with the rest of the people.[33]

In many cases, detainees admit their affiliations in the course of seeking to minimize their roles. For example, Salim Hamdan, the detainee whose challenge to military commissions went all the way to the Supreme Court, did not deny that he served as Osama bin Laden's driver. But he said he was "forced" to do so.[34] Several admitted members of the Taliban argued that their work for the militia was purely civilian in nature. These include Abdul Haq Wasiq, the Taliban's deputy minister of intelligence, who describes being forcibly pressed into service and then promoted when his boss became ill. "[He] told me to take his position until he got better. He got sick and didn't get better, so I continued doing the job. I confessed this and I will confess again. My job was against thieves and bribes; I was fighting against those kinds of people."[35] More plausibly, Mullah Norullah Noori acknowledged to his CSRT that he joined the Taliban and sometimes called himself a "soldier" but described his role as something closer to that of a civilian security guard. "I assured under the oath that against the United States or its allies, I never thought about fighting against them and I'm not thinking in the future to ever fight against them," he said.[36] At the margins, some of these cases may present a question under the laws of war, which do not treat civilian government workers as enemy fighters. In the case of the Taliban, which is a militia, that line is exceptionally difficult to draw. The type of hearing that might probe it meaningfully would require something far more calibrated and adversarial than the CSRTs.

A more sympathetic group is the thirteen detainees, nearly all Afghans, who claim — some quite plausibly — to have been forced against their will into low-level Taliban service. Abdul Rauf Aliza, for example, claimed that the Taliban threatened to take away his land unless he served them, so he carried food from a bakery to Taliban members.[37] Dawd Gul describes having been a brick maker whom the Taliban kidnapped and gave a gun. Since he could not shoot, he became an assistant to a Taliban cook.[38] Mohammed Sharif describes being taken forcibly by the Taliban

[33] CSRT hearing for Adnan Mohammed Ali, ISN #105, CSRT Set 10, 1126-32.

[34] CSRT hearing for Salim Ahmed Salim Hamdan, ISN #149, CSRT Set 51, 3538-46.

[35] CSRT hearing for Abdul Haq Wasiq, ISN #4, CSRT Set 16, 1375-86.

[36] CSRT hearing for Mullah Norullah Noori, ISN #6, CSRT Set 42, 2730-33.

[37] CSRT hearing for Abdul Rauf Aliza, ISN #108, CSRT Set 50, 3478-80; ARB I hearing, ARB 1 Set 3,874-80.

[38] CSRT hearing for Dawd Gul, ISN #530, CSRT Set 44, 3014-20.

from his village, something the Taliban did frequently to young men there. He would work twenty days or so every three months as a security guard, a cleaner, and a food and firewood carrier.[39] Under the rules of warfare, such people are ripe for capture and detention, just as they are — tragically — legitimate targets on the battlefield. As a matter of policy, however, assuming one believes their stories, locking them up for long periods of time makes little sense. The CSRT process treated them as enemy combatants. The ARB process, however, seemed relatively sensitive to the fact that impressed Taliban pose little danger to American forces. ARB hearings or other review mechanisms seem to have cleared all but two members of this group for either release or transfer.

A somewhat more complicated group of detainees — sixty-four in all — actively, sometimes passionately, denies affiliation with the Taliban or Al Qaeda yet nonetheless admits facts that strongly support their categorizations as enemy combatants. These detainees range a great deal in terms of the threat they likely pose. Fahed Nasser Mohamed, a Saudi detainee, denied in strong terms during his CSRT hearing that he had any relationship with the Taliban or Al Qaeda or that he had ever been to a terrorist training camp. He admitted, however, that he had gone to Afghanistan because "I met a man who told me about the idea of jihad" and "gave me the idea about fighting." While he claimed that his "opinion changed" after he got there and saw Afghans worshipping at graves, a practice he found religiously offensive, he nonetheless went to "a house" in Kabul "that was a cooking facility for the front line" and trained there on an AK47. He was captured as part of a surrender to Northern Alliance forces, escaped, and turned himself in again the following day.[40] Mohammed Ali Abdullah Bwazir of Yemen also refused to concede any affiliation with the enemy but did acknowledge traveling to Pakistan on a passport with a changed name, staying at a Taliban house in Quetta, and traveling to the front lines for humanitarian purposes in connection with an Al Qaeda-linked charity. "Sometimes we visited the Taliban trenches" to preach, he told his ARB. "Yes, I've seen the Taliban and all I have for them is respect and love. They are not my enemies."[41] At the more dangerous end of the spectrum is Hafez Qari Mohamed Saad Iqbal Madni of Pakistan. He disclaimed to his CSRT any relationship with Al Qaeda, but acknowledged hanging out with

---

[39] CSRT hearing for Mohammed Sharif, ISN #532, CSRT Set 33, 2312-21; ARB I hearing, ARB I Set 7, 2055-68.

[40] CSRT hearing for Fahed Nasser Mohamed ISN #13 CSRT Set 50 3462-66 ARB I hearing, ARB I Set 2, 624-29.

[41] ARB I hearing for Mohammed Ali Abdullah Bwazir, ISN #440, ARB I Set 6, 20430-44.

major terrorist figures in Indonesia and boasting to them of his high-level Al Qaeda contacts. "To show that I was such a big person, I talked about Osama bin Laden and they asked me, did I see Osama bin Laden and I told them yes, when I was coming from Pakistan, I heard one of his announcements, in which he announced that the Muslims should not travel on non-Muslim air lines." His contacts, in turn, told him of their operational plans, including an effort the previous year to "blow up the American embassy in Jakarta." They also took him to a meeting where they were planning terrorist acts against hotels: "An American ambassador had a program in one of the hotels."[42] At the less dangerous end, a Pakistani named Zia Ul Shah acknowledged that he worked for the Taliban as a truck driver but only because they were the available employer; he always refused to enter combat areas, he claimed, and quit after September 11. Yet he also acknowledged driving a large group of Taliban fighters to surrender to Northern Alliance forces.[43]

Legally speaking, these sorts of admissions make detention decisions pretty easy. The laws of war permit the government to lock up the enemy, and these groups — even those claiming Taliban impressments — all acknowledge a level of affiliation with the enemy sufficient that the military would reasonably regard them as either fighting for the other side or directly and materially supporting the other side's fight. What's more, any regime the government might employ in place of or in addition to the laws of war — and I argue for a civilianized administrative detention regime in Chapter 7 — would likewise permit noncriminal detention of many members of these groups. While in some instances, particularly the Taliban impressment cases, the policy and humanitarian arguments against long-term detention outweigh the security and intelligence benefits of holding people, these are prudential, not legal, considerations. Under one set of rules or another, American law does and should consider such people detainable for as long or as short a time as necessary to protect the country from them. There is, after all, no real dispute about the key fact at issue in any detention judgment: whether they have aligned themselves with the enemy. In the midst of an armed conflict, only a society whose Constitution truly is a suicide pact would require their freedom as a matter of law.

---

[42] CRST hearing for Hafez Qari Mohamed Saad Iqbal Madni, 15N #743, CSRT Set 1, 46-58.

[43] CSRT hearing for Zia Ul Shah, ISN #15, CSRT Set 42, 2752-68.

The legal question starts to get more difficult with the next group down the totem pole of admissions: those who deny membership but admit some nontrivial and yet nondispositive measure of affiliation. Some fourteen detainees, for example, admit to having stayed in Taliban or Al Qaeda housing but to nothing else. An additional fifteen admit to having spent time — often very short periods — in a training camp but not to any other activity indicative of membership. Thirty-three more admit to some other type of associational activity. Some claim to be refugees from the fighting in Afghanistan who traveled or camped with armed men fleeing the war zone. A Palestinian named Mahrar Rafat Al Quwari, for example, says he went to Afghanistan because he could live there without identification but fled to Tora Bora when the bombing started and Afghans began turning on Arabs. He worked briefly distributing food around the caves at Tora Bora but says he was never a part of the jihad.[44]

In many of these cases, it is easy to imagine that the government's classified evidence, were it available, would persuade one of a detainee's being properly categorized — there being a relatively narrow gap between a detainee's admissions and facts adequate to establish enemy combatant status. Yet unlike the cases of clearer admissions, there are at least some material issues of fact in dispute. Not everyone who spent time taking military-style training in Afghanistan was necessarily a Taliban fighter, after all. It's certainly possible that some recruits showed up, tested the waters, and realized that jihad was not for them. Likewise, some people who stayed in guest houses could have been prospective recruits, not actual ones, or even just guests. And some genuine refugees probably did get mixed in with the fighters in flight. In this group of cases, the government can draw partial support for its detention judgments from the statements of the detainees, but the statements don't get the military all the way home.

We come, then, to the many cases in which the detainees admit nothing. There are a few common themes among these 184 detainees, 160 of whom the CSRTs classified as enemy combatants. Twenty-three claim to have been doing charitable work, another 19 to have been teaching or studying the Koran. The rest are a mishmash of tales, plausible and tall. One man says he traveled to Afghanistan to escort his sister to her husband there.[45] Several say they went there to find better jobs.[46] Others traveled

---

[44] SRT hearing for Mahrar Rafat Al Quwari, ISN #519, CSRT Set 31, 2145-52.

[45] CSRT hearing for Mohammed Ahmad Said Al Edah, 15N #33, CRST Set 47, 1970-78.

[46] See, for example, CSRT hearing for Samir Naji Al Hasan Moqbel, ISN #43, CSRT Set 47, 3192-98.

to Afghanistan or Pakistan for medical care.[47] Some went for family reasons,[48] out of attraction to the pure Islamic lifestyle of the Taliban's Afghanistan,[49] even for sightseeing purposes.[50] Compared to the detainee population at large, the deniers as a group seem to comprise a considerably smaller concentration of people whom the government portrays as foreign jihadist fighters and a significantly higher concentration of those it regards as Taliban operatives or leadership. Two of the high-value detainees transferred to Guantánamo in 2006 from the CIA's secret detention program — including Hambali, the operational chief of Al Qaeda's Indonesian affiliate, Jemaah Islamiyah — deny the gravamen of government's allegations against them.[51] So do the preponderance of those the government set free as "no longer enemy combatants."

Many of the denying detainees are undoubtedly lying. In some cases, their stories are patently absurd; in others the circumstances under which American or allied forces captured the detainee belie his denial. An example of a simply incredible story is that of Bessam Muhammed Saleh Al Dubaikey, who claimed he traveled to Pakistan in the wake of September 11 to buy rare artifacts such as old coins. He ended up, however, buying a pair of mummies, which he sold on the Internet for a large sum of cash. He later hooked up with a man at a mosque, who turned out to be a leader in an Al Qaeda-linked charity, and the two traveled together looking for a group to which to donate the proceeds of the mummy sale — until they got arrested with ninety thousand dollars.[52] A Tajik man named Omar Hamzayavich Abdulayev was captured with three handwritten notebooks full of information about weapons systems, counterintelligence methods, chemistry, and poisons, and a small book listing the members of a jihadist group and the serial numbers of their weapons. Abdulayev claimed Pakistani intelligence officers forced him to copy down all this information, telling him he would go free if he did and beating him when he refused.[53] In many other cases, the stories have no obvious absurdities; they just ring

---

[47] See, for example, CSRT hearing for Ab Aljallil Allal, ISN #156, CSRT Set 8, 971-79.

[48] See, for example, ARB I hearing for Muhammad Ben Moujan, ISN #160, ARB I Set 1, 483-89.

[49] See, for example, CSRT hearing for Ridouane Khalid, ISN #173, CSRT Set 7, 792-804.

[50] See, for example, CSRT hearing for Salih Uyar, ISN #298, CSRT Set 29, 2015-21.

[51] CSRT hearing for Riduan Bin Isomuddin, ISN #10019, available at http://www.defenselink .mil/news/transcript_ISN10019.pdf; CSRT hearing for Majid Khan, ISN #10020, available at http://www.defenselink.mil/news/transcript_ISN10020 .pdf.

[52] CSRT hearing for Bessam Muhammed Saleh Al Dubaikey, ISN #340, CSRT Set 29, 2022-29A.

[53] CSRT hearing for Omar Hamzayavich Abdulayev, ISN #257, CSRT Set 20, 1606-13.

false, and it's therefore easy to imagine the classified record resolving the preponderance of these cases on the government's side. In many instances, a more robust, more independent review mechanism would likely have made the same decisions as did the CSRTs but would have done so with far greater prestige.

This is not to say that all detainees are where they belong. In some instances, detainees' denials seemed alarmingly credible — particularly when coupled with especially thin government allegations. U.S. District Judge Joyce Hens Green, in one judicial opinion, expressed particular concern about the case of Murat Kurnaz, a Turk who lived as a permanent resident in Germany and whom the government accused of being a friend of a would-be suicide bomber and a part of a missionary organization called Jammat al Tabliq that Al Qaeda has infiltrated.[54] Kurnaz told his CSRT: "Now I hear Jamaat al Tabliq supports terrorism. I never knew that. . . . My reason for going to Pakistan wasn't to kill anyone or learn about weapons, it was to study Islam. In Germany, Islam was only taught on weekends; therefore, it would take a few years to learn what would only take a month in Pakistan." Kurnaz acknowledged a relationship with Selcuk Bilgin, the man suspected of participating in a suicide attack, but described the relationship as purely religious and nonviolent.[55] Bolstering the credibility of Kurnaz's statement is the fact that the government's classified evidence, which became public in 2005, seems terribly weak. In an excellent *Washington Post* article, reporter Carol D. Leonnig quoted accidentally declassified documents from American military intelligence, which had concluded that it had "no definite link/evidence of detainee having an association with Al Qaida or making any specific threat against the U.S." and was "not aware of evidence that Kurnaz was or is a member of Al Qaeda." Another document in Kurnaz's file, the *Post* reported, made clear that the "Germans confirmed this detainee has no connection to an al-Qaida cell in Germany." Even the suggestion that Bilgin was dirty turned out to be thin. German authorities never made a case against him. The German prosecutor who investigated him told the *Post* that there was no evidence of his being a suicide bomber and that authorities there had to drop the case. "We don't have proof the two wanted to go to Afghanistan or had any terrorist plans," he told Leonnig.[56] Kurnaz, after being found an enemy combatant by his CSRT and subject to continued detention in

---

[54] See *In Re Guantanamo Detainee Cases*, 355 F. Supp. 2d 443 (D.D.C. 2005).
[55] CSRT hearing for Murat Kurnaz, ISN #61, CSRT Set 9, 1055-64.
[56] Carol D. Leonnig, "Panel Ignored Evidence on Detainee." See also Carol D. Leonnig, "Evidence of Innocence Rejected at Guantánamo," *Washington Post*, December 5, 2007, Al.

the first round of ARB hearings, was transferred to Germany and released following the second round of ARB hearings.[57]

Kurnaz's is not the only case in which a detainee's denial seems non-frivolous. The government alleged that Abdul Razzak, an Afghan detainee, served as an "Al Qaida facilitator and smuggler," conducted an "escort mission" for Bin Laden, fought against the United States, "was a commander of a Taliban terrorist cell in Afghanistan," and "was involved in assassination attempts against Afghani government officials.["][58] The detainee denied the allegations; while he acknowledged he had been forced to serve the Taliban as a driver early in the militia's rule, he claimed he had broken major opponents of the Taliban out of prison, opponents who later became significant figures in the government of Hamid Karzai. After that incident, he said, he fled the country and was abroad until after the Karzai government came to power.[59] Abdul Razzak never made headway with these claims in the military's review systems, and other detainees described serving under a Taliban commander named Abdul Razzak.[60] The detainee died of cancer at Guantánamo in late 2007. After his death, however, the *New York Times* published a report indicating that the man the paper called Abdul Razzaq Hekmati might have been telling the truth. Senior Afghan officials, including those whom the detainee had busted out of prison, described his case as a gross error and described him as a war hero against the Russians and a courageous opponent of the Taliban.[61] Given the shifting allegiances of Afghan factions, the murk[]y evidence, and the limitations of the CSRTs as a fact-finding mechanism, it would be surprising if more such cases did not exist.

In the majority of the denial cases, in fact, the detainee's statements are at least plausible, and the CSRTs were left resolving genuinely contested issues of fact, mostly in the government's favor. Particularly when dealing with detainees captured far from anything resembling a traditional battlefield setting, the tribunals had little credibility in carrying out this task. Perhaps the most troubling example of their failure here involved a

---

[57] See "Administrative Review Board Assessment and Recommendation ICO ISN 061 (Turkey/Germany)," ARB II Decision Memos, 39-46. See also Mark Landler, "Guantánamo Prisoner Goes Home," *New York Times*, August 26, 2006, A2.

[58] CSRT Summary of Evidence for Abdul Razzak, ISN #942, 670.

[59] CSRT hearing for Abdul Razzak, ISN #942, CSRT Set 18, 1517-21. See also ARB Round I hearing for Abdul Razzak, ARB I Transcripts, Set 9, 21288-301.

[60] See, for example, CSRT h[e]aring for Nasrullah, ISN #886, CSRT Set 33, 2336-57; CSRT hearing for Ismat Ullah, ISN #888, CSRT Set 31, 2234-50.

[61] Carlotta Gall and Andy Worthington, "Time Runs Out for an Afghan Held by U.S.," *New York Times*, February 5, 2008, A1.

group of six Algerian natives living in Bosnia. Bosnian authorities arrested them as an alleged Al Qaeda terrorist cell. And while the allegations against them were severe — one was supposedly a high-ranking operative in phone contact with Abu Zubaydah, and the group was suspected of plotting to bomb the American embassy in Sarajevo — the Bosnian courts ordered them freed for lack of evidence. Instead, authorities turned them over to the United States, which shipped them to Guantánamo, where the military held them based on intelligence data they could not attack. This evidence persuaded their CSRT panels, notwithstanding the detainees' strenuous denials. But the outsider has little basis to evaluate the integrity of what appears to be a series of civilian arrests outside of any combat setting.[62] In some instances, the CSRTs clearly struggled with the plausibility of detainee denials, and relatively weak evidence provoked dissents in the three-member CSRT panels' determination that a detainee met the criteria for detention. One such case involved Hassan Adel Hussein, a Sudanese man accused of working for a pair of organizations the government later lamely claimed "may" be connected to Al Qaeda.[63] The detainee acknowledged in his ARB hearing that in his work in refugee camps, he saw Khalid Sheikh Mohammed from a distance and at one point worked for an organization run by Mohammed's brother, but he denied any connection to Al Qaeda.[64] The CSRT voted 2-1 to consider him an enemy combatant, though he was cleared for transfer by the first round of ARB hearings.[65] In some cases, CSRTs initially believed detainee denials and determined those detainees not to be enemy combatants, only to have the Pentagon order a do-over. New tribunals hearing new classified evidence then came to different conclusions.[66] Some of the cases, in short, are hard. Some-

---

[62] See CSRT records for Bensayah Belkacem, ISN #10001, Publicly Filed CSRT Records, 4851-90; Sabir Mahfouz Lahmar, ISN #10002, Publicly Filed CSRT Records, 4891-946; Mohammad Nechle, ISN #10003, Publicly Filed CSRT Records, 4947-5000; Mustafa Alt Idr, ISN #10004, Publicly filed CSRT Records, 5001-53; Lakhdar Boumediene, ISN #10005, Publicly Filed CSRT Records, 5054-68; and Boudella Al Hajj, ISN #10006, Publicly Filed CSRT Records, 5069-134.

[63] "Unclassified Summary of Evidence for Administrative Review Board in the Case of Adel Hussein, Hassan," ISN #940, ARB Round I Factors, 749-51.

[64] ARB I hearing for Hassan Adel Hussein, ISN #940, ARB I Set 9, 21260-76.

[65] CSRT record for Hassan Adel Hussein, ISN #940, Publicly Filed CSRT Records, 4287-315. See also "Administrative Review Board Assessment and Recommendation ICO ISN 940 (Sudan)," ARB I Decision Memos, 625-31.

[66] See CSRT record for Hassan Anvar, ISN #250, Publicly Filed CSRT Records, 1734-67. Anvar is a Uighur, which probably explains the CSRT's difficulty with his case. See also CSRT record for Abdullah Mohammad Khan, ISN #556, Publicly Filed CSRT Records, 2835-68. Khan's case is particularly interesting. It was sent back twice after two successive

times the CSRTs own processes and outcomes reflect the difficulty. In some cases, like Kurnaz's and Abdul Razzak's, the panels seem to have missed the difficulty. While I suspect that a more rigorous process would, in many cases, have ended up validating the government's detention choices, this is only an instinct — one based on seeing so many detainees telling such similar stories and the fact that it would have been an extraordinary coincidence indeed for the military's roundup of the enemy to have netted such a concentration of relief workers, students, teachers, job seekers and tourists as the detainees claim to be. I concede, however, that the facts do not compel this instinct. It is certainly possible that a significant fraction of these detainees are telling the truth, and it is positively likely that among those who are lying are a significant number about whom the government's classified evidence would fail to impress a reasonable fact finder under a more adversarial process.

The final large group of detainees is the 161 who have given no statement at all. For these detainees, we have only one side of the story: the government's. It is therefore difficult in general to draw conclusions about them. In some instances, as with the denials, the circumstances of a detainee's capture offer strong indication that his detention would pass muster. Some were captured with large groups of other fighters.[67] Others were part of significant Taliban surrenders.[68] Still others were captured in raids on safe houses in Pakistan, sometimes after firefights and sometimes

---

CSRTs determined him to be no longer an enemy combatant. A third determined him to be an enemy combatant. The circumstances of capture in Khan's case, at least as described in his subsequent ARB proceeding, seem to back this designation: He was allegedly captured with explosives residue on his hands. See "Unclassified Summary of Evidence for Administrative Review Board in the Case of Khan, Abdullah Mohammad," ARB I Factors, 929-31. See also CSRT record for Abdullah Hamid Abdalsalam Alghazawy, ISN #654, Publicly Filed CSRT Records, 3244-90. The record states: "On 24 November 2004, a Tribunal unanimously determined that the detainee was not properly designated as an enemy combatant. Following that Tribunal, CSRT intelligence personnel conducted another search of the Government Information for evidence relevant to ISN #654's status. They collected additional evidence which eventually became exhibits R-17 through R-20. . . . [T]he additional evidence, along with the original evidence and original Tribunal Decision Report, was presented to Tribunal panel #32 to reconsider the detainee's status. Following their consideration of the new information, along with the original information, the second Tribunal unanimously determined that the detainee was properly classified as an enemy combatant."

[67] See, for example, "Unclassified Summary of Evidence for Administrative Review Board in the Case of Al Mudhaffan, Abdel Qadir Hussein," ISN #40, ARB I Factors, 48-50.
[68] See, for example, "Unclassified Summary of Evidence for Administrative Review Board in the Case of Al Shamyri, Mustafa Abdul/Qawi Abdul Aziz," ISN #434, ARB I Factors, 1075-77.

in the company of senior Al Qaeda figures.[69] In a few other instances, like that of September 11 conspirator Ramzi Binalshibh, one can safely assume based on the public record — including Binalshibh's own public statements — that the government would have no trouble establishing his amenability to detention, whatever process and standards it might use. All of these cases, however, represent the exceptions. In general, the cases without detainee statements represent a significant wild card. It is not clear how many of them would deny the allegations against them and how many are proudly enemies who simply chose not to dignify the CSRT and ARB processes with their participation. Nor do we know whether the government's evidence would satisfy a reasonable fact finder.

One final group of detainees warrants brief comment, for its members fit into none of the categories above: the Uighurs. In key respects, the Uighurs presented more of a policy problem than one of due process or fact-finding. In almost all of the twenty-two Uighur cases, the basic facts were not disputed: The Uighurs came to Afghanistan to train in order to fight for autonomy from the Chinese. By the standards to which the military subjected other foreign nationals who took training under the auspices of the Taliban, they clearly warranted the enemy combatant label. At the same time, they just as clearly had no interest in fighting against the United States and did not have much interest in international jihad either. Rather, they concerned themselves with their own regional conflict with a highly oppressive government. The CSRTs struggled with the Uighurs, some of whom they labeled as enemy combatants and some of whom they cleared; facing detainees who so tested the premises of the review mechanism, different tribunals reacted to them differently. That said, there was not much dispute over what should happen to them: Nobody really believed they should remain detained. The military itself had long been attempting to get rid of them and had cleared several for release or transfer even before the CSRTs took place. Effectuating this decision has presented a major logistical problem, because the Uighurs did not want to go back to China out of a reasonable fear of persecution and other countries proved unwilling to take them.[70] But from early on, in contrast to the other detainees, a basic consensus existed both as to who they were and as to what to do with them. By the time the first round of ARBs were completed, in fact, all but one of the Uighurs — the lone individual the government

---

[69] See, for example, "Unclassified Summary of Evidence for Administrative Review Board in the Case of Azani, Saad Masir Mukbl Al," ISN #575, ARB I Factors, 1048-49.

[70] See Neil A. Lewis, "Freed From Guantánamo but Stranded Far From Home," *New York Times*, August 15, 2006, A15.

seems to have regarded as a part of enemy forces — had been cleared to leave.

All told, the public record supports the following breakdown of the government's enemy combatant determinations. In 27 percent of cases, the detainee's own statement validates his designation. In 3 percent of cases, notwithstanding a denial or no statement by the detainee, the alleged circumstances of his capture are so suggestive of belligerence that it seems overwhelmingly likely that the government has pegged him properly. In 1 percent of cases, detainees who deny or offer no statement concerning the allegations against them have faced criminal charges before military commissions, either the pre-MCA commissions or the more recent statutory tribunals — and should thus be considered reasonably detained pending trial. In 31 percent of cases, therefore, the public record one way or another supports the government's position with relative clarity. In an additional 11 percent of cases, the detainee's statement partially supports the designation, though not adequately to say comfortably that he is properly detained.

In 28 percent of cases, by contrast, the detainee gave a statement in which he denied affiliation with hostile forces and a contested issue of fact remains about his status. In 27 percent of cases, the detainee gave no statement and there exists no other basis to validate the government's claims.

This picture changes remarkably little when one examines the subset of Guantánamo detainees whom the government regarded as still requiring detention after the second round of ARBs. The percentage of detainees staying mum has risen a bit. The percentage of those whose detention the public record justifies in whole or in part has inched up. The percentage of those denying all allegations, conversely, has declined marginally.

What does change considerably in the subset of the population not cleared for release following the second ARB review is the severity of the government's allegations against the detainees. The percentage of the population the government describes as Al Qaeda's leadership doubles from 4 percent in the population subjected to CSRTs to 8 percent in the group that survived the second ARB process. The percentage the government casts as Al Qaeda operatives grows from 32 percent to 45 percent of the total, while the concentration of foreign fighters shrinks from 42 percent to 34 percent. The concentration of Taliban operatives drops in half, from 16 percent to 8 percent, while the concentration of Taliban leadership rises a small amount. In other words, more than half the population at Guantánamo the government insisted upon holding past the second ARB round falls into the three most serious categories of detainees: Al Qaeda and Taliban leadership and Al Qaeda operatives.

The change here would probably appear more dramatic were ongoing detention judgments purely a function of the given detainee's individual circumstances, but they're not. A big factor in whom the military releases is which foreign governments are willing and able to take responsibility for managing the risks they pose. The result is that all British detainees, even some whose files are pretty scary, have gone home, and Saudi detainees — once the second largest group at the base — are now scarce. But Yemenis, even some who seem to pose a less obvious threat than some of the Saudis and British who have gone home, continue to languish.[71]

That said, the administration has clearly taken big steps to concentrate the hard core at Guantánamo and send the bit players home. Officials were certainly stretching the truth when they declared the detainees at the base the "worst of the worst" in 2002. While the phrase still smacks of hyperbole, as a description of the population the government believes itself to be holding it approximates the truth today far more closely than it did when the White House actually said it.

• • • •

In short, as a mechanism for adjudicating which detainees the government needed to hold on to and for how long, the review mechanisms the government set up almost certainly outperformed their dismal public reputation — probably by a country mile. The CSRT and ARB panels offered detainees a process considerably more generous than that required by the laws of war. Their members worked diligently and freed or transferred a lot of people. They also identified a large group of detainees about whose incarcerations no serious question of propriety should have existed. And they isolated that group of people about whom questions of fact remained. None of this comports with their public reputations as a meaningless layer of kangaroo court justice.

---

[71] Compare, for example, Faruq Mi Ahmed, ISN #32, the young Yemeni man discussed in the Introduction with British national Feroz Ali Abbasi, ISN #24. The former denied all suggestions of belligerency, of which evidence seemed relatively weak and associational, yet both rounds of ARB review have insisted on the necessity of continuing to hold him. By contrast, Abbasi acknowledged having gone to Afghanistan committed to jihad and participating in meetings with top Al Qaeda figures; he was even slated for trial by military commission, yet he was sent home as part of a blanket release of British detainees early in 2005. I describe this case in more detail in Chapter 6.

Yet if the goal was a review mechanism that would justify over the long term detention decisions to a public used to criminal justice norms and suspicious of arbitrary detentions of people not wearing enemy uniforms, these review processes failed utterly. They failed because detainees had too few procedural rights to challenge government allegations and offer their own evidence.[72] They failed because the government's evidentiary burden was so low that a finding that a given detainee was an enemy combatant meant literally no more than that he had failed to prove he was not one.[73] They failed because the decision-making panels had no independence from the military's chain of command ,and therefore could not credibly resolve contested factual matters in the government's favor without seeming merely to rubber stamp pre-existing conclusions.[74] Perhaps most importantly, they failed because they operated in secret, so that both striking detainee admissions and the actions the panels took to free people remained almost entirely beneath the public radar.

A mature legal architecture would have done better: It would have given detainees sufficient procedural protections and set the government's evidentiary burden high enough that a finding in the government's favor would have meant something substantial. It would have employed a decision maker with sufficient independence that such a finding would have carried prestige and institutional heft. And it would have produced a public document explaining each decision so that the public need not argue about the many cases in which there existed no real dispute between the parties and might have understood the precise parameters of the contested questions at issue where a genuine dispute did exist. Such a process would surely have complicated the government's task. Charles Stimson, who oversaw detainee matters at the Pentagon for a spell, estimates that a more rigorous process, the creation of which he supports, would have freed about 200 detainees, instead of the 38 the CSRTs let go. In 50 of these cases, he guesses, that judgment would have reflected the actual status of wrongly classified detainees. In 150 additional cases, he suspects, the gov-

---

[72] See Denbeaux and Denbeaux, "No-Hearing Hearings."

[73] The memorandum "Implementation of Combatant Status Review Tribunal Procedures for Enemy Combatants detained at Guantánamo Bay Naval Base, Cuba," issued on July 29, 2004, is available at http://www.defenselink.mil/news/Jul2004/d20040730comb.pdf.

[74] Even some of those who participated in the CSRT process had anxieties on this front. Lieutenant Colonel Stephen Abraham, who served on CSRT panels, complained in an affidavit filed in the Supreme Court's Guantánamo litigation both of serious inadequacies in tribunal access to intelligence information and of interference by the chain of command in CSRT findings. See "Declaration of Stephen Abraham," June 15, 2007, filed in *Khaled A.F. Al Odah et al. vs. United States*, No. 06-1196.

ernment had correctly identified detainees but would not have been able to prove a case adequately in a more court-like proceeding.[75] Other insiders believe this estimate high. But clearly, a fairer process that makes detention harder would generate less of it. Since the ARBs in any event sent home many of those whose detentions lay at the margins, those costs were probably not all that high in practice.

The administration's critics chronically portray the Guantánamo policy as lawless. This is the wrong vocabulary. The problems that plagued, and still plague, Guantánamo by and large did not stem from defiance of the law. They stemmed, rather, from a mismatch between the assumptions of the laws of war, which the administration tried to adapt for the task at hand, and the realities of that task, which required something more public, adversarial, and courtlike in character. This misunderstanding by administration critics of Bush's basic error led to a profound error in their own response: Instead of seeking to create a more appropriate regime, they went to court. In a perverse turn of their own, many critics actually came to *oppose* the creation of institutions better tailored to adjudicating war on terror detentions than the ones the administration had set up.[76] They came to see Congress, the one institution capable of delivering a system that might work better, as a device chiefly useful for giving judges free rein. And it was in those judges, not in the legislature, in whom they put their hopes.

---

[75] Stimson's estimate was given in a conversation on January 25, 2007.

[76] For a startling example, see the letter from a coalition of human rights and civil liberties groups to Senator Carl Levin (D-MI.), sent April 23, 2007. Levin had been contemplating legislation to beef up the CSRTs and give detainees more procedural protections within the CSRT process. The groups objected, arguing that "if Congress tinkers with the CSRT process in a way that gives it a greater veneer of due process respectability, it will be seen by some as an adequate substitute for habeas corpus, and the critical effort to restore habeas rights to detainees will flounder." The letter can be found at http://www.constitutionproject.org/pdf/Letter_to_Senator Levin_4-23-07.pdf.

SHAKESPEARE'S LEGAL ACQUIREMENTS

(continued from page 490)

John Lord Campbell

SHAKESPEARE'S WILL

Among Shakespeare's writings, I think that attention should be paid to his *Will*, for, upon a careful perusal, it will be found to have been in all probability composed by himself. It seems much too simple, terse, and condensed, to have been the composition of a Stratford attorney, who was to be paid by the number of lines which it contained. But a testator, without professional experience, could hardly have used language so appropriate as we find in this will, to express his meaning.

Shakespeare, the greatest of British dramatists, appears to have been as anxious as Sir Walter Scott, the greatest of British novelists, to found a family, although he does not require all his descendants to "bear the name and arms of Shakespeare." But, as far as the rules of English law would permit, he seeks to perpetuate in an heir male, descended from one of his daughters (his son having died in infancy, and there being no longer any prospect of issue male of his own), all the houses and lands he had acquired,— which were quite sufficient for a respectable Warwickshire squire. His favourite daughter, Susanna, married to Dr. Ball, an eminent physician, was to be the *stirps* from which this line of male heirs was to spring; and the testator creates an estate in tail male,— with remainders over, which, but for fines and recoveries, would have kept the whole of his property in one male representative for generations to come.

The will, dated 25th March, 1616, a month before his death, having given legacies to various friends and relations, thus proceeds:—

> "Item, I give, will, bequeath, and devise, unto my daughter, Susanna Hall, for better enabling of her to perform this my will and towards performance thereof, all that capital messuage or tenement, with the appurtenances, in Stratford aforesaid, called the New Place, wherein I now dwell, and two messuages or tenements with the appurtenances, situate, lying, and being in Henley Street, within the borough of Stratford aforesaid; and all my barns, stables, orchards, gardens, lands, tenements, and hereditaments whatsoever, situate, lying, and being, or to be had, received, perceived, or taken, within the towns, hamlets, villages, fields, and grounds of Stratford-upon-Avon, Old Stratford, Bishopton, and Welcombe, or in any of them, in the said county of Warwick; and also all that messuage or tenement, with the appurtenances, wherein one John Robinson dwelleth, situate, lying, and being in the Blackfriars in

London, near the Wardrobe; and all other my lands, tenements, and hereditaments whatsoever; to have and to hold all and singular the said premises, with their appurtenances, unto the said Susanna Hall, for and during the term of her natural life; and after her decease, to the first son of her body lawfully issuing, and to the heirs males of the body of the said first son lawfully issuing; and for default of such issue, to the said second son of her body lawfully issuing, and to the heirs males of the body of the second son lawfully issuing; and for default of such heirs, to the third son of the body of the said Susanna lawfully issuing, and to the heirs males of the body of the said third son lawfully issuing; and for default of such issue, the same so to be and remain to the fourth, fifth, sixth, and seventh sons of her body, lawfully issuing one after another, and to the heirs males of the bodies of the said fourth, fifth, sixth, and seventh sons lawfully issuing, in such manner as it is before limited to be and remain to the first, second, and third sons of her body, and to their heirs males; and for default of such issue, the said premises to be and remain to my said niece Hall, and the heirs males of her body lawfully issuing; and for default of such issue, to my daughter Judith, and the heirs males of her body lawfully issuing; and for default of such issue, to the right heirs of me the said William Shakespeare for ever."

In his will, when originally engrossed, there was no notice whatever taken of his wife; but immediately after these limitations he subsequently interpolated a bequest to her in the following words:—

"I give unto my wife my second best bed with the furniture."

The subject of this magnificent gift being only personal property, he shows his technical skill by omitting the word *devise*, which he had used in disposing of his reality.*

---

* The idolatrous worshippers of Shakespeare, who think it necessary to make his moral qualities as exalted as his poetical genius, account for this sorry bequest, and for no other notice being taken of poor Mrs. Shakespeare in the will, by saying that he knew she was sufficiently provided for by her right to dower out of his landed property, which the law would give her; and they add that he must have been tenderly attached to her, because (they take upon themselves to say) she was exquisitely beautiful as well as strictly virtuous. But she was left by her husband without house or furniture (except the second best bed), or a kind word, or any other token of his love; and I sadly fear that between William Shakespeare and Ann Hathaway the course of true love never did run smooth. His boyish inexperience was no doubt pleased for a short time with her caresses; but he probably found that their union was "misgraffed in respect of years," and gave advice from his own experience when he said,—

"Let still the woman take

RETROSPECT

Having concluded my examination of Shakespeare's juridical phrases and forensic allusions,— on the retrospect I am amazed, not only by their number, but by the accuracy and propriety with which they are uniformly introduced. There is nothing so dangerous as for one not of the craft to tamper with our free-masonry. In the House of Commons I have heard a county member, who meant to intimate that he entirely concurred with the last preceding speaker, say, "I join issue with the honourable gentleman who has just sat down;" the legal sense of which is, "I flatly contradict all his facts and deny his inferences." *Junius*, who was fond of dabbling in law, and who was supposed by some to be a lawyer (although Sir Philip Francis, then a clerk in the War Office, is now ascertained, beyond all doubt, to have been the man), in his address to the English nation, speaking of the House of Commons, and wishing to say that the beneficial interest in the state belongs to the people, and not to their representatives, says, "They are only *trustees*; the *fee* is in us." Now every attorney's clerk knows that when land is held in trust, the *fee* (or legal estate) is in the trustee, and that the beneficiary has only an equitable interest. While Novelists and Dramatists are constantly making mistakes as to the law of marriage, of wills, and of inheritance,— to Shakespeare's law, lavishly as he

---

An elder than herself; so wears she to him
So sways she level in her husband's heart.
    For, boy, however we do praise ourselves
Our fancies are more giddy and infirm,
More longing, wavering, sooner lost and worn
Than women's are. . . .
Then let thy love be younger than thyself
Or thy affection cannot hold the bent;
For women are like roses; whose fair flower,
Being Once displayed, doth fall that very hour."

To strengthen the suspicion that Shakespeare was likely not to have much respect for his wife, persons animated by the spirit of the late John Wilson Croker (although Shakespeare's biographers, in the absence of any register of his marriage, had conjectured that it took place in June, 1582), by searching the records of the Ecclesiastical Court at Worcester, have lately made the very awkward discovery that the bond given on grant of the licence for *William Shakespeare* to marry *Ann Hathaway* is dated 26th November, 1582, while the entry in the parish register of the baptism of Susanna, their eldest child, is dated 26th May, 1583. As Shakespeare, at the time of this misfortune, was a lad of eighteen years of age, and Miss Hathaway was more than seven years his senior, he could hardly have been the seducer; and I am afraid that she was "no better than she should be," whatever imaginary personal charms may be imputed to her.

propounds it, there can neither be demurrer nor bill of exceptions, nor writ of error.

He is no doubt equally accurate in referring to some other professions, but these references are rare and comparatively slight. Some have contended that he must have been by trade a gardener, from the conversation, in the "Winter's Tale," between Perdita, Polixenes, and Florizel, about raising *carnations* and *gilliflowers,* and the skilful *grafting* of fruit trees. Others have contended that Shakespeare must have been *bred to the sea,* from the nautical language in which directions are given for the manœuvring of the ship in the "Tempest," and from the graphic description in Henry IV.'s soliloquy of the "high and giddy mast," of the "ruffian billows," of the "slippery shrouds," and of "sealing up the ship boy's eyes." Nay, notwithstanding the admonition to be found in his works, "Throw physic to the dogs," it has been gravely suggested that he must have been initiated in medicine, from the minute inventory of the contents of the apothecary's shop in "Romeo and Juliet." But the descriptions thus relied upon, however minute, exact, and picturesque, will be found to be the result of casual observation, and they prove only nice perception, accurate recollection, and extraordinary power of pictorial language. Take the last instance referred to — Romeo's *photograph* of the apothecary and his shop.

> "Meagre were his looks,
> Sharp misery had worn him to the bones:
> And in his needy shop a tortoise hung,
> An alligator stuffed, and other skins
> Of ill-shaped fishes; and about his shelves
> A beggarly account of empty boxes.
> Green earthen pots, bladders and musty seeds,
> Remnants of packthread and old cakes of roses,
> Were thinly scattered to make up a show.

(Act V. Sc. 1.)

Any observing customer, who had once entered the shop to buy a dose of rhubarb, might have safely given a similar account of what he saw, although utterly ignorant of Galen and Hippocrates. But let a non-professional man, however acute, presume to talk law, or to draw illustrations from legal science in discussing other subjects, and he will very speedily fall into some laughable absurdity.

To conclude my summing up of the evidence under this head, I say, if Shakespeare is shown to have possessed a knowledge of law, which he might have acquired as clerk in an attorney's office in Stratford, and which he could have acquired in no other way, we are justified in believing the fact that he was a clerk in an attorney's office at Stratford, without any direct proof of the fact. Logicians and jurists allow us to infer a fact of which there is no direct proof, from facts expressly proved, if the fact to be inferred may have existed, if it be consistent with all other facts known to exist, and if facts known to exist can only be accounted for by inferring the fact to be inferred.

But, my dear Mr. Payne Collier, you must not from all this suppose that I have really become an absolute convert to your side of the question. *Æneas*, while in the shades below, for a time believed in the reality of all he seemed to see and to hear; but, when dismissed through the ivory gate, he found that he had been dreaming. I hope that my arguments do not "come like shadows, so depart." Still I must warn you that I myself remain rather sceptical. All that I can admit to you is that you may be right, and that while there is weighty evidence for you, there is nothing conclusive against you.

Resuming the Judge, however, I must lay down that your opponents are not called upon to prove a negative, and that the *onus probandi* rests upon you. You must likewise remember that you require us implicitly to believe a fact, which, were it true, positive and irrefragable evidence in Shakespeare's own handwriting might have been forthcoming to establish it. Not having been actually inrolled as an attorney, neither the records of the local court at Stratford, nor of the superior courts at Westminster, would present his name, as being concerned in any suits as an attorney; but it might have been reasonably expected that there would have been deeds or wills witnessed by him still extant;— and, after a very diligent search, none such can be discovered. Nor can this consideration be disregarded, that between Mash's Epistle in the end of the 16th century, and Chalmers's suggestion more than two hundred years after, there is no hint by his foes or his friends of Shakespeare having consumed pens, paper, ink, and pounce in an attorney's office at Stratford.*

I am quite serious and sincere in what I have written about Nash and Robert Greene having asserted the fact; but I by no means think that on this ground alone it must necessarily be taken for truth. Their statement that he had belonged to the profession of the law may be as false as that he was a plagiarist from Seneca. Nash and Robert Greene may have invented it, or repeated it on some groundless rumour. Shakespeare may have contradicted and refuted it twenty times; or, not thinking it discreditable, though untrue, he may have thought it undeserving of any notice. Observing what fictitious statements are introduced into the published

---

* "Three years I sat his smoky room in,
  Pens, paper, ink, and pounce consumin'."
  Pleader's Guide.

"Lives" of living individuals, in our own time, when truth in such matters can be so much more easily ascertained, and error so much more easily corrected, we should be slow to give faith to an uncorroborated statement made near three centuries ago by persons who were evidently actuated by malice.*

What you have mainly to rely upon (and this consideration may prevail in your favour with a large majority of the literary world) is the seemingly utter impossibility of Shakespeare having acquired, on any other theory, the wonderful knowledge of law which he undoubtedly displays. But we must bear in mind that, although he was a mortal man, and nothing miraculous can be attributed to him, he was intellectually the most gifted of mankind, and that he was capable of acquiring knowledge where the opportunities he enjoyed would have been insufficient for any other. Supposing that John the father lived as a gentleman, or respectably carried on trade as one of the principal inhabitants of the town, and that William the son, from the time of leaving the grammar-school till he went to London, resided with his father, assisting him in the management of his houses and land and any ancillary business carried on by him,— the son might have been in the habit of attending trials in the Stratford Court of Record, and when of age he might have been summoned to serve as a juryman there or at the Court Leet; he might have been intimate with some of the attorneys who practiced in the town and with their clerks, and while in their company at fairs, wakes, church ales, bowling-, bell-ringing-, and hurling-matches, he might not only have picked up some of their professional jargon, but gained some insight into the principles of their calling, which are not without interest to the curious.

---

* In several successive Lives of Lord Chief Justice Campbell it is related that, by going for a few weeks to Ireland as Chancellor, he obtained a pension of 4000l. a year, which he has ever since received, thereby robbing the public; whereas in truth and in fact, he made it a stipulation on his going to Ireland that he should receive no pension — and pension he never did receive — and, without pension or place, for years after he returned from Ireland he regularly served the public in the Judicial Committee of the Privy Council, and in the judicial business of the House of Lords. This erroneous statement is to be found in a recent Life of Lord C., which is upon the whole laudatory above due measure, but in which the author laments that there was one fault to be imputed to him which could not be passed over by an impartial biographer, viz., that he had most improperly obtained this Irish pension, which he still continues to receive without any benefit being derived by the public from his services.— Lord C. ought to speak tenderly of *Biographers*, but I am afraid that they may sometimes be justly compared to the hogs of Westphalia, who without discrimination pick up what falls from one another.

Moreover, it is to be considered that, although Shakespeare in 1589 was unquestionably a shareholder in the Blackfriars Theatre, and had trod the boards as an actor, the time when he began to write for the stage is uncertain; and we are not in possession of any piece which we assuredly know to have been written and finished by him before the year 1592. Thus there was a long interval between his arrival in London and the publication of any of the dramas from which my selections are made. In this interval he was no doubt conversant with all sorts and conditions of men. I am sorry to say I cannot discover that at any period of his life Lord Chancellors or Lord Chief Justices showed the good taste to cultivate his acquaintance.* But he must have been intimate with the students at the Inns of Court, who were in the habit of playing before Queen Elizabeth at Greenwich, as he took a part in these court theatricals; and the author, in all probability, was present among the lawyers when 'Twelfth Night' was brought out at the Readers' Feast in the Middle Temple, and when 'Othello' was acted at Lord Chancellor Ellesmere's before Queen Elizabeth.

Shakespeare, during his first years in London, when his purse was low, may have dined at the ordinary in Alsatia, thus described by Dekker, where he may have had a daily surfeit of law, if, with his universal thirst for knowledge, he had any desire to drink deeply at this muddy fountain:

> "There is another ordinary at which your London usurer, your stale bachelor and your *thrifty attorney* do resort; the price three-pence; the rooms as full of company as a gaol; and indeed divided into several wards, like the beds of an hospital. . . . If they chance to discourse, it is of nothing but of *statutes, bonds, recognizances, fines, recoveries,* audits, rents, subsidies, *sureties, enclosures, liveries, indictments, outlawries, feoffments, judgments, commissions, bankrupts, amercements,* and of such horrible matter."
>
> —*Dekker's Gull's Hornbook,* 1609.

In such company a willing listener might soon make great progress in law;— and it may be urged, that I have unconsciously exaggerated the difficulty to be encountered by Shakespeare in picking up his knowledge of that which I myself have been so long labouring to understand. Many may think that Shakespeare resembles his own Prince Hal, when reformed and become Henry V., who, notwithstanding his revels in East Cheap, and with no apparent opportunities of acquiring the knowledge he displayed, astonished the world with his universal wisdom:

---

* Although it is said that Shakespeare was introduced to Lord Chancellor Ellesmere, Lord Somers is the first legal dignitary I find forming friendships with literary men.

"Hear him but reason in divinity,
And, all-admiring, with an inward wish,
You would desire the king were made a prelate
Hear him debate of commonwealth affairs,
You would say, it hath been all-in-all his study.
List his discourse of war, and you shall hear
A fearful battle render'd you in music.
Turn him to any cause of policy,
The Gordian knot of it he will unloose
Familiar as his garter; that, when he speaks,
The air, a chartered libertine, is still,
And the mute wonder lurketh in man's ears
To steal his sweet and honeyed sentences;
So that the art, and practick part of life,
Must be the mistress to this theorick.

Henry V., Act I. Sc. 1.

We cannot argue with confidence on the principles which would guide us to safe conclusions respecting ordinary men, when we are reasoning respecting one of whom it was truly said:

"Each change of many-coloured life he drew,
Exhausted worlds, and then imagined new;
Existence saw him spurn her bounded reign,
And panting Time toiled after him in vain."

And now, my dear Hr. Payne Collier, I must conclude. Long ago, I dare say, you were heartily sorry that you ever thought of taking the opinion of counsel on this knotty point; and at last you may not only exclaim, "I am no wiser then I was," but shaking your head, like old *Demipho* in 'Terence,' after being present at a consultation of lawyers on the validity of his son's marriage, you may sigh and say, "Incertior sum multo quam dudum."

However, if my scepticism and my argumentation (worthy of Serjeant Eitherside) should stimulate you deliberately to reconsider the question, and to communicate your matured judgment to the world, I shall not have doubted or hallucinated in vain. By another outpouring of your Shakespearian lore you may entirely convince, and at all events you will much gratify,

Your sincere admirer and friend,

(Signed) CAMPBELL.

The End.

DECEMBER

THE MEASURE OF JUSTICE:
MEET HIM AT THE GATES

By John V. Orth, with the assistance of Joseph L. Hyde

When Duke Vincentio resumes his duties at the conclusion of *Measure for Measure*, he does so in an elaborate ceremony at the city gates. To the sound of trumpets, surrounded by his loyal retainers, he proclaims himself ready to redress any injustice committed in his absence. Since biblical times, justice has been administered at the city gates.[1] It is liminal space, the boundary between the wilderness of the country and the civilization of the city. But during his time in disguise the Duke had lifted the lid on Vienna: *I have seen corruption boil and bubble / Till it o'er run the stew.* The city walls can barely contain it. Only outside the city is there shelter from the toil and trouble: *the moated grange* where Mariana sits, listening to melancholy music and musing on old wrongs.

It is at the gates that the climactic trial of Angelo is held, *and the corrupt deputy scaled,* weighed in the balance and found wanting — but not ulti-

---

[1] See, e.g., Ruth 4:1-12 (Boaz gathered a group of elders at the gates to arrange his marriage to Ruth).

mately punished. Sexual desire had threatened to overbalance the established order, but in the end all the sexual miscreants — Claudio, Angelo, Lucio, and perhaps even the Duke himself — are safely housed in matrimony, sentenced to marriage rather than to death, to paraphrase W.H. Auden.[2] But the play's ending is actually no conclusion. As the astute German critic, A.W. Schlegel observed long ago, since the Duke "ultimately extends a free pardon to all the guilty, we do not see how his original purpose, in committing the execution of the laws to other hands, of restoring their strictness, has in any wise been accomplished."[3]

The debate between law and natural justice is not resolved. Yet some advance has been made. We have seen the quotidian business of justice being done. Escalus has given good counsel to Froth, committed the picklock Pompey to prison after fair warning, and started to reestablish the constabulary on its proper footing. The endless war on prostitution has gone on; some, at least, of the houses have been *plucked down*, and Mistress Overdone has been jailed, also after repeated warnings. A public spectacle has been made of several upper-class fornicators. Corruption in high places has been exposed. The Duke, who (as Escalus said) *contended especially to know himself*, has learned a lesson about the duty of princes. And all of us have learned many things, perhaps too many, about the difficulty of doing earthly justice.

continued on page 566 . . .

POLK V. STATE

2008 WL 5136318 & n.5 (Ct. Spec. App. Md. Dec. 3, 2008)

Charles E. Moylan, Jr., Judge

In the case of a knife, moreover, its handle is most assuredly a part of the weapon, just as the handle of a revolver or a rifle is a part of the weapon. A knife is not *ipso facto* concealed because its blade is in its sheath, any more than a six-gun is concealed because its barrel is in the holster or a sword concealed because its blade is in the scabbard. Though drawing an inference, perhaps, the reasonable observer knows when he has seen a knife, a six-gun, or a sword. Concealment "should be made of sterner stuff."[5]

---

[2] W.H. Auden, *Lectures on Shakespeare* 191 (Arthur Kirsch ed. 2002) ("In the play, in every case, marriage is substituted for the death penalty.").

[3] A.W. Schlegel, *Lectures on Dramatic Art & Literature* 388 (1811) (based on lectures originally delivered in Vienna) (John Black trans., 2d ed. rev. by A.J.W. Morrison) (1889).

[5] Marc Anthony's funeral oration from Shakespeare's *Julius Caesar*.

❧ DECEMBER ❧

SUN	MON	TUES	WED	THUR	FRI	SAT
		1	2	3	4	5
6	7	8	9	10	11	12
13	14	15	16	17	18	19
20	21	22	23	24	25	26
27	28	29	30	31		

THE FIRST THING WE DO . . .

Bryan A. Garner
Garner on Language and Writing xxi (ABA 2008)

2000: "Why are you going to a used-book store?" the cab driver asked. We were on our way to my favorite bookstore in Sacramento.

"I'm a book collector," I responded.

"What do you collect?"

"Law dictionaries."

"Me too!" I was surprised, and I didn't really believe him. But he continued, "I like Bouvier's Law dictionary." I began to believe him: few people know the legal lexicographer John Bouvier.

"Why do you collect law dictionaries?" I asked.

"Because I'm fascinated by law. The *real* law. The *original* law. We've gotten away from that. Most of the law today is bogus. So you have to go to Bouvier to get the real law. Law dictionaries today are no good. *Black's Law Dictionary*, for example. The editors have been bought off. There's a conspiracy to get people to think that the Internal Revenue Code is valid, when in fact it's unconstitutional. The government has paid off the editors of *Black's* to support the idea that there's a legal basis for the IRS! That's a documented fact."

"Really?" I was incredulous.

"Whoever is responsible for *Black's Law Dictionary* should be shot. If I could find the editor, I'd do it myself."

Just then, we arrived at Beer's Books, down the street from California's capitol. I paid and started getting out of the cab.

"Why do you collect law dictionaries?" the cabbie asked as I was getting out.

"Just a hobby."

540

THE GREEN LIGHT

Philippe Sands[†]

The abuse, rising to the level of torture, of those captured and detained in the war on terror is a defining feature of the presidency of George W. Bush. Its military beginnings, however, lie not in Abu Ghraib, as is commonly thought, or in the "rendition" of prisoners to other countries for questioning, but in the treatment of the very first prisoners at Guantánamo. Starting in late 2002 a detainee bearing the number 063 was tortured over a period of more than seven weeks. In his story lies the answer to a crucial question: How was the decision made to let the U.S. military start using coercive interrogations at Guantánamo?

The Bush administration has always taken refuge behind a "trickle up" explanation: that is, the decision was generated by military commanders and interrogators on the ground. This explanation is false. The origins lie in actions taken at the very highest levels of the administration — by some of the most senior personal advisers to the president, the vice president, and the secretary of defense. At the heart of the matter stand several political appointees — lawyers — who, it can be argued, broke their ethical codes of conduct and took themselves into a zone of international criminality, where formal investigation is now a very real option. This is the story of how the torture at Guantánamo began, and how it spread.

"CRYING. ANGRY. YELLED FOR ALLAH."

One day last summer I sat in a garden in London with Dr. Abigail Seltzer, a psychiatrist who specializes in trauma victims. She divides her time between Great Britain's National Health Service, where she works extensively with asylum seekers and other refugees, and the Medical Founda-

---

[†] Philippe Sands is an international lawyer at the firm Matrix Chambers and a professor at University College London. His latest book is *Torture Team: Rumsfeld's Memo and the Betrayal of American Values* (Palgrave Macmillan). *The Green Light* was originally published in the May 2008 issue of *Vanity Fair*. Copyright © 2008 by Philippe Sands. Reprinted by permission of the author and the publisher.

tion for the Care of Victims of Torture. It was uncharacteristically warm, and we took refuge in the shade of some birches. On a table before us were three documents. The first was a November 2002 "action memo" written by William J. (Jim) Haynes II, the general counsel of the U.S. Department of Defense, to his boss, Donald Rumsfeld; the document is sometimes referred to as the Haynes Memo. Haynes recommended that Rumsfeld give "blanket approval" to 15 out of 18 proposed techniques of aggressive interrogation. Rumsfeld duly did so, on December 2, 2002, signing his name firmly next to the word "Approved." Under his signature he also scrawled a few words that refer to the length of time a detainee can be forced to stand during interrogation: "I stand for 8-10 hours a day. Why is standing limited to 4 hours?"

The second document on the table listed the 18 proposed techniques of interrogation, all of which went against long-standing U.S. military practice as presented in the Army Field Manual. The 15 approved techniques included certain forms of physical contact and also techniques intended to humiliate and to impose sensory deprivation. They permitted the use of stress positions, isolation, hooding, 20-hour interrogations, and nudity. Haynes and Rumsfeld explicitly did not rule out the future use of three other techniques, one of which was waterboarding, the application of a wet towel and water to induce the perception of drowning.

The third document was an internal log that detailed the interrogation at Guantánamo of a man identified only as Detainee 063, whom we now know to be Mohammed al-Qahtani, allegedly a member of the 9/11 conspiracy and the so-called 20th hijacker. According to this log, the interrogation commenced on November 23, 2002, and continued until well into January. The techniques described by the log as having been used in the interrogation of Detainee 063 include all 15 approved by Rumsfeld.

"Was the detainee abused? Was he tortured?," I asked Seltzer. Cruelty, humiliation, and the use of torture on detainees have long been prohibited by international law, including the Geneva Conventions and their Common Article 3. This total ban was reinforced in 1984 with the adoption of the Convention Against Torture and Other Cruel, Inhuman or Degrading Treatment or Punishment, which criminalizes torture and complicity in torture.

A careful and fastidious practitioner, Seltzer declined to give a straight yes or no answer. In her view the definition of torture is essentially a legal matter, which will turn on a particular set of facts. She explained that there is no such thing as a medical definition of torture, and that a doctor must look for pathology, the abnormal functioning of the body or the mind. We reviewed the definition of torture, as set out in the 1984 Convention, which is binding on 145 countries, including the United States. Torture includes "any act by which severe pain or suffering, whether physical or mental, is intentionally inflicted on a person."

Seltzer had gone through the interrogation log, making notations. She used four different colors to highlight moments that struck her as noteworthy, and the grim document now looked bizarrely festive. Yellow indicated episodes of abusive treatment. Pink showed where the detainee's rights were respected — where he was fed or given a break, or allowed to sleep. Green indicated the many instances of medical involvement, where al-Qahtani was given an enema or was hospitalized suffering from hypothermia. Finally, blue identified what Seltzer termed "expressions of distress."

We talked about the methods of interrogation. "In terms of their effects," she said, "I suspect that the individual techniques are less important than the fact that they were used over an extended period of time, and that several appear to be used together: in other words, the cumulative effect." Detainee 063 was subjected to systematic sleep deprivation. He was shackled and cuffed; at times, head restraints were used. He was compelled to listen to threats to his family. The interrogation leveraged his sensitivities as a Muslim: he was shown pictures of scantily clad models, was touched by a female interrogator, was made to stand naked, and was forcibly shaved. He was denied the right to pray. A psychiatrist who witnessed the interrogation of Detainee 063 reported the use of dogs, intended to intimidate "by getting the dogs close to him and then having the dogs bark or act aggressively on command." The temperature was changed, and 063 was subjected to extreme cold. Intravenous tubes were forced into his body, to provide nourishment when he would not eat or drink.

We went through the marked-up document slowly, pausing at each blue mark. Detainee 063's reactions were recorded with regularity. I'll string some of them together to convey the impression:

> Detainee began to cry. Visibly shaken. Very emotional. Detainee cried. Disturbed. Detainee began to cry. Detainee bit the IV tube completely in two. Started moaning. Uncomfortable. Moaning. Began crying hard spontaneously. Crying and praying. Very agitated. Yelled. Agitated and violent. Detainee spat. Detainee proclaimed his innocence. Whining. Dizzy. Forgetting things. Angry. Upset. Yelled for Allah.

> The blue highlights went on and on.

Urinated on himself. Began to cry. Asked God for forgiveness. Cried. Cried.
Became violent. Began to cry. Broke down and cried. Began to pray and
openly cried. Cried out to Allah several times. Trembled uncontrollably.

Was Detainee 063 subjected to severe mental pain or suffering? Torture is not a medical concept, Seltzer reminded me. "That said," she went on, "over the period of 54 days there is enough evidence of distress to indicate that it would be very surprising indeed if it had not reached the threshold of severe mental pain." She thought about the matter a little more and then presented it a different way: "If you put 12 clinicians in a room and asked them about this interrogation log, you might get different views about the effect and long-term consequences of these interrogation techniques. But I doubt that any one of them would claim that this individual had not suffered severe mental distress at the time of his interrogation, and possibly also severe physical distress."

THE AUTHORIZED VERSION

The story of the Bush administration's descent down this path began to emerge on June 22, 2004. The administration was struggling to respond to the Abu Ghraib scandal, which had broken a couple of months earlier with the broadcast of photographs that revealed sickening abuse at the prison outside Baghdad. The big legal guns were wheeled out. Alberto Gonzales and Jim Haynes stepped into a conference room at the Eisenhower Executive Office Building, next to the White House. Gonzales was President Bush's White House counsel and would eventually become attorney general. Haynes, as Rumsfeld's general counsel, was the most senior lawyer in the Pentagon, a position he would retain until a month ago, when he resigned — "returning to private life," as a press release stated. Gonzales and Haynes were joined by a third lawyer, Daniel Dell'Orto, a career official at the Pentagon. Their task was to steady the beat and make it clear that the events at Abu Ghraib were the actions of a few bad eggs and had nothing to do with the broader policies of the administration.

Gonzales and Haynes spoke from a carefully prepared script. They released a thick folder of documents, segmented by lawyerly tabs. These documents were being made public for the first time, a clear indication of the gravity of the political crisis. Among the documents were the Haynes Memo and the list of 18 techniques that Seltzer and I would later review. The log detailing the interrogation of Detainee 063 was not released; it would be leaked to the press two years later.

For two hours Gonzales and Haynes laid out the administration's narrative. Al-Qaeda was a different kind of enemy, deadly and shadowy. It targeted civilians and didn't follow the Geneva Conventions or any other international rules. Nevertheless, the officials explained, the administration had acted judiciously, even as it moved away from a purely law-enforcement strategy to one that marshaled "all elements of national power." The authorized version had four basic parts.

First, the administration had moved reasonably — with care and deliberation, and always within the limits of the law. In February 2002 the president had determined, in accordance with established legal principles, that none of the detainees at Guantánamo could rely on any of the protections granted by Geneva, even Common Article 3. This presidential order was the lead document, at Tab A. The administration's point was this: agree with it or not, the decision on Geneva concealed no hidden agenda; rather, it simply reflected a clear-eyed reading of the actual provisions. The administration, in other words, was doing nothing more than trying to proceed by the book. The law was the law.

Relating to this was a second document, one that had been the subject of media speculation for some weeks. The authors of this document, a legal opinion dated August 1, 2002, were two lawyers in the Justice Department's Office of Legal Counsel: Jay Bybee, who is now a federal judge, and John Yoo, who now teaches law at Berkeley. Later it would become known that they were assisted in the drafting by David Addington, then the vice president's lawyer and now his chief of staff. The Yoo-Bybee Memo declared that physical torture occurred only when the pain was "equivalent in intensity to the pain accompanying serious physical injury, such as organ failure, impairment of bodily function, or even death," and that mental torture required "suffering not just at the moment of infliction but . . . lasting psychological harm." Interrogations that did not reach these thresholds — far less stringent than those set by international law — were allowed. Although findings that issue from the Office of Legal Counsel at Justice typically carry great weight, at the press conference Gonzales went out of his way to decouple the Yoo-Bybee Memo from anything that might have taken place at Guantánamo. The two lawyers had been asked, in effect, to stargaze, he said. Their memo simply explored "the limits of the legal landscape." It included "irrelevant and unnecessary" discussion and never made it into the hands of the president or of soldiers in the field. The memo did not, said Gonzales, "reflect the policies that the administration ultimately adopted."

The second element of the administration's narrative dealt with the specific source of the new interrogation techniques. Where had the initiative come from? The administration pointed to the military commander at Guantánamo, Major General Michael E. Dunlavey. Haynes would later describe him to the Senate Judiciary Committee, during his failed confirmation hearings for a judgeship in 2006, as "an aggressive major general." The techniques were not imposed or encouraged by Washington, which had merely reacted to a request from below. They came as a result of the identification locally of "key people" at Guantánamo, including "a guy named al-Qahtani." This man, Detainee 063, had proved able to resist the traditional non-coercive techniques of interrogation spelled out in the Army Field Manual, and as the first anniversary of 9/11 approached, an intelligence spike pointed to the possibility of new attacks. "And so it is concluded at Guantánamo," Dell'Orto emphasized, reconstructing the event, "that it may be time to inquire as to whether there may be more flexibility in the type of techniques we use on him." A request was sent from Guantánamo on October 11, 2002, to the head of the U.S. Southern Command (SouthCom), General James T. Hill. Hill in turn forwarded Dunlavey's request to General Richard Myers, the chairman of the Joint Chiefs of Staff. Ultimately, Rumsfeld approved "all but three of the requested techniques." The official version was clear: Haynes and Rumsfeld were just processing a request coming up the chain from Guantánamo.

The third element of the administration's account concerned the legal justification for the new interrogation techniques. This, too, the administration said, had originated in Guantánamo. It was not the result of legal positions taken by politically appointed lawyers in the upper echelons of the administration, and certainly not the Justice Department. The relevant document, also dated October 11, was in the bundle released by Gonzales, a legal memo prepared by Lieutenant Colonel Diane Beaver, the staff judge advocate at Guantánamo. That document — described pointedly by Dell'Orto as a "multi-page, single-spaced legal review" — sought to provide legal authority for all the interrogation techniques. No other legal memo was cited as bearing on aggressive interrogations. The finger of responsibility was intended to point at Diane Beaver.

The fourth and final element of the administration's official narrative was to make clear that decisions relating to Guantánamo had no bearing on events at Abu Ghraib and elsewhere. Gonzales wanted to "set the record straight" about this. The administration's actions were inconsistent with torture. The abuses at Abu Ghraib were unauthorized and unconnected to the administration's policies.

Gonzales and Haynes laid out their case with considerable care. The only flaw was that every element of the argument contained untruths.

The real story, pieced together from many hours of interviews with most of the people involved in the decisions about interrogation, goes something like this: The Geneva decision was not a case of following the logic of the law but rather was designed to give effect to a prior decision to take the gloves off and allow coercive interrogation; it deliberately created a legal black hole into which the detainees were meant to fall. The new interrogation techniques did not arise spontaneously from the field but came about as a direct result of intense pressure and input from Rumsfeld's office. The Yoo-Bybee Memo was not simply some theoretical document, an academic exercise in blue-sky hypothesizing, but rather played a crucial role in giving those at the top the confidence to put pressure on those at the bottom. And the practices employed at Guantánamo led to abuses at Abu Ghraib.

The fingerprints of the most senior lawyers in the administration were all over the design and implementation of the abusive interrogation policies. Addington, Bybee, Gonzales, Haynes, and Yoo became, in effect, a torture team of lawyers, freeing the administration from the constraints of all international rules prohibiting abuse.

KILLING GENEVA

In the early days of 2002, as the number of al-Qaeda and Taliban fighters captured in Afghanistan began to swell, the No. 3 official at the Pentagon was Douglas J. Feith. As undersecretary of defense for policy, he stood directly below Paul Wolfowitz and Donald Rumsfeld. Feith's job was to provide advice across a wide range of issues, and the issues came to include advice on the Geneva Conventions and the conduct of military interrogations.

I sat down with Feith not long after he left the government. He was teaching at the school of foreign service at Georgetown University, occupying a small, eighth-floor office lined with books on international law. He greeted me with a smile, his impish face supporting a mop of graying hair that seemed somehow at odds with his 54 years. Over the course of his career Feith has elicited a range of reactions. General Tommy Franks, who led the invasion of Iraq, once called Feith "the fucking stupidest guy on the face of the earth." Rumsfeld, in contrast, saw him as an "intellectual engine." In manner he is the Energizer Bunny, making it hard to get a word in edgewise. After many false starts Feith provided an account of the president's decision on Geneva, including his own contribution as one of its principal architects.

"This was something I played a major role in," he began, in a tone of evident pride. With the war in Afghanistan under way, lawyers in Washington understood that they needed a uniform view on the constraints, if any, imposed by Geneva. Addington, Haynes, and Gonzales all objected to Geneva. Indeed, Haynes in December 2001 told the CentCom admiral in charge of detainees in Afghanistan "to 'take the gloves off' and ask whatever he wanted" in the questioning of John Walker Lindh. (Lindh, a young American who had become a Muslim and had recently been captured in northern Afghanistan, bore the designation Detainee 001.)

A month later, the administration was struggling to adopt a position. On January 9, John Yoo and Robert Delahunty, at the Justice Department, prepared an opinion for Haynes. They concluded that the president wasn't bound by traditional international-law prohibitions. This encountered strong opposition from Colin Powell and his counsel, William H. Taft IV, at the State Department, as well as from the Tjags — the military lawyers in the office of the judge advocate general — who wanted to maintain a strong U.S. commitment to Geneva and the rules that were part of customary law. On January 25, Alberto Gonzales put his name to a memo to the president supporting Haynes and Rumsfeld over Powell and Taft. This memo, which is believed to have been written by Addington, presented a "new paradigm" and described Geneva's "strict limitations on questioning of enemy prisoners" as "obsolete." Addington was particularly distrustful of the military lawyers. "Don't bring the Tjags into the process — they aren't reliable," he was once overheard to say.

Feith took up the story. He had gone to see Rumsfeld about the issue, accompanied by Myers. As they reached Rumsfeld's office, Myers turned to Feith and said, "We have to support the Geneva Conventions If Rumsfeld doesn't go along with this, I'm going to contradict them in front of the president." Feith was surprised by this uncharacteristically robust statement, and by the way Myers referred to the secretary bluntly as "Rumsfeld."

Douglas Feith had a long-standing intellectual interest in Geneva, and for many years had opposed legal protections for terrorists under international law. He referred me to an article he had written in 1985, in *The National Interest,* setting out his basic view. Geneva provided incentives to play by the rules; those who chose not to follow the rules, he argued, shouldn't be allowed to rely on them, or else the whole Geneva structure would collapse. The only way to protect Geneva, in other words, was sometimes to limit its scope. To uphold Geneva's protections, you might have to cast them aside.

But that way of thinking didn't square with the Geneva system itself, which was based on two principles: combatants who behaved according to its standards received P.O.W. status and special protections, and everyone else received the more limited but still significant protections of Common Article 3. Feith described how, as he and Myers spoke with Rumsfeld, he jumped protectively in front of the general. He reprised his "little speech" for me. "There is no country in the world that has a larger interest in promoting respect for the Geneva Conventions as law than the United States," he told Rumsfeld, according to his own account, "and there is no institution in the U.S. government that has a stronger interest than the Pentagon." So Geneva had to be followed? "Obeying the Geneva Conventions is not optional," Feith replied. "The Geneva Convention is a treaty in force. It is as much part of the supreme law of the United States as a statute." Myers jumped in. "I agree completely with what Doug said and furthermore it is our military culture It's not even a matter of whether it is reciprocated — it's a matter of who we are."

Feith was animated as he relived this moment. I remained puzzled. How had the administration gone from a commitment to Geneva, as suggested by the meeting with Rumsfeld, to the president's declaration that none of the detainees had any rights under Geneva? It all turns on what you mean by "promoting respect" for Geneva, Feith explained. Geneva didn't apply at all to al-Qaeda fighters, because they weren't part of a state and therefore couldn't claim rights under a treaty that was binding only on states. Geneva did apply to the Taliban, but by Geneva's own terms Taliban fighters weren't entitled to P.O.W. status, because they hadn't worn uniforms or insignia. That would still leave the safety net provided by the rules reflected in Common Article 3 — but detainees could not rely on this either, on the theory that its provisions applied only to "armed conflict not of an international character," which the administration interpreted to mean civil war. This was new. In reaching this conclusion, the Bush administration simply abandoned all legal and customary precedent that regards Common Article 3 as a minimal bill of rights for everyone.

In the administration's account there was no connection between the decision on Geneva and the new interrogation rules later approved by Rumsfeld for Detainee 063; its position on Geneva was dictated purely by the law itself. I asked Feith, just to be clear: Didn't the administration's approach mean that Geneva's constraints on interrogation couldn't be invoked by *anyone* at Guantánamo? "Oh yes, sure," he shot back. Was that the intended result?, I asked. "Absolutely," he replied. I asked again: Under the Geneva Conventions, no one at Guantánamo was entitled to any protection? "That's the point," Feith reiterated. As he saw it, either you were a detainee to whom Geneva didn't apply or you were a detainee to whom Geneva applied but whose rights you couldn't invoke. What was the difference for the purpose of interrogation?, I asked. Feith answered with a certain satisfaction, "It turns out, none. But that's the point."

That indeed was the point. The principled legal arguments were a fig leaf. The real reason for the Geneva decision, as Feith now made explicit, was the desire to interrogate these detainees with as few constraints as possible. Feith thought he'd found a clever way to do this, which on the one hand upheld Geneva as a matter of law — the speech he made to Myers and Rumsfeld — and on the other pulled the rug out from under it as a matter of reality. Feith's argument was so clever that Myers continued to believe Geneva's protections remained in force — he was "well and truly hoodwinked," one seasoned observer of military affairs later told me.

Feith's argument prevailed. On February 7, 2002, President Bush signed a memorandum that turned Guantánamo into a Geneva-free zone. As a matter of policy, the detainees would be handled humanely, but only to the extent appropriate and consistent with military necessity. "The president said 'humane treatment,'" Feith told me, inflecting the term sourly, "and I thought that was O.K. Perfectly fine phrase that needs to be fleshed out, but it's a fine phrase — 'humane treatment.'" The Common Article 3 restrictions on torture or "outrages upon personal dignity" were gone.

"This year I was really a player," Feith said, thinking back on 2002 and relishing the memory. I asked him whether, in the end, he was at all concerned that the Geneva decision might have diminished America's moral authority. He was not. "The problem with moral authority," he said, was "people who should know better, like yourself, siding with the assholes, to put it crudely."

"I WAS ON A TIMELINE"

As the traditional constraints on aggressive interrogation were removed, Rumsfeld wanted the right man to take charge of Joint Task Force 170, which oversaw military interrogations at Guantánamo. Two weeks after the decision on Geneva he found that man in Michael Dunlavey. Dunlavey was a judge in the Court of Common Pleas in Erie, Pennsylvania, a Vietnam veteran, and a major general in the reserves with a strong background in intelligence.

Dunlavey met one-on-one with Rumsfeld at the end of February. They both liked what they saw. When I met Dunlavey, now back at his office in Erie, he described that initial meeting: "He evaluated me. He wanted to know who I was. He was very focused on the need to get intelligence. He wanted to make sure that the moment was not lost." Dunlavey was a strong and abrasive personality ("a tyrant," one former jag told me), but he was also a cautious man, alert to the nuances of instruction from above. Succinctly, Dunlavey described the mission Rumsfeld had given him. "He wanted me to 'maximize the intelligence production.' No one ever said to me, 'The gloves are off.' But I didn't need to talk about the Geneva Conventions. It was clear that they didn't apply." Rumsfeld told Dunlavey to report directly to him. To the suggestion that Dunlavey report to South-Com, Dunlavey heard Rumsfeld say, "I don't care who he is under. He works for me."

He arrived at Guantánamo at the beginning of March. Planeloads of detainees were being delivered on a daily basis, though Dunlavey soon concluded that half of them had no intelligence value. He reported this to Rumsfeld, who referred the matter to Feith. Feith, Dunlavey said, resisted the idea of repatriating any detainees whatsoever. (Feith says he made a series of interagency proposals to repatriate detainees.)

Dunlavey described Feith to me as one of his main points of contact. Feith, for his part, had told me that he knew nothing about any specific interrogation issues until the Haynes Memo suddenly landed on his desk. But that couldn't be right — in the memo itself Haynes had written, "I have discussed this with the Deputy, Doug Feith and General Myers." I read the sentence aloud. Feith looked at me. His only response was to tell me that I had mispronounced his name. "It's Fythe," he said. "Not Faith."

In June, the focus settled on Detainee 063, Mohammed al-Qahtani, a Saudi national who had been refused entry to the United States just before 9/11 and was captured a few months later in Afghanistan. Dunlavey described to me the enormous pressure he came under — from Washington, from the top — to find out what al-Qahtani knew. The message, he said, was: "Are you doing everything humanly possible to get this information?" He received a famous Rumsfeld "snowflake," a memo designed to prod the recipient into action. "I've got a short fuse on this to get it up the chain," Dunlavey told me, "I was on a timeline." Dunlavey held eye contact for more than a comfortable moment. He said, "This guy may have been the key to the survival of the U.S."

The interrogation of al-Qahtani relied at first on long-established F.B.I. and military techniques, procedures sanctioned by the Field Manual and based largely on building rapport. This yielded nothing. On August 8, al-Qahtani was placed in an isolation facility to separate him from the general detainee population. Pressure from Washington continued to mount. How high up did it go?, I asked Dunlavey. "It must have been all the way to the White House," he replied.

Meanwhile, unbeknownst to Dunlavey and the others at Guantánamo, interrogation issues had arisen in other quarters. In March 2002 a man named Abu Zubaydah, a high-ranking al-Qaeda official, was captured in Pakistan. C.I.A. director George Tenet wanted to interrogate him aggressively but worried about the risk of criminal prosecution. He had to await the completion of legal opinions by the Justice Department, a task that had been entrusted by Alberto Gonzales to Jay Bybee and John Yoo. "It took until August to get clear guidance on what Agency officers could legally do," Tenet later wrote. The "clear guidance" came on August 1, 2002, in memos written by Bybee and Yoo, with input from Addington. The first memo was addressed to Gonzales, redefining torture and abandoning the definition set by the 1984 torture convention. This was the Yoo-Bybee Memo made public by Gonzales nearly two years later, in the wake of Abu Ghraib. Nothing in the memo suggested that its use was limited to the C.I.A.; it referred broadly to "the conduct of interrogations outside of the United States." Gonzales would later contend that this policy memo did "not reflect the policies the administration ultimately adopted," but in fact it gave carte blanche to all the interrogation techniques later recommended by Haynes and approved by Rumsfeld. The second memo, requested by John Rizzo, a senior lawyer at the C.I.A., has never been made public. It spells out the specific techniques in detail. Dunlavey and his subordinates at Guantánamo never saw these memos and were not aware of their contents.

The lawyers in Washington were playing a double game. They wanted maximum pressure applied during interrogations, but didn't want to be seen as the ones applying it — they wanted distance and deniability. They also wanted legal cover for themselves. A key question is whether Haynes and Rumsfeld had knowledge of the content of these memos before they approved the new interrogation techniques for al-Qahtani. If they did, then the administration's official narrative — that the pressure for new techniques, and the legal support for them, originated on the ground at Guantánamo, from the "aggressive major general" and his staff lawyer — becomes difficult to sustain. More crucially, that knowledge is a link in the causal chain that connects the keyboards of Feith and Yoo to the interrogations of Guantánamo.

When did Haynes learn that the Justice Department had signed off on aggressive interrogation? All indications are that well before Haynes wrote his memo he knew what the Justice Department had advised the C.I.A. on interrogations and believed that he had legal cover to do what he wanted. Everyone in the upper echelons of the chain of decision-making that I spoke with, including Feith, General Myers, and General Tom Hill (the commander of SouthCom), confirmed to me that they believed at the time that Haynes had consulted Justice Department lawyers. Moreover, Haynes was a close friend of Bybee's. "Jim was tied at the hip with Jay Bybee," Thomas Romig, the army's former judge advocate general, told me. "He would quote him the whole time." Later, when asked during Senate hearings about his knowledge of the Yoo-Bybee Memo, Haynes would variously testify that he had not sought the memo, had not shaped its content, and did not possess a copy of it — but he carefully refrained from saying that he was unaware of its contents. Haynes, with whom I met on two occasions, will not speak on the record about this subject.

THE GLASSY-EYED MEN

As the first anniversary of 9/11 approached, Joint Task Force 170 was on notice to deliver results. But the task force was not the only actor at Guantánamo. The C.I.A. had people there looking for recruits among the detainees. The Defense Intelligence Agency (D.I.A.) was interrogating detainees through its humint (human intelligence) Augmentation Teams. The F.B.I. was carrying out its own traditional non-aggressive interrogations.

The source of the various new techniques has been the stuff of speculation. In the administration's official account, as noted, everything trickled up from the ground at Guantánamo. When I suggested to Mike Dunlavey that the administration's trickle-up line was counter-intuitive, he didn't disabuse me. "It's possible," he said, in a tone at once mischievous and unforthcoming, "that someone was sent to my task force and came up with these great ideas." One F.B.I. special agent remembers an occasion, before any new techniques had been officially sanctioned, when military interrogators set out to question al-Qahtani for 24 hours straight — employing a variation on a method that would later appear in the Haynes Memo. When the agent objected, he said he was told that the plan had been approved by "the secretary," meaning Rumsfeld.

Diane Beaver, Dunlavey's staff judge advocate, was the lawyer who would later be asked to sign off on the new interrogation techniques. When the administration made public the list, it was Beaver's legal advice the administration invoked. Diane Beaver gave me the fullest account of the process by which the new interrogation techniques emerged. In our lengthy conversations, which began in the autumn of 2006, she seemed coiled up — mistreated, hung out to dry. Before becoming a military lawyer Beaver had been a military police officer; once, while stationed in Germany, she had visited the courtroom where the Nuremberg trials took place. She was working as a lawyer for the Pentagon when the hijacked airplane hit on 9/11, and decided to remain in the army to help as she could. That decision landed her in Guantánamo.

It was clear to me that Beaver believed Washington was directly involved in the interrogations. Her account confirmed what Dunlavey had intimated, and what others have told me — that Washington's views were being fed into the process by people physically present at Guantánamo. D.I.A. personnel were among them. Later allegations would suggest a role for three C.I.A. psychologists.

During September a series of brainstorming meetings were held at Guantánamo to discuss new techniques. Some of the meetings were led by Beaver. "I kept minutes. I got everyone together. I invited. I facilitated," she told me. The sessions included representatives of the D.I.A. and the C.I.A. Ideas came from all over. Some derived from personal training experiences, including a military program known as sere (Survival, Evasion, Resistance, and Escape), designed to help soldiers persevere in the event of capture. Had sere been, in effect, reverse-engineered to provide some of the 18 techniques? Both Dunlavey and Beaver told me that sere provided inspiration, contradicting the administration's denials that it had. Indeed, several Guantánamo personnel, including a psychologist and a psychiatrist, traveled to Fort Bragg, sere's home, for a briefing.

Ideas arose from other sources. The first year of Fox TV's dramatic series *24* came to a conclusion in spring 2002, and the second year of the series began that fall. An inescapable message of the program is that torture works. "We saw it on cable," Beaver recalled. "People had already seen the first series. It was hugely popular." Jack Bauer had many friends at Guantánamo, Beaver added. "He gave people lots of ideas."

The brainstorming meetings inspired animated discussion. "Who has the glassy eyes?," Beaver asked herself as she surveyed the men around the room, 30 or more of them. She was invariably the only woman present — as she saw it, keeping control of the boys. The younger men would get particularly agitated, excited even. "You could almost see their dicks getting hard as they got new ideas," Beaver recalled, a wan smile flickering on her face. "And I said to myself, You know what? I don't have a dick to get hard — I can stay detached."

Not everyone at Guantánamo was enthusiastic. The F.B.I. and the Naval Criminal Investigative Service refused to be associated with aggressive interrogation. They opposed the techniques. One of the N.C.I.S. psychologists, Mike Gelles, knew about the brainstorming sessions but stayed away. He was dismissive of the administration's contention that the techniques trickled up on their own from Guantánamo. "That's not accurate," he said flatly. "This was not done by a bunch of people down in Gitmo — no way."

That view is buttressed by a key event that has received virtually no attention. On September 25, as the process of elaborating new interrogation techniques reached a critical point, a delegation of the administration's most senior lawyers arrived at Guantánamo. The group included the president's lawyer, Alberto Gonzales, who had by then received the Yoo-Bybee Memo; Vice President Cheney's lawyer, David Addington, who had contributed to the writing of that memo; the C.I.A.'s John Rizzo, who had asked for a Justice Department sign-off on individual techniques, including waterboarding, and received the second (and still secret) Yoo-Bybee Memo; and Jim Haynes, Rumsfeld's counsel. They were all well aware of al-Qahtani. "They wanted to know what we were doing to get to this guy," Dunlavey told me, "and Addington was interested in how we were managing it." I asked what they had to say. "They brought ideas with them which had been given from sources in D.C.," Dunlavey said. "They came down to observe and talk." Throughout this whole period, Dunlavey went on, Rumsfeld was "directly and regularly involved."

Beaver confirmed the account of the visit. Addington talked a great deal, and it was obvious to her that he was a "very powerful man" and "definitely the guy in charge," with a booming voice and confident style. Gonzales was quiet. Haynes, a friend and protégé of Addington's, seemed especially interested in the military commissions, which were to decide the fate of individual detainees. They met with the intelligence people and talked about new interrogation methods. They also witnessed some interrogations. Beaver spent time with the group. Talking about the episode even long afterward made her visibly anxious. Her hand tapped and she moved restlessly in her chair. She recalled the message they had received from the visitors: Do "whatever needed to be done." That was a green light from the very top — the lawyers for Bush, Cheney, Rumsfeld, and the C.I.A. The administration's version of events — that it became involved in the Guantánamo interrogations only in November, after receiving a list of techniques out of the blue from the "aggressive major general" — was demonstrably false.

"A DUNK IN THE WATER"

Two weeks after this unpublicized visit the process of compiling the list of new techniques was completed. The list was set out in a three-page memorandum from Lieutenant Colonel Jerald Phifer, dated October 11 and addressed to Dunlavey.

The Phifer Memo identified the problem: "current guidelines" prohibited the use of "physical or mental torture, threats, insults, or exposure to inhumane treatment as a means of or aid to interrogation." The prohibition dated back to 1863 and a general order issued by Abraham Lincoln.

The list of new interrogation techniques turned its back on this tradition. The 18 techniques were divided into three categories and came with only rudimentary guidance. No limits were placed on how many methods could be used at once, or for how many days in succession. The detainee was to be provided with a chair. The environment should be generally comfortable. If the detainee was uncooperative, you went to Category I. This comprised two techniques, yelling and deception.

If Category I produced no results, then the military interrogator could move to Category II. Category II included 12 techniques aimed at humiliation and sensory deprivation: for instance, the use of stress positions, such as standing; isolation for up to 30 days; deprivation of light and sound; 20-hour interrogations; removal of religious items; removal of clothing; forcible grooming, such as the shaving of facial hair; and the use of individual phobias, such as the fear of dogs, to induce stress.

Finally came Category III, for the most exceptionally resistant. Category III included four techniques: the use of "mild, non-injurious physical contact," such as grabbing, poking, and light pushing; the use of scenarios designed to convince the detainee that death or severely painful consequences were imminent for him or his family; exposure to cold weather or water; and waterboarding. This last technique, which powerfully mimics the experience of drowning, was later described by Vice President Cheney as a "dunk in the water."

By the time the memo was completed al-Qahtani had already been separated from all other detainees for 64 days, in a cell that was "always flooded with light." An F.B.I. agent described his condition the following month, just as the new interrogation techniques were first being directed against him: the detainee, a 2004 memo stated, "was talking to non-existent people, reporting hearing voices, [and] crouching in a corner of the cell covered with a sheet for hours on end."

ENDS AND MEANS

Diane Beaver was insistent that the decision to implement new interrogation techniques had to be properly written up and that it needed a paper trail leading to authorization from the top, not from "the dirt on the ground," as she self-deprecatingly described herself. "I just wasn't comfortable giving oral advice," she explained, as she had been requested to do. "I wanted to get something in writing. That was my game plan. I had four days. Dunlavey gave me just four days." She says she believed that senior lawyers in Washington would review her written advice and override it if necessary. It never occurred to her that on so important an issue she would be the one to provide the legal assessment on which the entire matter would appear to rest — that her word would be the last word. As far as she was concerned, getting the proposal "up the command" was victory enough. She didn't know that people much higher up had already made their decisions, had the security of secret legal cover from the Justice Department, and, although confident of their own legal protection, had no intention of soiling their hands by weighing in on the unpleasant details of interrogation.

Marooned in Guantánamo, Beaver had limited access to books and other documents, although there was Internet access to certain legal materials. She tried getting help from more experienced lawyers — at South-Com, the Joint Chiefs, the D.I.A., the JAG School — but to no avail.

In the end she worked on her own, completing the task just before the Columbus Day weekend. Her memo was entitled "Legal Review of Aggressive Interrogation Techniques." The key fact was that none of the detainees were protected by Geneva, owing to Douglas Feith's handiwork and the president's decision in February. She also concluded that the torture convention and other international laws did not apply, conclusions that a person more fully schooled in the relevant law might well have questioned: "It was not my job to second-guess the president," she told me. Beaver ignored customary international law altogether. All that was left was American law, which is what she turned to.

Given the circumstances in which she found herself, the memo has a certain desperate, heroic quality. She proceeded methodically through the 18 techniques, testing each against the standards set by U.S. law, including the Eighth Amendment to the Constitution (which prohibits "cruel and unusual punishment"), the federal torture statute, and the Uniform Code of Military Justice. The common theme was that the techniques were fine "so long as the force used could plausibly have been thought necessary in a particular situation to achieve a legitimate government objective, and it was applied in a good faith effort and not maliciously or sadistically for the very purpose of causing harm." That is to say, the techniques are legal if the motivation is pure. National security justifies anything.

Beaver did enter some important caveats. The interrogators had to be properly trained. Since the law required "examination of all facts under a totality of circumstances test," all proposed interrogations involving Category II and III methods had to "undergo a legal, medical, behavioral science, and intelligence review prior to their commencement." This suggested concerns about these new techniques, including whether they would be effective. But in the end she concluded, I "agree that the proposed strategies do not violate applicable federal law." The word "agree" stands out — she seems to be confirming a policy decision that she knows has already been made.

Time and distance do not improve the quality of the advice. I thought it was awful when I first read it, and awful when I reread it. Nevertheless, I was now aware of the circumstances in which Beaver had been asked to provide her advice. Refusal would have caused difficulty. It was also reasonable to expect a more senior review of her draft. Beaver struck me as honest, loyal, and decent. Personally, she was prepared to take a hard line on many detainees. She once described them to me as "psychopaths. Skinny, runty, dangerous, lying psychopaths." But there was a basic integrity to her approach. She could not have anticipated that there would be no other piece of written legal advice bearing on the Guantánamo interrogations. She could not have anticipated that she would be made the scapegoat.

Once, after returning to a job at the Pentagon, Beaver passed David Addington in a hallway — the first time she had seen him since his visit to Guantánamo. He recognized her immediately, smiled, and said, "Great minds think alike."

THE "VOCO"

On October 11, Dunlavey sent his request for approval of new techniques, together with Diane Beaver's legal memo, to General Tom Hill, the commander of SouthCom. Two weeks later, on October 25, Hill forwarded everything to General Myers, the chairman of the Joint Chiefs, in Washington. Hill's cover letter contains a sentence — "Our respective staffs, the Office of the Secretary of Defense, and Joint Task Force 170 have been trying to identify counter-resistant techniques that we can lawfully employ" — which again makes it clear that the list of techniques was no surprise to Rumsfeld's office, whatever its later claims. Hill also expressed serious reservations. He wanted Pentagon lawyers to weigh in, and he explicitly requested that "Department of Justice lawyers review the third category of techniques."

At the level of the Joint Chiefs the memo should have been subject to a detailed review, including close legal scrutiny by Myers's own counsel, Jane Dalton, but that never happened. It seems that Jim Haynes short-circuited the approval process. Alberto Mora, the general counsel of the navy, says he remembers Dalton telling him, "Jim pulled this away. We never had a chance to complete the assessment."

When we spoke, Myers confessed to being troubled that normal procedures had been circumvented. He held the Haynes Memo in his hands, looking carefully at the sheet of paper as if seeing it clearly for the first time. He pointed: "You don't see my initials on this." Normally he would have initialed a memo to indicate approval, but there was no confirmation that Myers had seen the memo or formally signed off on it before it went to Rumsfeld. "You just see I've 'discussed' it," he said, noting a sentence to that effect in the memo itself. "This was not the way this should have come about." Thinking back, he recalled the "intrigue" that was going on, intrigue "that I wasn't aware of, and Jane wasn't aware of, that was probably occurring between Jim Haynes, White House general counsel, and Justice."

Further confirmation that the Haynes Memo got special handling comes from a former Pentagon official, who told me that Lieutenant General Bantz Craddock, Rumsfeld's senior military assistant, noticed that it was missing a buck slip, an essential component that shows a document's circulation path, and which everyone was supposed to initial. The Haynes Memo had no "legal chop," or signature, from the general counsel's office. It went back to Haynes, who later signed off with a note that said simply, "Good to go."

Events moved fast as the process was cut short. On November 4, Dunlavey was replaced as commander at Guantánamo by Major General Geoffrey Miller. On November 12 a detailed interrogation plan was approved for al-Qahtani, based on the new interrogation techniques. The plan was sent to Rumsfeld for his personal approval, General Hill told me.

Ten days later an alternative plan, prepared by Mike Gelles and others at the N.C.I.S. and elsewhere, using traditional non-aggressive techniques, was rejected. By then the F.B.I. had communicated its concerns to Haynes's office about developments at Guantánamo. On November 23, well before Rumsfeld gave formal written approval to the Haynes Memo, General Miller received a "voco" — a vocal command — authorizing an immediate start to the aggressive interrogation of al-Qahtani. No one I spoke with, including Beaver, Hill, and Myers, could recall who had initiated the voco, but an army investigation would state that it was likely Rumsfeld, and he would not have acted without Haynes's endorsement.

Al-Qahtani's interrogation log for Saturday, November 23, registers the immediate consequence of the decision to move ahead. "The detainee arrives at the interrogation booth His hood is removed and he is bolted to the floor."

REVERSAL

Four days after the voco, Haynes formally signed off on his memo. He recommended, as a matter of policy, approval of 15 of the 18 techniques. Of the four techniques listed in Category III, however, Haynes proposed blanket approval of just one: mild non-injurious physical contact. He would later tell the Senate that he had "recommended against the proposed use of a wet towel" — that is, against waterboarding — but to the contrary, in his memo he stated that "all Category III techniques may be legally available." Rumsfeld placed his name next to the word "Approved" and wrote the jocular comment that may well expose him to difficulties in the witness stand at some future time.

As the memo was being approved, the F.B.I. communicated serious concerns directly to Haynes's office. Then, on December 17, Dave Brant, of the N.C.I.S., paid a surprise visit to Alberto Mora, the general counsel of the navy. Brant told him that N.C.I.S. agents had information that abusive actions at Guantánamo had been authorized at a "high level" in Washington. The following day Mora met again with Brant. Mike Gelles joined them and told Mora that the interrogators were under extraordinary pressure to achieve results. Gelles described the phenomenon of "force drift," where interrogators using coercion come to believe that if some force is good, then more must be better. As recounted in his official "Memorandum for Inspector General, Department of the Navy," Mora visited Steve Morello, the army's general counsel, and Tom Taylor, his deputy, who showed him a copy of the Haynes Memo with its attachments. The memorandum describes them as demonstrating "great concern." In the course of a long interview Mora recalled Morello "with a furtive air" saying, "Look at this. Don't tell anyone where you got it." Mora was horrified by what he read. "I was astounded that the secretary of defense would get within 100 miles of this issue," he said. (Notwithstanding the report to the inspector general, Morello denies showing Mora a copy of the Haynes Memo.)

On December 20, Mora met with Haynes, who listened attentively and said he would consider Mora's concerns. Mora went away on vacation, expecting everything to be sorted out. It wasn't: Brant soon called to say the detainee mistreatment hadn't stopped. On January 9, 2003, Mora met Haynes for a second time, expressing surprise that the techniques hadn't been stopped. Haynes said little in response, and Mora felt he had made no headway. The following day, however, Haynes called to say that he had briefed Rumsfeld and that changes were in the offing. But over the next several days no news came.

On the morning of Wednesday, January 15, Mora awoke determined to act. He would put his concerns in writing in a draft memorandum for Haynes and Dalton. He made three simple points. One: the majority of the Category II and III techniques violated domestic and international law and constituted, at a minimum, cruel and unusual treatment and, at worst, torture. Two: the legal analysis by Diane Beaver had to be rejected. Three: he "strongly non-concurred" with these interrogation techniques. He delivered the draft memo to Haynes's office. Two hours later, at about five p.m. on January 15, Haynes called Mora. "I'm pleased to tell you the secretary has rescinded the authorization," he said.

The abusive interrogation of al-Qahtani lasted a total of 54 days. It ended not on January 12, as the press was told in June 2004, but three days later, on January 15. In those final three days, knowing that the anything-goes legal regime might disappear at any moment, the interrogators made one last desperate push to get something useful out of al-Qahtani. They never did. By the end of the interrogation al-Qahtani, according to an army investigator, had "black coals for eyes."

The Great Migration

Mike Gelles, of the N.C.I.S., had shared with me his fear that the al-Qahtani techniques would not simply fade into history — that they would turn out to have been horribly contagious. This "migration" theory was controversial, because it potentially extended the responsibility of those who authorized the Guantánamo techniques to abusive practices elsewhere. John Yoo has described the migration theory as "an exercise in hyperbole and partisan smear."

But is it? In August 2003, Major General Miller traveled from Guantánamo to Baghdad, accompanied by Diane Beaver. They visited Abu Ghraib and found shocking conditions of near lawlessness. Miller made recommendations to Lieutenant General Ricardo Sanchez, the commander of coalition forces in Iraq. On September 14, General Sanchez authorized an array of new interrogation techniques. These were vetted by his staff judge advocate, who later told the Senate Armed Services Committee that operating procedures and policies "in use in Guantánamo Bay" had been taken into account. Despite the fact that Geneva applied in Iraq, General Sanchez authorized several techniques that were not sanctioned by the Field Manual — but were listed in the Haynes Memo. The abuses for which Abu Ghraib became infamous began one month later.

Three different official investigations in the space of three years have confirmed the migration theory. The August 2006 report of the Pentagon's inspector general concluded unequivocally that techniques from Guantánamo had indeed found their way to Iraq. An investigation overseen by former secretary of defense James R. Schlesinger determined that "augmented techniques for Guantanamo migrated to Afghanistan and Iraq where they were neither limited nor safeguarded."

Jim Haynes and Donald Rumsfeld may have reversed themselves about al-Qahtani in January 2003, but the death blow to the administration's outlook did not occur for three more years. It came on June 29, 2006, with the U.S. Supreme Court's ruling in *Hamdan* v. *Rumsfeld,* holding that Guantánamo detainees were entitled to the protections provided under Geneva's Common Article 3. The Court invoked the legal precedents that had been sidestepped by Douglas Feith and John Yoo, and laid bare the blatant illegality of al-Qahtani's interrogation. A colleague having lunch with Haynes that day described him as looking "shocked" when the news arrived, adding, "He just went pale." Justice Anthony Kennedy, joining the majority, pointedly observed that "violations of Common Article 3 are considered 'war crimes.'"

Jim Haynes appears to remain a die-hard supporter of aggressive interrogation. Shortly after the Supreme Court decision, when he appeared before the Senate Judiciary Committee, Senator Patrick Leahy reminded him that in 2003 Haynes had said there was "no way" that Geneva could apply to the Afghan conflict and the war on terror. "Do you now accept that you were mistaken in your legal and policy determinations?," Leahy asked. Haynes would say only that he was bound by the Supreme Court's decision.

As the consequences of *Hamdan* sank in, the instinct for self-preservation asserted itself. The lawyers got busy. Within four months President Bush signed into law the Military Commissions Act. This created a new legal defense against lawsuits for misconduct arising from the "detention and interrogation of aliens" between September 11, 2001, and December 30, 2005. That covered the interrogation of al-Qahtani, and no doubt much else. Signing the bill on October 17, 2006, President Bush explained that it provided "legal protections that ensure our military and intelligence personnel will not have to fear lawsuits filed by terrorists simply for doing their jobs."

In a word, the interrogators and their superiors were granted immunity from prosecution. Some of the lawyers who contributed to this legislation were immunizing themselves. The hitch, and it is a big one, is that the immunity is good only within the borders of the United States.

A Tap on the Shoulder

The table in the conference room held five stacks of files and papers, neatly arranged and yellow and crisp with age. Behind them sat an elderly gentleman named Ludwig Altstötter, rosy-cheeked and cherubic. Ludwig is the son of Josef Altstötter, the lead defendant in the 1947 case *United States of America* v. *Josef Altstoetter et al.*, which was tried in Germany before a U.S. military tribunal. The case is famous because it appears to be the only one in which lawyers have ever been charged and convicted for committing international crimes through the performance of their legal functions. It served as the inspiration for the Oscar-winning 1961 movie *Judgment at Nuremberg,* whose themes are alluded to in Marcel Ophuls's classic 1976 film on wartime atrocities, *The Memory of Justice,* which should be required viewing but has been lost to a broader audience. Nuremberg was, in fact, where Ludwig and I were meeting.

The Altstötter case had been prosecuted by the Allies to establish the principle that lawyers and judges in the Nazi regime bore a particular responsibility for the regime's crimes. Sixteen lawyers appeared as defendants. The scale of the Nazi atrocities makes any factual comparison with Guantánamo absurd, a point made to me by Douglas Feith, and with which I agree. But I wasn't interested in drawing a facile comparison between historical episodes. I wanted to know more about the underlying principle.

Josef Altstötter had the misfortune, because of his name, to be the first defendant listed among the 16. He was not the most important or the worst, although he was one of the 10 who were in fact convicted (4 were acquitted, one committed suicide, and there was one mistrial). He was a well-regarded member of society and a high-ranking lawyer. In 1943 he joined the Reich Ministry of Justice in Berlin, where he served as a *Ministerialdirektor,* the chief of the civil-law-and-procedure division. He became a member of the SS in 1937. The U.S. Military Tribunal found him guilty of membership in that criminal organization — with knowledge of its criminal acts — and sentenced him to five years in prison, which he served in full. He returned to legal practice in Nuremberg and died in 1979. Ludwig Altstötter had all the relevant documents, and he generously invited me to go over them with him in Nuremberg.

I took Ludwig to the most striking passage in the tribunal's judgment. "He gave his name as a soldier and a jurist of note and so helped to cloak the shameful deeds of that organisation from the eyes of the German people." The tribunal convicted Altstötter largely on the basis of two letters. Ludwig went to the piles on the table and pulled out fading copies of the originals. The first, dated May 3, 1944, was from the chief of the SS intelligence service to Ludwig's father, asking him to intervene with the regional court of Vienna and stop it from ordering the transfer of Jews from the concentration camp at Theresienstadt back to Vienna to appear as witnesses in court hearings. The second letter was Altstötter's response, a month later, to the president of the court in Vienna. "For security reasons," he wrote, "these requests cannot be granted." The U.S. Military Tribunal proceeded on the basis that Altstötter would have known what the concentration camps were for.

The words "security reasons" reminded me of remarks by Jim Haynes at the press conference with Gonzales: "Military necessity can sometimes allow . . . warfare to be conducted in ways that might infringe on the otherwise applicable articles of the Convention." Haynes provided no legal authority for that proposition, and none exists. The minimum rights of detainees guaranteed by Geneva and the torture convention can never be overridden by claims of security or other military necessity. That is their whole purpose.

Mohammed al-Qahtani is among the first six detainees scheduled to go on trial for complicity in the 9/11 attacks; the Bush administration has announced that it will seek the death penalty. Last month, President Bush vetoed a bill that would have outlawed the use by the C.I.A. of the techniques set out in the Haynes Memo and used on al-Qahtani. Whatever he may have done, Mohammed al-Qahtani was entitled to the protections afforded by international law, including Geneva and the torture convention. His interrogation violated those conventions. There can be no doubt that he was treated cruelly and degraded, that the standards of Common Article 3 were violated, and that his treatment amounts to a war crime. If he suffered the degree of severe mental distress prohibited by the torture convention, then his treatment crosses the line into outright torture. These acts resulted from a policy decision made right at the top, not simply from ground-level requests in Guantánamo, and they were supported by legal advice from the president's own circle.

Those responsible for the interrogation of Detainee 063 face a real risk of investigation if they set foot outside the United States. Article 4 of the torture convention criminalizes "complicity" or "participation" in torture, and the same principle governs violations of Common Article 3.

It would be wrong to consider the prospect of legal jeopardy unlikely. I remember sitting in the House of Lords during the landmark Pinochet case, back in 1999 — in which a prosecutor was seeking the extradition to Spain of the former Chilean head of state for torture and other international crimes — and being told by one of his key advisers that they had never expected the torture convention to lead to the former president of Chile's loss of legal immunity. In my efforts to get to the heart of this story, and its possible consequences, I visited a judge and a prosecutor in a major European city, and guided them through all the materials pertaining to the Guantánamo case. The judge and prosecutor were particularly struck by the immunity from prosecution provided by the Military Commissions Act. "That is very stupid," said the prosecutor, explaining that it would make it much easier for investigators outside the United States to argue that possible war crimes would never be addressed by the justice system in the home country — one of the trip wires enabling foreign courts to intervene. For some of those involved in the Guantánamo decisions, prudence may well dictate a more cautious approach to international travel. And for some the future may hold a tap on the shoulder.

"It's a matter of time," the judge observed. "These things take time." As I gathered my papers, he looked up and said, "And then something unexpected happens, when one of these lawyers travels to the wrong place."

MEASURE FOR MEASURE IN COURT

By John V. Orth, with the assistance of Joseph L. Hyde

Editor's note: This is the final installment of Professor Orth's treatment of *Measure for Measure*. See also pages 46, 161, 205, 231, 275, 309, 341, 393, 419, 447, 477, 493, and 537.

Shakespeare and the Bible, once part of Americans' common culture, were often quoted in legal argument. Even today, *Measure for Measure* with its legal themes continues to provide judges the opportunity to enliven otherwise routine judicial opinions. Aside from the 49 times specific passages were quoted — indicated in the footnotes — the play was referred to in general terms an additional seven times. Judge Richard Posner, author (among many other titles) of *Law and Literature: A Misunderstood Relation*, turned naturally to *Measure for Measure* in a case involving solicitation for sex in return for official favors, particularly when the defendant was named DeAngelo,[1] and again in a case involving the sudden revival of a long forgotten law carrying harsh penalties.[2] A federal district court judge followed Posner's lead in the latter case, citing his use of the play on the question of desuetude.[3] Another scholar-judge on the U.S. Court of Appeals, Judge John Noonan, was also reminded of the play's theme of sex for favors in a case of official misconduct.[4] In addition, two federal district court judges mentioned the play in explanation of the need for secular study of the Bible: "Some of the better known works which rely heavily on allusions from the Bible include . . . the plays of Shakespeare, especially *Measure for Measure* . . . ."[5] Finally, a Pennsylvania judge, somewhat surprisingly, mentioned the play for its recognition of

---

[1] Alexander v. DeAngelo, 329 F.3d 912, 917 (7th Cir. 2003).

[2] Central Nat'l Bank of Mattoon v. U.S. Dept. of Treasury, 912 F.2d 897, 906 (7th Cir. 1990). Judge Posner quoted lines from the play to similar effect in Connecticut General Life Ins. Co. v. Chicago Title & Trust Co., 690 F.2d 115, 116 (7th Cir. 1982) (quoting *Our decrees, / Dead to infliction, to themselves are dead, / And Liberty plucks Justice by the nose*).

[3] United States v. Jones, 347 F.Supp.2d 626, 629 (E.D.Wis. 2003) (Callahan, J.) (citing *Central Nat'l Bank of Mattoon*).

[4] People of Guam v. Camacho, 103 F.3d 863, 867 (9th Cir. 1996). Judge Noonan quoted a line from the play in his dissenting opinion in U.S. v. Chischilly, 30 F.3d 1144, 1163-64 (9th Cir. 1994) (quoting *It is the law, not I, condemn your brother*).

[5] Crockett v. Sorenson, 568 F.Supp. 1422, 1427 (W.D. Va. 1983) (Kiser, J.); Gibson v. Lee County School Board, 1 F.Supp.2d 1426, 1431 (M.D. Fla. 1998) (Kovachevich, J.) (quoting *Crockett*).

the right of constables to appoint deputies.[6]

The lines most frequently quoted by American judges — nine times, most recently in the Microsoft Antitrust Case[7] — are Isabella's counsel of humility to Angelo: *Oh, it is excellent / To have a giant's strength, but it is tyrannous / To use it like a giant.*[8] Runners-up are the quotations illustrating the law's disuse: *The law hath not been dead, though it hath slept* — six times[9] — and *We must not make a scarecrow of the law* — five times.[10] *Drest in a little brief authority,* describing a judge's temporary hold on power, was quoted six times, but five of the six were by one judge, Justice Eugene F. Black of the Michigan Supreme Court.[11] Also cautioning about the fallibilities of the judicial system were the lines: *The jury, passing on the prisoner's life, / May in the sworn twelve have a thief or two / Guiltier than him they try* — quoted four times.[12]

Perhaps the oddest use of a line from *Measure for Measure* was the quotation by a New Jersey Superior Court Judge of the lines *Laws for all faults / But faults so countenanced that the strong statutes / Stand like the forfeits in a barber's shop / As much in mock as mark* to illustrate "the laxity of law enforcement in the area of barber shops."[13]

CASES CITING MEASURE FOR MEASURE

Aguirre v. State, 22 S.W.3d 463 (Tex. Crim. App. 1999)
Air Terminal Services, Inc. v. United States, 330 F.2d 974 (Ct. Cl. 1964)
Alexander v. DeAngelo, 329 F.3d 912 (7th Cir. 2003)
Application of Allen S., 387 A.2d 271 (Md. 1978)
Central Nat'l Bank of Mattoon v. U.S. Dept. of Treasury, 912 F.2d 897 (7th Cir. 1990)
Collazo v. Estelle, 940 F.2d 411 (9th Cir. 1991)
Committee on Legal Ethics v. Printz, 416 S.E.2d 720 (W. Va. 1992)
Commonwealth v. Blessing, 29 Pa. D. & C.3d 356 (1984)
Commonwealth v. Vallone, 32 A.2d 889 (Pa. 1943)
Connecticut General Life Ins. Co. v. Chicago Title & Trust Co., 690 F.2d 115 (7th Cir. 1982)
Cooney v. Park County, 792 P.2d 1287 (Wyo. 1990)

---

[6] Petition of Preno, 77 Pa. D. & C. 193, 195 (1952) (Flood, J.).
[7] New York v. Microsoft Corp., 224 F.Supp.2d 76, 103 (D.C. Cir. 2002) (Kollar-Kotelly, J.).
[8] See page 84, note 28, supra.
[9] See page 83, note 27, supra.
[10] See page 67, note 14, supra.
[11] See page 84, note 29, supra.
[12] See page 67, note 15, supra.
[13] Tomasi v. Wayne, 313 A.2d 229, 233 (N.J. Super. 1973) (Schwartz, J.). The reference to *forfeits* is generally understood to refer to teeth, extracted by the barber-surgeons of the day.

Crockett v. Sorenson, 568 F. Supp. 1422 (W.D. Va. 1983)

Davis v. Ohio Barge Line, Inc., 697 F.2d 549 (3rd Cir. 1983)

Denlinger v. Brennan, 87 F.3d 214 (7th Cir. 1996)

District Attorney for the Suffolk District v. Watson 411 N.E.2d 1274 (Mass. 1980)

Farr v. Designer Phosphate & Premix Int'l, Inc., 804 F.Supp. 1190 (D. Neb. 1992)

Fields v. Luther, 1988 U.S. Dist. LEXIS 5405 (D. Md. 1988)

Ford Motor Credit Co. v. Amodt, 139 N.W.2d 6 (Wis. 1966)

Ford v. Ford, 727 A.2d 254 (Conn. App. 1999)

Fritts v. Krugh, 92 N.W.2d 604 (Mich. 1958)

Gardiner v. A.H. Robins Co., Inc., 747 F.2d 1180 (8th Cir. 1984)

Gibson v. Lee Co. School Board, 1 F.Supp.2d 1426 (M.D. Fla. 1998)

Grant v. Pendley, 39 S.W.2d 596 (Tex. Comm'n App. 1931)

Grasso v. State, 857 P.2d 802 (Okla. Crim. App. 1993)

Hopkinson v. State, 632 P.2d 79 (Wyo. 1981)

In re Apportionment of Mich. Legislature, 140 N.W.2d 436 (Mich. 1966)

In re Finley, Kumble, Wagner, Heine, Underberg, Manley, Myerson & Casey, 160 B.R. 882 (Bankr. S.D.N.Y. 1993)

Labat v. Bennett, 365 F.2d 698 (5th Cir. 1956)

Leigh v. Perdue Farms, Inc., 2001 U.S. Dist. LEXIS 11986 (M.D. Ala. 2001)

Lewis v. Bill Robertson & Sons, Inc., 162 Cal.App.3d 650 (1984)

Magreta v. Ambassador Steel Co., 158 N.W.2d 473 (Mich. 1968)

Matteson v. Board of Education, 286 P. 482 (Cal. App. 1930)

Michigan State UAW Community Action Program Council (CAP) v. Austin, 198 N.W.2d 385 (Mich. 1972)

New York v. Microsoft Corp., 224 F.Supp.2d 76 (D.C. Cir. 2002)

Nigido v. First Nat. Bank of Baltimore, 288 A.2d 127 (Md. 1972)

People of Guam v. Camacho, 103 F.3d 863 (9th Cir. 1996)

People v. Fatone, 165 Cal.App.3d 1164 (1985)

People v. Lalka, 449 N.Y.S.2d 579 (N.Y. City Ct. 1982)

Petition of Preno, 77 Pa. D. & C. 193 (1952)

Summerlin v. Stewart, 267 F.3d 926 (9th Cir. 2001)

State v. Lanier, 273 S.E.2d 746 (N.C. App. 1981)

State v. Serra, 529 So.2d 1262 (Fla. Dist. Ct. App. 1988)

State v. Spicer, 2005 WL 742071 (Kan. App. 2005)

State v. Sykes, 104 S.E. 83 (N.C. 1920)

Taylor v. Auditor General, 103 N.W.2d 769 (Mich. 1960)

Tomasi v. Wayne, 313 A.2d 229 (N.J. Super. 1973)

United States v. Alkhabaz, 104 F.3d 1492 (6th Cir. 1997)

United States v. Apfelbaum, 445 U.S. 115 (1980)

United States v. Chischilly, 30 F.3d 1144 (9th Cir. 1994)

United States v. Elliott, 266 F.Supp. 318 (S.D.N.Y. 1967)

United States v. Jones, 347 F.Supp.2d 626 (E.D. Wis. 2003)

United States v. Lynch, 499 F.2d 1011 (D.C. Cir. 1974)

United States v. Matsumaru, 244 F.3d 1092 (9th Cir. 2001)

United States v. Worcester, 190 F.Supp. 548 (D.C. Mass. 1960)

Waldron v. British Petroleum Co., 231 F.Supp. 72 (S.D.N.Y. 1964)

Wollman v. Gross, 637 F.2d 544 (8th Cir. 1980)

ILLUSTRATIONS & CREDITS

ILLUSTRATIONS

Cover: William Shakespeare by Martin Droeshout. *From* THE FIRST FOLIO (1623).

Page i: *From A Midsummer Night's Dream, in* 1 THE SPIRIT OF THE PLAYS OF SHAKESPEARE, EXHIBITED IN A SERIES OF OUTLINE PLATES ILLUSRATIVE OF THE STORY OF EACH PLAY (1833) (drawn and illustrated by Frank Howard).

Page iv: Public domain.

Pages x & 570: The Judge. *From* H. Stacy Marks et al., MR. PUNCH IN WIG AND GOWN: THE LIGHTER SIDE OF BENCH AND BAR (ca. 1910).
Pages 6, 22, 40, 45, 160, 176, 192, 226, 274, 278, 295, 392, 400, 450, 476, and 490: *From* KENNY MEADOWS, ETCHINGS TO THE ILLUSTRATED SHAKESPEARE (1845).

Page 11: Bryan A. Garner. Reprinted by permission of Bryan A. Garner.

Page 23: John P. Elwood. Reprinted by permission of John P. Elwood.

Page 41: Tony Mauro. Reprinted by permission of Tony Mauro.

Pages 161, 205, 231, 275, 309, 341, 393, 419, 447, 477, 493, and 537: *From Measure for Measure, in* 1 THE SPIRIT OF THE PLAYS OF SHAKESPEARE, EXHIBITED IN A SERIES OF OUTLINE PLATES ILLUSRATIVE OF THE STORY OF EACH PLAY (1833) (drawn and illustrated by Frank Howard).

Page 169: *From* the opinion of the court in *FTC v. QT, Inc.,* 512 F.3d 858 (7th Cir. 2008).

Page 208: THE SHAKESPEARIAN ANNUAL ALMANAC 1872.

Page 312: *From* 1 JOHN CASSELL'S ILLUSTRATED HISTORY OF ENGLAND (1857).

Page 422: *Courtesy of* Library of Congress, Prints and Photographs Division, Work Projects Administration Poster Collection, reproduction no. LC-USZ62-59981 DLC (ca. 1936-38).

Page 480: Beaver and cat. *From* WEBSTER'S NEW INTERNATIONAL DICTIONARY OF THE ENGLISH LANGUAGE (3d ed. 1923).

Page 480: *From* the website of the Northwestern University School of Law. Reprinted by permission of the Northwestern University School of Law.

Page 528: *Courtesy of* Library of Congress, Prints and Photographs Division, Work Projects Administration Poster Collection, reproduction no. LC-USZC2-1143 DLC (ca. 1936-41).

Page 571: Andrew Heger, aboard *The Spectacle.* Reprinted by permission of Andrew Heger.

CREDITS

Michael Boudin, *Judge Henry Friendly and the Mirror of Constitutional Law,* 82 NEW YORK UNIVERSITY LAW REVIEW 975 (2007). Copyright © 2007 by Michael Boudin. Reprinted by permission of the author and the publisher.

Lee Epstein, Kevin Quinn, Andrew D. Martin, and Jeffrey A. Segal, *On the Perils of Drawing Inferences About Supreme Court Justices from Their First Few Years of Service,* 91 JUDICATURE 168 (Jan.-Feb. 2008). Copyright © 2008 by American Judicature Society. Reprinted by permission of the authors and the publisher, *Judicature,* the journal of the American Judicature Society.

Richard G. Kopf, *The Top Ten Things I Learned From Apprendi, Blakely, Booker, Rita, Kimbrough and Gall,* OSJCL Amici: Views from the Field (Jan. 2008), at http://osjcl.blogspot.com. Copyright © 2008. Reprinted by permission of the author and the publisher.

Charles Lane, *Chapter Six: Black Letter Law, from* THE DAY FREEDOM DIED: THE COLFAX MASSACRE, THE SUPREME COURT, AND THE BETRAYAL OF RECONSTRUCTION by Charles Lane. Copyright

. . . and a spectacularly

Happy New Year

to you, filled with clear skies,
blue seas, and fair winds.

Subscription Information

Domestic subscriptions to the *Green Bag, An Entertaining Journal of Law* cost $40 for one year (four issues), $80 for two years (eight issues), $120 for three years (twelve issues), and $200 for four years (sixteen issues). Foreign subscriptions are $60 per year. All subscriptions start with the next issue to be published after we receive payment. For gift subscriptions, please specify to whom renewal notices should be sent, and whether you'd like us to send a note informing the recipient of the gift. For back-issues, call Hein at (800) 828-7571. For other subscription matters, please email us at subscriptions@greenbag.org.

To subscribe by Paypal, please visit our web site, www.greenbag.org. Or send the following information, or a completed copy of this form, together with your check payable to the *Green Bag,* to the address below.

When you buy a subscription to the *Green Bag,* that is all you are buying — one copy of each issue of the journal for the duration of your order. Everything else we make is a gift we may or may not bestow on some or all of our subscribers (*e.g.,* a bobblehead or almanac) or a product you may purchase separately (*e.g., Judge Dave & the Rainbow People*). In addition, to the extent that the *Green Bag* does occasionally and arbitrarily give away goodies, we do not give multiple goodies to anyone carrying more than one *Green Bag* subscription.

Name: _____

Address: _____

City: _____

State/Zip: _____

Email: _____

The Green Bag, 6600 Barnaby Street NW, Washington, DC 20015

Thank you.